THE KU KLUX KLAN
An Encyclopedia

GARLAND REFERENCE LIBRARY
OF THE SOCIAL SCIENCES
(VOL. 499)

ALSO BY MICHAEL AND JUDY ANN NEWTON

Racial and Religious Violence in America
A CHRONOLOGY

The FBI Most Wanted
AN ENCYCLOPEDIA

THE
KU
KLUX
KLAN

An Encyclopedia

MICHAEL & JUDY ANN NEWTON

Garland Publishing, Inc.

NEW YORK & LONDON 1991

Newton, Michael. 1951-
    The Ku Klux Klan : an encyclopedia / by Michael and Judy Ann Newton.
    p. cm. — (Garland reference library of the social sciences : vol. 499)
    Includes bibliographical references and index.
    ISBN 0-8240-2038-3
    1. Ku Klux Klan (1866-   )—Dictionaries.   I. Newton, Judy Ann,
1952-   .   II. Title.   III. Series: Garland reference library of the social science
: v. 499.
HS2330.K63N49   1991
322.4'2'0973—dc20   90-14008

Printed on acid-free, 250-year-life paper
MANUFACTURED IN THE UNITED STATES OF AMERICA

CONTENTS

PREFACE   *vii*

LIST OF ENTRIES   *xv*

THE ENCYCLOPEDIA   *1*

BIBLIOGRAPHY   *632*

PREFACE

The world's oldest, most persistent terrorist organization is not European or even Middle Eastern in origin. Fifty years before the Irish Republican Army was organized, a century before Al Fatah declared its holy war on Israel, the Ku Klux Klan was actively harassing, torturing, and murdering in the United States. Today, as we approach the Klan's 125th year, its members remain fanatically committed to a course of violent opposition to social progress and racial equality in the United States. As Alphonse Karr declared in 1849, the more things change—at least, for members of the KKK—the more those things remain the same.

Ironically, the Klan was born from simple idleness, created as a social club by six young Confederate veterans of the Civil War. All six were educated, relatively affluent, and each had passed the war years as an officer. Boredom led them to create a secret lodge near Pulaski, Tennessee, in 1866, complete with mystic titles for the officers and ghostly costumes to enliven their nocturnal, boozy wanderings. They called their club the Ku Klux Klan, from *kuklos*—Greek for "circle," honored in the title of a then popular fraternity, Kuklos Adelphon. "Clan" was added as an afterthought, spelled with a *K* for uniformity, because the founders of the KKK were all Scotch-Irish.

It took a year for word of Ku Klux ramblings to spread beyond Pulaski and the state of Tennessee, and Southerners had much to ponder in the meantime. They had lost the Civil War and had seen slavery banned by law, but they still cherished hopes of turning back the clock to something that approximated antebellum life. Their readmission to the Union was assured under President Abraham Lincoln's policy of "malice toward none," but in the wake of Lincoln's assassination, a "radical" Congress had strikingly different ideas. To many congressmen, the Southern Black Codes, coupled with brutal race riots in Memphis and New Orleans, signaled a reversion to de facto slavery. The response from Washington was swift and stern: civil rights laws, troops, and new amendments aimed at guaranteeing the political equality of former slaves.

The prostrate South was stunned, but veterans of the recent War Between the States recovered quickly, organizing local paramilitary bands to deal with Northern bluecoats, radicals, and any "pushy" blacks. Pre-war slave patrols and violent action with the anti-Catholic Know-Nothing movement predisposed these men to armed reaction, and to these men the temper of the times demanded nothing less. The hallowed "Southern way of life" was under siege, and to a prejudiced Southerner's mind, it was a short step from the ballot to the bedroom, spelling ultimate destruction for the so-called master race.

In Tennessee, where charter Klansmen had been dressing as ghosts to frighten superstitious blacks for sport, the KKK was suddenly regarded in a different light, with a new potential as a secret army for the cause of white supremacy. In April 1867, delegates from several Southern states convened in Nashville to reorganize the Klan, where they prepared a noble sounding constitution and selected a leader for themselves. Their choice of Nathan Bedford Forrest—a Confederate cavalry hero and pre-war slave trader turned railroad PR man—guaranteed the KKK's loose organization along military lines and predisposed members toward nightriding violence in their local communities.

Between 1867 and 1869, the Klan put down roots in a dozen states, attracting an estimated half million members at its peak. Rebuffed in Virginia, Klansmen took up the slack by establishing themselves in Kentucky, the movement's only Reconstruction foothold outside the old Confederacy. Leadership generally rested in the hands of Southern gentry—attorneys and planters, ex-Confederate officers, past and future politicians—but the secrecy and decentralization of the Klan prevented their leaders from exercising much control over the rank and file. Predictable targets included active Republicans, U.S. Army or state militia officers, carpetbaggers from the North, Unionist "scalawags," and blacks who attended school or signed up to vote. The Southern Democratic Party sheltered Klansmen, nurturing the movement as its last and best hope of undermining state Republican administrations, but in time the violence went too far, as Klan leaders lost control and raiders lost their focus on the higher goal of Democratic rule. By January 1869, the bad publicity attending gang rapes, local feuds, and lynchings prompted Nathan Forrest to proclaim a general moratorium on Klan activity, suggesting that the KKK itself might punish those who continued to raid while in disguise.

While Forrest's order more or less dissolved the Klan in Arkansas and Tennessee, it had the opposite effect in other states, precipitating new, unprecedented violence as local Klansmen cast off all restraints from leaders they had previously recognized. In Alabama, Georgia, Mississippi, and the Carolinas, blacks and "radicals" were instantly confronted with a new reign of terror, while Kentucky Klansmen seemed to split their time between the persecution of minorities and the defense of bootleg whiskey stills. Congressional investigation and a set of federal "Ku Klux Acts" eventually jailed some Klansmen in the early 1870s, but the evaporation of the KKK had more to do with its success than pressure from the courts. In 1874, Democrats secured a majority in the U.S. House of Representatives, and by 1876 they had effectively restored one-party rule across the so-called Solid South. The KKK had done its job, outlived its usefulness, and in the process earned a lasting place in Southern folklore.

Over the next four decades, without the Klan, prejudiced sheriffs, local White Cap vigilantes, and the ad hoc lynch mobs murdered several dozen blacks each year. But memories of Ku Klux glory lingered on. Novelist Thomas Dixon lit a candle to that memory in 1905, with *The Clansman,* and ten years later this racist romance became Hollywood's first epic motion picture, D.W. Griffith's *Birth of a Nation.* The movie's pro-Klan theme provoked a storm of controversy nationwide, but with endorsements from the White House and the Chief Justice of the U.S. Supreme Court—a former Klansman from Louisiana—the film's success was guaranteed. Across the country the prospects of a KKK revival were discussed, but the first to act was William Simmons, an eccentric former minister residing in Atlanta.

Simmons timed his resurrection of the Klan to coincide with the Atlanta premiere of Griffith's blockbuster, cashing in on the free publicity. Some of Simmons' recruits included members of the Knights of Mary Phagan, the same group that lynched Jewish murder suspect Leo Frank in August 1915 and celebrated the event with America's first cross burning two months later. On Thanksgiving night, the Knights joined Simmons and a handful of others, including Atlanta's city clerk, for a ride to the summit of nearby Stone Mountain, where another giant cross was burned and the assembled Anglo-Saxons pledged their lives in the defense of God, country, and white womanhood as the Knights of the Ku Klux Klan.

Chartered as a "purely benevolent and eleemosynary" fraternal order, the modern Klan deliberately evoked memories of its Reconstruction ancestor. Simmons described his group as the "same soul in a new body," but there were obvious changes as well. To the original Klan's abbreviated list of black and "radical" enemies, modern recruiters added Catholics, Jews, most immigrants, and labor unions. An estimated 5,000 Klansmen had been recruited in Georgia and Alabama by the time the United States entered World War I, but the Klan's marginal role as a wartime vigilante force failed to attract new legions for the cause. At last, in 1920, Simmons hired a professional recruiting team, led by Edward Clarke and Elizabeth Tyler, to turn his fading dream around. By the following summer, 100,000 Klansmen had been enlisted at ten dollars a head, and the KKK was drawing national attention. A 1921 congressional investigation provided more free publicity, and the Klan grew to an estimated 4 million members by 1924. In retrospect, Simmons would tell the press, "Congress made us."

At the same time, various other factors combined to "make" the Klan. Prohibition's "noble experiment" sought to banish Demon Rum and legislate fundamentalist values across the United States, granting Ku Klux moralists a golden opportunity to spy on their neighbors. Echoes of Russia's Bolshevik Revolution were heard in a wave of anarchist bombings and violent strikes by radical left-wing unions. Unrestricted immigration brought 14.5 million newcomers to U.S. shores between 1900 and 1920, most of them from Southern and Eastern Europe. At the same time, a northward migration of Southern blacks sparked bloody race riots from Omaha and Chicago to Washington, D.C. By 1924, the Klan was a truly national phenomenon, with members in every state and a majority north of the Mason-Dixon Line. Indiana and California were among the most active Klan territories, and Ohio was the most populous, with an estimated half million Klansmen of its own.

Muscled out of office by Texas Klansman Dr. Hiram Evans, William Simmons was compelled to watch the Klan's growth from a distance. Inevitably, Klansmen turned to politics, infesting both major parties and flexing their electoral muscle from local precincts to the nation's capital. President Warren Harding was initiated in a special White House ceremony, while Klansmen turned out to elect their own into the governorships of Alabama, Georgia, Colorado, and Indiana; countless other Klansmen or Ku Klux allies were elected to Congress, and state and local offices. The KKK came close to getting parochial schools banned in Oregon, and Catholic presidential candidate Al Smith's religion became a major issue in the 1924 campaign. In August 1925, some 40,000 Klansmen marched down Pennsylvania Avenue in full regalia. But the movement had already passed its prime: When the march was repeated a year later, barely half as many Klansmen turned out, and by 1929 the Invisible Empire had withered to a bare 100,000 members nationwide.

Reasons for the Klan's abrupt decline were as diverse as the causes of its phenomenal growth. Endemic violence played a major role, initially attracting the adventurous and cruel, but then repelling thousands more as tales of torture, rape, and murder surfaced from the bayous of Louisiana to the California oil fields and the Hoosier plains. Extremists in the Klan became their own worst enemies, frightening the rank and file with their insistence that the only good Catholic was a dead Catholic. In addition, corruption, drunkenness, and immorality among the leaders of the KKK persuaded thousands of the faithful that they had been duped and robbed by hypocrites. Each time a ranking Klansman was arrested in his cups or split for parts unknown with stolen dues, rude headlines hammered at the Klan's prestige. When Dr. Hiram Evans finally resigned in 1939, the KKK was but a shadow of its former self. Evans' successor, James Colescott, tried to revive the organization with fresh infusions of anti-communism and anti-Semitism, but his efforts were too little, too late. In 1944, the Internal Revenue Service filed a lien against the Klan for $685,000 in back taxes, and Colescott officially disbanded the order, telling newsmen, "Maybe the government can make something out of the Klan. I never could."

A Georgia obstetrician, Dr. Samuel Green, worked overtime to hold the scattered remnants of the KKK together in the post-World War II era, launching his own Association of Georgia Klans with a Stone Mountain cross burning in October 1946. The "new" Klan emphasized white supremacy and opposition to "communistic" labor unions such as the CIO. But Dr. Green's Invisible Empire was torn by dissension as it competed for cash and recruits with at least six other Klans in Alabama, Georgia, Florida, and the Carolinas. Green's death, in 1949, left Atlanta policeman Sam Roper in charge, but his ineffective leadership opened the door for competitors. Independent Klans began crowding the headlines in several states with their violent outbursts, and their nightriding prompted state and federal investigations across the South, landing scores of Klansmen in prison. By 1953, progressive Southerners felt safe in saying that the Klan, if not precisely dead, was fading fast.

As if on cue, the civil rights movement provided a vital shot in the arm for the Klan. In May 1954, the U.S. Supreme Court's decision in favor of nationwide school integration caused a stir in the Jim Crow states and gave idle Klan recruiters an issue they could exploit. Affluent racists flocked to the banner of the "respectable" White Citizens' Councils by fighting integration by exerting economic pressure on their black employees, but the genteel approach ignored thousands of blue-collar whites. While the Southern gentry organized its garden parties and discussed political campaigns, the Klan addressed a different audience—the "crackers," "rednecks," and assorted "white trash."

Georgia native Eldon Edwards was the dominant Klansman of the late 1950s, claiming an estimated 15,000 members for his Atlanta-based U.S. Klans that had active chapters in nine states. He faced competition from at least fifteen rival groups, from Arkansas to Florida and the Carolinas, each with an average 1,000 to 1,500 members. As in the days of Reconstruction, decentralization magnified the potential for violence, with an increasing reliance on dynamite. Black-owned homes and integrated schools were favored targets, but synagogues also received substantial attention from Klansmen, who believed they had found an explanation for so-called black assertiveness in the guise of a Jewish conspiracy. Militant groups such as the National States Rights Party and American Nazis encouraged the Klan's anti-Semitism, swapping literature with the KKK and recruiting Klansmen to beef up their own slender ranks.

The 1960 death of Eldon Edwards roughly coincided with a new shift in the civil rights movement, from long-winded litigation to "direct action" in the form of marches, freedom rides, and sit-ins. Klan recruiters were the immediate beneficiaries of the move, with estimates of total membership nearing 50,000 by early 1961. The U.S. Klan was still dominant but seemed to drift aimlessly without its founder at the helm, and some dissatisfied members left in July 1961 to create the United Klans of America. Based in Tuscaloosa, Alabama, with Robert Shelton in charge, the United Klans expanded to plant chapters in eighteen states by 1966. At its peak, observers for the Anti-Defamation League of B'nai B'rith credited the United Klans with some 30,000 members and sympathizers, while the next largest of Shelton's seventeen competitors fell somewhere short of the 10,000 mark.

Violence in the 1960s flared across the South in direct response to civil rights campaigns, familiarizing television viewers in the North with communities such as Birmingham, St. Augustine, Selma, McComb, and Bogalusa. Klansmen and their allies were implicated in most of the decade's racial bombings and several notorious murders. All-white juries stubbornly failed to return convictions in most cases, and by mid-decade federal authorities had dusted off the Reconstruction "Ku Klux Acts," convicting a handful of Klansmen for violating the civil rights of their victims. By 1968, the light had dawned even in darkest Mississippi, as local courts began to hand down life sentences to Klansmen who had burned a black man to death in his home. A new congressional investigation exposed prominent Klan leaders as nothing more than greedy racists who often pled the Fifth Amendment to avoid prosecution, and several—including Robert Shelton—were ultimately jailed for contempt on the basis of their public performances.

The early 1970s witnessed a rapid decline in Klan membership nationwide, slipping to an estimated 1,500 hard-core loyalists in 1974. A new leader then appeared, David Duke. Soft-spoken, charismatic, and college educated, Duke became a fixture in the media appearing on talk shows, touring the country, and building his Louisiana-based Knights of the KKK into the United States' dominant Klan by 1980. Klan-watchers placed total membership close to 12,000 that year, with Duke's group leading in a field of twenty-odd competitors. Resigning at his peak of strength that summer to pursue political office from the helm of the new National Association for the Advancement of White People, Duke left the field to Bill Wilkinson, his closest competitor and the preeminent Klansman of the 1980s. By the time Wilkinson was exposed as an FBI informant in 1981, the movement had already veered off into more radical directions, embracing the neo-Nazi philosophy of the Aryan Nations and similar groups, while cloaking its violence in the religious disguise of the so-called Christian Identity movement. Rabid anti-Semitism remained the order of the day, with leaders in the reduced Invisible Empire—total membership estimated at around 6,000— issuing public declarations of war against the "Zionist Occupational Government" in Washington, D.C. Whatever the size of the modern Klan, however, it seems intent on living up to its own poetic slogan:

Yesterday, Today, Forever

Since Eighteen Hundred and Sixty-Six

the KU KLUX KLAN

has been riding and will

continue to do so as long as

the WHITE MAN liveth.

Since the end of World War II, "the Klan" has for the most part been a series of smaller groups, changing and dividing up with great frequency. Dissenting Klansmen quarrel with their elected leaders and strike off to organize new factions on their own. Klans rise and fall with such fluidity that they are sometimes gone before police and journalists are cognizant of their existence. On the fringes of the movement, native Nazi groups split up, reorganize, and change their titles with bewildering frequency. In any given year since 1945, at least five separate Klans have staked their claim to lineal descent from the original, with eighteen identified in 1966 and twenty-four in 1983, exclusive of affiliates and front groups. In some cases, the Klansmen have fought one another with the same zeal normally reserved for blacks and Jews, confounding the efforts to identify or separate the warring factions.

The present volume is an effort to bring some order out of the chaos, in the form of an encyclopedic reference work. Entries represent organizations (both pro- and anti-Klan), individuals (victims and opponents of the KKK, along with Klansmen and their allies), and various general topics (including Klan jargon and passwords). Geographical entries are included for nearly all of the United States and several foreign countries where Ku Klux factions have operated, along with some of the noteworthy battlegrounds where Klansmen have attempted to prevent the march of progress. Considerable space is also allotted to native Nazi groups, based on their persistent cooperation with the various Klans since the Great Depression. Reference notes have been abbreviated and replaced with numbers in most cases, coordinated with a full bibliography that follows the text. Multiple indices cover groups, individuals, geographical entries, and general topics.

In conclusion, we can do no better than to echo historian Walter Fleming's remark from his 1905 history of the KKK: "There is still much that is obscure about the Ku Klux Klan and I shall be glad to obtain additional information in regard to the order, and also to receive notice of mistakes and errors in this account."

LIST OF ENTRIES

The following lists contain all of this encyclopedia's entries. The lists include a General List, a Geographic List, an Organizational List, and a List of People.

GENERAL LIST

The General List contains those entries relating to ethnic groups and minorities; key events from the Klan's history; facilities and institutions; Klan beliefs; legislation aimed at stopping the Klan; publications and films related to the Klan (including Klan periodicals); Klan terminology; and the forms of violence employed by the Klan throughout its history.

ETHNIC GROUPS AND MINORITIES

Immigrants
Japanese-Americans
Lumbee Indians
Vietnamese refugees
Women

EVENTS

"Ax Handle Saturday"
"Black Monday"
Conference of Eastern Dragons
Cross burning
Freedom rides
Freedom summer
Hesper
Montgomery, Alabama,
    bus boycott
United States v. Williams

FACILITIES AND INSTITUTIONS

Camp My Lai
Camp Nordland
Camp Puller
Cane Branch Baptist Church
Carver Village
Hattie Cotton School
Klan Haven Home
Klan Krest
Koinonia Farm
Little Holiness Church
Pacifica Foundation
Silver Dollar Cafe
Valparaiso University

KLAN BELIEFS

Anti-Catholicism
Anti-Semitism
Klankraft

LEGISLATION

Anti-mask laws
"Ku Klux Acts"

PUBLICATIONS AND FILMS

Advocate, The
Birth of a Nation
Dawn
Fellowship Forum
Fiery Cross
Harold the Klansman
Kloran
Knighthawk, The
Kourier, The
National Kourier
Searchlight, The
Turner Diaries, The
X-Ray, The

TERMINOLOGY

"AKIA"
"Alien"
"AYAK"
Carpetbaggers
Degree team
Den
Dominion
Escaped nuns
Furies
Genii
Ghouls
Giant
Goblins
Grand cyclops
Grand dragon
Grand ensign
Grand exchequer
Grand giant
Grand guard

Grand magi
Grand monk
Grand scribe
Grand sentinel
Grand titan
Grand turk
Grand tycoon
Grand wizard
Great giant
Great titan
Hydras
Imperial giant
Imperial kloncilium
Imperial representative
Imperial tax
Imperial wizard
Invisible empire
Kalendar
Kardinal kullors
Klabee
Kladd
Klaliff
Klan
Klanburgesses
Klanton
Klarogo
Klavern
Kleagle
Klectoken
Klexter
Kligrapp
Klikon
Klokan
Klokann
Klokard
Klongress
Klonklaves
Klonversation
Klonverse
Klonvokation
Klorero
Kludd
Ku Klux Register
Lictor
Night run

Nighthawk
Province
Realm
Scalawags
Smith and Wesson Line
Wrecking crew
Yellow dog

VIOLENCE
Belt Line
Bombing
Castration
Lynching
Murder
Riots

GEOGRAPHIC LIST

The Geographic List contains listings by country, individual United States, and cities, towns, and counties that have played a role in the history of the Klan.

COUNTRIES
Austria
Canada
Canal Zone
Chile
Dominica
England
Germany

STATES
Alabama
Alaska
Arizona
Arkansas
California
Colorado
Connecticut
Delaware
Florida
Georgia
Idaho
Illinois
Indiana
Iowa
Kansas
Kentucky
Louisiana
Maine
Maryland
Massachusetts

Michigan
Minnesota
Mississippi
Missouri
Montana
Nebraska
Nevada
New Hampshire
New Jersey
New Mexico
New York
North Carolina
North Dakota
Ohio
Oklahoma
Oregon
Pennsylvania
Rhode Island
South Carolina
South Dakota
Tennessee
Texas
Utah
Vermont
Virginia
West Virginia
Wisconsin
Wyoming

CITIES, TOWNS, AND COUNTIES

Albany, Ga.
Athens, Ga.
Bogalusa, La.
Camilla, Ga.
Clinton, Tenn.
"Dynamite Hill" (Birmingham, Ala.)
Eutaw, Ala.
Greensboro, N.C.
Groveland, Fla.
Laurens County, S.C.
Little Rock, Ark.
McComb, Miss.
Meridian, Miss.
Mer Rouge, La.
Oxford, Miss.
Pulaski, Tenn.
St. Augustine, Fla.
Selma, Ala.
Stone Mountain, Ga.
Tuscaloosa, Ala.

ORGANIZATIONAL LIST

The Organizational List contains anti-Klan groups and those government agencies most involved in attempts to eliminate the Klan, as well as Klan factions, groups affiliated with the Klan, various Klan "fronts," and Nazi groups. Also listed are businesses, labor unions, political parties, and religious groups that have been involved in the history of the Klan.

ANTI-KLAN GROUPS

American Unity League
Anti-Klan Association
Black K.K.s
Committee of Notables
Dallas County Citizens League
Deacons for Defense and Justice
Detroit Anti-Klan Coalition
Freedmen's Bureau
John Brown Anti-Klan Committee
Knights of Liberty
Knights of the Blazing Ring
Knights of the Flaming Circle
Loyal Legion of Lincoln
Minute Men of the West
Mossy-Backs
National Anti-Klan Network
National Vigilance Association
Order of Anti-Poke Noses
Southern Poverty Law Center
Union League
United Coalition Against the Klan
Whangs
Wide Awakes
Wilmington 10

BUSINESSES

American Southern Publishing Company
Blackwell Real Estate
Dickey Clay Manufacturing Co.
Heritage Enterprises, Inc.

GOVERNMENT AGENCIES

Federal Bureau of Investigation
House Un-American Activities Committee
Southern Conference on Bombing

KLAN FACTIONS

Adamic Knights of the KKK
Alabama Knights of the KKK

Alabama KKK, Inc.
American Knights of the KKK
Ancient Order, Invisible Knights
    of the KKK
Aryan Knights of the KKK
Associated Klans of America
Assn. of Alabama Knights of
    the KKK
Assn. of Arkansas Klans
Assn. of Carolina Klans
Assn. of Florida KKK
Assn. of Georgia Klans
Assn. of South Carolina Klans
    (1950s–1960s)
Assn. of South Carolina Klans
    (1970s)
Bedford Forrest Klans
Black Shirts
Cahaba River Group
California Knights of the KKK
Camellia White Knights
Canadian Knights of the KKK
Carolina Knights of the KKK
Chessmen
Christian Knights of the KKK
    (1959–61)
Christian Knights of the KKK
    (1980s)
Confederate Independent Order
    Knights of the KKK
Confederate Knights of the KKK
    (1960s)
Confederate Knights of the KKK
    (1980s)
Confederate Vigilantes, Knights
    of the KKK
Confederation of Independent
    Orders-Invisible Empire-
    Knights of the KKK
Confederation of Klans
Cottonmouth Moccasin Gang
Council of Centaurs
Council of Yahoos
Crusaders of the North
Dixie Klans, Knights of the
    KKK, Inc.

Essex-Middle River Knights of
    the KKK
Federated Knights of the KKK
Federated Ku Klux Klans, Inc.
Florida Klans, Inc.
Florida KKK
Florida White Knights of the
    KKK
Grand Klan
Greenville County Klan
Gulf Coast KKK
Improved Order of the U.S.
    Klans, Knights of the
    KKK, Inc.
Independent Invisible Knights
    of the KKK
Independent Klan of America
Independent Knights of the KKK
Independent Mississippi Klan
Independent Northern Klans,
    Inc.
Independent Order Knights of
    the KKK
Interstate Klans, Knights of the
    KKK
Invincible Empire, Knights of
    the White Rose
Invisible Empire, Knights of the
    KKK (Wilkinson)
Invisible Empire, Knights of the
    KKK (Reusch)
Invisible Empire Knights of the
    KKK
Invisible Empire, Knights of the
    KKK, Realm of
    South Carolina
Invisible Empire, United Klans,
    Knights of the KKK of
    America, Inc.
Justice Knights of the KKK
Klan Air Force
Klan Beret
Klan of the North
Klan softball team
Klan Youth Corps

Klavalier Klub
Klavaliers
Knights of American
    Protestantism
Knights of the Air
Knights of the Golden Eagle
Knights of the Green Forest
Knights of the KKK
    (Florida:1955–?)
Knights of the KKK
    (South Carolina: 1955–?)
Knights of the KKK, Florida
Knights of the KKK, Inc.
    (1915–1944)
Knights of the KKK, Inc. (1960)
Knights of the KKK, Inc.
    (1975–)
Knights of the KKK of America
Knights of the KKK of the
    Confederacy
Konsolidated Ku Klux Klans of
    the Invisible Empire
Ku Klux Klan (1866–1872)
Ku Klux Klan of Florida, Inc.
Ku Klux Rangers
Ladies of the Golden Mask
Ladies of the Invisible Empire
Louisiana Knights of the KKK
Maryland Knights of the KKK
    (1966–1967)
Maryland Knights of the KKK
    (1969–1980)
Michigan KKK
Missouri Knights of the KKK
National Association of Ku Klux
    Klan
National Christian Knights
National Intelligence
    Committee
National Knights of the KKK
National KKK
National Order of Knights of
    the KKK, Inc.
National Women of the KKK
New Empire KKK

New Order, Knights of the KKK
New Order of Knights of the
    KKK
New Orleans KKK
Night Riders
North Carolina Knights of the
    KKK (1956–1958)
North Carolina Knights of the
    KKK (1969–1980)
Northern and Southern Knights
    of the KKK (1949–1952)
Northern and Southern Knights
    of the KKK (1977–?)
Northern Independent KKK of
    New York
Ohio Knights of the KKK
Original Knights of the KKK
Original KKK
Original KKK of America
Original KKK of the
    Confederacy
Original Southern Klans, Inc.
Palmetto Knights of the KKK
Queens of the Golden Mask
Red Caps
Secret Six
Silver Dollar Group
Sipsey Swampers
South Carolina Knights of the
    KKK, Inc.
Southern Knights of the KKK
Southern White Knights of the
    KKK
Texas Fiery Knights of the KKK
Triple-S Super Secret Society
Tri-State KKK
U.S. Klans of Georgia
U.S. Klans, Knights of the KKK,
    Inc.
Underground, The
United Empire, Knights of the
    KKK
United Klans of America, Inc.,
    Knights of the KKK
Universal Klans

Venango Gang
Vigilantes
White Band
White Crusaders of the North
White Heritage Knights of the
    KKK
White Knights of Alabama
White Knights of the KKK
    (Miss.)
White Knights of the KKK
    (Iowa)
White Knights of the KKK
    (Mich.)
White Knights of the KKK (Pa.)
White Knights of Liberty
White Knights of the New
    Jersey KKK
White Unity Party
York County Klan

KLAN-AFFILIATED GROUPS
    American Krusaders
    American Order of Clansmen
    Americans for Preservation of
        the White Race
    Black Legion
    California Anti-Communist
        League
    California Rangers
    Caucasian Clubs
    Chester Conservative Clan
    Christian Defense League
    Christian Freedom Council
    Christian Nationalist Alliance
    Christian Nationalist Crusade
    Christian Voters and Buyers
        League
    Christian-Patriots Defense
        League
    Citizens' Council
    Civilian Material Assistance
    Committee of One Million
        Caucasians to March on
        Congress

Confederate Underground
Conservative Clubs
Constitutional Union Guard
Council of Safety
Covenant, the Sword, and the
    Arm of the Lord
Defensive Legion of Registered
    Americans
Democratic Clubs
Devil's Advocates
Duck Club
Euro-American Alliance
Farmers Liberation Army
Georgians Unwilling to
    Surrender
Heggie's Scouts
Innocents Club
Jack Robinsons
Jackson County Citizens
    Emergency Unit
John Birch Society
Kamelia
Kappa Beta Lambda
Knights of Mary Phagan
Knights of the Black Cross
Knights of the Flaming Sword
Knights of the Rising Sun
Knights of the White Camellia
    (1867–1869)
Knights of the White Camellia
    (1934–1942)
Knights of the White Camellia
    (1950s)
Knights of the White Camellia
    (1980s)
Knights of the White Carnation
Knights of White Christians
Kuklos Adelphon
Liberty Net
Men of Justice
Minutemen (1920s)
Minutemen (1959–1973)
Nacirema, Inc.

National Association for the
    Advancement of White
    People
National Christian Conservative
    Society
National Emancipation of Our
    White Seed
National States Rights Party
Native Sons of the South
New South Freedom Fighters
North Alabama Citizens'
    Council
North American Alliance for
    White People
Order of Pale Faces
Patriotic Legal Foundation
Patriotic Legal Fund
Patriotic Interorganizational
    Communications Center
Posse Comitatus
Rights of White People
Royal Riders of the Red Robe
Seymour Knights
Skinheads
Southern Gentlemen, Inc.
Southern National Front
Southerners, The
Supreme Cyclopean Council
United Protestant Alliance
United Racist Front
Vigilantes, Inc.
Western Front
Western Guard
White America, Inc.
White American Political Assn.
White Aryan Resistance
White Brotherhood
White Caps (1888–1903)
White Christian Crusaders
White Confederacy of
    Understanding
White League
White Patriot Party
White People's Committee to
    Restore God's Laws

White Rose Society
White Students Union
Whiteman's Defense Fund
Wide Awake Club
Yellow Jackets

KLAN "FRONT" GROUPS

Action
Adams County Civic &
    Betterment Assn.
Alabama Rescue Service
Alpha Pi Sigma
Altamaha Men's Club No. 72
American Confederate Army
Ancient City Gun Club
Anson Sportsman Club
Anti-Communist
    Christian Assn.
Apex Ladies League
Apex Restoration Association
Arcadia Sportsman Club
Auburndale Fisherman's Club
Ayden Christian Fellowship
    Club
Ayden Garden Club
B. & H. Sporting Club
Back Swamp Hunting Club
Baker Hunting & Fishing Club
Bassett Creek Hunting Club
Benevolent Association
Benevolent Association Unit
    No. 53
Bernice Sportsman's Club
Better Citizens Club
Black River Club
Black River Improvement Club
Blanca Club
Blount County Hunters Club
Boeuf River Hunting Club
Bogue Homa Hunting &
    Rifle Club
Brotherhood of Jasper County
Broward Club
Broward Fellowship Club

Broward Rod & Reel Club
Brunswick Sportsman
Bunn Saddle Club
Burke County Improvement
    Society
Bush Hunting & Fishing Club
    No. 1055
Cairo Hunting Lodge
Caldwell Improvement Assn.
Calhoun Businessmen's Assn.
Camp Creek Club
Cane River Hunting &
    FishingClub
Capitol City Restoration Assn.
Capitol City Sportsmans Club
Cash Sportsman Club
Catahoula Sportsman Club
Catarrah Sports Club
Catawba Improvement Assn.
Central Carolina Ladies League
Central DeKalb Civic Club
Central Improvement Assn. of
    Lillington
Central Sportsmans Club
    No. 101
Charlotte County Anonymous
    Club
Chase City Fellowship Club
Chatham Citizens Club
Chatham Hunting & Fishing
    Club
Cherokee 92 Men's Club
Cherokee Sportsmans Club
Chesapeake Bar-B-Q Club
Chesterfield Sportsmans Club
Choudrant Rod & Gun Club
Chowan Boat Club
Christian Constitutional
    Crusaders
Chula Men's Club
Clark-Washington Hunting &
    Fishing Club
Clark's Game Bird Farm
Clayton Civic Club
Clinton Hunting & Fishing Club

Club No. 50
Columbus County Sportsman
    Club
Community Improvement
    Association
Confederate Club No. 38
Confederate Lodge No. 304
Confederate No. 14
Continental League for
    Christian Freedom
Coolidge Fishing Club
Coon Hunters Club
Copiah Rod & Gun Club
Cove City Hunting Club
Covington Hunting &
    Fishing Club
Craven County Improvement
    Association
Craven County Ladies
    Auxiliary
Craven Fellowship Club No. 1
Craven Fellowship Club No. 2
Cumberland County Patriots
Davidson County Rescue
    Service
Davidson County Sportsman
    Club
Deland Sportsmans Club
Delaware Birdwatchers
Delhi Sportsman Club
Delta Sportsman Club
Deville Hunting & Fishing Club
Dixie Belle Ladies Club
Dixie Travel Club
Donalsonville Lodge No. 3
Douglas Sportsman Club
Dover Community Club
Draper Hunting Club
Dubach Hunting & Fishing Club
Dudgemonice Hunting Club
Duval Fellowship Club
Early Lodge No. 35
East Hillsborough Sportsman's
    Club
East Side Fellowship Club

Eastern Triangle Ladies League
Echo Valley Club
Etowah Rescue Service
Family Improvement Club
Fayette S.A. Club
Fellowship Club
51 Club
Fine Fellows Club
Flint River Men's Club No. 8
Flint River Men's Group No. 30
Folson Sportsman's Club
Forrest Club No. 11
Franklin County Improvement
   Association
Friendly Circle
Friendship Club
Garden City Club
Garner Improvement
   Association
Gaston County Sportsman Club
Georgetown Tidewater Club
Gravel Ridge Hunters Lodge
Green Thumb Garden Club
Greene County Improvement
   Association
Grifton Christian Society
Guilford County Boosters Club
Halifax County Ladies Club
Hamburg Sportsman Club
Hannah Hawks Club
Harnett County Improvement
   Association
Harnett County Ladies League
Harriman Volunteer Club
Hartsville Sportsmans Club
Haw River Fishing Club
Hemingway Sportsmans Club
Henry County No. 49 Club
High Point Brotherhood Club
Highway 14 Hunting Club
Hineston Hunting &
   Fishing Club
Homer Hunting & Fishing Club
Horse Thief Detective Society
Houston County Committee for
   Law and Order

Hunters Club
Hunting Club
Impala No. 42
Imperial Club No. 27-1
Indian River Hunt Club
Jacinto City Citizens Committee
   for Law and Order
Jacksonville Sports Club
Jena Hunting & Fishing Club
Joseph E. Johnson Club No. 61
Junction City Sportsman's Club
Kemp Fishing Lodge
Keystone Club
Kingsville Hunt Club
Kon Klave Klub
Ladies Auxiliary of the Surf Club
Ladies Confederate Dixons
   Mills Unit
Ladies Confederates
Ladies of Savannah
Lake Wales Pioneer Club
   No. 5-4
Lakeview Men's Club
Lee County Improvement
   Association
Lenoir Fellowship Club
Lilburn Men's Club No. 29
Limestone Debating Club
Limestone Fishing Club
Lincoln County W.P. Lodge
Lithonia No. 57 Club
Little River Club No. 27
Little River Rod & Gun Club
Louisiana Rifle Assn.
Louisiana-Arkansas Law
   Enforcement League
Lynches River Hunting Club
M. Murphy Club
McDowell's Sportsman
Magic City Lodge
Magnolia Spotrsman Club
   No. 10
Many Hunting & Fishing Club
Marion County Catfish Club
Marion Hunting & Fishing Club

Martin County Ladies
    Improvement Club
Martin County Sportsman Club
Meadow Improvement
    Association
Mecklenburg Sportsman Club
Men's Club of Strong
    Community
Midway Club
Mississippi Constitution Party
Monroe Hunting &
    Fishing Club
Monticello Men's Club
Morehouse Hunt and Gun Club
Nansemond & Suffolk
    Hunt Club
Nash County Charter Service
National Christian Party
Neuse Hunting Club
Neuse Rescue Service
Never Club
New Hanover Improvement
    Association
New River Fishing Club
New River Rifle Club
Newport Fellowship Club
Northeast Gun Club
Nottoway Club
Oakville Outdoor Sports Club
Ocala Hunt Club
Odd Brother's Club No. 16 and
    No. 33
Okaloosa Hunting &
    FishingClub
Old Dominion Club
Old Hickory Club
Onslow County Improvement
    Association
Order of the Rattlesnake
Ormandsville Loyal Fellowship
    Association
Ouachita Parish Hunting &
    Fishing Club
Our Fishing Club
Pactolus Hunting Club

Paradise N. 115
Paul Revere Historical Society
Pearl River Gun & Rod Club
Pearl River Hunting & Fishing
    Lodge No. 1028
Pee Dee Gun Club
Pender County Improvement
    Association
Pitchett Club
Pin Hook Improvement
    Association
Pine Grove Hunting &
    Fishing Club
Pine Valley Lodge
Pinedale Saddle Club
Pioneer Sportsman Club
Pitt County Christian
    Fellowship Club
Pitt County Improvement
    Association
Poinsettia Unit 101
Pride Sportsman League
Pro-Southerners
Protestant War Veterans of
    America
Quilting Club
R.H. Volunteers of America
Rainbow Club
Ranch Gun Club
Red Bluff Hunting Club
Red River Club
Red Wood Lodge
Richburg Sportsman Club
Riverside Sportsman Club
Roseland Hunting Club
Round Hill Fishing Club
Rowan Sportsman's Club
Roxboro Fishing Club
Sand Hill Hunting Club
Sandhill Stag Club
Santee Sportsman Club
7-11 Sportsman Club
7-1 Club
772 Club
Sneads Ferry Fellowship Club

Sons of Democracy
Sophia Rebels Club
South Hill "85" Club
South Pike Marksmanship
    Association
South Rowan Gun Club
Southern Publicity Bureau
Southlands Sport Club of
    Fair Bluff
Southside Beagle Club
Southside Handcraft Club
Spencer Club
Sports, Inc.
Sportsman Club
Sportsmans Club
Sportsman's Club No. 3
Sportsman's Lakeside Lodge
Stanley Improvement
    Association
Sterlington Hunting &
    Fishing Club
Stonewall Jackson No. 1
Stork Club
Straight Arrow No. 17
Summerfield Fellowship Club
Summerfield Sewing Auxiliary
Sumter Sportsmans Club
Supply Improvement
    Association
Surry County Sportsman Club
Swansboro-White Oak
    Fishing Club
Swartz Hunting & Fishing Club
Tar Heel Development
    Association, Sampson
    County
Taylor Town Hunting Club
Tensas Sportsman Club
Texas Emergency Reserve
Thomasville Brotherhood Club
Tipton County Community
    Center
Top Sail Fishing Association
Town & Country Sportsman
    Club

Trent Community Club
Tri-City Lodge
Tri-County Sportsman Club
Triple Ace Club
Tri-Valley Sportsman Club
Tulls Mill Recreation Club
Turkey Creek Rod & Gun Clkub
211 Pointers Club
Tyrell County Men's Club
United Conservatives of
    Mississippi, Inc., No. 1
United Ladies Club
United Social Club
Varnado Sportsmans Club
Venus Rescue Service
Victoria Hunt Club
Vidalia Sportsman's Club
Virginia Hunting Club No. 1039
Virginia Rod & Gun Club
Wade Hampton Club
Wake Forest Restoration Service
Wa-Lin-Da Beach Club
Wallace Fellowship Club
W-A-M-B-A
Ward 10 Hunting Club
Warren County Improvement
    Association
Warren Women's Improvement
    Association
Warsaw Fellowship Club
Warwick Men's Club
Washington County Fellowship
    Club
Watson Hunting Club
Wayne County Improvement
    Association
Wayne County Sewing Circle
West Carroll Rifleman Club
West Columbia Club
West Duplin Boating &
    Fishing Club
West Melbourne Fellowship
    Club
West Orange Sportsman's
    Lodge No. 7-3

White Caps (1965)
White Citizens of Randolph
White Citizens of Whitsett
White Crusaders for God and
    Country
White Patriots
White People's March for
    Freedom
Wilder's Golf Club
Wildwood Sewing Auxiliary
Wildwood Sportsman Club
Wilkes County Club No. 301
Willow Springs Restoration
    Association
Wills Valley Hunting Club
Wilson County Improvement
    Association
Winfield Hunting &
    Fishing Club
Women's Activity Club
Young Men's Democratic Clubs
Young Men's Social Club

LABOR UNIONS

Congress of Industrial
    Organizations
International Brotherhood of
    Teamsters

NAZI GROUPS

America First Committee
American Nazi Party
Aryan Brotherhood
Aryan Nations
Chico Area National Socialists
Christian Anti-Jewish Party
Columbians, Inc.
German-American Bund
League of St. George
National Alliance
National American Socialist
    Renaissance Party
National Committee to Free
    America from Jewish
    Domination

National Party (Canada)
National Party (USA)
National Renaissance Party
National Socialist League
National Socialist Liberation
    Front
National Socialist Movement
National Socialist Party of
    America
National Socialist
    White People's Party
National Socialist White
    Workers Party
National White Americans Party
Ohio White Nationalist Party
Order, The
People's Movement
S.S. Action Group
Silver Shirts
Social Nationalist Aryan
    Peoples Party
Sons of Liberty
United Nordic Confederation
United White Party
Uptown Rebels
White Man's League

POLITICAL PARTIES

American Conservative Party
American Independent Party
Christian National Party
Commoner Party
Communist Workers Party
Constitution Party of the
    UnitedStates
Constitutional American Party
    of the United States
Populist Party
Progressive Party
States Rights Party

RELIGIOUS GROUPS

Anglos-Saxon Christian
    Congregation
Assembly of Christian Soldiers,
    Inc.

Black Muslims
Church of Jesus Christ Christian
Identity Church Movement
Mountain Church of
    Jesus Christ

National Christian Church
New Christian Crusade Church
Odinist Religion and Nordic
    Faith Movement
Shakers

LIST OF PEOPLE

The List of People includes Klansmen and their allies (including Nazis), those who have opposed the Klan, and victims and targets of the Klan. A list of law enforcement officials and one of public officals involved in the history of the Klan have also been included.

KLANSMEN

Abbott, Thomas
Adams, Dr. Clifford L.
Adams, David
Adams, Ellis
Adams, Kenneth
Adams, Sherman
Ainsworth, Kathryn M.
Aitcheson, William M.
Akin, Bernard
Alexander, Henry
Allen, Gerald
Allen, Rev. Keith
Allison, R.A.
Aloia, Dennis
Ambrose, Rev. F. Halsey
Anderson, Raymond
Anderson, William
Andes, Paul
Annable, Robert
Asher, Court
Atkins, F.W.
Avery, James
Babington, Robert
Bacon, Mary
Badon, Judy
Bailey, Charles
Bailey, Daniel
Bailey, Walter
Bailey, Wesley

Baldwin, William
Ballentine, Donald
Banks, J. Austin
Barnard, Elmo
Barnett, Ethel
Barnett, Lloyd
Barnette, W.C.
Bartlett, Charles
Bass, Fred
Beach, Phillip
Beall, Frank
Beam, Louis
Beckwith, Byron
Behringer, John
Bell, Arthur
Belser, Morgan
Bergeron, Sandra
Betts, Rev. James
Bickley, James
Bicknell, John
Bing, Robert
Birdsong, Billy
Bishop, Ronald
Black, Hugo
Black, Stephen
Black, William
Blessing, William
Bogar, William
Bogart, Joe
Bolen, Aubrey

Bonner, George
Booker, Ray
Borglum, Gutzon
Bossert, Walter
Bowers, Samuel H.
Boyd, James
Braddock, Wilson
Brandenberg, Clarence
Brassell, William
Bratton, Dr. J. Rufus
Britt, Raymond
Britton, Neumann
Broadway, Steve
Brock, John
Brook, Paul
Brooks, Early
Brown, G.T.
Brown, Harry
Brown, Jack
Brown, John
Brunson, R.J.
Bryant, George
Bryant, Joseph
Bryant, L.D.
Buckles, Billy
Buckley, Travis
Burros, Dan
Burton, Benjamin
Bush, Uriah
Bush, Wilson
Butterworth, Wallace
Byrd, Allen and Bobby
Byrd, Douglas
Cabiness, H.D.
Caffee, A.E.
Cagle, Charles
Caho, Steven
Caldwell, Lester
Callaway, Caleb
Campbell, Dennis
Campbell, Rev. Samuel
Cannon, Jack
Carlock, Rev. Richard
Carpenter, Rev. C.N.
Carr, Emmett

Carr, G.E.
Carroll, C.E.
Carter, Asa
Caudle, Roy
Chambliss, Robert
Chaney, William
Chase, L.W.
Cheney, Turner
Chopper, Phillip
Christians, George
Christmas, Charles
Church, William
Clanton, James
Clark, Walter
Clarke, Edward
Coburn, William
Cochran, Paul
Cockrill, Harrison
Cody, James
Coker, Billy
Coker, James
Coker, Rocky
Cole, Rev. James
Coleman, Bill
Coleman, Tom
Colescott, James
Coley, Sandy
Collier, Clarence
Collier, Ralph
Collins, Robert
Comer, James
Comer, Robbie
Compton, Dr. William
Constantineau, Richard
Converse, Frank
Cooksey, Alton
Corkern, Virgil
Cothran, Donald
Craig, Calvin
Cranford, Raymond
Crawford, John
Creekmore, Ricky
Creel, Robert
Cribbs, Charles
Crodser, W.H.

Cross, Donald
Cross, William
Crowe, James
Crowe, William
Cummins, Eli
Daniel, William
Davidson, Robert
Daview, Elmer
Davis, James
Davis, Roy
Davis, William
Dawson, Edward
Day, Robert
Dayvault, Wayne
Deatherage, George
Deese, Charles
Demarest, Horace
Dennis, Rev. Delmar
De Rosier, Harvey
Dibrell, G.G.
Dickerson, Lester
DiSalvo, Louis
Distel, Albert
Dixon, W. Lloyd
Doerfler, Rev. Raymond
Downs, Tommy
Drager, Frank
Drennan, William
Droege, Walter
DuBois, Joseph
DuBose, Dudley
Duke, David
Dunaway, Hilton
Dunaway, Hulon
Duncan, Dr. Amos
Duncan, Murphy
Dunning, M.O.
Durham, Plato
Dutton, Jerry
Earle, Joshua
Eaton, William
Echlin, Raymond
Edwards, Eldon
Edwards, James
Edwards, Xavier

Effinger, V.F.
Ellington, Doyle
Ellis, Dr. A.D.
Ellis, Claiborne
Elrod, Milton
Elwood, Charles
Emmons, Pat
Esdale, James
Etheridge, Paul
Evans, Dr. Hiram
Faggard, Jesse
Fallaw, Eunice
Farmer, Saxon
Farnsworth, Eugene
Faulkner
Felker, William
Fields, Dr. Edward
Fogel, Richard
Folendore, Thomas
Folks, Warren
Foreman, Gene
Foreman, Wilburn
Forrest, Nathan B.
Forrest, Nathan B., III
Foster, Paul
Fowler, William
Fox, Philip
Frankhouser, Roy
Fraser, J.E.
Frolich, James
Frost, Jonathan
Fuller, Edward
Fussell, Joseph
Gaille, Gordon
Garcia, George
Garner, Joe
Gaston, Frank
Gause, C.L.
Gayer, Dr. E.W.
Gholson, Samuel
Gifford, Fred
Gilbert, Ernest
Gilliam, Harry
Gilliam, Verlin
Gillis, Sterling

Gipson, John
Girgenti, Gladys
Glover, Nicholas
Glover, Robert
Gollub, Jordan
Gordon, George
Gordon, John
Grady, Henry A.
Grady, Henry W.
Grady, Joe
Grantham, Jack
Green, Dr. Samuel
Green, Samuel, Jr.
Griffin, Barton
Griffin, Virgil
Griffin, William
Guest, Herbert
Gulledge, Rev. A.H.
Gullion, Steward
Gustiatus, Bernard
Haggard, Rev. A.A.
Hall, Eugene
Hall, John
Hamby, Boyd
Hamilton, James
Hamilton, Thomas
Hammond, C.R.
Hampton, Stephen
Hancock, W.C.
Hand, B.J.
Hand, Karl
Handley, Roger
Hanley, James
Harold, Dr. C.L.
Harper, James
Harper, Julius
Harper, Ronnie
Harris, David
Harris, Jim
Harrison, Andrew
Harrison, McCord
Harry, James
Hart, Emmett
Hartley, A.I.
Harvey, Flynn

Harwood, Brown
Hawkins, Joe Daniel
Hawkins, Joe Denver
Hawkins, Dr. John
Hawkins, Lester
Hays, Bennie
Head, Daniel
Helm, Jack
Henderson, Jerris
"Hendrix, James"
Hendrix, William
Henry, R.L.
Henson, Don
Henson, Everett
Heredeen, H.H.
Herrington, A.C.
Higgins, George
Hightower, A.C.
Hill, H.G.
Hinshaw, Donald
Hodges, Robert
Hoff, William
Holcombe, Earl
Holden, Pete
Holder, James
Holland, Charles
Holland, David
Horn, Rev. Alvin
Horton, Rev. Jack
Howard, John
Howarth, Charles
Hoyt, Sharida
Huffington, Joe
Humphries, J.H.
Hunnicutt, John
Hunter, Dean
Hutto, Jimmy
Ingle, Harry
Jackson, Andrew
Jacobs, Lloyd
Jacobs, Marvin
James, Charles
Jarvis, Thomas
Johnson, Donald
Johnson, Richard

Johnston, Rev. Evall
Joiner, Lloyd
Jones, Calvin
Jones, H.H.
Jones, H.J.
Jones, Hamilton
Jones, Iredell
Jones, James
Jones, Kenneth
Jones, Tom
Juday, Robert
Kelly, Roger
Kelso, David
Kennedy, John B.
Kerr, John
Kersey, Jason
Kersey, Richard
Kidd, W.J.
Killen, Edgar
Kimble, Jules
Kimbro, George
Kinard, William
King, Cecil
King, L.J.
Kleist, John
Klipoth, Seth
Knox, James
Korman, Robert
Lackey, Gordon
Lacoste, Rene
Lambright, Oddist
Lane, David
Langley, Sara
LaRicci, Tony
Lea, John
Leazer, Donald
Ledford, David
Lee, Ellis
Lee, H.D.
Lee, Henry
Lee, Howard
Leland, Bobby
Leonard, Arthur
Lester, John
Lewallyn, Cecil

Lewis, Charles
Lewis, Howard
Lindsay, Jim
Livingston, William
Locke, Dr. John
Lollar, Coleman
Long, Jacob
Lumpkin, James
Lundahl, Bjoern
Lutterloh, Thomas
Lutterman, Harry
Luttrell, Roy
Lyle, J. Banks
Lynch, Charles
Lynch, Woodrow
Lyons, Robert
McAfee, Leroy
McBride, J.R.
McCall, Herschel
McCauley, John
McCollum, Stanley
McCord, Frank
McCorkle, Albert
McCullough, Charles
McDaniel, Edward
McGhee, Rev. Charles
McGriff, Colbert
McKellar, Kenneth
McKinney, James
McKoin, Dr. B.M.
McMennamy, T.J.
McNaught, Dr. C.E.
McNeely, George
McPahil, Royce
McRae, Dandridge
Maddox, Charles
Mahoney, Dr. William
Maitton, Horace
Mann, Arthur
Manucy, Holsted
Mars, Grady
Martin, James
Martin, Murray
Martz, Louis
Massengale, Pat

Means, Rice
Mendosa, Michael
Meriwether, Minor
Mettert, Larry
Metzger, Tom
Milam, Dennis
Miles, Robert
Miles, Uriel
Miller, Emmett
Miller, George
Miller, Glenn
Miller, Horace
Miller, William
Milliken, Carl
Mills, Raymond
Milteer, Joseph
Mims, Cecil
Miner, Roy
Minton, Will
Mitchell, Gerhart
Mitchell, John
Mixon, O.C.
Moore, Dr. John
Moore, Roger
Morgan, John
Morgan, M. Wesley
Morgan, P.L.
Morley, Clarence
Morris, Houston
Morris, William
Morrison, Aaron
Morton, Ernest
Mueller, L.A.
Muldrow, H.L.
Murphy, Matthew
Murphy, Robert
Murray, Harold
Myers, Cecil
Naimaster, Vernon
Nalls, Rev. L.A.
Nance, Silas
Neal, Coy
Neason, John
Nelson, Scott
New, Fred

Newberry, James
Nix, Deavours
Nix, Sybil
Orbison, Charles
Orwich, William
Osborn, Clyde
Ostwalt, Farrell
Otwell, B.G.
Otto, George
Ouzts, Thurman
Overton, Harold
Owens, Larry
Oxford, James
Page, Hubert
Parker, C.L.
Parker, Ernest
Parker, Lewis
Pate, Alton
Payne, Larry
Pecoraro, Clara
Peden, Alonzo
Pedigo, Amos
Pepper, George
Perkins, DeForest
Perkins, W.O.
Perry, J.W.
Peterson, Eric
Pettie, Virgil
Pettus, Edmund
Phillips, Denver
Pickett, A.C.
Pierce, Paul
Pike, Albert
Pitts, Billy
Porter, William
Poter, Olaf
Pottle, E.H.
Powell, Luther
Prins, Jack
Pruitt, Dr. E.P.
Pryor, Ralph
Puckett, Charles
Pyle, Henry
Ramsey, H.C.
Randolph, Ryland

Redwine, Clifford
Reed, John
Reed, Richard
Reisner, Harvey
Rester, Robert
Reusch, Dale
Reynolds, Edwin
Reynolds, James
Riccio, Bill
Rich, Sam
Riddlehoover, Charles
Ridley, Rev. Caleb
Rittenhouse, D.M.
Robinson, Coy
Rogers, John
Rogers, Walter
Roper, Samuel
Rosecrans, William
Rosenberg, Jimmy
Rotella, Frank
Roton, Ralph
Rowley, Ewell
Saddler, Tom
Sartin, Bennie
Saucier, Jack
Savage, Fred
Savina, Richard
Schenck, David
Schoonmaker, Earl
Schreffler, Frederick
Scoggin, Robert
Scott, Luther
Scott, Parkie
Sessum, Cecil
Sexton, Melvin
Shaffer, H.F.
Shaver, Robert
Shaw, Rev. Herbert
Shaw, Ian
Shearhouse, I.T.
Shelton, Robert
Shepard, Dr. William
Sherer, Mark
Shotwell, Randolph
Sickles, Charles

Silva, Frank
Simkins, W.S.
Simmons, William
Sims, Joseph
Skipper, Billy
Skipworth, J.K.
Sligh, George
Smith, Frederick
Smith, Jerry
Smith, John
Smith, Randall
Smith, Ray
Smithers, Dan
Snelson, Earl
Spears, Rev. James
Spinks, Lycurgus
Stapleton, Ben
Starling, Jacob
Stephens, Ed
Stephens, Thomas
Stephens, David
Stoball, George
Stoddard, Lothrop
Stokes, Wila
Stoner, Jack
Stoner, Jesse
Strayer, Rev. John
Strickland, Carey
Strickland, Paul
Strickland, Rev. Perry
Strudwick, Frederick
Styles, Hal
Summer, W.A.
Swenson, John
Swift, Wesley
Tackett, Elmer
Tarrants, Thomas
Taylor, Edgar
Taylor, Gilbert
Taylor, Ken
Taylor, John
Terbeck, Donald
Terry, Charles
Terwillinger, Lew
Thomas, Eugene

Thomas, Robert
Thompson, H. Roswell
Thompson, Robert
Thronhill, J. Emmett
Thrash, Marshall
Titus, Rev. George
Tracy, N.H.
Trosper, Don
Tucker, Gary
Turner, George Hampton
Tuttle, Douglas
Udgreen, Arthur
Upchurch, Z.R.
Vail, Vernon
Vance, Zebulon
Venable, James
Vernado, Devan
Vittur, Cliff
Wagner, Daniel
Walker, John
Walker, Morris
Wallace, Charles
Walraven, Gerald
Walton, Dale
Warner, James
Watkins, Orville
Weakland, Alfred
Weaver, Gerald
Webster, Clyde
West, Gene
Wheat, G. Clinton
White, Edward
White, Robert
White, Steven
Whitehead, Tom
Wiley, Frank
Wilkins, Collie
Wilkins, Fred
Wilkinson, Elbert ("Bill")
Williams, Bill
Williams, Furman
Williams, George
Williams, Joseph
Williams, W.J.
Wilson, Billy

Wilson, Charles
Wilson, Fred
Wilson, Paul
Wilson, William
Winter, Paul
Witte, Eloise
Woldanski, Paul
Woodle, Roy
Woods, Woodrow
Wydner, David
Xavier, Peter
York, James
Young, Royal
Young, S. Glenn
Yount, James

KLAN ASSOCIATES AND ALLIES

Aiken, D. Wyatt
Allen, Marilyn
Allen, Michael
Andrew, Dr. John
Angell, R.H.
Bagwell, Robert
Barker, Frank
Barnes, Sidney
Bassett, John
Baxter, C.M.
Benjamin, Rev. Dale
Bentcliffe, Howard
Bishop, Ann
Black, Jerrold
Bowles, Bryant
Branham, Billy
Bright, George
Brooks, Henry
Brown, Robert
Brown, T.A.
Brown, Walter
Bruce, Daniel
Bruce, Melvin
Bryant, John
Carmack, Barnie
Carroll, Joseph
Cash, Jack

Chase, William
Cobb, Alvin
Cole, Arthur
Corley, Luther
Cowan, Frederick
Cowan, Mrs. Peter
Crommelin, John
Croom, Henry
Crowder, H.L.
Crump, Richard
Culbert, James
Davis, Phil
DeBlanc, Alcibiade
Dennett, Daniel
DePugh, Robert
Dixon, Thomas
Dommer, Paul
Dormer, William
Dorsett, George
Drennan, Dr. Stanley
Dupes, Ned
Emry, Sheldon
Euliss, Eli
Fields, Dolores
Franklin, Joseph
Gale, William
Garland, William
Garvey, Marcus
Greaves, Elmore
Greene, Jerry
Griffin, Kenneth
Hanes, Arthur
Harrell, John
Hensley, Don
Jackson, Helen
Jones, Bob
Kahl, Gordon
Kanger, Thomas
Kasper, John
Kennedy, Jesse
Kurts, Daniel
Lauderdale, E.A.
Lewandoski, Ralph
Linderman, Frank
Luthardt, Charles

Mabry, H.P.
McClellan, James
McCorvey, Thomas
McGinley, Conde
McMichael, Obed
Mann, F. Allen
Manness, David
Miller, William
Mohr, Gordon
Moseley, George
Mower, Dennis
Munroe, A.
Patterson, James
Potito, Rev. Oren
Ray, Jerry
Rhody, Robert
Robinson, James
Rogers, Louis
Rucker, Elza
Russell, Katherine
Saufley, William
Sawyer, B.F.
Scaife, Dorothy
Shuler, Rev. A.C.
Sisente, Robert
Slaughter, G.H.
Smith, Bob
Smith, Gerald
Snell, Richard
Stanley, David
Thomas, William
Tucker, Rev. Buddy
Turner, Josiah
Tyler, Elizabeth
Vicks, Raymond
Walker, Edwin
Watson, Thomas
Whatley, Andrew
White, Alma
Wickstrom, James
Williams, Eldred
Williams, Londell and Tammy
Winrod, Gordon

KLAN OPPONENTS

Atkins, J.W.
Beckerman, Milton
Bellesen, Paul
Berry, Isaac
Beveridge, Albert
Brown, Rev. Kenneth
Carpenter, J.B.
Carter, W. Horace
Catterson, Robert
Cole, Willard
Dees, Morris
Faris, John
Fuller, Alfred
Gayman, Dan
Gibson, Leroy
Good, Jona
Gorman, J.C.
Hamilton, John
Harris, Julian
Imperiale, Anthony
Isbell, Joey
Jenkins, Jay
Johnson, Thomas
Jones, William
Kennedy, Stetson
King, George
Lindsey, Ben
McGill, Ralph
Melton, Quimby
Pearson, Drew
Philpott, Tom
Rose, E.M.
Seawell, Malcolm
Smith, Hazel
Thompson, Jerry
Tolliver, Ken
Treadway, F.N.
Vincent, Robert
West, J.W.
White, William
Williams, Robert
Zumbrunn, William

KLAN VICTIMS OR TARGETS

Aaron, Edward
Aaron, Ralph
Abrams, Morris
Addison, Joseph
Albright, William R.
Alexander, Jack
Allen, Sarah
Allen, Thomas
Allen, W.L.
Alston, James
Anderson, Bob
Arnell, Samuel
Ashburn, George
Ayer, Dr. Benjamin
Bailey, S.G.
Baker, Rev. James
Banks, Parks
Barker, E.G.
Barmore, Seymour
Bellows, Jim
Bentley, Emerson
Berg, Alan
Bergman, Walter
Bermanzohn, Dr. Paul
Berry, Mrs. Reaner
Best, H.D.
Bettis, Frank
Bigby, Herman
Biggerstaff, Aaron
Billups, Rev. Charles
Blackburn, W. Jasper
Blackford, William
Blumberg, Ralph
Boney, Leslie
Bowland, Walter
Boyd, Alexander
Boykin, Albert
Brewster, Willie
Brigan, Bill
Briley, Corine
Brinson, Willie
Brode, Fred
Brooks, James
Brown, Anderson

Brown, Ben
Brown, Dewitt
Brown, Mary
Brown, P. Rayfield
Brownlee, R. Wiley
Bryant, Charles
Bryant, Curtis
Burk, William
Burke, Rev. Richard
Burton, Irene
Burton, Pierce
Bussie, Victor
Byrd, Lillie
Byrd, Theon
Cabe, Brigido
Carey, Tim
Carey, Wilson
Cargell, Robert
Cathcart, Andrew
Champion, William
Charlton, Judge
Chase, Valentine
Choutteau, Dr. Gerard
Clarke, Charles
Clink, John
Cokely, Warren
Colby, Abram
Cole, Nat
Coleman, Guilford
Coleman, John
Coleman, William
Coley, John
Colgrove, O.R.
Collier, Charles
Collins, Addie Mae
Coney, Allen
Corliss, Alonzo
Crossland, M.P.
Cruell, Claude
Culbertson, Kirk
Culbreath, Lee
Curry, Rev. Michael
Curtis, Archie
Dahmer, Vernon
Dale, Arthur
Daniels, Jonathan

Dannons, Jake
Daponte, Dorothy
Darden, Dr. G.O.
D'Avy, Francois
Deason, Matt
Dee, Henry
Delaine, Rev. Joseph
Dennis, William
Dickinson, John
Diggs, Frank
Dollar, William
Donald, Michael
Dorman, Michael
Dove, Oscar
Drake, Clinton
Drennon, Thomas
Duckworth, Kaley
Dudley, Willie
Dunlap, J.C.
Dupree, Jack
Eager, Scipio
Edwards, Willie
Eilbeck, Ivan
Elduayan, Fidel
Ellington, Clarence
Ellison, Viola
Eubanks, Goldie
Evans, Lela
Evers, Charles
Evers, Medgar
Ferrel, Anderson
Finlayson, Dr. John
Fitzgerald, Charlie
Fitzpatrick, Henry
Fleishman, Samuel
Flournoy, Robert
Flowers, Evergreen
Floyd Esther
Foley, Albert
Folsom, Constance
Ford, Benton
Fortune, Emanuel
Foster, Anthony
Foster, Robert
Fowler, Wallace

Franklin, James
French, Peggy
Frost, L.S.
Fullerlove, Robert
Gallagher, John
Gappins, Mary
Garner, Artis
Garrett, D.B.
Gaston, A.G.
Gaston, Ike
Genobles, John
Gibson, W.H.
Gilliam, George
Glymph, C.L.C.
Good, Charles
Goodman, Flo
Goodman, Jessie
Gore, J.C.
Gould, Barbara
Grainger, Ben
Gregory, C.E.
Griffin, Spencer
Gunn, Dr. Howard
Gupton, Wilbur
Gutter, Booker
Hall, Rev. Enell
Hall, Maxine
Hall, Sam
Hamilton, Bill
Hamm, Willie
Harkey, Ira
Harris, Essic
Harris, R.E.
Harrison, W.H.
Harvey, Joseph
Hayling, Dr. Robert
Haynes, A.J.
Hays, Brooks
Hays, Charles
Hendricks, Charles
Hernandes, Harriet
High, Zeke
Hill, Elias
Hinds, James
Hines, Clifford

Hines, Tommy
Holliday, J.R.
Holt, Caswell
Holt, Sallie
Houston, George
Howle, William
Huggins, Allen
Huie, William
Humphries, Ban
Hurst, Charlie
Hutchins, Guy
Inge, Benjamin
Jackson, Matthew
Jackson, Opal
Jackson, Robert
Jackson, Wharlest
Jeffers, Perry
Jeter, Columbus
Johnson, Dr. A.M.
Johnson, E.G.
Johnson, Katherine
Johnson, Willis
Johnson, Woodrow
Joiner, Nelson
Jones, Warren
Jordan, Otis
Justice, James
Kelly, W.A.
Kent, Rev. Grady
King, A.D.
King, Dr. Martin Luther
Lakin, Rev. A.S.
Lane, Daniel
Lange, Otto
Langston, Dorothy
Lee, Roger
Lee, Rufus
Leech, Alex
Lentz, B.
Liuzzo, Viola
Logan, George
Lowther, Henry
Lucy, Autherine
Luke, William
McBride, Cornelius

McDanal, Mrs. Hugh
McGrone, Frank
McNair, Denise
Mallard, Robert
Marshlar, Steve
Martin, James
Martin, Jim
Mason, Simpson
Massel, Sam
Matthews, J.L.
Matthews, Otis
Meadows, William
Mendez-Ruiz, Juan
Metcalfe, George
Miglionico, Nina
Miller, Jacob
Mills, Letty
Mixon, Fred
Moore, Charles
Moore, Clayton
Moore, Harry
Moore, Jere
Moore, O'Neal
Mulligan, E.
Munsell, Charles
Nance, James
Nodine, John
Norman, Frank
Nussbaum, Perry
Oberholtzer, Madge
O'Berry, Clarence
Odom, Willie
Outlaw, Wyatt
Pace, Rev. Edward
Page, Alec
Parker, Albert
Parnell, Beverly
Patterson, Rev. Joe
Peck, James
Peek, James
Penn, Lemuel
Perrin, Wade
Perry, Samuel
Philpot, Kate
Pope, Henry

Potts, "Preacher"
Powell, Rev. Eugene
Powell, Mrs. Lewis
Puryear, William
Quinn, Aylene
Randolph, B.F.
Reeb, Rev. James
Richardson, Alfred
Robinson, Dorsey
Robinson, Will
Rogers, Calvin
Rogers, Ernest and Christine
Ross, Mike
Roundtree, Tom
Schwerner, Michael
Sellers, Clayton
Seward, William
Shepard, Rev. Bruce
Shepard, M.L.
Sheppard, Rev. Clifford
Shoemaker, Joseph
Shores, Arthur
Short, Rev. Jimmy
Shropshire, Wesley
Shuttlesworth, Rev. Fred
Sibley, J.D.
Simmons, Samuel
Sinclair, Joyce
Smith, David
Smith, George
Smith, Woodrow
Stallworth, Clarke
Stephens, John
Stewart, Aleck
Stovall, Bill
Studdard, Elizabeth
Surratt, Jackson
Thompson, Rev. Donald
Tippins, Bill
Toney, Pierce
Trawick, Paul
Turner, Abram
Turner, George
Turner, Porter
Tyson, Lee

Van Loon, Rev. Oren
Varnado, Jerry
Vincent, Willie
Wamble, Abraham
Ware, James
Ware, Jordan
Washington, Hugh
Watkins, Jack
Watley, Smith
Weir, James
Wesley, Cynthia
Wheeler, Stephen
White, Ben
White, Marlin
Williams, Allen
Williams, Franklin
Williams, Jim
Winfield, Roosevelt
Winsmith, Dr. John
Womack, Melvin
Woods, Jim
Wright, Anderson
Wright, Greer
Wright, William
Wyatt, William

LAW ENFORCEMENT OFFICERS
Baker, Wilson
Barnes, Sidney
Blackwell, Leo
Buchanan, Bob
Butler, George
Chisolm, W.W.
Clark, James
Connor, Theophilus ("Bull")
Cook, Thomas
Davis, L.O.
Edwards, Charles
Eidson, Herb
Goodwin, Charles
Grimsley, James
Guy, George
Heath, Donald
Huett, Joseph

Keeton, Ward
Kennard, Adam
Lingo, Albert
Littlejohn, Frank
Logan, B.F.
Lynch, John
McCall, Willis
Miller, Wallace
Millis, Marion
Murray, Albert
Nash, "Trigger"
Nigus, David
Norris, John
Patrick, N.W.
Peden, Bryant
Plogger, William
Price, Cecil
Rainey, Lawrence
Raley, John
Robinson, J.T.
Rogers, Leslie
Rowe, Gary
Sadewhite, Michael
Scarborough, W.W.
Semet, Ernest
Stanton, Richard
Stephens, Robert
Stirewalt, John
Taylor, Woodford
Webb, J.S.
West, Thomas
Willis, Richard
Young, Alex

NAZIS
Allen, Karl
Alt, Ed
Brannen, Robert
Burford, James
Burros, Robert
Butler, Richard
Carlson, Gerald
Collin, Frank
Covington, Harold
Cutler, Bud

Dorr, David
Dunn, Edward
Erlanger, Alezi
Forbes, Ralph
Fry, Mrs. Leslie
Gilbert, Keith
Grimstad, William
Hunt, Harold
Jones, Arthur
Kerr, Martin
Kuhn, Fritz
Lauck, Gary
Madole, James
Mason, James
Matthews, Robert
Patler, John
Pelley, William
Phelps, Coy
Pierce, William
Pires, Robert
Rockwell, George
Roeder, Manfred
Rust, David
Scutari, Richard
Smythe, Edward
Spisak, Frank
Tate, David
Tomassi, Joseph
Veh, Russell
Vincent, Allen
Warthen, Perry
Weber, Mark

PUBLIC OFFICIALS

Adkins, Joseph
Allen, Henry
Allen, James
Allen, Marion
Arnall, Ellis
Arnold, Luke
Baker, George
Barnett, Ross
Baxley, William
Beasley, Jere

Bilbo, Theodore
Boutwell, Albert
Bowles, Charles
Brady, Philip
Brewster, Ralph
Brownlow, William
Bucklew, Henry
Burbank, W.J.
Burns, Haydon
Byrd, Robert
Campbell, Philip
Carlin, Gen. W.P.
Carter, James Earl
Clayton, Powell
Colgrove, D.D.
Cox, Harold
Davis, John
Dennis, L.G.
Drake, C.L.
Duke, Dan
Duvall, John
Everett, R.O.
Faubus, Orval
Flowers, Richmond
Folson, James
Godwin, H.L.
Goodwin, Mills
Graham, Royal
Graves, Bibb
Hall, C.G.
Harding, Warren
Heflin, Thomas
Holden, William
Jackson, Ed
Johnson, Frank
Johnson, Lyndon
Johnson, Paul
Johnson, Rivers
Jones, Clayton
Kubli, K.K.
McAdoo, William
McCall, Charles
McRae, Thomas
Maddox, Lester
Mayfield, Earl

Mitchell, Parren
Patterson, John
Paulen, Ben
Peterson, Jim
Rarick, John
Rawls, Louis
Richardson, Friend
Rivers, E.D.
Rowbottom, Harry
Russell, Richard
Smith, Alfred
Steck, Daniel
Talmadge, Eugene
Talmadge, Herman
Truman, Harry
Underwood, Oscar
Walker, Clifford
Wallace, George
Waller, William
Waring, J. Waites
Warren, Fuller
Waters, H. Franklin

AARON, EDWARD ("JUDGE")

A black victim of Klan violence, Aaron was abducted from a Birmingham, Alabama, streetcorner on September 2, 1957, by members of Asa Carter's Original Ku Klux Klan of the Confederacy. (His abductors were also members of the local Citizens' Council.) The kidnappers included Joe Pritchett, exalted cyclops of the klavern; Grover McCullough; John Griffin; William Miller, recently appointed a Klan "captain" by Carter; Jesse Mabry, klabee and one of those who assaulted singer Nat "King" Cole in 1956; and newcomer Bart Floyd. Driven to the unit's "lair" near Chalkville, Aaron was castrated with a razor blade, his severed scrotum preserved by the Klansmen as evidence of their "achievement." Dumped beside a rural highway, Aaron nearly died from loss of blood before a motorist discovered him and drove him to a nearby hospital. In custody, Griffin and Miller turned state's evidence against their comrades and escaped with terms of probation. Upon conviction of mayhem, Pritchett, McCullogh, Mabry, and Floyd each drew twenty-year prison terms, exhausting their appeals late in 1959. Alabama law requires inmates to serve ten years or one third of their sentence, whichever is shorter, and in 1960 the state parole board ruled that the Klansmen would have to serve a full one third of their time—six years and eight months—before they were considered for parole. However, with the election of Governor George Wallace in 1962, the four got preferential treatment. The parole board's 1960 decision was reversed in July 1963, two weeks after Wallace's first appointee joined the panel. Mabry was released in February 1964, the others in 1965. [42]

AARON, RALPH

A Jewish resident of Paxton, Illinois, Aaron was abducted from his home by Klansmen in August 1924 and branded with the letters "KKK." [*NYT* 1924]

ABBOTT, THOMAS

A "martyr" for the Klan in the 1920s, Abbott was shot and killed in a riot in Carnegie, Pennsylvania, in September 1923. Marching through the heavily Catholic community in defiance of a mayoral restraining order, Klansmen were met by a mob armed with stones, clubs, and firearms. Abbott died in the first volley, and his "sacrifice" was memorialized in a Klan pamphlet, *The Martyred Klansman*. [10]

ABRAMS, MORRIS

As president of the American Jewish Committee, Morris was marked for assassination in 1965 by a Klan faction that called itself "The Secret Six." FBI agents discovered the conspiracy and prevented it by warning Abrams in advance. [33]

ACTION

In 1966 the House Un-American Activities Committee identified Action as a front group for the Galveston, Texas, klavern, United Klans of America. [38]

ADAMIC KNIGHTS OF THE KU KLUX KLAN

A small, violence-prone splinter group based in Maryland, the Adamic Knights was exposed for the first time on May 21, 1981, when U.S. Treasury agents staged coordinated raids on Klan hangouts in Maryland, Pennsylvania, Delaware, and New Jersey. Leader Charles Sickles, one of ten persons arrested in the sweep, was held on federal firearms charges in connection with an alleged conspiracy to bomb a Baltimore NAACP office. Several Klansmen were sentenced to prison, and the Adamic Knights had disappeared by the time the Anti-Defamation League published a new list of Klan factions in 1983. [2]

ADAMS, DR. CLIFFORD LEROY

A Klansman and prominent physician in Suwanee County, Florida, Adams was shot and killed in his office on August 3, 1952. His assailant, Ruby McCollum, was a black woman who was believed to be his secret lover and the mother of his illegitimate child. Recently elected to the state senate but not yet sworn in, Adams had promised patronage jobs to various supporters in the Klan, and Klansmen were enraged by his death. With threats of lynching in the air, "moderate" Klansmen in mufti patrolled the streets to "keep things quiet," and local police asked Klansman LaVergne Blue, a close friend of Adams, to show himself on the streets in the interest of peace. [41]

ADAMS, DAVID

In the summer of 1975, Adams was identified as the leader of the Decatur, Illinois, klavern, United Klans of America.[43]

ADAMS, ELLIS

A member of the Reconstruction KKK in Warren County, Georgia, Adams was implicated in the stabbing of a black man and various other crimes in 1868. On May 10, 1869, he was identified as the gunman who murdered Joseph Adkins, a Republican state senator, near Dearing, Georgia. He was never apprehended for that crime, and died in a shootout in December 1869. [87]

ADAMS, HUGH LYNN

See *Miller, Emmett.*

ADAMS, KENNETH

A resident of Anniston, Alabama, and a longtime Klansman, Adams was part of the group that assaulted singer Nat "King" Cole during a 1956 performance in Birmingham. Subpoenaed by federal authorities after one of the CORE Freedom Ride buses was burned outside Anniston in May 1961, Adams took the Fifth Amendment on advice from KKK attorney J.B. Stoner. Indicted along with eight others in that case, Adams won a directed verdict of acquittal, based on insufficient evidence, on November 3, 1961. In November 1963, Adams was described by National States Rights Party activist Joseph Milteer as "a mean damn man" and "one of the hard-core of the underground," desired as a recruit for Milteer's Constitutional American Party of the United States. On July 15, 1965, Adams shared the stage at an Anniston NSRP rally with Stoner and racist orator Connie Lynch; a short time after the rally, Willie Brewster, a black man, was shot and killed by white gunmen. One of the defendants in that case was a friend and employee of Adams. After quitting the Klan, Adams became head of the Anniston NSRP chapter. In 1965, he was charged with receiving explosives that had been stolen by James Roberts from the nearby Ft. McClellan army base, but a jury acquitted him on January 21, 1966. [NYT 1961, 1965; FOF 1966]

ADAMS, SHERMAN

As Kentucky grand dragon for the United Klans of America, Adams led an unauthorized parade of 260 robed Klansmen through Shepherdsville on

July 3, 1976. The parade was allowed to proceed, despite the lack of permits, since Klansmen outnumbered the local police force. On August 15, 1976, three masked horsemen led several hundred Klansmen on another march through the Louisville suburb of Okolona, a hotbed of white antibusing sentiment. Adams told newsmen that the march was held to demonstrate support for police and the U.S. Constitution. In March 1977, Adams was one of eleven Kentucky Klansmen indicted for staging a private drug raid during a teenage party held in a trailer. During the course of the raid, fifteen to twenty armed men, several wearing ski masks, kicked in the door and herded guests into a back bedroom, warning, "If somebody comes out, you'll be sorry." The raiders, who boasted they were Klansmen, ransacked the trailer and sprayed graffiti on the ceiling and walls before leaving. [NYT 1976; 84]

ADAMS, WALTON

See *Bigby, Herman.*

ADAMS COUNTY CIVIC & BETTERMENT ASSOCIATION

A 1967 report of the House Un-American Activities Committee identified this group as a cover for Natchez, Mississippi, Unit No. 719, United Klans of America. [38]

ADDISON, JOSEPH

A target of the Reconstruction Klan in Georgia, Addison was fired on, and the lives of his family were threatened, because he voted the Republican ticket. [93]

ADKINS, JOSEPH

A Republican state senator in Reconstruction Georgia, Adkins joined his colleagues by visiting Washington, D.C., in spring 1869 to report on Klan terror in his state. Returning home, he was ambushed and killed near Dearing, Georgia, by Klansman Ellis Adams, whom Adkins had reported to the law for stabbing a black man the previous year. [87]

ADVOCATE, THE

A Jackson, Mississippi, newspaper, *The Advocate* was targeted for KKK harassment in December 1981 and January 1982. Klansmen fired thirty-two shots into the paper's office during December 1981, returning a month later to fire eighty-four rounds at the building. Several Klansmen were arrested after the second attack, one of whom complained that the editors "had written some articles about myself and some friends." [NYT 1982]

AIKEN, D. WYATT

A prominent Reconstruction Democrat in Abbeville County, South Carolina, and later a congressman and leader of the South Carolina Grange movement. Aiken openly instigated Klan violence, including public advocacy of killing Republican state legislators. [87]

AINSWORTH, KATHRYN MADLYN

A Mississippi housewife and fifth grade teacher who once angrily protested the assignment of a black girl to her class, Ainsworth was also a nightriding member of the KKK. Her involvement in Klan violence led to her death during a shootout with police in Meridian, Mississippi, on June 30, 1968. With companion Thomas Tarrants, she was attempting to bomb the home of a Jewish businessman when police sprang a trap and gunfire erupted. In Ainsworth's purse detectives found an automatic pistol and membership cards for the United Klans of America and the Original Knights of the KKK. Papers recovered from her home indicated that she had also joined the White Knights of the KKK and the Americans for Preservation of the White Race. Other literature retrieved from the house included Minutemen survival manuals and issues of the National States Rights Party newspaper. Ainsworth's husband admitted knowing about her Klan membership, but claimed ignorance about any involvement of hers in terrorism. Tarrants, from his prison cell, described her as "a real worthwhile human being who was just misguided." [84]

AITCHESON, WILLIAM MARX

A student at the University of Maryland, Aitcheson was also a member of the Maryland Knights of the KKK until December 1976, when he led thirty to forty other members in defecting to form a rival splinter group. Aitcheson became exalted cyclops of the new Robert E. Lee Klavern in that group, and his move was followed by a rash of cross burnings and threats in the Maryland suburbs of Washington, D.C. In March 1977, he spoke at a Klan rally with Grand Dragon Tony LaRicci, saying

> We're going to have a little Bolshevik America unless we keep our powder dry, clean our weapons, and get ready to go into the streets. I tell you something. You got this robe, but it don't mean a thing unless you've got something to back it up. I mean a good weapon, a rifle, a good pistol. And ammunition . . . thousands of rounds, not hundreds. The next war is going to be a big one and it's going to last a long time. The only way this country can ever revive its laws, can ever revive the laws of God, is going to be through violence.

Aitcheson later sent a threatening letter to Coretta King ("Stay off the University of Maryland campus or you will die") and burned a cross on campus in conjunction with her scheduled appearance. Police discovered twenty-five identifiable fingerprints on the letter, which led to Aitcheson's arrest and confiscation of weapons—including nine pounds of black powder—at his home. Aitcheson was also charged in a string of incidents dating from the spring of 1976, including six cross burnings and the manufacturing of explosives without a license. Police suspected him of plotting to bomb the local NAACP office and communications facilities at Ft. Meade, but no charges were filed due to lack of evidence. On September 7, 1977, Aitcheson pled guilty to threatening Coretta King and was sentenced to ninety days in the Federal Treatment Facility at Springfield, Missouri. He also pled guilty in state court on two counts of cross burning and manufacturing explosives, drawing a two-year suspended sentence. Vernon Vail, grand dragon of Aitcheson's splinter group, said the case had "set the Klan back 50 years." [84].

"AKIA"

See "AYAK."

AKIN, BERNARD

A Mississippi Klansman linked to the 1964 murder of Michael Schwerner and two other civil rights workers, Akin sued *Life* magazine for libel over an article about the case. His suit was thrown out of federal court on February 9, 1966. [NYT 1966]

AKIN, JAMES M.

See *Columbians, Inc.*

ALABAMA

The first state to experience Reconstruction Klan activity outside of Tennessee, Alabama welcomed the KKK to Tuscaloosa County in the fall of 1867. Newspaper editor Ryland Randolph was its most visible and volatile leader—some sources name him as the state's grand dragon—and violence around Tuscaloosa was a constant fact of life through early 1871. Klansmen issued their first public warnings in Blount County during November 1867, and by the spring of 1868 dens were organized throughout the Tennessee Valley, in the northern part of the state, where Klan goals and membership overlapped those of the Knights of the White Camellia. Greene County Klansmen burned their local courthouse on March 20, 1868, to destroy criminal records, and a similar effort was foiled by Hale County authorities the following day. Northern and eastern counties were the center of Klan violence during the 1868 elections, with Tuscaloosa County rated among the worst. In that county, Ryland Randolph's campaign against "radicals" and carpetbaggers on the state university faculty would briefly result in the closing of the school, with its eventual reopening under a new, more conservative management. In 1869 and 1870, Ku Klux violence was more virulent and widespread in Alabama than in any other state, except for chaotic North Carolina. No precise casualty figures are available, but congressional investigators estimated that Klansmen in the state murdered at least 109 persons between 1868 and 1871, with many times that number beaten, mutilated, raped, or otherwise abused. Two major areas of activity were the western counties—including Fayette, Greene, Sumter, and Tuscaloosa—and the entire northern part of the state, including the mountain counties east of the city of Birmingham. Authorities noted a decline in violence after white Democrats swept the November 1870 elections, but scattered nightriding continued well into 1871. In that year, Democrats and Republicans alike were moved to denounce Klansmen as "the lowest-down, meanest characters that we have got among us." Public disapproval brought a marked decrease in violence by the summer of 1871, although mayhem continued in Choctaw County through early 1872.

With the revival of the Klan in 1915, sparks of memory were kindled into flames. A kleagle was dispatched to till the fertile ground in 1916, and Alabama joined neighboring Georgia as the only state with active klaverns prior to 1920. Klansmen were active throughout World War I, keeping an eye out for saboteurs and suspicious aliens, but the state's real growth occurred with the enlistment of publicists Edward Clarke and Elizabeth Tyler. By 1926, the Invisible Empire could boast an estimated 50,000 members in the state, and their strength was felt at the ballot box. Hundreds of Klansmen were elected to public office in that year's elections, including Bibb Graves (governor), Charles McCall (attorney general), and Hugo Black (U.S. senator). Graves—the exalted cyclops of Montgomery Klavern No. 3—got away with seating Imperial Wizard Hiram Evans and Grand Dragon James Esdale on the dais for his inauguration speech, but McCall, a member of the same klavern, raised a storm of protest when he tried to appoint Esdale as an assistant state attorney general. For all of Montgomery's prominence in state politics, the Klan was most firmly entrenched with blue-collar industrial workers around Birmingham, where the Knights controlled an estimated 18,000 of the city's 32,000 votes. Senator Oscar Underwood opposed the KKK at his peril, dooming his hopes for the 1924 presidential nod. He finally withdrew rather than face Klan opposition for reelection to the Senate in 1927. Senator Tom Heflin, meanwhile, became a staple on Klan lecture circuits, inciting Klansmen—and some Klan opponents—to acts of mayhem with his blatant anti-Catholicism. Inevitably, violence followed the growth of the modern Klan, with at least twenty victims flogged in Birmingham in 1921-1922, and over 100 beatings recorded statewide during a three-year period of the early 1920s. Bloodshed and blatant political cronyism produced a backlash by 1928, and Klan membership had shriveled to roughly 6,000 from its peak two years earlier.

Alabama Klansmen continued to ride in the 1930s and 1940s, primarily targeting CIO trade unionists and blacks, but the future lay in diversity. Hugh Morris chartered his Federated Ku Klux Klans in September 1946, and members were linked—without proper convictions—to a rash of Birmingham floggings in 1949 and 1950. (Bombings were also popular around Birmingham, where an estimated forty-nine racially motivated bombings would be linked to the Klan between the end of World War II and the summer of 1963.) Governor Jim Folsom was a staunch enemy of the KKK, urging residents to defend their homes "by any means necessary," but Alabama governors were forbidden by law from succeeding themselves in office, and the Klan was thus able to wait out Folsom's term, chafing at the imposition of a new anti-mask law. Splinter groups proliferated after "Black Monday," with the U.S. Klans, the Dixie Klans, Robert Shelton's Alabama Knights, Asa Carter's Original KKK of the Confederacy, and Mobile's Gulf Ku Klux Klan all exploiting the Supreme Court's decision to help build their ranks. Tuscaloosa was the scene of fleeting violence in 1956, after black coed Autherine Lucy enrolled at the state university, and increased after 1958, following the election of Governor John Patterson. A friend of the Klan, indebted to Robert Shelton for his election, Patterson favored the Alabama Knights with political patronage and financial rewards, publicly siding with white supremacist forces when violence was meted out to integrated freedom riders in 1961. The Klan counted on friends in law enforcement—men such as Col. Al Lingo, Birmingham's "Bull" Connor, and Selma's Jim Clark—to overlook nightriding and cover the KKK's track for its bombings or murders. By July 1961, Shelton's new United Klans of America was the dominant organization in the state, and Governor George Wallace courted KKK support in his successful 1962 campaign. By 1964, the United Klans had an estimated 1,200 members in Alabama, dispersed among forty active klaverns, while the Dixie Klans clung to a small unit in Anniston. Congressional investigations and public reaction to unbridled violence reduced the Klan's strength by 1970, but the order's "100% Americans" hung on, undaunted, into the new decade.

The 1970s and 1980s produced mixed blessings for the KKK in Alabama. Governor Wallace remained faithful through his 1968 and 1972 presidential campaigns, but his near-assassination in the latter race seemed to change things, and a Texas Klan leader was subsequently moved to complain that Wallace "isn't as white as he used to be." Still, there were other friends of the KKK in elective office. U.S. Senator James Allen sent a congratulatory telegram to the United Klans' 1970 klonvocation, and Lieutenant Governor Jere Beasley appeared as a featured speaker. On the flip side, Attorney General Bill Baxley was a die-hard opponent of the KKK, and played a large part in the conviction of a Klansman in the fatal 1963 church bombing in Birmingham. (The successful effort reportedly hurt Baxley's 1980 gubernatorial bid.) Sporadic violence continued, with riots in Decatur in 1979 (sparked by the case of a black rape suspect, Tommy Hines) and the lynching of a black man, Michael Donald, the following year, but juries were increasingly pronouncing convictions, and two Klansmen in the Donald case now occupy death row. In April 1979, twenty members of the United Klans were indicted for shooting at black homes in Talladega

County, with other attacks reported in Hayden and Muscle Shoals. By 1976, David Duke's Knights of the KKK had replaced Shelton's group as the dominant force in U.S. Klandom, and the reins were then passed to Alabama dragon Stephen Black in 1980. Following Black's 1981 conviction for plotting an invasion of Dominica, however, the Knights were torn apart by factional rivalries, with Alabama's wing led by Stanley McCollum and Thom Robb, competing for members and money with the home office in Metairie, Louisiana. Shrunken in size and battered by recent prosecutions, the Alabama Klans show no sign of fading gracefully from the scene. [2; 10; 87]

ALABAMA KNIGHTS OF THE KU KLUX KLAN

An active splinter group organized and led by Robert Shelton after his break with the U.S. Klans, in 1958. Shelton's group was one of three Klans hit with a restraining order from federal judge Frank M. Johnson, which barred violent interference with Freedom Ride demonstrations in May 1961. Two months later, Shelton merged his Klan with Georgia units led by Calvin Craig to form the United Klans of America. [10]

ALABAMA KU KLUX KLAN, INC.

Organized in 1957, this was one of seven splinter groups reported active in the state after the Supreme Court's "Black Monday" decision ordering desegregation of public schools. [6]

ALABAMA RESCUE SERVICE

Evidence presented before the House Un-American Activities Committee in 1965 identified this group as a front for the imperial treasury of the United Klans of America. [38]

ALASKA

In the early 1920s, a small chapter of the Knights of the Ku Klux Klan, Inc., was organized in the Alaska territory, but its appeal—with nearly no blacks and few Catholics or Jews in the territory—was strictly limited. Since the demise of the ill-conceived klavern, Alaska remains one of two states (Hawaii being the other one) apparently unfazed by the KKK phenomenon. [10]

ALBANY, GEORGIA

Georgia's fifth largest city in the early 1960s, Albany boasted a population of 38,000 whites and 18,000 blacks. White supremacists dominated the city government in 1961, when local blacks imported members of the Student Nonviolent Coordinating Committee (SNCC) to organize protest demonstrations. Violence followed, with a black church burned in Leesburg on August 15, 1961. By August 12, 1962, police reported various "outsiders" in the area, including Klan leaders Robert Shelton and Calvin Craig, in addition to a three-man "task force" from the American Nazi Party. On August 31, 1962, nightriders shot at four rural homes near Leesburg, targeting individuals active in black voter registration. On September 3, 3,000 persons gathered for a rally addressed by Craig and Shelton, who promised to fight "this blackboard jungle that is creeping up on the chastity of Southern womanhood." One Klansman was killed and six were arrested on September 5 when they stormed the home of a local black woman, Kate Philpot. Four days later, two churches, including one used for civil rights meetings, were burned near Sasser. At the site of one fire a white farmer was arrested for assaulting an FBI agent who had been sent to investigate. Yet another church was burned on September 17, with three whites pleading guilty on September 20. Local interest in the Klan declined as the furor eventually subsided, and only 300 spectators turned out for a rally on July 7, 1963, at which Calvin Craig shared the dais with city court judge Clayton Jones. [NYT 1962, 1963]

ALBRIGHT, WILLIAM R.

Invited to join the Reconstruction Klan in Alamance County, North Carolina, Albright later informed Congress that he was told "I had better join it for my own protection and that of my father, who [was] a member of the Republican party." [93]

ALEXANDER, HENRY

An Alabama Klansman jailed in 1957 for his role in bombings linked to the Montgomery bus boycott, Alexander faced capital charges, with accomplice James York, for dynamiting the home of Reverend Ralph Abernathy. The charges were later dismissed without prosecution, but Alexander was arrested once more, with Don Landers and J.M. White, for exploding gas-filled balloons outside a black Montgomery church on December 12, 1964. He paid a $200 fine and served ten days for that case, with another capital charge reduced to a misdemeanor count of "disturbing religious worship." On February 21, 1976, Alexander and two other Klansmen, Sonny Livingston and James York, were arrested for the 1957 murder of a black man, Willie Edwards. All three were indicted on March 5, but the case was dismissed on April 14, 1976, when authorities discovered their indictment did not specify a cause of death. At this writing, no new charges have been filed in the case. [NYT 1964, 1976]

ALEXANDER, JACK

One of three victims whipped by Alabama Klansmen on May 19, 1949, Alexander's case resulted in the state's first flogging conviction in two decades. A. Byrd Carradine, an officer of the Federated KKK's Stonewall Jackson klavern, was tried in state court that December, winning a mistrial on December 12, when the jury deadlocked 8–4 for acquittal. Carradine was convicted at his second trial, on October 6, 1950, on a federal charge of conspiring with seventeen other Klansmen to violate Alexander's civil rights. The defendant was sentenced to six months in jail. [*NYT* 1949; *FOF* 1950]

"ALIEN"

In Klan parlance, any person who has not been "naturalized" as a "citizen" of the Invisible Empire. [38]

ALLEN, GERALD

A member of the Confederation of Independent Orders, Knights of the KKK under Maryland Grand Dragon Tony LaRicci, Allen was one of three Klansmen convicted in the July 1978 attempted bombing of a synagogue in Lochearn, Maryland. Authorities charged the defendants with membership in a special Klan unit formed "with the intent and purpose of engaging in illegal violent acts aimed primarily at religious and ethnic targets." Upon conviction, Allen was sentenced to eight years in prison. [*NYT* 1979]

ALLEN, HENRY

A former editor of the *Wichita Beacon* and anti-Klan governor of Kansas in the 1920s, Allen ordered his attorney general to prosecute Klansmen in 1922. In numerous public speeches he denounced the Klan as the "greatest curse that comes to a civilized people" and a "travesty upon Americanism." [10]

ALLEN, JAMES

A former U.S. senator from Alabama and an open admirer of the KKK, Allen sent an autographed photograph of himself to the imperial wizard of the United Klans of America in August 1968, signed: "With sincerest best wishes to my good friend Robert M. Shelton." Two years later, while still in office, Allen also sent a friendly telegram to the United Klan's 1970 klonvocation. [84]

ALLEN, KARL

George Rockwell's second in command of the American Nazi Party, Allen organized a Wallace-for-President headquarters in Alexandria, Virginia, during 1967, promoting the national cause of the Alabama governor. [17]

ALLEN, REV. KEITH K.

An Oregon Klansman and chief investigator for the 1920s grand dragon, Allen left the United States for Vancouver, Canada, in 1924, to form a chapter of the Royal Riders of the Red Robe. [10]

ALLEN, MARILYN R.

A Salt Lake City resident and a Klan associate. In December 1949 Allen mailed out an open letter titled "In Defense of the Ku Klux Klan." [25]

ALLEN, MARION H.

As an Internal Revenue Service agent in Atlanta, Allen hit the Knights of the KKK with a substantial tax lien of $685,355 in 1944. In August 1949, when the Association of Georgia Klans was faced with a new lien of $9,332 for the years 1946-1948, Allen's office was flooded with telephone death threats. Georgia Klans leader Sam Roper paid "under protest" on September 12, but Allen soon filed yet another lien, for an additional $8,383. [NYT 1949; 25]

ALLEN, MICHAEL

As midwest coordinator for the National Socialist Party of America, Allen took control of the group and transferred their headquarters to his Chicago home when leader Harold Covington stepped down in April 1981. Cashing in on publicity from the assassination attempt on President Ronald Reagan, Allen announced that John Hinckley, Jr., had been ousted from the party in 1979 because "he wanted to shoot people and blow things up." In 1982, Allen was replaced by James Burford, who promptly rechristened the National Socialist Party as the American Nazi Party. [2]

ALLEN, SARAH

A "carpetbag" teacher from Geneseo, Illinois, Allen was visited by the Klan while working in Reconstruction Mississippi. She later told Congress, "They treated me gentlemanly and quietly, but when they went away I concluded that they were savages—demons!" [93]

ALLEN, THOMAS M.

A black politician, elected to the House of Representatives during Reconstruction, Allen was targeted by Klansmen, who killed his brother-in-law by mistake. [93]

ALLEN, W.L.

A white Georgia tenant farmer, Allen was flogged by Klansmen in 1939 because of his friendship with a black man. [93]

ALLEN, WALLACE

See *Bright, George.*

ALLIED KLANS

See *Knights of the Ku Klux Klan of America.*

ALLISON, R.A.

A Reconstruction Klan leader in Wayne County, Tennessee, Allison signed a pact with the authorities in August 1868 to eliminate violence and unmask his men, after which most local raiding effectively ceased. [87]

ALOIA, DENNIS

One of six Chicago policemen exposed as Klansmen in December 1967, Aloia was fired following a yearlong investigation. [*NYT* 1967]

ALPHA PI SIGMA

A cover for the New York Klan at its incorporation in 1923. This front name was discarded two years later. [10]

ALSTON, JAMES H.

An ex-slave and black Republican legislator in Macon County, Alabama, during Reconstruction, Alston was driven from the area in June 1870 by a Klan group led by his former master, Gen. Cullen Battle. [87]

ALT, ED

Alt was identified in 1983 as a Texas leader of the Aryan Nations. [2]

ALTAMAHA MEN'S CLUB NO. 72

In 1966 the House Un-American Activities Committee identified this group as a cover for a Baxley, Georgia, klavern, the United Klans of America. [38]

AMBROSE, REV. F. HALSEY

As pastor of the First Presbyterian Church in Grand Forks, North Dakota, Ambrose was also the driving force behind the state's 1920s Klan. In January 1923, he addressed the state legislature in a futile attempt to block passage of an anti-mask law. [10]

AMERICA FIRST COMMITTEE

A fascist splinter group created in 1982 by defectors from the American Nazi Party and led by Arthur Jones, the America First Committee remained on friendly terms with its parent organization. In 1983, advertisements promoting the AFC were regularly printed in the American Nazi Party's *Bulletin*. [2]

AMERICAN CONFEDERATE ARMY

A front for the Southern Knights of the KKK, led by Bill Hendrix, this group was formed at a July 1952 meeting in Orlando, Florida. Hendrix said that the ACA hoped to "organize all anti-communist organizations under one leadership and one program." [25]

AMERICAN CONSERVATIVE PARTY

An extremist group based in St. Louis, the party shared a mailing address with the local Workers for Wallace group. Its leader was Floyd Kitchen, president of the St. Louis Property Owners Association, which in 1968 sponsored a public appearance by J.B. Stoner. Another party leader was James Kernodle, an associate of Robert DePugh in the Minutemen. [27]

AMERICAN INDEPENDENT PARTY

Created in 1968 as the vehicle for George Wallace's presidential campaigns, the American Independent Party (AIP) drew heavily on the support and membership of racist/right-wing groups. In Florida, the John Birch Society and KKK cooperated to organize the AIP at the precinct level, financed by wealthy citrus growers working quietly to avoid publicity. The Florida AIP was dominated by Cecil King, a wealthy farmer and longtime Klansman from Parrish, Florida. In 1968, the head of the AIP central committee in Los Angeles was Kenneth Waite, who had attended secret Minutemen training camps. Georgia's 1968 AIP leader was Roy Harris, an officer of the Citizens' Council who told newsmen: "When you get right down to it, there's really only going to be one issue, and you spell it n-i-g-g-e-r." Members of the Citizens' Council also controlled the AIP in Bakersfield, California, where one faction was chaired by Reverend Alvin Mayall. In that election year, the party polled 9,446,167 votes, with 46 electoral votes from 5 Southern states. In 1970, Wallace's brother, Jack, paid for a twenty-four-page campaign brochure, "The Life of George C. Wallace," included in the May 1970 issue of *Fiery Cross*. That same year Michigan's AIP nominated United Klans of America Grand Dragon Robert Miles for secretary of state at its convention. Another Klansman ran for city commission in Pontiac, Michigan, but later withdrew from the race, citing threats on his life. On May 8, 1972, when Wallace failed to appear for an AIP rally at Farmington, Michigan, a known Klansman in the audience assaulted a regular Democratic party volunteer, shouting, "I'll make a vegetable out of you!" After Wallace was shot and crippled in Maryland a few days later, the August 1972 AIP convention nominated a California John Birch Society member, John G. Schmitz, as its presidential candidate. Schmitz won a paltry 993,199 votes in the election, and his defeat effectively finished the AIP as a national force. [*NYT* 1968, 1970, 1972]

AMERICAN KNIGHTS OF THE KU KLUX KLAN

Reported active in California during the 1980s, the American Knights were reportedly involved in harassing a black resident of Livermore in August 1985. By 1987, the faction claimed fewer than 100 members. [2]

AMERICAN KRUSADERS

A Klan-affiliated organization active in the state of Washington during the 1920s, the American Krusaders recruited naturalized citizens, as opposed to native-born Americans. In time, the group absorbed local units of the Royal Riders of the Red Robe. [10]

AMERICAN NATIONAL PARTY

See *Burros, Dan.*

AMERICAN NATIONAL SOCIALIST PARTY

See *Burros, Dan.*

AMERICAN NAZI PARTY

The most visible neo-Nazi movement in the United States was founded in November 1958, at Arlington, Virginia, by George Lincoln Rockwell. In his autobiography, *This Time the World*, Rockwell described his typical disciple when he wrote: "The anti-Jewish movement abounds with cowards, jerks, queers and fanatics. Many of the characters who were attracted to us were pretty sorry." The party's headquarters was purchased in 1959 by Floyd Fleming, former supporter of racist agitator John Kasper. In May 1961, the party's "hate bus" toured the South in protest against recent integrated freedom rides. Virginia revoked the party's charter on April 6, 1962, but Rockwell continued to operate unofficially. He sent a three-man delegation to Albany, Georgia, during a period of black demonstrations in September 1962, and Rockwell himself was on hand for joint demonstrations with robed Klansmen at Chicago's Marquette Park in July 1966. In the same month his followers joined Klansmen and members of the National States Rights Party for a joint rally in Cambridge, Maryland, haranguing an estimated audience of eighty people. With Rockwell's 1967 assassination, Matt Koehl emerged as heir apparent to the Führer's mantle, but was unable to hold the shrinking organization together. Various spin-off groups emerged as the party began to disintegrate. The most significant, founded by Chicago's Frank Colin in 1970, was the National Socialist Party of America, which was rechristened as the American Nazi Party in 1982. [2]

AMERICAN ORDER OF CLANSMEN

A short-lived San Francisco group organized after the 1915 California premiere of *Birth of a Nation*, the group was designed as "a nation-wide, patriotic, social and benevolent secret society" for the purpose of "uniting all loyal, white American citizens." Quickly upstaged by the Georgia-based Knights of the KKK, it never got off the ground. [93]

AMERICAN SOUTHERN PUBLISHING COMPANY

Based in Northport, Alabama, this company produced the *Fiery Cross* and other official literature for United Klans of America in the 1960s. Under Governor George Wallace, ASP also won a contract to publish textbooks for Alabama's schools. On April 12, 1966, the company issued a check for $1,077 to United Klans Imperial Wizard Robert Shelton, which Shelton deposited in his personal bank account. Congressional investigators were unable to determine the services performed by Shelton in return for that payment, and the wizard declined to explain on grounds of possible self-incrimination. [22; 38]

AMERICAN UNDERGROUND

See *Hendrix, Bill.*

AMERICAN UNITY LEAGUE

Founded in the summer of 1922 by Chicago attorney "Mad" Pat O'Donnell, the Unity League was a leading anti-Klan group of the 1920s. Its magazine, *Tolerance*, published the names of known and suspected Klansmen, sometimes making errors in the process. The South Bend, Indiana, chapter was sued in early 1923 for publishing the names of six non-Klansmen by mistake. (The group's biggest error was naming chewing gum magnate William Wrigley as a Klansman.) Eventually, the KKK managed to plant a spy in the League, foiling its organizational efforts and dissipating funds, with fatal results for the group. [10; 93]

AMERICAN WHITE NATIONALIST PARTY

See *Ohio White Nationalist Party.*

AMERICANS FOR PRESERVATION OF THE WHITE RACE

A front group for the White Knights of the KKK, it claimed 30,000 members in 1964. When newsman Ken Tolliver, of Greenville, Mississippi, planned to produce a series on the group in June 1964, he received an anonymous phone call. "We've killed other people," he was told. "You wouldn't be the first." The group's secretary-treasurer was Sybil Nix, wife of Klansman and convicted murderer Deavours Nix. The group backed segregationist Ross Barnett in the 1967 gubernatorial race, and J.B. Stoner addressed a group rally in Meridian during May 1968, at the height of racial bombings in the area. [17]

ANCIENT CITY GUN CLUB

Sometimes called the Ancient City Hunting Club, this group fulfilled its purpose as a cover for St. Augustine Klavern No. 519, United Florida Ku

Klux Klan. Reputed leader Holstead "Hoss" Manucy denied Klan membership on the basis of his nominal Catholicism, but evidence secured by the House Un-American Activities Committee in 1965 confirmed the club's KKK affiliation. Members were recruited by Sheriff L.O. Davis as "special deputies" to combat black demonstrators in 1963 and 1964, and the club was inseparably linked to outbursts of violence in St. Augustine during that time. Armed motorcades were a favorite pursuit of club members, and one participant was shot to death while cruising through a black neighborhood in October 1963. Public exposure apparently led to the club's dissolution in late 1964 or early 1965. [10; 38]

ANCIENT ORDER, INVISIBLE KNIGHTS OF THE KU KLUX KLAN

A North Carolina splinter group, based in Shelby and led by Grand Dragon Woodrow Lynch, the Ancient Order was reported active from 1968 to 1970. [NYT 1968; 84]

ANDERSON, BOB

A black Union veteran, Anderson lived five miles from Nashville, Tennessee, during Reconstruction. Klansmen raided his home on March 17, 1868, one of whom was killed by Anderson during the resulting shootout. The next day, a mob of fifty whites "arrested" Anderson and several black friends, giving them twenty-four hours to leave the area. [87]

ANDERSON, RAYMOND R.

A resident of Maryville, Tennessee, Anderson was elected Tennessee grand dragon for the United Klans of America in 1961, soon after the United Klans was organized by Robert Shelton and Calvin Craig. His efforts met with little success, recruiting an estimated 225 Klansmen for ten klaverns by 1967. [38]

ANDERSON, WILLIAM ALLISON

A resident of Decatur, Georgia, Anderson served as an instructor at a United Klans demolition school, held on the Georgia farm of O.C. Mixon in October 1961. In 1963, he was one of forty Klan members booked for operating a disorderly house at the local klavern in Dekalb County. He was also linked to the bombing activities of Nacirema, Inc. Anderson, an illiterate dropout, was unable to read a statement prepared by his attorney when appearing before the House Un-American Activities Committee in November 1965. [NYT 1965]

ANDES, PAUL G.

A Tennessee Klansman, Andes was one of three defendants who pled guilty in a December 1984 shooting incident at Murfreesboro, claiming that he believed that his target was a home used for the sale and distribution of illegal drugs. [*NYT* 1985]

ANDREW, DR. JOHN S.

A resident of Stone Mountain, Georgia, Andrew led the John Birch Society's Emory chapter, in Atlanta, until he resigned to run for the state legislature in 1965. Despite the resignation, he still retained membership, and the Society continued meeting at his home. After his defeat at the polls, he addressed an Atlanta rally of the United Klans on August 23, 1965, telling Klansmen he had been defeated by the "international banking conspiracy." On September 13, 1965, Andrew escorted the parents of John Birch to a rally at the Henry Grady Hotel, in Atlanta, where retired Gen. Edwin Walker told the audience, "There will be a KKK in the USA longer than there will be an LBJ!" [28]

ANGELL, R.H.

Virginia's Republican state chairman in 1928 and a part-owner of the bitterly anti-Catholic, pro-Klan *Fellowship Forum*, Angell sponsored articles attacking presidential candidate Al Smith on the basis of his religion. [10]

ANGLO-SAXON CHRISTIAN CONGREGATION

Based in Los Angeles and led by Wesley Swift, this "religious" group was founded 1945 and remained active into the early 1950s. With an estimated 200 to 300 members, it was rated by the Anti-Defamation League of B'nai B'rith as the strongest anti-Semitic group on the West Coast. [25]

ANNABLE, ROBERT

A known Klansman and the leader of a Cleveland-based Klan affiliate, the National Christian Conservative Society, Annable testified before the House Un-American Activities Committee in 1965, calling the KKK "a good organization." In 1968, he was identified as the leader of the North American Alliance of White People and the George Wallace Christian Conservative Party of Ohio. The latter group's platform called for total segregation of the races and an immediate repeal of Ohio's fair-housing laws. [*NYT* 1967; 17]

ANSON SPORTSMAN CLUB

In 1965 this group was identified as a cover for a Peachland, North Carolina, klavern, United Klans of America, in Anson County. [38]

ANTI-CATHOLICISM

Introduced as a selling point for kleagles in the early 1920s, anti-Catholicism soon became a staple of KKK doctrine. The specter of a papal plot to dominate the United States proved remarkably effective for gaining new recruits, drawing on the same reservoir of religious bigotry that fed the nativist Know-Nothing movement of the 1840s. In addition to standard anti-Catholic literature, Klan leaders recruited a stable of "escaped nuns," whose lectures featured tales of lustful priests, convent orgies, and that told of illegitimate infants consigned to furnaces in special leather bags. A forged Knights of Columbus Oath was circulated by Klan recruiters, asserting that every member donated rifles and ammunition to the local Catholic arsenal each time he fathered a child. Klansmen were implicated in the burning or vandalism of Catholic churches in both the United States and Canada. On one occasion, in North Manchester, Indiana, a lynching nearly resulted after a Klan orator told his audience, to "watch the trains" for a potential appearance by the Pope. Next day, 1,000 persons were waiting at the depot when a traveling corset salesman disembarked, who spent the next half hour persuading the anxious mob of his true identity. The major focus of KKK anti-Catholicism in the 1920s was New York State Governor Al Smith, whose presidential bids in 1924 and 1928 were frustrated by some voters' suspicion of his religion. Largely supplanted by anti-communism and anti-Semitism since the Depression, anti-Catholicism remains a standard tenet of some Klan groups. Major sources of anti-Catholic literature in the early 1950s were L.J. King's Book and Bible House, in Decatur, Georgia, and William Blessing's House of Prayer for All People in Denver. In April 1957, Bill Hendrix announced that Catholics were welcome in his Southern Knights, declaring that "the fight today is against integration, communism, and federal controls." In August 1960, Senator Estes Kefauver cited the KKK as a major source of the anti-Catholic propaganda opposing John Kennedy's presidential campaign. On September 9, 1960, a cross was burned at a Roman Catholic church in Tifton, Georgia, where a white priest had married a black couple hours earlier. One of five Klan bombs discovered in Birmingham, Alabama, on March 21, 1963—and the only one directed at a white target—was planted at a Catholic church. On June 24, 1966, a rural Catholic school for blacks was burned near Carthage, Mississippi; FBI agents noted previous bombing attempts related to civil rights activity by members of the congregation. On December 15, 1974, the National Knights of the KKK announced an intent to allow Catholics to become Klansmen, but there was no rush on the part of Catholics to respond. In May 1975, David Duke claimed nearly half his Louisiana Klansmen were Catholics. Five months later, Dale Reusch's new Invisible Empire of the KKK also welcomed Catholics into the ranks. [10; 84]

ANTI-COMMUNIST CHRISTIAN ASSOCIATION

Identified as a front for the KKK in Louisiana's 6th Congressional district, with its headquarters at Bogalusa, the Association emerged from a 1964 rift in the Original Knights of the Ku Klux Klan. Incorporated in January 1965, the Association declared its intent "to provide for the preservation of the Constitution of the State of Louisiana, the Constitution of the United States of America, as originally written, to establish justice, ensure domestic tranquillity, provide for the common defense, promote the welfare of Christians and Christian civilization, and to secure the blessings of liberty against encroachment by communism." Under the leadership of Klansmen Charles Christmas and Saxon Farmer, the group cherished some queer definitions of "justice" and "tranquillity," relying on its reference to the U.S. Constitution "as originally written" to cancel any progress made by blacks since the Civil War. Members of the Association were active in violent opposition to black demonstrations throughout 1965, and in December of that year the group was named in federal injunctions banning acts of terrorism and intimidation around Bogalusa. [38]

ANTI-KLAN ASSOCIATION

Active in Oklahoma during 1923, the Association was one of seven anti-Klan groups in America during the 1920s. [93]

ANTI-MASK LAWS

A series of state and local laws passed in response to outbreaks of KKK terrorism, anti-mask legislation typically forbids adults from donning disguises in public, particularly with intent to commit criminal acts of violence or intimidation. The Reconstruction Ku Klux Acts contain a provision against masked violence designed to deprive former slaves of their civil rights, and various states began to pass legislation of their own after the Klan was linked to various crimes. In November 1948, Wrightsville, Georgia, became the first Southern community to outlaw masked demonstrations. Atlanta passed a similar ordinance on May 2, 1949, fixing punishment at thirty days in jail and a $200 fine. The Alabama state legislature responded to an outbreak of KKK violence by passing an anti-mask law in June 1949, legislation which divided local Klan units, with leader Hugh Morris opposing the measure and his subordinate, Dr. E.P. Pruitt in favor. In Arkansas, two blacks became the first persons arrested under a new anti-mask law, charged with donning Klan-type hoods to frighten black girls out of dating white men. An anti-mask bill died in the Georgia assembly on February 18, 1950, but a new version was passed eleven months later that outlawed public masking or the burning of crosses on private property without the owner's prior consent. A South Carolina law was enacted on April 28, 1951, that provided penalties of one year in jail and a $500 fine for traveling masked or for burning unauthorized crosses on private property. Florida followed suit with a new anti-mask law on May 8, 1951. On October 31, 1951, fourteen Klansmen were arrested in Conway, South Carolina, for parading masked through the Cane Branch Baptist Church; a deacon of the church responded by swearing out arrest warrants on the deputies who made the collar. By 1967, twenty-two states and fifty-two Southern communities had anti-mask laws, and the legislation was fairly standard north of the Mason-Dixon Line. On July 3, 1966, a man and woman were arrested for wearing masks at a Klan rally near Lebanon, Ohio, led by James Venable, whereupon the angry crowd began pelting the arresting officers with stones. In most areas, Klansmen are able to circumvent anti-mask laws by meeting on private property, with the owner's prior consent, and prevailing legislation typically exempts occasions such as Mardi Gras and Halloween. [25; 26]

ANTI-SEMITISM

The Klan's first attack on Jews was recorded at Greensboro, Alabama, in the spring of 1868, when local Klansmen accused two Jewish merchants of overcharging their customers and attempted to drive them out of the community. Another Jewish storekeeper, Samuel Fleischman, was murdered by Klansmen in Marianna, Florida, in 1869, but his execution was apparently motivated more by his friendship with blacks than for religious reasons. Organized anti-Semitism did not emerge as a tenet of Klan doctrine until the 20th century, and the 1915 Georgia case of Leo Frank, a Jew convicted of murdering a child, led in part to the revival of the Klan. In October 1915, Frank was lynched by the Knights of Mary Phagan (named after the murdered child), and members of the group were among those who organized the new Knights of the KKK a month later. Anti-Semitism soon became a standard part of the Klan platform, as kleagles recognized the need for an appeal beyond that of white supremacy. Jews were linked to international communism through the person of Karl Marx, and Klansmen reprinted anti-Jewish propaganda such as *Protocols of Zion* and the writing of anti-Semites Gerald L.K. Smith and Conde McGinley, among others. Throughout the country, Jewish merchants were subjected to boycotts, threats, cross burnings, and sometimes acts of violence. In August 1923, police in Tulsa, Oklahoma, cooperated with Klansmen in the abduction and sexual mutilation of a Jewish landlord who was suspected of selling illegal drugs. The Klan's flirtation with neo-Nazi groups began in the late 1930s, with opinions divided over the wisdom of befriending groups such as the German-American Bund. In general, Northern Klansmen showed more sympathy for Nazi groups in the 1930s and 1940s, while hard-core Southern members dismissed the Aryan troops as "un-American." By the late 1950s, various Klan factions were cooperating openly with the anti-Semitic National States Rights Party, the American Nazi Party, and similar groups as the civil rights movement added fuel to their fire. Imperial Wizard Robert Shelton spoke for most Klansmen in the early 1960s when he said: "I don't hate niggers, but I hate the Jews. The nigger's a child, but the Jews are dangerous people. All they want is control and domination of the gentiles through a conspiracy with the niggers." In the 1970s and 1980s, Klan factions have openly affiliated themselves with rabid anti-Semitic groups such as the Aryan Nations, the Order, Posse Comitatus, and the Christian Identity movement, often seeking paramilitary avenues of response to the perceived threat from "ZOG," the "Zionist Occupational Government" in Washington, D.C. [2; 10; 13; 87]

APEX LADIES LEAGUE

In 1966 the House Un-American Activities Committee identified this group as a front for the Apex, North Carolina, ladies auxiliary, United Klans of America. [38]

APEX RESTORATION ASSOCIATION

Information collected by congressional investigators in 1966 identified this association as a cover for the Apex, North Carolina, klavern, United Klans of America. The group later went public as the Apex Unit, United Klans of America, Inc. [38]

ARCADIA SPORTSMAN CLUB

In 1966 congressional probers identified this club as a front for the Arcadia, Louisiana, klavern, Original Knights of the Ku Klux Klan, in Bienville Parish. [38]

ARIZONA

The Klan began in Arizona during 1922, but stalled early on. The order's early leader was Tom Akers, exalted cyclops of Kamelback Klan No. 6, in Phoenix, and former editor of the local *Gazette*. During their first year of activity, at least three floggings were reported and a school principal's face was scarred with acid. Akers fled the state following indictments for the beating of a black janitor. Governor George Hunt announced that he possessed a list of some 900 active Klansmen in his state but was loathe to publish names. The implied threat had little immediate impact on membership. Secure in his new position with the intelligence branch of the Klan at imperial headquarters in Atlanta, Akers felt it safe enough to return to Arizona in 1923 for the inauguration of his successor, Grand Dragon McCord Harrison. Under Harrison, the Arizona Klan was divided in two, with dual headquarters at Tempe and Winslow, but the move signaled no upsurge in membership. The KKK made its one and only political foray in 1924, surfacing as a key issue in the gubernatorial primary. In that election, anti-Klan incumbent Hunt easily retained his office, with the Klan candidate running a distant third. By 1926, few members remained, and the Arizona Klan faded. No significant KKK activity has been reported since that time, despite some anonymous threats against Jews in the Phoenix area by a self-styled Aryan Brotherhood in 1980, and no indigenous Klans were discovered in surveys conducted between 1965 and 1983. [2; 10]

ARKANSAS

The Reconstruction Klan reached Arkansas in March 1868, and competed with the Knights of the White Camellia around Little Rock and in the state's Southern counties. By May 1868, nocturnal violence in Crittenden County produced a call for federal troops, and that summer the state legislature granted Governor Powell Clayton's plea for twelve militia companies—two of which were black—to be ready for action in late August. Widespread violence continued through September and October, concentrated in the southern and northeastern counties; in contrast, nightriding was rare in the northern part of the state, where blacks were less plentiful and white Unionists held a comfortable majority. As in other states, no precise body count is available, but Arkansas Klansmen did claim Congressman James Hinds, who was assassinated in Little Rock in October 1868. In the same month, Klansmen hijacked the steamboat *Hesper* on the Mississippi River, routing her crew and destroying a shipment of weapons earmarked for the Arkansas militia. In November, Governor Clayton declared martial law over ten of the state's most violent counties, extending military rule to Conway County a month later. The move ignited a storm of controversy, but brutal violence gradually swayed public opinion against the Klan, as it did in Lewiston, where Klansmen torched a store owned by Radical Republicans and the flames spread to consume most of the town. The militia campaign was remarkably effective. Many Klansmen fled the state to avoid arrest, and martial law was lifted in March 1869. On March 13, new legislation specifically banned the Klan and the Knights of the White Camellia. Although few prosecutions resulted, the racist movement was already in decline, with Crittenden County, which was 80 percent black, standing as the last area of sporadic nightriding.

In the 20th century, the reborn Knights of the Ku Klux Klan, Inc., were active throughout Arkansas, their estimated membership topping the 40,000 mark by the end of 1922. Klansmen won most of the elective offices in Little Rock that year, and violence inevitably followed, with vigilante raids around Hot Springs and a pitched battle at Smackover, leaving one man dead and many wounded. By 1924, internal dissension was tearing the Razorback Klan apart, and thousands of Klansmen fled the imperious rule of Grand Dragon J.C. Comer and his wife. That year's elections were disastrous for the Klan, and by 1925 its membership had shrunk to an estimated 10,000 members, and continued to decline.

Quiescent during the Great Depression and World War II, Arkansas Klandom was revived by the U.S. Supreme Court's 1954 Black Monday ruling on school desegregation. The U.S. Klans were represented in the late 1950s, competing with the local Association of Arkansas Klans, and Klansmen saw action around Little Rock during the school integration crisis of 1957–1959. During the 1960s, Robert Shelton's United Klans of America boasted ten klaverns in six Arkansas counties, with an estimated 150 members overall, while the tiny Association of Arkansas Klans clung to life with its 25 members divided between Pine Bluff and Texarkana. Two alleged Klansmen were tried for the murder of a black paperboy in 1965, but most of the civil rights action was conducted on other battlefields in the Deep South states. Those who remained faithful to the Klan in the 1970s and 1980s were forced to seek their leadership out of state, cleaving to the various national Klans, or affiliated groups such as the Aryan Nations and The Covenant, the Sword, and the Arm of the Lord. [10; 87]

ARLEDGE, AUBREY EUGENE

See *Pace, Rev. Edward.*

ARLEDGE, RICKY

See *Pace, Rev. Edward.*

ARNALL, ELLIS

As Georgia's state attorney general in 1940, Arnall prosecuted Imperial Wizard Hiram Evans and a former purchasing agent for the state highway department on charges of price fixing and violating the Sherman Anti-Trust Act. Evans had been allowed to sell asphalt and paving materials to the state without competitive bids, a reward for the Klan's electoral support of Governor E.D. Rivers in 1936. Upon conviction, Evans was forced to pay the state $15,000 in refunds. Arnall later served as governor from 1943 to 1946, ordering legal moves to revoke the Association of Georgia Klans charter on May 30, 1946. That same year, Georgia's state legislature rescinded a seventy-five-year-old ban on black votes in the Democratic primary, a move upheld by the U.S. Supreme Court in April 1946. On June 21, 1946, Arnall announced that the FBI had uncovered "a well-organized plot" against his life by Atlanta Klansmen. The plot apparently had five prospects being drawn by lot from each klavern, with Dr. Samuel Green choosing the two triggermen from the finalists. The Klan retaliated by issuing unsubstantiated claims that Arnall had become a lifetime member of the order in 1942. [*NYT* 1946; 84]

ARNELL, SAMUEL M.

A Reconstruction congressman from Tennessee, Arnell was marked for murder by the Klan in June 1868. Klansmen armed with ropes and pistols stopped a train in Maury County during that month and searched its cars for Arnell, but he eluded them. When Arnell asked Governor Brownlow for troops to fight Klan violence in his district, he was told that no men were available. [87]

ARNETTE, MACK

See *Rogers, Ernest and Christine.*

ARNOLD, LUKE

An Atlanta judge, Arnold was also popular on the Association of Georgia Klans lecture circuit in 1946. [93]

ARP, WALTER

See *Lynch, John.*

ARYAN BROTHERHOOD

Generally identified as a racist prison gang involved in contract murders and the sale of narcotics, there is some evidence of involvement of hate activity. In May 1980, a Jewish businessman in Phoenix, Arizona, received an anonymous phone call, stating: "There is no reason that Hitler did not kill every fucking Jew that walked the earth. We are trying to remedy that, so go outside your house, you Jew, and see." Another call announced, "This is the Aryan Brotherhood. You are a dead man." [*UPI,* May 18, 1980]

ARYAN KNIGHTS OF THE KU KLUX KLAN

Based in Waco, Texas, this tiny splinter group was led by Horace Miller, a disabled veteran of World War I. Miller's literature has been found in the possession of neo-Nazis in Austria, England, and Chile. Miller published the newspaper *Here It Is!*, with the subtitle "White Folks News—There is no equality among men." A Waco journalist put the Aryan Knights in perspective when he explained that the group's membership consisted of Miller, one other man, and "maybe the immediate family." [14]

ARYAN NATIONS

Officially titled the Church of Jesus Christ Christian-Aryan Nations, this neo-Nazi group evolved directly from Wesley Swift's California "church." Reverend Richard Butler took over the congregation when Swift died in 1970, and moved the headquarters to a rural compound in Hayden Lake, Idaho. Committed to preparations for the coming race war and the overthrow of the so-called Zionist Occupational Government, Butler says, "If you believe in the Bible, you know that there is no peaceful solution." In the early 1980s, The Order served as a militant action wing of Butler's organization, and Aryan Nations literature was recovered at the scene of a Spokane, Washington, church bombing in 1981. Since 1982, the Aryan Nations compound has hosted annual rallies attended by members of various KKK and neo-Nazi groups, Posse Comitatus, the Mountain Church, and assorted survivalists groups. Affiliates of the Aryan Nations have been identified from coast to coast. The group claims 6,000 adherents nationwide, but observers place the average attendance at rallies between 150 and 200 persons. Principal financing is derived from sale of Butler's taped sermons, and from a requirement that members donate 10 percent of their annual income to the cause. Implicated in numerous acts of violence, with its leaders prosecuted unsuccessfully for sedition in 1988, the Aryan Nations remains a key element in the racist Christian Identity network. [2]

ASHBURN, GEORGE W.

A white Republican leader during Reconstruction, Ashburn was murdered by Klansmen in Columbus, Georgia, on March 31, 1868. A party of thirty to forty masked men invaded Ashburn's home shortly after midnight and shot him to death, the first recorded incident of Klan violence outside of Tennessee. A few days later, the militia arrested thirteen suspects, including three blacks. Their bond was raised by popular subscription, and none of them was convicted. [87]

ASHER, COURT

A former bootlegger and D.C. Stephenson's chief lieutenant in the Indiana Klan of the 1920's, Asher remained active during and after World War II, and published the racist newsletter *X-RAY* from his base in Muncie. Asher was one of twenty-eight neo-Nazis arrested by the FBI on charges of sedition in July 1942. [8; 10]

ASSEMBLY OF CHRISTIAN SOLDIERS, INC.

A "church" active by 1972, the Assembly claimed 3,000 members in Alabama, Georgia, and Mississippi. The group was led by a former imperial wizard of the Original Knights of the KKK of the Confederacy. Its lay arm was a group dubbed The Southerners, which was responsible for issuing bulletins and maintaining dial-a-message services. Denied federal tax exemption as a church, the Assembly borrowed $35,000 from a Birmingham physician to open a "commissary" stocking groceries. When the produce did not sell, the Assembly's creditor foreclosed and hauled away the groceries to cover the debt. Another group project was the drive for private white "academies," supported from church funds so that parents could transfer their children from integrated public schools at no extra cost. A widow in Mobile donated twenty acres, formerly a stockyard, for the Assembly's headquarters, and public rallies on the site drew an average audience of 300 persons. At one such meeting, observer Albert Foley, who was suspected as a FBI plant, was assaulted with a hammer, but he escaped serious injury. Twelve hundred members from three states were recruited to work on construction of the Assembly's Birmingham headquarters, but the group was soon evicted for nonpayment of rent. [23]

ASSOCIATED KLANS OF AMERICA

An insubstantial umbrella Klan, the AKA was created—at least on paper— in September 1949, when Sam Roper's Association of Georgia Klans theoretically merged with the Knights of the KKK of America, run by Lycurgus Spinks. Roper was listed as imperial wizard of the group, thus taking the first—and only—step toward his vision of a "United States of the Ku Klux Klan." [25]

ASSOCIATION OF ALABAMA KNIGHTS OF THE KU KLUX KLAN

Organized in 1957, this was one of seven Klan factions reported active in Alabama during the late 1950s in response to court-ordered school desegregation. [38]

ASSOCIATION OF ARKANSAS KLANS

One of three active groups reported in Arkansas during the summer of 1959, this association's chief activity seems to have been printing posters proclaiming the virtues of segregation and white supremacy. [33]

ASSOCIATION OF CAROLINA KLANS

Organized in November 1949 under Thomas L. Hamilton, this group consolidated independent Klan units in North and South Carolina, maintaining its headquarters at Leesville, South Carolina. In January 1950, Hamilton attended a Jacksonville, Florida, meeting with leaders of Alabama's Federated Klans and Florida's Southern Knights, where they issued a joint declaration of war on "hate groups" such as the NAACP and B'nai B'rith. During 1951 and 1952, 113 members of Hamilton's Klan were arrested on state and federal charges for their involvement in various abductions and floggings, including those of Evergreen Flowers, Woodrow Johnson, Ben Grainger, Esther Floyd, and Dorsey Robinson. Hamilton's Klansmen were also implicated in a Myrtle Beach, South Carolina, shootout at a dance hall owned by Charlie Fitzgerald, during which one Klansman was killed. During the summer of 1952, sixty-three Klansmen were convicted on various charges, drawing terms from eighteen months to six years in prison. [NYT 1951-1952]

ASSOCIATION OF FLORIDA KU KLUX KLAN

Organized by Tampa Klansman William Griffin in July 1953, this was one of five Klan factions reported active in Florida after the U.S. Supreme Court's 1954 Black Monday ruling on school desegregation. Griffin reportedly disbanded the group in August 1955. [38]

ASSOCIATION OF GEORGIA KLANS

Founded by Dr. Samuel Green in May 1946, this association was a direct descendant of the 1920s Knights of the KKK. Impetus for the new Klan's growth was provided by a number of factors, including the 1944 Supreme Court ruling against "white primaries," a new wave of post-war immigration, creation of the Fair Employment Practices Commission under President Truman, and the CIO's "Operation Dixie," which was designed to recruit new union members in the South. By September 1948, this Klan had at least one klavern in each of Georgia's 159 counties. A rally at Stone

Mountain on July 23, 1948, drew 10,000 people, and 7,000 turned out the following month for another gathering at Rossville. After his death in August 1949, Dr. Green was succeeded by Sam Roper, the politically connected Atlanta policeman. The disintegration of the group into rival factions, which began under Green accelerated with Roper at the helm. Roper's November 1949 announcement of a short-lived "working agreement" with Alabama's Federated Klans signaled no progress, and the new Associated Klans of America, with Roper serving as imperial wizard, existed for the most part on paper only. Unable to hold his subordinates in line, Roper named Tom Hamilton as the grand dragon of South Carolina, but Hamilton soon pulled out and became independent. During the closing months of 1949, the group was hit with two IRS tax liens, totaling more than $17,000. Three years later, Charles Klein, Roper's second-in-command, was arrested on charges of bombing a black family's home in Atlanta. Financial difficulties, adverse publicity, and Roper's inept leadership combined to drive the organization out of existence prior to the Supreme Court's 1954 Black Monday ruling on school integration. [10]

ASSOCIATION OF SOUTH CAROLINA KLANS (1950s–1960s)

One of seven Klans reported active in South Carolina after Black Monday, this group's formation was announced in the fall of 1955. The group's founders were identified as alumni of Tom Hamilton's defunct Association of Carolina Klans, which had been broken up by state and federal prosecution in 1952, and was represented by spokesman R.E. Hodges, secretary of of the Columbia unit. By April 1957, Klan-watchers were calling it the third largest faction in the South. A month later, several members of the Greenville unit were implicated and ultimately convicted in the flogging of a black resident. Rumors of cooperation with the Gulf KKK in Mobile, Alabama, bore no visible fruit for this Carolina organization. A klonvocation was scheduled for November 25, 1957, with installation of officers set for January 1958. In the early 1960s, this association affiliated itself with James Venable's National Association of Ku Klux Klan. From August to December 1961, the group cooperated with the Majority Citizens League of South Carolina to publish a newsletter, *Southland Standard*, which failed due to a lack of financial support. In 1965 congressional investigators identified 250 members of the group, which was divided into eight klaverns and located in six of the state's forty-six counties. [6; 38; 48; 74]

ASSOCIATION OF SOUTH CAROLINA KLANS (1970s)

A splinter group reported active in 1976, it was so secretive that professed member John Howard told interviewer Patsy Sims that "the members don't even know who their grand dragon is." Orders for the group were reportedly issued by a Grand Council of anonymous members. No group activities have been confirmed. [84]

ATHENS, GEORGIA

Located seventy miles northwest of Atlanta, Athens is the home of the University of Georgia, a target for black integrationists in the early 1960s. On January 11, 1961, Calvin Craig and other known Klansmen distributed literature to a riotous crowd that gathered to block the admission of two black students. Of the nine rioters who were jailed for their involvement in the outbreak, eight were admitted Klansmen. The violence resulted in the suspension of the two black students on January 12, but the incidents continued. On January 15, an armed man roamed the campus looking for one of the black students, but he was disarmed by security guards. Two university students and nine men from Atlanta, including the eight Klansmen, were indicted on riot-related charges on January 19, 1961. [NYT 1961]

ATKINS, F.W.

An Atlanta Klansman dispatched to organize the Pennsylvania realm in early days of the KKK revival, F.W. Atkins soon quarreled with Imperial Wizard William Simmons and King Kleagle Edward Clarke over management procedures, and he was dismissed in the latter part of 1921. Furious at his dismissal, Atkins destroyed local membership records and absconded with the Klan's state treasury, leaving the realm in chaos. [10]

ATKINS, J.W.

As editor of the Gastonia, North Carolina, *Gazette*, J.W. Atkins was a staunch opponent of the KKK. A cross was burned in front of his home in 1949 after he had denounced efforts to revive the local klavern. [25]

AUBURNDALE FISHERMAN'S CLUB

In 1966, the House Un-American Activities Committee identified this club as a front group for the Auburndale, Florida, klavern, United Florida Ku Klux Klan. [38]

AUSTRIA

On February 21, 1960, police in Vienna announced the discovery of a neo-Nazi cell there that had links to the Klan in the United States. Confiscated propaganda, inscribed "Ku Klux Klan of America," was subsequently traced to Horace Miller's Aryan Knights in Waco, Texas. [NYT 1960]

AVANTS, ERNEST

See *White, Ben Chester.*

AVERY, JAMES W.

A Reconstruction planter, prosperous merchant, and Klan leader in York County, South Carolina, Avery presided over an area of unequaled violence.

Between November 1870 and September 1871, authorities in Avery's district recorded at least eleven murders and more than 600 beatings, in addition to the destruction of five black schools and churches. (One structure was rebuilt, and then demolished by the Klan, four separate times.) In May 1871, Avery issued a statement condemning violence, but he was unable to control the rank and file. Refusing to appear before congressional investigators, he later fled to Ontario, Canada, where he found refuge with Carolina expatriates. [87]

"AX HANDLE SATURDAY"

On August 27, 1960, ten days of black sit-in demonstrations in Jacksonville, Florida, were capped by a riot. Evidence suggests that the outbreak was planned at a local meeting of the Florida Knights on August 23, with a call issued for Klan reinforcements from Florida and southern Georgia. Participants were urged to bring as many friends as possible and to leave their Klan IDs at home. Scores of Klansmen and associates gathered on the appointed day, with local stores selling out of ax handles and baseball bats. (One Sears outlet sold fifty ax handles in a period of fifteen minutes.) Mayor Haydon Burns was reportedly forewarned of the attack on August 26, but opted to let the riot proceed. By 8 a.m., white mobs began to assemble in Hemming Park, with Klansmen distributing ax handles. The mob began its march through the streets at 9:30 a.m., assaulting black pedestrians, while police watched impassively or openly joked with the rioters. (Police spokesmen later claimed that the initial group, estimated at sixty persons, was "too large" for officers to control.) Blacks retreated into their own neighborhoods as the riot developed, with an estimated 3,000 persons involved at the peak of violence. Fifty persons were reported injured during the outbreak of violence, the only fatality a black man, ex-convict Charlie Davis, who was shot while attacking a white-owned gas station. Police officers armed with shotguns finally intervened, arresting persons described by Mayor Burns as "more than 100 troublemakers of both races." Sporadic violence continued over the next several days, with Burns blaming out-of-town agitators, but the police chief declared that "all the fellows we arrested were local boys." On August 29, short jail terms and/or fines, ranging from $10–$250 were imposed against twenty-six whites and fifty-seven blacks. The stiffest sentence—ninety days—went to Richard Parker, a white university student and NAACP member who had been active in leading the sit-ins. [*Time,* Sept. 12, 1960; 70]

"AYAK"

A Klan password and recognition signal used to identify fellow Klansmen in strange surroundings, "AYAK" is an acronym for the phrase "Are you a Klansman?" The proper response is "AKIA" ("A Klansman I am"). In practice, the code words are inserted into common conversation, as: "Does a Mr. Ayak live in this neighborhood?" A typical response might be: "No, but a Mr. Akia lives just around the corner." Passwords are typically accompanied by secret Klan handshakes or other signs of recognition. [10]

AYDEN CHRISTIAN FELLOWSHIP CLUB

In 1966 congressional investigators identified this club as a front for the Ayden, North Carolina, klavern, United Klans of America. [38]

AYDEN GARDEN CLUB

Testimony offered in 1966 congressional hearings identified this club as a cover for the Ayden, North Carolina, ladies auxiliary, United Klans of America. [38]

AYER, DR. BENJAMIN

An elderly Georgia state legislator during Reconstruction, Ayer joined Joseph Adkins on a trip to Washington, D.C., in the spring of 1869, to report about Klan violence in his state. Around the time Adkins was killed, in May 1869, Ayer was also ambushed and shot dead near his home in Jefferson County. Authorities blamed his death on an unidentified "Negro robber," while local conservatives mounted a posthumous campaign of character assassination. [87]

AYSCUE, JACK

See *Caldwell, Lester.*

B

B. & H. SPORTING CLUB

In 1965 congressional investigators identified this group as a cover for the Lewiston, North Carolina, klavern, United Klans of America. [38]

BABINGTON, ROBERT

A Reconstruction officer of the Knights of the White Camellia in Washington Parish, Louisiana, Babington was also a merchant, postmaster, and chairman of the Democratic Party's central committee. These divided loyalties did not prevent him from serving as secretary of the local KKK at the same time, and Babington was known to issue "protection papers" for blacks who voted Democratic in the 1868 elections, exempting them from attacks by nightriders. Prior to the balloting, Babington was identified as a member of a hooded gang that rode through Franklinton on five successive nights, intimidating would-be voters. [87]

BACK SWAMP HUNTING CLUB

In 1966 investigators for the House Un-American Activities Committee identified this club as a front for a klavern of the United Klans of America in Chinquapin, North Carolina. [38]

BACON, MARY

A female jockey of some renown in the early 1970s, Bacon first went public as a Klanswoman on April 4, 1975, with her appearance at a rally of David Duke's faction in Walker, Louisiana. As a featured guest, she told the crowd of 2,700 persons, "We are not just a bunch of illiterate Southern nigger-killers. We are good white Christian people, hard-working people working for a white America. When one of your wives or one of your sisters gets raped by a nigger, maybe you'll get smart and join the Klan." Bacon's KKK affiliation cost her a lucrative television contract with Dutch Masters cigars, along with an endorsement contract for Revlon cosmetics. In July 1975, she complained of difficulty getting mounts in races; two horses she was scheduled to ride at Hollywood Park were scratched by their owners for "medical reasons." Unable to find thoroughbred mounts, by mid-July Bacon was reduced to riding quarter horses. She soon faded into obscurity. [NYT 1975]

BADON, JUDY

Active in David Duke's Klan at Denham Springs, Louisiana, she advertised a 10 percent discount for Klan members at her laundry and dry cleaning shop. Duke cited Badon as one example of the modern Klan's increasing reliance on female members. [NYT 1975]

BAGWELL, ROBERT

A native of either Tennessee or North Carolina (the sources are conflicting), Bagwell joined the Klan at age fourteen, later drifting into the National States Rights Party and wearing the party's initials tattooed, with a skull, on his arm. Moving to Roosevelt, Long Island, he joined the Minutemen there while working as a gardener. In October 1966, he was one of twenty Minutemen arrested by New York State Police on weapons charges. Bagwell unsuccessfully ran for a New York State congressional seat in 1970, representing the Minutemen's Patriot Party with the slogan "Send a Minuteman to Congress." [46; 90]

BAILES, GEORGE LEWIS

See *Federated Ku Klux Klans, Inc.*

BAILEY, CHARLES

An Alabama Klansman sentenced to federal prison in 1983 for setting fire to the Montgomery office of the Southern Poverty Law Center, Bailey was arrested again in July 1985 for burning a cross in front of the home of a black county commissioner. [NYT 1985]

BAILEY, DANIEL L.

A native of Norfolk, Virginia, and a corporal in the U.S. Marine Corps, Bailey served as David Duke's exalted cyclops at Camp Pendleton, California, during 1976. His unit, consisting of sixteen known members, was exposed on November 13, 1976, after black marines staged a commando-type raid on a Klan-occupied barracks. Military authorities found a list of Bailey's Klansmen the next day, which produced new publicity for Duke's Knights of the KKK. Racial brawls were common at Camp Pendleton, which had 6,000 blacks among its 32,000 marines; in 1975, Oceanside's police chief called black marines the main cause of violent crime in his town. Marine commanders took immediate steps to separate the identified Klansmen, and Bailey was arrested by military police on December 4, 1976, for refusing to obey a transfer order. Flown under guard to a base at New River, North Carolina, he blamed the Marine Corps for "reverse discrimination." Pfc. K.A. Lagerman, a former roommate of several Klansmen at Camp Pendleton, testified at a pretrial hearing of black marines charged with assault that he heard Klansmen threaten blacks and that he had observed illegal weapons in the barracks on various occasions. [NYT 1976]

BAILEY, ELMER

See *Federated Ku Klux Klans, Inc.*

BAILEY, S.G.

A white resident of Goodwater, Alabama, Bailey was abducted by Klansmen, tied to tree, and flogged on the night of July 19, 1949. S.J. Thomas, a black student and military veteran, was flogged at the same time. Authorities suspected members of the Federated Ku Klux Klans, but no one was specifically identified. [NYT 1949]

BAILEY, WALTER F.

In 1958, Bailey founded the Mississippi Knights of the Ku Klux Klan, based at Gulfport, with himself serving as imperial wizard. Never boasting more than twenty-five members, Bailey was reduced to a one-man operation after the White Knights emerged in early 1964. The Mississippi Knights disappeared with his death two years later. [38]

BAILEY, WESLEY GUY, III

A Georgia attorney and klokard of Clayton County Klavern No. 52, United Klans of America, Bailey appeared before the House Un-American Activities Committee in November 1965. A reluctant witness, he refused to answer questions about a June 29, 1964, meeting in the Lake City Community House, where Klansmen agreed that violence might be necessary to stop integration. Bailey's klavern also sponsored an October 1964 seminar on violent techniques for Klansmen interested in armed resistance to black progress. [38]

BAKER, GEORGE

As mayor of Portland, Oregon, Baker sought to run for the U.S. Senate in 1922, with backing from Grand Dragon Fred Gifford. His hopes collapsed when some members backed House Speaker K.K. Kubli, dividing Klan support. Grand Dragon Gifford wound up backing incumbent Sen. Charles McNary for his successful reelection bid, while Baker's campaign was sidelined and forgotten. [10]

BAKER, REV. JAMES

A black minister in McComb, Mississippi, Baker was the target of a KKK bombing that damaged his home on September 9, 1964. The leader of the attack was identified as Billy Wilson, a member of the United Klans of America, who had drawn lots with other Klansmen on September 1 to select local targets. The dynamite used on Baker's home was originally earmarked for a different target, which Klansmen failed to destroy. [38]

BAKER, WILSON

A captain in the Selma, Alabama, police department, Baker ran for sheriff against incumbent Jim Clark in 1958, and addressed a Klan rally outside of town during the last days of the campaign. The move backfired, however, as Baker gained few white votes and lost whatever black support he may have had. In 1964, Mayor Joe Smitherman appointed the moderate Baker as police chief in an effort to control Clark and his special posse of deputized racists within the city limits. Responsible for the arrest of Reverend James Reeb's murderers in 1965, Wilson was unable to prevent their acquittal by an all-white jury. [20]

BAKER HUNTING & FISHING CLUB

Testimony collected by the House Un-American Activities Committee in 1965 identified this group as a front for the Original Knights of the KKK in Baker, Louisiana. [38]

BALDWIN, WILLIAM

A former Klansman, Baldwin sparked controversy in 1930 when Senator Gerald Nye selected him as a chief aide to the Senate Election Expenditures Committee. [10]

BALLENTINE, DONALD J.

A defector from the United Florida Ku Klux Klan, Ballentine emerged as the imperial wizard of Jacksonville's Militant Knights when the splinter group was first organized in the spring of 1965. Still active in early 1967, Ballentine and his Klan disappeared by the time a new survey was completed in 1970. [38]

BANKS, J. AUSTIN

A resident of Montgomery, Alabama, and an officer of the Alabama Knights of the KKK, Banks sent a telegram to President John F. Kennedy in early 1961, denouncing Charles Merriwether—Kennedy's newly appointed member of the Export-Import Bank—as a "tool of the Jews." [14]

BANKS, PARKS

A black resident of Yazoo City, Mississippi, Banks was found hanging from a tree outside of town on August 22, 1922. Authorities reported that Banks had engaged in verbal altercations with local KKK leaders and had ignored subsequent warnings to leave town. His murder remains "unsolved." [*NYT* 1922]

BARFIELD, HARVEY

See *Floyd, Esther; Johnson, Woodrow.*

BARFIELD, MARSDEN

See *Rogers, Ernest and Christine.*

BARKER, E.G.

A one-armed Union veteran who, doubled as a state senator and an agent of the Freedmen's Bureau in Crittenden County, Arkansas, Barker was shot and seriously wounded by Klansmen in August 1868. Several arrests were made in the case, including the local sheriff (a Klansman), and three of the suspects were killed while trying to escape. A fourth defendant in the case was later convicted of several murders and hanged. [87]

BARKER, FRANK D.

Chairman of the 1968 Wallace-for-President Committee in Norwalk, Connecticut, Barker was also one of six Minutemen who were indicted for conspiracy to commit arson and assault with intent to kill after an August 1968 raid on a pacifist camp near Voluntown. Four of the raiders, one state trooper, and a female camper were wounded in the shootout. [17]

BARMORE, SEYMOUR

A former treasury agent hired by Governor William Brownlow to gather information on the Reconstruction KKK in Tennessee, Barmore was snatched from a train in Columbia after midnight on January 12, 1869, taken into the nearby woods, and shot to death. His body was recovered from the Duck River weeks later. [87]

BARNARD, ELMO C.

A Mobile, Alabama, Klansman and gunsmith whose shop was located half a block from the police station, Barnard killed Melvin Williams, a fifteen-year-old-black, during an alleged burglary on September 26, 1953. Barnard was later identified as the leader of the Klan group that visited a Loxley, Alabama, Missionary Baptist Church on October 15, 1955, where they received an enthusiastic welcome from the pastor after handing over a cash donation. In April 1957, Barnard was named as the leader of the Gulf Ku Klux Klan. At the time, he said "a little violence" might be needed to preserve segregation in the South. He also declared, "We're for free speech, free press, white supremacy, free public schools—be sure you put that white supremacy in there—just laws, the pursuit of happiness and no foreign creeds. One thing we don't like is social equality, and that's what the Supreme Court declared for. It's my information a lot of money changed hands in that deal. All this agitation in the South is communist-inspired." [NYT 1955; 48]

BARNES, SIDNEY

While serving as police chief of Savannah, Georgia, Barnes appeared at a United Klans rally of 3,000 persons on July 20, 1963, where he accepted a Bible and a copy of the U.S. Constitution from Grand Dragon Calvin Craig as the assembled Klansmen chanted "Barnes for mayor." Incumbent Mayor Malcolm MacLean had rejected a United Klans invitation and had banned a Klan parade in the wake of recent violence. [NYT 1963]

BARNES, SIDNEY CROCKETT

A resident of Mobile, Alabama, Barnes hosted group meetings at which anti-Semitic records were played and discussed during the 1960s. In the fall of 1963, he joined several Klansmen on a trip to Birmingham, hoping to kill Dr. Martin Luther King, but their target remained elusive. While visiting Birmingham, shortly before a church bombing killed four black children, Barnes participated in a secret conference with Klan associates John Crommelin and William Potter Gale. His Mobile home was the site of Kathy Ainsworth's first meeting with Thomas Tarrants. [39; 84]

BARNETT, ETHEL GLEN

Known to his friend as "Hop," Barnett preceded Lawrence Rainey as sheriff of Neshoba County, Mississippi. Like Rainey, he was a member of the White Knights of the KKK. In May 1962, Barnett was present, along with Rainey and another deputy, when Willie Nash, a black epileptic who had been secured with handcuffs, was riddled with police bullets. One of twenty-one Klansmen arrested by FBI agents on December 4, 1964, in connection with the Michael Schwerner case, Barnett was reelected as sheriff in 1967 despite his mistrial and pending charges that could have sent him to prison. The government dismissed its charges against Barnett on January 27, 1973. [96]

BARNETT, LLOYD

A Klansman from Algiers, Louisiana, Barnett was one of six arrested on June 21, 1966, and charged with participation in a series of New Orleans firebombings between March 1, 1956, and May 11, 1965, that damaged two churches, a furniture store, and several homes. [NYT 1966]

BARNETT, ROSS

An attorney from Jackson, Mississippi, Barnett defended racist agitator John Kasper at his trial in Tennessee during 1957. Elected governor of Mississippi in 1959, in part because of his promise to maintain segregation, he has often been held responsible for sparking the race riot at Oxford in 1962. Barnett's resistance to the court-ordered enrollment of black student James Meredith created an uneasy atmosphere at the state university campus, and his attempts to discourage offers of "help" from the Klan and the National States Rights Party did little to prevent the violence that claimed two lives. Barred by law from succeeding himself, Barnett ran unsuccessfully for office again in 1967, finding his warmest reception before gatherings of a Klan front group, Americans for Preservation of the White Race. [83]

BARNETTE, HORACE DOYLE

See *Schwerner, Michael.*

BARNETTE, TRAVIS MARYN

See *Schwerner, Michael.*

BARNETTE, W.C.

A former Shreveport judge, Barnette defended accused Klansmen in the 1922 Mer Rouge, Louisiana, murder case. In 1924, Klan headquarters named him as one of three Klansmen chosen to handle realm affairs after several leading officers were expelled for their support of state bills requiring the KKK to unmask and register lists of its members. The expulsions led to mass defections from the ranks, and the Louisiana realm fell into obscurity. [10]

BARTLETT, CHARLES

Bartlett served as an instructor at the October 17, 1964, "violence school" that was sponsored by the United Klans of America Clayton County

Klavern No. 52 on a farm owned by Klansman Robert Bing. Bartlett was also listed as the incorporator of a local KKK front group, the Clayton Civic Club. [NYT 1965]

BASS, FRED M.

A Tampa, Florida, kleagle, Bass was accused of plotting the 1935 slaying of Joseph Shoemaker with local police. At their trial, Bass and Tampa's police chief were acquitted, while five patrolmen were convicted and sentenced to jail. [93]

BASSETT, JOHN DAVID

In 1925, Bassett opposed Catholic incumbent John Purcell in the race for Virginia state treasurer. Klansmen endorsed him as the "100 percent candidate," but Bassett hedged on the question of whether he was a member of the KKK. Anti-Catholic propaganda was widely used in the campaign, and a Democratic Party investigation traced one shipment back to Klan "troubleshooter" James Esdale. Bassett was ultimately defeated by a narrow margin of votes. [10]

BASSETT CREEK HUNTING CLUB

In 1965 congressional investigators identified this club as a front group for the Wagarville, Alabama, klavern, United Klans of America. [38]

BATTLES, CHARLES R.

See *Pace, Reverend Edward.*

BAXLEY, WILLIAM J.

Elected as state attorney general in 1970 at age twenty-eight with the support of George Wallace, Baxley won 83 percent of the popular vote. He soon earned a reputation for prosecuting corrupt sheriffs and legislators, winning reelection without opposition in 1974. Despite his close friendship with Wallace and his obvious grooming for a gubernatorial race, Baxley was determined to pursue Klan terrorists on charges dating from the 1950s and 1960s. While a student at the University of Alabama in 1963, he had found himself especially disturbed by the Birmingham church bombing, and pursued the case as state attorney general, but refrained from any comment on the role played by Wallace or Colonel Al Lingo in the fourteen-year cover-up. Threats of adverse publicity finally jarred the reluctant FBI into cooperating with Baxley, and in 1977 he successfully prosecuted ex-Klansman Robert Chambliss for one murder in the Birmingham case. Baxley also won indictments in the 1957 Willie Edwards murder in Montgomery, but charges were ultimately dismissed on a technicality. In 1978, Baxley lost his race for the governor's office. [10]

BAXTER, C.M.

In 1958 Baxter was identified as Washington's state chairman for the neo-fascist National States Rights Party. [65]

BEACH, PHILLIP DANIEL

An Indiana KKK and Nazi activist, Beach was sentenced to prison in 1982 for vandalizing a synagogue and a Jewish cemetery. Following his release, in April 1985, he was arrested on charges of firing a rifle into a teenager's car in Evansville. Codefendant Cesare Motisi was also charged in the shooting. [NYT 1985]

BEALL, FRANK H.

One of Maryland's earliest Klan recruits in 1922 and the state's first exalted cyclops, Beall quit his job as chief inspector for the Baltimore City Highways Department to serve as grand dragon when the realm was chartered in 1923. He was quickly disillusioned by dishonest recruiting techniques, inflated membership estimates, and the low quality of recruits, leading to quarrels with the national headquarters in Atlanta. Internal clashes and confusion led to Beall's resignation in June 1926, with a parting blast at the Klan's national propagation department as "shamefully crooked" and "shockingly immoral." [10]

BEAM, LOUIS RAY, JR.

As a child growing up in Lake Jackson, Texas, Louis Beam attended an all-white school, and classmates recall that he was "very much against blacks." Military service in Vietnam did nothing to change his views, and when he returned home, Beam joined the Texas realm of the United Klans of America, then led by Grand Dragon Frank Converse. By 1971 he was a member of the United Klans's Klan Bureau of Investigation, serving as a self-styled public relations man. On June 11, 1971, Beam was one of four Texas Klansmen indicted on charges of mounting a terrorist campaign against the local Pacifica Foundation radio station, as well as other targets. Eluding conviction he shifted allegiance to David Duke's newly reorganized Knights of the KKK in 1976, emerging from the reorganization as Duke's grand titan for Texas. This post gave Beam responsibility for new recruitment, and his special targets during 1978 and 1979 were soldiers serving at Ft. Hood, Texas. When Duke and Beam addressed a rally at Euless, Texas, in the summer of 1979, their "honor guard" consisted of new recruits from Ft. Hood, dressed in paramilitary uniforms complete with pistols, rifles, and bayonets. Known for his extremism of word and deed, Beam ranted at one Texas Klan rally that "I've got news for you, nigger. I'm not going to be in front of my television set, I'm gonna be hunting you. I don't need any of the three Jewish-owned networks to tell me what I've got to do. I've got the Bible in one hand and a .38 in the other hand and I know what to do." One step toward the ultimate hunt was Beam's organization of the so-called Texas Emergency Reserve for paramilitary training of both adults and, in the case of one facility near Houston, teenage members of the Civil Air Patrol and Boy Scouts Explorer program. In early 1981 Beam's Klansmen targeted a Texas community of Vietnamese refugees, and consequently were sued by the Southern Poverty Law Center and the Vietnamese Fishermen's Association in April 1981. Beam and his followers were slapped with an injunction against acts of harassment in May, and a second lawsuit, aimed at the Klan's paramilitary training camps, led to the issuance of a permanent injunction in June 1982. Fresh from his defeats in court, Beam became a self-styled "ambassador at large" for the Aryan Nations, developing a point system for the qualification of "aryan warriors." In Beam's calculations—available to racists nationwide on computerized bulletin boards—killing a congressman was worth one fifth of a point, judges one sixth, federal agents one tenth, and newsmen or local politicians one twelfth. Instant qualification, with one full point, could be earned by killing the president. In April 1987, Beam was one of fourteen neo-Nazis indicted on federal sedition charges, after which he immediately disappeared. Added to the FBI's "Ten Most Wanted" list on July 14, 1987, he was traced to Guadalajara, Mexico, and captured there on November 6, after his wife engaged in a brief shootout with Mexican authorities. All fourteen defendants were acquitted at their trial in Ft. Smith, Arkansas, on April 7, 1988. Beam emerged from the courtroom triumphant, telling reporters, "There are over 150 other political prisoners being held in ZOG's jails that need to be freed. I think ZOG has suffered a terrible defeat here today. I think everyone saw through the charade and saw that I was simply being punished for being a vociferous and outspoken opponent of ZOG [Zionist Occupational Government in Washington, D.C.]." [NYT 1971, 1987, 1988; 2; 93]

BEASLEY, JERE L.

Alabama's lieutenant governor under George Wallace, Beasley appeared as a guest speaker at the United Klans of America 1970 klonvocation. [10]

BEAUFORT COUNTY HUNTING CLUB NO. 18

Known also simply as Hunting Club No. 18, this group was identified in 1965 as a cover for the Beaufort, South Carolina, klavern, United Klans of America. [38]

BEAVER CREEK MEN'S FELLOWSHIP CLUB

In 1966 congressional investigators named this club as a front for Unit No. 66, United Klans of America, in Kinston, North Carolina. [38]

BEAVERS, GRADON

See *Lauderdale, E.A.*

BECKERMAN, MILTON

As editor of the *Claxton Enterprise* in Claxton, Georgia, Beckerman was a staunch enemy of the local KKK. In August 1949, his editorials exposed a new businessman's club as a Klan front, prompting a series of telephone threats and an incident in which one Klansman attacked Beckerman with a hammer. In March 1950, the *Enterprise* called for a city anti-mask law and a ban on KKK meetings at the local Masonic lodge. Klansmen retaliated with a horn-blowing motorcade that drove across Beckerman's lawn, then fled when he opened fire with a rifle. The recommended anti-mask law was passed, with support from church and civic groups, but Beckerman refused to take the credit. "We wrote the stories," he said, "and the people did the work." [*Newsweek*, April 17, 1960]

BECKWITH, BYRON DE LA

Born in California, Beckwith, the son of Mississippi natives, returned with his family to the state when he was five years old. In 1957, working as a fertilizer salesman in Greenwood, Beckwith authored a letter to the editors of a Jackson newspaper that read: "I believe in segregation like I believe in God. I shall combat the evils of integration and I shall bend every effort to rid the U.S.A. of the integrationist whoever and wherever he may be." To that end, Beckwith first joined the local Citizens' Council, and later the KKK. When the National Council of the Protestant Episcopal Church announced a policy of nondiscrimination in its churches, Beckwith printed and distributed handbills attacking the church's policy (he once attended church with a revolver in his pocket, in case a black person should try to enter). In a January 1963 letter to the National Rifle Association, Beckwith wrote: "Gentlemen, for the next 15 years we here in Mississippi are going to have to do a lot of shooting to protect our wives, children and ourselves from bad niggers." After NAACP leader Medgar Evers was shot to death at his home in Jackson on June 12, 1963, two local cabbies identified Beckwith as the passenger who asked for directions to Evers' home. According to the witnesses, Beckwith explained, "I've got to find him in a couple of days." (After Beckwith's arrest, the Jackson *Clarion-Ledger* ran an ironic headline: "Californian Is Charged With Murder of Medgar Evers.") FBI agents uncovered evidence that Beckwith and two other men attended a mass meeting addressed by Evers the night before his murder, and left when an NAACP secretary asked their business. Held in the Rankin County Jail after his indictment, Beckwith was treated like a hero, permitted to keep his own television and his private gun collection with him in his cell. The Hinds County sheriff refused to allow the guns in his jail when Beckwith was transferred in November 1963, despite Beckwith's appeal that he might need them "mighty bad when I get out." The defendant's trial expenses were covered by an ad hoc White Citizens Legal Fund, with fourteen leading business and professional men on the board of directors. Byron's defense attorneys included a former district attorney, a leader of local citizens' council, and a member of Governor Ross Barnett's law firm. At his first trial, a Greenwood businessman and two policemen swore they were with Beckwith at the time when Evers was shot. Beckwith claimed that the murder weapon, a rifle linked to Evers by ballistics tests, was stolen from his home some time before the crime. On February 7, 1964, a mistrial was declared, with jurors deadlocked 7–5 for acquittal. Retired General Edwin Walker appeared in court to shake hands with Beckwith after the announcement, and Beckwith promptly joined the White Knights of the KKK after his release. (In 1968, FBI informant Delmar Dennis informed the author that Beckwith was previously a member of the Original Knights of the KKK.) Klansmen turned out in force for Beckwith's second murder trial in April 1964, with ten crosses burned statewide on the night of April 10, and seventy-five Klansmen packing the court when proceedings began the next day. A key witness, cab driver H.R. Speight, this time backed off from his positive identification of Beckwith, claiming that his passenger merely resembled Beckwith. Under cross-examination, Speight admitted receiving threats on his life. A second mistrial was declared on April 17, with jurors deadlocked 8–4 for acquittal. Beckwith returned to Greenwood in a triumphant procession, greeted by crowds with welcome signs. (Local blacks got a discouraging message after the trial, when the U.S. Post Office purchased land from Beckwith for $25,000.) Free on bond pending a third trial that never materialized, Beckwith joined other racists in harassing white patrons of a desegregated theater in Greenwood. Informant Delmar Dennis placed Beckwith at White Knights violence seminars held outside of Jackson, including one occasion when he confessed to the Evers murder. Beckwith told in the audience that "killing that nigger gave me no more inner discomfort than our wives endure when they give birth to our children. We ask them to do that for us. We should do just as much. So, let's get in there and kill those enemies, including the president, from the top down!" In May 1965 Beckwith helped kleagle Gordon Lackey paint a black ring around the home of man who hired "the wrong nigger" to paint his house. In 1966, Beckwith was identified as a part owner of *The Southern Review*, a local pro-Klan newspaper. He entered the race for lieutenant governor in February 1967, saying that the campaign "will provide me with the opportunity to repay the many kindnesses which I have received from my fellow Mississippians by offering myself as a candidate whose political position has already been clearly established." Voters rejected Beckwith at the polls, but he remained active in racist circles. In 1973 he was featured as a guest speaker at the National States Rights Party's annual convention. On October 1 of that year he was arrested in New Orleans on federal firearms and explosives charges, and was indicted on three counts on October 9. An informant had exposed Beckwith's plan to bomb the home of Anti-Defamation League director Adolph Blotnick. Klansmen came to Beckwith's defense, with David Duke announcing, "This penniless victim of government illegality and crime must be defended." Beckwith was acquitted on January 19, 1974, after a five-day trial. His attorney persuaded jurors that the bomb was planted in Beckwith's car without his knowledge, to frame or kill him, while the various guns were dismissed as instruments of self-defense. [NYT 1963-74; 38; 54]

BEDFORD FORREST KLANS

One of three Florida splinter Klans reported active in the early 1960s, this group had dissolved prior to congressional investigations in 1965. [14]

BEHRINGER, JOHN

An ex-policeman serving as grand dragon of New Jersey in 1968, Behringer told newsmen on June 23 of that year that he had inducted vigilante leader Anthony Imperiale into the Klan on April 19, 1967. Imperiale denied the charge, but admitted teaching karate to Klansmen. [NYT 1968]

BELL, ARTHUR H.

An attorney from Bloomfield, New Jersey, Bell also served as grand dragon for the Knights of the KKK during the 1920s and 1930s, while his wife handled affairs for the Tri-K Girls. In 1928, Bell rented a hotel room in Atlantic City and invited candidates to drop by and prove their Americanism before the pending election, but there were no takers. He arranged a joint rally of the Klan and the German-American Bund in New Jersey on August 18, 1940. Bell himself was a featured speaker at the gathering, denouncing the singing of "God Bless America" as a Jewish song fit only for brothels. Public outcry over the rally led Imperial Wizard James Colescott to remove Bell from his Klan office, citing Bell's failure "to adhere to the principles and ideals of the Klan." Called before a congressional panel investigating the Bund in October 1940, Bell said he thought the joint meeting was a good idea at the time, "but I don't now." [93]

BELLESEN, PAUL L.

A black Catholic from Nampa, Idaho, Bellesen joined the National Knights of the KKK by mail as a prank in 1965. Imperial Wizard James Venable appointed him grand titan for the state, sight unseen, with predictable embarrassment for all concerned when Bellesen took his story to the media. [93]

BELLOWS, JIM

A reporter for the *Columbus Ledger* (Georgia), Bellows was assigned, along with Carl Johnson and photographer Joe Talbott, to cover a Klan rally at Pine Mountain State Park on March 13, 1948. After hearing Dr. Samuel Green address 200 Klansmen, the journalists were assaulted, drugged, and forced to drink liquor, after which they were jailed overnight as drunks. Rally participants identified by Bellows included: Fred New, editor and publisher of the *Georgia Tribune*, a white supremacist weekly; Reverend E.G. Johnson, the *Tribune*'s former publisher; and Hollis Cooper, an Alabama resident employed as circulation manager for the *Ledger*. Confronted with evidence of his role in the frame-up of his three co-workers, Cooper resigned from his job with the paper. [*NYT* 1948]

BELSER, MORGAN S.

As attorney of record for the Association of Georgia Klans, Belser filed the group's state charter application on March 21, 1946, and paid back fees for the period of 1940–1946. Klan incorporation papers identify Belser as the secretary of the Knights of the Ku Klux Klan, Inc. [*NYT* 1946]

BELT LINE

A form of punishment reserved for Klansmen charged and convicted of violating KKK rules, the belt line is essentially a gauntlet run by the accused, while other members of his klavern whip the runner with their belts or leather straps. [38]

BENEVOLENT ASSOCIATION

A congressional report published in 1967 identified this group as a cover for the Winterville, North Carolina, klavern, United Klans of America. [38]

BENEVOLENT ASSOCIATION UNIT NO. 53

See *Pitt County Christian Fellowship Club.*

BENJAMIN, REV. DALE J.

In 1958 news reports identified Reverend Benjamin as the National States Rights Party's state chairman in Oregon. [65]

BENNETT, CLAUDE

See *Penn, Lemuel.*

BENNETT, TROY

See *Flowers, Evergreen.*

BENTCLIFFE, HOWARD

On February 26, 1958, Bentcliffe pled guilty to burning a cross illegally in Levittown, Pennsylvania, on September 6, 1957. Codefendant Eldred Williams pled guilty to the same charge at an earlier date. [NYT 1958]

BENTLEY, EMERSON

Bentley was a precocious eighteen year old who doubled as a teacher at a black school in St. Landry Parish, Louisiana, and as the editor of a local Republican newspaper during Reconstruction. On September 28, 1868, three members of the Knights of the White Camellia visited Bentley's school and demanded that he recant a recent article attacking their organization. When he refused, Bentley was beaten in front of his class. The attack nearly began a riot by blacks, but Bentley personally intervened and restored peace. [87]

BENTLEY, JACK

See Cruell, Claude.

BERG, ALAN

The Jewish moderator of a controversial radio talk show in Denver, Colorado, Berg was murdered by members of a neo-Nazi group, The Order, on June 18, 1984. Defendants in the case included former Klansman David Lane, Bruce Pierce, Richard Scutari, and Jean Craig. Lane and Pierce were convicted of Berg's murder on November 17, 1987, while Scutari and Craig were acquitted. On December 3, 1987, Lane and Pierce were sentenced to prison terms of 150 years without parole. [85]

BERGERON, SANDRA

Serving as a giant for David Duke's Knights of the KKK in Jefferson Parish, Louisiana, Bergeron was frequently cited as living proof of a women's role in the "new" Klan. Her husband once bailed Duke out of jail after his arrest in New Orleans for inciting a riot. [84]

BERGMAN, WALTER

A former director of the Detroit, Michigan, public school system, Bergman was a participant in the May 1961 Freedom Rides sponsored by the Congress of Racial Equality (CORE). Permanently injured and confined to a wheelchair from injuries received when Klansmen beat him in Birmingham, Bergman filed suit against the FBI in 1983, charging that it failed to prevent the attack despite prior notice from confidential informants. On February 7, 1984, a federal court ordered the FBI to pay Bergman damages totaling $45,000. [93]

BERMANZOHN, DR. PAUL

A resident of Durham, North Carolina, Bermanzohn participated in a November 1979 anti-Klan rally sponsored by the Communist Workers Party in Greensboro, North Carolina. Shot in the head when Klansmen attacked the march, Bermanzohn remains permanently confined to wheelchair. [*UPI*, June 16, 1980]

BERNICE SPORTSMAN'S CLUB

In 1965, congressional investigators identified this club as a front for the Bernice, Louisiana, klavern, United Klans of America. [38]

BERRY, ISAAC M.

With assistance from Republican Judge Charlton, Berry organized an anti-Klan group in Blount County, Alabama, during the fall of 1869. Several ex-Klansmen were recruited for the effort, with armed bands visiting the homes of known members to warn them from raiding in the future. The tactic was effective, and Klan terrorism in the region was substantially reduced. [87]

BERRY, JAMES ENFIELD

See *Lynch, John.*

BERRY, MRS. REANER

A Reconstruction target of the Klan in Broomtown, Alabama, Berry was victimized when Klansmen broke into her house, surprising her and her son George, his wife, and a neighborhood girl. The women were told that the raiders "wanted to bed with them"; when they refused, Berry's son received thirty lashes, while Berry and the neighborhood girl were gang-raped. Berry's daughter-in-law escaped a similar fate by saying she had recently miscarried and was still bleeding. [93]

BEST, H.D.

A victim of the Association of Carolina Klans, Best was abducted from his home by Klansmen who had asked to use his telephone. Accused of beating his wife, he was bent over a car fender and flogged by his kidnappers. [*Life*, March 31, 1952]

BETTER CITIZENS CLUB

A cover for the Mount Olive, North Carolina, klavern, United Klans of America, this group was publicly exposed by congressional hearings in 1965. [38]

BETTIS, FRANK

A white feed-and-flour merchant in Atlanta, Bettis earned Klan enmity in 1949 by complaining to police about a hooded parade through his neighborhood. Klansmen and police subsequently cooperated to frame him on a drunk driving charge, but jurors acquitted Bettis at his trial. [25]

BETTS, REV. JAMES L.

Identified as the grand dragon of the New Order of Knights of the KKK, in St. Louis, Missouri, Betts sported a Hitler-style haircut and mustache to match his neo-Nazi uniform and KKK armband. His chief activity was publication of the newspaper *White Liberty!*. In March 1976, Betts offered police a team of forty Klansmen to help patrol the streets, but the authorities declined his generosity. [NYT 1976; 44]

BEVERIDGE, ALBERT

An anti-Klan progressive who ran for the U.S. Senate in Indiana during 1922, Beveridge lost by a landslide of pro-Klan votes. [93]

BICKLEY, JAMES H.

Appointed as South Carolina's grand dragon for the U.S. Klans in September 1956, Bickley increased the state's number of klaverns from twenty to thirty-five by January 1957. Proud of his achievement, Bickley told the press, "I ain't got nothing against niggers. I don't believe most of them would be causing any trouble if it wasn't for the NAACP and the Jews. I understand there are a lot of communists behind this thing, trying to get us to integrate with the niggers so we'll breed down the race." [48]

BICKNELL, JOHN

A member of the Reconstruction Klan and Pale Faces in Maury County, Tennessee, Bicknell was robbed and killed by a black highwayman named Walker in late February 1868. Both groups paraded at his funeral, with Klansmen marching in full regalia. Bicknell's killer was subsequently taken from jail in Columbia and lynched. [87]

BIGBY, HERMAN

A resident of Royston, Georgia, Bigby was fatally wounded when Klansmen raided his home on the night of March 10, 1926. A friend of Bigby's, Walton Adams, was also killed in the attack. [NYT 1926]

BIGGERSTAFF, AARON

An elderly Unionist and resident of Rutherford County, North Carolina, during Reconstruction, Biggerstaff was despised by many of his neighbors. Accused of helping Northerners seize horses from Confederates in the county during the Civil War, he also opposed Klan efforts to intimidate blacks and Republicans. In early 1870, Biggerstaff helped track a party of Klan nightriders to the home of his own half brother, Samuel Biggerstaff. The affair resulted in Aaron's conviction of forcible trespass, after he and others fired on the house. On April 8, 1871, forty Klansmen raided Biggerstaff's home, and flogged him and his married daughter. He managed to identify several of the raiders and had them arrested. En route to testify at a pretrial hearing in Shelby, Cleveland County, Biggerstaff was ambushed and beaten a second time. Several Klansmen were eventually convicted and imprisoned for the assaults. [87]

BILBO, THEODORE

A former governor and longtime senator from Mississippi, Bilbo easily won his third Senate term in July 1946 despite his admission of Klan membership. Opponents said Bilbo was "clowning," and they denied the existence of any Klan in Mississippi since 1924, but Bilbo insisted, "I am a member of the Ku Klux Klan, Bilbo Klan No. 40, Mississippi. I don't know what the present Klan stands for." In a typical campaign speech, he proclaimed, "Mississippi is white. We got a right to keep it that way and I care not what [U.S. Attorney General] Tom Clark and [Supreme Court Justice] Hugo Black say. I'm calling on every red-blooded American who believes in the superiority and integrity of the white race to get out and see that no nigger votes. Use all the power, the legal power, lawful power, and persuasion." [FOF 1946]

BILLUPS, REV. CHARLES

A black minister in Birmingham, Alabama, and a charter member of the Alabama Christian Movement for Human Rights, Billups was abducted by Klansmen on the night of April 10, 1959. His kidnappers beat Billups with tire chains in an effort to extract information about the civil rights movement at Miles College, a black college in Birmingham, but the minister refused to talk. [64]

BING, ROBERT LEWIS

A Georgia farmer and exalted cyclops of Clayton County Klavern 52, United Klans of America, Bing played host to a United Klans violence seminar on October 17, 1964. His position on violence had apparently remained consistent since 1958, when he attended a meeting of various Klan factions convened by Hugh Morris at the Henry Grady Hotel in Atlanta to discuss the advisability of burning integrated schools. Congressional investigators named Bing as the organizer of a special United Klans action squad, designated the "White Band," but he refused to answer questions on this or other subjects when he was subpoenaed by the House Un-American Activities Committee in 1965. [38]

BIRDSONG, BILLY

A member of the White Knight of the KKK, Birdsong ran a motel in Meridian, Mississippi, and relayed communications to local Klansmen from Imperial Wizard Samuel Bowers. The relationship was severed in early 1965, and Birdsong was severely beaten when Bowers began to suspect that he was an FBI informant. [59]

BIRTH OF A NATION

The first epic movie, *Birth of a Nation,* directed by D.W. Griffith and based on Thomas Dixon's novel *The Clansman,* proved to be instrumental in reviving the Ku Klux Klan. The film's premiere in Los Angeles on January 8, 1915, earned critical raves and strident opposition from the recently formed NAACP. Dixon personally called on college classmate President Woodrow Wilson and arranged for a private screening at the White House, which was attended by the president and members of his cabinet. Afterward, Wilson declared, "It is like writing history with lightning, and my only regret is that it is all so terribly true." The next day, Dixon arranged a screening for other Washington notables, including Supreme Court Chief Justice Edward White, a former Klansman from Louisiana. The collected endorsements helped Griffith's film past the National Board of Censorship, but blacks continued their protests. A group of blacks were denied entry to Boston's Tremont Theater, some of whom then snuck in and hurled eggs at the screen. The film's March opening in Boston also led to critical attacks, and public hearings held on April 7 resulted in strategic deletions from the print. News of the protests led President Wilson and Justice White to recant their earlier endorsements, but the film went on to gross more than $60 million. Its December 1915 opening in Atlanta inspired William Simmons to hold a resurrection ceremony for the Klan atop nearby Stone Mountain. Considered a film classic, units of the United Klans used old prints as a recruiting device well into the 1960s, and the film still draws protests at some screenings. On June 10, 1980, a scheduled showing at the Richilieu Cinema, a San Francisco art house, led to picketing by the International Committee Against Racism and protestors vandalizing the theater, forcing it to close. [10; 93]

BISHOP, ANN

A resident of Little Rock, Arkansas, and active in the National States Rights Party, Bishop helped gather the 29,552 signatures required to put that party on the state ballot in 1960. (On election day, the party polled 28,952 votes in Arkansas.) In 1962, Bishop was identified as the NSRP's executive secretary. [14]

BISHOP, RONALD R., JR.

Identified as a Michigan Klan leader during the summer of 1980, Bishop was a weekend visitor to the Galveston, Texas, paramilitary training camp maintained by Louis Beam's Texas Emergency Reserve. In November 1980 Bishop was one of three Klansmen who pled guilty to shooting a black man for drinking in a "white" Detroit tavern. The guilty plea earned Bishop a sentence of one to four years in prison. [NYT 1980]

BLACK, HUGO L.

As, a young county prosecutor in Alabama, Black handled the case in 1916 of a kleagle who embezzled Klan funds. Five years later, he defended a Klansman responsible for the shooting of a priest who had married his daughter to a Puerto Rican by persuading the jury that the act constituted justifiable homicide. With an eye on politics, Black joined Birmingham's Robert E. Lee Klan No. 1 during a mass initiation held in September 1923. He resigned his membership in 1925 with the consent of Klan headquarters to avoid unpleasant questions in the 1926 Senate race. Elected to the U.S. Senate that year, Black was a guest of honor at a victory party held at the Birmingham klavern. His final break with the Klan occurred in 1928, when Black campaigned in Alabama for Catholic presidential candidate Al Smith. In 1937, Black was President Franklin Roosevelt's first nominee to fill a vacancy on the U.S. Supreme Court, winning Senate confirmation despite the controversy sparked by his Klan ties. Klansmen were generally displeased by Black's appointment, viewing any friend of Roosevelt with suspicion, and their worst fears were realized when Black often cast his vote with the court's liberal majority, supporting various rulings on behalf of black civil rights between World War II and his death in 1971. [10]

BLACK, JERROLD

A member of the National States Rights Party, Black was convicted on May 10, 1966, under an Ohio statute that bars the distribution of hate literature. A federal appeals court reversed his conviction on June 13, 1966, holding the law unconstitutional. [NYT 1966]

BLACK, STEPHEN DONALD

Black's anti-Semitic activities date from his high school years in Athens, Alabama, when he joined the National Socialist Youth Movement, a unit of the Virginia-based National Socialist White People's Party. At the same time, he was also active in supporting racist J.B. Stoner's unsuccessful Alabama gubernatorial campaign, a circumstance that Stoner later described as a deliberate effort by the National Socialists to infiltrate the National States Rights Party. In 1970 Black was shot and wounded by States Rights member Jerry Ray, during a break-in at Stoner's party headquarters in Savannah, Georgia. (Ray was acquitted on charges of aggravated assault on November 24, 1970, with Stoner serving as his attorney.) Black went on to hold membership in the White Youth Alliance and the National Party, later forming his own Klan chapter while enrolled at the University of Alabama (where he was forced out of the ROTC because of his racist activities). Black joined David Duke's Knights of the KKK in 1975, and by 1977 had risen to the rank of grand dragon, frequently joining Duke on trips around the country. When Duke resigned his leadership of the Knights in 1980, Black assumed control of the dwindling organization. In the spring of 1981, with nine others, he hatched a plot to overthrow the Dominican government, but the plan failed: Various "seamen" hired for the mission were federal agents working undercover, and Black and his guerillas were charged with violating the Neutrality Act. A conviction on those charges earned Black a three-year prison term. In 1982, before going to prison, Black was chosen to lead a new Confederation of Klans, which was made up of factions led by James Venable, Robert Miles, and Glenn Miller. Committed to prison in December 1982, he emerged in the spring of 1985 to announce the formation of a 120 man Klan unit, the Nathan Bedford Forrest Brigade, which was designed to aid the Contras in Nicaragua. Black announced that his group would engage in psychological warfare in Latin America while at the same time providing "a civil action unit to promote a stable economy." Klansmen apparently felt that they had the official blessings of the White House when President Ronald Reagan declared that it was "traditional" for American volunteers to join revolutionary movements abroad. At this writing, Black's "brigade" is apparently defunct. [93]

BLACK, WILLIAM C.

A former state legislator and wealthy landowner in Reconstruction York County, South Carolina, Black was identified as leader of the Klan council that ordered the murder of Tom Roundtree, a black man, in December 1870. [87]

BLACK K.K.s

A black anti-Klan group reported active in Tennessee during 1868, the organization apparently disbanded due to threats from the state's grand dragon. No details of its activities survive. [87]

BLACK KNIGHTS OF THE KU KLUX KLAN

See Black Shirts.

BLACK LEGION

A Klan look-alike, the Black Legion was organized in Detroit during the early 1930s by industrial workers transplanted from the South. Beginning as a social club with dues of ten cents per month, the organization's structure—and its future—were influenced by the prior Klan affiliation of some members. The Legion first turned to violence after two members were fired from their jobs, and then got them back after their boss was dragged to a Legion gathering and threatened with flogging or death. The word, along with new Legion chapters, quickly spread through Detroit's suburbs and to other industrial cities in Michigan, Indiana, and Ohio. Ex-Klansman V.F. Effinger, from Lima, soon took over as "brigade commander" of the group. In general, the Black Legion did not follow the Klan's path of financial exploitation, but marginal profits were derived from the sale of robes. Legion members cherished the same basic hatreds as Klansmen, and several Michigan units kept in touch with William Dudley Pelley and his Silver Shirts, heeding Pelley's advice for a move into politics. The group's power was growing until WPA worker Charles Poole was found shot to death, execution-style, in a Detroit suburb, late in the spring of 1936. Investigation led police to the Wolverine Club, soon identified as a Legion front. Exposure led to the dismissal of nearly 100 members who were on the Oakland County payroll, and eleven members were convicted of Poole's murder in the fall of 1936. The KKK tried desperately to disassociate itself from Michigan's nightriders. When Hollywood made *The Black Legion in* 1937, starring Humphrey Bogart, and used Klan insignia, KKK leaders filed suit for damages. [10]

"BLACK MONDAY"

On May 17, 1954, nicknamed "Black Monday" by segregationists, the U.S. Supreme Court issued its historic ruling in the Topeka, Kansas, case of *Brown v. the Board of Education,* which ordered U.S. schools to implement racial desegregation "with all deliberate speed." This controversial ruling rejuvenated dormant Klan factions and led to the birth of the new "upper class" Citizens' Councils. Within a year of the Brown decision, an estimated ninety resistance groups were organized, involving over 250,000 whites from all walks of life. Whatever their social station, the groups were encouraged by racist spokesmen such as Mississippi Senator James Eastland, who proclaimed in 1955: "You are not required to obey any court which passes out such a ruling. In fact, you are obligated to defy it." Klansmen were more eager to take Eastland at his word, and spokesmen such as James Venable advised their troops to deal aggressively with the threat of integrated schools. "Let's close them up," Venable demanded. "Let's burn them up, if it comes to that." Inevitably, the South's "respectable" leaders must share a portion of the blame for the outbreaks of violence that affected blacks and white moderates over the next fifteen years, when calls for defiance and resistance at last became the norm in Southern politics. [6; 52]

BLACK MUSLIMS

A black separatist group founded in the 1940s, the Black Muslims—formally known as the Nation of Islam—have enjoyed a curious love-hate relationship with the KKK and its affiliated groups since the early 1960s. George Lincoln Rockwell and his American Nazis were welcomed at Muslim rallies in Washington, D.C., in June 1961, and in Chicago a year later. Returning the favor in 1964, Grand Dragon Calvin Craig introduced Muslim spokesman Jeremiah X at a rally of the United Klans, held in Atlanta's Hurd Park. Conversely, when Muslims purchased a 1,000 acre farm from its white owner in Ashville, Alabama, in 1969, Klansmen violently opposed the sale. Workers at the farm were bombarded with telephone threats and harassed by arrests under a state law that required registration of Black Muslim members. On November 21, 2,200 angry whites rallied at the local high school gym to protest the sale, and nocturnal snipers killed six cows at the farm a few nights later. On December 8, arsonists caused heavy damage to a Pell City auto dealership run by the farm's former owner. Harassment continued into early 1970, with sixty-three cows killed by mid-March. Acid was poured over twelve cars at the Pell City dealership, and the proprietor reported that his business was down "at least 90 percent." United Klans leader Robert Shelton announced his intention to purchase the land surrounding the farm, so that the Klan could "keep an eye on things." On March 16, 1970, the Muslims announced their intent to sell the disputed property—even to the Klan, if they could find no other takers. [NYT 1969–1970]

BLACK RIVER CLUB

In 1965, congressional investigators identified this group as a cover for Unit No. 17, United Klans of America, in Kingstree, South Carolina. [38]

BLACK RIVER IMPROVEMENT CLUB

According to evidence gathered by a congressional panel in 1965, this title was simultaneously used as a front for klaverns of the United Klans of

America in Angier and Wendell, North Carolina. Although evidence is scarce, the two klaverns, located in neighboring Harnett and Wake counties, may well have cooperated on various "projects" during the early 1960s. (Ironically, although the South Black River borders Harnett County, it does not encroach on Wake County, to the north.) [38]

BLACK SHIRTS (1950s)

See *Chessmen.*

BLACK SHIRTS (1960s)

A secretive, violence-prone group within the National Knights of the KKK, the Black Shirts were first organized as the Vigilantes, near Barnesville, Georgia, in the latter half of 1964. National Knights Imperial Wizard James Venable denied any knowledge of the group, which, theoretically, operated without his prior approval. Leaders of the Black Shirts were identified as Earl Holcombe an ex-member of the U.S. Klans, who had been arrested during the 1961 riot in Athens, Georgia, and Colbert McGriff, expelled from the United Klans of America after a shooting incident in Griffin, Georgia. Prominent members of the Black Shirts included two more exiles from the United Klans, Cecil Myers and Joseph Sims, both of whom were later convicted on federal civil rights charges in the July 1964 murder of Lieutenant Colonel Lemuel Penn. Members of the elite action squad dressed all in black, stockpiling mobile arsenals of bludgeons, knives, and guns. When civil rights demonstrations began at Crawfordville, Georgia, in October 1965, the Black Shirts were on hand to harass protesters. Sims and Myers were arrested twice, on October 13 and 18, for assaulting black victims Brigido Cabe and George Turner, respectively, and a special team of state troopers were detailed to follow the pair around to prevent further trouble. [*NYT* 1965; 38]

BLACKBURN, W. JASPER

A Republican congressman elected from Claiborne Parish, Louisiana, in 1868, Blackburn also served as editor of the "radical" *Iliad* in Homer, Louisiana. In the spring of 1868, he visited New Orleans as a delegate to the state constitutional convention, but his return home was delayed by death threats from the local Klan. Blackburn's newspaper office was mobbed and demolished in July and November 1868. [87]

BLACKFORD, WILLIAM T.

A judge in Reconstruction Hale County, Alabama, Blackford was coerced by Klan threats into briefly recanting his Republican party allegiance. As a self-defense measure, he tried cultivating "quality" whites in the area, even joining Nathan Bedford Forrest on a tour to promote railroad expansion in the South. Tuscaloosa Klansman Ryland Randolph denounced Blackford's

association with Grand Wizard Forrest as "disgraceful and disgusting."
[87]

BLACKWELDER, HOMER
See *Dayvault, Wayne.*

BLACKWELL, J.B.
See *Hattie Cotton School.*

BLACKWELL, LEO
As police chief of Griffin, Georgia, Blackwell arrested five Klansmen for
illegally burning a cross outside a black-owned business on April 24, 1964.
A court order forced Chief Blackwell to return a small arsenal of weapons
confiscated from the Klansmen at the time of their arrest. [38]

BLACKWELL REAL ESTATE
A Jackson, Mississippi, firm that had sold houses to blacks, Blackwell's
office was bombed on March 7, 1968. On April 10, a county grand jury
indicted ten White Knights in the case, including: Imperial Wizard Sam
Bowers; James L. Harper, arrested with 115 sticks of dynamite; Joe Daniel
Hawkins; attorney Harry Kelly; Burris Leon Dunn, Jr.; L.E. Matthews, a
former province giant; William Pickle, an employee of the State Highway
Department; Jimmy Copeland; and William Watkins, former circulation
manager for the Jackson *Clarion-Ledger.* Harper's case ended in a mistrial
on July 31, 1968. Hawkins was acquitted on August 7, 1968, while charges
against Harper and Burris were dismissed two days later. [*NYT* 1968]

BLANCA CLUB
In 1965 congressional investigators named this group as a cover for the
Akron, Alabama, klavern, United Klans of America. The name was apparently
taken from *blanca*, the Spanish word meaning "white." [38]

BLANTON, ELBERT
See *Rogers, Ernest and Christine.*

BLESSING, WILLIAM L.
An admitted former Klansman, Blessing founded the so-called House of
Prayer for All People in Denver, Colorado, during the early 1950s. Fearful
of "wholesale mongrelization," Blessing called for the creation of "a 100
percent American Protestant organization like the Ku Klux Klan to rise in
order to protect Americans and our Christian way of life." [77]

BLEVINS, LEWIS

See *Brewster, Willie.*

BLOODY SHIRT

See *Huggins, Alan P.*

BLOUNT COUNTY HUNTERS CLUB

In 1966, congressional hearings identified this club as a front for Maryville Klavern No. 1, in the Tennessee realm of the United Klans of America. [38]

BLUE, LAVERGNE

See *Adams, Dr. Clifford.*

BLUMBERG, RALPH

As the owner of radio station WBOX in Bogalusa, Louisiana, Blumberg was driven out of business by Klan threats and boycotts in 1965. Klansmen marked Blumberg for being part of the group that invited liberal congressman Brooks Hays to speak in Bogalusa during January 1965. The scheduled speech was canceled because of anonymous threats, and Klan pressure soon cut WBOX's number of sponsors from seventy to four, three of which were located outside Bogalusa. Bricks were hurled through Blumberg's windows, tacks were spread on his driveway, and shots were fired at the station's transmitter. The campaign drove WBOX from its rented quarters to a trailer, and finally out of existence. Persistent threats against his family prompted Blumberg to resettle his wife and children in St. Louis. In October 1965, Blumberg received the annual Paul White award for distinguished service in broadcasting, but it was too late to save WBOX. Announcing his plans to sell the station, Blumberg said, "When you become a target of the Ku Klux Klan, you soon learn that if there ever was a devil on the face of this earth, it lives, it breathes, it functions in the cloaked evil of the leaders of the Ku Klux Klan." [*Time*, November 5, 1965]

BOEUF RIVER HUNTING CLUB

In 1965 congressional investigators identified this club as a front for a rural klavern, Original Knights of the KKK, in Richland Parish, Louisiana. [38]

BOGALUSA, LOUISIANA

In 1965, Bogalusa's population was 23,000, 40 percent of which was black. Militant whites were determined to hold their narrow margin of superiority. With an estimated 800 Klan members in town, Bogalusa boasted the largest per capita KKK membership in the nation, earning its dubious designation as "Klantown USA." In April 1964 hooded raiders abducted and flogged a local white man, Jerry Varnado. The following month, 300 armed and masked men received permission to gather on private property in a rally billed as a "religious ceremony." An FBI infiltrator in the local Klan once forewarned police of a planned illegal cross burning, but officers failed to respond. A speech by ex-congressman Brooks Hays, planned for January 5, 1965, was canceled in the face of Klan threats, and Klansmen targeted one of the event's sponsors, Ralph Blumberg, for a campaign of harassment that finally drove his radio station out of business. On April 4, 1965, a group of twenty Klansmen demonstrated with a coffin near a rally sponsored by the Congress of Racial Equality; the next night, shots were fired into a home housing CORE activists. On April 9, after Klansmen broke through police lines to assault black marchers and newsmen, local Klan leader Charles Christmas met with Bogalusa's mayor to discuss the Klan's role in coping with black demonstrations. Violence broke out again on May 24, when a mob of 300 whites tore down the gates of a city park closed to avert clashes over proposed desegregation. The county's first black deputy sheriffs, O'Neal Moore and Creed Rogers, were ambushed and shot on June 3, 1965, with Moore dying from his wounds. Klansman E.R. McElveen was charged in the case, but never convicted. On June 5, shots were fired into the home of an officer investigating the murder, but no further arrests resulted. At the peak of local violence, several newsmen called on Klansmen to rescue them from a hostile mob, noting that Bogalusa had thereby established "some kind of record in meanness." On July 8, 1965, after a white rioter was wounded by a member of the Deacons for Defense, J.B. Stoner came to Bogalusa and addressed a crowd of 1,500 persons at a National States Rights Party gathering. "The nigger is not a human being," Stoner told his audience. "He is somewhere between the white man and the ape. We don't believe in tolerance. We don't believe in getting along with our enemy, and the nigger is our enemy." Two thousand whites turned out for another rally the night of July 10, harangued by Stoner and his partner, Connie Lynch. Both sides marched in the streets on July 11, with Lynch sporting a Confederate flag vest and leading 500 whites with a chant of "Niggers! Jigaboos! Coons!" On July 16, whites made six attacks on black demonstrators at a Bogalusa shopping center, before state troopers intervened during a seventh assault. The following day, black marchers were pelted with stones, fruit, and firecrackers, prompting the U.S. Department of Justice to file suit, on July 19, against the Original Knights of the KKK, the Anti-Communist Christian Association, and thirty-eight individual Klansmen. During September 1965, hearings for this suit were held in New Orleans, where it was revealed that Bogalusa City Attorney Robert Rester and several auxiliary policemen were past of present Klansmen; defendants in the suit were represented by the same attorney defending Klansman McElveen against murder charges. Federal injunctions against further Klan violence were issued on December 1 and 22, but the nightriders of Bogalusa continued. On December 10, 1965, shots were fired at the home of Robert Hicks, a black leader of the Bogalusa Civic and Voters League, following a protest rally at the jail. Klansman Devan Vernado was reappointed to his post on the city housing authority five days later, despite his admitted Klan ties. On March 11, 1966, Captain Donald Sims, a black soldier, was shot and critically wounded while using a public phone booth in Bogalusa; a local white man was arrested the following day. Clarence Triggs, a black participant in the 1965 demonstrations, was killed outside of town on July 30, 1966. Two white men were arrested in the case; one defendant was acquitted in July 1967. A black march from Bogalusa to Baton Rouge in August 1967 was marked by cross burnings and mob assaults on the marchers in Holden, Satsuma, and Denham Springs. In April 1976, nine years later, Bill Wilkinson's Klan opened a new headquarters in Bogalusa, with thirty Klansmen and 100 spectators on hand. Mayor Louis Rawls agreed to cut the ribbon, remarking of the Klan, "They're citizens, just like anybody else." [NYT 1964–1967, 1976]

BOGAR, WILLIAM

The former exalted cyclops of an Apopka, Florida, klavern and a member of the Florida Klan's executive committee, Bogar was indicted June 3, 1953, on eight counts of perjury before a federal grand jury probing local violence since 1949. According to the charges, Bogar allegedly led the attempt to kidnap Franklin Williams and three other blacks near Tavares, Florida, in August 1949. He was also linked to the burning of a shack on the outskirts of Apopka, which was occupied by a black man accused of child molesting. [NYT 1953]

BOGART, JOE

An ex-marine and member of the Klan in Texas, Bogart was linked in November 1980 with the operation of Camp Puller, located near Houston, where paramilitary training was offered to teenagers, including Civil Air Patrol cadets and Boy Scout Explorers, without parental permission. [AP, November 25, 1980]

BOGUE HOMA HUNTING & RIFLE CLUB

In 1965 congressional investigators identified this group as a cover for Jones County Unit No. 1, White Knights of the Ku Klux Klan, based in Laurel, Mississippi. Between May 1964 and October 1965, Klansmen from the six Jones County klaverns were linked with more than forty local assaults, bombings, and incidents of arson. [38]

BOLEN, AUBREY E.

In the early 1960s, Bolen served as imperial wizard for the Association of South Carolina Klans, also holding a seat on the ASCK's four-man grand council. No trace of the group remained when a new survey was made in 1970. [38]

BOMBING

While nativist "Know Nothings" first used blasting powder against Catholic churches in the 1830s, demolition never caught on with their spiritual heirs in the Reconstruction Klan. Kluxers demolished or burned hundreds of buildings between 1867 and 1871—including the near destruction of the whole town of Lewiston, Arkansas—but dabbling in explosives was reserved for 20th-century nightriders. In the 1920s, doubtless influenced by "foreign" radicals and Prohibition gangsters, Klansmen in several realms tried their hand at bombing. A Brooklyn Klan leader was arrested with hand grenades in 1922, and a store outside Raleigh, North Carolina, was bombed the same year, when its owner refused to leave town on command. Grand Dragon D.C. Stephenson blamed rival Kluxers for the blast that scuttled his yacht in 1924, and two years later Canadian Klansmen were linked to the bombing of St. Mary's Roman Catholic Church. In 1925 the Dayton klavern bombed a Catholic university and—in a bid for sympathy—its own headquarters. Muskegon's Klan leader was responsible for three fatalities with a parcel bomb in 1926, but Klansmen were sometimes on the receiving end of explosive special deliveries. In 1921, Kansas City bombers struck at the Maxwellton Inn, following a KKK initiation ceremony. Over the next two years, several Klan-owned businesses were bombed in Chicago, along with the printing plant of the KKK's periodical *Dawn*. When the mayor of Youngstown, Ohio, refused to ban a Klan parade in 1923, his porch was blasted in protest.

The Great Depression and World War II called a temporary cease-fire in the Klan's bombing campaign, but race relations heated up after V-J Day, as determined blacks launched a nationwide "invasion" of all-white residential neighborhoods. Klansmen and their allies on the neo-Nazi fringe stood ready to repel intruders at any cost, and most of the targets in the new war were private homes. No Southern state was immune from the plague— and a few Northern blasts were also recorded—but Dallas, Atlanta, Chattanooga, Nashville, and Birmingham quickly emerged as the principal battlegrounds. Three Atlanta members of the Columbians, Inc., were jailed for illegal possession of explosives in December 1946, two months after the blasting of a black-owned home. Eight months later, bombers struck at the residence of a Georgia reporter covering political corruption in the Herman Talmadge administration. Birmingham, Alabama, logged thirteen explosions between 1948 and 1950, earning itself the nickname "Bombingham," with one black neighborhood dubbed "Dynamite Hill."

The early 1950s echoed with explosions in the South: at least fifty racial bombings were recorded between January 1950 and December 1952. Klansmen were not responsible for all of the attacks, but they did their share and more, with thirteen blasts around the Miami area between June and December 1951. At Mims, Florida, a Christmas explosion killed NAACP leader Harry Moore and his wife as they slept; thirty years would pass before a guilty conscience produced confessions implicating Klansmen and a local sheriff in the crime. Atlanta resident Charles Klein, imperial klaliff for the Association of Georgia Klans, was charged in the March 1951 bombing of a black family's home, but his January 1952 trial ended with a hung jury. That same month, bombers demolished a home in Ft. Payne, Alabama, but gunfire drove them away before they could light a cross planted in the yard.

The U.S. Supreme Court's 1954 Black Monday decision on school integration produced a new militance in the South, and bombings multiplied accordingly. No less than 227 racial bombings were recorded between 1954 and early 1965, with fifty-six suspects arrested and only twenty convicted. Across the South, police officials such as Birmingham's "Bull" Connor were notorious for dragging their feet on bombing investigations, blaming local explosions on lightning, leaky gas mains, or plots hatched by blacks and communists "to get publicity." A series of fourteen blasts between January and May 1958 led to creation of the Southern Conference on Bombing, with officers from several jurisdictions sharing information, but the conviction rate remained modest by any standards and was further diminished by the incidence of multiple convictions in individual bombings, leaving the vast majority of cases unsolved. (Authorities themselves were sometimes suspect. A witness in Birmingham blamed one 1963 bombing on uniformed policemen. Eight months later, in January 1964, Alabama National Guardsmen were indicted for planting a series of bombs around Birmingham and Tuscaloosa.) Prevention was another problem. When a dynamite control bill passed the lower house of the Alabama legislature in 1965, it was scuttled in the state senate by cronies of Governor George Wallace.

With the exception of Birmingham, where dedicated bombers set a record of forty-five blasts by 1965, outbreaks of bombings followed the movement of civil rights action during the late 1950s and 1960s. The Montgomery, Alabama, bus boycott produced at least ten bombings between January 1956 and January 1957. Eight bombs were detonated around Clinton, Tennessee, in 1956 and 1957, when John Kasper and Asa Carter joined forces to stall the integration of local schools. Little Rock, Arkansas, suffered a rash of explosions in 1958 and 1959, while an increase occurred in Georgia during 1961. Mississippi terrorists bombed or burned thirty-four churches and thirty-one other buildings during the Freedom Summer in 1964, and Alabama suffered a new spate of explosions the following year, during a statewide campaign to register black voters.

Although Klansmen were not alone responsible for the new wave of terror, investigators credit the several Klans and affiliated a groups with a majority of the bombings. (In October 1965, Alabama state attorney general Richmond Flowers blamed the KKK in forty of Birmingham's forty-five racial blasts.) Across the South, militant "wrecking crews" were organized between 1960 and 1964, stockpiling weapons and explosives, hosting seminars with military veterans to brief the faithful on marksmanship and demolitions. Some groups, such as Nacirema, Inc., were created with the knowledge and approval of established Klan leaders; others, such as the Cahaba River Group and Silver Dollar Group, spun off on their own, attracting the worst of the lunatic fringe in their search for "a little action." A sampling of Klan-related bombings from the troubled era includes the following:

> February 1957, Montgomery, Alabama: Five Klansmen are jailed in connection with recent bombings. Two sign confessions, but all are released in a general amnesty that also drops charges filed against black demonstrators for conducting an illegal boycott.

> September 1957, Nashville, Tennessee: Police arrest four men, including at least one Klansman, for bombing the Hattie Cotton School.

> December 1957, Birmingham, Alabama: A black home is bombed eight days after a cross is burned in the yard.

> March 1958, Charlotte, North Carolina: Three Klansmen are sentenced to prison for plotting to bomb a local school.

> June 1958, Birmingham: Reverend Fred Shuttlesworth's church is bombed. Klan leader J.B. Stoner is indicted in 1977 and convicted in 1980.

> July 1958, Birmingham: Three Klansmen are arrested for the bombing of a black home; all are convicted.

> October 1958, Atlanta, Georgia: Five members of the National States Rights Party are arrested for bombing a synagogue. Charges against four are dismissed after the 1959 acquittal of defendant George Bright.

> September 1959, Little Rock, Arkansas: Klan organizer E.A. Lauderdale and two other men are arrested in the wake of three local bombings. He is convicted and imprisoned.

> July 1960, Little Rock: Two Klansmen are arrested while planting a bomb at Philander Smith College. Charges are dismissed to protect FBI informants from exposure.

> September 1963, Birmingham: A church bombing kills four black children. Klansman Robert Chambliss is convicted of murder in 1977.

> February 1964, Jacksonville, Florida: A black home is bombed. One Klansman pleads guilty, while five others are acquitted.

> October 1964, McComb, Mississippi: Nine Klansmen plead no contest in a series of local bombings. A sympathetic judge issues suspended sentences on grounds of "undue provocation" by blacks.

December 1964, Montgomery, Alabama: Three men are jailed for detonating explosives outside a black church. One is a Klansman who had been held on bombing charges in 1957.

January 1965, New Bern, North Carolina: Three Klansmen are jailed in a series of local bombings; all three plead guilty in June.

February to August 1965, Bessemer, Alabama: Multiple blasts are detonated at the W.S. Dickey Clay Co. during a violent strike led by a Klan-dominated union local.

March to May 1965, New Orleans, Louisiana: A series of firebombs damage various targets, including two churches. Six Klansmen are arrested in June 1966.

August 1965, Natchez, Mississippi: NAACP leader George Metcalfe is crippled by a car bomb. FBI agents trace the blast to the Silver Dollar Group, but no prosecutions result.

September 1966, Milwaukee, Wisconsin: Illinois Grand Dragon Turner Cheney and two Wisconsin Klansmen are arrested in two local bombings.

February 1967, Natchez: NAACP officer Wharlest Jackson is killed by a car bomb. FBI agents link the blast to the secretive Silver Dollar Group.

March 1967, Jackson, Mississippi: The Blackwell Real Estate office is bombed for selling homes to blacks. Nine Klansmen are charged with the crime in April 1968.

July 1967, Salisbury, North Carolina: Eleven men, including at least eight Klansmen, are charged in a two-year reign of terror that climaxes on July 1 with five bombings.

September 1967, Mississippi: A new rash of bombings begins, aimed at synagogues and black churches. The attacks end in June 1968, after a shootout with police that leaves one Klansman wounded and his female accomplice dead.

October 1967, Bastrop, Louisiana: An explosive booby trap injures two boys at a local Klan meeting house.

August 1968, North Carolina: Homes owned by Klan officers are bombed in Charlotte and Shelby.

The climax of the 1960s did not break the Klan's connection with bombing. In 1970 and 1971, Houston Klansmen launched an explosive reign of terror against the local Pacifica Foundation radio outlet and various other "liberal" targets. August 1971 witnessed the bombing of ten school buses in Pontiac, Michigan; Grand Dragon Robert Miles and four other Klansmen were convicted of the bombing in May 1973, but the case was later overturned by the deathbed confession of a Klansmen stricken with terminal leukemia. In October 1973, Klansman Byron de la Beckwith was found with an active time bomb in his car, cruising the streets of New Orleans, but a jury accepted his lawyer's contention of a government frame-up. Pennsylvania's grand dragon was indicted for receiving stolen explosives in March 1974, but was saved from conviction by the fact that he was acting in his role as a federal informant. Two years later, in May 1976, Indiana's grand dragon was jailed for bombing the establishment of a former employer. In July 1978, three Maryland Klansmen were convicted of attempting to bomb a synagogue.

Increasing militance in the 1980s has kept Klan bombers in the news. At Hayden Lake, Idaho, residents of the Aryan Nations compound stand accused of blasting their critics with more than strong rhetoric, resulting in destruction or damage of several stores. In July 1980, three Chattanooga Klansmen were jailed for possessing explosives, with one convicted at trial. September saw the Illinois grand dragon and one of his followers charged with burglary in the theft of blasting materials. In March 1981, a mixed bag of Klansmen and Nazis were charged with plotting to blow up selected portions of Greensboro, North Carolina, and all six defendants have since been convicted. Two months later, ten Maryland Klansmen were jailed for plotting to bomb the Baltimore NAACP headquarters, and the chief of the Adamic Knights was sentenced to prison in October 1981. In a separate case, the leader of another Maryland Klan was also jailed after a botched bombing attempt. In May 1981, six persons were arrested for trying to bomb a Nashville synagogue; two of those convicted and sentenced to prison were verified Klan members. [2; 10; 65; 72; 93; 84]

BONEY, LESLIE L.

A YWCA swimming instructor in Sumter, South Carolina, Boney happened on a gathering of the Association of Carolina Klans, near Bishopville, on August 12, 1950. Suspected of being a spy, he was dragged from his car and beaten by the assembled Klansmen. Grand Dragon Tom Hamilton was indicted on September 18, 1950, for conspiracy to incite mob violence in Boney's case. [NYT 1950]

BONNER, GEORGE

A resident of Monroe, Louisiana, Bonner was listed as vice president when the Original Ku Klux Klan of America, Inc., was chartered in Ouachita Parish, on January 26, 1965. [38]

BOOK AND BIBLE HOUSE

See *King, L.J.*

BOOKER, RAY

A resident of Vidor, Texas, Booker was identified as one of two grand dragons serving David Duke's Klan in the Lone Star State during the mid-1970s. Booker's activities included operating a KKK bookstore in Vidor, and a campaign to keep blacks out of of local restaurants by posting signs that read: "10% of All Our Profits Go to the KKK." [84]

BORGLUM, GUTZON

The sculptor of Mt. Rushmore and the Confederate memorial on Stone Mountain, Georgia, Borglum was also a high ranking Klansman in the 1920s. He participated in strategy meetings between Hiram Evans and Indiana's D.C. Stephenson prior to the Evans ouster of Imperial Wizard William Simmons in 1921, and in the same year he reportedly arranged a White House meeting between Evans and President Warren Harding. One of six Klansmen selected for the Imperical Kloncilium of 1923, Borglum helped settle the Evans-Simmons dispute over ownership of Klan ritual, regalia, and funds. Borglum once described the Klan as a movement expressing the "minds of the villagers and agrarians" in the United States without resort to foreign creeds. [10]

BOSSERT, WALTER

In 1924, after a publicized rift between Imperial Wizard Hiram Evans and Indiana Grand Dragon D.C. Stephenson, Bossert was chosen by Atlanta headquarters to take Stephenson's place. Stephenson retaliated by suing Bossert for libel, also seeking damages for a bombing that wrecked Stephenson's yacht. Bossert joined Evans to lead a sixty-man delegation at the 1924 Republican convention in Cleveland, later serving as one of five men on the Klan's strategy board at the Democratic convention in New York City. Retired from the Klan by 1938, he was defeated that year in the Republican senatorial primary. [10]

BOTSFORD, BRUCE

See *Pace, Reverend Edward.*

BOUTWELL, ALBERT

Elected mayor of Birmingham, Alabama, after Arthur Hanes, Boutwell defeated police commissioner Eugene "Bull" Connor in the April 1963 runoff election that also discarded Birmingham's three-man commission form of government. Connor fought the election results in court, hanging onto his job while black demonstrations and Klan violence continued through May. Despised by local Klansmen, Mayor Boutwell was the target of a bomb found at his home on April 1, 1965. [*NYT* 1965]

BOWDEN, CLEM

See *Champion, William.*

BOWERS, SAMUEL HOLLOWAY, JR.

Born in New Orleans in August 1924, Bowers was the grandson of a distinguished Mississippi lawyer who served four terms in Congress; he was also a direct descendant of the first president of the Virginia House of Burgesses. His parents divorced when Bowers was fourteen, and he followed his father around the South on business trips. Dropping out of high school to join the Navy soon after Pearl Harbor, Bowers was honorably discharged in 1945. He earned his high school diploma through a state equivalency test, attending Tulane University in New Orleans before he transferred to the University of Southern California School of Engineering. After graduation, he settled in Laurel, Mississippi, and established the Sambo Amusement Company, sharing the quarters behind the shop with his partner until 1970, when Bowers was committed to federal prison. A lapsed Catholic, Bowers showed little interest in religion until 1966, when he joined the local Southern Baptist Church in the wake of a murder indictment, authorities dismissing the move as an attempt to influence potential jurors. Around the house, Bowers sometimes wore a Nazi armband and posed before a full-length mirror, clicking his heels and shouting, "Heil Hitler!" (Conversely, FBI informant Delmar Dennis claims that Bowers kept photographs of Marx, Lenin, and the Pope on his mantle, once professing membership in the Communist Party during 1947, while a student at USC.) In early 1964, Bowers was elected imperial wizard of the Mississippi White Knights, organizing his Klan along authoritarian lines that required his personal approval for major acts of violence. Personally implicated in at least four murders, Bowers surrendered to FBI agents for the murder of Vernon Dahmer on March 31, 1966, two days after agents reported finding a "small arsenal" at his home. On October 20, 1967, Bowers was convicted on federal civil rights charges in the triple murder of Michael Schwerner, Andrew Goodman, and James Chaney, and sentenced to ten years in prison. Three weeks later, Bowers and two other Klansmen were charged with kidnapping ex-convict Jack Watkins, a prosecution witness in the Vernon Dahmer murder case. On December 21, 1967, Klansman Thomas Tarrants was stopped for reckless driving in Collins, Mississippi, with Bowers in the car, and both men were arrested when police found a submachine gun in the car. Bowers was acquitted of possessing the submachine gun on January 18, 1968, and his first trial in the Dahmer case ended in a mistrial seven days later, with jurors deadlocked 10–2 for conviction. Murder charges were eventually dismissed, following a fourth mistrial declared in July 1969. Bowers entered the federal prison at McNeil Island, Washington, on April 3, 1970, to begin serving his ten-year sentence in the Schwerner case. Federal charges in the Dahmer incident were dismissed in 1973, and Bowers was paroled in March 1976. Mississippi sources stated that a small, hard-core unit of the White Knights revived "within 2 days" of Bowers' release. [59; 84; 96]

BOWLAND, WALTER

A high school athletic coach in Lakeview, Georgia, Bowland became the target of a Klan harassment campaign in early 1947, the reason for which was never clear. On January 16, while Bowland was away from home, a gang of eighteen hooded Klansmen burned a cross on his front lawn. Bowland's wife emerged from the house, kicked the cross over, and berated the Klansmen as a group of "yellow cowards." When Bowland sought police protection, the local sheriff told him, "I'm just as scared of the Ku Klux Klan as you are. You should conduct yourself in such a way that the Ku Klux Klan wouldn't appear in front of your house." Bowland's principal resisted Klan demands that Bowland be fired, and the furor gradually subsided as Klansmen went in search of targets more susceptible to personal intimidation. [NYT 1947]

BOWLES, BRYANT

A Baltimore resident and blatant anti-Semite, he was known to have addressed several Klan rallies as a guest speaker. Bowles was identified as a leader of the National Association for the Advancement of White People in the late 1950s. His short-lived prominence on the racist scene was terminated by his imprisonment in Texas for murdering his brother-in-law. [45; 55]

BOWLES, CHARLES

A prominent Detroit attorney, Bowles ran for mayor in 1924, in a special election precipitated by the resignation of the ailing incumbent. As the only protestant candidate, he drew the local Klan's endorsement. Bowles denied being a Klansman, but the venom of the KKK campaign cost him crucial votes among minorities and labor unions. Ironically, the Klan tried to court Jewish votes by pointing out that anti-Semite Henry Ford opposed Bowles, but the tactic failed. Bowles was successful in his second gubernatorial bid in 1929, but was recalled a year later amid charges of graft and corruption. [10]

BOWLING, RICHARD

See Bright, George.

BOWLING, ROBERT

See *Bright, George.*

BOYD, ALEXANDER

A Republican county solicitor in Eutaw, Alabama, during Reconstruction, Boyd was shot and killed at his hotel, March 31, 1868, by a Klan hit team imported from neighboring Greene County. [87]

BOYD, JAMES E.

As a young attorney and officer in the North Carolina Reconstruction Klan, Boyd was one of the first Klansmen to defect and testify before congressional investigators. He reported that the Klan was meant "to ride around the country and whip a little, and go about the houses of the Negroes and tell them if they went to election they [the Klansmen] would meet them on the way." After his own confession, he persuaded fifteen other members to turn state's evidence in various criminal trials. [87]

BOYKIN, ALBERT

A black resident of Apopka, Florida, Boykin was targeted by the local Klan in 1950 because of his union activities. He avoided one kidnapping attempt, but was snatched and beaten by nightriders that summer. Federal agents accused Klansmen Robert Juday and Harvey Reisner of participating in the crime. [*NYT* 1953]

BRADDOCK, WILSON

In March 1975, Braddock was identified as the grand titan for northern Indiana, representing the United Klans of America. On March 29, he was featured as a guest speaker at a United Klans organizational meeting in Kankakee, Illinois. [43]

BRADDY, MALCOLM

See *Peterson, Jim.*

BRADY, PHILIP

While serving as a selectman in McComb, Mississippi, in the spring of 1964, Brady introduced Imperial Wizard Robert Shelton to an audience of 700 persons at a rally of the United Klans of America. [9]

BRANDENBERG, CLARENCE

A Cincinnati, Ohio, Klan leader, Brandenberg was arrested August 7, 1964, on charges of criminal syndicalism and illegal masking, related to a June 28 cross burning at a local amusement park. Brandenberg was convicted despite his denials of being present at the scene. On June 9, 1968, the U.S. Supreme Court overturned his conviction and declared unconstitutional the Ohio syndicalism law. [*NYT* 1964, 1968]

BRANHAM, BILLY

A member of the National States Rights Party in Atlanta, Georgia, Branham accompanied George Bright and Leslie Rogers on a trip to greet John Kasper when Kasper was released from federal prison in 1957. [*NYT* 1958]

BRANNEN, ROBERT

A resident of Cincinnati, Ohio, Brannen was identified in 1983 as leader of a neo-Nazi splinter group, the National Socialist Movement. Brannen is an ex-Klansman and former associate of George Lincoln Rockwell in the American Nazi Party who joined the National Socialist Movement in the mid-1970s, serving as an aide to founder James Mason. When Mason left to form the competing National Socialist Liberation Front, Brannen replaced him. [2]

BRASFIELD, FRED

See *Federated Ku Klux Klans, Inc.*

BRASSEL, WILLIAM

On January 1, 1966, Brassel replaced Robert Creel as Alabama grand dragon for the United Klans of America, serving in that capacity until James Spears was elected at the state klonvocation, on June 19. [38]

BRATTON, DR. J. RUFUS

A Reconstruction Klansman in York County, South Carolina, Bratton was identified as the leader of a gang that hanged ex-militia Captain Jim Williams on March 6, 1871. Bratton also helped organize black political meetings in his area, manipulating the selection of "Uncle Tom" spokesmen who called on Republican officials to resign from office. In May 1871 he published a renunciation of further nightriding, but the ban proved ineffective. One of 200 Klansmen who fled the state to avoid prosecution, he was brought back from Canada in June 1872, but managed to escape a second time, remaining in Ontario until 1877, when the demise of Radical Reconstruction canceled further trials. [87]

BREWIS, ALEXANDER

See *Federated Ku Klux Klans, Inc.*

BREWSTER, RALPH OWEN

A descendant of *Mayflower* pilgrims, hero of World War I, and a Harvard educated attorney, Brewster was prominent in Maine politics during the 1920s. His first alliance with the Klan was formed when the Roman Catholic bishop in Portland requested that towns be allowed to use their money for support of parochial schools. Brewster fired back with a constitutional amendment to make such expenditures illegal, and Klansmen were delighted. Elected governor with Klan support in 1924, Brewster ran for the U.S. Senate in a special 1926 election occasioned by the retirement of incumbent William Patangall. He met with Imperial Wizard Hiram Evans and Grand Dragon DeForest Perkins to concoct a smear campaign, accusing rival Arthur Gould of illegal overspending in the primary, but the move backfired following the exposure of Brewster's Klan connections, and Gould easily won the election. Brewster ran for the Senate again, in 1928, but he was defeated in primary balloting. [10]

BREWSTER, WILLIE

A black resident of Anniston, Alabama, Brewster was shot while driving through town on July 15, 1965, two hours after a National States Rights Party rally at the local courthouse. When he died on July 18, three white men—Damon Strange, Johnny Defries, and Lewis Blevins—were indicted for murder. Strange was at the time employed by Kenneth Adams, a notorious Klansman who had been featured as a speaker at the NSRP rally the night on which Brewster was shot. J.B. Stoner defended Strange at his trial, and professing himself "stunned" when his client was convicted on December 2 and sentenced to ten years in jail. "I've been fighting niggers and Jews since I was 17," Stoner declared, "and I'll keep on." A second jury acquitted Defries of all charges on February 17, 1966. [*NYT* 1965–1966]

BRIDGES, CHARLES

See *Carter, Asa.*

BRIDGES, WINFRED

See *Dayvault, Wayne.*

BRIGAN, BILL

A Reconstruction victim of the KKK in Wilkinson County, Georgia, Brigan was abducted from his home, tied to a log, and beaten so badly on the genitals with a buggy trace that he lost one of his testicles. [87]

BRIGHT, GEORGE MICHAEL

A member of the National States Rights Party (NSRP) in Atlanta, Bright was one of four neo-Nazis arrested in July 1958 while picketing the Atlanta *Journal and Constitution* with anti-Semitic signs. When a local synagogue was bombed on October 12, 1958, and an anonymous call warning, "This is the last empty building I'll blow up in Atlanta," was received, police jailed five suspects, including NSRP members Bright, Wallace Allen, Kenneth Griffin, Luther Crowley, and brothers Richard and Robert Bowling. A raid on Allen's home turned up literature from the National States Rights Party, an Anniston, Alabama, Klan unit, and the Knights of the White Camellia. Police spokesmen also dropped hints of an anti-Semitic "fat cat" supporting the group. In addition, the police revealed correspondence between the alleged bombers and George Rockwell's National Committee to Free America From Jewish Domination. Rockwell admitted writing a letter to Allen, complete with references to a "big blast," but he denied any knowledge of the Atlanta bombing. The suspects were denied bail after members of a grand jury probing the case received threatening calls from the Confederate Underground. Bright's trial opened on December 1, 1958, with Klan attorney James Venable defending. The prosecution noted Bright's May 1958 disruption of a protestant ministers' meeting where Rabbi Jacob Rothschild—of the bombed temple—had been scheduled as a guest speaker. Bright had also discussed plans to burn a swastika on the temple's lawn, and a note found in Bright's home, addressed to Rabbi Rothschild, included the following threat: "You are going to experience the most terrifying thing in your life." Prosecution witness Leslie Rogers, an FBI informant in the U.S. Klans and NSRP, gave evidence against Bright, and a prison cellmate repeated Bright's alleged confession of participation in the bombing. Defense witnesses included Imperial Wizard Eldon Edwards, Edward Fields, Matt Koehl, NSRP chairman Arthur Cole, and a mental patient testifying during a period of "temporary lucidity," but none could place Bright after midnight on the night in question (the bomb had detonated at 3:37 a.m.). A mistrial was declared on December 10, with jurors deadlocked 9–3 for conviction. After Bright's acquittal in a second trial in January 1959, charges against his fellow defendants were dismissed. Bright subsequently joined John Crommelin, Bill Hendrix, John Hamilton, and others to greet racist agitator John Kasper on his release from federal prison. [14]

BRILEY, CORINE

The wife of Reverend George Briley, a black minister in Atlanta, Corine was killed when nightriders shot up her home on January 29, 1967. The unsolved shooting occurred several hours following attempts to burn Reverend Briley's church. [*NYT* 1967]

BRINSON, WILLIE LEE

A black resident of Dublin, Georgia, Brinson and his wife were hospitalized October 2, 1951, after they were abducted and beaten by Klansmen. Both victims were beaten with ax handles and leather straps by robed Klansmen who ordered them to "get out of Jackson County by night." [*NYT* 1951]

BRITT, RAYMOND C., JR.

A Montgomery, Alabama, Klansman charged with participation in bombings linked to a black bus boycott in 1956 and 1957, Britt was named by a confessed bomber as the wheelman in the bombing of Reverend Ralph Abernathy's home. Britt was acquitted at his trial despite confessions signed by himself and his accomplices. In 1976, he emerged as the chief prosecution witness in the January 1957 murder of Willie Edwards, naming three fellow Klansmen as the killers. Murder indictments were issued, then dismissed due to the failure to list cause of death. Britt later admitted a case of mistaken identity in naming one of the alleged killers. [*NYT* 1976]

BRITTON, NEUMANN

Active in opposition to black civil rights during the 1960s, Britton was identified as a Klan grand dragon in 1976. He was also publicly associated with the National States Rights Party and the National Emancipation of Our White Seed. [84]

BROADWAY, STEVE

A 1955 Klan recruit in South Carolina, Broadway was one of six Camden Klansmen arrested for the December 1956 beating of high school band director Guy Hutchins. In the late 1970s, he was identified as a member of the United Klans of America state board in South Carolina. [*NYT* 1957; 84]

BROCK, ELMER BAILEY

See *Federated Ku Klux Klans, Inc.*

BROCK, JOHN L.

While serving as grand klokard for the United Klans of America, Brock was arrested on March 16, 1963, with Georgia Klansmen William Anderson, William Crowe, and thirty-seven others—including ten children—during a wild party at Klan headquarters in DeKalb County. Identified as a member of Nacirema, Inc., he was also active with Grand Dragon Calvin Craig in violence against black demonstrators in Crawfordsville, Georgia, in October 1965. [*NYT* 1965; 38]

BRODE, FRED

As chairman of the Houston Committee to End the War, Brode became a target of KKK terrorism in the latter half of 1970. Between June and October of that year, a total of twenty shots were fired into his home by nightriders and an attempt was made to burn his house. The same Klansmen linked with the harassment of Brode were also involved in a local reign of terror against a Pacifica Foundation radio station and other Houston targets. [*NYT* 1970]

BROOK, PAUL

Identified as Indiana's grand dragon in 1968, Brook was the target of arsonists who burned his home on September 14, 1968, during the second night of racial unrest in Kokomo, Indiana. [*NYT* 1968]

BROOKS, BOBBY

See *Grainger, Ben.*

BROOKS, EARLY L.

Brooks served as police chief of Fair Bluff, North Carolina, until 1947, when he was charged with shooting a fellow officer. Despite his acquittal in court, public opinion forced his resignation, and he became a lightning rod salesman, moonlighting as a local constable. On the side, he also served as exalted cyclops of the Fair Bluff klavern, Association of Carolina Klans. On February 16, 1952, Brooks was arrested by FBI agents on federal kidnapping charges, resulting from the October 1951 flogging of Ben Grainger and Dorothy Martin. Eleven days later, along with ten other Klansmen, he was charged in the case of Esther Floyd, who had been taken from her home with her hair cut in the shape of a cross on November 14, 1951. On May 8, 1952, Brooks entered a plea of no contest for the December 8, 1951, flogging of Woodrow Johnson, drawing a two-year prison term. On May 13, 1952, he was convicted on two federal counts in the Grainger-Martin case, and sentenced to five years on each count. [*NYT* 1952]

BROOKS, HENRY

An ex-detective in Savannah, Georgia, Brooks also served as leader of a local Klan-like group, the Cavalcade of White Americans. On July 13, 1962, after two days of white rioting against black demonstrators, he addressed a rally of 300 persons in Forsythe Park, telling the crowd: "The white people have shown remarkable restraint in not killing niggers wholesale." Sporting a pistol on his belt, Brooks then led sixty persons on a march through the downtown business district, where they were turned back by police. He retaliated by leading a motorcade through the heart of town, with drivers blowing horns and waving rebel flags to protest a black boycott led by the Chatham County Crusade for Voters. [*NYT* 1963]

BROOKS, JAMES

A Republican politician in Reconstruction Arkansas, Brooks was shot and wounded in a Klan ambush that killed Congressman James Hinds in Monroe County on October 22, 1868. He survived his wounds and was later elected governor of the state. [87]

BROTHERHOOD OF JASPER COUNTY

In 1965, congressional investigators identified this group as a cover for the Ridgeland, South Carolina, klavern, United Klans of America. [38]

BROWARD CLUB

Testimony heard by the House Un-American Activities Committee in 1965 identified this club as a front for one of two Ft. Lauderdale, Florida, klaverns affiliated with the United Klans of America. [38]

BROWARD FELLOWSHIP CLUB

Prior to 1965 this club operated as a front for the Davie, Florida, klavern, United Klans of America. In the summer of that year, Klansmen led by Charles Riddlehoover quarreled with United Klans of America Grand Dragon Donald Cothran, and the Davie klavern defected with membership and cover name intact to form a new splinter group, the United Knights of the Ku Klux Klan. [38]

BROWARD ROD & REEL CLUB

According to congressional reports issued in 1966, this group was a front for the second Ft. Lauderdale, Florida, klavern, United Klans of America. [38]

BROWN, ANDERSON

A black arson suspect in York County, South Carolina, Brown was taken from jail by Klansmen and shot to death on February 25, 1871. [87]

BROWN, ARTHUR, JR.

See *Caldwell, Lester.*

BROWN, BEN

As the black president of the Republican Grant and Colfax Club in Sumter County, Alabama, during the 1868 elections, Brown ignored Klan warnings to halt political meetings. A raiding party of thirty Klansmen raided his home and murdered him on October 2, 1868. [87]

BROWN, DEWITT C.

While serving as an agent of the Freedmen's Bureau in Paris, Texas, in November 1868, Brown was driven from his outlying home by Klan harassment and forced to take refuge in town. [87]

BROWN, G.T.

A member of the 1920s Klan, Brown later served as grand titan of the Association of Georgia Klans in Georgia's fifth province. State attorney general Dan Duke publicly identified Brown as a ranking official of this Klan. [NYT 1946]

BROWN, HARRY LEON

A Chattanooga Klansman, Brown was expelled from Klavern No. 1 of the U.S. Klans in 1957. On October 25, 1957, Brown and his brother Jack became an incorporator and ranking officer of the new Dixie Klans, Knights of the Ku Klux Klan, Inc. [38]

BROWN, JACK WILSON

The operator of a gas station in a Chattanooga suburb and Klansman, Brown arranged for the KKK to enter the local softball playoffs in 1956. He was also active in the United White Party, and once served the National States Rights Party as a presidential elector. In 1957, with his brother Harry and other several others, Brown was expelled from Klavern No. 1 of the U.S. Klans. That October, he chartered the rival Dixie Klans and emerged as imperial wizard, a post he held until his death in the summer of 1965. Identified as a suspect in the September 1963 bombing of a Birmingham, Alabama, church that killed four children, Brown was also implicated by Joseph Milteer in continuing plots to kill Dr. Martin Luther King, Jr. [38; 95]

BROWN, JOHN C.

An ex-Confederate general from Tennessee and the brother of an antebellum governor, Brown was identified as Tennessee grand dragon of the KKK during part of Reconstruction. On August 1, 1868, he joined Grand Wizard Nathan Forrest and eleven other ex-generals (all of whom were Klansmen) at a Nashville meeting, where protests were issued against Governor William Brownlow's attempt to organize a state militia. Brown denied any knowledge of a Klan conspiracy to topple the state government, maintaining that the militia units were unnecessary. On Christmas Eve 1868, at a public meeting in Pulaski, Brown joined KKK founder Frank McCord in denouncing mob violence, a step that effectively ended nightriding in the vicinity. Elected governor in 1870, Brown also served as Masonic Grand Master in Tennessee and president of the Tennessee Coal and Iron Company. [87]

BROWN, REV. KENNETH

A Methodist minister in Atlanta, Brown touched off a 1948 grand jury probe with accusations that police actively joined in a local Klan parade. [*Christian Century,* Jan. 5, 1949]

BROWN, MARY

A black witness to the Klan murder of a revenue agent in White County, Georgia, in November 1870, Brown was warned to keep silent by Klansmen who unsuccessfully attempted to drive her from the area. On May 21, 1871, raiders staged a predawn attack on her home, stripping and flogging both Brown and her husband and briefly hanging both victims with chains around their necks. Brown was interrogated on her knowledge of the earlier slaying, after which all females in the house, including her mother and young daughter, were forced to undress and lie in the road while Klansmen danced around, prodded them with sticks, and "laughed and made great sport." As Brown told congressional investigators, "Some of them just squealed the same as if they were stable horses just brought out." After an hour of abuse, the raiders left their victims with warnings to leave the county or die. [87]

BROWN, P. RAYFIELD

As leader of the Office of Economic Opportunity in Monroe, Louisiana, Brown became a target of Klan harassment from 1966 to 1968. The campaign included telephone threats, a cross burned on his on lawn, and a bomb wired under the hood of his car. Around Christmas 1968, a shot fired into his home narrowly missed his wife. Police arrested a member of the White Knights of the KKK, but the gunman was freed on a legal technicality in February 1969. [*NYT* 1969]

BROWN, ROBERT KENNETH

An army captain stationed at Ft. Benning, Georgia, in December 1963 Brown told FBI agents that he had been active in anti-Castro activities for several years. His activities included visits to National States Rights Party headquarters in Los Angeles, where members discussed the need to eliminate "[President] Kennedy, the Cabinet, all the members of the Americans for Democratic Action, and maybe 10,000 other people." Brown's statements were revealed during the probe of President John F. Kennedy's death. [90]

BROWN, T.A.

Identified as a Cullman, Alabama, Klan leader in the summer of 1980, Brown was present at the July meeting where David Duke allegedly offered to sell his membership list to rival Bill Wilkinson for the sum of $35,000. [*UPI,* July 23, 1980]

BROWN, WALTER

See *Odom, Willie.*

BROWN, WALTER

A South Carolina member of the United Klans of America, Brown was elected to serve as imperial klarogo in September 1964. [38]

BROWNLEE, R. WILEY

As principal of Willow Run High School in Ypsilanti, Michigan, Brownlee was active in promoting racial harmony on campus. On April 2, 1971, while driving home to Plymouth, he was waylaid by six Klansmen packing shotguns, dragged from his car, and tarred and feathered. Grand Dragon Robert Miles and four other United Klans of America members were indicted on federal charges in the case on June 22, 1972. [*NYT* 1971–1972]

BROWNLOW, WILLIAM G.

Nicknamed "Parson" from his days as a circuit-riding Methodist preacher, Brownlow was a staunch Unionist and editor of the Knoxville *Whig* before and during the Civil War. Prior to General Lee's surrender, he led a group that captured control of state government from diehard Confederates; his election as governor made Tennessee the only Southern state immune from later military occupation during Reconstruction. Ex-Confederates were disfranchised under Brownlow's administration, with the Fourteenth Amendment accepted and Tennessee quickly restored to the Union. An enemy of the Klan, Brownlow pushed for legislation to punish masked violence and nightriding and later organized an anti-Klan militia in the summer of 1868, both with mixed results. He briefly declared martial law over parts of the state in early 1869, but resigned on February 25 to run for the U.S. Senate. From his new post in Washington, Brownlow urged remanding Tennessee to federal control when Klan violence continued, but the effort was frustrated—and most of the violence ended—when Democrats elected ex-Klansman John C. Brown as governor in 1870. [87]

BRUCE, DANIEL

A Georgia Klansman and incorporator of the Clayton County Civic Club, Bruce was also identified as an instructor at the "violence school" sponsored by United Klans of America Clayton County Klavern No. 52, conducted on the farm of Robert Bing in October 1964. [*NYT* 1965]

BRUCE, MELVIN

Once a chauffeur for George Lincoln Rockwell, Bruce was arrested during the September 1962 race riot in Oxford, Mississippi, armed with a rifle bearing a John Birch Society sticker on its stock. Tried in connection with the Ole Miss riot, he retained J.B. Stoner as his defense attorney, winning acquittal after Stoner produced a Mississippi National Guardsman to testify that he saw Bruce beaten by federal marshals. [*NYT* 1963; 18]

BRUNSON, R.J.

An early Klan member in Pulaski, Tennessee, Brunson was dispatched to South Carolina in July 1868, on orders from George W. Gordon, and spent three months organizing dens in the Palmetto State. [87]

BRUNSWICK SPORTSMAN

In 1965 congressional investigators identified the Brunswick Sportsman as a cover for the Lawrenceville, Virginia, klavern, United Klans of America. [38]

BRYANT, ARTHUR

See *Bryant, Joseph.*

BRYANT, CHARLES

A black supporter of the civil rights activities in McComb, Mississippi, Bryant became a target of Klan violence when his home was bombed on July 26, 1964. The bombers were subsequently identified as members of the United Klans of America. [38]

BRYANT, CURTIS

The brother of Charles Bryant and a local NAACP leader in McComb, Mississippi, Bryant was targeted by Klan bombers who wrecked his house on April 28, 1964. Members of the United Klans of America later pleaded guilty to the crime, receiving a suspended sentence. [38]

BRYANT, GEORGE

A 1920s Klan leader from Buffalo, New York, and grand titan for the western part of the state, Bryant was wounded in a 1924 shootout that killed a police undercover agent and a private detective employed by the KKK. He was briefly charged with murder in the case, but prosecutors dropped the charges. Later tried and convicted under the Walker Law, which required registration of Klan members, Bryant took his case to the U.S. Supreme Court, which ruled in 1928 that groups such as the KKK have no consti-tutional right to privacy. Meanwhile, in 1926, Bryant was nearly mobbed by a group of Klansmen in Batavia, New York, after he was forced to tell them that their money that was to be spent on robes had been misused by local officers. [10]

BRYANT, JOHN

Convicted in 1979 of illegal automatic weapons sales, Bryant was linked in 1980 to operation of Camp Puller, near Houston, where the Klan and Veterans for Victory Over Communism ran paramilitary exercises, including instruction of Civil Air Patrol cadets and Boy Scout Explorers without parental knowledge. [AP, Nov. 25, 1980]

BRYANT, JOSEPH

Following the U.S. Supreme Court's Black Monday ruling in 1954, Bryant and his brother, Arthur, tried to organize their own Klan faction in North Carolina. Both were arrested the following year for possession of dynamite and sending anonymous anti-Semitic and anti-Catholic literature through the mail. The brothers were acquitted, but the investigation had already publicized their past criminal records: Arthur for larceny and bad checks convictions, and Joe for juvenile rape and adult solicitation for prostitution. By 1969, employed as a naturopath in Charlotte, Joseph was chosen to serve as acting North Carolina grand dragon for the United Klans of America, while the elected dragon, J.R. Jones, served a prison sentence for contempt of Congress. On July 4, 1969, a rally shootout at Swan Quarter, North Carolina, led to the arrest of Bryant and sixteen others. One rifle, one automatic rifle, two shotguns, and several pistols were confiscated by police from the assembled Klansmen. Defended by attorney Arthur Hanes, the seventeen were fined $1,000 each, with jail terms suspended on charges of inciting a riot. Bryant publicly accused acting Imperial Wizard Melvin Sexton of running scared during the shootout, and their quarrel broadened into charges of mismanagement under Sexton's administration. On September 16, 1969, Bryant led a rally where United Klans membership cards were nailed to a cross and burned. Bryant led his supporters into a new splinter group, the North Carolina Knights of the KKK, based at Concord, North Carolina, which was organized in cooperation with Klansman Edward Dawson. Unable to control the rank and file, Bryant was subsequently ousted by his own members and replaced by Virgil Griffin. [NYT 1969]

BRYANT, L.D.

An ex-Confederate captain and active member of the Reconstruction Klan, Bryant was captured by the Arkansas militia in October 1868. In custody, he was suspended by a rope around his neck until he confessed Klan membership and revealed various internal secrets, including details of militia Captain Simpson Mason's murder. En route to Salem, Arkansas, with fellow prisoner Uriah Bush, Bryant was "liberated" from custody by a masked gang, and was later found hanging in the woods, his body partially devoured by vultures. (Bush was shot to death nearby.) Militia officers insisted the prisoners were killed by Klansmen; the Klan responded with accusations of summary execution by the militia, and the case remains unsolved. [87]

BUCHANAN, BOB

As sheriff of McLennon County, Texas, Buchanan tried to stop an unauthorized Klan parade through the streets of Lorena in 1921. Urged by spectators, the Klansmen responded with violence, one of them clubbing Buchanan over the head with a cross. A riot broke out. One man was stabbed to death, Sheriff Buchanan and ten others were wounded by gunfire before order was restored. White citizens signed a complaint against Buchanan, and a Klan-dominated grand jury formally rebuked him for "interfering with something that wasn't his business." [93]

BUCKLES, BILLY

Identified as Mississippi grand giant of the White Knights under Imperial Wizard Sam Bowers, Buckles addressed a Jackson rally after the Neshoba County murders of Michael Schwerner and two other civil rights workers in 1964, telling assembled Klansmen, "Now they know what we will do. We have shown them what we can do, and we will do it again if necessary." [38]

BUCKLEW, HENRY

As mayor of Laurel, Mississippi, a former vice president of the National Evangelist Association, and director of George Wallace's 1964 presidential campaign in Maryland, North Carolina, and Virginia, Bucklew had all the credentials of a prime Klan supporter in the early 1960s. Although a staunch segregationist himself, he did not agree with the bombings and other acts of violence perpetrated by the White Knights of the KKK in Jones County. On October 18, 1965, Bucklew appeared on television and denounced the White Knights with charges that would later be substantiated in police and congressional investigations. Sam Bowers and his followers responded with a special issue of *The Klan Ledger*, in which they denied Bucklew's charges and accused the mayor of malice based on his failure to obtain KKK contributions and his personal involvement in a Jewish conspiracy with "LBJ and Katzenback [sic] and the source of all cash." [38]

BUCKLEY, TRAVIS

A Mississippi lawyer and active member of the White Knights, Buckley served as chief defense attorney for Klansmen indicted in the deaths of Vernon Dahmer, Michael Schwerner, and two other civil rights workers in Neshoba County. On March 9, 1967, he was arrested in Pascagoula, Mississippi, and charged with kidnapping Jack Watkins, a key prosecution witness in the Dahmer case. Ten months later, on January 25, 1968, a judge in Hattiesburg ordered Buckley held on arson charges in the Dahmer slaying. The following month, a jury deliberated for only two hours before convicting Buckley of the Watkins kidnapping. In addition, Buckley was charged with attempted jury-fixing in Pascagoula, where District Attorney Donald Cumbest said, "These people have been terrorizing, kidnapping and murdering, and I'm damn sick of it." [*Time,* Feb. 23, 1968]

BUNN SADDLE CLUB

In 1965 congressional investigators identified this group as a cover for the Bunn, North Carolina, klavern, United Klans of America. [38]

BURBANK, W.J.

A former Iowa state treasurer, Burbank waged an unsuccessful gubernatorial campaign, with backing from the Klan, in 1924. [10]

BURFORD, JAMES

In 1982 Burford replaced Michael Allen as head of the National Socialist Party of America, formally renaming his group the American Nazi Party. A few months later, the party was split by internal dissension, and Burford was replaced by ex-Klansman Dennis Milam. [2]

BURK, WILLIAM

A black leader in Cornersville, Tennessee, during Reconstruction, Burk advocated armed self-defense against nightriders. Described by Klansmen as "a vicious and dangerous Negro," he was shot and killed at his home on July 4, 1868. [87]

BURKE, EMORY

See *Columbians, Inc.*

BURKE, REV. RICHARD

One of three black legislators elected from Sumter County, Alabama, during Reconstruction, Burke was killed by Klansmen at his Gainesville home on August 18, 1870. [87]

BURKE COUNTY IMPROVEMENT SOCIETY

In 1965 congressional investigators identified this group as a front for the Morganton, North Carolina, klavern, United Klans of America. [38]

BURNS, HAYDON

As the staunch segregationist mayor of Jacksonville, Florida, Burns overcame his passion for "massive resistance" long enough to found the Southern Conference on Bombing in 1958. His reluctance to act on advance warnings of violence prior to the August 1960 riots on "Ax Handle Saturday" no doubt encouraged local Klansmen, and the KKK openly supported his 1964 gubernatorial race. In May 1964, Klansmen lounging outside the Burns campaign headquarters in St. Augustine told black demonstrators, "If our man's in, you niggers have had it." [64]

BURROS, DAN

One of the soldiers who helped integrate Little Rock's Central High School in 1957, Burros allegedly quit the army in disgust at his assignment of "protecting niggers." In fact, he was judged unfit for service after attempting suicide and leaving a note signed "*Heil Hitler*," and received an honorable discharge "by reasons of unsuitability, character, and behavior disorder." By December 1958, he was in touch with various Nazi groups, signing his letters with a red swastika stamp and the name of the nonexistent "American National Socialist Party." In June 1960, he moved to American Nazi Party headquarters in Arlington, Virginia. A month later he was arrested with George Rockwell and fifteen others in a brawl during one of Rockwell's speeches on the Mall in Washington, D.C. Burros was arrested again, the same month, for pasting Nazi stickers on the Anti-Defamation League's headquarters in Washington with fellow Nazi Party member John Patler. In May 1961, Burros toured the South with Patler in the party's "hate bus," protesting the Freedom Rides sponsored by the Congress for Racial Equality. He defected from Rockwell's party in November 1961, joining Patler in New York to publish *Kill!*, a magazine "dedicated to the annihilation of the enemies of the white people." They named their two-man group the American National Party. In the spring of 1963, Burros joined the National Renaissance Party in New York and there met future Klansman Frank Rotella. In July 1963, Burros and other NRP members were arrested for brawling with blacks at a New York City diner. He served ten days in Sing Sing. Recruited for United Klans of America by Roy Frankhouser in July 1965, Burros overcame Imperial Wizard Robert Shelton's initial reluctance at accepting Nazis. He was soon named grand dragon and king kleagle of New York, commanding two rival klaverns in New York City. The "uptown" klavern had thirty-odd members, mostly clerks and office workers, and was dubbed the "panty Klan" by members of the "downtown" group, made up primarily of dock workers who were more prone to violent action. Merging Klan and Nazi philosophies, Burros carried as his good luck piece a bar of soap stamped "From the finest Jewish fat." In October 1965, *The New York Times* discovered Burros' Jewish background and announced its intention to publish the story. At the same time, Burros was dodging subpoenas from the House Un-American Activities Committee, which was investigating various Klans. On October 31, 1965, Burros shot and killed himself at Roy Frankhouser's home in Reading, Pennsylvania. Seven days later, a four-foot memorial cross was burned in his honor at a United Klans of America rally near Rising Sun, Maryland. The *NRP Bulletin* published an editorial praising Burros for his willingness to "blast himself into oblivion as final proof of his loyalty." [75]

BURROS, ROBERT

A member of of the National Renaissance Party in New York City and of no relation to United Klans member Dan Burros, Robert was exposed by the local media as a Jew in 1965. [75]

BURTON, BENJAMIN F.

Identified as grand titan of the Essex-Middle River Knights of the KKK, Burton was sentenced to a year in prison on November 20, 1984, following his conviction in two local cross burning incidents. (Four other Klansmen received sentences of sixty days each.) At the time of his conviction, Burton and another Klansman were awaiting trial on charges of attempted murder, stemming from a knife attack on two black patrons in a bar. [*NYT* 1984]

BURTON, IRENE

A white widow in Dora, Alabama, Burton was the target of Klansmen—for alleged "immortality"—who raided her home on June 3, 1949. While one daughter was forced to watch with a noose around her neck, Mrs. Burton, a second daughter, and three male guests were flogged, with a Klansman reciting prayers between the beatings. Members of the Federated Klans were suspected in the case, but none were prosecuted. [*NYT* 1949]

BURTON, PIERCE

As editor of the *Southern Republic*, published in Demopolis, Alabama, during Reconstruction, Burton was an obvious target for the local Klan. Attacked and beaten by Klansmen on the main street of Eutaw in May 1870, he sustained permanent injuries. [87]

BUSH, URIAH

An Arkansas Klansman captured by the state militia in October 1868, Bush was identified by fellow prisoner L.D. Bryant as one of the plotters who killed militia Captain Simpson Mason. "Liberated" from custody by a masked gang while traveling to Salem, Arkansas, Bush was taken into the woods and shot. Bryant was later found hanged. Militia officers and Klansmen blamed each other for the unsolved killings. [87]

BUSH, WILSON D.

A Brooklyn Klan leader in the 1920s, Bush convened KKK meetings in the local traffic court after-hours, presiding from the magistrate's bench. After exposure of this practice, the district attorney upheld the right of Klansmen to peaceably assemble, but police soon found a cache of weapons—including hand grenades—at Bush's home. In 1946, he surfaced as New York grand dragon for the Association of Georgia Klans. In August 1946, Georgia State Attorney General Dan Duke reported that "a leading candidate for governor" in Georgia—presumed to be former Klansman Eugene Talmadge—had recently visited Bush in New York, seeking financial support for his campaign. [NYT 1946]

BUSH HUNTING & FISHING CLUB NO. 1055

In 1966 congressional investigators identified this group as a cover for the Bush, Louisiana, Original Knights of the KKK. [38]

BUSSIE, VICTOR

As Louisiana president of the AFL-CIO, Bussie was the target of a bomb that destroyed one car, damaged another, and blew out the windows of his Baton Rouge home on July 19, 1967. The home of a black retired school principal, Viola Logan, was bombed the same night in suburban Port Allen, with Bussie blaming the KKK for both explosions. [NYT 1967]

BUTLER, GEORGE

As a lieutenant on the Dallas police force in 1963, Butler was placed in charge of transferring alleged presidential assassin Lee Harvey Oswald from the city lockup to the county jail. He gave the "all-clear" signal that brought Oswald to the basement, where he was shot and killed moments later by Jack Ruby. After the shooting, Midlothian newsman Penn Jones recounted an incident from 1961, in which Butler sought to have a Klan newsletter printed on Jones's press. According to Jones, "He told me that half of the Dallas police were members of the KKK." [89]

BUTLER, RICHARD GIRNT

A former aircraft engineer and self-ordained minister in the Church of Jesus Christ Christian, Butler is also the founder and leader of the Aryan Nations, based at Hayden Lake, Idaho. One of thirteen white supremacists indicted on sedition charges in 1987, Butler was acquitted on all counts in April 1988. He continues to declare that "there is a war going on for the extinction of our race and faith. There's only two sides, no middle of the road. If it comes down to violence in defense of liberty and life, violence is quite necessary." [2]

BUTTERWORTH, WALLACE

A former "vox pop" radio announcer, Wally Butterworth served as public relations director and an imperial board member of the United Klans of America, where he made the acquaintance of Imperial Klonsel James Venable. In April 1962, he helped Venable organize the Defensive Legion of Registered Americans and its subsidiary, the Christian Voters and Buyers League, as well as the coordination of anti-Semitic radio broadcasts from Atlanta during the next two years. When Venable defected from the United Klans to form his own National Knights of the KKK in November 1963, Butterworth signed on as one of the four incorporating officers. Three months later, he joined Venable in creating the Committee of One Million Caucasians to March on Washington, but the scheduled July 4 protest failed to materialize, and Butterworth soon broke with Venable, and left the Klan ranks. [38]

BYRD, ALLEN AND BOBBY

Brothers and residents of Mississippi, the Byrds were arrested by the FBI at Meridian on January 4, 1966, after firing shots at federal agents observing a cross burning. Five other Klansmen were also arrested, in a truck with two crosses prepared for ignition. Authorities reported that crosses were burned in nine Mississippi counties that night. [NYT 1966]

BYRD, DOUGLAS

In the fall of 1963, Byrd was appointed temporary grand dragon of Mississippi for the Louisiana-based Original Knights of the Ku Klux Klan. That December a controversy erupted when Byrd and Klansman Edward McDaniel accused Original Knights leader J.D. Swenson of pocketing profits from the sale of Klan robes. Swenson responded by charging Byrd and McDaniel with slander, threatening Klan leaders, and encouraging mutiny among the rank and file. Both men were expelled, with 200 Original Knights following Byrd into his new White Knights of the KKK, formed at a Brookhaven, Mississippi, conference in February 1964. Two months later, the reins of leadership passed to Imperial Wizard Sam Bowers, and Byrd promptly faded into obscurity. [38]

BYRD, LAWRENCE

See *Dahmer, Vernon.*

BYRD, LILLIE

The widow of a black civil rights activist in Florence, Mississippi, Byrd became the target of Klansmen who bombed her home on the night of June 6, 1968. [NYT 1968]

BYRD, ROBERT C.

A Democratic senator from West Virginia, elected as the majority whip in February 1971, Byrd is also a former Klansman who once held the rank of kleagle in his home state. According to Byrd, he joined the Klan in World War II while working as a shipyard welder, and claimed that he belonged to the hooded order only in 1942 and 1943, saying: "Those were my dues-paying years, and after that I lost interest." In 1946, however, he wrote a letter to Grand Dragon Samuel Green in Atlanta, stating: "I am a former kleagle of the Ku Klux Klan in Raleigh County. . . . The Klan is needed today as never before and I am anxious to see its rebirth in West Virginia. It is necessary that the order be promoted immediately and in every state in the union." Asked about the correspondence later, Byrd replied, "I had completely forgotten that letter." Briefly considered for a U.S. Supreme Court appointment by President Richard Nixon in October 1971, Byrd was finally rejected on the basis that he had no law degree and faced stiff opposition from civil rights groups. [*NYT* 1971]

BYRD, THEON V.

A fireman at Lookout Mountain, Tennessee, Byrd was abducted from his home by four nightriders in the spring of 1948, driven over the state line into Georgia, and flogged. [*NYT* 1949]

BYRD, WM. ALLEN

See *Federated Ku Klux Klans, Inc.*

C

CABE, BRIGIDO

A black photographer employed by the Southern Christian Leadership Conference, Cabe was beaten by members of the National Knights of the KKK at Crawfordsville, Georgia, on October 13, 1965. His attackers were Cecil Myers and Joseph Sims, who became angry when Cabe tried to take their picture near the scene of black protest demonstrations. [*NYT* 1965]

CABINESS, H.D.

An attorney, Democratic politician, and a high-ranking Klansman in Reconstruction Cleveland County, North Carolina, Cabiness conferred with Rutherford County Klan leaders to help reduce violence in March 1871. The compact reduced local nightriding and resulted in reorganization of the Rutherford County KKK under Randolph Shotwell. [87]

CAFEE, A.E.

A member of the Knights of the White Carnation in Tuskegee, Alabama, from the time of its organization in 1865, Cafee participated in nightriding against local blacks through the period when his group merged with the KKK. He was later elected judge. [87]

CAGLE, CHARLES ARNIE

An Alabama member of the United Klans of America, Cagle was arrested with a concealed weapon en route to a Tuscaloosa KKK rally on June 8, 1963. Three months later, after defecting to the rival Cahaba River Group, he was jailed with fellow members Robert Chambliss and John Hall for illegal possession of dynamite, in the wake of Birmingham's September 1963 bombings. All three men were sentenced to six months in jail and fined $100, but Cagle's conviction was thrown out in June 1964, on grounds that prosecutors never proved he had the dynamite inside city limits. [*NYT* 1963–1964]

CAHABA RIVER GROUP

Similar in form and function to the Silver Dollar Group or Nacirema, Inc., this Alabama splinter group was organized by violence-prone ex-Klansmen and defectors from Birmingham's Eastview Klavern No. 13, United Klans of America. Self-styled bombing specialists, the Cahaba River Group maintained links with Nacirema and conducted demolition seminars to prepare its members for violent action against blacks. Suspected of involvement in the September 1963 church bombing that killed four children, three members of the group—Charles Cagle, Robert Chambliss, and John Hall—were arrested by Alabama state police on September 30 and charged with misdemeanor counts of possessing dynamite without a permit. FBI reports declassified in 1988 reveal that Imperial Wizard Robert Shelton and two other United Klans officials actively cooperated with Colonel Al Lingo's troopers, indicating members of the renegade Cahaba faction in the fatal church bombing. In 1977 Chambliss was finally convicted of first-degree murder in the case, drawing a sentence of life imprisonment. [68]

CAHO, STEVEN

Identified in July 1975 as an Illinois member of the United Klans of America, Caho subsequently organized a United Klans klavern in Chicago Heights. [43]

CAIRO HUNTING LODGE

In 1965 congressional investigators identified this lodge as a front for Unit No. 2, United Klans of America, in El Dorado, Arkansas. [38]

CALDWELL, LESTER FRANCIS

While serving as the imperial wizard of a KKK splinter group in Charlotte, North Carolina, Caldwell and Klansman Jack Ayscue were arrested February 15, 1958, while attempting to plant a bomb at a local integrated school. Other Klansmen arrested the same day included David Quick, William Spencer, Arthur Brown, and H.E. Meyers. Convicted on February 21, 1958, with five other Klansmen on charges of forming a secret society with the purpose of breaking the law, Caldwell was fined and held over for trial on pending felony counts. At Caldwell's trial, demolition expert Robert Kindley testified that he had infiltrated Klavern 22 at the request of

Charlotte's police chief, and had uncovered the bomb plot and reported it to authorities. (Caldwell and four of his codefendants were earlier charged with burning a cross at the school.) Upon his conviction in March, Caldwell was sentenced to a prison term of five to ten years for the attempted bombing, with two to five years for conspiracy. Defendants Brown and Spencer each drew terms of two to five years for conspiracy alone. [*NYT* 1958]

CALDWELL IMPROVEMENT ASSOCIATION

As a 1960s cover for the Whitnel, North Carolina, klavern, United Klans of America, this association actively solicited contributions from prominent Lenoir County businessmen who sympathized with the KKK but who shied away from making donations directly to the Klan out of fear of public exposure. [38]

CALHOUN BUSINESSMEN'S ASSOCIATION

In 1965 congressional investigators identified this group as a front for the Choudrant, Louisiana, klavern, United Klans of America. [38]

CALIFORNIA

California was a major success story for the 1920s Klan, with dual headquarters located in San Francisco and Los Angeles. Infiltration of law enforcement was a top priority for recruiters in the Golden State, and Sacramento's kleagle was identified as a deputy sheriff. At least a score of policemen joined the Klan in San Francisco, and recruiting drives bore similar fruit around Los Angeles. Bakersfield's police chief was a Klansman, as were most of the officers in nearby Taft. Thus protected, nightriders were free to operate with impunity in some parts of the state, and nocturnal floggings held at Taft's ballpark drew audiences that included uniformed patrolmen. In June 1922, the Elduayan kidnapping case produced the indictments of thirty-seven Klansmen, but a judge sympathetic to the Klansmen made sure that none were convicted. Membership was declining by 1924, when the state legislature passed a strict anti-mask law, but Klansmen hung on through the Depression, making California one of thirteen states in which the KKK retained significant strength in the 1930s. Official disbandment of the Klan in 1944 left California Klansmen at loose ends, but Jewish merchants around Los Angeles were targeted for cross burnings in the summer of 1945. A year later, when the Association of Georgia Klans was reorganized in Atlanta, stirrings in southern California brought Attorney General Robert Kenny into court to revoke the Klan's charter. Ex-kleagle Ray Snyder, testifying in October 1946, declared that Klansmen had simply gone underground in the guise of so-called card clubs, with one of the state's largest klaverns located in Compton. Another 1946 development was the creation of ex-Klansman Wesley Swift's Church of

Jesus Christ Christian. Based in Lancaster until Swift's death in 1970, the church maintained close ties to the KKK, the National States Rights Party, and various far-right paramilitary groups. In the 1960s, divergent groups such as the Minutemen, the California Rangers, and the American Nazi Party were active in California, but a joint rally of the KKK, Nazis, and Minutemen drew only 250 persons—including journalists—in 1965. In the 1970s, David Duke's Knights of the KKK made inroads in southern California, recruiting a handful of Marines at Camp Pendleton and achieving somewhat greater success around San Diego, where Grand Dragon Tom Metzger made a career of running (unsuccessfully) for public office. Metzger's eventual defection to head his own White Aryan Resistance left the shrunken Klan in disarray. By 1983, the miniscule California Knights of the KKK were reduced to the status of a parlor debating society closely watched by law enforcement agencies. [2; 10]

CALIFORNIA ANTI-COMMUNIST LEAGUE

A front group for the anti-Semitic activities of Wesley Swift and Dennis Mower, the League was based in Lancaster, California, during 1971. [90]

CALIFORNIA KNIGHTS OF THE KU KLUX KLAN

Organized by Tom Metzger in the summer of 1980, this independent faction remained active until late 1982, when its founder severed his Klan ties to create a neo-Nazi splinter group, the White Aryan Resistance. Reports of the California Klan's survival on a local level are ambiguous. Police informants in the group linked Metzger's Klan with violent harassment of Hispanic residents around San Pablo, reporting that members boasted of decapitating an unnamed Mexican victim. [NYT 1980; 2]

CALIFORNIA RANGERS

Organized by retired Lieutenant Colonel William P. Gale in the late 1950s, this paramilitary private army did most of its early recruiting through veterans groups. In 1963, the press exposed Gale's efforts to take over the American Legion post in Signal Hill, California, and one Ranger was arrested for selling automatic weapons to an undercover officer. Gale later moved on to join the Christian Defense League, and a 1965 report by the California state attorney general reveals that the Rangers "have intimate connections with the Ku Klux Klan, the National States Rights Party, the Christian Defense League, and the Church of Jesus Christ Christian." [90]

CALLAWAY, CALEB

An Atlanta judge and member of the Association of Georgia Klans in the late 1940s, Callaway once received a letter of commendation from the KKK for rendering judgments "conforming with the principles of Klannishness." [93]

CAMELLIA WHITE KNIGHTS

Identified as an independent KKK splinter group, the Camellia White Knights were reported active in Texas during 1987, with an estimated membership of less than 100. [*NYT* 1987]

CAMILLA, GEORGIA

On September 19, 1868, a Republican rally in this small, south Georgia town attracted a sizeable crowd of blacks, causing alarm among some of the local whites. Klansmen and their sympathizers swiftly organized a posse, with the county sheriff at its head, and launched a day-long "hunt" that resulted in the deaths of at least seven blacks and the wounding of thirty to forty others. Six whites reportedly suffered minor injuries in the outbreak. [87]

CAMP CREEK CLUB

According to congressional testimony received in 1965, this group was a cover for a Lancaster, South Carolina, klavern, Association of South Carolina Klans. [38]

CAMP MY LAI

Operated by Bill Wilkinson's Klan Youth Corps, Camp My Lai—named for the site where U.S. troops massacred unarmed civilians in Vietnam—was a Louisiana center for indoctrination and paramilitary training of white teenagers. Campers received training in marksmanship and survival techniques, along with lectures from Wilkinson that included the following advice: "Many things your teachers tell you are not true, they're just lies." The camp closed down in the early 1980s rather than fight an expensive lawsuit filed by the Southern Poverty Law Center. [93]

CAMP NORDLAND

See *German-American Bund.*

CAMP PULLER

A paramilitary training facility for right-wing survivalists, Camp Puller was located at Double Bayou, Texas, forty-three miles west of Houston, between 1978 and 1980. The operators, husband-wife team Robert and Pat Sisente, of Deer Park, Texas, reported in late 1980 that the camp was sponsored by a group called Veterans for Victory Over Communism. Instructors included Klansmen Joe Bogart and John Bryant, who had been convicted of federal weapons charges in 1979. The camp's existence was revealed in November 1980, after Klansman Louis Beam delivered nine teenage Explorer Scouts to the facility, one that the boy's parents did not realize had Klan connections. The boys learned weapons training, instruction in the methods of decapitation with a machete, and heard lectures on communism, skyjacking, and the hunting of illegal aliens. Contacted by the press, Beam said, "Instead of playing baseball or football, they are learning how to survive. I'd even like to start them a little younger." Protests by the Anti-Defamation League and Austin's John Brown Anti-Klan Committee led to a lawsuit by the Southern Poverty Law Center in 1982, which secured an injunction against such camps under an obscure Texas law banning private armies. [*Newsweek*, Dec. 15, 1980; 93]

CAMPBELL, DENNIS L.

A private first-class in the U.S. Marine Corps and a member of David Duke's Knights of the KKK at Camp Pendleton, California, Campbell was transferred to another base in November 1976 following an outbreak of violence between Klansmen and black marines. [*NYT* 1976]

CAMPBELL, PHILIP

A Kansas City congressman and chairman of the House Rules Committee, Campbell chaired a brief congressional investigation of the KKK in 1921. When he was defeated for reelection the following year, Klansmen publicly took credit for his opponent's victory. [10]

CAMPBELL, REV. SAMUEL

An Atlanta-based Klan orator in the 1920s, Reverend Campbell traveled as far as Illinois to spread the gospel of the KKK. [10]

CANADA

There were rumors of Klan organizational drives throughout Canada in the early 1920s, allegedly linking the Klan with a series of arson attacks on Roman Catholic churches, including the historic Quebec Cathedral. No link was proven until 1926, when Klansmen were identified as the bombers of St. Mary's Church in Barrie, Ontario. Imperial Wizard Hiram Evans promptly disclaimed any ties with the Canadian Klan, which was based in Toronto, where an imperial palace was established. Much of the Klan activity took place in Saskatchewan, where Hoosier Klansman Pat Emmons lent a hand to the recruiting efforts by stirring up antipathy toward Southern European immigrants. Within two years, the KKK could boast of 40,000 members in Saskatchewan, a province with only 750,000 inhabitants, but the movement was doomed by the exposure of financial irregularities within the group. Emmons himself was indicted for misappropriating Klan funds. He voluntarily returned from the United States and and was found innocent by demonstrating that his contract allowed him to spend the money however he pleased. Canadian Klansmen were left to elect their own leader, but membership was already slipping. Four decades later, the neo-Nazi Western Guard was brought to court and formally barred from using the mail to distribute its hate literature. Leader John Ross Taylor maintained close ties with the National States Rights Party in the United States, and J.B. Stoner was invited to address the Western Guard's annual banquet in March 1974. Another Western Guard associate, Toronto resident Jack Prins, was identified as grand dragon of Canada's Klan in the mid-1970s. In June 1980, British Columbian Wolfgang Droege emerged as spokesman for the Canadian Knights of the KKK, which was affiliated with Stephen Black's Knights of the Ku Klux Klan in the United States. That same year, seventy-five Canadian representatives of the Western Guard and Nationalist Party of Canada attended the first annual congress of the National Socialist Party of America, held in Raleigh, North Carolina. Localized recruiting for the KKK and its affiliated neo-Nazi groups apparently still continues. [*NYT* 1980; 2; 10; 84]

CANADIAN KNIGHTS OF THE KU KLUX KLAN

Based in British Columbia and led by neo-Nazi Wolfgang Droege, the Canadian Knights are affiliated with the Knights of the Ku Klux Klan in the United States. In June 1980, Canadian Klansmen reportedly launched a Toronto recruiting drive, without significant success. [2]

CANAL ZONE

In the early 1920s, when the Knights of the KKK, Inc., were at their peak of strength, a small klavern was reportedly organized among U.S. citizens living in the Panama Canal Zone. No traceable activities were reported, and the group was apparently short-lived. [10]

CANE BRANCH BAPTIST CHURCH

On October 31, 1951, fourteen Klansmen were arrested for parading masked through this Conway, South Carolina, church. Four days later, Deacon A.L. Tyler swore out warrants for the arrest of the six deputies who had arrested the Klansmen. The pastors and deacons of other area churches raised bail for the officers, but the congregation of Cane Branch Baptist remained adamant, with spokesmen Arthur Tyler and N.E. Tyler announcing that members had adopted a resolution approving of the Klan's conduct in church. [*NYT* 1951]

CANE RIVER HUNTING & FISHING CLUB

In 1965 congressional investigators identified this club as a front for the Natchitoches, Louisiana, klavern, Original Knights of the Ku Klux Klan. [38]

CANNON, JACK

Cannon replaced Royce McPhail as Texas grand dragon for the United Klans of America in April 1966, after McPhail resigned and denounced the United Klans as "bent on violence." Cannon's chief publicity stunt was an attempt to schedule a Klan rally near the ranch of President Lyndon Johnson, but his efforts were blocked by what he called "federal harassment." [NYT 1966]

CAPE FEAR FISHING CLUB

See *Pin Hook Improvement Association.*

CAPITOL CITY RESTORATION ASSOCIATION

In 1965 congressional investigators identified this group as a cover for Unit No. 100, United Klans of America, in Raleigh, North Carolina. [38]

CAPITOL CITY SPORTSMANS CLUB

Testimony offered before the House Un-American Activities Committee in 1965 identified this club as a front for United Klans of America Unit No. 9, in Columbia, South Carolina. [38]

CAREY, TIM

A black resident of Cedartown, Georgia, eighteen-year-old Carey was attacked by several Klansmen in April 1984, while riding his bicycle on a city street. He was beaten with brass knuckles and sprayed with Mace, which resulted in the May 1985 arrest of Klansman Randall Wiley Smith. [NYT 1985]

CAREY, WILSON

A black state legislator and the second most powerful Republican in Reconstruction Caswell County, North Carolina, Carey was driven out of the area by Klan death threats in 1870. [87]

CARGELL, ROBERT

A resident of St. Petersburg, Florida, Cargell was kidnapped and castrated by nightriders in 1935. Several known Klansmen were accused of the crime in April 1936. [NYT 1936]

CARLIN, GEN. W.P.

As Tennessee state commander of the Freedmen's Bureau during Reconstruction, Carlin reported in 1868: "The Ku Klux organization is so extensive, and so well organized and armed, that it is beyond the power of anyone to exert any moral influence over them. Powder and ball is the only thing that will put them down." [87]

CARLISLE, CHARLES, JR.

See *Hurst, Charles.*

CARLOCK, REV. RICHARD E.

A resident of Cicero, Illinois, Carlock was identified as a guest speaker at a March 29, 1975, organizational meeting of the KKK in Kankakee, Illinois. According to evidence gathered by a state legislative investigating committee, Carlock was affiliated with both the United Klans of America and the New Christian Crusade Church, founded by James Warner. [43]

CARLSON, GERALD RUSSELL

A neo-Nazi activist in Lansing, Michigan, Carlson held membership in the Klan, the National States Rights Party, the John Birch Society, and the American Independent Party before he professed "disenchantment" with existing groups and founded his own National Christian Democratic Party in 1978. His activities included the establishment of a "White Power Hot Line," featuring recorded telephone messages denouncing blacks and Jews. (The service was discontinued when Carlson refused a demand from Michigan Bell that his personal address be included in every message.) In August 1980, Carlson won the 15th Congressional District's Republican primary with a total of 3,759 votes, defeating his opponent by more than 700 votes. Republican leaders instantly withdrew their support from Carlson, and he lost the general election that November, but his total of 53,570 votes led Anti-Defamation League spokesmen to express "deep concern." In February 1981, Carlson was soundly defeated in another political race, this time in Michigan's 4th Congressional District, but the trouncing left him undiscouraged. Shifting to Pennsylvania for a special congressional election in June 1981, Carlson was scratched from the ballot due to his false claims of residence in Philadelphia. In August 1982, Carlson tried his luck again in Michigan's 15th Congressional District, this time as a Democrat, but primary balloting left him with only 7,486 votes. [2]

CARMACK, BARNIE, JR.

A member of the National States Rights Party in Birmingham, Alabama, Carmack was one of eight racists indicted on September 23, 1963, for violent interference with local school desegregation. [*FOF 1963*]

CAROLINA KNIGHTS OF THE KU KLUX KLAN

A small North Carolina splinter group led by Glenn Miller, the Carolina KKK participated in violence around Greensboro, North Carolina, which culminated in the November 1979 murders of five persons. Federal authorities allege that Miller's Klan also received illegal "donations" in the form of money stolen from various banks by neo-Nazi members of The Order in 1980. In January 1983, four Carolina Knights sought to bail out a black man jailed on rape charges in Iredell County, but the prisoner declined their generosity. Miller's subsequent indictment and imprisonment on federal charges led the Klan to seek cover by repeatedly changing names. Variously known as the Confederate Knights, the White Patriot Party, and the Southern National Front, the group tenuously continued to exist with an estimated 300 members in 1987. [2]

CARPENTER, REV. C.N.

As pastor of the Capitol Hill Church of Christ in Des Moines, Iowa, Carpenter also served as the leader of the local Klan in the 1920s. He created a brief sensation with one of his sermons, "Why I Am a Member of the Klan," and called on the Knights of Columbus to publish their membership list. The excitement blew over when Carpenter's challenge was met, and the list contained no startling revelations. [10]

CARPENTER, J.B.

As the superior court clerk of Rutherford County, North Carolina, and editor of the Rutherford *Star*, Carpenter was an outspoken critic of the Reconstruction Klan. In June 1871, he testified before a congressional panel investigating the KKK, and Klansmen took advantage of his absence to demolish his newspaper office. [87]

CARPETBAGGERS

An insult directed at Northerners who visited the Reconstruction South to participate in politics or work for black civil rights, the term originated because some of the newcomers carried their personal belongings in then-popular suitcases made from carpeting material. White teachers in black schools were a favorite Klan target, along with Republican activists, revenue officers, and agents of the Freedmen's Bureau. As one Tennessee Klansman proudly reported, "Carpetbaggers lived in constant dread of a Ku Klux visit and were in great measure controlled through their fears." [87]

CARR, EMMETT ANDREW

A resident of Louisville, Kentucky, who once described himself as a Klansman in a radio interview, Carr was indicted on October 1, 1952, for failure to list his KKK affiliation on an application for employment at an atomic energy plant in Paducah. The indictment resulted from the recent inclusion of the Klan and several affiliated groups on the U.S. Attorney General's list of subversive organizations, placing Klansmen and neo-Nazis in the same class with the groups on the far left of the political spectrum that they opposed. [*NYT* 1952]

CARR, G.E.

As grand dragon of Michigan in the 1920s, Carr once issued a Christmas message urging Klansmen to "evidence their devotion to our Lord through their activities in making this great day a bright one for all they can consistently reach." The order produced some rare good publicity for the KKK, with numerous reports of Klansmen giving food and clothing to needy persons of all races. [93]

CARRADINE, A. BYRD

See *Alexander, Jack; Federated Ku Klux Klans, Inc.*

CARROLL, C.E.

A resident of Pensacola, Florida, Carroll was identified in 1975 as titan for Florida provinces five and six, United Klans of America. As such, he launched a new recruiting drive in May 1975, capitalizing on black protests over alleged police brutality and the suspicious deaths of five black fishermen that had been ruled accidental by local authorities. [*NYT* 1975]

CARROLL, JOSEPH

A spokesman for the National States Rights Party, Carroll was one of three party orators banned from Baltimore by an August 1966 court order following a July 29 rally of 1,000 persons that erupted into violence against blacks. (Connie Lynch and Richard Norton were also included in the ban.) On November 21, 1966, Carroll was sentenced to jail in Baltimore for disorderly conduct, inciting a riot, conspiracy to riot, and violation of city park rules. [*NYT* 1966; *FOF* 1966]

CARTER, ASA EARL

An Alabama native, Carter received radio training in the navy and later at the University of Colorado. Following his discharge from the service, he stayed in school, receiving a "certificate of journalism" in 1949. Carter worked briefly with professional anti-Semite Gerald L.K. Smith, and later held jobs as a radio newscaster in Colorado, Mississippi, and Alabama. While employed in Birmingham in 1955, his anti-Semitic broadcasts during Brotherhood Week sparked protests from the National Conference of Christians and Jews, prompting his summary dismissal. An early member of the Alabama Citizens' Council, Carter soon broke with leader Sam

Englehardt over Carter's insistence that "the mountain people—the real red neck—is our strength." Carter organized a competing North Alabama Citizens's Council in October 1955, excluding Jews from membership and publishing a magazine, *The Southerner,* that attacked rock 'n' roll as "sensuous Negro music," eroding "all the white man has built through his devotion to God." Sam Englehardt countered by calling Carter a "fascist," and Carter's group swiftly veered into violent confrontation with blacks. Six of his members assaulted singer Nat "King" Cole during a Birmingham performance in April 1956. Carter believed that Cole was "a vicious agitator for integration" and sponsored a White People's Defense Fund for the defendants. (A sign displayed at Carter's headquarters on Bessemer Road bore the legend: "Be Bop Promotes Communism.") Later in April 1956, retired admiral John Crommelin introduced Carter to racist agitator John Kasper. Their early partnership resulted in the formation of a White Youth League, and their subsequent harassment of blacks led to seventeen arrests for contempt of court. Carter also helped Kasper organize the Seabord White Citizens' Council in Washington, D.C., and they shared the dais at a September 1956 Council rally in Alabama, where hooded Klansmen were welcomed in the audience. Two months later, Carter formally announced the creation of his own Original Ku Klux Klan of the Confederacy, divided into "squads and platoons with areas of responsibility." Thirty-five Klansmen were initiated in Birmingham on November 15 before a bonfire of skulls, with Carter exhorting his recruits to "fight the enemies of Jesus Christ to the bitter end and after." In December Carter announced plans for a troop of white minutemen to patrol city buses and enforce segregation in the face of a black boycott. On January 22, 1957, Carter interrupted a Klan meeting with gunfire, wounding members J.P. Tillery and Charles Bridges after they protested his "one-man rule." Police arrested Carter the following day; others charged with assault in the case included Klansmen Harold McBride, Loney Curry, and Mira Evans. In September 1957, while four of his Birmingham disciples were awaiting trial for the castration of Edward Aaron, Carter joined John Kasper for riotous demonstrations in Clinton, Tennessee, and Charlotte, Virginia. In 1961, Carter was appointed as special assistant to Alabama Governor George Wallace, and was paid from a private slush fund for writing the governor's speeches and performing other unspecified tasks. In later years, he served as an organizer of Wallace-for-President clubs, and sent out the invitations to the several dozen men who met at Montgomery's Woodley Country Club to launch the ex-governor's 1968 presidential race. [*FOF* 1957; 17]

CARTER, JAMES EARL

A former governor of Georgia and U.S. President, Carter was despised by Klansmen for his liberal policies. Robed members demonstrated outside Carter's family church in Plains, Georgia, on November 14, 1976, after the congregation voted to lift a long-standing ban on black members. During the 1976 presidential campaign, literature published by the KKK and National States Rights Party branded Carter as an illegitimate son of Massachusetts millionaire Joseph Kennedy. [*NYT* 1976]

CARTER, ROY

See *Flowers, Evergreen.*

CARTER, W. HORACE

As editor of Tabor City (North Carolina) *Tribune,* Carter won the 1952 Pulitzer and Sidney Hillman journalism awards for a series of articles that eventually led to the conviction of more than 100 Association of Carolina Klans members on various criminal charges. [*NYT* 1953]

CARVER VILLAGE

A Miami housing project built during World War II for low income whites, Carver Village was once described as the worst white slum in the South. It became a target of repeated KKK demonstrations and bombings after black families started moving in during the summer of 1951, with dynamite blasts recorded on September 22, November 30 (causing $20,000 damage), and December 2. [*NYT* 1951–1953]

CASH, JACK

A Birmingham, Alabama, member of the National States Rights Party, Cash was one of eight racists indicted on September 23, 1963, for violent interference with desegregation of local schools. [*FOF* 1963]

CASH SPORTSMAN CLUB

In 1965 congressional investigators identified this group as a cover for Unit No. 36, United Klans of America, at Society Hill, South Carolina. [38]

CASTILLE, FRANK

See *Klein, Charles.*

CASTRATION

Often considered a typical Klan punishment, castration by Klansmen has in fact been documented on only a handful of occasions. Sketchy records from the Reconstruction era make precise tabulation impossible, but three definite cases are traceable to the KKK in Wilkinson County, North Carolina. All the victims were black, and one died from his injuries. The two others, Bill Briggan and Henry Lowther, survived to describe their ordeal for congressional investigators. In August 1923, the sexual mutilation of a Tulsa Jew led Oklahoma Governor Jack Walton to declare martial law against the Klan, and the same year saw Colorado Grand Dragon John Locke accused of forcing a "shotgun" wedding with threats of castration against a Denver youth. Policemen were implicated when members of the Orange County, Florida, klavern tortured and castrated union organizer Joseph Shoemaker in 1935. When he died nine days later, the charge was changed to murder, and several officers were sentenced to jail as accessories. St. Petersburg Klansmen were involved in the 1935 abduction and mutilation of Robert Cargell. Several Klansmen were charged in April 1936. Perhaps the worst case on record is that of Edward Aaron, a black man abducted by Birmingham Klansmen in September 1957 who was beaten, castrated, and had his wounds doused with turpentine in a ritual ceremony designed to test the courage of a newly promoted Klan officer. The shocking episode left four Klansmen facing twenty-year prison terms, but Governor George Wallace reduced their sentences and gave them early parole. [10; 87]

CATAHOULA SPORTSMAN CLUB

A front group for the Original Knights of the KKK in Catahoula Parish, Louisiana, this group was exposed in 1965 during an investigation by the House Un-American Activities Committee. [38]

CATARRAH SPORTS CLUB

In 1966 congressional investigators identified this group as a front for the Jefferson, South Carolina, klavern, United Klans of America. [38]

CATAWBA IMPROVEMENT ASSOCIATION

During the 1960s, this group served as a cover for Unit No. 83, United Klans of America, in Hickory, North Carolina. [38]

CATHCART, ANDREW

An elderly black resident of Reconstruction South Carolina, Cathcart saved enough money to buy a ninety-eight-acre plantation and built a schoolhouse for blacks on the property. He was subsequently whipped by Klansmen, who stole his money and burned the school. [93]

CATTERSON, ROBERT F.

A Union officer and later an Arkansas state legislator, Catterson was placed in charge of anti-Klan militia units in the southwestern part of the state when martial law was declared in November 1868. At Center Point on November 13, 1868, his troops defeated a force of 400 men and effectively crushed white resistance to Reconstruction in that sector. Catterson later executed two Klansmen for a murder committed in Little River County, then moved on in December to reinforce the militia in southeastern Arkansas. By early 1869, the Razorback Klan was effectively eradicated. [87]

CAUCASIAN CLUBS

A cover name applied to several Louisiana chapters of the Knights of the White Camellia after January 1869, the new designation fooled few, if any, local residents. [87]

CAUDLE, ROY

A Klansman involved in the November 1979 Greensboro, North Carolina, shootout that left five persons dead, Caudle reportedly carried Klan weapons to the scene in the trunk of his car. [10]

CAVALCADE OF WHITE AMERICANS

See *Brooks, Henry.*

CENTRAL CAROLINA LADIES LEAGUE

In 1965 congressional investigators identified this group as the cover for a United Klans of America ladies auxiliary unit, in Goldston, North Carolina. [38]

CENTRAL DEKALB CIVIC CLUB

Located in Decatur, Georgia, this group was identified in 1966 as a front for the local klavern of the United Klans of America. [38]

CENTRAL IMPROVEMENT ASSOCIATION OF LILLINGTON

Created as a cover for the Lillington, North Carolina, klavern, United Klans of America, this group was exposed by the House Un-American Activities Committee in 1965. [38]

CENTRAL SPORTSMANS CLUB NO. 101

In 1965 this group was identified as a front for the Haines City, Florida, klavern, United Florida Ku Klux Klan. [38]

CHAMBLISS, ROBERT E.

A native of Pratt City, Alabama, Chambliss joined the Knights of the KKK, Inc., in 1924. Eleven years later, he logged his first arrest, for a liquor law violation, and in 1936 he was charged with desertion and nonsupport of his first wife and children. As a member of the Federated Ku Klux Klans, Chambliss was indicted in July 1949 with sixteen others for a flogging. Two months later, on September 24, he assaulted newsman George Cook at a Klan rally in Warrior, Alabama, smashing Cook's camera. A city worker, Chambliss once had been suspended for ten days after threatening a black resident whose house was bombed. The Cook assault resulted in his dismissal from the city job, but Chambliss remained active in Klan circles, with Birmingham police dubbing him "Dynamite Bob" after he boasted about his skill with TNT. In the summer of 1963, he led defecting members of the United Klans of America into a splinter organization, the Cahaba River Group, that specialized in racial bombings. With fellow Klansmen Charles Cagle and John Hall, Chambliss was found in possession of unregistered dynamite on September 4, 1963, following a blast at the home of black attorney Arthur Shores. Chambliss claimed that the explosives were intended for clearing land at the site of a new KKK headquarters, but the lack of official permits led to his conviction on misdemeanor charges, with a sentence of six months in jail and a $100 fine. Fourteen years later, in September 1977, Chambliss was indicted on four counts of first-degree murder for the September 15, 1963, church bombing that killed four black girls. Tried first for the slaying of victim Denise McNair, Chambliss was defended by ex-mayor Arthur Hanes. At the trial, his niece testified for the prosecution, calling Chambliss "a racial fanatic" who once said he had "enough stuff put away to flatten half of Birmingham." Prior to the fatal church bombing, Chambliss told her, "You just wait until after Sunday morning, and they will beg us to let them segregate." Watching the television news after the blast, Chambliss said, "It wasn't supposed to hurt anybody; it didn't go off when it was supposed to." The FBI reported the discovery in the rubble of a fishing float, used as the crude timer of the "drip bomb" (which employed a leaking bucket) that Chambliss had openly discussed with Birmingham detectives. Convicted of murder on Denise McNair's twenty-sixth birthday, Chambliss was sentenced to life imprisonment, with a minimum of ten years to be served before parole. Departing the courtroom, he told reporters, "This is a terrible thing to do to a seventy-three-year-old-man." [10; 15; 68]

CHAMPION, WILLIAM

A Unionist "scalawag" in Spartanburg County, South Carolina, prior to the Civil War, Champion was an active Republican during Reconstruction, allowing a school for blacks to be built on his land. Appointed as a local election commissioner, he opposed the KKK, declaring that "no Christian-hearted or civilized man" would join such an organization. In October 1871, a party of fifty Klansmen raided his home, wounding a male visitor with gunfire and then binding both men before marching them into the woods, where another group of Klansmen was waiting with two elderly blacks, Clem Bowden and his wife. Champion and both Bowdens were severely beaten, with Champion forced to perform degrading acts before the assembled Klansmen. In parting, all four victims were ordered to refrain from voting Republican in the future. After Champion reported the attack, he soon received a letter which read: "We have been told that our visit to you was not a sufficient hint. We now notify you to leave the country within thirty days from the reception of this notice, or abide the consequences. K.K.K." Champion and the Bowdens moved to Spartanburg, abandoning their lands and escaping any further attention from the KKK. [93]

CHANEY, JAMES

See *Schwerner, Michael.*

CHANEY, WILLIAM MARSHALL

The Kentucky-reared son of a Baptist minister and a veteran of the Pacific in World War II, Chaney moved to Indianapolis in 1959. Appointed Indiana's grand dragon for the United Klans of America in January 1967, Chaney scheduled a statewide rally for August 11, but the meeting was banned by order of the Johnson County Superior Court. In 1968, Chaney addressed several state rallies supporting the presidential candidacy of Alabama Governor George Wallace. Not at all ashamed of his racist views, he told an interviewer in March 1973 that "people are tired of seeing our white women escorted on the street by nigger bucks." On August 24, 1974, following two shooting incidents that left Klansmen wounded during the midst of a Kokomo recruiting drive, Chaney advised his followers to "arm every household with shotguns." In May 1976, Chaney was arrested for the firebombing of an Indianapolis advertising company where he had once served as an employee and union leader. Defended by attorney J.B. Stoner, he was convicted on three felony counts. Chaney's break with Imperial Wizard Robert Shelton and the United Klans of America occurred at a May 31, 1976, rally in Pulaski, Tennessee. Shelton blamed Chaney's dismissal on drinking and womanizing, while the ousted dragon cited clashes over the use of Klan funds and Shelton's tendency toward tough talk rather than action. As a free agent, Chaney organized his own Confederation of Independent Orders-Invisible Empire-Knights of KKK, while also serving as national coordinator for an affiliated group, the Northern and Southern Knights of the KKK. His election to the latter post occurred at a June 5, 1977, "unity conference," where Robert Scoggin, Dale Reusch, and Bill Wilkinson all lost out during a three-way bid for control of the new Klan. An appeal of Chaney's bombing conviction produced an order for a new trial, and he was convicted for a second time in November 1977. [26; 84]

CHARLOTTE COUNTY ANONYMOUS CLUB

Identified as a 1960s front for the United Klans of America in Charlotte County, Virginia, this group's name bears testimony to the Klansmen's preoccupation with secrecy. [38]

CHARLTON, JUDGE

A leading Republican during Reconstruction in Morgan County, Alabama, Charlton was a Klan target. Klansmen invaded his Decatur home and threatened his life in October 1868. He responded by organizing, with the cooperation of Isaac Berry, a local anti-Klan organization in the fall of 1869, but this effort failed to save him: Charlton was assassinated by Klansmen on March 18, 1870. [87]

CHASE, L.W.

A Georgia Klansman arrested for trying to block the Congress of Racial Equality's Freedom Rides in Lagrange, Georgia, Chase was fined $135 for loitering on May 29, 1961. [FOF 1961]

CHASE, VALENTINE

A judge in St. Mary's Parish, Louisiana, during Reconstruction, Chase was ambushed and assassinated on October 17, 1868, by a party of Klansmen and Knights of the White Camellia. Sheriff Henry Pope was killed in the same attack. [87]

CHASE, WILLIAM SHEAFE

While serving as the Episcopal Canon for Brooklyn, New York, Chase praised the 1920s Klan because it was "organized to resist the corruption of politics and the lawlessness of our times." [93]

CHASE CITY FELLOWSHIP CLUB

In 1965 congressional investigators identified this group as a cover for the Chase City, Virginia, klavern, United Klans of America. [38]

CHATHAM CITIZENS CLUB

In 1966 congressional investigators exposed this group as a cover for Unit No. 19, United Klans of America, including Klansmen from the towns of Bynum and Pittsboro, North Carolina. [38]

CHATHAM HUNTING & FISHING CLUB

A 1960s front for the Chatham, Louisiana, klavern, United Klans of America, this group was publicly identified by the House Un-American Activities Committee. [38]

CHAVIS, REV. BEN

See *Wilmington 10.*

CHENEY, TURNER

While serving as the grand dragon of Illinois, Cheney was arrested on September 26, 1966, for participation in two Milwaukee, Wisconsin, bombings. Klansmen Robert Schmidt and Robert Long were also linked to the crimes—the July 1 bombing of a linoleum store owned by the former president of the Wisconsin Civil Rights Congress and the August 9 blast at the Milwaukee NAACP office. On May 1, 1967, Cheney was charged with solicitation to commit murder in a plot to keep Schmidt from testifying for the prosecution at Cheney's bombing trial. [*NYT* 1966–1967]

CHEROKEE 92 MEN'S CLUB

In 1966 congressional investigators identified this group as a front for the Roswell, Georgia, klavern, United Klans of America. [38]

CHEROKEE SPORTSMANS CLUB

A 1960s cover for the Gaffney, South Carolina, klavern, United Klans of America, this group was exposed by congressional probers in 1965. [38]

CHESAPEAKE BAR-B-Q CLUB

In 1965 the House Un-American Activities Committee identified this group as one of three Chesapeake, Virginia, klaverns linked to the United Klans of America. [38]

CHESSMEN

A violent Klan faction active in the Carolinas during the late 1950s, the Chessmen were nicknamed "Blackshirts" after the black masks and shirts of their standard uniform. In the spring of 1959, members expressed their objection to the employment of blacks at a sawmill in Richfield, North Carolina, by pouring sand and sugar in the gas tank of an expensive engine at the mill. Police investigation also implicated Chessmen in the 1959 bombing of a North Carolina home. [38]

CHESTER CONSERVATIVE CLAN

Organized in Chester County, South Carolina, in the spring of 1868, this group spread to neighboring York County in June. One of the original founders was also a Klansman, and membership of the two organizations generally overlapped. [87]

CHESTERFIELD COUNTY SPORTSMANS CLUB

In 1966 congressional investigators exposed this group as a cover for the Cheraw, South Carolina, klavern, United Klans of America. [38]

CHICO AREA NATIONAL SOCIALISTS

A small, California-based affiliate of the National Socialist White People's Party, this group apparently dissolved after leader Perry Warthen was convicted of murdering a teenage follower in 1982. [NYT 1982]

CHILDERS, JAMES R.

See *Hines, Clifford.*

CHILE

On May 24, 1958, police in Santiago arrested several members of a local KKK chapter who were accused of launching a terror campaign against Jewish residents. Investigators said that the Chilean Klansmen drew their inspiration from Horace Miller's Aryan Knights of the KKK based in Waco, Texas. [NYT 1958]

CHISOLM, W.W.

As sheriff of Reconstruction Kemper County, Mississippi, Chisolm used troops to make arrests after Klan violence broke out in early 1869. Until his subsequent assassination, Chisolm's efforts maintained Kemper as the most peaceful of the seven Klan-infested counties along the Alabama border. [87]

CHOPPER, PHILLIP

As Kentucky's grand dragon, Chopper held two joint rallies with David Duke in August 1975, sharing the stage with Robert Scoggin and James Warner. Afterward, he publicly accused Duke of making off with the $4,000 collected from the rallies and denounced his Louisiana associate as a "fraud." Duke responded by calling Chopper a "self-appointed" dragon who lacked authority and members. On September 6, 1975, Chopper was one of seventy-five persons arrested in a white anti-busing march in Louisville. The demonstration followed a day of rioting by whites in working class neighborhoods during which one school bus was burned, thirty others were heavily damaged, and extensive damage was suffered by stores along Preston Highway near the campus of Southern High School (where the buses were attacked). At nearby Valley High School, 2,500 rioters nearly overran police lines, leading to the deployment of National Guard units on September 6. In the aftermath of violence, Mayor Harvey Sloane cited evidence that proved the riots were deliberately organized by racist agitators. A month later, in October 1975, Chopper was extradited to Louisiana for prosecution on a bad check indictment. [NYT 1975; 84]

CHOUDRANT ROD & GUN CLUB

In 1965 congressional investigators exposed this group as a front for the Choudrant, Louisiana, klavern, Original Knights of the KKK. [38]

CHOUTTEAU, DR. GERARD

A white Republican in Reconstruction Sumter County, Alabama, Choutteau was constantly harassed by Klansmen during the 1868 election campaign. On November 14, 1868, a gunman fired shots at Choutteau's children while they were in their front yard. The next evening, nightriders surrounded his home and fired weapons through the night to keep the family awake. In December, the raiders returned while Choutteau was away and drove his mother-in-law from the house before burning it down. Klansmen also whipped four blacks on the same plantation and warned them to leave the area or die. Choutteau moved to the county seat at Livingston, but the harassment followed him. On August 12, 1869, during state elections, Klansmen stormed his house and killed John Coblentz, a white security guard. The local Democratic newspaper blamed Choutteau for the violence, stating that his "incendiary conduct for many months past had filled the public mind with apprehensions of danger." Following the death of Coblentz, Choutteau and his family left Alabama. [87]

CHOWAN BOAT CLUB

In 1965 the House Un-American Activities Committee identified this group as a front for the Edenton, North Carolina, klavern, United Klans of America. [38]

CHRISTIAN ANTI-JEWISH PARTY

Based in Atlanta, Georgia, this neo-Nazi party was organized by J.B. Stoner and Edward Fields in 1952. Stoner and four other members picketed the White House with anti-Semitic placards in 1954, and two identified members, brothers Richard and Robert Bowling, were indicted with George Bright four years later for the bombing of an Atlanta synagogue. [*Life*, Jan. 27, 1958; 14]

CHRISTIAN CONSTITUTIONAL CRUSADERS

In early 1964, when internal dissension created rifts in the Original Knights of the KKK, Grand Dragon Murray Martin rallied members from Shreveport and Bossier City, Louisiana, under the banner of the "Christian Constitutional Crusaders," using the title to cover financial transactions with local banks. In the fall of 1964, when a new three-way split developed in the Klan, Martin's loyalists continued to use the Crusaders front. [38]

CHRISTIAN DEFENSE LEAGUE

Originally created by ex-Klansman Wesley Swift in California, the Christian Defense League (CDL) maintained close ties with other racist groups. Klan orator Connie Lynch was a leading CDL figure in the early 1960s, and another director, based in San Diego, was Bertrand Comparet, attorney for the National States Rights Party and the Minutemen. In 1964, police in Cucamonga, California, raided the home of a CDL member, seizing eight machine guns, incendiary bombs, and a quantity of blasting caps. A driving force behind the CDL in its early days was retired Lieutenant Colonel William P. Gale, founder of the California Rangers. Police infiltrators reported that the CDL welcomed Klansmen and members of other extremist groups into its ranks, making it "the central group, the reporting group, for all these organizations. The very sister and co-worker in this, of the CDL on the West Coast, is the National States Rights Party." In June 1964, Swift and other CDL officers met with George Lincoln Rockwell to exchange information on suspected police informants. In 1963 and 1964, the CDL held meetings in the Los Angeles home of Klansman G. Clinton Wheat, and California Attorney General Thomas McDonald announced that there was a "real coalescence" between the CDL, the National States Rights Party, and other Klan-type groups in southern California. Aging anti-Semite John Crommelin was listed as the group's eastern coordinator in 1971, but the seat of operations had already shifted to Louisiana, with offices established in Baton Rouge and Arabi. Ex-Klansman James K. Warner was listed as the CDL's leader as late as 1983, combining the group's operations with those of his New Christian Crusade Church. It remains uncertain whether the relocated CDL constitutes a new organization or a mere continuation of Swift's original clique. [2; 90]

CHRISTIAN FREEDOM COUNCIL

Organized in 1979 by Michigan Congressman Mark Siljander, the Christian Federation Council was created to purge "obscene" books from public libraries in Niles and Three Rivers, Michigan. Leaders of the group were embarrassed when Klansmen flocked to the effort, with a spokesman branding the KKK as "disgustingly more immoral than any pornographic book or magazine could ever be." [93]

CHRISTIAN KNIGHTS OF THE KU KLUX KLAN (1959–1961)

Created in 1959 and based in Atlanta, Georgia, this splinter faction was led by Imperial Wizard J.B. Stoner. In August 1959, Stoner sent a letter to New York City's police commissioner, offering 5,000 Klansmen for a drive to "clean up Harlem." (The offer was ignored.) Stoner's group was excluded, along with the U.S. Klans, from a February 1960 Atlanta meeting that created the Knights of the KKK, Inc. By the following year, the Christian Knights had been effectively reduced to a paper organization, as recruiting failed and Stoner devoted more of his time to the National States Rights Party. [FOF 1960; 38]

CHRISTIAN KNIGHTS OF THE KU KLUX KLAN (1980s)

Based in North Carolina, the Christian Knights enjoyed marginal success in recruiting members outside of the Tarheel State. As of 1987, the group's strength was estimated to be at most 250 members. [NYT 1987]

CHRISTIAN NATIONAL PARTY

An anti-Semitic vehicle created and led by Gerald L.K. Smith, the group ran its founder for president of the United States in 1952 (polling 13,883 votes) and again in 1956 (returns unavailable). [NYT 1952, 1956]

CHRISTIAN NATIONALIST ALLIANCE

Based in Lancaster, California, during 1971, this group was yet another front for the anti-Semitic activities of Wesley Swift and cohort Dennis Mower. [90]

CHRISTIAN NATIONALIST CRUSADE

Organized by anti-Semite Gerald L.K. Smith in the 1930s, the Christian National Crusade welcomed Klansmen such as Wesley Swift into membership and positions of authority. As a far-right propaganda mill based in Eureka Springs, Arkansas, the group provided literature to groups ranging from the KKK to the Citizens' Council and John Birch Society, and served as an early bridge between white supremacist groups and anti-Semitic philosophy. The Crusade's magazine, *The Cross and the Flag*, openly sided with Klan terrorists during the 1960s, decrying their "persecution" by agents of the federal government who brought them to trial. After Smith's semi-retirement in the early 1970s, the group's headquarters was shifted to Glendale, California, under the leadership of former secretary R.L. Morgan. [90]

CHRISTIAN VOTERS AND BUYERS LEAGUE

Organized by Klansman James Venable in the early 1960s to attack the "kosher food racket," the League labeled Heinz Foods a Zionist front, accusing the company of using too little pork in its canned pork and beans. Venable warned buyers to look for a tiny letter "k" buried in the small print on packages, denoting kosher products, and boycott manufacturers who were thus identified as participants in this "Zionist conspiracy." Appearing before the House Un-American Activities Committee in 1965, Venable publicly apologized for the campaign, saying, "Some of the best friends I got are Jewish people." [38; 93]

CHRISTIAN-PATRIOTS DEFENSE LEAGUE

Based in Flora, Illinois, the group is an anti-Semitic survivalist group with Klan affiliations and was founded in 1977 by John Harrell. Spokesmen for the organization present a conspiracy theory of U.S. history, anticipating "an almost certain and inescapable collapse of the present structure" caused by insidious agents of "the Pharisaical anti-Christ system." In 1979, Harrell announced the group's intention of preparing whites for a coming race war, sparked by the "Christ-hating International Jewish Conspiracy," which would be part of the collapse. Since then the group has hosted a semi-annual "Freedom Festival" at Harrell's fifty-five-acre estate in Louisville, Illinois. The second festival, convened in September 1979, was climaxed by the first conference of Harrell's "Citizens Emergency Defense System," which produced a list of approved "Christian-Patriotic" groups that included the United Klans of America. At the 1980 summer festival, more than 1,000 persons attended seminars on firearms, archery, and knife-fighting. Also in 1980, Harrell announced the creation of a 232 acre "permanent base" in the Ozark region of Missouri, some twenty-five miles from Ft. Leonard Wood (this "permanent base" would be the site of his 1983 festival), with a second base located in West Virginia. The group's ultimate goal is the creation of a white "survival area" in the U.S. heartland, comprising a quadrangle spanning parts of twenty states, with its four corners at Atlanta, Pittsburgh, Scottsbluff, Nebraska, and Lubbock, Texas. [2]

CHRISTIANS, GEORGE W.

A former Klansman, Christians emerged as leader of the fascist White Shirts in the 1930s. [10]

CHRISTMAS, CHARLES

Born in Meridian, Mississippi, Christmas moved to Louisiana in 1956 and reportedly joined the Original Ku Klux Klan of America three years later. After the group split in 1964, he emerged as the ranking Klansman in the 6th Congressional District, which includes Bogalusa. His Klansmen were among the most violent in the South, largely ignoring Christmas's April 1965 agreement with Bogalusa's mayor, promising that police would be allowed to handle black protests without Klan interference. At the height of local rioting in 1965, Christmas reportedly ran transient agitators J.B. Stoner and Connie Lynch out of town in an effort to restore order. Still serving as grand dragon for the withered Original Knights in 1976, Christmas, in an interview with journalist Patsy Sims, claimed a vastly inflated membership of 1,500 Klansmen. [NYT 1965; 84]

CHULA MEN'S CLUB

In 1966 congressional investigators identified this group as a cover for the Amelia, Virginia, klavern, United Klans of America. [38]

CHURCH, WILLIAM

Identified as the imperial wizard of the Justice Knights of the KKK, Church was charged with shooting four black women (some accounts list five victims) in Chattanooga, Tennessee, during April 1980. He was acquitted by a jury three months later, a verdict that touched off black rioting. In November 1982, Church was jailed in Amelia County, Virginia, for the rape of a seven-year-old girl. [NYT 1980, 1982]

CHURCH OF JESUS CHRIST CHRISTIAN

Originally dubbed the Anglo-Saxon Christian Congregation when founded by ex-Klansman Wesley Swift in 1946, the Church of Jesus Christ Christian maintains that pure-blooded whites are the lost children of Israel. By the early 1960s, a string of "parishes" in California and a small-station radio network carried Swift's message to an estimated one million listeners. Klan agitator Connie Lynch was an ordained minister of the church, while another "reverend" was Dennis Mower of Lancaster, California, an associate of the National States Rights Party and close friend of White Knights Imperial Wizard Sam Bowers. Reverend Oren Potito, head of the church's "eastern conference" in St. Petersburg, Florida, was a former NSRP organizer and campaign manager for anti-Semite John Crommelin's 1962 political campaign. In 1965, a report issued by the California state legislature found the church working in close cooperation with the KKK, the National States Rights Party, the Minutemen, and the California Rangers. On Swift's death in 1970, disciple Richard Butler took over the church, subsequently shifting its headquarters to a survivalist compound in Hayden Lake, Idaho, where it was renamed the Aryan Nations-Church of Jesus Christ Christian. In its new guise, the church remains a keystone of the modern "Identity Church" movement in the United States. [2; 90]

CITIZENS' COUNCIL

Often called the White Citizens' Council despite the protests from "respectable" leaders, this movement had its roots in Sunflower County, Mississippi, where the first chapter was organized after the U.S. Supreme Court's 1954 Black Monday ruling on school integration. Florida Klan leader Bill Hendrix instantly denounced the competing Council as a movement "full of Jews," but various chapters distributed anti-Semitic literature along with their other racist broadsides gleaned from sources such as Gerald Smith's Christian Nationalist Crusade. Southern gentlemen and politicians tried to draw a line between these Councils—allegedly opting for "peaceful" economic pressure in the form of boycotts or firings—and the more violence-prone groups such as the KKK. Both black and white critics dismissed the cosmetic differences, dubbing the Council a "white-collar Klan" whose members remained emotionally unstable under pressure. One

Southern spokesman called the Councils "watchdogs of segregation in the Deep South—but when the going gets tough and they need bulldogs with that instinct for the jugular, the Klan will be there to step in." Some of the Councils were in fact secretly, or sometimes openly, allied with Klan factions in their localities. The membership of Asa Carter's North Alabama Citizens' Council, created in October 1955, was more or less interchangeable with that of his Original Ku Klux Klan of the Confederacy, organized a year later. Carter's followers assaulted black singer Nat "King" Cole during a Birmingham performance in April 1956, and nineteen months later four of Carter's followers were jailed for castrating Edward Aaron, a black man. In 1956, at the height of the Montgomery, Alabama, bus boycott, Mississippi Senator James Eastland addressed a Council crowd of 12,000 persons in the Alabama capital, while teenagers distributed handbills reading as follows:

> When in the course of human events it becomes necessary to abolish the Negro race, proper methods should be used. Among these are guns, bows and arrows, sling shots and knives. We hold these truths to be self-evident, that all whites are created equal with certain rights, among these are life, liberty and the pursuit of dead niggers.
>
> In every stage of the bus boycott, we have been oppressed and degraded because of black, slimy, juicy unbearably stinking niggers. Their conduct should not be dwelt upon because behind them they have an ancestral background of Pygmies, Head Hunters and snot suckers. My friends, it is time we wised up to these black devils. I tell you they are a group of two-legged agitators who persist in walking up and down our streets protruding their black lips. If we don't stop helping these African flesh eaters, we will soon wake up and find Reverend [Martin Luther] King in the white house.
>
> LET'S GET ON THE BALL WHITE CITIZENS.

In June 1956 racist agitator John Kasper organized his own Seabord White Citizens' Council in Washington, D.C. A year later, in Louisville, Kentucky, Edward Fields worked for the local Council before moving on to the United White Party and its successor, the National States Rights Party. In the winter of 1958–1959, Council spokesmen in South Carolina charged that Klansmen were trying to subvert their organization by concealing their KKK membership to join the Council and pervert their lofty purpose for the KKK's own "cowardly, secretive" ends. In 1959, the secretary-treasurer of Florida's Association of Citizens' Councils was Homer Barrs, a close friend of Florida Ku Klux Klan leader J.E. Fraser, who described Fraser as a "fine, right-thinking boy." In media interviews, Barrs made a point of emphasizing that Klansmen were not barred from joining the Council. In 1960, Emmett Miller, founder of the Crittenden County Citizens' Council in Little Rock, Arkansas, was arrested for trying to bomb all-black Philander Smith College; he later went on to serve as a Klan recruiter and officer in the

National States Rights Party. In November 1960, rioting by New Orleans segregationists followed a Council meeting of 5,000 persons where political kingmaker Leander Perez warned his audience, "These Congolese rape your daughters." A year later, the Louisiana Council was already dwindling, a virulent anti-Semitic group repudiated by other Councils for its close resemblance to the KKK. At a June 7, 1963, Council rally in Birmingham addressed by Police Commissioner "Bull" Connor, KKK leaflets were openly distributed and an announcement was made from the dais for a rally planned by the United Klans of America. Later that month the assassination of NAACP leader Medgar Evers in Jackson, Mississippi, was traced to Byron de la Beckwith, a prominent member of the Citizens' Council in Greenwood; Council leaders helped organize a White Citizens' Legal Fund to help Beckwith defray the costs of his several trials. Other Council members joined robed Klansmen to picket a meeting of Birmingham's biracial commission on July 13, 1963. By 1964, the original Councils in Mississippi were losing strength in favor of a revived KKK and the Americans for Preservation of the White Race, as well as crumbling under pressure from the "Freedom Summer" project and the Councils' failure to block integration after ten years of trying. Mississippi's White Knights of the KKK reportedly made a concerted effort to infiltrate the Councils between 1964 and 1966 with some success. In November 1965, the Council sponsored a speech by Selma, Alabama, Sheriff Jim Clark in San Diego. Three years later, the Councils vigorously supported George Wallace and the American Independent Party, with Council leader Roy Harris serving as Georgia's state chairman. Members of the Councils began stumping their districts for Wallace's 1972 presidential race on the night of his 1968 defeat, and remained loyal when his near-assassination passed the candidacy to Representative John Schmitz of California. In September 1970, Council members joined Klansmen in marches before school board and newspaper officers in Memphis, Tennessee, to protest new "awareness" programs in the local grade schools. At one such rally robed Klansmen urged parents to withdraw their children from the public schools as a hedge against "communistic brainwashing." Today, the Councils are reportedly defunct. [FOF 1963; NYT 1970; 61]

CIVILIAN MATERIEL ASSISTANCE

Organized by residents of Alabama in 1983 for the purpose of shipping food, clothing, and medical supplies to anti-communist Contra guerilla fighters in Central America, by 1986 this group had been transformed into an extralegal paramilitary group bent on stalking illegal aliens along the United States' southern border. In July 1986, Hispanic civil rights groups filed formal complaints against the group, charging its members with setting booby traps along the border and with holding several Mexicans at gunpoint before delivering them to officers of the Border Patrol. Texas state officials announced their intention of filing charges against the group, and its national director Tommy Posey declared that they would continue the border patrols. A policy rift was revealed during the group's first national convention held in Memphis, Tennessee, July 25–27, 1986, when Texas state coordinator D.L. ("Pappy") Hicks announced the immediate suspension of the vigilante patrols and denied any alleged links between his organization and the Texas Klan. Hicks told the press, "Most of us believe that we've distracted from what we were set up for: to give aid to the freedom fighters in Nicaragua." [AP, July 27, 1986]

CLANTON, JAMES H.

An ex-Confederate general, Alabama Reconstruction Klan leader, and state Democratic Party chairman, Clanton was also a minority member of the congressional panel that investigated KKK violence during 1871 and 1872. When Klan victims testified about the scope of the KKK's Southern terrorism, Clanton issued a fruitless public call for other witnesses "to disprove the statements of those fellows." [87]

CLARK, JAMES G.

Entering Alabama politics as Governor Jim Folsom's 1956 campaign manager in Dallas County, Clark was appointed sheriff when the incumbent sheriff died of a heart attack in 1957, and won the next two elections in 1958 and 1962. In 1958, he was opposed by Selma police captain Wilson Baker, who sought Klan support without much success, and afterward raised a charge of vote-count irregularities in Clark's victory. When civil rights activists targeted Selma for a black voter registration campaign in 1962, Clark recruited a special posse that allegedly included many Klansmen, arming them with clubs and electric cattle prods for use against demonstrators. The posse's most infamous foray occurred on "Bloody Sunday," March 7, 1965, when deputies and state troopers violently blocked a march from Selma to Montgomery, sending more than sixty blacks to the hospital. Alleged to have maintained close ties with the KKK, Clark declared on March 27, 1965, that Klan victim Viola Liuzzo "might not have been murdered" if the FBI had warned him that a particular Klan vehicle was under surveillance; FBI agents responded by calling Clark's statement a "malicious lie" and "typical of his weakness in handling his responsibilities." On April 16, 1965, a federal court ordered Clark to stop using his special posse in racial confrontations, but the action was already waning in Selma. In November 1965, the Citizens' Council sponsored a speech by Clark in San Diego, but he was shouted down by hecklers, and complained that it "wouldn't happen in Selma." He received a warmer welcome in Los Angeles, where the Greater L.A. Council presented him with a pistol belt inscribed: "Courage, Strength, Wisdom." When the Klan killers of Reverend James Reeb were on trial in Selma, Clark paid a mysterious visit to the jury room on December 12, 1965, moments before the panel returned with a verdict of acquittal. When Police Chief Wilson Baker filed to run against Clark in the 1966 sheriff's race, "special deputies" tried to undermine Baker by passing out copies of a KKK membership application, allegedly signed by Baker in 1958. Baker denounced the document as a "clever copy," asserting that Clark's supporters had access to Klan files "because some of them are Klansmen." Defeated in the Democratic primary, Clark attempted a write-in campaign catering to blacks in the November election, but did poorly. Unemployed for the first time in a decade, he joined the John Birch Society's lecture bureau as a traveling expert on the perils of communism. In May 1978, Clark was charged with marijuana smuggling after authorities seized three tons of the drug from an airplane in Montgomery. Pleading guilty, the ex-sheriff drew a two-year prison term. At the time of his sentencing in December 1978, four charges of fraud and one of racketeering were pending against Clark in an unrelated New York City case. [20; 61; 63]

CLARK, JOE

See *Harris, Essic.*

CLARK, WALTER

A resident of Atlanta, Georgia, Clark was a member of the party that followed William Simmons up nearby Stone Mountain for a ceremony reviving the KKK on Thanksgiving Day 1915. [93]

CLARK-WASHINGTON HUNTING & FISHING CLUB

In 1965 congressional investigators identified this group as a cover for the Jackson, Alabama, klavern, United Klans of America. [38]

CLARKE, CHARLES

A black rape suspect, Clarke was taken from jail and lynched by Klansmen in Morgan County, Georgia, in 1871. [87]

CLARKE, EDWARD YOUNG

A partner with Elizabeth Tyler in the Atlanta-based Southern Publicity Association, Clarke was arrested with Tyler in a local bawdy house, intoxicated and half-dressed, in 1919. His punishment was fixed at a five dollar fine, but the publicity returned to haunt him years later, after Clarke had risen to power in the Knights of the KKK, Inc. Hired by William Simmons to promote the Klan in June 1920, Clarke became the first imperial kleagle, in charge of recruiting new members. His propagation department received eight dollars from each new Klansman's ten dollar klectoken, with four dollars paid to the local kleagle, one dollar reserved for the state's king kleagle, 50 cents earmarked for the resident grand goblin, and $2.50 split between Clarke and Tyler. (The remaining two dollars went to Imperial Wizard Simmons.) In less than a year, Clarke had 1,100 kleagles recruiting among the Masons or other established lodges, simultaneously shifting the emphasis in Klan literature toward nativism, anti-Catholicism, and other "selling points" for a non-Southern audience. In the first fifteen months of Clarke's tenure, Klan membership leaped from 3,000 to nearly 100,000 dues-paying Klansmen. On the side, Clarke owned a real estate company created to manipulate Klan holdings for his personal profit. In September 1921, a congressional probe of the Klan exposed his 1919 arrest and produced a call for the dismissal of Clarke and Tyler, a move Simmons staunchly resisted. While denouncing violence, Clarke also offered Tulsa, Oklahoma, Klansmen a special "third degree" for those who liked a bit of the "rough stuff." In the summer and fall of 1922, Clarke served as imperial wizard pro tem while Simmons took a long vacation, but the publicist's time was running out. His contract was canceled "for the good of the order" in March 1923, three months after Hiram Evans seized power from Simmons. Pending indictments for violation of the Mann and Volstead Acts prevented Clarke from fighting his dismissal, but he escaped with a fine on conviction of the federal charges. On January 11, 1924, a convention of grand dragons formally banished him from the KKK; Clarke retaliated with a public letter to President Calvin Coolidge, calling for federal dissolution of the Klan as "a cheap political machine." Meanwhile, he tried to organize his own competing groups, an effort capped by Clarke's indictment for mail fraud. [10]

CLARK'S GAME BIRD FARM

In 1966 congressional investigators exposed this "farm" as a front for the Beulaville, North Carolina, klavern, United Klans of America. [38]

CLAY, MAMIE

See *Lynch, John.*

CLAYTON, POWELL

As the Reconstruction governor of Arkansas, Clayton broke the Klan's power in early 1869 by employing the militia, martial law, and undercover spies. Klansmen initially retaliated by burning most of Lewisburg in November 1868 and seizing a consignment of militia weapons from the steamship *Hesper* on the Mississippi River a month later, but their efforts were largely wasted. Pressure from Clayton's militia—including unrefuted allegations of torture to gain confessions and the deaths of several Klansmen, who were shot "while trying to escape"—led Democratic leaders to sue for peace, using their own influence to suppress Klan violence. [87]

CLAYTON CIVIC CLUB

A front group for Clayton County Klavern No. 52, in Jonesboro, Georgia, the Clayton Civic Club was utilized to purchase a new Klan headquarters in January 1964, later renting office space to the Federal Aviation Administration and various private firms. On occasion, when the members felt a bit more daring, they referred to their group as the Klayton Men's Club. [38]

CLEVENGER, ORLISS WADE

See *Cole, Nat ("King")*.

CLINK, JOHN

A black resident of Athens, Georgia, Clink was blinded in one eye when Klansmen shot up his apartment on June 20, 1964. Alice Fair, a thirteen-year-old girl, suffered facial wounds in the same attack. Herbert Guest, Denver Phillips, and Paul Strickland—all members of Clarke County Klavern No. 244, United Klans of America—were arrested in the case. On June 30, 1964, Guest and Strickland were fined $105 each for firing guns inside the city limits. More serious charges of assault with intent to kill were never prosecuted. [38]

CLINTON, TENNESSEE

Located in Anderson County, fifteen miles northwest of Knoxville, Clinton had a population of 3,712 persons in 1956, only 220 of whom were black. In January 1956, a district court ordered desegregation of the local schools, and the town remained peaceful until agitator John Kasper arrived on August 25, two days before the scheduled first day of school. Arrested for disturbing the peace on August 27, Kasper was freed the following day and led a mob demonstration of 100 persons at the town's high school on August 29. The mob returned the following day, nearly three times as large, as federal hearings convened on the recent unrest, and Kasper was jailed for another eight days for violating an injunction against rabble-rousing. Klansman Asa Carter took Kasper's place on the dais at a rally on August 31, departing before the crowd began to chant, "We want Kasper!" Angry whites marched on the mayor's home, threatening to blow it up if Kasper was not released, and black motorists were attacked by the mob while the town's six-man police force stood by, powerless to act. On September 1, the town board of aldermen declared an emergency and petitioned the governor for help. A citizens' posse held the mob at bay with guns and tear gas until reinforcements arrived—100 state police, 633 guardsmen, and seven tanks. Admirers bailed Kasper out of jail on September 6, and he was under a permanent injunction barring any interference with desegregation. On September 25, he was held for arraignment in Anderson County's criminal court, facing charges of sedition and inciting a riot, with his trial set for

November 5. Violence continued in Clinton that month, including the bombing of a black-owned home, and anti-Semite John Crommelin was imported from Alabama to address the racist gatherings. In mid-October, 125 carloads of hooded Klansmen paraded through town, burning four crosses and chasing newsmen away from the site of their rally. Kasper's two-week trial in November was a curious proceeding, with no stenographic record maintained. Crommelin was called as a defense witness, and the notes taken by a Birmingham detective, listing Kasper's inflammatory remarks, were lost in the course of the trial. Jurors deliberated less than an hour before acquitting Kasper on November 20, and he emerged from court to announce his plans for continued resistance. A white minister, Reverend Paul Turner, was mobbed and beaten on December 4 while escorting black children to school in Clinton, and the town's fourth bombing, near the integrated high school, occurred a month later. Three more bombings had been logged by February 14, 1957, when a suitcase filled with dynamite exploded on a Clinton Street, shattering the windows in more than twenty homes. On July 23, 1957, Kasper and six others were convicted of violating a federal court's restraining order. Three months later, Carter joined Kasper in Clinton for another series of rallies, but Kasper's time was running out. He entered federal prison that November, carrying a copy of *Mein Kampf.* A postscript was written on October 5, 1958, when three blasts virtually demolished Clinton High School. [*NYT* 1956–1958; 66]

CLINTON HUNTING & FISHING CLUB

In 1965 congressional investigators exposed this club as a front for the Clinton, Louisiana, klavern, Original Knights of the Ku Klux Klan. [38]

CLUB NO. 50

In 1965 the House Un-American Activities Committee identified this club as a front for the Cuba, Alabama, klavern, United Klans of America. [38]

COBB, ALVIN A.

A resident of New Orleans, Cobb founded a short-lived Klan clone, the Knights of White Christians, during 1955. [61]

COBLENTZ, JOHN

See *Choutteau, Dr. Gerard.*

COBURN, WILLIAM S.

The Klan's grand goblin in southern California, Coburn was arrested when police raided the KKK's Los Angeles headquarters in 1922. Before he was captured, he managed to slip past the raiders and drop a list of local Klansmen in the mailbox, safe from the authorities. Later employed as the personal attorney for Imperial Wizard William Simmons in Atlanta, Coburn was shot and killed by a Hiram Evans loyalist and speechwriter Philip Fox, in 1923. Coburn's murder finally convinced Simmons to abandon the imperial palace, declaring that "I didn't want to fight men who could kill that way." [10; 93]

COCHRAN, PAUL

A Jacksonville, Florida, Klan leader, Cochran was arrested in St. Augustine for cross burning on July 24, 1964. Other Klansmen jailed in the same incident included J.B. Stoner, Connie Lynch, Barton Griffin, and Bill Coleman. [NYT 1964]

COCKRILL, HARRISON

A Kentucky state senator during Reconstruction, Cockrill was publicly identified as a Klan leader with authority over a four-county area. [87]

CODY, JAMES

Cody and his two brothers were identified as the Klansmen who ambushed Sheriff John Norris in Warren County, Georgia, in December 1868. He also led the mob that lynched Dr. G.W. Darden in March 1869. Although arrested in both cases, Cody was never indicted by local grand juries. [87]

COGGINS, JOHN

See *Lauderdale, E.A.*

COINTELPRO

See *Federal Bureau of Investigation.*

COKELY, WARREN

A black resident of Tallapoosa, Georgia, who was married to a white woman, Cokely was attacked in his home and beaten by six masked men during February 1983. Four known Klansmen were later convicted in the case. [NYT 1983]

COKER, BILLY

Son of James Coker, a Reconstruction Klan leader in Jackson County, Florida, Billy was identified as the ringleader in numerous murders and other crimes, including the harassment and the 1870 assassination of black constable Calvin Rogers in Marianna. [87]

COKER, JAMES P.

A wealthy shopkeeper in Marianna, Florida, Coker also served as chief of the Reconstruction KKK in Jackson County. Rated as Florida's most violent county and one of the worst in the South, Jackson County was once described by a black minister as the place "where Satan has his seat." An estimated 179 murders, most of the victims black, were recorded in the area by late 1871, and a Klan intimidation campaign forced the sheriff to resign in March of that year. The only Republican officer left in the county, John Dickinson, was murdered by Klansmen a month later. Coker was arrested on December 11, 1871, and taken to Tallahassee for trial under the new federal Ku Klux Act, but his case was dismissed following a year of delays. [87]

COKER, ROCKY LEE

The self-proclaimed imperial wizard of the United Empire of the KKK, Coker was jailed during an outbreak of rioting in Chattanooga, Tennessee, on July 26, 1980. Along with fellow Klansman Larry Owens, he was convicted of unlawfully possessing explosives and conspiring to commit an illegal act. Coker drew a prison term of two to four years on each count. In 1984, Coker and several other Klansmen were charged with the murder of a local businessman in Dunlap, Tennessee. Coker was convicted in the case, and received the death sentence in July 1986. [NYT 1980, 1986]

COLBY, ABRAM

A black state legislator from Reconstruction Warren County, Georgia, Colby was beaten by Klansmen after he rejected a $5,000 bribe to resign his post in October 1869. Some twenty-five Klansmen lined up to deliver an estimated 1,000 lashes, leaving Colby permanently crippled. No prosecutions resulted, although Colby identified several of his assailants, including some prominent locals and others "not worth the bread they eat." Colby later acquired a small plantation, retiring to private life, but continued harassment forced him to spend most of his time in Atlanta. [87]

COLE, ARTHUR

A resident of LaFollete, Tennessee, Cole was identified as chairman of the National States Rights Party in 1958. That winter he was called as a defense witness in the synagogue bombing trial of National States Rights Party member George Bright. [14]

COLE, REV. JAMES W.

Known to his associates as "Catfish," Cole was an ex-carnival barker, patent medicine salesman, and Free Will Baptist minister who emerged as a KKK celebrity in the late 1950s. (He also boasted a police record dating from 1940, with several arrests for assault.) In the latter part of 1956, Cole defected from the U.S. Klans to form his own North Carolina Knights of the KKK. His chief publicity gimmick was a campaign against the Lumbee Indians in Robeson County, where a three-way system of segregation already existed to separate whites, Indians, and blacks. Beginning on January 13, 1958, Cole's Klansmen burned several crosses on property owned by Lumbee Indians, culminating with a rally in Lumberton on January 18. Armed Lumbee Indians raided the gathering that night, capturing the Klan's banner and public address system while Klansmen quickly dispersed, leaving several bullet-punctured vehicles behind. State police declared Reverend Cole a fugitive on January 21. Two thousand people turned out for a Klan rally in Burlington four days later, but Cole failed to appear, bent on fighting extradition from South Carolina. Convicted of inciting a riot on March 13, 1958, he drew a prison term of eighteen months to two years, with his appeal rejected in March 1959. In 1967, Cole joined forces with George Dorsett, banished imperial kludd for the United Klans of America to create a new splinter group, the Confederate Knights. Unknown to Cole, the FBI was also instrumental in launching the Knights, and thus the group was doomed from its beginning. [10; 84]

COLE, NAT ("KING")

A popular black singer, Cole was assaulted by six members of Asa Carter's North Alabama Citizens' Council during an April 1956 performance at the Birmingham municipal auditorium. His assailants included Anniston Klansmen Jesse Mabry, Kenneth Adams, Mike Fox, E.L. Vinson, and Orliss Clevenger. Mabry was sentenced to 180 days in jail for conspiracy and disorderly conduct, in addition to a fine of ten dollars and court costs. The other defendants paid $100 fines and court costs for charges of disorderly conduct. [*FOF* 1956; 42]

COLE, WILLARD

As editor of the Whiteville (North Carolina) *News Reporter*, Cole won the 1952 Pulitzer Prize and Sidney Hillman award for his series of articles that led to the conviction of more than 100 Klansmen on various criminal charges. [*NYT* 1953]

COLEMAN, BILL

A St. Augustine leader of the Florida Ku Klux Klan, Coleman was arrested in his home city for cross burning on July 24, 1964. Other Klansmen arrested in the case included J.B. Stoner, Connie Lynch, Barton Griffin, and Paul Cochran. [*NYT* 1964]

COLEMAN, GUILFORD

A black Republican leader during Reconstruction in Greene County, Alabama, Coleman was abducted from his home by Klansmen and murdered in September 1870, his body mutilated almost beyond recognition.[87]

COLEMAN, JOHN

A white mail agent on the railroad line between Selma, Alabama, and Meridian, Mississippi, Coleman was hired as a replacement for Frank Diggs, a black mail agent murdered by the KKK at Kewaunee, Mississippi. Previously accosted by Klansmen in February 1876 near the site where Diggs was murdered, Coleman was warned to remain east of Sumter County in the future or he would be killed. [87]

COLEMAN, TOM

A militant Klansman in Hayneville, Alabama, Coleman was an engineer with the Alabama Highway Department and the member of a prominent family in Lowndes County. His father was a state trooper who later served as county superintendent of schools until his death, when Coleman's sister took over the job. Maintaining the family tie to law enforcement, Coleman served as a special unpaid deputy in Lowndes County, but his activities were geared more to subversion of law and order. On August 10, 1965, he confronted state attorney general Richmond Flowers with the warning, "If you don't get off the Klan investigation, we'll get you off." On August 20, 1965, he killed seminarian Jonathan Daniels and wounded Reverend Richard Morrisroe in an unprovoked shotgun attack, afterward phoning state police commander Al Lingo to say, "I just shot two preachers. You better get down here." Lingo drove to Hayneville with a bail bondsman identified as a KKK member, and he stonewalled other investigators during the probe, defiantly insisting, "I'm not giving you or the damn attorney general or the damn FBI or anybody any information until I'm good and ready." The material was never forthcoming, but Coleman was indicted for manslaughter in the Daniels case on September 15, 1965. At his trial, laughter filled the court when Coleman's own name turned up on a list of prospective jurors. The court clerk was married to one of Coleman's cousins, and his defense counsel was a nephew. (On September 13, another grand jury, composed of eleven blacks and seven whites, refused to charge Coleman in the wounding of Morrisroe.) An all-white jury accepted Coleman's statement that he shot Daniels, an unarmed civil rights activist, in self-defense, and Coleman was acquitted on September 30, 1965. Richmond Flowers described the verdict as a "license to kill" in Lowndes County. [NYT 1965; 62]

COLEMAN, WILLIAM

A black resident of Winston County, Mississippi, during Reconstruction, Coleman was flogged and left for dead by the Klan after buying eighty acres of farm land. [93]

COLESCOTT, JAMES A.

An Ohio veterinarian and early member of the 1920s Klan, Colescott was elected grand dragon of the state in 1925. Fourteen years later, in June 1939, he replaced Hiram Evans as imperial wizard, announcing that his administration would be one of action. Violence and intimidation increased under Colescott. Klansmen threatened black voters in Florida and South Carolina, and mounted determined resistance to CIO recruiting efforts throughout the South. Colescott told reporters he was interested in "mopping up the cesspools of communism in the United States," but added that "anyone who flogs, lynches or intimidates ought to be in the penitentiary." The latter message was taken with a grain of salt by Klansmen in Georgia, where nightriding produced at least three deaths, and eight Klansmen, including several deputies, were sentenced to jail. Colescott was embarrassed by Klan flirtation with the German-American Bund in New Jersey during 1940, and moved to tone down anti-Semitism following the Pearl Harbor attack, announcing the withdrawal of all KKK literature "of a controversial nature." In 1944, the IRS slapped Colescott's knights with a lien in excess of $685,000 for back taxes, and the Klan folded when a special klonvokation voted for disbandment on April 23, 1946. Stowing his royal robe in mothballs, Colescott told newsmen, "Maybe the government can make something out of the Klan. I never could." Working in Miami during 1946, he denied current links to the Klan, but Colescott was still listed as president when the back dues were paid in Georgia that March. Chairing a board of trustees, he signed a July 1946 statement asking Georgia to drop its charter revocation suit because the Klan had "ceased to exist" in 1944. [10]

COLEY, JOHN L.

A Georgia victim of the Reconstruction Klan, Coley was flogged by nightriders for selling a pistol to a black man. [93]

COLEY, SANDY

In the spring of 1965, while serving as interim grand dragon for the United Klans of America, Coley organized several klaverns around Portsmouth and Chesapeake, Virginia. His recruiting drive was relatively unsuccessful, and in the late summer Coley was replaced by Marshall Kornegay. [38]

COLGROVE, D.D.

A state senator during Reconstruction in Jones County, North Carolina, Colgrove called on Governor Holden for troops after his brother, Sheriff O.R. Colgrove, was murdered by the Constitutional Union Guard in May 1869. Colgrove's letter to Holden read, in part, "We cannot tell at night who will be living in the morning." Troops were dispatched to Jones County for a period of six weeks but never left camp, and Colgrove soon fled the area, fearing for his life. [87]

COLGROVE, O.R.

The Republican sheriff in Jones County, North Carolina, during Reconstruction, Colgrove arrested several members of the Constitutional Union Guard for terrorizing local blacks. The Union Guard put a price on his head, and on May 28, 1869, an ambush killed Colgrove and a black companion. In a bid to justify their crime, Union Guard leaders manufactured a false New York prison record for Colgrove, then hosted a barbecue to celebrate his death. [87]

COLLIER, CHARLES A.

A resident of St. Albans, Queens, New York, and executive secretary of the City-Wide Citizens Committee on Harlem, Collier was one of several blacks who received threatening messages in July 1946. The postcards read: "District of St. Albans. Warning to Negroes entering St. Albans. Beware. Signed, Ku Klux Klan." Three white teenagers were arrested for mailing the notes on August 1. [NYT 1946]

COLLIER, CLARENCE

A Klansman during Reconstruction in Crittenden County, Arkansas, Collier was identified as a participant in at least one murder and various other crimes. He fled the area when martial law was imposed in 1868, and returned when the decree was lifted. In July 1869, he murdered Captain A.J. Haynes on the main street of Marion, shooting him in the back before emptying a revolver into the prostrate body and leaving town. Thrilled by this act of "heroism," the Memphis *Public Ledger* editorialized: "Gallant Clarence Collier! The blessings of an oppressed people go with you, and wherever the clouds lift you shall be known and honored throughout the land as the William Tell of Crittenden County, Arkansas." [87]

COLLIER, RALPH T.

A member of the Association of Carolina Klans under Tom Hamilton, Collier was convicted of a North Carolina flogging in 1952, drawing a sentence of eighteen to twenty months in prison. On September 1, his punishment was commuted to a $1,000 fine: the authorities cited a diagnosis of shell shock that had led to Collier's psychiatric discharge from the military in 1945. [NYT 1952]

COLLIN, FRANK

A member of the National Socialist White People's Party, Collin was expelled in 1970 when party leaders discovered his Jewish ancestry. (FBI agents later claimed credit for the leak, as part of their COINTELPRO campaign against domestic hate groups.) Founding his own National Socialist Party of America in Chicago in 1970, Collin was more or less ignored by an apathetic public until 1977, when he sought permission for parades in suburban Skokie, an area occupied by many Jewish holocaust survivors. The demonstrations were ultimately banned by court order, but Collin had scored international publicity, and a television movie starring Danny Kaye was made based on the incident. Convicted of child-molesting in the spring of 1980, Collin was sentenced to prison, and his dubious leadership role passed to subordinate Harold Covington. [2]

COLLINS, ADDIE MAE

Collins was one of four black girls killed when Alabama Klansmen bombed Birmingham's 16th Street Baptist Church on September 15, 1963. In 1977, ex-Klansman Robert Chambliss was convicted of murdering Collins, drawing a sentence of life imprisonment. [93]

COLLINS, ROBERT

A Georgia Klansman, Collins was elected imperial klokard at the United Klans of America's 1964 klonvocation in Birmingham, Alabama. He retained that office during the period of congressional investigations into Klan violence and corruption in 1965 and 1966. [38]

COLORADO

A boom state for the 1920s Klan, Colorado welcomed its first klavern to Denver in 1921. Four years later, one in every seven Denver residents was listed on the Klan rolls, and a series of threatening letters prompted a grand jury to investigate the KKK, exposing the Denver Doers Club as a Klan cover. By that time, Klansman Ben Stapleton had been elected mayor, and used his appointive powers to fill city offices with his fellow knights. Grand Dragon Galen Locke had a private box at the state Republican convention in 1924, and Klansmen swept the state in elections that year. Governor-elect Clarence Morley was a Klansmen, as were Secretary of State Carl Milliken, U.S. Senator Rice Means, many state officers, and a majority of the legislature's lower house. A month later, Locke was in jail, charged with kidnapping a local boy and using threats of castration to make the youth marry his pregnant girlfriend. Further controversy erupted over Locke's appointment as an officer in the Colorado National Guard, and IRS agents were suddenly interested in his tax returns. Investigation revealed that Locke had handpicked Denver's police chief, with his choice approved by Mayor Stapleton. Imperial Wizard Hiram Evans sought to cut his losses by replacing Locke, but the defiant dragon took his case to the membership, addressing a crowd of 30,000 supporters on July 1, 1925. Many of them followed Locke into his new, short-lived Minutemen organization, leaving the Colorado Klan by 1926 with only one third of its previous strength and no longer able to carry a single election campaign in the state. Quiescent for half a century following its first bid for power, the Denver Klan showed faint signs of life in the late 1970s. Fred Wilkins managed to organize a small klavern in Denver threatening Jewish radio host Alan Berg's life in 1979. But the neo-Nazi gunmen who killed Berg in 1984 came from out of state. [10; 85]

COLUMBIANS, INC.

One of the first neo-Nazi groups organized after V-J Day, the Columbians were chartered in Georgia on August 17, 1946. According to official documents, the group's stated purpose was "to encourage our people to think in terms of race, nation and faith and to work for a national moral reawakening in order to build a progressive white community that is bound together by a deep spiritual consciousness of a common past and determination to share a common future." In practice, potential recruits were asked three questions: "Do you hate Jews? Do you hate Negroes? Do you have three dollars?" Leaders of this small group included Emory Burke, Homer L. Loomis, Jr., and John H. Zimmerlee, Jr. Burke, the self-described "sole authority" on policy decisions for the Columbians, was an architect reared in Montgomery, Alabama. Affecting a British accent, he had worked for *The Storm*, a New York racist paper, in the 1930s. Loomis, a New York native, claimed to be a graduate of Princeton University, but his credentials proved elusive. The Columbians' attorney, Vester Ownby, was a veteran far-right activist who chartered a Georgia group called We the People in 1944. Members of the Columbians sported khaki uniforms with a red lightning bolt insignia borrowed from Hitler's SS. Both the outfits and the Columbians' newspaper title, *The Thunderbolt*, were later absorbed by the National States Rights Party. Organizational guidelines were lifted from a book entitled *Klan Building*, published by a midwestern KKK unit in 1937 and 1938. By the fall of 1946, out-of-state chapters were reported from Indianapolis and Gary, Indiana, Philadelphia, Minneapolis, and New York City, with others authorized in Florida, Tennessee, Texas, and Wisconsin. In October, the Columbians were linked with the patrolling of Atlanta neighborhoods that led to beatings and intimidation of blacks, and the bombing of a black-owned home on Halloween. On November 2, four Columbians—Loomis, James Akin, Jack Price, and R.L. Whitman—were arrested for disorderly conduct and inciting a riot while picketing a black home in a white district of Atlanta. State authorities moved to revoke the group's charter three days later. More charges were leveled on November 10, when Burke and Loomis were charged with misdemeanor counts of usurping police powers and James Childers faced a felony charge of rioting. State Attorney General Dan Duke took a personal interest in the Columbians, reporting that Emory Burke's name had appeared on the masthead of "nearly every fascist organization in the country prior to World War II." On November 23, Duke punched Burke during a confrontation in judge's chambers, earning himself a spot on the Columbians "lynch list" that was revealed by infiltrators from the Anti-Nazi League. On December 13, 1946, Columbians Burke, Loomis, and Ira Jett were indicted for unlawful possession of dynamite and were linked to a bomb plot that targeted city hall, Atlanta's municipal auditorium, police headquarters, and the offices of two daily newspapers. On February 16, 1947, Loomis was convicted of inciting a riot in the beating of an Atlanta black. On March 27, 1947, a conviction of usurping police powers earned him a thirty-month prison term. Emory Burke was convicted of three misdemeanor counts on February 21, 1947, and drew a three-year sentence. Stripped of their Georgia charter on June 27, 1947, the Columbians had ceased to exist by December 4, when they were added to the U.S. Attorney General's list of subversive organizations. [NYT 1946–1947]

COLUMBUS COUNTY SPORTSMAN CLUB

In 1965 congressional investigators exposed this group as a cover for the Whiteville, North Carolina, klavern, United Klans of America. [38]

COMER, JAMES C.

A judge in Little Rock and Arkansas grand dragon for the 1920s Klan, Comer was an intimate friend of Hiram Evans and was active in helping Evans replace William Simmons as imperial wizard in 1922. One of six Klansmen named to the Imperial Kloncilium in 1923, he helped settle the yearlong dispute over ownership of Klan regalia and ritual in favor of Evans. Comer briefly dominated the Women of the KKK through his wife's position as leader of that group, but opposition to his personal style and his wife's high living sparked a virtual mutiny within the Little Rock klavern by 1924. [10]

COMER, ROBBIE GILL

The wife of Arkansas grand dragon James Comer, she was appointed to lead the new Women of the Ku Klux Klan in 1922 as part of the payoff for her husband's backing of Hiram Evans in his successful attempt to replace Imperial Wizard William Simmons. [10]

COMMITTEE OF NOTABLES

An organization of college presidents and Protestant bishops created in 1924, the group's sole function was to support the addition of an anti-Klan plank to the Democratic national platform in that presidential election year. The plank was narrowly defeated at the party's chaotic nominating convention in Madison Square Garden. [10]

COMMITTEE OF ONE MILLION CAUCASIANS TO MARCH ON CONGRESS

Conceived by Klansmen James Venable and Wallace Butterworth in February 1964, this extravagantly named "mass movement" was designed to "wrest control of the U.S. government from the Communist hands of foreign Asiatic Jews and African Negroes" by countering the 1963 march on Washington, D.C. Despite their title, Venable and Butterworth hoped to gather 200,000 marchers in the capital on July 4, but the public endorsement of George Lincoln Rockwell's American Nazi Party proved unpopular. No one showed up for the "monster" rally except Venable, Rockwell, a few stormtroopers, and a handful of curiosity seekers. This pitiful turnout prompted Rockwell to declare, "Our cause is almost ridiculous. *We* are ridiculous." [38; 78]

COMMONER PARTY

A front group for the Columbians, Inc., in 1946, the party was organized in a futile attempt to create a "gigantic powerhouse" of anti-Semitic votes. Attempts to solicit support from recognized "nationalist leaders" such as Gerald L.K. Smith and Tulsa attorney Phil Davis were ultimately fruitless, and the party died with its parent organization. [*New Republic*, Nov. 23, 1946]

COMMUNIST WORKERS PARTY

A Maoist radical group, the Communist Workers Party was a spin-off from the old Students for a Democratic Society when that group disbanded in 1969. The Greensboro, North Carolina, chapter formed an Asian studies group in the early 1970s, and quickly broadened its interest to include organized labor. Short on members and publicity, the party hoped to win some headlines by attacking local Klan groups in the summer of 1979. After several confrontations, Communist Workers Party members sponsored an anti-Klan rally scheduled for November 3, 1979. Open letters to the Federated Knights of the KKK and the rival White Knights of Liberty announced that the rally would expose Klan cowardice for all the world to see. If that was insufficient, members of the Party were prepared to "physically smash the racist KKK wherever it rears its ugly head. Death to the Ku Klux Klan." The rally ended in gunfire, with five Party members dead and nineteen Klansmen or neo-Nazis facing indictment on various state and federal charges. The Party later announced its intent to block a Klan parade in Kokomo, Indiana, in April 1980, but no members appeared. Three members were arrested on June 16, 1980, in a scuffle with police at the trial of Klansmen charged with murder in the November 1979 shootings. Various courtroom observers suggest that the group's strident radicalism was a major factor in the all-white jury's vote of acquittal for all concerned, allowing defense attorneys to characterize the dead as subversives who "got what they asked for." [10]

COMMUNITY IMPROVEMENT ASSOCIATION

In 1965 congressional investigators exposed this group as a cover for a Jacksonville, North Carolina, klavern, United Klans of America. [38]

COMPTON, DR. WILLIAM M.

The editor of a Democratic newspaper and grand giant of the KKK during Reconstruction in Marshall County, Mississippi, Compton shifted sides in 1871 to edit the Republican *Leader* in Jackson. He was later appointed superintendent of the state insane asylum. [87]

CONEY, ALLEN

A black school principal in Magnolia, Mississippi, Coney was targeted by the McComb klavern of the United Klans in 1964. On September 7, 1964, his home was firebombed by Klansmen who had drawn lots for the assignment. Several of the bombers were convicted, but all received suspended sentences on the grounds that they had been "provoked" by blacks. [38]

CONFEDERATE CLUB NO. 38

A front for the Dade City, Florida, klavern, United Florida Ku Klux Klan, this group was exposed by the House Un-American Activities Committee in 1966. [38]

CONFEDERATE INDEPENDENT ORDER KNIGHTS OF THE KU KLUX KLAN

A Maryland splinter group reported active in 1987, this Klan faction claimed fewer than 100 active members. [*NYT* 1987]

CONFEDERATE KNIGHTS OF THE KU KLUX KLAN (1960s)

Organized in North Carolina during 1967, the Confederate Knights were founded by Reverend James Cole and George Dorsett, a former imperial kludd for the United Klans of America and FBI informant, with covert backing from the FBI. This splinter group, based in Greensboro, was supported with FBI funds in order to create a rift within the existing Carolina Klans, and FBI agents drafted the organization's first recruiting letter. The FBI also circulated another letter among known Klansmen, signed by the "National Intelligence Committee," alleging that United Klans officers Robert Shelton and James R. Jones had been suspended for mishandling Klan funds. Dorsett played his part in the undercover operation by claiming that the National Intelligence Committee was a secret KKK intelligence agency, unknown to ranking Klan leaders and formed in 1964 "by the people to protect them from the leadership." [84]

CONFEDERATE KNIGHTS OF THE KU KLUX KLAN (1980s)

See *Carolina Knights of the Ku Klux Klan.*

CONFEDERATE LODGE NO. 11

In 1965 congressional investigators identified this "lodge" as a Bessemer, Alabama, klavern, United Klans of America. [38]

CONFEDERATE LODGE NO. 304

A 1960s cover for the Gadsden, Alabama, klavern, United Klans of America, this group was publicly exposed by the House Un-American Activities Committee in 1965. [38]

CONFEDERATE NO. 14

Evidence collected by congressional investigators has identified Confederate No. 14 as a front for the Tarrant City, Alabama, klavern, United Klans of America. [38]

CONFEDERATE UNDERGROUND

Reported active during 1958, this group—if indeed it was a group—claimed credit for various Southern bombings, in Jacksonville, Florida, and Atlanta, Georgia. Anonymous phone calls to news agencies or local Jewish leaders were the normal means of communication, with the last reported call placed to United Press International following the October 1958 bombing of an Atlanta synagogue. The caller identified himself as "General Gordon of the Confederate Underground," stating: "We have just blown up the temple. This is the last empty building I'll blow up in Atlanta." No members of the Underground were ever identified, but disciples of the fledgling National States Rights Party were charged in the Atlanta case. Despite "Gen. Gordon's" threat of future bombings and the fact that numerous blasts were detonated across the South, no further communications from the Confederate Underground have been received to date. [70]

CONFEDERATE VIGILANTES, KNIGHTS OF THE KU KLUX KLAN

A Tennessee splinter group, the Confederate Vigilantes dissolved in May 1981, after cofounder Gladys Girgenti and five other members were jailed on charges of attempting to bomb a local synagogue. The defendants were also named in felony counts alleging conspiracy to dynamite a local television tower and several Jewish-owned businesses. Girgenti received a fifteen-year prison term. [*NYT* 1981]

CONFEDERATION OF INDEPENDENT ORDERS-INVISIBLE EMPIRE-KNIGHTS OF THE KU KLUX KLAN

Organized under the leadership of Imperial Wizard William Chaney, this umbrella group was the result of a Klan "unity conference" held on June 5, 1977. Chaney described the group as a loose confederation of twenty-six independent Klans, with Northern and Southern subdivisions. Each member group, regardless of size, paid a $100 annual assessment to the Confederation. In July 1978, three members of a Maryland faction led by Grand Dragon Tony LaRicci were jailed on charges of plotting to bomb a synagogue in Lochearn, Maryland. All three were convicted and two of the defendants sentenced to eight years in prison. An Anti-Defamation League survey conducted in 1983 reported that the Confederation was still active but dwindling in size due to traditional rivalries and factionalism among the splinter groups. [NYT 1978; 84]

CONFEDERATION OF KLANS

This loose coalition of seven independent factions was created in September 1982 from a gathering of Klan leaders at Stone Mountain, Georgia. Participants in the merger included: David Duke, of the National Association for the Advancement of White People; Stephen Black, Duke's successor as head of the Knights of the KKK; Edward Fields, of the New Order, Knights of the KKK; convicted bomber Robert Miles, of the Mountain Church; James Venable, leader of the National Knights of the KKK; and North Carolina KKK leader Glenn Miller. Black was elected to lead the Confederation, retaining his office when the same group met again in September 1983. Conspicuously missing from the group was Bill Wilkinson, chief of the Invisible Empire Knights. According to Black, Wilkinson was deliberately excluded in an effort to avoid "bad publicity." [2]

CONFERENCE OF EASTERN DRAGONS

Convened by Robert Scoggin in Spartanburg, South Carolina, in 1976, this onetime meeting was designed to bring order out of the prevailing chaos in the Invisible Empire. Identified participants included Earl Schoonmaker of New York, Tony LaRicci of Maryland, Dan Smithers of Texas, Wilbur Forman of Illinois, Virgil Griffin of North Carolina, Albert McCorkle of Missouri, Buddy Tucker of Tennessee, Neuman Britton of Arkansas, Raymond Doerfler of Pennsylvania, and Imperial Wizard Bill Wilkinson. A highlight of the rally was the auction sale of Roy Frankhouser's glass eye, purchased by Schoonmaker for five dollars. [84]

CONGRESS OF INDUSTRIAL ORGANIZATIONS (CIO)

Targeted by Imperial Wizard Hiram Evans in 1937 as "infested with communists," the CIO's Southern campaign to create a Textile Workers'

Organizing Committee and a Steel Workers' Organizing Committee gave Klan membership its biggest boost in fifteen years. Several union organizers were abducted and beaten in Georgia following the *Fiery Cross* headlines that read, "CIO Wants Whites and Blacks on Same Level." Klansmen were ready again in June 1946, when the CIO's "Operation Dixie" was launched in twelve target states. By January 1947, eighteen union-related floggings were reported in the South. In Lanett, Alabama, bricks with the message "Vote No for CIO" were hurled through the windows of sympathetic merchants. A racist newspaper in Arkansas, the *Orthodox Baptist Searchlight*, ran an editorial that stated, "Am I opposed to labor organizations? Certainly not. But I am glad that the Ku Klux Klan is coming back to power. I never heard of anybody being flogged by the Klan but if they went to work on a CIO organizer, that might be just the medicine he needs." A police official in Payne City, Georgia, announced his plan to help organize a Klan unit in Macon that would concentrate on labor organizers. In 1947, the pregnant wife of Mike Ross, a Macon CIO activist, suffered a miscarriage after hooded nightriders invaded her home. At Parson, Tennessee, the mayor personally led a mob of fifty men that drove four labor organizers out of town. In Evergreen, Alabama, a pair of CIO recruiters were ambushed by Klansmen, their car riddled with bullets and burned. Organizer Ben Bibb was beaten by a deputy sheriff in Montgomery, and others were mobbed while passing out leaflets at the Beacon Manufacturing Company in Sylacauga, Alabama. Organizer Tom Prosser, a disabled veteran of World War II, was abducted and beaten by Klansmen near the Avondale Mill Company. In June 1947, CIO spokesmen blamed the failure of their May 1946 packinghouse workers strike in Smithfield, Virginia, on Klan intimidation. [*FOF* 1947; 98]

CONNECTICUT

Led by Grand Dragon Harry Lutterman of Darien, Connecticut, the Connecticut Klan boasted 18,000 members by 1925, but by then dissension was already thinning the ranks. A year earlier, Klansmen grew suspicious when the imperial headquarters canceled its policy of mailing financial reports to individual realms, and protests from Connecticut fell on deaf ears in Atlanta. In January 1926, Connecticut's mother klavern in New Haven voted to disband, with Exalted Cyclops Arthur Mann publicly blasting the Klan for corruption. Membership swiftly declined after that. A brief resurgence occurred in September 1980, when Bill Wilkinson brought his Invisible Empire Knights to Scotland, located in Windham County. Three days of cross burnings and scuffling with hecklers won the Klan an estimated 500 members and sympathizers, with six persons injured and eight more arrested—Wilkinson among them—in a series of free-swinging brawls. However, when Wilkinson returned for new rallies in August 1982, policemen outnumbered the gathered Klansmen. Unable to salvage the realm, the Invisible Empire withdrew, charging "police harassment." [2; 10]

CONNOR, REX

See *Johnson, Woodrow*.

CONNOR, THEOPHILUS EUGENE ("BULL")

A former baseball announcer and symbol of segregation in Birmingham, Alabama, "Bull" Connor was first elected in 1937 as the city's public safety commissioner, giving him ultimate authority over the police and fire departments. Connor once arrested a U. S. senator for accidentally walking through a door marked "Colored," and was fond of predicting that "blood would run in the streets" before Birmingham desegregated. A master of malapropism, Connor once disrupted a meeting of the Southern Conference on Human Welfare with the remark, "We ain't gonna segregate no niggers and whites together in this town." Under Connor's administration, violent Klansmen were given a free reign in their harassment of blacks, earning the city the nickname of "Bombingham" following a long series of unsolved racial bombings. (When three black churches were bombed in January 1962, Connor told the press that there were no firm leads, but, "We know Negroes did it. Everybody we talk to who knows anything about it says they saw Negroes running away from the churches." In May 1963, uniformed policemen were identified as the bombers of a black-owned motel.) In May 1961, Connor and a group of pro-Klan police officers negotiated with KKK leaders to plan a riotous reception for integrated freedom riders. Klansmen and members of the National States Rights Party were guaranteed fifteen minutes in which to beat demonstrators, free of police interference, with some of them even driven to their destination in police cars. (As Connor told Klansmen before the riots, "By God, if you are going to do this thing, do it right.") When mass demonstrations began in Birmingham in the spring of 1963, Connor earned worldwide notoriety by unleashing police dogs and high-pressure fire hoses on peaceful protestors. By that time, however, Connor and Mayor Arthur Hanes had already been voted out of office in a November 1962 election, but had refused to step down pending the resolution of their protests in court. Staking his hopes on a mayoral runoff election, Connor was defeated again, this time by Albert Boutwell. His challenge to the November 1962 election was ultimately rejected in court. In the meantime, however, Connor had become a fixture at local rallies of the Citizens' Council, including a June 7, 1963, gathering when announcements were broadcast for a Klan rally the following night. [*NYT* 1962–1963; 18; 68]

CONSERVATIVE CLUBS

Organized and armed to resist "Negro rule" in Alabama after January 1869, the Conservative Clubs overlapped local Klan units both in ideology and membership. An active unit was reported outside of Alabama in Marion

County, Texas, where blacks who enlisted to vote Democratic received "protection papers" to ward off nightriders and offers of preferential treatment in hiring. [87]

CONSTANTINEAU, RICHARD

A Wilmington, North Carolina, gun dealer and member of the state's grand klokann for the United Klans of America, Constantineau specialized in selling weapons to his fellow Klansmen. Resigning from the United Klans because it did not have "a program that was satisfactory" and because his wife was "worried about my activities," he delivered his firearms sales records to the House Un-American Activities Committee in 1965. [38]

CONSTITUTION PARTY OF THE UNITED STATES

An extreme right-wing/racist political group active in the early 1960s, the Constitution Party welcomed members of various Klans, the National States Rights Party, and Minutemen into the fold. In 1962, the party's candidate for governor of California was William Gale, the anti-Semitic founder of the California Rangers. More recently, the party has fielded Wisconsin Posse Comitatus leader James Wickstrom as its candidate for U.S. senator (1980) and governor of the state (1982), candidacies that both showed poorly. [2; 90]

CONSTITUTIONAL AMERICAN PARTY OF THE UNITED STATES

Organized by Klansman Joseph Milteer in October 1963, the Constitutional American Party was conceived after Milteer's formal reprimand for falsely representing himself as a regional director of the Constitution Party of the United States. Veering away from politics toward more direct action, Milteer envisioned his group—in the words of a declassified FBI report—as "a front to form a hard-core underground for possible violence in combatting integration." During this same period Milteer was also active in recruiting members for the National States Rights Party. [95]

CONSTITUTIONAL UNION GUARD

A militant group organized to support white supremacy during Reconstruction, the Constitutional Union Guard frequently overlapped local KKK units (in fact, its various chapters were called "klans"). Founded in the winter of 1867–1868, this group was chiefly confined to North Carolina, where it existed simultaneously with—and outlasted—the White Brotherhood. The group expanded during the 1868 presidential election, and was credited with lynching five black prisoners at Kinston, North Carolina, in January 1869. Members joined Klansmen to assassinate Jones County's "carpetbag" sheriff, O.R. Cosgrove, in May 1869, and later drove his brother, state senator D.D. Cosgrove, from the area. In August 1869, Union

Guard gunmen assassinated Republican leader M.L. Shepard. Investigators persuaded three members of the group to turn state's evidence, and twenty-five suspects were indicted and held over for trial in October. The group officially dissolved in 1870, after Klan leader James Boyd persuaded several officers to join him in renouncing violence. [87]

CONTINENTAL LEAGUE FOR CHRISTIAN FREEDOM

Led by Millard Grubbs of Louisville, Kentucky, the League was described in November 1946 by Georgia State Attorney General Dan Duke as a Klan front that sought war veterans who despised blacks, Jews, and Catholics. [*NYT* 1946]

CONVERSE, FRANK

A Texas gun dealer, Converse also served as grand dragon for the United Klans of America in the early 1970s. In 1971, he declined to answer a Houston grand jury's questions about attacks aimed at a Pacifica Foundation radio station and other Klan targets. In June 1971, Converse announced plans to run for sheriff on a platform of "sheets and sawed-off shotguns," but voters somehow missed the campaign's appeal. Interviewed by Patsy Sims in 1977, Converse alleged that the CIA had approached him in 1969, trying to arrange a car-bomb "contract" on an unnamed Panamanian general, but the project was reportedly canceled when the White House refused financial backing. [*NYT* 1971; 84]

COOK, ELMER

See *Reeb, Reverend James.*

COOK, THOMAS H.

A sergeant with the Birmingham, Alabama, police force, Cook was identified in FBI reports as a special associate of Police Commissioner "Bull" Connor who "took most of his orders directly from Connor and not from Chief [of Police Jamie] Moore." In that capacity, Cook served as a contact between Connor's office and the local KKK and leaked classified FBI documents to the Klan. On one occasion, Cook reportedly opened two drawers of his personal filing cabinet for Klansman Gary Rowe, instructing Rowe to help himself to any available information "for the use of the Klan in general." Klansmen, in return, assisted the police by maintaining surveillance on civil rights groups, reporting on the movements of "radical" blacks, and recording the license plate numbers of "suspect" vehicles. In May 1961, Cook reportedly acted as liaison between Connor's office and the Klan, arranging "spontaneous" riots against the integrated freedom riders three weeks before their arrival in Birmingham. FBI agents were disgruntled by the continued leaks of information concerning potential violence given to Cook by the Birmingham FBI office, but the flow of material continued. Cook, in a move to regain the favor of the FBI, tipped agents to the fact that Edward Fields, a leader of the National States Rights Party, habitually carried a pistol with the hope of killing FBI personnel. [68]

COOKSEY, ALTON

A resident of Jacksonville, Florida, Cooksey was elected klaliff of the United Florida Ku Klux Klan in June 1961. He retired from the post in September 1965, refusing to seek reelection. [38]

COOLIDGE FISHING CLUB

In 1966 congressional investigators identified this "club" as a front for the Coolidge, Georgia, klavern, United Klans of America. [38]

COON HUNTERS CLUB

North Carolina Klansmen chose this tongue-in-cheek cover for a United Klans of America klavern in Rutherfordton. [38]

COOPER, HOLLIS

See *Bellows, Jim.*

COPIAH ROD & GUN CLUB

In 1965 the House Un-American Activities Committee exposed this club as the front for a Crystal Springs, Mississippi, klavern of the White Knights. [38]

CORKERN, VIRGIL

A member of the Original Knights of the KKK in Bogalusa, Louisiana, Corkern was identified as the Klansman who led an attack on black demonstrators in Cassidy Park on May 9, 1965. [69]

CORLEY, LUTHER KING

An early member of the National States Rights Party, Corley was one of four racist picketers with anti-Semitic signs arrested outside the Atlanta *Journal and Constitution* offices in July 1958. Three months later, he was indicted along with George Bright and others for the bombing of a local synagogue. Charges against Corley were dropped after Bright's acquittal in 1959. [65]

CORLISS, ALONZO B.

As a "carpetbag" teacher at a Quaker-backed school for blacks in Company Shops, North Carolina—now Burlington—Corliss soon became a target for the local KKK. On November 26, 1869, Klansmen dragged him from his home, whipped him, shaved half of his head and painted it black, and warned him to leave the area. Corliss tried to carry on with military protection, but his landlord soon evicted him for fear of damage to the property, and he left. [87]

COTHRAN, DONALD

In the fall of 1964, Robert Shelton appointed Cothran as grand dragon for the new Florida realm of the United Klans of America. Cothran's attempts to organize klaverns outside his native Jacksonville were generally unsuccessful, with fewer than 100 members registered statewide in 1965. In October, 1965, Broward County Klansmen accused Cothran of "dictatorial tactics" and financial mismanagement, and left to organize the United Knights of the KKK. [38]

COTTONMOUTH MOCCASIN GANG

A Mississippi Klan faction linked to the White Knights of the KKK, this group was responsible for the murder of Ben White in 1966. [NYT 1967]

COUNCIL OF CENTAURS

One of two tribunals established by the prescript of the Reconstruction Klan, this body was set up to try ghouls accused of violating Klan rules and regulations. Another committee existed to try ranking officers. [87]

COUNCIL OF SAFETY

A militant white group formed to combat "Negro uprisings" during Reconstruction in Columbia, South Carolina, the Council of Safety was created in December 1870, and its constitution prepared a month later. Despite apparent overlapping membership between the Council and the Klan, little activity was reported before the group dissolved. [87]

COUNCIL OF YAHOOS

Another tribunal established by the prescript of the Reconstruction KKK, this body existed—at least in theory—to try ranking officers accused of crimes. No evidence exists to indicate that the council was ever convened. [87]

COVE CITY HUNTING CLUB

In 1965 congressional investigators exposed this group as a cover for the Cove City, North Carolina, klavern, United Klans of America. [38]

COVENANT, THE SWORD, AND THE ARM OF THE LORD

Founded in 1971, this group is a paramilitary survivalist "church," based since 1976 at a communal settlement dubbed Zarephath-Horeb (after the biblical place of purging) near the Arkansas-Missouri border. The 100-odd residents, including men, women, and children, believe that U.S. society is nearing the point of a collapse into chaos and racial warfare and are preparing for the breakdown by stockpiling weapons, food, and wilderness survival gear. As spokesman Kerry Noble explains, "We are Christian survivalists who believe in preparing for the ultimate holocaust." To that end, this group's leaders operate the "Endtime Overcomer Survival Training School," which offers members and selected outsiders advanced training in marksmanship, survival techniques, and "Christian martial arts." Leader Jim Ellison reportedly founded the Missouri compound after a personal conversation with God, and his disciples spread the group's gospel in "self-protection" seminars throughout the South and Midwest. In 1981 and 1982, armed members served as security guards for "Freedom Festivals" sponsored by the Christian-Patriots Defense League in Louisville, Illinois. Blatantly racist and anti-Semitic, the group's ministers preach the "Identity Church" doctrines popularized by Wesley Swift and his Church of Jesus Christ Christian since the 1940s. As summarized by one spokesman, "We believe the Scandinavian-Germanic-Teutonic-British-American people to be the Lost Sheep of the House of Israel which Jesus was sent for." Group elder Kerry Noble explains that "we do believe non-whites and Jews are a threat to our Christian, white race," and that "Jews are financing the training of blacks to take over most of our major cities." Past and present Klansmen are frequently identified as participants in this group's ceremonies and training seminars. In August 1983, members burned a Jewish community center in Bloomington, Indiana, and others bombed a gas pipeline along the Red River in Arkansas three months later. In April 1985, a federal raid on the group's Arkansas compound netted several fugitive members of The Order, in addition to large quantities of illegal weapons. [2; 13]

COVINGTON, HAROLD

A resident of Raleigh, North Carolina, affiliated with the National Socialist Party of America, Covington identified several of his members as participants in the Greensboro, North Carolina, shootout of November 1979. In 1980, he took over leadership of the party after founder Frank Collin was sentenced to prison for child-molesting, and in April he organized a joint Klan/neo-Nazi "Hitlerfest" at Benson, North Carolina. In the November 1980 election, Covington polled 5,400 votes in his campaign to become North Carolina's state attorney general. Covington retired from the National Socialist Party in April 1981 and was replaced as *fuhrer* by Chicago neo-Nazi Michael Allen. [*AP*, April 20, 1980; 2; 93]

COVINGTON HUNTING & FISHING CLUB

In 1966 congressional probers identified this club as a front for the Covington, Louisiana, klavern, Original Knights of the KKK. [38]

COWAN, FREDERICK W.

A resident of New Rochelle, New York, and a member of the National States Rights Party, the 250 pound Cowan was an ardent body builder and gun collector who decorated his attic apartment with Nazi posters, once telling a friend, "I should have been born forty years ago so that I could have been in the SS." Employed at a local moving company, Cowan quarreled with his Jewish supervisor and was suspended from work in early February 1977. On the morning of February 14, he turned up on the job with a rifle and two automatic pistols, intent on killing his foreman. Instead, he murdered three black employees and an Indian immigrant and shot a policeman as squad cars arrived on the scene. More than 300 local officers and FBI agents surrounded the warehouse and maintained a six-hour vigil, which ended when Cowan committed suicide. Speaking for the National States Rights Party, J.B. Stoner told newsmen, "The FBI caused niggers to start harassing Cowan on the job. Apparently the FBI's to blame for the whole incident." [*Newsweek*, Feb. 28, 1977]

COWAN, MRS. PETER

A resident of Indiana, Mrs. Cowan was identified in 1958 as vice-chairman of the National States Rights Party. [65]

COX, BENJAMIN FRANKLIN

See *Donald, Michael.*

COX, HAROLD

A federal judge in Mississippi who was appointed by President John F. Kennedy, Cox made no secret about his staunch support for racial segregation. In February 1965, he dismissed the indictments of twenty-one Klansmen charged in the Michael Schwerner case, insisting there was no evidence of any federal violation in the triple homicide. In October 1966, Cox threw out the indictments a second time, on the grounds, ironically, that a federal grand jury had excluded blacks and women. Three months later, he refused to convene a new grand jury in the Schwerner or Vernon Dahmer cases unless the U. S. Justice Department also launched an investigation of the Child Development Group of Mississippi, a Head Start project. Cox dropped his objection when funding for the Child Development Group was discontinued due to financial irregularities, and a new grand jury was convened in the Klan cases on February 20, 1967. In October 1967, Cox surprised his fellow segregationists by refusing to declare a mistrial after jurors reported that they were deadlocked on the Schwerner case. His issuance of the so-called dynamite charge—instructing jurors to resume deliberations and break their deadlock—prompted threats against Cox from members of the White Knights. Cox responded by voiding several defendants' bail and handing down stiff prison sentences when seven of the accused were convicted on civil rights charges. [42; 96]

CRAIG, CALVIN FRED

Encouraged by his mother, Craig and his wife joined the U.S. Klans in Georgia during 1960. On February 21, 1961, Craig was second in command when Robert "Wild Bill" Davidson chartered his new United Klans in Fulton County. Assuming full control when Davidson bailed out two months later, Craig merged his Klan with Robert Shelton's Alabama Knights to create the United Klans of America in July 1961. Failing to qualify for a state senate race in 1962, he later ran (unsuccessfully) for a seat on the Fulton County Democratic executive committee. Conscious of media impact, Craig told his Klansmen in 1963, "Let's be nonviolent. We've got to start fighting just like the niggers." On July 4, 1964, he shared the stage with Lester Maddox and Alabama Governor George Wallace at an Atlanta segregationist rally where two blacks were mobbed and beaten by the audience. The following year, in Crawfordsville, Georgia, Craig was jailed for assaulting a black demonstrator on the street. Fined $1,000 for contempt of Congress following his appearance before the House Un-American Activities Committee in 1965, Craig managed to escape the jail time that was levied against Shelton and other United Klans officers. Elected to a policymaking position on Atlanta's federally funded Model Cities program in January 1968, the grand dragon initially shifted seats each time a black panelist sat beside him, but Craig's views were already shifting toward moderation. On April 28, 1968, he announced his resignation from the United Klans, stating that all races should "stand shoulder to shoulder in a united America." Three months later, he ran unsuccessfully for sheriff in Fulton County, promising to hire blacks and "not to hesitate one minute to arrest a Klansman who's committed a crime." By the time of his 1976 campaign for a seat on the Clayton County commission, Craig had rejoined the United Klans; some members, however, reportedly considered him a "sell-out." [10; 84]

CRANFORD, RAYMOND

In 1966 Cranford was identified as a major in the United Klans of America security guard and the exalted cyclops of the United Klan's klavern in Greene County, North Carolina. He once referred to Washington, D.C., as "Hersheytown—90 percent chocolate and 10 percent nuts," and told the press, "If I'm gonna burn a cross, I ram it through the man and burn it." [1]

CRAVEN COUNTY IMPROVEMENT ASSOCIATION

As a cover for North Carolina's New Bern Klavern No. 33, United Klans of America, the Craven County Improvement Association sheltered Klansmen convicted of bombing black-owned homes and businesses in 1965. [38]

CRAVEN COUNTY LADIES AUXILIARY

In 1965 congressional investigators exposed this group as the ladies auxiliary of New Bern Klavern No. 33, United Klans of America. [38]

CRAVEN FELLOWSHIP CLUB NO. 1

Congressional investigators identified this club in 1965 as a front for one of two Vanceboro, North Carolina, klaverns, United Klans of America. [38]

CRAVEN FELLOWSHIP CLUB NO. 2

This group was identified as the 1960s cover for a second Vanceboro, North Carolina, klavern of the United Klans of America. [38]

CRAWFORD, JOHN

An ex-Confederate officer, Crawford was arrested in a militia raid on Klan headquarters at Center Point, Arkansas, in November 1868. He later served as state auditor, elected on the Democratic ticket, but soon defaulted and resigned from office under charges of financial irregularity. [87]

CREEKMORE, RICKY L.

An Alabama Klansman, Creekmore pled guilty in January 1980 to charges of intimidating and injuring two black ministers at a Muscle Shoals restaurant. On the basis of his plea, he was sentenced to a year in prison. [NYT 1980]

CREEL, ROBERT

While serving as Alabama grand dragon for the United Klans of America between March 1964 and January 1966, Creel told newsmen, "I don't believe in segregation; I believe in slavery." The tough-talking grand dragon's resignation roughly coincided with his January 5, 1966, arrest for drunken driving and for possession of a rifle and two pistols that were found in his car. Convicted of driving-while-intoxicated and carrying concealed weapons, Creel was fined $300 and given a suspended sixty-day jail sentence. At the time, his wife held office as exalted cyclops of United Klans of America Ladies Auxiliary Unit One. [FOF 1966]

CRIBBS, CHARLES C.

A Klansman from Hialeah, Florida, Cribbs was one of twelve persons questioned by a 1952 federal grand jury in Miami probing recent acts of terrorism, including the bombing of synagogues and Carver Village. [*NYT* 1952]

CRIMMONS, VENSON A.

See *Hattie Cotton School.*

CRODSER, W.H., JR.

A resident of Columbus, Georgia, and self-described president of the Original Southern Klans in 1949, Crodser signed the application for Bill Hendrix's appointment as the Original Southern Klan's resident agent in Florida. [25]

CROMMELIN, JOHN

An admiral in the U.S. Navy who was pressured to retire in 1950 because of a front-page controversy between the Navy and Air Force, Crommelin was also a blatant anti-Semite linked with propagandists Gerald L.K. Smith and Conde McGinley. Retired to Montgomery, Alabama, Crommelin became a perennial candidate for elective office. Defeated in four senatorial bids—1950, 1954, 1956, and 1960—he also ran for mayor of Montgomery in 1959, for governor of Alabama in 1958 and 1962, and for Vice President of the United States on the National States Rights Party ticket in 1960. In 1955 Crommelin launched a drive to obtain 10 million signatures on a petition protesting the censure of right-wing Senator Joseph McCarthy. A year later, while addressing rallies of Asa Carter's North Alabama Citizens' Council, Crommelin met John Kasper and welcomed the New Yorker on board for his latest senatorial campaign. Several times Crommelin accompanied Kasper to the "riot zone" in Clinton, Tennessee, appearing as a defense witness at Kasper's subsequent trial. The testimony did not help, but Crommelin was on hand to welcome Kasper when he was released from prison. Crommelin was also questioned by FBI agents after an Atlanta synagogue had been bombed in October 1958. Crommelin's electoral showings were unpredictable; he ran eleventh in a field of fourteen candidates that sought the Alabama governor's post in 1958 with only 2,245 votes, but ran second in the 1956 and 1960 senatorial campaigns. His typical campaign speeches called for deportation of Jews and blacks, declaring that "90 percent of the Jews are mongoloids. That's why they're particular to Asiatic communism." (He also coined the term "Jewlatto," to indicate his belief that Jews are really black.) Crommelin's 1962 campaign manager, Reverend Oren Potito, was later identified as a National States Rights Party recruiter in Florida. In September 1963, shortly before a local church bombing killed four black children, Crommelin attended a secret conference in Birmingham, Alabama, with Klan associates Sidney Barnes and William Potter Gale. Undaunted by age, Crommelin was recognized as the eastern regional director of the Christian Defense League in 1971; six years later, he was linked with the production of David Duke's Klan newspaper, *The Crusader*. [14; 84; 90]

CROOM, HENRY

A bootlegger and member of the Constitutional Union Guard during Reconstruction in Alamance County, North Carolina, Croom traded whiskey to his fellow members in return for raw corn and protection for his still. In August 1869, he was one of twenty-five members indicted on murder and other charges. [87]

CROSS, DONALD

An applicant for Klan membership in New Orleans, Cross was arrested with five others on June 21, 1966, and charged in a series of firebombings aimed at churches, homes, and businesses between March and May of 1965. [*NYT* 1966]

CROSS, WILLIAM, JR.

A New Orleans Klansman, Cross was one of five members jailed on June 21, 1966, and charged with participation in the firebombing of various stores, churches, and homes between March and May 1965. [*NYT* 1966]

CROSS BURNING

Cross burning was reportedly practiced by Scottish clans in the fourteenth century as a means of signaling in the Highlands. Although never practiced by Reconstruction Klansmen, the technique was introduced after the fact by author Thomas Dixon in his 1905 novel *The Clansman*. The first actual cross burning on U.S. soil was conducted by members of a Georgia lynch mob, the Knights of Mary Phagan, who lit a giant cross atop Stone Mountain on October 16, 1915. Members of the Knights were reportedly on hand when William Simmons and other founders of the reborn Ku Klux Klan burned another cross on Stone Mountain on Thanksgiving Day 1915. Often described by Klansmen as a "religious ceremony," cross burnings on a smaller scale soon became a traditional form of KKK intimidation. Many communities on both sides of the Mason-Dixon Line have outlawed cross burning, unless it takes place on private property with the prior consent of the owner, prompting Klansmen to employ electric crosses and other devices to circumvent local ordinances. In the 1970s, David Duke and other Klan leaders began to speak of "cross lightings," a gentler term designed to illustrate their contention that "Christ is the light of the world." Klansmen complained that anyone can set a cross on fire, and numerous arrests in local cases have revealed the perpetrators to be teenagers unconnected with the KKK. This antiquated custom, however, shows no signs of disappearing— 301 cross burning incidents were recorded between 1980 and 1986. [93]

CROSSLAND, M.P.

A Republican state legislator during Reconstruction in Alabama, Crossland was ambushed and killed by Klansmen in Tuscaloosa County during September 1868. A male traveling companion died in the same attack. [87]

CROWDER, H.L.

A Nashville, Tennessee, businessman, Crowder ran for governor in 1966 with Klan support, pledging himself to drive communists from the state and issue a "shoot to kill" order against black rioters. Running as an independent candidate, he was soundly defeated. [NYT 1966]

CROWE, JAMES R.

One of six original Klansmen in Pulaski, Tennessee, Crowe is credited with coining the term "kuklux" from the Greek *kuklos*, or "circle." Serving as the first grand turk of the order, he attended the Klan's April 1867 reorganization meeting at the Maxwell House in Nashville. After Reconstruction, Crowe was elected Masonic Grand Master of Tennessee. [87]

CROWE, WILLIAM B.

A resident of Decatur, Georgia, Crowe served as an instructor at a United Klans of America demolition class held in October 1961 on the Georgia farm of Klansman O.C. Mixon. In 1963 he was arrested with Klansman William Anderson and thirty-eight other persons in DeKalb County, Georgia, and briefly charged with operating a disorderly house. Identified as a member of Nacirema, Inc., Crowe was an illiterate dropout who could not read a statement prepared by his attorney when called before the House Un-American Activities Committee in November 1965. [NYT 1965; 38]

CRUELL, CLAUDE

A black resident of Greenville, South Carolina, Cruell was flogged by Klansmen on July 23, 1957. Defendants sentenced to prison in January 1958 for the attack included: Marshall Rochester, exalted cyclops of Greenville (six years); Wade Howard (three years); Jack Bentley and Robert Waldrop (one year each). [14]

CRUMLEY, ALFRED

See *Goodman, Jessie Lee.*

CRUMP, RICHARD P.

A prominent resident of Reconstruction Jefferson County, Texas, Crump was an early member of the Knights of the Rising Sun. He led the party that tried to assassinate carpetbagger George Smith on the night of October 3, 1868. He then had Smith arrested for assault when he fired back at the mob in self-defense. After Smith was lynched, Crump and three other members were tried and acquitted on murder charges. [87]

CRUSADERS OF THE NORTH

A white supremacist group organized in rural Cumberland County, New Jersey, by ex-Klansman Frank Rotella, the Crusaders went public on November 5, 1966, when Rotella led seventy-five men in a cross burning ceremony outside Cedarville. [NYT 1966]

CULBERT, JAMES J.

A Klan associate from St. Claire, Pennsylvania, Culbert was indicted for receiving, selling, and disposing of stolen high explosives on March 1, 1974. Defendants Roy Frankhouser and Thomas Kanger were charged in the same case. [NYT 1974]

CULBERTSON, KIRK

A black garage owner in Philadelphia, Mississippi, Culbertson was beaten by Sheriff Lawrence Rainey and Deputy Cecil Price in 1964, suffering a skull fracture that left him with blinding headaches and unable to work. Later that year a federal grand jury indicted both officers for violating Culbertson's civil rights. [Life, Dec. 18, 1964]

CULBREATH, LEE EDWARD

A fourteen year old, black newspaper delivery boy, Culbreath was shot and killed in Hamburg, Arkansas, on December 5, 1965. Two white brothers, Ed and James Vail, were arrested by state troopers and charged with the murder. Both allegedly confessed to Klan membership. At his trial in February 1966, however, Ed Vail admitted attending Klan rallies but denied actual membership. He was convicted of second-degree murder. [NYT 1966]

CUMBERLAND COUNTY PATRIOTS

In 1965 congressional investigators identified this group as a front for Klavern No. 89, United Klans of America, in Fayetteville, North Carolina. [38]

CUMMINS, ELI

An ex-Confederate officer and attorney during Reconstruction in Wilkinson County, Georgia, Cummins was also a leader of the local KKK. In August 1871, he contrived the false arrest of black Republican Henry Lowther, resulting in Lowther's subsequent abduction from jail and castration by Klansmen. [87]

CURRY, LONEY

See *Carter, Asa.*

CURRY, REV. MICHAEL

A Methodist minister in Smithburg, West Virginia, Curry was harassed, threatened, and ultimately driven from the community after he rejected a Klansman's request to speak from the pulpit of his church in June 1980. Assaulted by a gang of hooded men on one occasion, Curry and his wife finally left Smithburg in November 1980. [NYT 1980]

CURTIS, ARCHIE

A black mortician in Natchez, Mississippi, Curtis was lured to a rural road by reports of a dying woman in February 1964, and was then beaten by hooded Klansmen. Six months later, a party of nightriders shot up his funeral home. [NYT 1964]

CUTLER, BUD

A former security chief for the Aryan Nations in Idaho, Cutler was jailed in August 1985 after he offered an undercover policeman $1,800 to arrange the decapitation of suspected informant Thomas Martinez. Upon conviction, Cutler was replaced in his security position by David Dorr. [NYT 1985]

D

DAHMER, VERNON

A black civil rights activist in Hattiesburg, Mississippi, Dahmer was an early target of surveillance by the White Knights of the KKK. Klan leaders voted a death sentence against Dahmer in December 1965 after he began collecting poll taxes from local blacks at his store to spare them from intimidating visits to the sheriff's office. On January 10, 1966, Klansmen staged a predawn raid on Dahmer's home and nearby store, setting both buildings on fire and exchanging gunfire with Dahmer as he attempted to defend his family. In the confusion, the Klansmen shot up one of their own cars and were forced to ditch it nearby. Dahmer was left with fatal burns. On March 28, 1966, the FBI arrested thirteen Klansmen on various charges. They included: Cecil Sessum, former exalted cyclops of the Jones County klavern; Howard Giles, ex-cyclops of the Ellisville klavern; Lawrence Byrd; Deavours Nix; Henry DeBoxtel; Clifton Lowe and his son Charles; James Lyons; Melvin Martin; Emanuel Moss; Charles Noble; Billy Roy Pitts; and William Smith. On June 23, 1966, a federal grand jury indicted sixteen Klansmen on civil rights charges, adding Imperial Wizard Sam Bowers to the list of those accused. Five months later, on November 10, Bowers, Nix, and Sessum were jailed on charges of abducting and attempting to intimidate prosecution witness Jack Watkins. Meanwhile, Klan attorney Travis Buckley encountered problems of his own: on January 25, 1967, he was charged with arson in the Dahmer case. By March 10, 1967, Buckley and defendant Billy Pitts were added to the list of those indicted for kidnapping Jack Watkins. Pitts pled guilty to charges of arson and murder on March 8, 1968, drawing a sentence of life imprisonment. Cecil Sessum was convicted of murder and sentenced to life on March 13, the same day that defense witness James Yount was arrested for perjury for denying his membership in the KKK. A mistrial was declared for Henry DeBoxtel on March 21, and six days later a federal grand jury returned conspiracy indictments against sixteen White Knights. Sam Bowers faced his first set of charges in May 1968, which ended in a mistrial when jurors failed to agree on a verdict. Convicted on the federal conspiracy charge, Billy Pitts drew another five-year term on July 15, 1968. Four days later, William Smith was convicted of murder and sentenced to life, while Charles Wilson's trial ended in a mistrial on July 28. Jurors deliberated for twelve minutes before convicting Lawrence Byrd of arson on November 10, handing down a ten-year sentence, while James Lyons escaped with a mistrial four days later. Sam Bowers was charged with murder on November 18, 1968, raising the ante from a previous charge of simple arson. At his murder trial in January 1969, Klansmen Billy Pitts and T. Weber Rogers testified that Bowers ordered "a Number 3 and a Number 4"—arson and murder—against Dahmer on December 13, 1965, in a meeting held at Lawrence Byrd's farm outside of Laurel, Mississippi. A mistrial was declared on January 25, the jury deadlocked 10–2 for conviction. Charles Wilson, however was convicted and sentenced to life imprisonment six days later. The federal conspiracy trial of ten Klansmen opened on April 28, 1969; on May 10, jurors acquitted Lester Thornton, Howard Giles, and James Lyons, and failed to reach a verdict on seven others. By July 1969, Sam Bowers had survived four mistrials in the Dahmer case, and the charges against him were finally dismissed in 1973. [NYT 1966–1969; FOF 1966–1969; 84; 96]

DALE, ARTHUR

A black inmate in a Missouri state prison, Dale was murdered by two convict members of the Aryan Nations in 1984. [NYT 1984]

DALLAS COUNTY CITIZENS LEAGUE

The first formal anti-Klan group of the 20th century, this group was organized in Texas on April 4, 1922. A typical piece of its literature posed the question: "Who can teach Americanism, tried patriots or the Night Prowlers?" [93]

DANIEL, WATT

See Mer Rouge, Louisiana.

DANIEL, WILLIAM A., SR.

Public documents identified Daniel as a founding member of the U.S. Klans in October 1955. In early 1961, the Georgia native joined Robert Davidson, Calvin Craig, and others in resigning from the U.S. Klans to create the

United Klans of America. Daniel was listed as one of four original incorporating officers for the United Klans. [38]

DANIELS, JONATHAN

A seminary student, Daniels was one of several hundred Northern whites who volunteered their time and risked their lives to register black voters in Alabama during 1965. Traveling south on the same flight that carried the Reverend James Reeb, he was assigned to work in Lowndes County, where Klansmen sported "Open Season" bumper stickers following the first mistrial in the Viola Liuzzo murder case. Arrested with other demonstrators in a march to the Hayneville courthouse, Daniels was released without bail on August 20, 1965. Moments later, he was dead, shot in a nearby store by Klansman Tom Coleman; Reverend Richard Morrisroe was critically wounded in the same shooting. After the shooting, Coleman telephoned Colonel Al Lingo, in charge of the state police, to announce, "I just shot two preachers. You better get down here." The local sheriff was out of town, but Coleman—an unpaid "special deputy"—reached his office in time to answer the first call reporting the shooting. Coleman was arraigned on August 21 in the office of Assistant County Solicitor Carlton Purdue, who told a grand jury, "If they [the victims] had been tending to their own business, like I was tending to mine, they'd be living and enjoying themselves." State Attorney General Richmond Flowers told the press that Al Lingo had made his own investigation of the case and refused to share information with the prosecutor's office. On September 15, 1965, Coleman was indicted for first-degree manslaughter, defined in Alabama as killing "intentionally but without malice." On September 27, 1965, Flowers requested a postponement of the trial so that Morrisroe could recover and testify for the prosecution, but the presiding judge refused, calling the motion "frivolous." Coleman's trial opened the next day, with Assistant Attorney General Joe Gannt standing in for Flowers (who feared for his life in Lowndes County, following numerous death threats—including one from Coleman). When potential jurors were asked if they had any preconceived ideas about the case, one replied, "I do, sir. Not guilty!" On September 29, several witnesses charged that Daniels and Morrisroe were armed at the time they were shot, although no weapons had been found in the store. Joe Gannt denounced the remarks as "perjured testimony obtained by Al Lingo," refusing to proceed without Morrisroe. The judge promptly removed Gannt from the case, with censure for "trifling with the court," and turned the proceedings over to local prosecutors. The trial instantly degenerated into a dark farce, with a deputy sheriff testifying that he saw Daniels kiss a black girl "on the mouth," while a spokesman for the state crime laboratory was called to testify that the victim's undershorts smelled of urine after he was shot. A cousin of Coleman insisted both victims were armed with knives, presumably hidden by black accomplices after the shooting. Circuit Solicitor Arthur

Gamble joined the defense in laughing at black witnesses and twice referred to "that knife," while Carlton Purdue spoke of Daniels "attempting to force his way into" the store. Coleman's lawyer told the jury, "You can believe that knife was there or not. I believe it was there whether it was or not." Filing out of court to deliberate on September 30, one juror openly winked at Coleman, and the panel returned ninety minutes later with a verdict of acquittal. A second grand jury declined to indict Coleman in the wounding of Morrisroe. [*NYT* 1965; 63]

DANNONS, JAKE

A black blacksmith during Reconstruction in Walton County, Georgia, Dannons was shot dead by Klansmen after refusing to work for a white man who had cheated him on previous jobs. [93]

DAPONTE, DOROTHY

A white resident of Mobile, Alabama, Daponte tried to enroll her black maid's daughter at a white school in September 1955. On the night of September 18, an eighteen-car caravan delivered 100 robed Klansmen to her house, where they burned a ten-foot cross on the lawn. A second cross was burned at the home of a friend on September 25. [*NYT* 1955]

DARDEN, DR. G.O.

A Republican and practicing physician during Reconstruction in Warrenton, Georgia, Darden shot and killed Charles Wallace—a Democratic newspaper editor—in a personal feud during March 1869. Jailed on a murder charge, he was subsequently dragged from his cell and lynched by masked men. The six Klansmen arrested in June included James Cody and his two brothers, John Raley, and A.I. Hartley—Wallace's successor as editor of the *Clipper*. All six were released on a writ of habeas corpus, issued by a judge who had no authority to hear such cases. None of them were ever brought to trial. [87]

DAVIDSON, MEYER

See *Tarrants, Thomas.*

DAVIDSON, ROBERT LEE ("WILD BILL")

Serving as Georgia grand dragon for the U.S. Klans under Eldon Edwards, from 1957 to 1960, Davidson earned his nickname from the fringed leather jacket he wore in his daily employment as an insurance salesman prior to joining his father in the operation of a bag-salvaging plant. In January 1960, he announced plans for private a Klan school in Atlanta to help white families avoid court-ordered desegregation. Assuming the title of imperial wizard when Edwards died that August, Davidson said of the KKK, "I'm trying to bring it out of the darkness and make it a progressive movement, not just a protest movement." In that light, he publicly rejected Robert Shelton, John Kasper, George Lincoln Rockwell, and the National States Rights Party as too extreme. "I don't get myself connected with any fanatical movement," Davidson told the press. "I can't go around lambasting Jews, Negroes, and Catholics and expect to get a national following." By November, his stance had become more militant, complete with warnings that Klansmen would use buckshot, if necessary, to prevent integration, but his hopes of a national movement were already fading. Harassed and handcuffed by lawsuits from the widow of Eldon Edwards and would-be wizard E.E. George, Davidson resigned from the U.S. Klans on February 18, 1961. Three days later, acting in conjunction with Klansman Calvin Craig, Davidson announced the formation of a new Invisible Empire, United Klans, Knights of the Ku Klux Klan of America, Inc. Davidson held office in the new Klan as imperial wizard until April 1, 1961, when he resigned in the midst of a dispute over KKK involvement in riots at the state university in Athens, Georgia [14; 38]

DAVIDSON COUNTY RESCUE SERVICE

In 1965 congressional investigators identified this group as a cover for the Nashville, Tennessee, klavern, United Klans of America. [38]

DAVIDSON COUNTY SPORTSMAN CLUB

A 1960s front for the Lexington, North Carolina, klavern, United Klans of America, this club was exposed by the House Un-American Activities Committee in 1965. [38]

DAVIES, ELMER

A former Klansman, Davies was appointed as a federal judge in Tennessee in 1939. Senators tried to withdraw their confirmation of the appointment when Davies's KKK ties were revealed, but their efforts proved fruitless. [10]

DAVIS, JAMES WAYNE

A member of the United Klans of America, Davis was elected recorder of deeds in Rowan County, North Carolina, in 1966. In July 1967, he was one of twelve Klansmen arrested for interfering with school desegregation through acts of bombing and terrorism. Davis and seven other defendants were acquitted at their trial in January 1968. [NYT 1967–1968]

DAVIS, JOHN W.

A West Virginia native, U.S. ambassador, and Democratic presidential candidate in 1924, Davis was nominated at the party's convention in New

York City on the 104th ballot, after a rancorous floor fight over proposed anti-Klan resolutions doomed the hopes of candidates William Gibbs McAdoo and Oscar Underwood. A move to denounce the KKK by name was defeated by a single vote at the convention, but Davis went on to attack the Klan anyway. In a speech given in Sea Girt, New Jersey, he told a cheering audience, "If any organization, no matter what it chooses to be called, whether Ku Klux Klan or by any other name, raises the standard of racial and religious prejudice or attempts to make racial origins or religious beliefs the test of fitness for public office, it does violence to the spirit of American institutions and must be condemned by all those who believe, as I do, in American ideals." Imperial Wizard Hiram Evans had vowed not to take sides between Davis and incumbent Calvin Coolidge, but after the Sea Girt speech Evans threw the Klan's weight behind Coolidge, later taking credit for his reelection. [10]

DAVIS, L.O.

As sheriff of St. John County, Florida, which included St. Augustine, Davis rivaled "Bull" Connor and Selma Sheriff Jim Clark as a symbol of diehard segregationist sentiment in the 1960s. In September 1963, he arrested Dr. R.N. Hayling and three other blacks who were beaten at a KKK rally, telling the press, "I don't know what got into them niggers, going down that dirt road when they knew a Klan meeting was going on." When black demonstrations began in St. Augustine the following spring, Davis banned night marches and jailed protesters in open-air pens, cramming some into an eight-foot sweat box. His force of 100-plus "special deputies" included members of the United Florida Ku Klux Klan and its local front group, the Ancient City Gun Club. Hauled into federal court before Judge Bryan Simpson in early June 1964, Davis denied membership in the Klan, but admitted that some of his deputies might be members, explaining that "I couldn't look into it when I put them on." The final list of names, delivered under court order, included convicted felon Holstead Manucy, leader of the Ancient City Gun Club, as well as known Klansmen Barton Griffin, Robert Gentry, and Donald Spegal. [38]

DAVIS, PHIL

A Tulsa, Oklahoma, attorney and associate of anti-Semite Gerald L.K. Smith, Davis visited Atlanta to defend members of the Columbians, Inc., in 1946. [*New Republic*, Nov. 23, 1946]

DAVIS, ROY E.

A native of Dallas, Texas, Davis organized the Original Ku Klux Klan in 1960, recruiting followers not only in his home state but in Arkansas and Louisiana as well. Unable to control the scattered klaverns, Davis soon resigned as imperial wizard. His organization disintegrated, with the Louisiana realm finding new life as the Original Knights of the KKK. [38]

DAVIS, WILLIAM B.

A resident of Anderson, South Carolina, Davis was identified in 1967 as one of five Klansmen who made up the ruling grand council of the Association of South Carolina Klans. [38]

D'AVY, FRANCOIS

A Republican leader during Reconstruction in St. Landry Parish, Louisiana, D'Avy was targeted for assassination by the Knights of the White Camellia in September 1868. Gunmen missed him on their first attempt as he lay sleeping in his bed. D'Avy fled the parish to avoid further incidents. [87]

DAWN

A weekly publication of the Knights of the Ku Klux Klan, Inc., in the 1920s, *Dawn* was instrumental in spreading the doctrines of white supremacy, anti-Semitism, and anti-Catholicism to Klansmen and prospective members. [10]

DAWSON, EDWARD

A native of New Jersey, Dawson was working as a self-employed contractor in Greensboro, North Carolina, when he joined the United Klans of America in 1964. Once a member of the United Klan's state board and an officer in the Klan security guard, he was arrested and sentenced to jail for destruction of property in Alamance County. Dawson was also involved in the July 1969 shootout in Swan Quarter, North Carolina, when a black girl was wounded and a police car was riddled with bullets. After serving nine months, Dawson was recruited as an FBI informant in the Klan, and later served in the same capacity for the Greensboro police. A cofounder, along with Joe Bryant, of the North Carolina Knights, he was also elected imperial kladd for the new Confederation of Independent Orders. Although uncertain of his loyalty, Greensboro detectives showed Dawson a copy of the parade permit for a Communist Workers Party anti-Klan demonstration in November 1979. The documents revealed the starting point of the parade, along with the fact that Communist Workers Party members would be unarmed. Dawson immediately began agitating for Klansmen to meet the parade, making personal contacts with various groups and putting up posters. As one Klansman later told the press, "We'd never have come to Greensboro if it wasn't for Ed Dawson berating us." On October 31, 1979, and again on November 3, Dawson told police that Klansmen were coming to the protest heavily armed, but his warnings failed to avert the shooting that claimed five lives. [93]

DAY, ROBERT

An ex-member of the U.S. Klans in Georgia, during 1961, Day was listed as one of four original incorporating officers for the new United Klans of America. [38]

DAYVAULT, WAYNE

A North Carolina state secretary for the United Klans of America, Dayvault declined to answer questions before the House Un-American Activities Committee in October 1965. Arrested by FBI agents in Salisbury, North Carolina, on July 18, 1967, he was one of twelve Klansmen charged with conspiracy to block school integration following a twenty-one-month-long series of terrorist acts in Anson, Rowan, and Cabarus counties. The most recent incident was on June 30, 1967, when bombs damaged property owned by five Anson County school officials in Wadesboro. Various other acts included bombings of churches and businesses, shooting into homes, and cross burnings. Dayvault's codefendants included: James Davis, Rowan County recorder of deeds; Charles Outen; Robert Hill; Ray Hornbeak; Ronald Mullis; Winfred Bridges; Nolan Safrit; Donald Stewart; Clifton Shaver; Homer Blackwelder; and Bobby Wagoner. Nine of the Klansmen were tried in January 1968, with Dayvault, Hornbeak, Safrit, Shaver, Bridges, Stewart, Wagoner, and Outen acquitted on January 19. No verdict was reached on Mullis. [NYT 1965, 1967–1968]

DEACONS FOR DEFENSE AND JUSTICE

A black group organized in Jonesboro, Louisiana, to oppose Klan violence in the summer of 1964, the Deacons reportedly engaged in several skirmishes with nightriders around Bogalusa and elsewhere. On one occasion, members took a black youth into protective custody after he was accused of stealing a kiss from a white girl. The "victim" later recanted her story and charges were dropped. [NYT 1964–1965]

DEARTH, CLARENCE W.

A judge in Muncie, Indiana, Dearth was impeached when his Klan connections were revealed in the late 1920s. [93]

DEASON, MAT

As sheriff of Wilkinson County, Georgia, during Reconstruction, Deason took a black mistress after his wife was confined to an insane asylum. When the local KKK took an interest in his domestic arrangement, the sheriff threatened to kill anyone who harmed his family. In August 1871, Deason and his lover were beaten and shot to death by Klansmen, their bodies weighted with iron bars and dumped in a creek. [87]

DEATHERAGE, GEORGE

A resident of St. Albans, West Virginia, and an engineer by profession, Deatherage was a Klansman in the 1920s, prior to reviving the Knights of the White Camellia in 1934. A proponent of "Constitutional Fascism," he openly affiliated the Knights with Nazi propagandists from Germany and Britain, suggesting a switch from cross burnings to fiery swastikas that would strike "terror and fear into the hearts of many." Deatherage claimed that German Nazis had copied their anti-Semitic policies and straight-arm salute from the KKK. By 1936, as founding father of the American Nationalist Federation, Deatherage was entertaining army officers at his home, briefing them on the prospects of fascist revolution, and writing speeches for Atlanta neo-Nazi George Van Horn Moseley. A year later, Deatherage and his military consorts were directly in touch with Hitler's government, a circumstance that led to his January 1943 indictment on sedition charges. The case, which involved thirty-three alleged conspirators, ended with a mistrial for all concerned in November 1943. Maintaining his Klan ties as late as 1960, Deatherage was invited as guest speaker at a poorly attended meeting of the Duval Fellowship Club, a Jacksonville front for the United Florida Ku Klux Klan. [8; 10]

DeBLANC, ALCIBIADE

An ex-Confederate officer, DeBlanc was a founder of the Knights of the White Camellia in St. Mary Parish, Louisiana, in May 1867. Believed to be the order's grand commander, DeBlanc never publicly acknowledged the office. [87]

DeBOXTEL, HENRY E.

See *Dahmer, Vernon.*

DEE, HENRY HEZEKIAH

A black resident of Meadville, Mississippi, Dee disappeared with a friend, Charlie Eddie Moore, on May 2, 1964. In early July, during a general search for Michael Schwerner and two other missing civil rights workers, the remains of Dee and Moore were found in the Old River, near Tallulah, Louisiana. An FBI investigation revealed that Doe and Moore had been murdered by members of the White Knights of the KKK, on suspicion of smuggling guns to the Black Muslims in a nonexistent plot against local whites. Klansmen James Seale and Charles Edwards were arrested in the case, and Edwards admitted that the two blacks were whipped on May 2, describing Dee as an alleged Peeping Tom. Murder indictments lodged against Seale and Edwards were dismissed on January 11, 1965. [*NYT* 1965; 96]

DEES, MORRIS

As chief legal counsel for the Southern Poverty Law Center and a driving force behind the Center's Klanwatch Project, Dees first became a target for Klan vituperation and violence in 1981, when his efforts won an injunction against Louis Beam and others, preventing the KKK harassment of Vietnamese refugees. Since that time, Dees has led the Center in successful suits against various Klans in Alabama, Georgia, Kentucky, North Carolina, and Texas. [93]

DEESE, CHARLES DOUGLAS

A native of North Carolina, "Bud" Deese came to the Klan with a prior record of felony convictions for breaking and entering, larceny, robbery, and assaulting a woman. In January 1964, less than two years after the latter conviction, he was elected as North Carolina's grand kligrapp for the United Klans of America. A month later, Deese was arrested during a civil rights demonstration and convicted of carrying a concealed weapon. At the time that he was booked, officers also listed charges of causing a riot, interfering with a police officer, and using indecent and profane language. In June 1965 Deese was again convicted for assaulting a woman. Summoned before the House Un-American Activities Committee in October 1965, he relied on the Fifth Amendment throughout. [38]

DEFENSIVE LEGION OF REGISTERED AMERICANS

One of several organizations founded by Klansman James Venable in the 1960s, the Legion was chartered in Georgia on April 11, 1962. Three months later, on July 4, members joined the United Klans of America and the National White Americans Party for a rally at Stone Mountain, Georgia. Chartered for thirty-five years, the Legion apparently dissolved sometime during 1964, after two years of circulating anti-black and anti-Semitic propaganda that predicted a war to "take back our country" from the "tyrannical" government in Washington. "Blood will surely flow in the streets," the Legion advised, adding: "Let it flow! Let us arm our homes to make sure that Negro-Jew blood flows—not ours." Legion authors recommended rifles with telescopic sights "for distance shooting," using hollow-point bullets that "go clear through your game, whether two-legged or four." [NYT 1962; 38]

DEFRIES, JOHN IRA

See Brewster, Willie.

DEGREE TEAM

In some Klans, a select "degree team" is appointed to perform the task of initiating new members into the Invisible Empire. [38]

DELAINE, REV. JOSEPH A.

A black minister who advocated school desegregation in South Carolina beginning in the early 1940s, Delaine was driven out of Clarendon County in 1949 by death threats. He moved to Summerton, South Carolina, where his home was burned by nightriders, and from there to Lake City. In September 1955, a KKK motorcade circled Delaine's house, smashing windows with bricks and bottles. Although Delaine recorded the license number of one car, the local sheriff remained inactive. Delaine's church was burned by arsonists on October 6, and two days later he exchanged gunfire with eight carloads of Klansmen at his home. On that occasion, Delaine claimed to recognize the sheriff as a member of the raiding party. Delaine and his family fled to New York in November 1955. [*NYT* 1955]

DeLAND SPORTSMANS CLUB

In 1965 congressional probers exposed this club as a front for the Samsula, Florida, klavern of the United Florida Knights of the Ku Klux Klan. [38]

DELAWARE

By the end of 1922, the Klan had gained substantial membership in the vicinity of Laurel, but opposition was already growing. In the summer of 1923, protesters stormed a KKK initiation ceremony near New Castle, with three men shot and fifty others injured in the riot that ensued. Klansmen remained active through the late 1920s, concentrated chiefly in the rural counties of Kent and Sussex, but their strength withered away with the advent of the Great Depression. Thirty years later, in the summer of 1965, Grand Dragon Ralph Pryor tried to spark new interest in the United Klans of America, but his efforts ran aground amid charges of fraternization with the American Nazi Party. Even at its peak, the new Klan in Delaware barely numbered 100 members, scattered among five klaverns. [10; 38]

DELAWARE BIRDWATCHERS

According to congressional reports issued in 1967, this group served as a statewide front for the United Klans of America's Delaware realm. [38]

DELHI SPORTSMAN CLUB

In 1965 the House Un-American Activities Committee identified this group as the front for the Delhi, Louisiana, klavern, Original Knights of the KKK. [38]

DELTA SPORTSMAN CLUB

This "club" was a 1960s cover for the Delta, Louisiana, klavern, Original Knights of the Ku Klux Klan. [38]

DEMAREST, HORACE A.

One of New York State's original Klansmen, Demarest chartered the KKK as the Alpha Pi Sigma fraternity in 1923, finally dropping the pretense two years later. In 1946, while serving as deputy state motor vehicle commissioner and a Republican leader in Queens, Demarest was embarrassed by exposure of his Klan background. Denying any links with the post-war Association of Georgia Klans, he was dismissed from his job on May 5, 1946, on the basis of "discrepancies" in his answers about past KKK affiliations. [NYT 1946]

DEMOCRATIC CLUBS

A network of paramilitary groups with numerous links to the KKK, the Democratic Clubs first surfaced in South Carolina during February 1868, when ex-Governor Benjamin Perry called on whites to organize against Radical Reconstruction. (The South Carolina Klan announced its first meeting a month later.) An Abbeville County Klansman later told authorities that the KKK and Democratic Clubs were one and the same. By election time that year, the clubs were widely organized in Louisiana, issuing "protection papers" to blacks who agreed to vote Democratic. A major project of the New Orleans faction was the disruption of the Republican-dominated city police force. The Democratic Club, organized in Fulton County, Arkansas, during September 1868, was generally accepted as a part of the Ku Klux Klan, and the same understanding prevailed when clubs were organized in northern Florida in 1869 and 1870. [87]

DEN

The official designation for local Klan unit or meeting place during Reconstruction, the term has generally been supplanted by "klavern" in 20th-century Klan jargon. [87]

DENNETT, DANIEL

A leader of the Knights of the White Camellia during Reconstruction in St. Mary Parish, Louisiana, Dennett also served as editor of the Planter's Banner in Franklin. [87]

DENNIS, REV. DELMAR

A Protestant minister in Meridian, Mississippi, Dennis was introduced to the White Knights of the KKK when a friend, T.C. Dixon, took him to a local meeting in March 1964. Dennis promptly joined the group and was appointed chaplain at his second meeting, but he was soon disillusioned by the Klan's preoccupation with violence. Dennis was on the verge of dropping out when the FBI recruited him as a confidential informant inside the Klan, and he paid up his back dues to remain a member on the FBI's behalf. Elevated to the rank of titan in November 1964, he met with Grand Dragon E.L. McDaniel of the rival United Klans of America three months later, and for a time Dennis belonged to both groups simultaneously. In October 1967, he appeared as a key prosecution witness in the federal trial of Klansmen accused in the murders of Michael Schwerner, Andrew Goodman, and James Chaney. A target of continuing Klan threats for his "betrayal," Dennis hit the road a year later, traveling widely as a member of the John Birch Society's lecture bureau. Following the John Birch party line, he maintained that the Klans and black civil rights groups were all controlled by communist agents, utilized as part of a sinister pincers movement to revolutionize blacks while at the same time discrediting white "patriots." [59; 96]

DENNIS, L.G.

A Republican state senator during Reconstruction in Florida, Dennis was sentenced to hang by a Klan mock court in Gainesville in 1871. He had the Klansmen arrested for disturbing the peace, but they were acquitted and returned the same night to assault Gainesville's mayor outside the courthouse. [87]

DENNIS, WILLIAM

A Republican activist in Mississippi during Reconstruction, Dennis survived one attempt on his life before Democrats had him jailed in Meridian in 1871 for making incendiary speeches. Wounded by gunshots at a preliminary court hearing on March 6, Dennis was held "in protective custody" at the local jail, but his guards withdrew that night, and Klansmen entered and murdered Dennis. Violence by armed whites following his murder soon escalated into a full-scale race riot, with other blacks killed in the melee. [87]

DePUGH, ROBERT BOLIVAR

A native of Independence, Missouri, DePugh graduated from a local high school in 1941 and served in the army until 1944, when he was discharged on medical grounds. In 1952, he ran for office in Missouri's 4th Congressional District, finishing fourth in a field of five candidates. Turning from politics to chemistry, he created Biolab Corporation, a drug manufacturing firm, and moved his home and business to Norborne, Missouri, in 1960. He founded the Minutemen in Norborne, a prototype of the modern paramilitary survivalist groups that first drew attention with a guerilla warfare seminar conducted in Shiloh, Illinois, in October 1961. In the mid-1960s, DePugh several times had discussed the possibility of forming a right-wing underground network with Robert Shelton's United Klans of America. In 1966, he announced that his group would accept Klansmen; the Minutemen also absorbed a group of twenty American Nazis, following their assurance that they would recognize George Lincoln Rockwell's "ideological errors." (Rockwell complained that DePugh had also "stolen" three of the party's chief financial supporters.) One of eight Minutemen indicted by a federal grand jury for plotting to rob a Washington bank, DePugh went underground in February 1968. Prior to his June 1969 capture in New Mexico, DePugh issued political appeals on behalf of George Wallace, providing some unorthodox support that Wallace was pleased to accept in his race for the White House. In July 1969, DePugh was sentenced to eleven years in jail for jumping bond and violating federal firearms laws. While imprisoned, he lent his name to the National Association to Keep and Bear Arms, a right-wing consortium opposed to gun control legislation that featured Robert Shelton on its board of directors. Paroled in May 1973, DePugh replaced the defunct Minutemen with a new Patriots Inter-Organizational Communications Center staffed by members of various right-wing groups and serving as a communications link between them. In 1975, at one of DePugh's annual Patriot's Leadership Conferences held in Kansas City, he met with Shelton, David Duke, James Warner and others to discuss strategies for the future. One result was DePugh's Committee of Ten Million, created in 1978 and headquartered at Independence, Missouri, with nationwide chapters financially supporting appearances by Shelton and their founder. By December 1980, DePugh and his committee were announcing plans for a paramilitary training seminar and coming full-circle. [2; 46; 84; 90]

DER DEUTSCHE ORDEN DES FUERIGEN KREUZES

See *Germany*.

DeROSIER, HARVEY

A postal worker and Klansman in Hialeah, Florida, De Rosier was indicted by federal authorities on December 10, 1952, on two counts of making false statements to the Post Office loyalty board. Specifically, De Rosier admitted belonging to a Klan front, Sports, Inc., but claimed to have resigned in May 1950 when he learned the group's true nature. The indictments charged that he not only had kept his membership intact, but that he was elected kludd in January 1951. [*NYT* 1952]

DETROIT ANTI-KLAN COALITION

Members of the tiny coalition assaulted Klansmen and Nazis at a meeting of the Detroit city council, held on June 26, 1980, after racist spokesmen requested permission for a downtown parade. Ten demonstrators were arrested in the clash. [*AP,* June 27, 1980]

DEVILLE HUNTING & FISHING CLUB

In 1965 congressional investigators identified this group as a cover for the Deville, Louisiana, klavern of the Original Knights of the KKK. [38]

DEVIL'S ADVOCATES

A Kankakee, Illinois, motorcycle gang notorious for its racist views, the Devil's Advocates participated in a May 1975 organizational meeting of the United Klans of America, held at the Kankakee Ramada Inn. Of the twenty-five people present—including three police informants—ten were identified as members of the gang. [43]

DIBRELL, G.G.

A Tennessee native and ex-Confederate general, Dibrell was a delegate to KKK's April 1867 reorganization conference in Nashville. Elected grand titan of the new order, he assumed responsibility for Klan recruiting in the eastern half of the state. Dibrell was one of thirteen ranking Klansmen who met in Nashville on August 1, 1868, to protest formation of a state militia and assure Republicans that the KKK had no intention of overthrowing the state government. [87]

DICKERSON, LESTER

A New Orleans Klansman, Dickerson was one of five arrested on June 21, 1966, for participating in a series of firebombings aimed at local churches, homes, and businesses between March and May of 1965. [NYT 1966]

DICKEY CLAY MANUFACTURING COMPANY

Located in Bessemer, Alabama, the W.S. Dickey Co. employed mostly black workers, supervised by white inspectors, in the early 1960s. Late in 1964, a group of sixteen inspectors, including at least two Klansmen, petitioned the National Labor Relations Board for representation by the United Brick and Clay Workers Union. Although labor issues were advanced to justify their request, the inspectors actually sought to form a local independent of black workers. Contract demands by the new United Brick and Clay Workers local precipitated a strike against Dickey in February 1965, but 90 percent of the firm's black employees, represented by the United Steelworkers, continued working under the terms of their prevailing contract. As the strike began, United Brick and Clay Workers Local 827 was led by James Whitefield, exalted cyclops for Bessemer Klavern No. 20, United Klans of America, and the job action quickly assumed the flavor of a KKK operation. From the start of picketing on February 8, Klansmen not employed by Dickey, including murder defendant Collie Leroy Wilkins, assumed a prominent role in the strike, and violence began erupting at the plant. On February 18, the factory was bombed and a worker's car was blasted with shotgun pellets. Before Dickey secured an injunction on March 12 against unlawful acts, company property and employee vehicles were extensively damaged by bombs, the gas mains to the factory kilns were sabotaged, and sugar was poured in gasoline tanks. Despite the injunction, nine more bombs exploded at the plant between March 12 and August 9, 1965, and several employee automobiles were damaged by gunfire. Congressional investigators identified six members of the United Klans involved in violence at the Dickey factory, but none were ever prosecuted for their crimes. [38]

DICKINSON, JOHN Q.

The foremost Republican in western Florida during Reconstruction, Dickinson was active in the Freedmen's Bureau while serving as a clerk for Jackson County. Once assaulted on a Marianna Street by Klan leader James Coker, Dickinson was shot and killed in the town square on the night of April 3, 1871. His death removed the last Republican official in the county. [87]

DIGGS, FRANK

A black mail agent on the railroad line between Selma, Alabama, and Meridian, Mississippi, Diggs was murdered by Klansmen in the latter part of 1870, when his train stopped at Kewaunee, Mississippi. [87]

DiSALVO, LOUIS ANTHONY

A barber and licensed firearms dealer in Waveland, Mississippi, DiSalvo joined the White Knights of the KKK in 1964 and once served as exalted cyclops of a klavern in Hancock County. In his capacity as a gun dealer, DiSalvo supplied firearms to fellow White Knights and members of the competing United Klans of America, including individuals later arrested for bombings around McComb, Mississippi. His efforts to recruit a Klan firing squad at Poplarville, with the blessings of Imperial Wizard Sam Bowers, prompted several White Knights to defect and join the United Klans. In September 1964, DiSalvo tried unsuccessfully to recruit other Klansmen for his scheme to dynamite a campaign train carrying President Lyndon Johnson's wife through Mississippi. Other activities on behalf of the White Knights included DiSalvo's private seminars on how to use venomous snakes as lethal weapons. In July 1965, DiSalvo appeared on the dais at a United Klans rally near Poplarville, and three months later he served as master of ceremonies for a United Klans rally at Bay St. Louis, Mississippi. At the time, he claimed to hold membership in the White Knights and the United Klans simultaneously. [38]

DISTEL, ALBERT

Father of Klansman and accused bomber Alexander Distel, Albert was arrested with four others in Pontiac, Michigan, on September 7, 1971, for causing racial disturbances at at school bus depot. [NYT 1971]

DIXIE BELLE LADIES CLUB

In 1965 congressional investigators identified this club as a front for the Sophia, North Carolina, ladies auxiliary, United Klans of America. [38]

DIXIE KLANS, KNIGHTS OF THE KU KLUX KLAN, INC.

The Dixie Klans traced its origins to the summer of 1957, when several Klansmen were expelled from Klavern No. 1 of the U.S. Klans in Chattanooga, Tennessee. Among the group of ousted knights were brothers Harry and Jack Brown, collectively the driving force behind a new group chartered in Tennessee on October 13, 1957. The group's small membership was concentrated around Chattanooga, but active klaverns were also reported in Anniston, Alabama, and in two counties of northwestern Georgia. Members of the Dixie Klans generally kept a low profile. The threat of a liberal Democrat's election, however, prompted the Klan to buy television time in November 1962. The same year saw the United Klans of America emerge as Tennessee's dominant racist group, and the Dixie Klansmen responded by joining seven other independent orders in a loose confederation chaired by James Venable, the so-called National Association of Ku Klux Klan. Jack Brown held the reins as imperial wizard until his death in the summer of 1965; within a year, successor Charles Roberts was discussing a merger of his 150 remaining members with the United Klans. Congressional investigators found that the Dixie Klans had grown so small by 1966 that none of its members were subpoenaed for its ongoing investigation of Ku Klux violence. The group soon disappeared. [10; 38]

DIXIE TRAVEL CLUB

In 1965 this group was publicly exposed as a front for the Mount Holly, North Carolina, klavern, United Klans of America. [38]

DIXON, THOMAS, JR.

Born in 1864 in North Carolina, Dixon was a classmate of Woodrow Wilson at Johns Hopkins University. Elected to the North Carolina state legislature before he reached voting age, Dixon soon resigned his post to enter the Baptist ministry, with financial backing from John D. Rockefeller. In later years, he authored two novels about Reconstruction, *The Leopard's Spots* (1902) and *The Clansman* (1905). The latter volume introduced the United States to the myth of Klan cross burning, a practice never witnessed during Reconstruction. Screen rights for *The Clansman* were sold in April

1914 for $2,500 and one fourth of the movie's profits. The story was filmed in 1915 and released as *Birth of a Nation*, a title suggested by Dixon after a preview showing in New York City. Initially proud of the new KKK, Dixon changed his tune after Klan violence and corruption were exposed in 1922, remarking to an interviewer: "There can be but one end to a secret order of disguised men. It will grow eventually into a reign of terror which only martial law will be able to put down." [10]

DIXON, W. LLOYD

According to testimony heard by congressional investigators, Dixon was a member of Klavern No. 297, U.S. Klans, and Clayton County Klavern No. 52, United Klans of America, while serving as sheriff of Clayton County from 1961 through 1964. Dixon left office on January 1, 1965, but he was still active in the United Klans klavern when congressional hearings convened ten months later. [38]

DIXON, T.C.

See *Dennis, Delmar.*

DOERFLER, REV. RAYMOND

Roy Frankhouser's replacement as grand dragon of Pennsylvania in the 1970s, Doerfler addressed Robert Scoggin's Conference of Eastern Dragons in 1976. In the same year, he was publicly associated with William Chaney's Confederation of Independent Orders, greeting Klansmen at one rally as "fellow terrorists." Around the same time, Doerfler persuaded Klansman Jimmy Mitchell to infiltrate the Anti-Defamation League of B'nai B'rith, reporting back to the Klan on their activities. [84]

DOLLAR, WILLIAM

A deputy sheriff during Reconstruction in Monticello, Arkansas. In October 1868, Dollar was taken from his home by Klansmen with a rope tied around his neck and with Fred Reeves, a black man, bound at the other end. They were marched 300 yards from Dollar's house, where they were shot and killed, their bodies tied in an embrace and left there for two days as a spectacle for the curious. [87]

DOMINICA

A Caribbean island nation, Dominica became the target of a plot involving Klansmen in the spring of 1981. The scheme originated with deposed Domincan prime minister Patrick John and one of his U.S. contacts, Texas mercenary Mike Perdue. Klansmen and neo-Nazis were recruited for the venture with a promise that the new regime would shelter right-wing fugitives and grant them land for the establishment of an international training facility. The plot hit a snag when two merchant seaman, hired by the conspirators to transport supplies, turned out to be agents of the U.S. Treasury Department. The ten men arrested at Slidell, Louisiana, in April 1981, were charged with violating the Neutrality Act, and included Stephen Donald Black, successor to David Duke as leader of the Knights of the KKK; Joe Daniel Hawkins, a longtime Mississippi Klansman; former neo-Nazi William Prichard, Jr.; and Wolfgang Droege, a Canadian Klansman linked to the extremist Western Front. The defendants were convicted and sentenced to three years imprisonment in a case that *Time* magazine referred to as the "Bayou of Pigs." [93]

DOMINION

According to the prescript of the Reconstruction KKK, a dominion was equivalent to a state congressional district, with Klan business supervised therein by an officer dubbed the grand titan. In modern Ku Klux jargon, the term has been replaced with "province," carrying a flexible—but often identical—definition. [38]

DOMMER, PAUL

Arrested with William Hoff on August 26, 1968, after giving an undercover officer a can of TNT to blast the home of a draft resistance leader in New York City, Dommer was charged with plotting to kill 158 "leftists" and civil rights activists. Both defendants had been frequently linked to meetings with leaders of the Klan, the National States Rights Party, the American Nazi Party, and the Minutemen. Dommer pled guilty to third-degree conspiracy in February 1969. [*NYT* 1969]

DONALD, MICHAEL

A black teenager in Mobile, Alabama, Donald was abducted on the street by Klansmen in March 1981, and then beaten, strangled to death, his throat slashed, with his body left hanging from a tree. Authorities began their search for suspects just across the street, where Klansman Henry Francis Hays occupied an apartment overlooking the crime scene. Another Klansman, James ("Tiger") Knowles, was charged with the slaying and entered a plea of guilty, receiving a life sentence in return for his promise of testimony against other participants. As Knowles said of Donald, "We didn't know him. We just wanted to show Klan strength in Alabama." Henry Hays was convicted on the basis of Knowles's testimony in February 1984, and was sentenced to death by the judge despite a jury recommendation of life without parole. The defendant's father, Bennie Jack Hays—identified as the highest ranking member of the United Klans in southern Alabama—was indicted for Donald's murder in August 1987, along with Mobile Exalted Cyclops Benjamin Franklin Cox. A mistrial was declared for both defendants in February 1988, on the basis of Hays' poor health, but Cox was retried and convicted of murder in May 1989. Meanwhile, a federal jury awarded Donald's mother $7 million in damages, to be paid by the nearly destitute United Klans and six individual Klansmen. In lieu of the nonexistent cash, Donald's family took possession of the United Klans headquarters and land in Tuscaloosa, selling the nine-year-old building to satisfy a small portion of the Klan's debt. [NYT 1981–1989]

DONALSONVILLE LODGE NO. 3

In 1965 congressional investigators identified this lodge as a front for the Donalsonville, Georgia, klavern, United Klans of America. [38]

DORMAN, MICHAEL

A reporter for Newsday during the 1963 integration crisis at the University of Alabama, Dorman uncovered and published the story of Governor George Wallace's military discharge on grounds of mental disability. A short time later, two strangers began following Dorman around Tuscaloosa; a U.S. marshal identified them as members of the United Klans of America, warning Dorman that his life might be in danger. United Klans Imperial Wizard Robert Shelton subsequently tried to pick a fight with Dorman at the local Stafford Hotel, but bystanders separated the men before anyone was injured. [17; 18]

DORMER, WILLIAM

A Klansman, karate enthusiast, and past president of a motorcycle gang in Aurora, Illinois, Dormer participated in a May 1975 organizational meeting of the United Klans of America, held at the Kankakee Ramada Inn. Dormer's prior associations include an intimate friendship with a drug dealer killed by agents of the Illinois Bureau of Investigation. Following that incident, Dormer reportedly swore vengeance on the agents involved, but he was subsequently distracted by Klan activities around Aurora. [43]

DORR, DAVID

Bud Cutler's replacement as Idaho security chief of the Aryan Nations in 1985, Dorr was one of several members jailed a year later in connection with bombings around Coeur d'Alene. [NYT 1986]

DORSETT, GEORGE FRANKLIN

A Greensboro, North Carolina, house painter, Dorsett was elected imperial kludd at the 1964 national convention of the United Klans of America. Also serving as North Carolina's titan and as chaplain for the United Klans security guard, Dorsett was fond of telling rallies that the "message of Christian love is a tool in communist hands." In 1965 Dorsett was transferred to Florida, joining kleagle Boyd Hamby in establishing a new

United Klans headquarters in Titusville. Banished by Imperial Wizard Robert Shelton on April 4, 1966, for allegedly disclosing "secret information" on the Klan, Dorsett surfaced days later at another United Klans rally, where his car was rocked and pelted with stones by the crowd. A secret FBI informant, Dorsett secured federal backing when he and James Cole organized the Confederate Knights of the KKK in 1967. Moving on to join the North Carolina Knights, Dorsett was finally exposed as an FBI plant in 1975. On January 12, 1976, the North Carolina state board of the United Klans belatedly issued a notice of exile on Dorsett, with members voting nine to one in favor of his banishment "forever." [NYT 1966, 1976; 84]

DOUGLAS SPORTSMAN CLUB

In 1965 congressional investigators identified this group as a cover for Clarendon County, South Carolina, Unit No. 34, United Klans of America. [38]

DOVE, OSCAR

A black mortician and NAACP member in New Bern, North Carolina, Dove was active in civil rights work around Craven County in the early 1960s. On January 24, 1965, his funeral home was one of three local targets damaged in racial bombings. Three members of the Craven County Improvement Association, a front for the United Klans of America, pled guilty in the bombings and received suspended sentences. [38]

DOVER COMMUNITY CLUB

A 1960s front for the Dover, North Carolina, klavern, United Klans of America, this group was publicly exposed by federal investigators in 1965. [38]

DOWNS, TOMMY

An Alabama Klansman who was sentenced to federal prison in 1983 for his role in torching the Southern Poverty Law Center's office in Montgomery, Downs was also linked with a 1983 cross burning at the home of a black Montgomery County commissioner. [NYT 1983]

DRAGER, FRANK

A resident of Trenton, New Jersey, and that state's grand dragon in the 1960s, Drager was arrested in September 1973 for purchasing a gun without a permit. On November 6, 1976, he was sentenced to six months in jail. [NYT 1976]

DRAKE, C.L.

As the mayor of Iron City, Georgia, Drake was a staunch opponent of the post-World War II Klan. On July 17, 1949, eight carloads of armed Klansmen approached his home, but they were driven off by gunfire. Grand Dragon Samuel Green denied responsibility for the attack, and blamed a rival faction based in Columbus, Georgia. On the night of August 6, 1949, Drake and a posse of friends exchanged shots with a caravan of sixteen Klan vehicles, wounding one of the raiders. Florida Klansman Bill Hendrix visited a local justice of the peace to file charges against Drake for disturbing the peace, but he fled across the border to Dothan, Alabama, when Drake and his friends arrived, seeking "protection" in the Dothan police station. Undaunted, Drake followed Hendrix into Alabama and had him arrested, publicly identifying Hendrix as the leader of the latest motorcade. [NYT 1949]

DRAKE, CLINTON

A black Union veteran in Tennessee, Drake was taken from his home in 1868 and lynched by Klansmen, who threatened to do the same to all other Unionists. [87]

DRAPER HUNTING CLUB

In 1966 congressional investigators identified this club as a front for the Leadsville, North Carolina, klavern, United Klans of America. [38]

DRENNAN, DR. STANLEY L.

Identified as a leader of the National States Rights Party in North Hollywood, California, in the 1960s, Drennan was active with army Captain Robert Brown and others in covert campaigns against Fidel Castro. According to FBI reports filed in December 1963, Drennan once told Brown that "what the organization needed was a group of young men to get rid of [President John F.] Kennedy, the Cabinet, and all the members of the Americans for Democratic Action, and maybe ten thousand other people." According to the FBI, Brown "gained the impression that Drennan may have been propositioning him on this matter." Possible connections between the National States Rights Party and Kennedy's assassination were not pursued by the Warren Commission prior to the issuance of its "lone assassin" report. [90]

DRENNAN, WILLIAM

A resident of Houston, Texas, Drennan was appointed as state representative for the United Klans of America in August 1965, thereafter competing with kleagle George Otto for the disputed title of acting grand dragon. When

Imperial Wizard Robert Shelton visited Texas a month later, he found the tiny membership split between factions supporting Drennan and Otto. Drennan's followers were not represented when the Texas realm was finally chartered on December 11, 1965. [38]

DRENNON, THOMAS M.

A blacksmith, wagonmaker, and active Republican during Reconstruction in Georgia, Drennon was visited by Klansmen on February 6, 1871, at his home outside of Rome. He talked his way out of a whipping by denying sympathy with the Republican party's radical wing. [87]

DROEGE, WALTER WOLFGANG

Identified as a leader of the Canadian Knights of the KKK in British Columbia, Droege actively sought recruits in Toronto during June 1980. In April 1981, he was one of ten men arrested for plotting an invasion of Dominica. Convicted with Klansmen Stephen Black, Joe Hawkins, and others, Droege was sentenced to three years in prison for violating the Neutrality Act. In February 1985, Droege pled guilty to federal drug, weapons, and illegal alien charges, drawing a new prison term of thirteen years. [NYT 1980, 1985; 2]

DUBACH HUNTING & FISHING CLUB

In 1965 congressional investigators identified this club as a front for the Dubach, Louisiana, klavern, United Klans of America. [38]

DuBOIS, JOSEPH G.

While serving as klabee of a Goldsboro, North Carolina, klavern, United Klans of America, DuBois appeared as the first cooperative witness in a probe of Klan violence by the House Un-American Activities Committee. Testifying on October 22, 1965, he resigned from the United Klans on the witness stand, and delivered Klan records to the committee. Disillusioned by the refusal of United Klans leaders to answer the Committee's questions, DuBois told the panel, "Anyone who takes the Fifth Amendment either has something to hide, or is a communist." Following his testimony, DuBois received several anonymous death threats. [NYT 1965]

DuBOSE, DUDLEY M.

An ex-Confederate general, DuBose also served as grand titan of the 5th Congressional District in Georgia during Reconstruction, which included some of the more violence-plagued counties in the state. A son-in-law of antebellum Senator Robert Toombs, DuBose was himself elected to Congress in 1870, with support from his fellow Klansmen. [87]

DUCK CLUB

A nationwide anti-Semitic movement founded by Florida millionaire Robert White in the late 1970s, the Duck Club draws its title from a speech by the late Senator Joe McCarthy, who once advised his followers on the method of spotting a secret communist: "If it looks like a duck and walks like a duck and flies like a duck and quacks like a duck, then it's probably a duck." In 1985, Seattle Duck Club member David Lewis Rice celebrated Christmas Eve by slaughtering four members of the Goldmark family, believing he had killed the "head Jew" and "top communist" in the Pacific Northwest. (In fact, the Goldmarks were Protestants.) At the time of Rice's trial and ultimate conviction, Robert White claimed to have 1,000 chapters of his organization from coast to coast. [13]

DUCKWORTH, KALEY

A black resident of Hattiesburg, Mississippi, active in the NAACP and Project Head Start, Duckworth stood guard at the home of a local NAACP leader after nightrider attacks in February 1968. On May 15, 1968, Duckworth was injured by a bomb wired to the horn of his car. Klansmen were suspected in the case, but never prosecuted. [NYT 1968]

DUDLEY, WILLIE

A black laborer in Gordon, Georgia, Dudley was abducted from his job at the P.W. Martin Clay Company by four masked Klansmen in the predawn hours of June 9, 1946. Ordered to sign a letter of resignation from the United Cement, Lime and Gypsum Workers union, Dudley was beaten with rubber hoses when he refused, then threatened with death to insure his silence before releasing him. [NYT 1946]

DUGDEMONICE HUNTING CLUB

In 1965 congressional investigators identified this group as a cover for the Jonesboro, Louisiana, klavern, United Klans of America. [38]

DUKE, DAN

As Georgia's state attorney general, Duke prosecuted Atlanta Klansmen accused of flogging in 1940, sending eight Klansmen to prison. In December 1941, he publicly clashed with Governor Eugene Talmadge over Talmadge's decision to pardon the defendants, a move that proceeded despite protests from churches and newspapers. Duke served with the marines in World War II and returned to his job after the war. In 1946, he spearheaded moves against the Association of Georgia Klans, calling it "the ragtag and bobtail of the old order." He also prosecuted the Columbians, Inc., calling them the "juvenile delinquents of the Klan." Seeking revocation of the Klan's state charter under Governor Ellis Arnall, Duke told reporters, "The Klan contains the germs of an American Gestapo." [10; 93]

DUKE, DAVID ERNEST

Born of affluent middle-class parents in Tulsa, Oklahoma, Duke attended elementary school in the Netherlands before moving on to a private academy in Georgia. His parents settled in New Orleans in the 1960s, where Duke graduated from high school. Entering Louisiana State University in 1968, he organized the White Youth Alliance (later rechristened the National Party) a year later, recruiting members on several college campuses. Working in open cooperation with James Warner's National Socialist White People's Party, Duke donned a Nazi-style uniform and took up a picket sign—GAS THE CHICAGO SEVEN—to protest a 1969 appearance by attorney William Kunstler at Tulane University. During the 1971-1972 school year, Duke's National Party was accused of fomenting racial tension at two New Orleans high schools. Duke and two of his followers were arrested in January 1972 for manufacturing Molotov cocktails; six months later, while collecting money for the George Wallace presidential campaign, Duke and several others were again jailed on charges of theft by fraud and contributing to the delinquency of a minor. By 1973, Duke was listed as national information director and Louisiana grand dragon for the Knights of the KKK. Duke's graduation from LSU with a degree in history was delayed until 1974 due to a year's hiatus from study, during which he served the U.S. State Department teaching English to native officers in Laos. When white Bostonians rioted against court-ordered busing to integrate schools in September 1974, Duke was on hand to harangue angry crowds. His audience responded by spray painting walls in South Boston with graffiti reading "This is Klan Country." In the same year, Duke and a colleague appeared before the judiciary committee of the Louisiana House, denouncing a proposed anti-discrimination bill that subsequently died in committee. Taking over control of the Knights when its founder was murdered in June 1975, Duke dropped the imperial wizard title to call himself the Klan's national director. (Around the same time, he was named an honorary colonel in the Alabama state militia under Governor Wallace, as a reward for past support.) In a typical speech to his Klansmen, Duke proclaimed, "We say give us liberty and give them [blacks] death. There's times I've felt like picking up a gun and going shooting a nigger. We've got a heritage to protect. We're going to do everything to protect our race." At the same time, he sought an appearance of distance from older, established Klans, seeking to recruit "other intellectuals." At Duke's Klan rallies, "The Old Rugged Cross" was replaced by rock bands and bluegrass music, while Catholics were welcomed into the fold and the Knights freely promoted women into leadership positions. (Duke's wife, Chloe, served as grand geni for the Knights.) The new approach brought marginal success by 1975, with Duke hosting the nation's largest Klan rally in a decade—2,700 persons in attendance—in Walker, Louisiana. Managing his own advertising agency on the side, Duke ran for the Louisiana state senate that year, polling 11,079 votes, or one third of all ballots cast. Also in 1975, he met with James Warner, Robert DePugh, Robert Shelton, and other leaders of far-right organizations for a covert strategy session in Kansas City. Arrested September 13, 1976, following a scuffle with deputies in Metairie, Louisiana, Duke was charged with inciting a riot. Three months later, on December 7, he was mobbed by hostile pickets while visiting Klansmen on the Marine Corps base at Camp Pendleton, California. Defeated in another race for the Louisiana state senate in 1979, Duke saw his Klan membership wither to an estimated 1,000 by 1980. On July 21, 1980, Duke and rival Klan leader Bill Wilkinson met for a secret discussion attended by Klansmen Stephen Donald Black, T.A. Brown, and Roger Handley. Duke offered Wilkinson a deal: his own resignation as leader of the Knights, delivery of Duke's mailing list (with 3,000 names), and public recognition of Wilkinson as the "most effective and capable" Klan leader in the United States. In return, Duke would receive $35,000 and Wilkinson's promise to refrain from creating any non-KKK groups in the future. Wilkinson flatly rejected the offer, accusing Duke of selling out his followers for cash; Duke responded by calling Wilkinson a "dishonorable liar," but their conversation had been taped for posterity, and Duke's days as a Klansman were numbered. On July 24, 1980, Duke announced his resignation from the Knights, together with creation of a new National Association for the Advancement of White People. As Duke described the NAAWP in interviews, "It would be more of a racialist movement, more of a high-class thing, mainly upper-middle-class people." In September 1982, Duke participated in ceremonies in Stone Mountain, Georgia, heralding the foundation of the Confederation of Klans, theoretically uniting seven factions led by Robert Miles, Don Black, James Venable, Edward Fields, and others. In January 1989, Duke astounded critics by winning a Republican primary race for the Louisiana House in Metairie, a suburb of New Orleans. Republican leaders, including President Ronald Reagan and Vice President George Bush, denounced Duke's candidacy, but he managed a narrow 227 vote victory in the February election, despite the withdrawal of party support. Sworn in on February 22 following unsuccessful challenges to his election, Duke told the press, "I repudiate any racial or religious intolerance. Any group—racial or religious—has nothing to fear from David Duke." Eight days later, Duke was foiled in his first official action, attempting to defeat a minority set-aside program on grounds that it would discriminate against "the more qualified white contractors" in state hiring. [NYT 1989; 2; 84; 93]

DUNAWAY, HILTON

A member of the McComb, Mississippi, klavern, United Klans of America, Dunaway was identified by federal agents as one of four Klansmen who bombed Charles Bryant's home on July 26, 1964. [38]

DUNAWAY, HULON

The grandson of a Reconstruction Klansman, Dunaway joined the KKK in the early 1960s, swiftly rising to the rank of kleagle. He helped organize the Original Knights of the Ku Klux Klan in Louisiana during 1963, and two years later he was named in a federal injunction barring violence against blacks around Bogalusa. Dropping out of the Klan in 1969, Dunaway rejoined when Bill Wilkinson opened a klavern of his new Invisible Empire at Bogalusa in the spring of 1976. [84]

DUNCAN, DR. AMOS

Duncan served as North Carolina's grand dragon during the Great Depression, under Imperial Wizard James Colescott. [10]

DUNCAN, MURPHY JOHN, JR.

Federal agents have identified Duncan as one of three Klansmen responsible for burning the black Sweet Home Missionary Baptist Church near McComb, Mississippi, on July 18, 1964. At the time, Duncan served as klabee for Ray Smith's local klavern, United Klans of America, and he was later named grand klabee for the Mississippi realm. In September 1964, Duncan was a delegate to the United Klans national klonvocation in Birmingham, Alabama. [38]

DUNLAP, J.C.

The "carpetbag" teacher at a black school in Shelbyville, Tennessee, during Reconstruction, Dunlap received 200 lashes from Klansmen on July 4, 1868, along with a threat of being burned at the stake if he did not leave town. The attack turned local sentiment against the Klan, but nightriding continued. One night in early January 1869, a group of twenty-five to thirty Klansmen rode into Shelbyville, calling for "Dunlap and fried nigger meat," but they retreated when Dunlap and friends opened fire, killing one member of the party. Local Unionists threatened dire reprisals against conservatives if Dunlap was further harassed, and Klansmen afterward left him in peace. [87]

DUNN, BURRIS, JR.

See *Blackwell Real Estate.*

DUNN, EDWARD

Identified as co-chairman of the Security Services Action Group, a neo-Nazi faction based in Michigan, Dunn has cooperated with the KKK in demonstrations around Detroit and elsewhere. With other members of the S.S.

Action Group, he has attended cross burning ceremonies at a farm owned by ex-Klansman and convicted bomber Robert Miles, in Howell, Michigan. [2]

DUNNING, M.O.

A ranking Georgia Klansman in the 1920s, Dunning led the state's knights in backing Calvin Coolidge against Democrat John Davis in the 1924 presidential election. His reward from the White House was an appointment as federal collector of customs for the port of Savannah. [10]

DUPES, NED

A resident of Knoxville, Tennessee, Dupes was identified as secretary-treasurer of the National States Rights Party in 1962. [14]

DUPREE, JACK

The president of a black Republican club in Monroe County, Mississippi, during Reconstruction, Dupree was taken from his home and whipped by Klansmen in 1871. Unsatisfied with the punishment administered in Dupree's front yard, the raiders carried him into the woods several miles from the scene, and there beat him a second time before disemboweling him. [87]

DURHAM, PLATO

An ex-Confederate officer, Durham also served as a ranking Klansman during Reconstruction in Cleveland County, North Carolina. In March 1871, he secretly conferred with Democratic leaders in violence-plagued Rutherford County, seeking unsuccessfully a means to reduce Klan nightriding. [87]

DUTTON, JERRY

A Georgia native, Dutton organized the Knights of the Confederacy while still in school. He moved to Birmingham, where he joined the National States Rights Party and was one of eight members indicted on September 23, 1963, for violent interference with school desegregation. Eight years later, Dutton surfaced as grand wizard of the Knights of the Ku Klux Klan, under national director David Duke. Visiting Denver, Colorado, on October 9, 1976, he was summoned to the office of District Attorney Dale Tooley and was informed that Dutton and the KKK were unwelcome in Denver. (The American Civil Liberties Union supported his protest against the illegal ban.) Dutton left the Knights in 1977, after James Warner accused him of trying to steal the group's mailing list, putting the Klan's post office box in his own name, and trying to siphon off cash from the Patriot Press for his personal use. Undaunted by the charges, Dutton went on to affiliate himself with Bill Wilkinson's competing Invisible Empire. [FOF 1963; NYT 1976; 84]

DUVAL FELLOWSHIP CLUB

Identified as a front group for Jacksonville Klavern No. 502 of the United Florida Ku Klux Klan, the Duval Fellowship Club sponsored a local appearance by ex-Klansman and longtime neo-Nazi George Deatherage in 1960. That August, members were linked to anti-black riots on "Ax Handle Saturday," and the klavern nurtured a reputation for violent words translated into action. Transient agitator Connie Lynch was a registered member in 1962, and he returned for several meetings in the latter part of 1965. In the spring of that year, dissatisfied members defected to form their own Militant Knights of the KKK under Imperial Wizard Donald Ballentine. [10; 38]

DUVALL, JOHN

Elected mayor of Indianapolis with Klan backing in the early 1920s, Duvall signed a secret pledge reading: "In return for the political support of [grand dragon] D.C. Stephenson, in the event that I am elected Mayor of Indianapolis, Indiana, I promise not to appoint any person as a member of the board of public works without they first have the endorsement of D.C. Stephenson. I fully agree and promise to appoint Claude Worley as Chief of Police and Earl Klinck as a captain." Exposure of the pledge, following Stephenson's murder trial in 1925, produced a political firestorm in Indianapolis. [93]

DYNAMITE HILL

A disputed neighborhood of Birmingham, Alabama, where the Klan believed blacks to be encroaching on white residents in the 1950s and 1960s, Dynamite Hill was so nicknamed for the frequency of bombings aimed at black homes and churches. At least twenty-eight racial bombings were recorded in Birmingham between December 1956 and October 1963, but Commissioner "Bull" Connor's police managed to solve only one—when Klansmen were captured by blacks at the scene. [NYT 1963]

E

EAGER, SCIPIO

A black Republican during Reconstruction in Washington County, Georgia, Eager was abducted from his home and flogged by Klansmen in April 1871. One of Eager's brothers, described by Klansmen as "too big a man" because he could read and write, was shot and killed in the same attack. Klansmen returned to kill Eager in July 1871, but he hid in the woods and from there watched the nightriders ransack his house. Following the July attack, Eager fled to Atlanta and there found sanctuary. [87]

EARLE, JOSHUA F.

An ex-Confederate officer and prominent Democrat in Crittenden County, Arkansas, during Reconstruction, Earle was also recognized as the leader of the local KKK. When Governor Powell Clayton declared martial law and unleashed his militia on the Klan in November 1868, Earle fled to Memphis, but Tennessee's governor approved his extradition in February 1869. A letter found on Earle at the time of his arrest was addressed to Crittenden County Klansmen, calling on them to disband. [87]

EARLY LODGE NO. 35

In 1965 congressional investigators identified this lodge as a front for the Blakely, Georgia, klavern, United Klans of America. [38]

EAST HILLSBOROUGH SPORTSMAN'S CLUB

A 1960s cover for the Plant City, Florida, klavern of the United Florida Ku Klux Klan, this group was exposed by federal investigators in 1966. [38]

EAST SIDE FELLOWSHIP CLUB

In 1965 the House Un-American Activities Committee identified this club as the front for a Fayetteville, North Carolina, klavern, United Klans of America. [38]

EASTERN TRIANGLE LADIES LEAGUE

A 1967 congressional report identified this group as a front for the Raleigh, North Carolina, ladies auxiliary, United Klans of America. [38]

EATON, WILLIAM ORVILLE

A former steelworker and member of the Bessemer, Alabama, Klavern No. 20, United Klans of America, Eaton was one of three Klansmen charged with the March 1965 murder of civil rights activist Viola Liuzzo. With codefendants Eugene Thomas and Collie Leroy Wilkins, Eaton was also linked to bombings and other acts of violence perpetrated by the United Klans during a bitter strike at the W.S. Dickey Clay Manufacturing Company, outside of Bessemer. In September 1965, Eaton withdrew his son from Bessemer High School after the school was desegregated by court order. Three months later, on December 3, he was convicted of civil rights violations in the Liuzzo case and sentenced to ten years in prison. A heart attack claimed Eaton's life on March 10, 1966, while his appeal of the conviction was in progress. [NYT 1965–1966; 38]

ECHLIN, RAYMOND

In November 1980, Echlin and two other Michigan Klansmen pled guilty to shooting a black man who patronized a "white" Detroit tavern. Echlin received a prison term of one to four years. [NYT 1980]

ECHO VALLEY CLUB

In 1965 congressional investigators identified this group as a cover for the Oconee, South Carolina, klavern, United Klans of America. [38]

EDGE, JOHN

See *Peterson, Jim.*

EDMOND, STEVE

See *Grainger, Ben; Johnson, Woodrow.*

EDWARDS, CHARLES

A policeman from Grimesland, North Carolina, Edwards was identified in

January 1966 as an officer in the United Klans of America. According to congressional investigators, Edwards was responsible for sending Klansmen in August 1965 to Plymouth, North Carolina, during civil rights demonstrations there that led to violent assaults on black protesters. [38]

EDWARDS, CHARLES MARCUS

See *Dee, Henry*.

EDWARDS, ELDON LEE

A resident of College Park, Georgia, Edwards worked as a paint sprayer at the General Motors Fisher Body Plant in Atlanta before devoting his life full-time to the KKK. In 1953, he gathered remnants of the old Association of Georgia Klans into a new U.S. Klans, publishing and copyrighting a revised version of the Kloran authored by William Simmons in 1915. Recruitment was sluggish until Black Monday, and Edwards formally chartered the U.S. Klans in October 1955. Two months later, on December 27, he was jailed in Atlanta for drunk driving, disorderly conduct, assaulting an officer, and resisting arrest. The latter charges were dismissed, and Edwards had only a $50 fine to pay. Called as a defense witness at the George Bright bombing trial in 1958, Edwards was clearly the nation's preeminent Klansman, with an estimated 15,000 followers in ten states. He died of a heart attack on August 1, 1960, at age fifty-one. Robert "Wild Bill" Davidson inherited the wizard's robes, but bitter arguments with Edwards's widow produced a rift that doomed the U.S. Klans in 1961, propelling Davidson, Calvin Craig, and others into formation of the United Klans of America. [10; 93]

EDWARDS, JAMES MALCOLM

Elected as Louisiana grand dragon for the United Klans of America in 1964, Edwards presided over the realm's greatest period of growth. In 1965, he addressed a letter to the House Un-American Activities Committee, urging its chairman "to investigate the United Klans and make your findings public as soon as possible." Presumably, Edwards believed an investigation would clear the Klan's name, but his superiors felt otherwise. In December 1965, shortly before his own congressional testimony, Edwards was removed from office and replaced by ex-grand klaliff Jack Helm. [38]

EDWARDS, HENRY

See *Johnson, Woodrow*.

EDWARDS, WILLIE

A black resident of Montgomery, Alabama, Edwards disappeared from his job as a grocery deliveryman on January 22, 1957; three months later, his body was pulled from the Alabama River, twenty miles downstream. Suspected of "annoying white women," Edwards had been kidnapped from his route by Klansmen and forced to leap from a bridge at gunpoint in an execution Klansmen later described as a case of "mistaken identity." Authorities took no action in the case until February 1976, when state attorney general William Baxley filed murder charges against Klansmen Sonny Livingston, James York, and Henry Alexander. Eyewitness Raymond Britt had turned state's evidence, describing how he and his fellow Klansmen— all indicted for bombings that occurred during the 1950s Montgomery bus boycott—abducted Edwards, beat him as they "interrogated" him, and finally forced him to jump from the bridge when he denied their accusations. Charges were dismissed against the three defendants on April 14, 1976, when a judge ruled that no cause of death was stated in the indictment, making a murder charge legally insupportable. Baxley planned to seek new indictments, but the case fell apart on June 1, when Britt announced he had been wrong in naming Livingston as one of Edwards's killers. [NYT 1976]

EDWARDS, XAVIER

As a kleagle for the United Klans of America, Edwards began organizing the Maryland realm in August 1965, soon after an inspirational rally in neighboring Delaware. Early in 1966, Edwards was linked to the harassment of Robert Lee's left-wing New Era Bookshop in Laurel, Maryland, telling reporters: "Wherever the store goes, they can expect to find the Ku Klux Klan." If and when Lee closed his shop, Edwards planned to direct his attentions toward Jewish merchants in the area. On March 27, 1966, after a weekend of cross burning incidents, Edwards announced his resignation from the United Klans, saying that he feared the Klan was turning toward violence and he wanted no part of criminal activity. United Klans leaders responded with charges that Edwards was banished for fraternizing with members of the American Nazi Party and recruiting them into the Klan. In either case, the defection of his loyal supporters split the tiny realm, with Edwards founding his own Maryland Knights of the KKK—also known as the Interstate Knights of the KKK—in Laurel. His stint as a Klan leader was short lived, and by the time journalist Patsy Sims interviewed leaders of the Maryland Knights in 1977, Edwards had faded from the scene. [NYT 1966; 38]

EFFINGER, V.F.

An electrical contractor from Lima, Ohio, and a high-ranking Klansman as late as 1931, Effinger took command of the rival Black Legion when that group expanded from its original base in the Detroit suburbs. [10]

EIDSON, HERB

A deputy sheriff in Fulton County, Georgia, Eidson was also a Klansman who participated in numerous floggings in 1939 and 1940. One of the eight floggers—including three deputies—convicted by state attorney general Dan Duke in 1940, Eidson was pardoned by Governor Eugene Talmadge and released from prison a year later. [93]

EILBECK, IVAN

A resident of Apopka, Florida, Eilbeck was snatched from his home in the summer of 1950 and beaten by a party of Klansmen that included Robert Juday and Harvey Reisner. [NYT 1953]

ELDUAYAN, FIDEL

A Mexican rancher in Inglewood, California, Elduayan was fingered by Klansmen as a bootlegger in 1922. Raiding his home one night, Klansmen bound Fidel and his brother, and they searched for a jailer willing to accept their prisoners. Meanwhile, a neighbor had reported the disturbance, and a marshal arrived on the scene. Gunfire erupted when the Klansmen refused to surrender their prisoners, and the marshal was forced to retreat after killing one raider (a local constable) and wounding two others (the constable's son and a deputy sheriff). The Elduayan brothers were released later that night, and the resultant investigation led to raid on Klan headquarters in Los Angeles, with the seizure of state records and the arrest of Grand Goblin William Coburn. The Los Angeles city council passed a strong anti-mask law, and a grand jury subpoenaed Klansmen listed on the membership rolls. In June 1922, Coburn and thirty-six others were indicted for kidnapping with intent to murder. At their trial, the presiding judge—who had opposed investigation of the Klan from the beginning—ordered jurors to acquit the defendants if they that determined the raiders were led by a policeman in pursuit of lawbreakers. The Klansmen were duly exonerated, stopping by the judge's chambers to pick up his campaign literature before leaving the courthouse. [10]

ELLINGTON, CLARENCE

A black insurance salesman from South Carolina, Ellington was driving through Colbert, Georgia, when Klansmen fired shotguns at his car on July 10, 1964. Lemuel Penn was killed in a similar incident the following day. [NYT 1964]

ELLINGTON, DOYLE

A resident of Brownsville, Texas, Ellington was identified in 1968 as grand dragon for the Texas realm, United Klans of America. [31]

ELLIS, DR. A.D.

An Episcopal minister in Beaumont, Texas, Ellis was also the first grand dragon of the modern Texas realm, elected in 1922. His klavern was the first in Texas to make headlines with floggings and other acts of violence, including tar and feather "parties." (One of their victims included a local doctor accused of performing abortions.) Bad publicity, however, soon forced imperial headquarters in Atlanta to lift the Beaumont klavern's charter. [10]

ELLIS, CLAIBORNE P.

As exalted cyclops of the Durham, North Carolina, klavern, United Klans of America, C.P. Ellis was a study in contradictions. Soon after his election in the early 1970s, he began to resent the Klan's role as a tool of wealthy whites, used by the local establishment to counteract black progress. "We would show up with our guns in our belts," Ellis told an interviewer, "and the next day I would see the same city official on the street and expect him to come up and thank me. And instead, he would cross to the other side of the street to keep from meeting me. I found out that we were being used to keep those folks in power. And I decided we weren't going to be used any more." Ellis encouraged his Klansmen to participate openly in politics, presenting a Klan position on public issues. Convinced that blacks and poor white children faced identical discrimination from "liberal" teachers in Durham's schools, Ellis won support from several influential blacks in his unsuccessful 1972 campaign for a seat on the school board. Excluded from United Klans state klonvocations in 1972 and 1973, the rebellious cyclops hung onto his office with support from Klansmen who shared his view of wealthy white merchants as the chief enemies of both blacks and blue-collar whites. Late in 1972, Ellis was invited to join the Durham Human Relations Commission, a move that he described as an attempt to coopt his leadership, using the Klan influence to neutralize blacks on the panel, but Ellis confounded his critics by siding with blacks to oppose housing discrimination. "I turned on them that put me there," he said, "and now they don't know what to do with me." By 1973, still clinging to his Klan office and his seat on the commission, Ellis also emerged as a leader of the International Union of Operating Engineers, representing service workers at Duke University. [57]

ELLISON, JIM

See *Covenant, the Sword, and the Arm of the Lord.*

ELLISON, VIOLA

One of four black women shot and wounded by Klansman Marshall Thrash in Chattanooga, Tennessee, on April 19, 1980, Ellison survived and pressed charges against her assailant. [*AP*, April 20, 1980]

ELROD, MILTON

As editor of *Fiery Cross* and an itinerant troubleshooter for the midwestern Klan in the 1920s, Elrod also served as a member of the KKK strategy board at the 1924 Democratic convention in New York City. [10]

ELWOOD, CHARLES

A resident of Camden, South Carolina, Elwood was identified as grand klabee of the South Carolina realm, United Klans of America. Summoned before the House Un-American Activities Committee in October 1965, he refused to answer any questions on the grounds of possible self-incrimination. [38]

EMMONS, PAT

As exalted cyclops of the South Bend, Indiana, klavern under Grand Dragon D.C. Stephenson, Emmons was cut adrift when Stephenson's feud with Imperial Wizard Hiram Evans divided the Indiana realm. In the later 1920s, Emmons moved to Canada, recruiting Klansmen there without much success. [10]

EMRY, SHELDON

A native of Minneapolis, Minnesota, Emry first drew public attention in 1962, as chairman of the Twin Cities Committee to Warn of the Arrival of Communist Merchandise on the Local Business Scene. Transplanted to Arizona in the mid-1960s, Emry founded the Lord's Covenant Church, considered an integral part of the modern Identity movement. In addition to his church activities and broadcasts of the "America's Promise" radio program, Emry is also linked with the Citizens Emergency Defense System, created by John Harrell, founder of the Christian-Patriots Defense League. [2]

ENGLAND

The KKK made its first appearance in England during April 1957, with widespread rumors of pamphleteering and recruitment campaigns. Within a month, Scotland Yard reported that it was keeping tabs on sympathizers who had organized klatsches in Birmingham, Liverpool, Fleetwood, Southend, Bishop's Castle, and the London workers' suburbs of Kilburn and Brixton. Police estimated that there might be 1,000 Klansmen in England, affiliated with Horace Miller's Aryan Knights of the KKK of

Waco, Texas. Alarmed by the influx of 30,000 nonwhite immigrants per year, British Klansmen wrote menacing letters to landlords of minority tenants and tried, with little success, to organize boycotts of nonwhite merchants. The movement had almost disappeared by April 1965, when Imperial Wizard Robert Shelton visited London and predicted a Klan resurgence. On June 7, 1965, a cross was burned at the home of an Indian immigrant in Birmingham, and the Klan's first public meeting was held six days later, disrupted by a Birmingham pub owner who regretted renting his upstairs room to Klansmen. Before the meeting was dispersed, Klansman George Newey addressed a group of thirteen men and three women, promising that the Klan would "rid this country of filthy niggers." On the same day, a cross was burned at the home of a Pakistani merchant in East London, with others reported at the homes of colored immigrants around the city. Active dens were reported by authorities in London, Birmingham, Manchester, Liverpool, and Leicester. A June 14 cross burning, at another black-owned home, marked England's sixth in a week, the second in London. On June 15, the government banned further visits by Shelton, but sporadic Klan activities continued. In mid-August, 100 West Indians from London and Birmingham met to organize an anti-Klan resistance movement, claiming that police were reluctant to move against the Klan. By the mid-1970s the Klan had again nearly disappeared, but race remained a volatile issue in Britain. Hundreds were injured in London riots during the summers of 1976 and 1977. A domestic fascist group, the National Front, claimed 10,000 members by September 1977, and the opportunity was too much for U.S. Klan leaders to resist. In March 1978, David Duke arrived in England, recruiting "several dozen" Klansmen and blitzing the media with interviews before authorities could order his deportation. Undaunted, Duke led policemen on a merry chase that spanned several weeks, once posing for snapshots in full regalia by the Tower of London, before he was finally captured and expelled from the country. As of this writing, there is no evidence of active klaverns surviving in England. [*NYT* 1957, 1965, 1977–1978]

ENTERPRISE CLUB
See *West Duplin Boating & Fishing Club.*

ENZOR, ROSS
See *Grainger, Ben.*

ENZOR, T.L.
See *Flowers, Evergreen.*

ERLANGER, ALEZI

A neo-Nazi propagandist from Buffalo, New York, Erlanger has been identified as a participant in racist gatherings hosted by the Aryan Nations at their fortified compound near Hayden Lake, Idaho. [2]

ESCAPED NUNS

In the 1920s, the KKK maintained a stable of female orators, billed as retired or "escaped" nuns, who specialized in regaling audiences with tales of alleged convent horrors. Masquerading as authorities on the Roman Catholic church, these itinerant lecturers lent an aura of authenticity to the Klan's virulent anti-Catholicism, perpetuating tales of priestly lust and brutality among gullible listeners. As typified by headliner Helen Jackson, the "nuns" normally segregated their audiences by sex, regaling women with the "inside" scoop on brainwashing in parochial schools, while the men would be titillated with lectures verging on the pornographic. Props included leather bags equipped with drawstrings in which the newborn offspring of lusty priests and submissive nuns were allegedly carried to the convent furnace and would be cremated alive. Catholics were further supposed to be stockpiling weapons in church basements, with each male member of the church required to donate a rifle and supply of ammunition upon the birth of a male child. By the early 1930s, media exposure had generally discredited the Klan nuns. As late as 1970, however, tape recordings prepared by an "ex-nun" were played for teenaged students at a Seventh Day Adventist school in Bakersfield, California, prompting several boys to visit a neighborhood Catholic church and peep through its basement windows in search of the cells allegedly reserved for Protestants in the forthcoming Catholic revolution. [10]

ESDALE, JAMES

Alabama's grand dragon in the 1920s, Esdale was attacked by Birmingham newspapers for his speeches advocating the flogging of Klan opponents. A close associate of Governor Bibb Graves, Esdale was also linked to out of state political efforts, including the circulation of anti-Catholic literature in an effort to defeat incumbent Virginia state treasurer John Purcell. [10]

ESSEX-MIDDLE RIVER KNIGHTS OF THE KU KLUX KLAN

A small New Jersey splinter group, the Essex-Middle River Knights was exposed in 1984 when Great Titan Benjamin Butler and five other members were sentenced to prison for illegal cross burnings and the attempted murder of a black man. [NYT 1984]

ETHERIDGE, PAUL S.

A longtime member of the Fulton County commission in Atlanta, Georgia, Etheridge was one of the 20th century Klan's first recruits in November 1915. While holding public office he doubled as imperial klonsel for the Knights of the KKK and later served as Klan chief of staff. In 1923, he was one of six Klansmen chosen for the imperial kloncilium formed to settle the power struggle between William Simmons and Hiram Evans. In 1932, Etheridge briefly headed the Roosevelt Southern Clubs, previous to the Klan's opposition to Franklin Roosevelt's New Deal. [10]

ETOWAH RESCUE SERVICE

In 1965 congressional investigators identified this group as a cover for Etowah, Tennessee, Unit No. 4, United Klans of America. [38]

EUBANKS, GOLDIE

As an officer of the NAACP in St. Augustine, Florida, Eubanks became a natural target for local Klansmen in the 1960s. Sit-in demonstrations were in progress around St. Augustine when nightriders fired on his home in June 1963, with armed guards returning the fire. Four months later, shooting erupted when a Klan motorcade passed within a block of Eubanks's home. One Klansman was killed in the exchange. [*Harper's*, January 1965]

EULISS, ELI

A leader of the Constitutional Union Guard during Reconstruction in Alamance County, North Carolina, Euliss retained his friendship with Republican T.M. Shoffner when the state senator became a target of Klan assassins. In December 1869, Euliss learned of a plot against Shoffner's life, helping Shoffner escape from the county before gunmen could track him down. [87]

EURO-AMERICAN ALLIANCE, INC.

Based in Milwaukee, Wisconsin, the Euro-American Alliance was founded in 1976 by Aryan propagandist Donald V. Clerkin. Characterized as a "nationalist front" of "Christian soldiers," the Alliance is publicly affiliated with the Mountain Church of Jesus Christ in Cohoctah, Michigan, led by former Klansman and convicted bomber Robert Miles. In April 1982, Miles hosted a series of meetings attended by spokesmen for the Alliance. Other participants included members of the Aryan Nations, the Knights of the Ku Klux Klan (then led by Stephen Black), the National Socialist White People's Party, and the National Alliance. [2]

EUTAW, ALABAMA

On October 24, 1870, 2,000 blacks turned out for a Republican rally in downtown Eutaw, provoking local Klansmen and KKK sympathizers to respond with jeers and catcalls. When this failed to break up the rally, Klan hecklers opened fire on the crowd, killing four blacks and wounding fifty others. Two white men reportedly suffered minor injuries in the outbreak when blacks struck back in self-defense. [87]

EVANS, DR. HIRAM WESLEY

A Dallas dentist and exalted cyclops of the state's largest klavern after World War I, Evans later served as grand titan of Province No. 2. Congressional testimony linked him personally to the flogging and acid-branding of a black hotel bellhop in Dallas. In 1921, Evans was summoned to Atlanta headquarters by Edward Clarke and elevated to the rank of imperial kligrapp in charge of the Klan's thirteen chartered realms. Evans traveled widely, forging alliances with Indiana's D.C. Stephenson and others, plotting to advance himself over Klan founder William Simmons. In November 1922, they muscled Simmons out of power as imperial wizard, with Evans assuming the throne, but disputes over cash and Klan regalia dragged on into early 1924. The following year, with an estimated 4 million Klansmen under his nominal control, Evans marched with 30,000 of his members through the streets of Washington, D.C. In 1927, he was invited to sit on the dais at Georgia Governor Charles McCall's inauguration as a gesture of gratitude for Klan support in the election. Unable to reverse the Klan's eventual decline, Evans ordered his knights to unmask in the summer of 1928. Eight years later, he announced that the KKK was deemphasizing "racial and religious matters" to concentrate on "communism and the CIO." Late in 1936, an insurance company bought the Klan's imperial palace on Peachtree Street in Atlanta, then embarassed Evans by selling it to the Catholic church. Hard-core Klansmen were furious when Evans accepted an invitation to the grand opening of the new rectory for the Cathedral of Christ the King in 1939, but Evans considered the event "a good exit." Retiring from Klan affairs that June as Klan membership plummeted, Evans was replaced by chief of staff James Colescott. When Dr. Samuel Green tried to revive the moribund Georgia Klan following World War II, Evans wistfully declared, "You can't start a fire in wet ashes." [10; 93]

EVANS, LELA MAE

One of four black women shot and wounded by Klansman Marshall Thrash in Chattanooga, Tennessee, on April 19, 1980, Evans survived to press charges against her attacker. [*AP*, April 20, 1980]

EVANS, MIRA

See *Carter, Asa.*

EVERETT, R.O.

In 1923, Everett—a state legislator from Durham, North Carolina—helped pass a law requiring the registration of Klan members and banning masked parades. After the vote, Everett told newsmen that initially he opposed the bill, until a Durham Klan leader warned him not to change his mind if he wanted to remain in office. [10]

EVERS, CHARLES

A brother of civil rights activist Medgar Evers, Charles has also been active in politics and black protest throughout Mississippi. On March 3, 1967, nightriders fired on his home in Jackson, retreating when armed guards responded in kind. In September 1968, while running for governor of Mississippi, Evers received an anonymous phone call warning him of a plot against his life, describing three alleged participants and their vehicles. On September 9, police arrested Dale Walton—ex-member of the United Klans and former imperial wizard of the Knights of the Green Forest—outside of a store owned by Evers, in Fayette, Mississippi. A search of Walton's car turned up three shotguns, a carbine, and a pistol, and he was arrested on charges of carrying concealed weapons. On September 10, authorities cited federal firearms charges in the arrest of Klansmen Pat Massengale in Hattiesburg and Bobby Haywood in Tupelo. No stranger to the courtroom, Massengale had earlier been charged with jury tampering in the Vernon Dahmer case, a trial that ended in a hung jury. [*NYT* 1969]

EVERS, MEDGAR

In January 1954, Evers was the first black student to apply for admission to the University of Mississippi. Eight years later, when a race riot had left two persons dead and James Meredith had enrolled at the Oxford campus, Evers was leading the state's NAACP chapter. The carport of his Jackson home was firebombed in May 1963, and a sniper murdered Evers in his driveway on June 12. Federal agents identified Klansman Byron de la Beckwith as the killer (Beckwith reportedly boasted of committing the murder at Klan rallies) but all-white juries twice failed to reach a verdict in the case, leaving the murder technically unsolved. [63]

F

FAGGARD, JESSE

An Alabama Klansman, Faggard and his father were arrested during riots that greeted the integrated Freedom Rides in May 1961. Both were held on charges of grand larceny and assault with intent to kill. [NYT 1961]

FAIR, ALICE

See *Clink, John.*

FALLAW, EUNICE ("GENE")

A Jacksonville, Florida, officer in the United Florida Ku Klux Klan, Fallaw sometimes referred to his unit simply as the Knights of the KKK or the North Florida Klan. In June 1964, Anti-Defamation League observers called the group "violently excitable," and their opinion was borne out three months later when Fallaw introduced traveling agitator Connie Lynch to a Klan audience outside of St. Augustine. On that occasion, four blacks were found spying on the rally, one of whom was identified as NAACP officer R.N. Hayling. Fallaw was identified as one of at least six Klansmen who joined in beating the blacks before Sheriff L.O. Davis arrived on the scene. [NYT 1964; 38]

FAMILY IMPROVEMENT CLUB

In 1965 congressional investigators identified this group as a cover for the Henderson, North Carolina, ladies auxiliary, United Klans of America. [38]

FARIS, JOHN R.

A white resident of York County, South Carolina, Faris was chosen in October 1869 to lead the nearly all-black militia in its local anti-Klan campaign. On February 10, 1871, a mob of fifty Klansmen raided his home, confiscating a stockpile of rifles collected to arm the militia. [87]

FARMER, SAXON

A resident of Bogalusa, Louisiana, Farmer served as grand titan in the Original Knights of the KKK prior to the three-way rift that tore that group apart in the fall of 1964. Remaining active in the 6th Congressional District, he joined Grand Dragon Charles Christmas to create a front group, the Anti-Communist Christian Association, in January 1965. Active in violent opposition to civil rights protesters during that year, Farmer was named as a defendant when the U.S. Justice Department filed suit to enjoin Klansmen from terrorizing blacks. Called to testify in New Orleans during the summer of 1965, Farmer swore that the Klan had disbanded in Bogalusa, but federal judges were unimpressed by his argument, and granted a permanent injunction against further acts of violence. Farmer subsequently shifted his allegiance to the United Klans of America, luring his fellow knights into the new group that soon became Washington Parish's dominant Klan. [38; 84]

FARMERS LIBERATION ARMY

A midwestern paramilitary group, the Farmers Liberation Army joined members of Posse Comitatus in guerilla training exercises near Weskan, Iowa, in 1982. [2]

FARNSWORTH, EUGENE

An ex-member of a Salvation Army band, Farnsworth emerged as the 1920s grand dragon of Maine, with additional responsibility for Klan activities in Vermont and New Hampshire. Operating from the tri-state headquarters on his estate in Bangor, Farnsworth drew national attention with his 1924 announcement that he would personally select Maine's next governor. Party regulars were outraged, and when Farnsworth failed to deliver, his days as grand dragon were numbered. His successor, Dr. E.W. Gayer, moved the Klan's regional office to New Hampshire, but the membership had already faded. [10]

FAUBUS, ORVAL

As governor of Arkansas between 1955 and 1958, Faubus became a national symbol of defiance during the Little Rock school integration crisis. Prior to his inauguration, the NAACP hailed Arkansas as "the bright spot of the South" for desegregation, but a new governor's intransigence altered this praise. In 1960, the National States Rights Party nominated Faubus, against his will, for president, with retired admiral John Crommelin as the vice presidential candidate. When Faubus publicly declined the nomination, National States Rights Party candidates were removed from the ballot in Florida, but the neo-Nazi option was still offered in four other states, with Faubus polling 7 percent of the vote in Arkansas, 1 percent in Tennessee, and less than 1 percent in both Alabama and Delaware. [61]

FAULKNER

First name unrecorded, this Reconstruction Klansman was wounded and captured during an 1871 raid against a black county commissioner in Newberry, South Carolina. Suspected of divulging Klan secrets while in custody, after his release he was followed to Edgefield, and was murdered there by his fellow Klansmen. [87]

FAYETTE S.A. CLUB

In 1965 congressional investigators identified this club as a front for the Fayette, Alabama, klavern, United Klans of America. The significance of the initials "S.A." remains a mystery. [38]

FEDERAL BUREAU OF INVESTIGATION

FBI agents got their first crack at the Klan in 1922, when the governor of Louisiana complained of widespread KKK conspiracies, including interception of the mails. Contrary to popular myth, inspired by actor James Stewart's performance in *The FBI Story*, the investigation of the notorious Mer Rouge murders produced no evidence of federal violations, and the FBI's only victory against the 1920s Klan consisted of a Mann Act charge filed against Edward Clarke. Klan leaders reportedly tried to have FBI Director J. Edgar Hoover dismissed in the early 1930s, but the FBI had already moved on to other targets, gathering evidence for the abortive sedition trial of thirty-three Nazi sympathizers (including ex-Klansman George Deatherage and several other KKK associates). In July 1946, spokesmen for the U.S. Justice Department announced a new probe of resurgent Klans in California, Florida, Georgia, Michigan, Mississippi, New York, and Tennessee, but no prosecutions resulted. Federal agents were more successful with Georgia Sheriff John Lynch, in 1949, but the prosecution of those wanted for flogging incidents near Soperton, Georgia, the following year fell short of bringing Klansmen to trial. The FBI proved successful in 1952 and 1953, crippling the Association of Carolina Klans with mass arrests, and later winning indictments of ten Florida Klansmen involved in terrorism in the Miami area. Southern violence increased after the U.S. Supreme Court's Black Monday ruling in 1954, but Hoover's FBI regime was reluctant to move in defense of black civil rights. At a March 1956 cabinet meeting, Hoover blamed the Supreme Court and the media's "lack of objectivity" for the Southern crisis, describing Citizens' Council members as "some of the leading citizens of the South." Agents kept an eye on the Klan—described by Hoover as "pretty much defunct"—and one of their infiltrators surfaced as a prosecution witness at the George Bright bombing trial in 1958. Three years later, FBI agents deliberately suppressed reports of a Klan conspiracy against the integrated Freedom Rides, supplying Klansmen on the Birmingham police department with a bus itinerary that enabled Klansmen to select their targets more precisely. (Twenty years later, one of the freedom riders crippled by Klansmen during a riot filed suit against the FBI in federal court, winning a judgment of $45,000 on grounds of official malfeasance.) On the other side of the coin, an agent was assaulted by a group of racists in September 1962 while investigating the burning of a black church in Sasser, Georgia, and FBI agents gathered voluminous evidence against Klansman Byron de la Beckwith in the June 1963 murder of NAACP leader Medgar Evers. In 1964, under pressure from the White House, Hoover launched his COINTELPRO campaign to infiltrate and disrupt the Klans, resulting in the federal prosecution of several notorious cases over the next three years. As a September 2, 1964, memo from Assistant Director William Sullivan explained, "The purpose of this program is to expose, disrupt and otherwise neutralize the activities of the various Klans and hate organizations, their leadership and adherents." Agents targeted seventeen Klans and nine other "hate" groups such as the American Nazi Party in a program that resulted in 255 separate actions. By 1965, the FBI had 2,014 informants in the various Klans, including high-ranking officers in seven groups and the grand dragon of one realm. (By September 1972, FBI infiltration in the Klan had become so widespread that Imperial Wizard Robert Shelton purchased lie detectors for use on new recruits.) As one infiltrator was told by his control agents, "You can do anything to get your information. We don't want you to get involved in unnecessary violence, but the point is to get the information." Informant Gary Rowe reportedly was told to seduce Klan wives in an effort to disrupt marriages, while fabricated news items and anonymous letters accused known Klansmen of adultery, alcoholism, theft of Klan money, and other various crimes. (Critics charged that FBI agents also suppressed evidence of crimes committed by informants, including Gary Rowe's alleged murder of a black man in Birmingham in 1963.) At the same time, Hoover and his successors stubbornly refused to cooperate with Alabama state attorney generals Richmond Flowers and Bill Baxley in their own KKK investigations, suppressing for fourteen years crucial evidence in a fatal Birmingham church bombing. (FBI agents quickly broke the 1963 case, but Hoover twice denied requests for prosecution from the Birmingham office. One of the killers was later retained as a paid FBI informant.) In March 1965, hours after Klansmen murdered Viola Liuzzo, Hoover sent a memo to President Lyndon Johnson that read, in part: "A Negro was with Mrs. Liuzzo and reportedly sitting close to her." In a later memo to his aides, Hoover explained that he told President Johnson that "she was sitting very, very close to the Negro in the car; that it had the appearance of a necking party." In July 1967, FBI agents arrested twelve North Carolina terrorists, including at least nine Klansmen. But the FBI's methods appeared to some as entrapment. The following year, after a new rash of Mississippi bombings, FBI agents put murder suspect Alton Roberts in touch with Jewish leaders in order to arrange a trap for Klan nightriders; one retired agent, acting as an intermediary on the deal, pocketed $2,000 of the $36,500 reward after Thomas Tarrants was captured and his female companion was killed by police. When newsman Jack Nelson exposed the FBI's role in arranging the trap, Hoover tried to have him fired, sending agents to visit Nelson's editor and circulating unfounded rumors about his private life. Two years later, the FBI claimed credit for driving Frank Collin out of the National Socialist White Peoples' Party by leaking details of his Jewish ancestry. [*FOF* 1975, 1978; 16; 68; 69; 91]

FEDERATED KNIGHTS OF THE KU KLUX KLAN

In 1983, Anti-Defamation League investigators identified this group as a splinter faction active on a local scale in North Carolina and South Carolina. [2]

FEDERATED KU KLUX KLANS, INC.

Founded by William Hugh Morris in Birmingham, Alabama, on June 21, 1946, the Federated KKK claimed 30,000 members by the end of the decade, but this self-serving estimate was vastly inflated. A suggestion of the group's true strength is found in the fact that its newspaper, *Uxtra*, managed to sell out only one issue before it folded in 1949. In July 1949, seventeen Birmingham members were indicted on forty-four criminal counts, including twenty-eight floggings, eight illegal boycotts, six burglaries, one count of carnal knowledge, and two misdemeanors. Morris was jailed for contempt on July 14 when he refused to produce a list of his dues-paying Klansmen. The next day, grand jury hearings were briefly sidetracked when one member, Alexander Brewis, was identified as a Klansman, and several others were found to have criminal records. On July 18, presiding judge George Bailes admitted Klan membership during the 1920s, maintaining that he resigned in 1925. Klansmen indicted—but never convicted—in the local reign of terror included: Coleman ("Brownie") Lollar, a former special deputy, named as the Birmingham ringleader; A. Byrd Carradine; Richard Lollar, exalted cyclops of the Adamsville klavern; Moody Nations; James Shaffer, a part-time Brookside policeman; Elmer Bailey Brock, Brookside's police chief; Robert Chambliss; Mel Fields; William Allen Byrd; Albert Swindle; Roy Landrum; Fred Brasfield; C. Dozier; Henry Nelson, a constable in Flat Creek; high school football coach Valcus McCluskey; and Reverend R.C. Lyons, a Holiness preacher doubling as the Klan's chaplain. In and out of jail during August, Morris finally claimed that burglars had stolen Klan membership lists from his home, and won his freedom by "recreating" an abbreviated roster from memory. Meanwhile, his wife joined rival Klan leader Lycurgus Spinks for a Talladega motorcade on August 21, heralding a short-lived bid for unity among competing Klans. In January 1950, Morris attended a Jacksonville, Florida, meeting with representatives of the Southern Knights and the Association of Carolina Klans. A joint declaration of war was issued against "hate groups" such as the NAACP and B'nai B'rith. After almost a decade of inactivity, Morris revived the Federated Klans in 1959, recruiting a few small units in neighboring Georgia. Clinging to tenuous life through the early 1960s, the Federated Klans were one of three groups hit with an injunction from federal judge Frank Johnson after opposition to the integrated Freedom Rides turned violent in May 1961. Private investigations disclose no visible activity by the Federated Klans after 1961, and Morris himself, resettled in Georgia, emerged in November 1963 as an officer of James Venable's National Knights. Congressional hearings on the Martin Luther King assassination brought Morris back into the spotlight for a moment in 1978, allowing him to "revive" the Federated Klans, claiming in testimony that there were 1,000 members scattered over seven states. [*NYT* 1949–1950, 1961; 38]

FELKER, WILLIAM

A Reconstruction storekeeper and moonshiner in Walton County, Georgia, Felker was also repeatedly identified as the leader of local KKK raids. A black employee of Felker's advised congressional investigators of the merchant's advice on peaceful coexistence with whites. "He told me how to do," the witness testified. "He said if I always raised my hat to the people when I passed, and was always polite to them, I would not be bothered." [87]

FELLOWSHIP CLUB

In 1965 congressional investigators identified this group as the cover for a Mount Olive, North Carolina, klavern, United Klans of America. [38]

FELLOWSHIP FORUM, THE

A pro-Klan, anti-Catholic magazine that was widely circulated in the 1920s, the *Forum* was published in Washington, D.C., by drugstore impresario James S. Vance. Part-owners of the magazine included Virginia Republican Party chairman R.H. Angell, of Roanoke, and West Virginia's 1928 Democratic candidate for governor. A prominent mouthpiece for the drive to defeat Al Smith's presidential hopes, the *Forum* specialized in headlines such as "Roman Catholic Clerical Party Opens Big Drive To Capture America For The Pope." [10]

FERREL, ANDERSON

A black Georgia resident, Ferrel was whipped by Reconstruction Klansmen in an effort, as they explained to him, "to teach you the difference between a white man and a nigger." [93]

FIELDS, DOLORES

A resident of Louisville, Kentucky, Fields was identified as state chairman of the National States Rights Party in 1958. [65]

FIELDS, EDWARD R.

Introduced to Nazi philosophy at age 14 when he attended an Atlanta meeting of the Columbians, Fields later worked with George Van Horn Moseley on a Free Emory Burke Committee. In October 1950, when the first desegregation lawsuit was filed in Atlanta, Fields responded by handing out anti-Semitic pamphlets headlined: "Jewish Communists Behind Atlanta's School Segregation Suit." While attending law school in Atlanta during 1951 and 1952, he teamed with J.B. Stoner to form the Christian Anti-Jewish Party in 1952. An Iowa chiropractic school consumed Fields's time between 1953 and 1956, and by 1957 he was practicing in Louisville, Kentucky, using his spare time to recruit members for the Citizens' Council and the United White Party, which became the National States Rights Party in 1958. Copying the National States Rights Party's thunderbolt insignia from the defunct Columbians, Fields sponsored a local "Anti-Jew Week," covering the windows of Jewish-owned shops with anti-Semitic posters. In 1958, he testified as a defense witness at the George Bright bombing trial, and three years later, with another States Rights member, he was cited for contempt of court after proceeding with a racist rally at Fairfield, Alabama, that had been banned. (The U.S. Supreme Court reversed the contempt convictions on December 16, 1963.) In September 1963, Fields was one of eight party members indicted for violent interference with school desegregation. When state attorney general Bill Baxley reopened the files on a fatal Birmingham church bombing after thirteen years, Fields fired off a letter of protest. Baxley wrote back: "My response to your letter of February 19, 1976, is—kiss my ass." In 1980, Fields attended the first national conference of Stephen Black's Knights of the KKK in Alabama, and a year later he hosted a banquet in Marietta, Georgia, honoring Klansmen and neo-Nazis accused of murdering five persons in Greensboro, North Carolina. In 1982 and 1983, representing both the National States Rights Party and his own Georgia-based New Order, Knights of the KKK, Fields attended Labor Day rallies that resulted in a new Confederation of Klans, which merged seven regional groups. [2; 38]

FIELDS, MEL

See *Federated Ku Klux Klans, Inc.*

FIERY CROSS, THE

An official KKK periodical in the 1920s, *The Fiery Cross* was published in Indianapolis and edited by Klansman Milton Elrod. Since 1961, the same title has been used for a newsletter published by the United Klans of America. [10]

51 CLUB

In 1966 congressional investigators identified this group as a cover for the Columbia, Alabama, klavern, United Klans of America. [38]

FILLINGAME, EDWARD

See *Mills, Raymond.*

FILLINGAME, LAURIE L.

See *Mills, Raymond.*

FINE FELLOWS CLUB

In 1965 the House Un-American Activities Committee exposed this group as a front for the Reidsville, North Carolina, klavern, United Klans of America. [38]

FINLAYSON, DR. JOHN

A Republican clerk in Jackson County, Florida, during Reconstruction, Finlayson was murdered by Klansmen in Marianna on February 26, 1869, killed by the same bullet that wounded state senator W.J. Purman. [87]

FITZGERALD, CHARLIE

A black dance hall proprietor in Myrtle Beach, South Carolina, Fitzgerald was targeted by Klansmen who mistook his light-skinned wife for a white woman. (Some sources say that Klansmen were used to drive blacks away from desirable beachfront property, so that whites could purchase the land.) When an initial motorcade drove past his establishment, Fitzgerald phoned the sheriff and Myrtle Beach police to warn that there would be trouble if the nightriders returned. On August 26, 1950, a caravan of 150 robed Klansmen launched an assault on the dance hall, firing an estimated 300 shots that left one of their own members, Conway patrolman James Johnston, dead at the scene. Fitzgerald was carried away by the raiders, beaten, and had his ear notched with a knife before being dumped along the roadside. Grand Dragon Tom Hamilton, of the Association of Carolina Klans, was jailed on August 31, 1950, for "conspiracy to stir up mob violence," with eight of his followers picked up the next day. One of the Klansmen, Constable T.M. Floyd, was dismissed when his link to the Klan was revealed. [*NYT 1950*]

FITZPATRICK, HENRY

A black resident of Tennessee who was suspected of burning two barns in 1868, Fitzpatrick received 200 lashes from a gang of Klansmen at his home. The raiders returned a few nights later and lynched Fitzpatrick. [87]

FLEISHMAN, SAMUEL

The Klan's first Jewish victim, Fleishman was ordered out of Marianna, Florida, in August 1869 for befriending local blacks. Refusing to leave his home and family, he was forcibly escorted to the Alabama border and left there with orders not to come back. Returning home a few days later, Fleishman was attacked by Klansmen and killed outside of town. [87]

FLEMING, FLOYD

See *American Nazi Party*.

FLINT RIVER MEN'S CLUB NO. 8

In 1965 congressional investigators exposed this club as a front for the Albany, Georgia, klavern, United Klans of America. [38]

FLINT RIVER MEN'S GROUP NO. 30

A 1960s cover for the Bainbridge, Georgia, klavern, United Klans of America, this group sometimes used an alternate title, posing as the Flint River Sportsman Club. [38]

FLINT RIVER SPORTSMAN CLUB

See *Flint River Men's Group No. 30*.

FLORIDA

The Reconstruction KKK invaded Florida in April and May 1868, often hiding behind aliases such as the Young Men's Democratic Club. Little violence was reported in the early months of operation, but nightriding intensified during the fall, as the crucial presidential election drew near. State legislators passed a militia bill to combat white terrorism in August 1868, but the law was difficult to implement. Governor Harrison Reed visited New York a month later, purchasing 2,000 muskets and 40,000 rounds of ammunition for his troops, but Klansmen were waiting when the arms arrived. On November 5, raiding parties boarded the train between Jacksonville and Tallahassee, tossing the muskets overboard while military guards slept unaware. When the train arrived at the next stop, the Klansmen disembarked and doubled back and spent the night destroying the weapons. Nightriders were active in ten Florida counties during 1869 and 1870, with the most deaths reported in Jackson County, on the Georgia-Alabama State line. (As early as June 1868, a state convention of black Methodists urged all freedmen who valued their lives to vacate Jackson County without delay.) Jackson and a half dozen other counties witnessed sporadic violence through mid-1871, and state authorities issued conservative reports listing 235 racist murders over the preceding four years. Still, congressional investigation and the passage of the Ku Klux Acts had an effect, and by December 1871, Jackson County's black majority was able to elect two Republican officers with no reports of white intimidation.

The 20th century Klan began in Jacksonville and spread, entering politics by 1922 and scoring a clean sweep in the Volusia County primary elections in June 1922. Violence inevitably followed, with at least four floggings reported in Kissimmee in the spring of 1923. Later in 1923, a series of whippings were reported in Tampa, Sanford, and Miami. A Putnam County grand jury was moved to investigate masked violence in September 1926, which revealed at least sixty-three floggings in the past year, with two victims fatally injured. Still, this evidence of racial violence failed to excite widespread opposition in Florida, and Klansmen would endure through the Depression, flexing their muscles most frequently in the central part of the state. Brothels were sometimes burned in and around Gainesville in the 1930s, but union organizers were the most frequent targets of Klan violence, typified by the torture-slaying of Joseph Shoemaker in 1935. Disbandment of the national Klan in April 1944 left Florida Klansmen to shift for themselves, and the Ku Klux Klan of Florida, Inc., was chartered in September 1944.

The post-war Klan revival met with opposition from Governor Fuller Warren, who branded Klansmen as "hooded hoodlums and sheeted jerks," but south of Tallahassee the atmosphere was more favorable. In July 1949, with the Groveland rape case making headlines, Klansmen pitched in to inaugurate a local reign of terror, shooting at and burning black-owned homes until militia units finally arrived. One lynching was averted only when Sheriff Willis McCall decided to take matters into his own hands and shoot the suspects himself. Cashing in on the atmosphere of racial tension, Bill Hendrix led his Southern and Northern Knights of the KKK in a drive to purge blacks and Jews from Miami. Over the next two years, bombs were detonated at local synagogues, a Catholic church, and several times at Carver Village, a black housing project. On Christmas 1951, a Klan bombing claimed the life of NAACP leader Harry Moore and his wife in their home in Mims.

The U.S. Supreme Court's Black Monday decision of 1954 breathed new life into the Florida Klan, with at least five splinter groups reported active in the late 1950s. Jacksonville Klansmen made headlines in August 1960, with their riot against black demonstrators on "Ax-Handle Saturday," and the United Florida Ku Klux Klan was organized ten months later, a merger of two splinter groups into a unit that would dominate Florida Klandom for the next three years. Around September 1963, outsiders J.B. Stoner and Connie Lynch began their efforts to build "a rough and tough Klan, looking for action," with marathon rallies outside Jacksonville and St. Augustine that lasted until 2 a.m. By Easter 1964, North Florida Klansmen had been loosely reshuffled into a regional group dubbed "Providence No. 41," which claimed an estimated 1,000 members by the time rioting rocked St. Augustine in June and July. Recruiters for the United Klans of America made their appearance that fall, organizing twenty-seven klaverns statewide, but internal dissension was a fact of life in the Florida Klan, with bitter arguments over money and policy leading to rifts in the United Klans and the United Florida KKK. Jacksonville's Militant Knights and Melbourne's United Knights of the KKK were organized in 1965, but the Florida realm was already past its prime, with membership rapidly declining. By 1983, despite some widely scattered klaverns of the United Klans, Florida had no domestic Klan. [2; 10; 38; 87]

FLORIDA KLANS, INC.

A short-lived spin-off from the Association of Georgia Klans, this faction was organized in 1948 by locals whom Dr. Samuel Green described as "three sharp fellows," bent on fleecing the faithful. [93]

FLORIDA KU KLUX KLAN

Organized in 1955, this was one of five Klan factions active in Florida after Black Monday. A year later, in October 1956, members raided the jail at Wildwood to "punish" a black who had requested confinement for his own protection. In 1957, led by J.E. Fraser, the Florida KKK ran second in statewide membership to the U.S. Klans, but claims of 30,000 dues-paying members were doubtless inflated for publicity's sake. Through Fraser, the Klan enjoyed close relations with the more "respectable" Association of Citizens' Councils of Florida. On June 25, 1961, representatives of the Florida KKK met with spokesmen for the rival United Ku Klux Klan, agreeing to a merger that created the United Florida KKK. [6; 38; 48]

FLORIDA WHITE KNIGHTS OF THE KU KLUX KLAN

An independent splinter group reported active in 1987, the Florida White Knights reportedly had fewer than 100 active members. [NYT 1987]

FLOURNOY, ROBERT W.

A Georgia native who relocated in Pontotoc, Mississippi, during 1856, Flournoy opposed secession but briefly led a Confederate company during the Civil War, later resigning from service because of his Unionist sympathies. Serving as Pontotoc's superintendent of schools during Reconstruction, he soon emerged as a prominent Republican and editor of a local newspaper, *Equal Rights*. By May 1871, he had established fifty-two white and twelve black schools in the county, marking himself as a target for local Klansmen. Nightriders came to get him on May 12, but Flournoy was forewarned by friends and had gathered reinforcements, including a judge and a deputy sheriff, to meet the raiders with armed force. One Klansman was killed in the shootout before his companions fled, and they never returned. The Columbus *Index* lamented their failure in an editorial that read: "Flournoy was not captured. For the Ku Klux this was a very badly managed affair, and there is something so at variance with the usual daring and success of the mysterious brotherhood, that we cannot but receive the account with some grains of allowance. We are opposed to lawlessness, but we could have heard of the hanging of this ungodly wretch with a very great degree of fortitude, consoling ourselves with the conviction that 'his loss was Mississippi's gain.'" [87]

FLOWERS, EVERGREEN

A black resident of Chadbourn, North Carolina, Flowers was beaten by Klansmen who invaded her home on January 18, 1950. Investigators traced the raid to the Association of Carolina Klans, and in May 1952 a series of indictments were handed down, implicating the following: Grand Dragon Tom Hamilton and ten of his Klansmen, including Ernest Hardee, Joe Hardee, Troy Bennett, J.D. Nealey, Roy Carter, Russell Hammacher, Sid Scott, Jule Richardson, Jenrick Hammonds, and T.L. Enzor. At their trial in July 1952, the defendants all pled guilty or no contest and received prison terms. [*NYT* 1950, 1952]

FLOWERS, RICHMOND

A staunch segregationist, elected as Alabama's state attorney general in 1962, Flowers surprised his colleagues and constituents three years later by calling on Governor George Wallace to join him in a probe of Ku Klux Klan activities. (For the record, Flowers voiced his belief that communists might have infiltrated the Klan, as they had the civil rights movement, to pervert its "patriotic" ideals.) Rebuffed by Wallace, Flowers announced in June 1965 that his investigation was stalled by FBI refusal to cooperate; despite their massive infiltration of the Klan, FBI agents responded to his plea for inside information with a few old news clips and a Florida grand jury report dating from 1953. Two months later, Lowndes County Klansman Tom Coleman approached Flowers and told him, "If you don't get off this Klan investigation, we'll get you off." Wallace chimed in a short time later, calling for the attorney general's impeachment on charges of "collaborating with the federal government." Frustrated in his efforts to convict the Klan killers of Jonathan Daniels and Viola Liuzzo, Flowers still managed to collect substantial information on the Alabama realm. His final report, issued in October 1965, linked Klansmen with forty of Birmingham's forty-five racist bombings since World War II, in addition to being involved in twelve of the South's seventeen civil rights murders recorded since 1963. (As a sidelight of the probe, Flowers also learned that the Mississippi White Knights had recently huddled with Alabama Klan leaders to discuss his own assassination.) Flowers was assaulted by two racists at a Montgomery football game, on October 30, 1965, but rebounded a year later with an unsuccessful gubernatorial campaign against favorite Lurleen Wallace. His election defeat was closely followed by his conviction on extortion charges, described by friends and family as a Klan-inspired frame-up. Flowers was eventually pardoned by President Jimmy Carter. Now retired from public life, he resides in Dothan, Alabama, where he practices law and teaches part-time at, ironically, George C. Wallace State Community College. [*NYT* 1965–1967, 1988; 22]

FLOYD, BART

See *Aaron, Edward.*

FLOYD, ESTHER LEE

A black resident of Chadbourn, North Carolina, Floyd was dragged from her parents' home by Klansmen on November 14, 1951. Pregnant at the time of the attack, she was spared from a whipping, but the raiders cut her hair in the shape of a cross and warned her to stop "going with white men." (She was also threatened with death if she wore a hat or otherwise attempted to cover her head.) Investigators traced the raid to the Association of Carolina Klans, and twenty-seven Klansmen—including Early Brooks—were charged by April 28, 1952. [*NYT* 1952]

FLOYD, T.M.

See *Fitzgerald, Charlie.*

FOGEL, RICHARD

In June 1988, Fogel was identified as the reigning grand dragon of the Pennsylvania KKK. [*UPI*, June 22, 1988]

FOLENDORE, THOMAS ("HORSEFLY")

A teenaged member of the United Klans in Athens, Georgia, Folendore was called as a prosecution witness in the 1964 murder trial of Klansmen Joseph

Sims and Cecil Myers. On the stand he described watching Sims and Myers carry shotguns into defendant Herbert Guest's garage the morning that Lieutenant Colonel Lemuel Penn was shot and killed outside of town. Folendore also heard his fellow Klansmen discussing the murder—a fact corroborated by one of Guest's employees—but jurors chose to ignore the truth, returning a verdict of acquittal. [33]

FOLEY, ALBERT S.

In 1972, Foley was the director of Spring Hill College Human Relations Center, Mobile, Alabama. While attending a rally of the Assembly of Christian Soldiers, Inc., he was singled out as a possible FBI informant and assaulted with a hammer. Foley escaped, but was threatened with further beatings if he returned. Later, Foley heard that a gunman had been hired to kill him. A gunman did appear on the Spring Hill campus, disguised as a gardener and working in flower beds outside of Foley's office. Foley, however, was out of town. This gunman had been observed by a federal agent, who had a talk with him and warned the Christian Soldiers' leader not to harm Foley. [23]

FOLKS, WARREN

A Jacksonville, Florida, Klansman, Folks was arrested on July 18, 1966, while trying to "serve a Klan warrant" on NAACP president Rutledge Pearson, the leader of black protest marches that had led to racial clashes. [NYT 1966]

FOLSOM, CONSTANCE

A black resident of Wrightsville, Georgia, Folsom was nine years old when nightriders shot and wounded her in April 1980. Klansmen Danny Foskey and Herschel Hall were identified and ultimately prosecuted in the shooting, which sparked a series of local race riots. [NYT 1980]

FOLSOM, JAMES

During his two terms as Alabama's governor (1947–1950 and 1955–1958), Folsom emerged as a staunch opponent of the KKK. When Birmingham Klansmen kicked off a series of floggings in early 1949, Folsom declared open season on nightriders with the announcement that "Your home is your castle; defend it in any way necessary." That July, one day after passage of a statewide anti-mask law, the governor issued a ringing denunciation of these "would-be Hitlers," ordering his attorney general to file a charter revocation suit against the Federated Ku Klux Klans. In the wake of Black Monday, Folsom relied on urban votes to secure his reelection, which was achieved by the largest winning margin in Alabama's history. One of six Southern governors who refused to sign a formal protest statement against school integration, Folsom vetoed segregationist bills from the Black Belt, invited black congressman Adam Clayton Powell to the governor's mansion, and supported the creation of a biracial commission to ease mounting tensions. Dismissing calls for "nullification" of the U.S. Supreme Court's ruling as so much "hogwash," he compared the defiant state legislature to "a hound dog baying at the moon." In June 1955, Folsom was outraged by an incident in Wadley, where thirty Klansmen invaded an integrated meeting of the International Relations Institute at Southern Union College, ordering blacks to vacate the chapel or "we'll blow the place up." The governor ordered an immediate crackdown on "hooded terrorism," and there were ten arrests. (Klan leader Asa Carter was so disturbed by Folsom's conduct in office that he launched an abortive drive to impeach the governor in March 1956, based on Folsom's failure to "respect and enforce" state segregation laws.) Hedging his bets in September 1957, Folsom told the press that "I have a lot of good friends in the Klan." He stopped short of endorsing the KKK, but remarked that it "could be a good, genuine fraternal organization" if properly handled. Alabama Klansmen remained unimpressed, drawing comfort from the fact that their state's constitution forbade Folsom from succeeding himself in office. The subsequent administrations of John Patterson and George Wallace would prove more congenial to the Klan. [NYT 1955; 81]

FOLSOM SPORTSMAN'S CLUB

In 1965 congressional investigators identified this group as a cover for the Folsom, Louisiana, klavern, Original Knights of the KKK. [38]

FORBES, RALPH P.

As a member of the American Nazi Party, Forbes picketed screenings of *Exodus* in 1961 and had his nose bloodied a year later while picketing the White House with anti-Semitic placards. Moving to California in 1963, he was elevated to the rank of captain, but his recruiting efforts gathered few converts for the cause. Two decades later, he was identified as the prime mover behind the Sword of Christ, a racist group based in London, Arkansas. His front group, the Shamrock Society, urged patriots to "Kick the Jew Habit" at Christmas by spending their money on anti-Semitic literature, tapes, and membership dues in "God's White Army," which was led, of course, by Forbes. [2]

FORD, BENTON

A Depression-era victim of the Georgia KKK, Ford was beaten to death along with his girlfriend Sarah Rawls by Klansmen who caught them parked on an Atlanta "lover's lane" in March 1939. Both victims were white. [93]

FOREMAN, GENE

In 1966, Foreman was identified as grand dragon of the Jacksonville, Florida, Militant Knights of the KKK. In that capacity, he served as second-in-command to Imperial Wizard Donald Ballentine. [38]

FOREMAN, WILBURN

A resident of Aurora, Illinois, Foreman launched his campaign to organize a local klavern around 1966. His progress was marginal until early 1974, when he enlisted the assistance of Indiana Grand Dragon William Chaney, representing the United Klans of America. The Aurora klavern was chartered on March 1, 1974, and by the fall Foreman had extended his recruiting efforts to Joliet. In May 1975, he joined other United Klans leaders and members of the Devil's Advocates motorcycle gang for an organizational meeting in Kankakee, but his relationship with the United Klans leaders was already strained. Within days, Imperial Wizard Robert Shelton stripped Foreman of his title as imperial representative, and Foreman soon cast his lot with Robert Scoggin's Invisible Empire Knights, based in Spartansburg, South Carolina. By the end of the month, he had signed on fifty recruits for the new Klan, but most left once they had paid dues, and only fifteen hardcore members remained through summer. In 1976, Foreman attended Scoggin's Conference of Eastern Dragons, but his small band of Klansmen barely qualified him for the title that he bore. [43; 84]

FORREST, NATHAN BEDFORD

A millionaire slave trader and cotton planter before the Civil War, Forrest was commissioned as a Confederate general and left his mark on history as a cavalry leader who traditionally offered opponents a choice of unconditional surrender or annihilation. On April 12, 1864, his troops captured the Union garrison at Ft. Pillow, Tennessee, and proceeded to massacre 250 black prisoners of war, including some who were crucified or burned alive. His semiliterate report read, in part: "We bust the fort at ninerclock and scattered the niggers. The men are still a killenem in the woods." Later, with ample time to clean up his grammar, Forrest wrote, "The river was dyed with the blood of the slaughtered for two hundred yards. It is hoped that these facts will demonstrate to the Northern people that Negro soldiers cannot cope with Southerners." An unconditional pardon from President Andrew Johnson left Forrest at liberty after the war, and he was subsequently named the first—and only—Grand Wizard of the Reconstruction KKK. Although he missed the Klan's April 1867 organizational congress in Nashville, Forrest signed on a month later and was elevated to the post of leadership by acclamation. (Around the same time, he also joined the paramilitary Order of Pale Faces.) Traveling through the South as a railroad insurance representative, Forrest was "coincidentally" present when Klan dens were organized in Alabama, Arkansas, Georgia, Mississippi, and North Carolina. By 1868, he claimed a following of 40,000 Klansmen in Tennessee, with some 550,000 in the South overall. In a Memphis interview on August 28, 1868, Forrest staunchly denied any racist motivation, concentrating on the battleground of Southern politics. "I have no powder to burn killing Negroes," he proclaimed. "I intend to kill the radicals. There is not a radical leader in this town but is a marked man, and if trouble should break out, none of them would be left alive." Forrest denied Klan membership, but allowed that he was "in sympathy and will cooperate with them." Five months later, on January 25, 1869, Forrest issued "General Order Number One"—the only dictum ever traced to Klan headquarters—proclaiming that evil men had perverted the high-minded aims of the KKK. He ordered disguises to be "entirely abolished and destroyed" in the presence of local Klan officers, adding that anyone seen in disguise thereafter would be considered an enemy of the KKK and treated accordingly. Public demonstrations were forbidden unless ordered by the grand titan or some higher officer. Despite contrary interpretations, Forrest's order specifically denied intent of disbanding the Klan; rather, Klansmen were merely enjoined to reserve their energies for local emergencies. In practice, the dictum merely served to release local Klans from the already tenuous discipline of their parent organization. By 1870, as an apostle of the "New South," Forrest was traveling on railroad business with Alabama Republican William Blackford, a circumstance that diehard Klansmen found "disgraceful and disgusting." At the same time, North Carolina Klansmen helped the wizard out by discouraging black competitors from recruiting railroad workers. A year later, Forrest told Congress that the KKK grew out of "insecurity felt by many Southern people. Many Northern men were coming down there, forming Leagues all over the country. The Negroes were holding night meetings; were going about; were becoming very insolent; and the Southern people were very much alarmed. Parties organized themselves so as to be ready in case they were attacked. Ladies were ravished by some of those Negroes. There was a great deal of insecurity. This organization was got up to protect the weak, with no political intention at all." Excused from prosecution while a number of his Klansmen went to federal prison over the next twelve months, Forrest was fond of telling friends that he had "lied like a gentleman" before the congressional panel. [10; 87]

FORREST, NATHAN BEDFORD, III

A grandson of the Klan's first wizard, Forrest was also a high school classmate of James Venable and an aide to William Simmons in the 1915 KKK revival. Launching his career in Atlanta as the exalted cyclops of Nathan Bedford Forrest Klan No. 1, he was later elevated to serve as Georgia's grand dragon. One of six Klan leaders chosen for an Imperial Kloncilium to settle financial disputes between Simmons and Hiram Evans in 1923, a year later Forrest sat on the Klan's strategy board at the

Democratic convention in New York City. A moderate as Klansmen go, he once complained of twenty calls per week from persons hoping that the Klan would flog their enemies; one woman even asked him to arrange a lynching. Forrest's death, near the end of the Depression, marked a day of mourning for Klansmen from coast to coast. [10; 93]

FORREST CLUB NO. 11

In 1965 congressional investigators identified this club as a front for the Lakeland, Florida, klavern, United Florida KKK. [38]

FORTUNE, EMANUEL

A black legislator during Reconstruction in Jackson County, Florida, Fortune fled the county in 1869 after Klansmen threatened his life. [87]

FOSKEY, DANNY

See *Folsom, Constance.*

FOSTER, ANTHONY

A "scalawag" during Reconstruction in South Carolina, Foster was accosted by Klansmen and forced to dance at gunpoint after voting the Republican ticket in November 1868. [93]

FOSTER, PAUL L.

A resident of Natchez, Mississippi, Foster was identified as grand kludd for the White Knights of the KKK in 1964, when that group formally incorporated as the Adams County Civic Betterment Association. [38]

FOSTER, ROBERT S.

A planter in Chattooga County, Alabama, Foster was repeatedly harassed and threatened by Reconstruction Klansmen after he and his sons attempted to prosecute the killers of a black farmhand. [87]

FOWLER, JACK WILSON

See *Greensboro, North Carolina.*

FOWLER, ROSCOE

See *Stallworth, Clarke.*

FOWLER, WALLACE

A black victim of the Reconstruction Klan, Fowler was murdered after complaining that a Klansman's son stole watermelons from his property. [93]

FOWLER, WILLIAM

A former California Klan leader, in the early 1980s Fowler was identified as an officer of the Aryan Nations, residing at that group's fortified compound near Hayden Lake, Idaho. [2]

FOX, MIKE

See *Cole, Nat ("King")*.

FOX, PHILIP

A former editor of the Dallas *Times-Herald*, Fox moved to Atlanta when Hiram Evans replaced William Simmons as imperial wizard of the KKK in 1922. He soon advanced from a job as imperial speechwriter to become editor of *The Knight Hawk* and the national Klan's chief publicity agent. In 1923, Fox shot and killed William Coburn, Simmons's lawyer, in Atlanta. At his trial, he escaped the death penalty by pleading that he was a dangerous paranoid, thus not responsible for his actions. Sentenced to a life term, Fox served ten years before gaining parole under Governor Eugene Talmadge and a complete pardon under Governor E.D. Rivers (both of whom were former Klansmen). Fox returned to Texas and handled the publicity for Lyndon Johnson's 1948 senate race. Later, he created a television documentary, "The Port Arthur Story," which described a supposed influx of communists into Texas and aired in support of Ralph Yarborough's 1956 gubernatorial campaign. [10; 80]

FRANKHOUSER, ROY E.

The product of a bitter parental custody fight and three years in a state children's home, as a young adult Frankhouser searched for a sense of belonging in the American Nazi Party, the National States Rights Party, the National Renaissance Party, the Minutemen, and the United Klans of America. With over sixty arrests on charges ranging from inciting a riot to conducting disorderly Klan rallies, he was dubbed "Riot Roy" by his fellow Klansmen. A typical case occurred on September 4, 1961, when Frankhouser was arrested for disturbing the peace and assaulting a police officer at a United Klans rally in Atlanta. In his hometown of Reading, Pennsylvania, Roy lost his right eye in a 1965 tavern brawl. That summer of 1965, he was appointed grand dragon of the United Klans's Pennsylvania realm, and began actively recruiting Klansmen in New York, New Jersey, Maryland, and Delaware. (One of his early recruits was Dan Burros, later king kleagle for New York, who killed himself at Frankhouser's home in October 1965.) With widespread contacts on the neo-Nazi fringe, Frankhouser enlisted friendly brownshirts as Klansmen, sometimes arranging joint rallies to pad the turnout. Imperial Wizard Robert Shelton was initially reluctant to deal with neo-Nazis, but he soon realized that the Northern Klan would have to draw its hard-core membership from existing like-minded groups. On October 24, 1965, Frankhouser reported an attempt on his life in Reading, but no suspects were identified. Six months later, Delaware's attorney general stated that Roy effectively controlled the state's United Klans organization, with Grand Titan Bennie Sartin "just a puppet goose-stepping along behind Frankhouser." To garner publicity, Frankhouser announced a June 1966 march from Gettysburg to Washington, D.C., protesting James Meredith's "walk against fear" in Mississippi. Only seven Klansmen turned out for the event. On October 8, Roy and two out-of-state Klansmen were jailed for disorderly conduct during an NAACP demonstration at Girard College in Philadelphia. In the spring of 1972, when New York City passed a law forbidding the public appearance of Nazi-style uniforms, Frankhouser and fourteen members of the National Renaissance Party appeared at the Rhodesian National Tourist Board in Nazi uniforms, in an attempt to challenge the law's constitutionality. On March 1, 1974, a Philadelphia grand jury indicted Frankhouser, James Culbert, and Thomas Kanger on charges of receiving, selling, and disposing of stolen explosives. According to the indictment, 240 pounds of high explosives had been tendered to a former bodyguard of Klansman and convicted bomber Robert Miles. This latest indictment ended Frankhouser's long career as a federal informant. He boasted of a previous assignment, undertaken with blessings from the White House, that involved the infiltration of a Canadian-based Black September unit plotting to murder U.S. Zionist leaders. Cleared on the explosives charges, Frankhouser was still involved with the Pennsylvania United Klans in the early 1980s, describing himself as the Klan's "counterintelligence and informational officer." At the same time, he led a Reading congregation of the Mountain Church of Jesus Christ, founded by Robert Miles in Michigan. In February 1983, Frankhouser raised eyebrows by cooperating with black community activists in a drive to reduce local crime and unemployment. When journalists questioned his "credibility and sincerity in working with blacks," the Klansman replied, "Make no mistake about it, I don't renounce my past associations or affiliations. I was dedicated to them when I belonged, and I still belong to them in one way or another." In December 1987, while serving as an aide to extremist presidential candidate Lyndon LaRouche, Frankhouser was convicted in Boston of plotting to obstruct a federal investigation into a purported multimillion-dollar credit card fraud. [*NYT* 1961, 1966, 1972, 1974; 2; 38; 84]

FRANKLIN, JAMES

A black who resided in Bedford County, Tennessee, during Reconstruction, Franklin was flogged by Klansmen and eventually fled the county following continued threats by the Klan. [87]

FRANKLIN, JOSEPH PAUL

Born James Clayton Vaughn, Jr., in Mobile, Alabama, Franklin was the eldest son of an alcoholic drifter who often abandoned his family for months or years at a time. Siblings remember that James Vaughn, Sr., would celebrate infrequent homecomings by beating his children, with James, Jr., absorbing the worst punishment. As a youth, Franklin went in for food fads and fringe religions, dropping out of high school after an accident left him with severely impaired eyesight. The injury exempted Franklin from military conscription, and he married in 1968, at an age when many young men worried about the draft lottery and serving in Vietnam. Soon after the wedding, Franklin's bride noted a change in his personality, "like night and day." He began to beat her, emulating the father he hated, and on other occasions she would find him inexplicably weeping. Around the same time, their all-white neighborhood was racially integrated, and Franklin began to veer toward pathological bigotry. The next few years were marked by ugly racial incidents and sporadic arrests for carrying concealed weapons. Franklin joined the American Nazi Party, lapsing into the segregationist movement full-time after his mother's death in 1972. Moving to Atlanta, he joined the neo-fascist National States Rights Party, simultaneously holding membership in the local Ku Klux Klan. Franklin began insulting interracial couples in public, and on Labor Day 1976, he trailed one such couple to a dead-end street in Atlanta, where he sprayed them with Mace. Around this time, Franklin legally changed his name, shedding the last links with his former life. Federal prosecutors allege that he spent the years 1977 to 1980 wandering across the South and Midwest, employing eighteen pseudonyms, changing cars and weapons frequently, and dying his hair so often that it nearly fell out. Along the way, he killed thirteen persons in a frenzied, one-man war against minorities. According to the FBI, Franklin launched his campaign in the summer of 1977, bombing a Chattanooga synagogue on July 29. Nine days later, investigators say, he shot and killed Alphonse Manning and Toni Schwenn, an interracial couple, in Madison, Wisconsin. On October 8, Gerald Gordon was killed by sniper fire as he left a bar mitzvah in the St. Louis suburb of Richmond Heights. Harold McIver, the black manager of a fast-food restaurant in Doraville, Georgia, was working the night-shift when a sniper took his life on July 22, 1979. Three months later, in Oklahoma City, another interracial couple came under attack from the itinerant gunman. Jesse Taylor was killed by three bullets from a high-powered rifle, and his wife, Marian Bresette, was shot and killed when she went to the aid of her husband. Franklin struck twice in Indianapolis during January 1980, killing black men with long-distance rifle fire in two separate attacks. On May 3, he allegedly killed a young white woman, Rebecca Bergstrom, and dumped her body near Tomah, in central Wisconsin. On June 8 he surfaced in Cincinnati, murdering cousins Darrell Lane and Dante Brown from his sniper's perch on a nearby railroad trestle. A week later, in

Johnstown, Pennsylvania, Franklin shot and killed a black couple, Arthur Smothers and Kathleen Mikula, as they crossed a downtown bridge. On August 20, joggers Ted Fields and David Martin were cut down by rifle fire in Salt Lake City, Utah. Franklin was arrested in September 1980, but escaped to Florida, where he was recaptured a month later. Franklin faced a marathon series of state and federal trials, with mixed results. He was acquitted of the shooting that had left civil rights leader Vernon Jordan critically injured in May 1980, but Utah juries found him guilty of murder and civil rights violations, and handed down a sentence of life imprisonment. He also stands convicted of the Chattanooga bombing and the double murder in Wisconsin, described by prosecutors as "the closest thing to killing for sport." [*NYT* 1979–1984]

FRANKLIN COUNTY IMPROVEMENT ASSOCIATION

In 1965 congressional investigators identified this group as a cover for Louisburg, North Carolina, Unit No. 121, United Klans of America. [38]

FRASER, J.E. ("FROG")

A nurseryman in MacClenny, Florida, Fraser emerged in 1957 as the spokesman for the Florida Ku Klux Klan, although he denied serving as imperial wizard. A Klansman since 1923 and a self-described "cracker," he told newsmen, "We're for segregation and white supremacy and upholding the law. There's plenty of ways to do things within the law and sometimes we have to straighten up officials. Fellow sells his house to a nigger in a white neighborhood and we just spread the word. He loses his business and his friends. That ol' boy better just get out of this state." [48]

FRATERNAL ORDER OF RANGERS

See *Indiana*.

FREEDMEN'S BUREAU

Created by Congress near the end of the Civil War, the Bureau of Refugees, Freedmen, and Abandoned Lands—more commonly called the Freedmen's Bureau—was attached to the army and primarily designed to care for newly freed slaves. Bureau agents distributed food and clothing, arranged employment contracts, established hospitals, schools, and colleges for blacks with aid from Northern charitable groups. At the time it represented an unprecedented extension of federal authority over individuals, regulating economic, social, and legal affairs in the South. The Bureau's carpetbag agents and "white nigger" teachers soon became prime targets for the Reconstruction Klan from Texas to the Carolinas. [87]

FREEDOM RIDES

Sponsored by the Congress of Racial Equality in 1961, the Freedom Rides were designed to test federal court rulings that required desegregation of buses and bus stations used by interstate passengers. The ill-fated experiment began on May 4, when two buses—one a Greyhound and the other a Trailways—left Washington, D.C., with integrated complements of passengers, bound for the South. The first violence occurred on May 9, in Rock Hill, South Carolina, where three riders were assaulted by whites. Local police were slow in responding to the attack. On May 14, the Greyhound bus's tires were slit near Anniston, Alabama, stopping the bus six miles from town. A lone state trooper prevented carloads of Klansmen from boarding the bus, but a firebomb was tossed through a window, severely damaging the Greyhound bus and sending twelve riders to the hospital for treatment of smoke inhalation. The Trailways bus then arrived, and was boarded by eight men who beat three of the riders and rode with their victims the rest of the way into Birmingham. One rider required fifty stitches in the head. At the Trailways bus depot, members of the KKK and National States Rights Party were waiting, having been given a fifteen-minute "head start" by Police Commissioner "Bull" Connor before his offers would interfere with the Klan's disruptions. Klansmen drove the riders from the bus and into the arms of the mob. Beatings ensued, leaving one rider crippled for life. After reluctantly jailing three Klansmen who lingered too long at the scene, Connor declared, "Our people of Birmingham are a peaceful people, and we never have any trouble unless some people come into our city looking for trouble." Governor John Patterson, elected with Klan support in 1958, added his own advice to the riders: "Get out of Alabama as fast as possible." On May 20, despite two advance warnings from the FBI, Montgomery's Police Commissioner Lester Sullivan had no officers at Union Terminal when the Freedom Bus arrived. Three hundred Klansmen were on hand, however, and White House observer John Siegenthaler was one of those beaten unconscious by the mob. Secure at his headquarters, Sullivan told newsmen, "We have no intention of standing police guard for a bunch of troublemakers coming into our city." When officers arrived ten minutes after the bus's arrival, over 1,000—many of them armed—had gathered to confront the freedom riders. It took police over an hour to restore some order. On the night of May 21, 3,000 whites besieged and stoned a local church where Dr. Martin Luther King and several freedom riders were scheduled to address a black audience. President John F. Kennedy dispatched 600 U.S. marshals to the scene, and a federal court responded the same day, handing down an injunction against further violence by the the U.S. Klans, the Alabama Knights, the Federated Klans, and individuals including Robert Shelton and Reverend Alvin Horn. In hearings on the case, J.B. Stoner served as legal counsel for some of the Klansmen involved, and Shelton drew a warning from the court for evasive answers, at one point claiming that he could not identify Klansmen in the riots because he kept no records of his membership. (A Birmingham newsman had no trouble fingering Shelton as one of those present at the Trailways terminal on May 14.) On May 22, FBI agents arrested four Klansmen for burning the Greyhound bus outside Anniston; three days later, police in Lagrange, Georgia, jailed five men for trying to intercept a Freedom Bus near the Alabama border. All five arrested carried KKK membership cards or application blanks. In one Klansman's car, police found three pistols, a hammer, and a blackjack, while another had a permit for the gun hidden under his jacket. Two of the Klansmen were charged with rioting, and three others paid fines on lesser counts of idling, loitering, and violating local anti-pamphleteering laws. On May 26, interstate cooperation paid off with the arrest of a Rome, Georgia, Klansman for assaulting a Birmingham newsman during the May 14 riot. A week later, Judge Frank Johnson continued his injunction against terrorism, but dropped the near-defunct Federated Klans from his list. The freedom riders entered Monroe, North Carolina, on August 21 on an invitation from local blacks, and by August 24 they were under attack. One rider was wounded in a drive-by shooting on August 25, with two others assaulted and beaten on the street. Yet another was beaten in jail by a white prisoner, who later admitted that policemen had offered him dismissal of his charges in return for the beating. On August 26, Klan motorcades raided a black neighborhood, with residents erecting barricades and exchanging gunfire with Klansmen throughout the night. Six days later, a federal grand jury in Birmingham indicted nine men on various charges related to the Anniston bus-burning. Eight defendants went on trial October 31, with the presiding judge reporting efforts to intimidate the jury. A mistrial was declared for seven defendants on November 3, while Anniston Klansman Kenneth Adams won a directed verdict of acquittal based on insufficient evidence. One juror, Klansman Lewis Parker, was jailed November 28 on perjury charges, stemming from his denial of KKK membership at the time he was selected. Over the next four days, freedom riders were sporadically assaulted, including an incident in McComb, Mississippi, where the mob was estimated at 700 persons. Convicted in January 1962, five of the Alabama bus-burners drew terms of one year's probation in return for their promise to sever all ties with the Klan. On July 7, 1962, a burning cross was suspended from a turnpike overpass near Nashau, New Hampshire, the day before a scheduled visit by the freedom riders, but it was not proven whether Klansmen were involved. [NYT 1961–1962; 68]

FREEDOM SUMMER

Characterized by one observer as a "closed society," Mississippi was the most difficult state for civil rights activists in the 1960s. Statewide, Mississippi's 1.257 million whites were numerically superior, but blacks outnumbered them two-to-one in some counties. Illegal bars preventing blacks from voting were rigorously maintained, "for the sake of white civilization." Late in 1963, leaders of two civil rights groups—the Congress of Racial Equality (CORE) and the Student Nonviolent Coordinating Committee (SNCC)—combined to target Mississippi as their major project for 1964. The new Council of Federated Organizations (COFO) trained volunteers that spring on campuses in the North, announcing their intention to educate and register black voters throughout Mississippi, effecting a political revolution by peaceful, constitutional means. Opposition was organized and waiting when the volunteers began to arrive in June. A decade of ineffective rhetoric had undermined the Citizens' Council's authority in its home state, and angry, frightened whites sought help from more action-prone groups such as the White Knights of the KKK, the United Klans of America, and Americans for Preservation of the White Race. The Freedom Summer was not without its casualties. At least seven blacks and two white civil rights workers were killed during the campaign, with five of the deaths traceable to identified White Knights. Three other volunteers were wounded. An estimated thirty-five shooting incidents occurred, and eighty volunteers were beaten in numerous attacks. A total of thirty-seven churches and thirty-one homes were bombed or burned between April and September, with twenty-five of those attacks recorded within the vicinity of McComb. (In October 1964, nine McComb Klansmen pled no contest on bombing charges and were promptly released, the sympathetic judge declaring they had been "unduly provoked" by blacks and outsiders.) Mississippi sheriffs and police—where they did not actually join the Klan or Americans for Preservation of the White Race—killed an unarmed black man, beat dozens of others, and arrested over 1,000 volunteers on charges ranging from the dubious to the nonexistent. In Philadelphia, Mississippi, where past or present Klansmen held office as sheriff from 1960 to 1971, a Methodist minister proclaimed, "For all practical purposes, the Klan has taken over the guidance of thought patterns in our town. It has controlled what was said and what was not said." To that end, Klansmen attacked "moderate" newspapers, "liberal" whites, the mayor of Natchez (whose property was bombed on two occasions), and anyone else who dared speak out against the violence. [FOF 1964; NYT 1964; 4; 58]

FRENCH, PEGGY JO

A white resident of Waco, Texas, French was whipped by nightriders in November 1982 as punishment for her friendship with several blacks. Four known Klansmen were later convicted of the attack. [NYT 1982–1983]

FRIENDLY CIRCLE

A front for the United Klans of America ladies auxiliary in Durham, North Carolina, this group was exposed in 1967. [38]

FRIENDS OF RHODESIA

See *Swift, Reverend Wesley.*

FRIENDSHIP CLUB

In 1966 the House Un-American Activities Committee identified this club as a front for the Klavern No. 2 Women's Auxiliary, United Klans of America, in Jacksonville, Florida. [38]

FROLICH, JAMES

An ex-Confederate officer and editor of the Searcy, Arkansas, *Record*, Frolich was also grand giant of the Reconstruction Klan in White County. In October 1868, he participated in a conspiracy to murder detective Albert Parker, after Parker was assigned to infiltrate the KKK. [87]

FROST, JONATHAN

A charter member of the KKK in November 1915, Frost also edited a racist magazine in Atlanta. His influence helped shift the early Klan away from pure fraternalism and into more aggressive racist and nativist channels. His suggestion of hiring professional advertizers led William Simmons to employ Edward Clarke and Elizabeth Tyler in 1920, which began the Klan's greatest membership boom. Dispatched by Simmons to organize the Alabama realm, Frost tried to claim the state as his private preserve, finally absconding with several thousand dollars and leaving the Klan in serious financial straits. [93]

FROST, L.S.

A "carpetbag" teacher in Tennessee during Reconstruction, Frost was flogged by Klansmen, his body then coated with a mixture of turpentine, tar, and lampblack. [93]

FRY, MRS. LESLIE

A prominent Nazi propagandist during the Great Depression, Fry escaped to Hitler's Germany before she could be tried on charges of sedition. Congressional testimony indicated that she once offered Imperial Wizard Hiram Evans $75,000 in cash in a bid to purchase the KKK. [8; 10]

FULLER, ALFRED

As president of the Fuller Brush Company, Fuller publicly denounced 1920s Klansmen as "fools and radicals." His statement provoked a KKK boycott, which was lifted when he apologized to the Klan a month later. [93]

FULLER, CLAUDE

See *White, Ben.*

FULLER, EDWARD WILLARD

Between 1947 and 1958, Fuller was arrested nine times on charges of drunkenness, fighting and disorderly conduct, carrying concealed weapons, gambling, reckless driving, and suspicion of rape, although none of the charges led to a conviction. Fuller joined the Klan in 1964, when he took over as exalted cyclops of a White Knights klavern in Louisiana, near the Mississippi border. A gambler by trade, he was employed as the manager of a roadhouse specializing in gambling and prostitution. In April 1964, he assaulted a local black man with a shotgun. He reportedly beat up two more persons in early 1965, firing a gun into one victim's car, and near the end of 1965, he again was arrested, on charges of aggravated assault. Summoned before the House Un-American Activities Committee in January 1966, he declined to answer any questions about his past. [38]

FULLERLOVE, ROBERT

A black resident of Reconstruction Choctaw County, Alabama, Fullerlove attracted the Klan's attention when he purchased 400 acres of farmland. In 1870, he was coerced into signing a Democratic party pledge and promised protection in return. But the sporadic attacks continued over the next year. Between April and October 1871, his family slept in the woods at night, fearful of being trapped inside their home by nightriders. Subpoenaed to appear before a congressional subcommittee in Livingston, Alabama, in October 1871, Fullerlove was confronted by Klansmen en route to the hearings on Klan violence and beaten. [87]

FURIES

In the Reconstruction Klan, furies were the six officers appointed to aid a grand titan in commanding a dominion. In modern parlance, there are seven furies, detailed to assist a great titan in ruling his province. By their specific titles, the modern furies include three great klaliffs, one great kligrapp, one great klabee, one great kludd, and one great nighthawk. [43; 87]

FUSSELL, JOSEPH

An ex-Confederate officer, Fussell was identified as the grand titan in charge of a Klan district covering Reconstruction Marshall and Maury counties in Tennessee [87]

G

GAILLE, GORDON

In 1976, Gaille was identified as grand dragon for the Mississippi realm of Bill Wilkinson's Invisible Empire, Knights of the KKK. [84]

GALE, WILLIAM POTTER

After training Filipino guerillas to resist the Japanese in World War II, Gale retired from the army as a lieutenant colonel. He was briefly affiliated with the John Birch Society before moving toward more extreme right-wing groups. Recruiting from veterans' organizations, he founded the paramilitary California Rangers in the late 1950s, teaching his soldiers that communists were tools of "the international Jewish conspiracy. You got your nigger Jews, you got your Asiatic Jews, and you got your white Jews. They're all Jews, and they're all the offspring of the devil." Gale's favorite comment at the time was, "Turn a nigger inside-out and you've got a Jew." Pamphlets published by the Rangers under Gale's by-line further claimed that the 6 million Jews "allegedly" murdered by Nazis in World War II were actually living in the United States. In 1963, Gale joined the Christian Defense League and began making regular speeches before ex-Klansman Wesley Swift's Church of Jesus Christ Christian. Both the Rangers and the Defense League were known to cooperate with, and recruit members from, the KKK, the National States Rights Party, the Minutemen, and similar groups. In September 1963, shortly before a local church bombing killed four black children, Gale attended a secret meeting with Klan associate Sidney Barnes and John Crommelin in Birmingham, Alabama. A month later, on October 15, 1963, he addressed a private anti-Semitic gathering at the William Penn

Hotel, in Whittier, California; members of the audience included Klan "evangelist" Connie Lynch and at least two undercover policemen. A close associate of North Hollywood States Rights leader Dr. Stanley Drennan, allegedly involved in CIA anti-Castro activities during the early 1960s, Gale ran for governor of California in 1966, his handful of votes lost in the Ronald Reagan landslide. In 1971, a year after Wesley Swift's death, Gale authored a pamphlet outlining the aims and tenets of Swift's "Identity" movement, maintaining that Aryan people constitute the Biblical lost tribe of Israel. In April 1972, he addressed a Los Angeles gathering of James Warner's New Christian Crusade Church on the theme of "How to Survive the Coming Anti-Christian Bloodbath." A typical 1970s "sermon" from Gale included this advice: "If the Jews ever fool around with us, or try to harm us in any way, every rabbi in Los Angeles will die within 24 hours. Let 'em start." A 1980 issue of the Aryan Nations newsletter named Gale as one of "our Aryan Racial Comrades in the battle for the Resurrection of our Nation." Heading up the U.S. Christian Posse Association—a branch of Posse Comitatus—in the early 1980s, Gale was featured as an instructor at the Posse's survival school near Weskan, Kansas, in March 1982. Participants were treated to racist, anti-Semitic lectures during the seminar, along with more practical schooling in the "proper explosives needed to demolish roadways, dams and bridges." On the spiritual side, Gale has also taped messages for The National Identity Broadcast, sponsored by Posse Comitatus and aired from Dodge City, Kansas. In October 1986, Gale and several other Posse members were jailed in Nevada on charges of threatening to kill IRS agents and a federal judge. [2; 67; 90]

GALLAGHER, JOHN C.

A one-armed Confederate veteran living in Sandersville, Georgia, Gallagher was visited in 1871 by Klansmen who accused him of deserting his wife and children in Tennessee and then settling in Georgia with a mistress he acquired in Alabama. The raiders carried him off, bent on whipping or killing him, but Gallagher escaped and was found the next day, alive but with serious wounds. [87]

GAPPINS, MARY

A backwoods brothel madam during Reconstruction in Alamance County, North Carolina, Gappins became a target of Klan harassment in 1870. When she ignored various warnings to leave the county, Klansmen turned out in force to demolish her house. [87]

GARCIA, GEORGE

In the 1930s Garcia served as Florida grand dragon for the Knights of the KKK, under Imperial Wizard Hiram Evans. [10]

GARDEN CITY CLUB

In 1965 congressional investigators identified this club as a front for the Orangeburg, South Carolina, klavern, United Klans of America. [38]

GARDNER, RUFUS C.

See *Rogers, Ernest and Christine.*

GARDNER, RUFUS M.

See *Rogers, Ernest and Christine.*

GARDNER, WOODROW

See *Rogers, Ernest and Christine.*

GARLAND, WILLIAM H.

A member of Wesley Swift's Christian Defense League in Cucamonga, California, Garland was arrested in 1964 when police raided his home, seizing eight machine guns and several incendiary bombs and explosive caps. At the time of his arrest, he told police the weapons had been stockpiled to repel "invaders." [90]

GARNER, ARTIS

A black resident of McComb, Mississippi, his home bombed by Klansmen on September 23, 1964. [38]

GARNER, JOE

An Alabama Klansman sentenced to federal prison for his role in a 1983 arson attack on the Southern Poverty Law Center, Garner was also implicated in an illegal cross burning at the home of a black Montgomery County commissioner. [*NYT* 1983]

GARNER IMPROVEMENT ASSOCIATION

In 1965 congressional investigators identified this group as a cover for the Garner, North Carolina, klavern, United Klans of America. [38]

GARRETT, D.B.

A black teacher during Reconstruction in Marshall County, Tennessee, Garrett was driven from his home and school by Klansmen, and warned to tip his hat and call them "master" if they met again. [93]

GARVEY, MARCUS

An early black separatist and founder of the Universal Negro Improvement Association in the 1920s, Garvey was praised by Klan leaders for his attempts to repatriate American blacks in Africa. Garvey took advantage of the Klan's support, fraternizing with Klansmen in a tenuous alliance, while using the KKK as a prime example of why blacks should leave the United States. As black historian W.E.B. DuBois explains, "Garvey's motives were clear. The triumph of the Klan would drive Negroes to his program in despair." When black leaders pressured President Calvin Coolidge to denounce the Klan, Garvey wired Coolidge a message that he had "the full sympathy of 4 million of our organization in your refusal to be drawn into the Ku Klux controversy." In 1923, Garvey was convicted of mail fraud after an estimated 1 million persons donated cash to his nonexistent Black Star steamship line. Sentenced to five years in prison, he was pardoned by President Coolidge in 1927 and deported to his native Jamaica as an undesirable alien. [93]

GASTON, A.G.

A black businessman supportive of civil rights activities in Birmingham, Alabama, Gaston became a target of Klan violence in 1963. His motel was bombed on May 12, shortly after a local rally of the United Klans, and the blast—along with another at the home of Reverend A.D. King—touched off a black riot that was suppressed by Colonel Al Lingo's state troopers. [*NYT* 1963]

GASTON, FRANK L.

In August 1964, Gaston was listed as one of the original incorporators of the "Adams County Civic & Betterment Association," a recognized front for Natchez, Mississippi, Unit No. 719, United Klans of America. [38]

GASTON, IKE

A black barber in Atlanta, Georgia, Gaston was flogged by Klansmen in March 1939, and left naked and unconscious in the woods near town. His death was blamed on shock and exposure. [93]

GASTON COUNTY SPORTSMAN CLUB

In 1965 congressional investigators identified this group as a cover for Cherryville, North Carolina, Unit No. 34, United Klans of America. [38]

GAUSE, C.L.

A Confederate veteran and member of the Reconstruction Klan in Woodruff County, Arkansas, Gause was later elected to Congress from his district. [97]

GAYER, DR. E.W.

As the 1920s successor to Eugene Farnsworth in control of the Klan's tri-state realm that included Maine, New Hampshire, and Vermont, Gayer moved the KKK headquarters from Portland, Maine, to Rochester, New Hampshire, and presided over the order's swift decline. [10]

GAYMAN, DAN

A former high school principal and self-proclaimed "bishop" in the Identity movement, Gayman alternates national speaking tours with leadership duties for his own Church of Israel, located near Schell City, Missouri. Between 1973 and 1976, Gayman was publicly affiliated with anti-Semite Buddy Tucker and his Louisiana-based National Emancipation of Our White Seed. He also maintains working links to James Warner's New Christian Crusade Church and the Aryan Nations, and addressed a 1979 conference at Hayden Lake, Idaho, on the topic of "The Aryan Warrior's Stand." [2]

GENII

In the Reconstruction Klan, there were ten genii, serving as policy advisors to the grand wizard. In the modern United Klans of America, a similar function is performed by fifteen genii who, collectively, make up the imperial kloncilium, advising the imperial wizard as necessary. By title, the United Klans genii include the imperial klaliff, imperial klokard, imperial kludd, imperial kligrapp, imperial klabee, imperial kladd, imperial klarogo, imperial klexter, imperial klonsel, imperial nighthawk, and five members of the imperial klokann. [43; 93]

GENOBLES, JOHN

A sixty-nine-year-old farmer in Spartanburg, South Carolina, Genobles was whipped by Klansmen in 1871 and ordered to publicly renounce his Republican affiliation. After he complied, with an announcement in the village marketplace, several prominent Democrats stepped up to shake his hand. [87]

GENTRY, EARL

See *Oberholtzer, Madge.*

GENTRY, ROBERT

See *Gilliam, George.*

GEORGE, REV. E.E.

Backed by the widow of Eldon Edwards, George challenged Imperial Wizard Robert Davidson for control of the U.S. Klans in the winter of 1960, assuming command when Davidson resigned in February 1961. On October 26, 1963, Klansmen in College Park, Georgia, advised Reverend George that a secret klonvocation had voted his removal from office, due to charges of financial irregularity. George responded by leading the bulk of the U.S. Klans membership into a new organization, the Improved Order of the U.S. Klans, Knights of the KKK, based in Lithonia, Georgia. At its peak, the new Klan boasted klaverns in Georgia, Alabama, and Florida, but most had gone out of business by 1967, when the House Un-American Activities Committee estimated their total membership at about 100. By the early 1970s, George and his Klan were totally inactive. [38]

GEORGETOWN TIDEWATER CLUB

In 1965 congressional investigators identified this group as a cover for the Georgetown, South Carolina, klavern, United Klans of America. [38]

GEORGIA

The Reconstruction Klan first surfaced in Columbus, Georgia, during March 1868, and the order spread statewide with the approach of November's presidential election. No portion of the state was immune from Klan violence that year, but most of the bloodshed occurred in the eastern counties, along the Alabama and Florida state lines. Between August and October 1868, the Freedmen's Bureau recorded thirty-one racist murders, forty-three nonfatal shootings, five stabbings, fifty-five beatings, and eight floggings. Countless other crimes were committed by Klansmen through 1871, and the published estimate of seventy-four Klan murders in a four-year period doubtless falls short of the mark. Whether they rode by night or turned out in broad daylight, as they did in the Camilla riot of September 1868, Klansmen were successful in their primary goal of intimidating black and Republican voters. Republican margins fell sharply throughout Georgia in 1868, and eleven counties recorded no Republican votes whatsoever. Warren County was the KKK's primary stronghold in Reconstruction Georgia, and Sheriff John Norris waged a two-year guerilla war against the Klan before he was finally framed on a bribery charge and removed from office in 1870. Democrats captured the state legislature that December, but sporadic nightriding continued into 1871, with Klansmen in Floyd and Chatooga counties enlisting aid from dens in neighboring Alabama when their ranks were lean.

For all of its post-war activity, Georgia never played the preeminent role during Reconstruction Klandom that it has in the 20th century. Stone Mountain witnessed the KKK's revival in November 1915, and Atlanta would remain the citadel of Klan power for most of the next half-century. White Georgians easily led the nation in lynchings each year, and the new Klan early on adopted a vigilante role in Georgia, although realms such as Texas, Oklahoma, and Louisiana soon proved themselves more lethal.

Sweeping the polls in 1922, Klansmen gloried in the achievement of electing a brother, Clifford Walker, as Georgia's governor. The Klan also maintained a cozy relationship with Richard Russell, chief justice of the state supreme court, and at least two more past or present Klansmen—Eugene Talmadge and E.D. Rivers—would occupy the governor's mansion prior to World War II. With the Association of Georgia Klans gaining strength following the war, Talmadge tried a comeback at the ballot box, but his death shifted Klan support to his son. Maintaining the family's traditional friendship with Georgia Klan leaders, Herman Talmadge would soon surpass his father's greatest achievement with his election to the U.S. Senate.

Far from dying out, the late 1940s and 1950s found Georgia with a confusion of Klans. Following Black Monday, the U.S. Klans rose to dominate smaller, independent operations, choosing Atlanta as the seat of an invisible empire that covered ten states. The death of Imperial Wizard Eldon Edwards led to schism in the ranks, and the organization of a new United Klans of America, with headquarters in Alabama, shifted the action away from Georgia for the first time since World War I. Still, the 1960s Georgia realm remained larger than any other except North Carolina, with an estimated fifty-seven active klaverns. At least five other Klans were also active in the state, with a combined membership approaching 2,000. Sporadic violence, including the 1961 riot at Athens and the 1964 murder of Lemuel Penn, gave Klansmen the chance to flex their muscles, but Grand Dragon Calvin Craig increasingly called on his followers to "be nonviolent, just like the niggers." The election of a president from Georgia did nothing to lift Klan spirits in 1976; Jimmy Carter was liberal even by Northern standards, and Klansmen had to be content with circulating pamphlets that described Carter as the illegitmate son of the Massachusetts Kennedys. At least three Klans clung stubbornly to life in the 1980s, along with the Georgia-based National States Rights Party, but in general the Klan in Georgia had all but disappeared. [2; 10; 84; 87]

GEORGIANS UNWILLING TO SURRENDER

A segregationist group led by Atlanta restaurateur (and future governor) Lester Maddox in 1960, GUTS, as it was called, reportedly maintained friendly ties with Grand Dragon Calvin Craig's realm of the U.S. Klans, later the United Klans of America. [NYT 1960]

GERMAN-AMERICAN BUND

Organized as the Association of the Friends of the New Germany in July 1933, the Bund was one of several pro-Nazi factions active during the Great Depression. Reorganized and renamed after ex-auto worker Fritz Kuhn took the helm in March 1936, the group was essentially a foreign arm of Adolf Hitler's Reich, receiving financial support and its orders directly from Berlin. By November 1938 the Bund had recruited an estimated 100,000 members. Klansmen were bitterly divided on the Nazi question, with Southern and midwestern members generally opposed to the Bund, while the brownshirts—then, as in the 1960s—received more favorable attention from Klan leaders in New Jersey, New York, and along the West Coast. Negotiations with the New Jersey Klan bore fruit on August 18, 1940, when several hundred Klansmen turned out for a joint rally at the Bund's Camp Nordlund, near Andover, New Jersey. Grand Dragon Arthur Bell and middleman Edward Smythe shared the dais with Deputy *Bundesfuhrer* August Klapprott, beaming as Klapprott proclaimed, "The principles of the Bund and the principles of the Klan are the same." Adverse publicity moved Imperial Wizard James Colescott to dismiss Bell and New Jersey Kligrapp A.M. Young, but the damage to Klan prestige was already done. With Kuhn serving time in Sing Sing Prison on a larceny conviction, the Bund's days were numbered, and the outbreak of hostilities with Nazi Germany a year later soon brought the group to its end. [8; 10]

GERMANY

Inspired by the Klan's financial and political success, naturalized U.S. citizens Reverend Otto Strohschein and his son returned to their native Berlin in 1923, founding *Der Deutsche Orden des Fuerigen Kreuzes* (the German Order of Fiery Crosses). Three hundred merchants, mechanics, clerks, and laborers were soon committed to "ridding the country of undesirables by fighting the Jews," but internal conflict split the order and its founders were expelled, the details of which found their way to the headlines. One newspaper called the Order "silly rather than dangerous," noting that Germany was "full of such groups of ill-balanced and romantic youths." Soon following the KKK's 1924 klonvokation in the United States, a Leipzig magazine was moved to praise the hooded knights: "Thus, then, we greet the gallant men of the Ku Klux Klan with our warmest sympathies and cherish the hope to find such cordial expressions of feeling with them in the accomplishment of our mutual aims, as are necessary to victory over the powerful enemy." Despite their ideological similarities, the Order of Fiery Crosses offered unwelcome competition to Hitler's Nazi movement, and the Order soon disappeared during the general drive against secret societies. Four decades later, in the spring of 1970, New York Representative Seymour Halpern received a complaint that one of his constituents, Spec. 4 Edward Kaneta, had been beaten by fellow soldiers for crossing the color line to associate with black soldiers in Frankfurt. Kaneta described his assailants as four white sergeants, members of an on-base klavern said to number forty-seven men. An army report, issued on June 3, denied any evidence of Klan activity in West Germany, but the furor prompted Imperial Wizard Robert Shelton to claim extensive infiltration of the military, both at home and abroad. No evidence was found to back up Shelton's boast, and when an active military klavern was discovered six years later at Camp

Pendleton, California, neither Shelton nor his United Klans of America were involved. [*NYT* 1970; 10]

GHOLSON, SAMUEL J.

An attorney and ex-Confederate general, Gholson was also identified as a Reconstruction Klan leader in Monroe County, Mississippi, and its surroundings. In June 1871, he represented twenty Klansmen charged with the murder of a black man, Alec Page. [87]

GHOULS

The original prescript of the Reconstruction KKK applied this designation to rank-and-file Klansmen. In Maury County, Tennessee, during 1867 and early 1868, curious and confusing attempts were made to adapt the title for members of higher rank, but the designation was never clarified or officially sanctioned. Published sources differ on whether the term still applies to modern Klansmen, but it does not appear in the Kloran or in any current constitution of the various competing Klans. [87]

GIANT

In United Klans parlance, this is a purely honorary title reserved for retired officers of various levels, with a Klansman's prior status determined by prefix. Thus, a Klan giant is a retired exalted cyclops; a great giant is a former great titan; a grand giant is a retired grand dragon; and an imperial giant is a former imperial wizard. Contradictory press reports indicate that other Klans may use the title for active officers, but specific duties and definitons remain undefined. [43; see also *Grand Giant*]

GIBSON, LEROY

A twenty-year Marine Corps veteran, Gibson was identified in October 1971 as the leader of a militant racist group, the Rights of White People, located in Wilmington, North Carolina. A resident of Jacksonville, fifty miles away, Gibson told the press that his group was prepared to deal forcefully with the "communist-inspired black revolutionaries" he blamed for recent violence in Wilmington. He explained further, "Our organization is growing, and not just in the South. If necessary, we'll eliminate the black race. What are we supposed to do while these animals run loose in the streets? They'll either abide by the law, or we'll wipe them out." In May 1973, Gibson was jailed in Wilmington for bombing a local bookstore. [*NYT* 1971; 26]

GIBSON, W.H.

A black postal agent on the Louisville & Lexington Railroad, in Kentucky, Gibson was assaulted by Klansmen while his train was stopped at North

Benson on January 26, 1871. Soldiers were detailed to protect Gibson over the next month, but mail service was finally discontinued in the area after Klansmen threatened to storm the train in force. [87]

GIFFORD, FRED

A Portland, Oregon, power company employee, Gifford became Oregon's grand dragon in 1921 and soon emerged as the top Klan leader west of the Rocky Mountains. As his power increased, he was elected to sit on the board of Oregon's Federation of Patriotic Societies, which was created to endorse "American" candidates for office. Gifford's authoritarian attitude and mishandling of cash prompted Klansmen around Salem, Oregon, to resign from the order en masse. In one notorious case, he swindled Klansmen out of their investments in Skyline Corporation, which was created to build a Klan skyscraper that never materialized, and several similar schemes included a nonexistent Women's Christian Temperance Union children's camp near Corvallis. Further criticized for his domination of the Ladies of the Invisible Empire, Gifford refused to surrender his post, creating internal dissension that eventually doomed the Oregon Klan. [10]

GILBERT, ERNEST S.

When the White Knights of the KKK were incorporated in April 1964, Gilbert was identified as chief of the group's Klan Bureau of Investigation. [38]

GILBERT, KEITH

An ex-convict from Idaho and associate of the Aryan Nations, Gilbert founded his own Social Nationalist Aryan People's Party in 1979. In 1982, Gilbert conducted a yearlong harassment campaign against the children of Kootenai County resident Connie Fort, whose ex-husbands were American Indian and black, respectively. The campaign included hate mail, death threats, and personal confrontations, including an attempt to run over one of her children with a car. When racist serial killer Frank Spisak was sentenced to death in Ohio in 1983, Gilbert claimed him as a lieutenant in the Social Nationalist Aryan People's Party, asserting that Spisak was "acting under direct orders from the party" when he killed three persons in Cleveland. His orders, according to Gilbert were, "Kill niggers until the last one is dead." [*People Magazine,* Aug. 29, 1983]

GILES, HOWARD TRAVIS

See *Dahmer, Vernon.*

GILLIAM, GEORGE

A black resident of Jacksonville, Florida, whose grandson enrolled in a white school, Gilliam became the target of Klan violence in early 1964. His home was bombed on February 16, and six members of the United Florida Ku Klux Klan were indicted for the bombing. The defendants included William Rosecrans, Barton Griffin, Jacky Harden, William Wilson, Donald Segal, and Robert Gentry. Rosecrans pled guilty in March 1964 and was sentenced to seven years in prison. Four months later, he appeared as the key prosecution witness when his five fellow Klansmen faced trial on charges of conspiracy and interference with a federal court order. Attorney J.B. Stoner defended the five Klansmen, exhorting jurors to "stand up for white rights" by acquitting his clients. In the end, Harden was acquitted on both counts, Gentry was acquitted on one count with a mistrial on the other, and the other three defendants had mistrials on both charges. A November 1964 retrial for Gentry, Griffin, Siegel, and Wilson resulted in verdicts of acquittal for all of the defendants on all counts. [NYT 1964]

GILLIAM, HARRY

A grand klaliff of the United Klans and a next-door neighbor of Robert Scoggin in Spartanburg, South Carolina. Gilliam replaced Scoggin as acting grand dragon while Scoggin was imprisoned in 1969 on a conviction for contempt of congress. His refusal to surrender the office after Scoggin's release sparked a bitter power struggle which resulted in Scoggin's banishment from the United Klans. Gilliam, in turn, was soon replaced as grand dragon by Dean Williams. [84]

GILLIAM, VERLIN U.

A member of the National Knights of the KKK and identified as klaliff of the Columbus, Ohio, klavern, Gilliam was arrested and charged with robbery in 1965. Summoned before the House Un-American Activities Committee in February 1966, he pled the Fifth Amendment when confronted with evidence that he obtained dynamite from Georgia klansmen—including Joseph Sims and Cecil Myers—and transported it to Ohio in the hope of inciting "civil war." [38]

GILLIS, STERLING ("BUBBA")

A member of the United Klans of America in McComb, Mississippi, Gillis was arrested on October 5, 1964, in connection with racial bombings in and around that city. An arsenal of twenty-one firearms—in addition to knives, brass knuckles, and other weapons—was confiscated in a police raid on his home. Convicted for his part in the bombings, Gillis received a suspended sentence from a judge who decided that the Klansmen had been "provoked" by black civil rights workers. [38]

GIPSON, JOHN

An ex-Klansman from Slidell, Louisiana, Gipson joined the Pearl River Union Klavern of the Original Knights in 1963. Indicted in a flogging case, he resigned from the Klan on January 4, 1966, and turned state's evidence. His court testimony helped convict two Klansmen. In late January 1966, Gipson appeared before the House Un-American Activities Committee, and described the Klan's role in the flogging of a white youth, Clarence O'Berry, and the burning of two Slidell churches on August 2, 1965. Gipson admitted to his role in the whipping, but said he had balked at committing arson. Following his congressional testimony, he said, "Right now, I feel like my life is not worth two cents." [38]

GIRGENTI, GLADYS

Identified as a co-founder of a Tennessee splinter group, the Confederate Vigilantes, Knights of the KKK, Girgenti was one of six persons jailed after a bungled synagogue bombing in Nashville, Tennessee, in May 1981. The defendants were also charged with conspiring to blast a local television tower and several Jewish-owned shops. [NYT 1981]

GLOVER, NICHOLAS

A New Orleans Klansman, Glover was one of five arrested on June 21, 1966, in connection with a series of firebombings aimed at churches, homes, and businesses between March and May 1965. [NYT 1966]

GLOVER, ROBERT

Identified as a member of Tony LaRicci's Maryland unit in the Confederation of Independent Orders, Knights of the KKK, Glover and two other Klansmen were convicted in July 1978 of attempting to bomb a synagogue in Lochearn, Maryland. Authorities believe that the terrorists also planned to dynamite the home of a Maryland congressman. [NYT 1978]

GLYMPH, C.L.C.

A black grocer in Gaffney, South Carolina, Glymph entered the 1952 Democratic primary for city council. He withdrew on February 11 after he received a letter on the stationery of the Association of Carolina Klans, which read: "It is not customary, as you know, for the colored race of South Carolina to hold public office. Now is the time you should realize your defeat and let your withdrawal before Feb. 12 be your protection for now and hereafter." [NYT 1952]

GOBLINS

In the Reconstruction KKK, four goblins were elected as aides to the grand giant of each province. No corresponding rank exists in the modern Klan. [87]

GODFREY, GLEN

See *Stallworth, Clarke.*

GODWIN, H.L.

An ex-congressman from Dunn, North Carolina, Godwin led the lobbying effort that scuttled state anti-Klan legislation in 1927. [10]

GOLLUB, JORDAN

A resident of Poplarville, Mississippi, and identified as leader of the Mississippi Christian Knights of the KKK, Gollub was deposed in May 1989 after Klansmen discovered he was raised in Philadelphia, Pennsylvania, by Jewish parents. Gollub staunchly maintained his personal commitment to Christianity, and blamed his ouster on national Klan leader Virgil Griffin, who allegedly disliked Gollub's "background and the fact that I'm against Catholics joining the Klan." In parting, Gollub announced his intent to form a new Klan faction of his own. [*UPI,* May 12, 1989]

GOOD, CHARLES

A black resident of York County, South Carolina, during Reconstruction, Good was whipped by Klansmen in an effort to elicit his promise that he would vote the Democratic ticket in the future. When Good refused to recant his Republican membership, he was murdered. [87]

GOOD, JONA

A World War II veteran residing in Princeton, North Carolina, Good was infuriated when Klansmen erected signs reading "This is Klan Country" on local highways in June 1969. He responded by putting up signs of his own that read "This is Not Kooks, Krooks and Kowards Country! No Hate Here!" An attempt to burn his signs failed; the second attempt also failed: Good, waiting for another attempt, fired on the nightriders when they approached. Several nights later, gunmen sprayed bullets at the signs and Good's home. On July 5, both sides removed their signs in response to a plea from the mayor and the local paper, citing violence as harmful to Princeton's image and any hopes of attracting new industry. Klansmen staunchly denied any role in the raids against Good. [*NYT* 1969]

GOODMAN, ANDREW

See *Schwerner, Michael.*

GOODMAN, FLO

A white widow residing in Columbiana, Alabama, Goodman was flogged by masked Klansmen in June 1949. [NYT 1949]

GOODMAN, JESSIE LEE

A black tenant farmer in Eastman, Georgia, Goodman was twice flogged by Klansmen in early 1950. The second time, on March 2, Goodman's landlord, Otho Wiggins, drove the seven carloads of nightriders away with gunfire. Three days later, the county sheriff arrested Klansmen Theo Lewis and Alfred Crumley. A local newspaper identified three local flogging victims in the proceeding four months. [NYT 1950]

GOODWIN, CHARLES

A deputy sheriff in Wilmington, North Carolina, Goodwin was one of several officers allegedly assigned to infiltrate the United Klans of America, and who then retained his membership when officers on the force were ordered to resign. In January 1964 he was elected grand klaliff for the realm, collecting dues at the sheriff's office and storing the cash in the safe. [NYT 1965]

GOODWIN, MILLS E.

As governor of Virginia, Goodwin offered a standing $1,000 reward for illegal cross burners on December 7, 1966. The move was prompted by a recent Klan resurgence, with eighteen crosses burned in Richmond alone. Another was burned an hour after Goodwin announced the reward, at the home of a white high school student who wrote an anti-Klan letter to his local newspaper. On December 10, a cross was burned near the governor's mansion. Journalists reported at least 175 Virginia Klan rallies in the previous eighteen months, with Klan membership estimated at 2,000, and 8,000 to 10,000 sympathizers. [NYT 1966]

GORDON, GEORGE W.

An ex-Confederate general and one of the earliest Klan members in Tennessee during Reconstruction, Gordon is generally credited with drafting the KKK's original prescript. He was also the chief organizer of the April 1867 conference in Nashville, which reorganized the Klan as an instrument of resistance to Radical Reconstruction. In July 1868, Gordon dispatched R.J. Brunson to organize dens in South Carolina, but Gordon was soon repulsed by the Klan's undisciplined violence. Gordon joined Grand Wizard Nathan Forrest and others in pleading with Governor Brownlow to disband the state militia, citing black troops as an irritant bound to provoke further unrest. On August 3, 1868, he addressed a crowd in Pulaski with a plea to curb nightriding, and his influence soon helped to minimize masked violence. [87]

GORDON, JOHN B.

An ex-Confederate general and Reconstruction grand dragon of the Georgia KKK, Gordon was also the Conservative candidate for governor in 1868. He severed his connection with the Klan soon after the election, citing Klan violence as his reason, and thereafter pretended that the order had ceased to exist. Gordon was later elected to serve in the U.S. Senate. [87]

GORE, J.C.

A white, disabled veteran of World War II, Gore was dragged from his Conway, South Carolina, home by Klansmen on January 17, 1950. A crippled uncle, Sam Gore, was seized in the same raid, and both men were flogged on accusations of neglecting their families. Local patriots were outraged by the attack, and nine Klansmen were arrested by January 21. [NYT 1950]

GORMAN, JOHN C.

The editor of the Raleigh, North Carolina, *Telegram,* Gorman was identified as the founder of White Brotherhood during the 1868 election campaign. [87]

GOULD, BARBARA AYRTON

A member of parliament from London, in May 1947 Gould received an anonymous letter headed "Klavern Eight," warning her against publicly mentioning or antagonizing the KKK. The message made reference to a "certain Jew who had a very nasty experience and received medical attention last week." The comment was apparently referring to an assault on Lewis Lipstein, a forty-one-year-old barber in Edgewood-Middlesex, adjoining Gould's Northwest London parliamentary district, but a police investigation of the case failed to reveal any organized Klan activity. [NYT 1947]

GRADY, HENRY A.

A superior court judge and grand dragon of North Carolina from 1922 to 1927, Grady was a member of the court-approved board that supervised the transfer of power from Imperial Wizard William Simmons to Hiram Evans. In 1926, he clashed with Evans on the issues of masked demonstrations and Klan involvement in politics. Grady was finally banished when he refused to support a package of "silly, unseemly, and unconstitutional" bills proposed by imperial headquarters aimed at blacks and Catholics. Still occupying the bench in New Bern in February 1952, he personally announced the arrest of floggers linked to the Association of Carolina Klans, declaring, "There is no place in North Carolina for the Ku Klux Klan." [*Nation*, March 8, 1952]

GRADY, HENRY W.

Editor of the Rome, Georgia, *Commercial* during Reconstruction, Grady was identified by a rival newsman as a participant in a January 1871 Klan demonstration. When a grand jury opened its probe of masked violence a month later, the *Commercial* urged all members of secret societies "to remain perfectly quiet and orderly, for the present at any rate." The editorial advised that Klansmen should ride again only "if an inexorable necessity calls for action." [87]

GRADY, JOE

Identified as a leader of the White Knights of Liberty in Greensboro, North Carolina, Grady ignored a public challenge from the Communist Workers Party that led to a shootout and the deaths of five people in November 1979. Attending the murder trial of five Klansmen and Nazis in 1980, he described the prosecution as "a shaft job from the beginning." [*UPI*, Aug. 5, 1980; 10]

GRAHAM, ROYAL

A Denver judge, Graham ran against anti-Klan incumbent Ben Lindsey for a seat on the children's court in 1924. After he lost, Graham filed a lawsuit (with KKK support), claiming that ballots from a predominantly Jewish district had been fraudulently marked for Lindsey. The case was thrown out of court, and Graham's attorney was forced to sue for his fee. Judge Graham subsequently killed himself rather than face a state bar association investigation of his link to the Klan. [10]

GRAHAM GAME CLUB

In 1965 congressional investigators identified this group as a cover for United Klans of America Unit No. 50, in Graham, North Carolina. [38]

GRAINGER, BEN

A white resident of Fair Bluff, North Carolina, Grainger and his girlfriend, Dorothy Martin, were abducted by Klansmen on October 6, 1951. The couple was driven across the state line into Horry County, South Carolina, where they were flogged. FBI agents traced the crime to the Fair Bluff klavern, Association of Carolina Klans, and eleven members were arrested on federal kidnapping charges. The defendants included: Early L. Brooks, Fair Bluff's exalted cyclops, constable, and ex-police chief; his son, Bobby Brooks; Ross Enzor; brothers George and Sherwood Miller; Steve Edmond;

Horace Strickland, a deputy sheriff and ex-police chief of Tabor City; James R. Hayes; Pittman F. Strickland (no relation to Horace); L.C. Worley; and Carl Richardson. At their trial in May 1952, George Miller was acquitted, while the other ten Klansmen were convicted on various charges. Sentences included three years probation (Edmond, Worley, Sherwood Miller, and Bobby Brooks); two years each on two counts (Richardson); three years each on two counts (Enzor, Hayes, and both Stricklands); and five years each on two counts (Early Brooks). [NYT 1952]

GRAND CYCLOPS

In the Reconstruction Klan, this officer commanded a local den, assisted by two nighthawks. [93]

GRAND DRAGON

Throughout Klan history, this title has applied to the chief officer of a realm. During Reconstruction, the grand dragon was advised by eight hydras, a number increased to nine for the 20th century Klan. [38]

GRAND ENSIGN

In the Reconstruction Klan, the grand ensign was a local officer in charge of the Klan banner for a particular den. Today, the kladd fulfills that function, while the term "grand ensign," at least in the United Klans of America, is reserved for the banner itself. [93]

GRAND EXCHEQUER

During Reconstruction, the grand exchequer was a Klan treasurer, serving at various levels from individual dens to imperial headquarters without different titles to designate rank. His modern equivalent would be the klabee. [93]

GRAND GIANT

In the Reconstruction Klan, this title designated the chief officer of a province who was advised by four goblins. Some modern groups retain the office, while the United Klans of America has added a unique twist, treating "grand giant" as an honorary title sometimes (but not always) bestowed on retired grand dragons. [43; 87]

GRAND GUARD

Selected as sentries for the original KKK, members of the grand guard were chosen by a den's grand sentinel to stand watch during meetings. Their symbolic function is fulfilled in modern times by the klexter, but Klans of significant size normally maintain a special, uniformed security force to patrol public rallies and demonstrations. [93]

GRAND KLAN

A special gathering convened in Spartanburg County, South Carolina, in the spring of 1871, this meeting included delegates from Spartanburg, York, Union, and Chester counties, along with some representatives from North Carolina. The convention issued a decree forbidding future raids without specific orders from the Grand Klan itself, establishing penalties for same, but the gesture was fruitless and ultimately unenforceable. [87]

GRAND MAGI

During Reconstruction, this officer served as second in command of a den, presiding in the absence of the grand cyclops. Today, the klaliff holds an equivalent rank as vice president of a klavern. [93]

GRAND MONK

In the original Klan, this officer was third in command of a den, presiding when both the grand cyclops and the grand magi were absent. There is no equivalent rank in the 20th century KKK. [93]

GRAND SCRIBE

As secretary of the Reconstruction Klan, the grand scribe served at various levels from local dens to imperial headquarters without further differentiation in title. His modern equivalent is the kligrapp. [87]

GRAND SENTINEL

During Reconstruction, this officer held responsibility for den security, including selection and assignment of the grand guard. The modern KKK divides this task between the klexter and klarogo, with occasional assistance from special security squads. [87]

GRAND TITAN

The commanding officer of a dominion during Reconstruction, this officer was advised by six furies. [87]

GRAND TURK

In the Reconstruction Klan, the grand turk served as a den's executive officer, charged with informing the rank and file of any irregular or informal gatherings called by the grand cyclops. [93]

GRAND TYCOON

The anonymous signatory of an alleged Klan circular published in Lebanon, Tennessee, in September 1868, the grand tycoon advised Klansmen that

"Our mission on earth, to some extent, is ended. Quiet and peace must be cast abroad in the land." Although neither the title nor dateline of the circular bore any resemblance to an established format from the Klan prescript, it still had the effect of ending nocturnal raids in Wilson County. [87]

GRAND WIZARD

As supreme leader of the Reconstruction Klan, the grand wizard was advised and assisted by ten genii. Retired cavalry general Nathan Bedford Forrest was the one and only wizard of Reconstruction times, and his control over local Klansmen was minimal, at best. In modern times, the supreme rank has generally been altered to "imperial wizard," although a few smaller Klans have retained the original title. [38; 87]

GRANTHAM, JACK

Identified as the exalted cyclops of the Miami klavern, United Knights of the KKK, Grantham was arrested with Grand Dragon Charles Riddlehoover on October 29, 1965, and charged with speeding and reckless driving. A search of Grantham's vehicle turned up documents indicating that the United Knights had broken off from the United Klans of America in a feud involving money. [*NYT* 1965]

GRAVEL RIDGE HUNTERS LODGE

In 1965 congressional investigators identified this group as a cover for the Hermitage, Arkansas, klavern, United Klans of America. [38]

GRAVES, BIBB

A former state adjutant general and colonel of an Alabama regiment in World War I, Graves was one of the most successful politicians in Alabama's history. As an avowed Klansman, he was elected governor in 1926, joining Senator-elect Hugo Black and Imperial Wizard Hiram Evans for a victory celebration at the Birmingham klavern. (At the height of the festivities, both winners received lifetime passes to the Invisible Empire.) At his inauguration, Graves invited Evans and Alabama Grand Dragon James Esdale to sit beside him on the podium. Still faithful to the Klan in August 1927, he pushed for the passage of the Graves-Klan Muzzling Bill, which proposed $25,000 fines for the libelous criticism of public officials. Nightriders flourished with Graves in the statehouse, and the governor actively obstructed the prosecution of Klansmen, slashing trial budgets to an average of $15 per case. By late 1927, Klan violence led civic leaders to call on Graves to disband the KKK, but he had no such power. [10]

GREAT GIANT

In the United Klans of America, this honorary title is reserved for certain retired great titans. [43]

GREAT TITAN

The modern commanding officer of a Klan province, a great titan is assisted in his duties by a staff of seven furies. [43; see also *Grand Titan*]

GREAVES, ELMORE D.

A resident of Jackson, Mississippi, Greaves edited *The Southerner*, an "unofficial" publication of the White Knights, in 1965 and 1966. In January 1965, he was appointed chairman of the White Christian Protective and Legal Defense Fund by Imperial Wizard Sam Bowers. [59]

GREEN, DR. SAMUEL

An Atlanta obstetrician, Green joined the KKK in the early 1920s and worked his way up during the Great Depression to the post of grand dragon, serving as Imperial Wizard James Colescott's righthand man. A month after Colescott's April 1944 disbandment order, Green organized his own Association of Georgia Klans, holding together a loose network of klaverns in Georgia, Alabama, Tennessee, South Carolina, and Florida. This association's existence was publicly announced with a cross burning ceremony at Stone Mountain in October 1945, and Green presided over the Klan's greatest period of growth in the late 1940s. In Georgia politics, he maintained close ties with the Talmadge family, and Green was treated to a lively ovation when he addressed the South Carolina state legislature in 1948. The tide had begun to turn by 1949, with rival Klans competing for members and money, and politicians and journalists raising their voices in opposition to Klan violence. In Columbia, South Carolina, a student audience heckled Green and pelted him with stink bombs. In July 1949, while being interviewed by a black reporter, he explained, "If God wanted us all to be equal, He would have made all people white men." Formally dubbed the grand dragon after Georgia revoked his Klan's charter in 1946, Green was elevated to the rank of imperial wizard during an early August 1949 klonkave. His reign was brief, however. On August 18, he died of a heart attack. He was replaced by ex-policeman Sam Roper on August 27, but the Association would never fully recover. [10; 38]

GREEN, SAMUEL, JR.

The son of Dr. Samuel Green, Sr., and a loyal Klansman, Green served as an attorney for Eldon Edwards when he incorporated the U.S. Klans in October 1955. [*NYT 1955*]

GREEN THUMB GARDEN CLUB

In 1965 congressional investigators identified this group as a cover for Ladies Auxiliary No. 4, United Klans of America, in Monroe, Louisiana. [38]

GREENE, JERRY

A former grand dragon of New Jersey, Greene moved to South Carolina in 1976 and launched an unsuccessful campaign for elected office in the 37th Congressional District. [84].

GREENE, JOE

See *Peterson, Jim.*

GREENE COUNTY IMPROVEMENT ASSOCIATION

A 1960s front for the Snow Hill, North Carolina, klavern, United Klans of America, this group was publicly exposed in 1966. [38]

GREENSBORO, NORTH CAROLINA

In 1979, Greensboro members of the Communist Workers Party selected the local KKK as a symbol of "capitalist America," and deliberately sought a violent confrontation for its publicity value. On July 8, Workers Party members disrupted a Klan rally in China Grove, seventy miles from Greensboro, where Klansmen had gathered to watch *Birth of a Nation*. A Klan banner was burned while Workers Party members chanted "Kill the Klan." The Klansmen responded with racial epithets and by brandishing their guns. Hoping for a more newsworthy showdown, the Workers Party addressed an open letter to area Klansmen, which read in part: "The KKK is one of the most treacherous scum elements produced by the dying system of capitalism. We challenge you to attend our rally in Greensboro." Joe Grady's White Knights of Liberty chose to ignore the challenge, but members of the North Carolina Knights and the affiliated National Socialist Party of America chose not to ignore it. In retrospect, police informant Edward Dawson seems to have been instrumental in drawing Klansmen to Greensboro on the appointed day. Police contacts told Dawson where the procession would begin, and they assured him that the Workers Party members would be unarmed. A second informant, Bernard Butkovich— employed by Treasury's Bureau of Alcohol, Tobacco, and Firearms—had infiltrated a local National Socialist Party chapter, where he worked overtime to coordinate a neo-Nazi/Klan alliance, urging members to stockpile their arsenals. Like Dawson, Butkovich attended strategy sessions prior to the rally, urging Klansmen to attack the Workers Party at their first opportunity. On October 31 and again on rally day, November 3, Dawson warned Greensboro police that Klansmen and neo-Nazis, all heavily armed, were bent on disrupting the march. Despite this advance notice, police were nowhere in sight when the one-sided shootout began. Four Workers Party members were killed, including Dr. James Waller (a physician who gave up his practice to serve as president of the local textile workers' union); Bill Sampson (a union organizer with a master of divinity degree from Harvard); Cesar Cauce (a Cuban immigrant who graduated magna cum laude from Duke University); and Sandi Smith (a black civil rights activist). A fifth victim, Dr. Michael Nathan, chief of pediatrics at Durham's Lincoln Community Health Center, died from his wounds on November 6. Of the forty Klansmen and neo-Nazis in the firing squad, sixteen were identified from videotapes and arrested for murder. Conspiracy charges were dropped by the state, thus eliminating Dawson and Butkovich as potentially embarassing witnesses. Greensboro's general attitude was reflected in the comments of prospective jurors. One declared, "The only thing the Klan is guilty of is poor shooting," while another said, "I don't think we are out a lot because those people aren't with us anymore. I think we are better off without them." The 1980 trial last twenty-two weeks, one of the longest in North Carolina's history. The six defendants included Klansmen Jerry Smith, Coleman Pridmore, Lawrence Morgan, and David Matthews, along with neo-Nazis Jack Fowler and Roland Wood. Jerry Cooper, a Greensboro patrolman who followed the Klan motorcade, described Fowler as the first man to fire on the unarmed marchers, but his testimony was ignored by the jury. All six defendants were acquitted on November 17, 1980, with jurors accepting their plea of self-defense. Nine days later, charges were dismissed against thirteen other Klansmen, neo-Nazis, and Workers Party members. Returned to court on federal civil rights charges in 1985, the six accused sat through another fourteen weeks of testimony, which ended with five acquittals and one Klansman sentenced to six months in a prison work-release program. As Grand Dragon Virgil Griffin voiced his jubilation—"I felt like I died and went to heaven"—spouses of the Greensboro victims were left to seek monetary damages in civil suits against the gunmen already twice acquitted. [10; 93]

GREENVILLE COUNTY KLAN

A small and ineffective splinter group, this was identified as one of seven competing Klans active in South Carolina during the late 1950s. [6]

GREGORY, C.E.

A reporter for the Atlanta *Journal*, Gregory escaped injury when Klansmen bombed his home on August 23, 1947. The bomb was thrown at an open window, but it missed and fell back on the porch. Gregory became a Klan target after writing an exposé of corruption in the Herman Talmadge political campaign, including the time-honored practice of allowing the dead to vote in Telfair County. He was also working on a book-length exposé of Georgia demagogues and race-baiters. [*NYT* 1947]

GRIFFIN, BARTON

As exalted cyclops of Jacksonville Klavern 13, United Florida KKK, Griffin was one of six Klansmen charged with bombing George Gilliam's home in February 1964. When Griffin's own house was wrecked and burned in an April 25 explosion, attorney J.B. Stoner publicly blamed blacks and agents of the FBI. A mistrial was declared on Griffin's federal bombing charges, July 5, 1964, and he was acquitted at his second trial, on November 25. Between trials, Griffin—along with four other Klansmen, including Stoner and Connie Lynch—was arrested for burning a cross at a St. Augustine bakery on July 24. [*NYT* 1964]

GRIFFIN, JOHN

See *Aaron, Edward.*

GRIFFIN, KENNETH CHESTER

Identified as Georgia state chairmain of the National States Rights Party in 1958, Griffin was one of four men arrested in July 1958 while picketing the *Journal and Constitution* offices with anti-Semitic placards. Three months later, he was indicted with George Bright and other States Rights members for bombing an Atlanta synagogue. The case against Griffin was dropped after Bright's acquittal in 1959. [65]

GRIFFIN, SPENCER

A black resident of Spencer County, Tennessee, during Reconstruction, Griffin received 150 lashes from Klansmen seeking to teach blacks "that they had to do what they were told." [93]

GRIFFIN, VIRGIL

A high school dropout and textile mill worker, Griffin succeeded Joe Bryant as grand dragon for the North Carolina Knights of the KKK. He attended Robert Scoggin's Conference of Eastern Dragons in 1976, and two years later met with Greensboro members of the National Socialist Party of America to create the United Racist Front. Griffin's Klansmen accepted a public challenge from the Communist Workers Party to attend an anti-Klan rally in November 1979, which resulted in five deaths. After the gunmen were acquitted of the murder charges, Griffin declared, "I don't see any difference between killing communists in Vietnam and killing them here." [10; 93]

GRIFFIN, WILLIAM J.

As founder in July 1953 of the Association of Florida Ku Klux Klans, Griffin reportedly disbanded the group two years later. By 1960, however, he was competing with Bill Hendrix for dominance of the Florida realm. His public endorsement of Richard Nixon for president became an embarrassing public issue in Nixon's televised debate with John Kennedy in October 1960. On October 13, in the crucial third debate, Kennedy was asked about a statement from his publicist that "all bigots will vote for Nixon." He replied, "Well, Mr. Griffin, I believe, who is the head of the Klan, who lives in Tampa, Florida, indicated in a statement, I think, two or three weeks ago, that he was not going to vote for me, and that he was going to vote for Mr. Nixon. I do not suggest in any way—nor have I ever—that that indicates that Mr. Nixon has the slightest sympathy in regard to the Ku Klux Klan." Nixon echoed the rejection from Los Angeles, but in an election in which the black vote made a crucial difference, the disavowal was too little and too late. In Tampa, Griffin told the press, "I don't give a damn what Nixon said. I'm still voting for him." [10; 93]

GRIFTON CHRISTIAN SOCIETY

In 1965 congressional investigators identified this group as a cover for the Grifton, North Carolina, klavern, United Klans of America. [38]

GRIMSLEY, JAMES IRA

As sheriff of Jackson County, Mississippi, in 1962, Grimsley led a mob of seventy whites from Pascagoula to Oxford for the riot against black student James Meredith. The rioters were summoned by radio bulletins and transported to Oxford in chartered buses, with Grimsley and his chief deputy in command. On their return, they were treated as heroes. Grimsley chartered his group as the Jackson County Citizens Emergency Unit, and began local intimidation campaigns and a boycott of moderate newspaper editor Ira Harkey. On one occasion an anonymous caller warned Harkey that "some people would like to see you dead," advising him to "ask the sheriff" for details. Late in 1963, an FBI probe revealed links between Grimsley's Unit and the resurgent Mississippi Klan, but Grimsley's group soon withered under federal scrutiny. When the sheriff ran for state office in 1964, his margin of support was insufficient to carry the vital Democratic primary in Jackson County. [37]

GRIMSTAD, WILLIAM N.

A professional anti-Semite and at one time a registered foreign agent for Saudi Arabia, Grimstad launched his career by joining the National Socialist White People's Party in 1971. Within a year he had risen to the post of managing editor for the party's official newspaper, *White Power*. By 1977, he had authored numerous anti-Semitic articles and several books, including one outlining the "Zionist myth" of the Nazi holocaust. Late in 1979, Grimstad joined David Duke's Knights of the KKK, emerging as corresponding editor for Duke's periodical, *The Crusader*. [2]

GROVELAND, FLORIDA

In July 1949, Groveland was transformed into a war zone by reports of a white woman being kidnapped and raped by four blacks. On July 16, a mob of 100 whites—which included members of the Ku Klux Klan of Florida, Inc.—converged on Tavares, seeking two suspects recently removed from the Groveland jail. Sheriff Willis McCall dispersed the would-be lynchers, and turned them back toward Groveland. On their return, they raided a black neighborhood and shot up a restaurant patronized by blacks. On July 17, Groveland was the scene of a Klan parade. Governor Fuller Warren dispatched National Guard units to Groveland as 400 blacks evacuated the town. On July 18, truckloads of Klansmen raided the rural village of Mascotte, forcing police and Guardsmen to withdraw, and searched outbound vehicles for fleeing blacks. Three homes were burned in the raid, including one owned by the father of one of the rape suspects. Klansmen continued their raid into some adjacent small towns. Order was restored by July 19, with three of the rape suspects indicted on capital charges; a fourth was killed by a posse in Perry, Florida, on July 26. The convictions of two of the defendants were overturned by the U.S. Supreme Court in 1951, with orders for a new trial. On November 6, while transporting the defendants from Raiford state prison to Tavares, Sheriff McCall shot them both "in self-defense," leaving one dead and the other critically wounded. [*NYT* 1949, 1951]

GRUBBS, MILLARD

See *Continental League for Christian Freedom*.

GUEST, HERBERT

An illiterate mechanic and gun collector in Athens, Georgia, Guest was a member of Clarke County Klavern No. 44, United Klans of America. On March 7, 1964, Guest sent black garage employee "Preacher" Potts to start a car reportedly stalled on a rural highway near Athens. At the alleged breakdown site, Potts was overpowered and whipped by robed Klansmen. When Potts returned to the garage, Guest met him with a smile and asked, "Your tail sore, Preacher? You want a cushion to sit on?" Arrested on June 21, 1964, for firing shots into black homes and wounding two persons, Guest was ultimately fined $105 on conviction of disorderly conduct. In mid-July, FBI agents named Guest as a suspect in the Lemuel Penn murder case, but state charges were dropped to allow Guest to testify against Joseph

Sims and Cecil Myers. On the witness stand, Guest admitted signing a statement, read to him by federal agents, but he denied knowledge of its contents, claiming he had "blacked out" while in custody. Tried on federal charges of conspiring to violate Penn's civil rights, Guest was acquitted in July 1966. [33; 88]

GUILFORD COUNTY BOOSTERS CLUB

In 1965 congressional investigators identified this club as the front for a Greensboro, North Carolina, klavern, United Klans of America. [38]

GULF COAST KU KLUX KLAN

Based in Mobile, Alabama, this group was one of six Klans active in the state after Black Monday. Gun dealer Elmo Barnard was the Gulf Klan's leader, with an estimated 1,000 members enrolled by early 1957. Smaller than some competing groups, Barnard's faction cherished its reputation for aggressiveness, and maintained a loose working agreement with Robert Hodges and his Association of South Carolina Klans. In Alabama, Barnard's chief competition came from Reverend Alvin Horn's U.S. Klans, which promised to push the Gulf Coast Klan "right into the Gulf." Time and attrition, however, ended the Mobile faction, which ceased to exist by the early 1960s. [6; 48]

GULLEDGE, REV. A.H.

A Klansman and minister from Columbus, Ohio, Gulledge participated in the Klan's 1925 march on Washington, D.C. When rain began to drench the faithful, Gulledge led his congregation in a special weather prayer, trying to stop the downpour, which promptly increased. [93]

GULLION, STEWARD R.

With James Venable, Gullion was an original incorporating officer of the Defensive Legion of Registered Americans in April 1962. [38]

GUNN, DR. HOWARD

A black leader of the United League in Tupelo, Mississippi, Gunn drew the Klan's attention in 1978 while leading protests over the death of black man killed in police custody. That August, gunmen shot out his windshield while Gunn was driving near town. Two weeks later, Bill Wilkinson held a rally of his Invisible Empire Knights with national television coverage, announcing, "We hurt some niggers. We shot up Gunn's car and we're not ashamed of it." Two participants in the rally later removed their robes, revealing deputy sheriffs' uniforms underneath. [93]

GUNN, ROY

See *Tarrants, Thomas.*

GUPTON, WILBUR

A CIO organizer in Lagrange, Georgia, Gupton and his wife were abducted and flogged by Klansmen in August 1947. [*NYT* 1947]

GUSTIATUS, BERNARD

A factory worker in Danville, Illinois, Gustiatus was identified in 1975 as the organizer and exalted cyclops of a local klavern, United Klans of America. [43]

GUTS

See *Georgians Unwilling to Surrender.*

GUTTER, BOOKER T.

A black grocer in Summit, Mississippi, Gutter became a target for Klansmen from McComb, who bombed his market in September 1964. [38]

GUY, GEORGE

As police chief of McComb, Mississippi, in 1964, Guy also served as president of the local Americans for Preservation of the White Race. [83]

H

HAGGARD, REV. A.A.

A Tennessee evangelist and Klansman, Haggard was the principal speaker at a Knoxville rally of the Association of Georgia Klans in June 1946. Although he denied a leadership role, his public statements claimed 10,000 members for the group. [NYT 1946]

HALIFAX COUNTY LADIES CLUB

In 1965 congressional investigators identified this group as a cover for a ladies auxiliary unit, United Klans of America, serving klaverns in Enfield and Weldon, North Carolina. [38]

HALL, C.G.

As the Arkansas secretary of state, Hall issued a June 8, 1959, announcement that he would use every legal means available to block the filing of Klan incorporation papers. Arsonists set fire to his front porch the next day, but rain extinguished the flames. Embarrassed by the attack, Grand Dragon A.C. Hightower said, "We don't have people who would do such a thing as that." [NYT 1959]

HALL, REV. ENELL

A black minister in Hickory Hills, Illinois, Hall was the target of a bomb in August 1984. The unexploded bomb, found in his home, was ultimately traced to Willis Pernic, who was indicted in June 1985. A search of Pernic's home revealed a Klan robe, but the suspect eluded capture and disappeared, and is believed to be in hiding underground. [*NYT* 1985]

HALL, EUGENE S.

Arrested in connection with bombings related to the Montgomery, Alabama, bus boycott in 1957, Hall was released without trial in a general amnesty that dismissed charges against black demonstrators and Klansmen. The author of a pamphlet titled "The Bible Answers Racial Questions," Hall was affiliated with James Venable's National Knights by 1976, addressing rallies as a keynote speaker. [84]

HALL, HERSCHEL

See *Folsom, Constance.*

HALL, JOHN WESLEY

Nicknamed "Nigger" by his fellow Klansmen in Birmingham, Hall was a member of the United Klans of America when he volunteered to murder black minister Fred Shuttlesworth. The assassination never took place, and Hall later shifted his allegiance to the violence-prone Cahaba River Group, a band of United Klans defectors blamed for the September 1963 church bombing in Birmingham that killed four black children. Fingered by Imperial Wizard Robert Shelton, Hall was arrested by Alabama state police on September 30, along with Robert Chambliss and Charles Cagle. The three were found with a case of dynamite on September 4—the same night on which bombers struck the home of black attorney Arthur Shores—but prosecutors pressed only misdemeanor charges of possessing explosives without legal permits. All were convicted, drawing terms of six months in jail and $100 fines, but the sentences were later overturned on jurisdictional grounds. State Attorney General Richmond Flowers complained that premature arrests in the case, orchestrated by Shelton and Colonel Al Lingo, had ruined any hopes of prosecuting the three men for murder. In November 1963, after polygraph tests convinced FBI agents of Hall's complicity in the fatal bombing, he was placed on the federal payroll as a confidential informant, reporting to the FBI on activities of the Klan. J. Edgar Hoover twice refused local requests to prosecute the church bombers, on grounds that Hall would be compromised as an informant. Years later, Attorney General Bill Baxley identified Hall as the builder of the lethal church bomb, but Hall died before FBI headquarters released enough information to Baxley to allow him to prosecute the 1963 case. [*NYT* 1963; 10; 68]

HALL, MAXINE

A black resident of Indianapolis, Indiana, Hall won an urban homestead house in a 1984 civic contest, investing $10,000 to make the home liveable.

In June 1984, her contractor found a threatening note in his car, signed "KKK," and Hall's new house was destroyed by arsonists the following day. [*NYT* 1984]

HALL, SAM J.

As Alabama secretary of the American Communist Party, Hall was a natural target both for policemen and Klansmen. In 1950, Birmingham police commissioner "Bull" Connor launched a personal campaign against Hall, resulting in the secretary's conviction on vagrancy charges. Several known Klansmen were spotted in court on the day of Hall's trial, and a cross was burned at his home on July 15. A note recovered at the scene, signed by the Federated Ku Klux Klans, read: "There is no room in this country for rattlesnakes, mad dogs or communists." [*NYT* 1951]

HAMBURG SPORTSMAN CLUB

In 1965 congressional investigators identified this group as a cover for the Hamburg, Arkansas, klavern, United Klans of America. [87]

HAMBY, BOYD LEE, SR.

A native of North Carolina, Hamby served as grand nighthawk for the United Klans of America under Grand Dragon J.R. Jones until late 1965. In September of that year, after Reverend Roy Woodle resigned from the United Klans and offered embarrassing testimony to the House Un-American Activities Committee, Hamby reportedly visited the minister's home and told Woodle he had been given "the authority to do away with me." A few weeks later, Hamby and George Dorsett were transferred to Florida by Imperial Wizard Robert Shelton to recruit members for a new United Klans realm. Establishing headquarters in Titusville, Hamby soon emerged as grand dragon of the state. [38]

HAMILTON, BILL

A resident of Coalburg, Alabama, Hamilton was dragged from his home by members of the Federated Ku Klux Klans in May 1949, and received twenty lashes with a belt. A crippled neighbor, William Rochester, was also abducted and forced to observe the flogging, and was threatened with a worse punishment "if you do just one thing." [*NYT* 1949]

HAMILTON, JAMES

A perennial loser in Michigan politics, Hamilton waged his various 1920s campaigns on the single issue of a constitutional amendment banning parochial schools. In 1920, as head of the Wayne County Civic Association, he ran for governor and was soundly defeated. By 1924, Hamilton was a

Klansman and leader of the Michigan Public School Defense League. Both he and his proposed school law were on the ballot that year, and both were rejected by state voters. Hamilton's pet issue was finally settled two years later, when the U.S. Supreme Court struck down a similar law in Oregon. [10]

HAMILTON, JOHN W.

As editor of *The White Sentinel* in the late 1950s, Hamilton was part of the delegation that greeted John Kasper upon his release from federal prison in August 1958. [14]

HAMILTON, THOMAS

An Atlanta wholesale grocer and onetime aide to Dr. Samuel Green in the Association of Georgia Klans, Hamilton moved to Leesville, South Carolina, in 1948, dividing his time between business and the Invisible Empire. Within a year, Hamilton's Association of Carolina Klans demanded his full attention, with Klansmen kicking off a two-year reign of terror that spanned portions of two states. By the summer of 1950, state and federal authorities were close to arresting Hamilton and his group. On August 31, 1950, after a Klan raid on Charlie Fitzgerald's Myrtle Beach dance hall, Hamilton was arrested for conspiracy to incite mob violence. He was jailed again on September 18 on identical charges for the August 1950 whipping of Leslie Boney. A new state law against cross burnings resulted in Hamilton's next arrest, on May 19, 1951, after he led a motorcade through Conway, South Carolina, with an electric cross mounted on his car. Five months later, on October 30, 1951, Hamilton was convicted of criminal libel for his published attacks on a newsman in Anderson, South Carolina, and forced to pay a $1,000 fine. On May 24, 1952, the portly grand dragon was held for conspiracy in two North Carolina floggings; indictments issued on June 19 charged Hamilton and twenty-three others with kidnapping, conspiracy, and assault in the whippings of five blacks and two whites. Hamilton pled no contest on conspiracy charges in the case of victim Evergreen Flowers, and received a four-year prison sentence in July. In prison Hamilton formally renounced his Klan membership and on October 22, 1953, urged his followers to disband. By that time, however, there were few if any active members left to heed his call. As the Greensboro *Daily News* gloated, the "Tarheelias *Fuhrer* of the meat counter and vegetable bins" had received his comeuppance. Released on parole in February 1954, Hamilton apparently made good on his promise to stay clear of the Klan. [10]

HAMM, WILLIE J.

A black resident of Asbury Park, New Jersey, Hamm was the target of a cross burning incident in 1972. Four Klansmen were identified as suspects in the case, three of whom were given only $500 fines in return for testifying against their leader. Tried as the "moving spirit" behind the attack, Joseph Kusch was convicted and sentenced to six months in January 1973. A year later, his conviction was affirmed on appeal. [*NYT* 1973–1974]

HAMMACHER, RUSSELL

See *Flowers, Evergreen.*

HAMMOND, C.R.

A Newnan, Georgia, Klansman, Hammond was armed when police arrested him in Lagrange in May 1961 for attempting to block the integrated Freedom Rides. On May 29, a judge ordered Hammond held over for trial on charges of inciting a riot. [*FOF* 1961]

HAMMONDS, JENRICH

See *Flowers, Evergreen.*

HAMPTON, STEPHEN

In the summer of 1975, Hampton was identified as the exalted cyclops of a Decatur, Illinois, klavern, United Klans of America. [43]

HANCOCK, W.C.

A Harpeville, Georgia, Klansman, Hancock was armed when arrested in May 1961 in La Grange for trying to block the integrated Freedom Rides. On May 29, he was ordered held over for trial on charges of inciting a riot. [*FOF* 1961]

HAND, B.J.

With brothers Fred and Henry, Hand was identified as one of the original incorporators of the Clayton Civic Club in January 1965. Congressional investigators subsequently identified the club as a front for Clayton County Klavern No. 52, United Klans of America, in Jonesboro, Georgia. [38]

HAND, FRED

See *Hand, B.J.*

HAND, HENRY

See *Hand, B.J.*

HAND, KARL, JR.

A member of David Duke's Knights of the KKK, Hand was one of three New Jersey Klansmen indicted in February 1980 after shots were fired into the home of Joseph and Shirley Sanders, a black couple in Barnegat Township. Hand pled innocent to the charges in March, then went underground in a bid to escape prosecution. While hiding from the law, he attempted suicide by drinking antifreeze, and spent the next several months in and out of hospitals. In January 1981, Hand changed his plea to guilty on a charge of attempted bodily harm with a weapon, but sentencing was deferred until April. In the meantime, Hand resigned from the Klan and joined the National Socialist Party of America, for which he planned a neo-Nazi rally in Buffalo, New York, on January 15, to "celebrate" the birthday of Dr. Martin Luther King. The rally attracted two Nazis, 100 reporters, and 500 protesters. In February 1981, Hand defected from the National Socialist Party to accept a leadership post in the National Socialist Liberation Front. Two months later, he was sentenced to six months in jail for the Barnegat shooting, with three months suspended and two years probation. Free on bond pending an appeal of his conviction, Hand moved to Metairie, Louisiana, billing himself as the commanding officer of the National Socialist Liberation Front, a group he describes as "a revolutionary movement that has repudiated mass tactics and has instead embraced armed struggle and political terrorism." Hand's appeal was rejected in October 1982, and he was ordered to begin serving his three-month sentence in April 1983. Defiant to the last, he accused the court of "headhunting" and shouted "White Power!" as bailiffs led him away. [2]

HANDLEY, ROGER

In 1979, Handley was identified as the Alabama grand dragon of Bill Wilkinson's Invisible Empire Knights. Active in fomenting violent rallies around Decatur, Alabama, in connection with the rape trial of black defendant Tommy Lee Hines, Handley also donated forty-seven acres of land near Cullman for the establishment of a paramilitary training center known as Camp My Lai. In statements to the press Handley described the camp as one of several facilities maintained in Alabama, noting that the locations are changed every three months to maintain tight security. In July 1989, as losers of a federal lawsuit, Handley and nine other Klansmen were ordered to pay $11,500 each to blacks injured in the Decatur riots. They were also ordered to attend classes in race relations, to be taught by leaders of the Southern Christian Leadership Conference. This verdict was denounced by Imperial Wizard James Farrands as "cruel and unusual punishment." [UPI, July 26, 1989; 2]

HANES, ARTHUR, SR.

A former mayor of Birmingham, Alabama, Hanes was voted out of office in the same November 1962 special election that ousted police commissioner "Bull" Connor. Both men refused to surrender their offices pending a long-winded battle in court, and their reign extended through the period of black civil rights demonstrations in early 1963. Declassified FBI files from the period identify Hanes as "a very strong supporter" of Connor's violent tactics and "a fellow who has certainly a strong smell of the Klan about him." When Birmingham moderates negotiated a desegregation agreement in 1963, Hanes complained that "These traitors have sold their birthrights to negotiate with these niggers." When Imperial Klonsel Matt Murphy died in an August 1965 auto accident, Hanes served as a pallbearer at his funeral, afterward taking over the legal defense of three Klansmen charged in the Viola Liuzzo murder. Hanes still denied any KKK connection, telling the press, "I was hired by these boys, but as far as I know, the Klan has nothing to do with paying me." In his summation at the trial of Collie Wilkins, Hanes told jurors, "Maybe the murderer is from the Watts area of Los Angeles or over in Crawfordville, Georgia, trying to produce a body to raise money for their nefarious schemes." Briefly retained to defend James Earl Ray in 1968 on charges of assassinating Dr. Martin Luther King, Hanes rejected J.B. Stoner's offer of support through a nationwide fund-raising campaign by the National States Rights Party. At the same time, Midwestern Klan leader George Wilson testified that Hanes accepted a $10,000 retainer in Ray's case from the United Klans of America. Congressional investigators documented two meetings between Hanes and United Klans Imperial Wizard Robert Shelton, in June and August 1968, but the topics of discussion remain uncertain. In 1969 Hanes joined acting wizard Melvin Sexton and others for a meeting of the United Klans imperial board, at which Klan leaders discussed his $12,500 fee for defending members jailed in North Carolina. With his son, Hanes went on to defend lifelong Klansman Robert Chambliss in 1977, dismissing evidence of his client's involvement in a fatal church bombing with the claim that everyone "talked tough" in 1963. [68]

HANLEY, JAMES H.

Publicly identified as the "great kligrapp" of New York, Handley's threatening letter to Dorothy Langston, mailed on April 5, 1946, sparked a state investigation into renewed Klan activity since World War II. [*NYT* 1946]

HANNAH HAWKS CLUB

In 1965 congressional investigators identified this club as a front for the Florence, South Carolina, klavern, United Klans of America. [38]

HANSEN, ROBERT SCOTT

See *McKinney, James.*

HARDEE, CLAUDIS
See *Rogers, Ernest and Christine.*

HARDEE, ERNEST
See *Flowers, Evergreen.*

HARDEE, JOE
See *Flowers, Evergreen.*

HARDEN, JACKY DON
See *Gilliam, George.*

HARDING, WARREN GAMALIEL
As the Republican victor in 1920's presidential campaign, Harding may have benefited from Klan demonstrations on election eve warning blacks in various parts of the South not to vote. Shortly after his inauguration, Harding was initiated as a Klansman in the Green Room of the White House, with William Simmons leading the five-man imperial induction team. The nervous Klansmen forgot their Bible, required for the final oath, and Harding sent for the White House Bible to complete the ceremony. Afterward, Simmons and company received special War Department license tags, thereby securing immunity for them against traffic citations. On August 2, 1923, while returning from a tour of Alaska, Harding fell ill and died in San Francisco, not long before scandals rocked his corrupt administration. Rumors of his Klan membership leaked out as early as 1924, and Imperial Klokard Alton Young, a member of the induction team, described the ceremony for journalist Stetson Kennedy on his deathbed in the late 1940s. Interviewed by Patsy Sims in 1976, Imperial Wizard James Venable claimed to possess—but never produced—photographs of a Klan funeral ceremony conducted for Harding in Marion, Ohio, in August 1923. [10; 84; 93]

HARKEY, IRA B., JR.
Settling in Mississippi during 1949, Harkey edited the Pascagoula *Chronicle*, and earned a reputation for liberalism in a region dedicated to preservation of the racial status quo. Pascagoula witnessed a rash of cross burnings on September 1, 1954, shortly before schools were scheduled to open, one of which was planted at Harkey's beach house with a sign reading: "We do not appreciate niggerlovers. We are watching you. KKK." A few days later, Klan spokesman Tommy Harper visited Harkey's office and warned him that blacks would not be the primary target if Pascagoula was forced to desegregate. "The one we'll get is the white man that's behind them,"

Harper cautioned, "and we know who he is." By 1962, Harkey was running editorials critical of Governor Ross Barnett and the Oxford rioters, and referring to blacks as "Mr." and "Mrs." in print. A new antagonist was the Jackson County Citizens Emergency Unit, a Klan-affiliated group led by Sheriff James Grimsley and his chief deputy. On the night of the Unit's second meeting, October 15, 1962, a rifle shot was fired through the *Chronicle* front door. Days later, at another meeting, Grimsley named Harkey's paper as "the state's leading niggerlover." *Chronicle* newsboys were harassed by Grimsley and other whites, chased off their delivery routes, and local stores were threatened with boycotts if they purchased ads in the paper. FBI agents launched an investigation after Harkey's windows were shattered by shotgun blasts on November 1, and Grimsley's Unit soon faded in the face of federal investigation. By that time, however, a new, more violent Klan was putting down its roots in Mississippi. Harkey left Mississippi in July 1963. [37]

HARMONY CLUB

See *West Duplin Boating & Fishing Club.*

HARNETT COUNTY IMPROVEMENT ASSOCIATION

In 1965 congressional investigators identified this group as a cover for Dunn, North Carolina, Unit No. 22, United Klans of America. [38]

HARNETT COUNTY LADIES LEAGUE

A front for the United Klans of America ladies auxiliary in Dunn, North Carolina, this group was publicly identified in 1965. [38]

HAROLD, DR. C.L.

A dentist and grand goblin for the 1920s Ohio KKK, Harold conducted Klan business from his State Street office in Columbus. [10]

HAROLD THE KLANSMAN

A pro-Klan novel authored by George Alfred Brown and published by the Western Baptist Publishing Company in 1923, *Harold the Klansman* was a surprisingly literate effort, complete with reasonably well-developed characters. The story line pits Harold and his brother knights against evil Roman Catholic priests plotting to "put out propaganda to discredit the Klan." In the final scene, Harold and his wife admire a fiery cross that "represents a wonderful movement. A movement that will mean better citizenship." [93]

HARPE, J.L.

See *Hawkins, Joe Denver.*

HARPER, JAMES D.

A Miami Klansman, Harper was one of twelve called before a federal grand jury probing local terrorism in October 1952. [*NYT* 1952]

HARPER, JAMES L.

See *Blackwell Real Estate.*

HARPER, JULIUS

In 1964, Harper was identified as grand dragon of the White Knights of the KKK, serving as second in command to Imperial Wizard Sam Bowers. In October 1964, following the arrest of several Klan bombers in McComb, he cautioned other White Knights to bury any explosives they might have on hand, thereby preserving them for future use. [38]

HARPER, RONNIE M.

A Marine Corps private first-class and member of the Knights of the KKK, Harper was assigned to new living quarters at Camp Pendleton after a clash with black marines left thirteen whites wounded in December 1976. [*NYT* 1976]

HARRELL, JOHN R.

As leader of the extremist Christian-Patriot Defense League, Harrell participated in May 1978 gatherings of the United Klans of America in Orlando and Plant City, Florida. [2]

HARRIMAN VOLUNTEER CLUB

In 1965 congressional investigators identified this group as a cover for Harriman, Tennessee, Unit No. 2, United Klans of America. [38]

HARRINGTON, E.P.

See *Rogers, Ernest and Christine.*

HARRINGTON, P.M.

See *Rogers, Ernest and Christine.*

HARRIS, DAVID

Identified as Wisconsin's grand dragon in 1966, Harris was the target of gunmen who fired into his Waukesha home on October 8. Denouncing the police investigation as a "whitewash" and vowing retaliation, Harris posted armed guards—including bombing suspect Robert Long—around his house. [*NYT* 1966]

HARRIS, ESSIC

A black resident of Chatham County, North Carolina, Harris was "insolent" enough to buy another shotgun after Klansmen confiscated his in December 1870. The raiders returned a few nights later, firing into the house, and Harris answered in kind. The sound of shots attracted landlord Ned Finch, who pleaded with Klansmen to leave his tenant alone. Ignoring Finch's plea and threatening his life when he persisted, the nightriders fought for thirty minutes with Harris, wounding him several times before being driven away. Harris severely wounded Klansmen Joe Clark and Barney Bridges before they withdrew. Several Klansmen were arrested during February 1871 and charged with the raid against Harris, but all were released after producing "airtight" alibis. [87; 93]

HARRIS, JAMES

See *Hattie Cotton School.*

HARRIS, JIM

A resident of Cincinnati, Harris was selected to replace Flynn Harvey as Ohio grand dragon for the United Klans of America in late 1965. On September 11, 1972, he announced Imperial Wizard Robert Shelton's order for all Klansmen to undergo polygraph examinations to weed out any government informants. According to Harris, the United Klans had already purchased several lie detectors, and operators were being trained to administer the tests. [*NYT* 1972; 38]

HARRIS, JULIAN

As editor of the Columbus, Georgia, *Enquirer-Sun*, Harris was the only Georgia newsman to reprint a series of Klan exposés published by the New York *World* in 1921. Four years later, he won the Pulitzer prize for his coverage of black community news and exposure of local KKK activities. In stinging editorials, Harris attacked Georgia Klansmen as "grafters, blackmailers, spy-chiefs," and sometimes simply as "cluck-clucks." His paper named various public officials as Klansmen, including Georgia's governor, attorney general, commissioner of agriculture, commissioner of fish and game, the superintendent of public education, and the chief justice of the state supreme court. H.L. Mencken described Harris's 1925 Pulitzer selection as "the most intelligent award the committee has yet made." [10; 93]

HARRIS, R.E.

A Republican congressman in Alabama during Reconstruction, Harris was dragged from a train with Senator Lentz in October 1868 and flogged by Klansmen. [87]

HARRISON, ANDREW JACKSON

In 1976, Harrison was identified as the teenaged leader of the Junior Order, United Klans of America. [84]

HARRISON, LOUIS

See *Hurst, Charlie.*

HARRISON, McCORD

A resident of Phoenix, Arizona, Harrison served as king kleagle and editor of *Arizona Klankraft* in the early 1920s. He was elected grand dragon at a statewide rally in the summer of 1923. [10]

HARRISON, W.H.

A black state legislator in Hancock County, Georgia, during Reconstruction, Harrison was defeated after a Klan-led riot prevented blacks from voting in 1870. A year later, he told congressional investigators that he still spent one night of every three in the woods to avoid Klan raiders. [87]

HARRY, JAMES

Identified as a Klan leader in west Georgia, Harry was arrested in West Point in 1984, and charged with carrying and displaying a firearm during a public demonstration. He pled guilty that September and was fined $105. [*NYT* 1984]

HART, EMMETT

A member of the Apopka, Florida, klavern, Hart was indicted on June 3, 1953, for perjury before a federal grand jury that had been probing Klan violence since 1949. Independent testimony identified Hart as a member of the team that tried to kidnap NAACP lawyer Franklin Williams in August 1949. [*NYT* 1953]

HARTLEY, A.I.

Employed as editor of the Warrenton, Georgia, *Clipper*, Hartley was one of six Warren County Klansmen arrested in June 1869 for the murder of state senator Joseph Adkins. He was subsequently freed without indictment in the case. [87]

HARTLINE, WILLIAM

See *Lynch, John.*

HARTSVILLE SPORTSMANS CLUB

In 1965 congressional investigators identified this group as a cover for Hartsville, South Carolina, Unit No. 24, United Klans of America. [38]

HARVEY, FLYNN

A resident of Columbus, Ohio, Harvey was recruited into the National Knights of the KKK in September 1963. Returning home to incorporate the Buckeye realm, he was appointed as James Venable's Ohio grand dragon in the fall of 1964. Charges of inefficiency, drunkenness, and financial mismanagement drove him out of the National Knights in May 1965, but Harvey soon resurfaced as Robert Shelton's grand dragon for the United Klans of America. A change of Klans did not produce a change of luck, however, and Harvey was removed from office before year's end and replaced by Grand Dragon Jim Harris. [38]

HARVEY, JOSEPH

A black resident of Alamance County, North Carolina, Harvey was visited by Klansmen and administered 150 lashes in March 1869. The Klansmen then clubbed Harvey's infant child to death. [87]

HARWOOD, BROWN

In 1922 Harwood replaced Dr. A.D. Ellis as Texas grand dragon for the Knights of the Ku Klux Klan, Inc. [10]

HATTIE COTTON SCHOOL

Located in Nashville, Tennessee, the Hattie Cotton School was bombed in September 1957 in an effort to forestall court-ordered desegregation. Suspects arrested in the case included Charles Reed (a participant in local Klan demonstrations), Venson Crimmons, James Harris, and J.B. Blackwell. [*NYT* 1957]

HAW RIVER FISHING CLUB

In 1965 congressional investigators identified this club as the front for a Greensboro, North Carolina, klavern, United Klans of America. [38]

HAWKINS, JOE DANIEL

A second-generation Mississippi Klansman, Hawkins was indicted during 1967 on three counts of assault and battery with intent to kill for the beating and shooting of black civil rights workers. Tried twice on one count, he walked away from mistrials on each occasion when jurors failed to agree on a verdict. On September 18, 1967, Hawkins and his father were arrested in Jackson for assaulting FBI agents. In November 1968 he and Thomas Tarrants were indicted in a Meridian bomb plot that led to the police killing of Klanswoman Kathy Ainsworth. Still at large in April 1981, Hawkins was arrested with Imperial Wizard Stephen Black and eight neo-Nazi associates for plotting an invasion of Dominica. Convicted of violating the federal Neutrality Act, Hawkins was sentenced to three years in prison. [NYT 1967, 1981–1982]

HAWKINS, JOE DENVER

A Jackson, Mississippi, Klansman and member of the board of directors of Americans for Preservation of the White Race, Hawkins was arrested for assaulting FBI agents on September 18, 1967. His son, Joe Daniel, and Klansman Julius L. Harper were jailed in the same incident. Federal agents were investigating the bombing of a local synagogue when the assault took place near Hawkins's home. [NYT 1967; 96]

HAWKINS, DR. JOHN

A former exalted cyclops in Solebury, Pennsylvania, during the 1920s, Hawkins broke with the Klan by publicly supporting Catholic Al Smith's presidential candidacy in 1928. [10]

HAWKINS, LESTER C.

An Alabama Klansman specifically named in Judge Frank Johnson's May 21, 1961, injunction barring violent interference with the Freedom Rides, Hawkins was dropped from the list when the order was extended on June 2, 1961. [FOF 1961]

HAYES, JAMES ROBERT

See *Grainger, Ben.*

HAYLING, DR. ROBERT N.

A black dentist and civil rights activist, Dr. Hayling moved to St. Augustine, Florida, in 1959. Elected to lead the local NAACP, he encouraged sit-in demonstrations by black college students in 1961. Along with three other blacks, he was caught spying on a rally of the United Florida Ku Klux Klan, on September 19, 1963, and was beaten by Klansmen (including Connie Lynch) before Sheriff L.O. Davis arrived to arrest the victims. Four Klansmen were later charged with assault, one of whom was acquitted on November 5, 1963. Charges against the others were subsequently dismissed. Hayling and the other blacks were convicted of assaulting Klansmen after an unregistered pistol was "found" in their car. On February 8, 1964, nightriders fired shotgun blasts into Hayling's home, killing the family dog. [*NYT* 1963–1964]

HAYNES, A.J.

A captain of the Arkansas militia during 1868 and early 1869, Haynes was accused of murder by prominent Democrats after his troops, in the line of duty, killed Klansmen. In July 1869, Haynes was killed on the main street of Marion, Arkansas, by Klansman Clarence Collier. [87]

HAYS, BENNIE JACK

A high-ranking member of the United Klans in Mobile, Alabama, Hays and his wife were convicted of mail fraud, wire fraud, and conspiracy in October 1984. Three years later, Hays was charged in the 1981 murder of black teenager Michael Donald, a case that saw both his son and son-in-law convicted of first-degree murder. Hays's own trial in the case during February 1988 was aborted on grounds of his age and poor health. [*NYT* 1984, 1987–1988]

HAYS, BROOKS

An ex-congressman from Arkansas, Hays was known as a moderate on racial matters during the 1960s. In January 1965, he was invited to address an audience in Bogalusa, Louisiana. The Original Knights of the KKK distributed more than 6,000 handbills, advising Bogalusans that Hays was coming "to convince you that you should help integration by sitting in church with the black man, hiring more of them in your businesses, serving and eating with them in your cafes, and allowing your children to sit by filthy, runny-nosed, ragged, ugly little niggers in your public schools." Klansmen warned that anyone attending the meeting would "be tagged as integrationists and will be dealt with accordingly." The speech was canceled after a series of telephone bomb threats and a cross burning at the church where Hays was scheduled to appear. [*NYT* 1965; 93]

HAYS, CHARLES

As a Republican congressman from Alabama during Reconstruction, Hays was a natural target for Klan harassment. In October 1868, Klansman Ryland Randolph led a mob that broke up a Republican rally addressed by Hays and Senator Willard Warner in Tuscaloosa. Defeated for reelection in August 1869, an election in which the Klan's terrorism prevented blacks in his district from voting, Hays requested federal troops to patrol Sumter County during the 1870 election campaign. The request was denied, and Klan threats became so persistent that Hays was afraid to appear in the county, thus permitting his opponent to carry the race by default. [87]

HAYS, HENRY FRANCIS

See *Donald, Michael.*

HAYWOOD, BOBBY D.

See *Evers, Charles.*

HEAD, DANIEL

A leader of the Reconstruction Klan in Haralson County, Georgia, Head was also the father of a Democratic candidate for the state legislature in 1871. [87]

HEATH, DONALD

A policeman assigned to the predominantly black Philmore District on Chicago's West Side, Heath was also a member of the National Knights of the KKK in 1967. A yearlong probe identified several Klansmen on the force, and a raid on Heath's home turned up various weapons—including a bazooka—and 200,000 rounds of ammunition. Authorities alleged that the weapons had been stockpiled in a plot to kill Mayor Richard Daley and various other public figures. Heath was immediately relieved of duty, and two other Klan cops resigned from the force. [*NYT* 1967]

HEATH, REV. ROY

See *Hurst, Charlie.*

HEFLIN, THOMAS

A U.S. Senator from Alabama and one of America's leading anti-Catholic spokesmen in the 1920s, Heflin was also a closet Klansman who later emerged as a full-time orator on the Klan lecture circuit. Dakota Klansmen pegged Heflin as their presidential candidate in 1928, against New York Catholic Al Smith, and produced pamphlets headlined "Swat Smith and put Heflin in the White House." Heflin recognized the hopelessness of a personal campaign, but he did his part to defeat Smith that year, touring the country and addressing Klan rallies for $150 or $250 a throw, assuring Klansmen that Smith would go down to defeat in November. Some receptions were tougher than others, and Catholics in Brockton, Massachusetts, disrupted two scheduled appearances with showers of rocks, bottles, and mud. Heflin overstepped his bounds when he broke party ranks to support Herbert Hoover in 1928, and Alabama's state Democratic committee used the transgression to unseat Heflin in his own reelection bid that year. In 1929, the city fathers of Portland, Maine, denied Klansmen the use of city hall for a Heflin speech, and his next two senate races, including one as a Republican, were unsuccessful. Klan leaders finally admitted Heflin was one of their own after he lost the race for a senate seat vacated by new Supreme Court Justice Hugo Black, in 1937. The same year, Heflin and another Klansman faced new opposition when they were appointed as as special assistants to the U.S. Attorney General. [10]

HEGGIE'S SCOUTS

A Reconstruction white supremacist group with apparent ties to the KKK, the Scouts were active during 1867 and 1868 in Holmes, Carroll, and Montgomery counties, Mississippi. [87]

HELM, JACK

Appointed as grand klaliff for the Louisiana realm, United Klans of America, in 1965, Helm replaced James Edwards as grand dragon early the following year. His reign was short-lived, and internal dissension led him to resign in March 1967. He then led most of the United Klans south Louisiana provinces into a new Universal Klans, also known as The South. On February 23, 1967, a few days before making his break with the United Klans, Helm and Klansman Jules Kimble reportedly visited the New Orleans apartment of Kennedy assassination suspect David Ferrie. (Ferrie, an associate of Lee Harvey Oswald and New Orleans Mafia boss Carlos Marcello, had died the previous day, from a "stroke.") According to Kimble, Helm removed a valise filled with documents from Ferrie's apartment, and took them to a local bank, where they were stored in a safe deposit box. The documents in question were never retrieved. [21; 38]

HEMINGWAY SPORTSMANS CLUB

In 1965 congressional investigators identified this group as a cover for Hemingway, South Carolina, Unit No. 17, United Klans of America. [38]

HENDERSON, JERRIS

A member of the Invisible Empire KKK, Henderson was jailed in Hall County, Georgia, during 1985, for "making terroristic threats" against a young man who ridiculed the Klan. [NYT 1985]

HENDRICKS, CHARLES

An election manager in Gwinnett County, Georgia, during Reconstruction, Hendricks was shot and wounded by Klansmen. He survived the attack, but immediately retired from political activity. [93]

"HENDRIX, JAMES J."

In 1965 congressional investigators identified this name as an alias used by Betty Shelton, wife of Imperial Wizard Robert Shelton, in co-signing various checks drawn on the account of the Alabama Rescue Service. In this manner, Shelton was able to tap the United Klans of America's bank account for personal gain while circumventing a requirement of the Klan constitution that all checks be co-signed by the imperial klabee. Despite public exposure of the "Hendrix" scam in October 1965, Betty Shelton continued using the pseudonym on checks as late as May 1966. [38]

HENDRIX, WILLIAM ("BILL")

A plumbing contractor from Tallahassee, Florida, Hendrix organized the Southern Knights of the KKK in January 1949, with an estimated 200 members. In April, he published his one and only issue of *The Klansman*, emerging a month later as Florida grand dragon of Jack Johnston's Original Southern Klans. When the Georgia home office folded, Hendrix was on his own, hosting a June 11 ceremony that drew 1,000 Klansmen from Florida, Alabama, and Georgia, with 250 new members sworn in beneath a fiery cross. Hendrix soon changed the name of his group to the more expansive Northern and Southern Knights of the KKK, with a Jacksonville mailing address. On August 28, 1949, after a secret klonvocation in Jacksonville, he announced his own election as "national adjutant," serving under an anonymous—and probably nonexistent—"Permanent Emperor Samuel II." The elusive emperor was soon replaced by an unnamed imperial wizard, whom Hendrix designated as "Number 4-006800." Speaking from parts unknown—presumably Hendrix's office—the wizard issued an edict advising Klansmen to await orders on how they could best preserve "the American way of life," since "a state of emergency exists in the Invisible Empire." A prime Hendrix target was the "communist-inspired income tax," but he also mailed thousands of letters in 1949 supporting a bill introduced by Mississippi Representative John Rankin, calling for one year in jail and a $10,000 fine for anyone joining the Anti-Defamation League of B'nai B'rith. The August 1949 Peekskill, New York, riots against black singer Paul Robeson allowed Hendrix to claim members north of the Mason-Dixon Line, but his public call for a week of nationwide cross burnings "to light up the skies of America in protest of communism" produced only six crosses—five in Florida, and one in Valdosta, Georgia. Visiting Montgomery, Alabama, in December 1949, Hendrix met with William Morris and Thomas Hamilton to form "the governing body" of an alleged national Klan, pointedly excluding Sam Roper's Association of Georgia Klans. On February 12, 1952, Hendrix was arrested in Tallahassee for mailing material "too libelous" to appear in court records, specifically defaming Governor Fuller Warren, columnist Drew Pearson, a state legislator, and a local attorney. Denouncing his trial as a "a case of outright persecution,"

Hendrix was convicted of obscene mailings on February 20, ordered to pay a $700 fine with one year's jail time suspended on his promise to refrain from similar pursuits. Five months later, he announced the formation of a new American Confederate Army, kicking off a gubernatorial campaign that won him 11,200 votes in November. General apathy led to disbandment of the Southern Knights in 1953, but Black Monday gave Hendrix a shot in the arm, and he launched a new recruiting drive in the fall of 1956. Undaunted when the competing Florida KKK denounced him as a "swindler" using the Klan "for personal gain only," Hendrix sought to make up for his lack of membership with a diversity of organizations, including at various times the Knights of the White Camellia, the Order of the Rattlesnake, and the Konsolidated Ku Klux Klans of the Invisible Empire. In August 1958, he joined J.B. Stoner to address a National States Rights Party convention in Louisville, Kentucky. Two years later, on December 29, 1960, Hendrix resigned from the Klan, declaring integration inevitable and adding that "I cannot agree to go outside the law to maintain segregation." He apparently changed his mind by July 24, 1964, announcing the creation of an American Underground, which would cooperate with the Klan and other groups in defying the new civil rights act. As Hendrix told the press, "We will fight legally so far as we can, and violently when necessary." In January 1967, congressional investigators linked Hendrix with the tiny Knights of the Ku Klux Klan, Florida, which boasted ten "active" members in his home town of Oldsmar. By 1970, it had failed completely. [*NYT* 1952, 1960, 1964; 38; 48]

HENRY, R.L.

A Texarkana, Texas, Klansman, Henry served his town as mayor and congressman before he ran for governor in 1922. He secured the public endorsement of imperial headquarters in Atlanta, but the voting ran against him in November, and Klansman Earl Mayfield was elected instead. [10]

HENRY, RAYMOND

See *Moore, Harry.*

HENRY COUNTY NO. 49 CLUB

In 1965 congressional investigators identified this group as a cover for the Abbeville, Alabama, klavern, United Klans of America. [38]

HENSLEY, DON

In 1958, Hensley was identified as the Tennessee state chairman of the National States Rights Party. [65]

HENSON, DON

Identified as the grand dragon of Tennessee, Henson visited Indiana in September 1977 to help out with a statewide recruiting drive. [WRTV Channel 6 News, Indianapolis, Sept. 29, 1977]

HENSON, EVERETT

A Lakeside, California, Klansman, Henson was murdered on April 27, 1978. Fellow Klansmen Terry Martin was sentenced to life imprisonment for the slaying on June 15, 1979, convicted of killing his "friend" after Henson informed police of Martin's illegal drug transactions. [FOF 1979]

HEREDEEN, H.H.

In January 1965, Heredeen was appointed by Imperial Wizard Sam Bowers to serve as secretary-treasurer of the White Christian Protective and Legal Defense Fund. [59]

HERITAGE ENTERPRISES, INC.

Imperial Wizard Robert Shelton organized this corporation in the 1960s, with 51 percent of its stock owned by the United Klans of America and 49 percent held by personal friends of Shelton. Subsidiaries included Heritage Garment Works (which produced United Klans regalia) in Columbia, South Carolina, and Heritage Insurance Company, in Bessemer, Alabama. In 1965, congressional investigators discovered that Shelton received a commission on robe sales from Heritage Garment Works, in addition to his share of the company's profits. The ultimate rift between Heritage and the United Klans was attributed to Shelton's suspicion that manager Younger Newton had delivered names of robe buyers to the FBI. Newton also continued business relations with Robert Scoggin after Scoggin was banished from the United Klans, a connection viewed by Shelton as outright betrayal. Following the United Klans-Heritage break, production of Klan robes was delegated to the various realms. [84]

HERLTH, CLARENCE

See *New York*.

HERNANDES, HARRIET

A black resident of South Carolina during Reconstruction, Hernandes and her child were whipped by Klansmen after she refused to break her labor contract with one white man to work for another. [93]

HERRINGTON, A.C.

A resident of Ruth, Mississippi, Herrington was identified as state organizer of the White Knights of the KKK in 1964. [38]

HESPER

Captain Sam Houston and his brother, commanders of the steamboat *Hesper*, were known during Reconstruction as the only Republican boatmen on the Mississippi River. On October 15, 1868, they stopped in Memphis to load a cargo of 4,000 rifles, ammunition, and other supplies purchased by the Arkansas militia for use in suppressing the Klan. When the *Hesper* had traveled twenty-five miles downriver, it was overtaken by a party of armed Klansmen aboard the tug *Netty Jones*. Houston ran the boat aground on the Arkansas shore to avoid being rammed in midstream, and escaped with his brother while the crew surrendered. The *Hesper* was then towed back into midstream, where the arms were tossed overboard and the boat cut adrift and was later reclaimed by its owner when it drifted ashore. [87]

HIGGINS, GEORGE, JR.

Identified in 1976 as the Mississippi grand dragon for the United Klans of America, Higgins made headlines when his wife's election as a delegate to the National Women's Conference outraged liberal supporters of the Equal Rights Amendment. [84]

HIGH, ZEKE

A black resident of Livingston, Alabama, High killed a white man who invaded his home during the Klan-led riots of October 1870. Charged with murder, he spent nearly a year in jail before he was lynched by Klansmen in September 1871. [87]

HIGH POINT BROTHERHOOD CLUB

In 1965 congressional investigators identified this club as a front for the High Point, North Carolina, klavern, United Klans of America. [38]

HIGHTOWER, A.C.

A Little Rock, Arkansas, barber, Hightower chartered the Arkansas branch of the U.S. Klans on June 5, 1959. Two months later, on August 10, he resigned as grand dragon after clashing with members who "wanted to take action" against local school integration. [*FOF 1959*]

HIGHWAY 14 HUNTING CLUB

In 1966 congressional investigators identified this group as a cover for Eutaw, Alabama, Unit No. 47, United Klans of America. [38]

HILBURN, HUBERT

See *Floyd, Esther.*

HILL, ELIAS

A black Baptist minister and active Republican in Clay Hill, South Carolina, during Reconstruction, Hill opened a school for blacks after the Civil War. Accused by local whites of inciting black arsonists, the invalid minister—paralyzed since age seven—was dragged from his home on May 5, 1871, and whipped by Klansmen, who ordered Hill to renounce his Republican membership. Five months later, Hill led a party of 136 Carolina blacks to Liberia, where they founded a settlement and spent the rest of their lives. [87]

HILL, H.G., SR.

A resident of Atlanta, Georgia, Hill was an original incorporating officer of the National Knights of the KKK in November 1963. Ten months later, when Imperial Wizard James Venable united eight independent factions in his National Association of Ku Klux Klan, Hill was elected kludd of the umbrella organization. In April 1965, Hill joined Venable, William Morris, and other Klansmen in forming the unincorporated Knights of the KKK, sponsoring a series of Ohio rallies during that summer. [38]

HILL, ROBERT

See *Dayvault, Wayne.*

HINDS, JAMES M.

A Republican congressman from Arkansas and the highest-ranking victim of the Reconstruction Klan, Hinds was shot to death in Monroe County on October 22, 1868. Future governor James Brooks was wounded in the same attack. [87]

HINES, CLIFFORD

A black Atlanta, Georgia, resident, Hines was assaulted and beaten on October 28, 1946. His assailant, seventeen year old James Childers, told arresting officers that he was "on assignment" from the Columbians, Inc. At a November 6 court hearing, Childers wore a "medal of honor" awarded by the Columbians for his attack on Hines. He was indicted for rioting on November 18, and with Columbians officer Henry Loomis, Jr., was convicted of inciting a riot in the same case on February 16, 1947. [NYT 1946–1947]

HINES, TOMMY LEE

A young, retarded black with a tested IQ of 39, Hines was charged with robbing and raping three white women in Decatur, Alabama, during 1979.

Black protests against his indictment prompted counterdemonstrations by Bill Wilkinson's Invisible Empire Knights, with crowds of 5,000 and 10,000 persons turning out for the biggest Klan rallies since the 1920s. Publicity resulted in a change of venue to nearby Cullman, where Hines was convicted by an all-white jury and sentenced to thirty years. The conviction was overturned on appeal, and maneuvers preceding a new trial kept the Klan active in Decatur. In the summer of 1979, Klansmen and blacks clashed outside a supermarket where a black man had been arrested for shoplifting. Decatur's city council banned armed processions, and the Klan responded with a motorcade of pickups past the mayor's house with their weapons displayed. As Wilkinson told the press, "If the mayor wants our guns, he'll have to come and get them." Reverend R.B. Cottonreader's local demonstrators were soon supplemented by advisers from the Southern Christian Leadership Conference, and the stage was set for massive confrontation. When 1,000 blacks marched through downtown Decatur, they found their way blocked by 250 Klansmen armed with pipes, baseball bats, and ax handles, shouting, "Niggers, that's as far as you go." Police tried to hold the hostile groups apart, but gunfire erupted, leaving four persons wounded. Klansmen soon became fixtures at the county courthouse, carrying clubs and picket signs, chanting "White Power!" whenever a television camera appeared. Rallies and cross burnings became regular weekend events in Decatur, with Klansmen stopping cars on the highway and soliciting money "to fight the niggers." State and federal investigations led to the conviction of several Klansmen for firing into homes owned by blacks or mixed couples, as the violence spread across central Alabama. The state legislature pitched in with a law banning guns within 1,000 feet of public demonstrations, and numerous weapons were seized during Wilkinson's recreation of the 1965 march from Selma to Montgomery. A lawsuit filed by the Southern Christian Leadership Council against the Invisible Empire Knights was finally settled in July 1989. Grand Dragon Roger Handley and nine others were ordered to pay injured marchers $11,500, to resign from the KKK, perform specified community service, and attend a two-hour course on race relations taught by the Leadership Council. James Farrands, Wilkinson's replacement as imperial wizard, was predictably outraged by the verdict, calling the race relations class an example of "cruel and unusual punishment." [*NYT* 1989; 10]

HINESTON HUNTING & FISHING CLUB

In 1965 congressional investigators identified this group as a cover for the Hineston, Louisiana, klavern, Original Knights of the KKK. [38]

HINSHAW, DONALD

A former titan of the White Knights who defected to the United Klans of America, Hinshaw was abducted on December 21, 1967, then released unharmed on a highway south of Heidelberg, Mississippi. Authorities suspect White Knights in the case, but Hinshaw was unable or unwilling to identify the kidnappers. [*NYT* 1967]

HODGES, ROBERT E.

A New York native, Hodges was attending Columbia, South Carolina, Commercial College in 1957, when he was identified as spokesman for the Columbia klavern, Association of South Carolina Klans. Identified as the state kligrapp three years later, he actively opposed the presidential candidacy of Senator John F. Kennedy on religious grounds, telling interviewers, "You cannot afford to support or vote for anyone or group that represents the Roman Catholic Church. Heaven help your soul if you vote away your religious liberty." In 1967, the House Un-American Activities Committee identified Hodges as a grand council member for the Association of South Carolina Klans, simultaneously serving as a nighthawk for James Venable's National Knights. As late as 1976, employed as a postal worker, he remained active in the same Klan, its leader still unnamed. [38; 84; 93]

HOFF, WILLIAM

Appointed as king kleagle for the United Klans of America in New York during 1965, Hoff served concurrently as state director of the National States Rights Party. During the April 1968 race riots in Newark, New Jersey, Hoff threw a concussion grenade into a bar patronized by blacks, wounding two persons. Arrested in New York City in August 1968, after giving an undercover officer a can of dynamite to blast the home of a local draft resistance leader, Hoff was charged with conspiring to murder 158 leftists and civil rights activists. Investigation of the charges revealed continuing links with leaders of the Klan, the National States Rights Party, the Minutemen, and the American Nazi Party. On August 21, 1969, Hoff pled guilty on two of nine felony counts lodged against him. [*NYT* 1969; 38]

HOGGLE, WILLIAM S.

See *Reeb, Reverend James.*

HOLCOMBE, EARL

While a member of the U.S. Klans in 1961, Holcombe participated in violent demonstrations at Georgia's state university in Athens. Gravitating into the United Klans of America later that year, he was expelled by Imperial Wizard Robert Shelton after a 1964 shooting incident produced bad publicity for the United Klans. Recruited for James Venable's National Knights, he served as a member of that Klan's degree team, later joining Colbert McGriff to form the secretive, ultra-violent Black Shirts. [38; 84]

HOLDEN, PETE

In 1976, Holden was identified as Louisiana's new grand dragon for the United Klans of America. [84]

HOLDEN, WILLIAM W.

As the Reconstruction governor of North Carolina, Holden was a staunch opponent of the KKK. By 1869, he claimed that there were 40,000 Klansmen in his state, cooperating with groups such as the Constitutional Union Guard, whose terrorism prevented sheriffs and grand juries from punishing crimes committed against blacks and Republicans. In August 1869, Holden employed a private detective to gather evidence which resulted in the indictment of Union Guard leaders and he also organized a militia to fight Klansmen on their own terms. The Shoffner Act of January 1870 allowed Holden to proclaim a state of insurrection in lawless counties, but the blunders and public excesses of some militia officers produced a political backlash, and Democrats swept the state in that year's elections. Holden advised Washington that "this organized conspiracy is in existence in every county of the state. And its aim is to obtain the control of the government. It is believed that its leaders now direct the movements of the present legislature." In effect, he was right; the new Democrat-dominated legislature voted to impeach Holden in November 1870, and his trial before the state senate began a month later, ending with his conviction and removal from office in February 1871. The Klan was thus responsible for impeaching the first state governor in U.S. history. [87]

HOLDER, JAMES

A sergeant in Glenn Miller's Confederate Knights of the KKK, Holder shot and killed fellow Klansman David Wallace in November 1983, during an argument following a Klan rally. Convicted of murder in July 1984, he was sentenced to eighteen years in prison. [NYT 1984]

HOLLAND, CHARLES

A guard at New York's Wallkill Prison, Holland was exposed as a Klansman when he addressed a Pennsylvania rally in December 1974. Following a state investigation, Holland was allowed to keep his job because his Klan activities did not appear to affect his performance. [NYT 1974]

HOLLAND, DAVID W.

Identified as grand dragon of the Southern White Knights of the KKK, Holland was one of eleven Klansmen convicted of assaulting black civil rights marchers in Forsyth County, Georgia, during 1987. The verdict, delivered in October 1988, required the Southern White Knights to pay

$400,000 in damages, for division among fifty plaintiffs. Holland was fined another $50,000. [*NYT* 1988]

HOLLIDAY, J.R.

A plantation owner in Jackson County, Georgia, during Reconstruction, Holliday threatened to prosecute nightriders who began harassing his black tenants in the spring of 1871. In July 1871, following numerous threats and a boycott of his mill, armed Klansmen stormed his home one night and were turned back following a battle. Holliday claimed to have killed at least two assailants in the struggle and later filed criminal charges against thirteen Klansmen. The Klan's campaign continued, however. Holliday's mill and cotton gin were destroyed by arsonists and his black tenants were driven away by raiding parties, but local Conservative leaders promised the troubles would cease if he dropped prosecution of the indicted Klansmen. Holliday eventually came to terms with this, and the case was dismissed. [87]

HOLT, CASWELL

A black man suspected of theft, Holt was one of the Reconstruction Klan's first victims in Alamance County, North Carolina. Dragged from his home in December 1868, Holt was beaten and several times hoisted off the ground with a rope around his neck in a futile effort to make him confess. Holt was unimpressed with his former master's opinion that ghosts had perpetrated the attack, and retained attorney Henry Badham to prosecute the nightriders. The Klansmen appeared in court with alibi witnesses, and the case was dismissed. A year later, Klansmen again raided Holt's home. Holt was wounded several times by shots fired through a bolted door, and Klansmen made it inside the home and terrorized his daughters. A note was left for Henry Badham, warning him against further attempts to prosecute Klansmen in Alamance County. [87]

HOLT, SALLIE

A backwoods brothel madam in Alamance County, North Carolina, during Reconstruction, Holt was raided and put out of business by Klansmen in September 1869. During the attack, which left her whorehouse in a shambles, Holt's daughter was sexually abused by Klansmen. [87]

HOMER HUNTING & FISHING CLUB

In 1965 congressional investigators identified this group as a cover for the Homer, Louisiana, klavern, Original Knights of the Ku Klux Klan. [38]

HONEYCUTT, JOHN, JR.

See *Johnson, Woodrow*.

HONEYCUTT, LEROY

See *Johnson, Woodrow*.

HORN, REV. ALVIN

Reverend Horn joined the Federated Ku Klux Klans in 1948, rising to the post of kleagle and a seat on the Klan's board of directors that same year. A resident of Talladega, where he owned substantial farm land, by 1950 Horn was dividing his time between the KKK and the three churches for which he served as pastor. In February 1950, he was implicated in the Klan slaying of Charlie Hurst at Pell City, but a state murder charge was dismissed in October 1952. Horn had quarreled with Federated Klans leader William Morris, branding him a traitor and defecting to Imperial Wizard Sam Roper's Association of Georgia Klans in early 1950. That pledge of allegiance lasted until the summer of 1956, when Eldon Edwards recruited Horn as Alabama grand dragon for the growing U.S. Klans. Horn soon emerged as the new Klan's most effective organizer, increasing the realm from two klaverns to an estimated 100 by early 1957. In January 1957, he told a Birmingham rally of 235 members (including women and children) that the Klan would "not give another inch or another concession" on desegregation in Alabama. A short time later, however, Horn's personal life disrupted his Klan duties. Horn's wife, despondent over recent surgery, committed suicide, leaving Horn to raise their six children on his own. Horn's new wife was a fifteen-year-old girl, who was pregnant and thus making the annulment of their marriage impossible. The resultant scandal destroyed Horn's standing in the U.S. Klans. Replaced by up-and-comer Robert Shelton as the Alabama dragon, Horn languished on the sidelines, watching as his successor quarreled with Edwards and broke away to organize the Alabama Knights. When Eldon Edwards died in August 1960, Horn eagerly answered a summons from Imperial Wizard Robert ("Wild Bill") Davidson to head up the realm, which was shrinking from competition with Shelton. Davidson did not last with the U.S. Klans, but Horn remained steadfast, earning individual mention in Judge Frank Johnson's May 1961 injunction barring violent interference with the integrated Freedom Rides. [*NYT* 1957; *FOF* 1961; 10; 48]

HORNEBEAK, RAY

See *Dayvault, Marx*.

HORSE THIEF DETECTIVE SOCIETY

A vigilante group organized in Indiana around 1908, the Horse Thief Detectives were revived by Klan leaders D.C. Stephenson and E.A. Watkins in 1922 and served as the Klan "police" in Indiana and Ohio. This group was especially active in Indiana, where vigilante movements were legalized in 1852. Members raided the homes of alleged bootleggers, patrolled highways adjacent to Klan rallies, and terrorized black neighborhoods on election days with armed motorcades. Authorized to carry guns in their role as "special constables," the Horse Thief Detectives stopped and searched so many cars in Indiana that national auto clubs filed formal protests. When kleagles sought to revive the Indiana Klan in 1946, state authorities moved to revoke the society's charter, thereby preventing further abuses. [10]

HORTON, REV. JACK

As pastor of the Calvary Baptist Church in South Bend, Indiana, Horton also served his local klavern of the KKK as kligrapp in the 1920s. When Notre Dame students registered their objection to a Klan parade by storming Klan headquarters on May 17, 1924, it was Horton who held the collegiates at bay with a drawn revolver. South Bend Klansmen finally agreed to a truce, promising to march unmasked if the irate students would refrain from beating and stoning them along the way. [93]

HORTON, WILLIAM C.

See *Peek, James.*

HOUSE OF PRAYER FOR ALL PEOPLE

See *Blessing, William.*

HOUSE UN-AMERICAN ACTIVITIES COMMITTEE

Created in the latter 1930s to investigate domestic fascist movements, the House Un-American Activities Committee (HUAC) soon took a sharp left-hand turn, launching a forty-year search for communists, dangerous liberals, and "fellow travelers" in U.S. society. Once the German-American Bund and similar groups disappeared during World War II, HUAC members showed little enthusiasm for investigating right-wing extremist groups, and some of the panelists, such as Mississippi's anti-Semitic Representative John Rankin, were frankly sympathetic to the Klan. In January 1946, with the Justice Department probing a newly active Klan, HUAC counsel Ernest Adamson announced that the committee had tried to collect information on the KKK, but could find no material more current than news clips from the Great Depression. Six months later, HUAC flatly refused to launch an investigation of its own; Rankin spoke for the majority when he said that the committee had no mandate to "interfere" with the Klan. HUAC's reticence produced criticism from columnist Walter Winchell, who said destroying the Bund and leaving the Klan at large "is comparable to licking the German army and then not doing anything about the Gestapo." With a nod toward public pressure, a HUAC subcommittee briefly examined native fascist groups, reporting in May 1947 that the Klan and Columbians, Inc., were of "no consequence." In the committee's sage opinion, communists were behind the public demands for investigation of far-right groups, seeking to divert attention from their own conspiracies. By 1965, with Klan violence making daily headlines, HUAC's Southern chairman was clearly embarrassed by the bloody excesses of his fellow segregationists. Five days after Viola Liuzzo was murdered by Klansmen in Alabama, the committee voted to undertake a formal investigation of the KKK. Scrutiny was finally narrowed to the seven largest and most active factions for hearings conducted between October 1965 and February 1966. Congressmen interviewed 187 witness, and collected thousands of documents, photographs, canceled checks, membership lists, police records, and other items of documentation. Even though most of the subpoenaed Klansmen refused to testify (several officers of the United Klans were cited for contempt of Congress), HUAC did an adequate job of exposing Klan brutality, infiltration of Southern law enforcement, and financial improprieties. Ironically, while some Klansmen resigned after watching their leaders plead the Fifth Amendment "like communists," publicity generated by the HUAC hearings—like earlier congressional hearings in October 1921—actually served to increase Klan membership over the coming year. [*FOF* 1946–1947, 1965–1966; 38]

HOUSTON COUNTY COMMITTEE FOR LAW AND ORDER

In 1966 congressional investigators identified this group as a cover for the Crockett, Texas, klavern, United Klans of America. [38]

HOUSTON, GEORGE W.

A black state legislator during Reconstruction from Sumter County, Alabama, Houston was shot and wounded, along with his son, when Klansmen raided his home on August 12, 1869. Threats continued after the attack, and Houston finally left the area. [87]

HOWARD, JOHN

Once a member of James Venable's National Knights, Howard joined Dale Reusch and three other grand dragons in a September 1975 defection from that Klan. Accusing Venable of senility, they organized the new Invisible Empire, Knights of the KKK, with Howard established as grand dragon of the South Carolina realm. [84]

HOWARD, WADE HENRY

See *Cruell, Claude.*

HOWARTH, CHARLES

Heading up the United Klans of America in Colorado Springs, Colorado, during 1982, Howarth was arrested in May 1982, on charges of illegally transporting explosives and conspiring to blow up the federal courthouse in Denver. Seven members of Posse Comitatus were also charged in the case, with Howarth and Posse member Wesley White convicted and sentenced to jail terms. [85]

HOWLE, WILLIAM R.

An active Republican and contractor in charge of a railroad construction camp in Chatham County, North Carolina, during Reconstruction, Howle was threatened several times by Klansmen in the fall of 1870, and his black workers were chased from their jobs. In April 1871, a band of fifty Klansmen raided the camp, whipping several men and women and raping an eighteen-year-old black girl. Howle went to the state capital, obtained a commission as a U.S. marshal, and returned to arrest three of the Klansmen involved. He still did not spend his nights in the county, however. Railroad construction was critically disrupted, and Howle was finally forced into bankruptcy, forfeiting his contract with a loss of $2,200. [87]

HOYT, SHARIDA

In 1975, college student Sharida Hoyt was identified as the exalted cyclops for a New Orleans klavern of David Duke's Knights of the KKK. Her selection was frequently cited as evidence of the opportunities available to women in the "new Klan." [NYT 1975]

HUDGINS, ROBERT EUGENE

A resident of North Carolina, Hudgins served as imperial kladd for the United Klans of America in the 1960s. His refusal in 1965 to cooperate with the House Un-American Activities Committee by delivering Klan documents led to a citation for contempt of congress, but the criminal charges were later dismissed. In September 1969, Hudgins moved to Richmond, Virginia, and replaced Marshal Kornegay as grand dragon of the Old Dominion realm. The statewide Klan revival included a ban on drinking by Klansmen, announced at a Victoria rally on September 6, when Hudgins reminded the knights that "This is a Christian organization." A year later, in September 1970, Hudgins made headlines with his unsuccessful attempt to have federal judge Robert Merhige, Jr., arrested for ordering busing to achieve school integration in Richmond. [NYT 1969–1970; 38]

HUETT, JOSEPH THOMAS, SR.

The police chief of Mt. Dora, Florida, Huett was subpoenaed as part of the House Un-American Activities Committee's Klan investigation in February

1. Klansman, North Carolina, ca. 1870. *(North Carolina State Archives)*

2. Knights of Mary Phagan lynch Leo Frank in Cobb County, Georgia, August 17, 1915. The lynchers later burned the first cross on U.S. soil and became charter members of the Knights of the KKK. *(Georgia Department of Archives and History)*

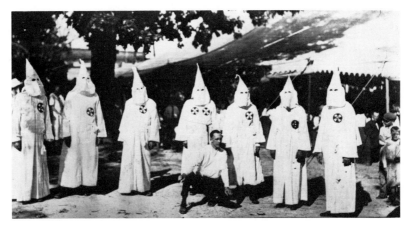

3. Klansmen at tent meeting near Hamlet, North Carolina, ca. 1915.
(North Carolina State Archives)

4. D. William Simmons, in mask, led first Klan revival in Alabama. *(Culver Pictures)*

5. Knights of KKK hold initiation ceremony at Stone Mountain, Georgia.

6. Klan outing in Virginia, 1920. *(Culver Pictures)*

7. D. William Simmons at rally of Knights of KKK. *(Culver Pictures)*

8. New members being sworn in at Knights of KKK rally in New Brunswick, Maryland, June 1922. *(Culver Pictures)*

9. Knights of KKK ceremony, Valdosta, Georgia, 1922.
(Georgia Department of Archives and History)

10. Frank Jones, Sr., a member of the KKK drum and bugle corps, poses with his drum in Atlanta, Georgia, 1923. *(Georgia Department of Archives and History)*

11. Frank Jones, Jr., a child, poses in his KKK uniform, Atlanta, Georgia, 1923.
(Georgia Department of Archives and History)

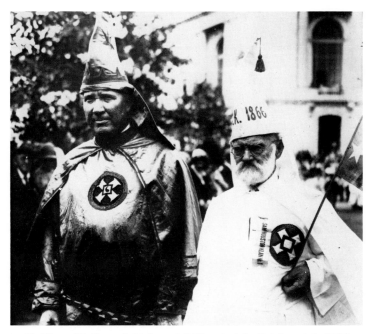

12. Hiram W. Evans (left), Imperial Wizard of the Knights of the KKK (1923–1939), poses with an unidentified veteran of the Reconstruction Texas Klan, ca. 1924. *(National Archives)*

13. KKK members parade down Pennsylvania Avenue in Washington, D.C., in 1925. *(National Archives)*

14. German-American Bund parade at "Camp Nordland," near Andover,
New Jersey, ca. 1940. The camp was also used for a joint Bund-KKK rally that
summer, resulting in severe embarrassment to the Klan and the subsequent ouster
of New Jersey's grand dragon. *(American Jewish Historical Society)*

15. Dr. Samuel Green (with glasses, holding sword) presides over the initiation of new members into the Association of Georgia Klans, ca. 1946. *(National Archives)*

16. Members of the Association of Georgia Klans, led by Dr. Samuel Green (in foreground, wearing glasses), rally in Wrightsville, Georgia, in 1948. The rally was an attempt to intimidate black voters on the eve of a state Democratic primary election. *(National Archives)*

17. Cross burned by United Klans of America Klavern No. 310, the "Sportsmans Club," to intimidate blacks in Waynesboro, Georgia, ca. 1961. *(Georgia Department of Archives and History)*

18. United Klans of America rally, Burke County, Georgia, ca. 1962–1964.
(Georgia Department of Archives and History)

19. Viola Gregg Liuzzo, who was killed by Klansmen while transporting civil rights' marchers on the Selma Highway, Selma, Alabama, March 25, 1965.

20. Robert Shelton of the United Klans of America, in robe and hood, Tuscaloosa, Alabama, 1965. *(UKA Klansman Manual)*

21. Rally of the Invisible Empire in Huntsville, Alabama, January 1979.
Bill Wilkenson is in the suit.

22. Dave Holland and Steve Miller at a White Patriot Party Rally in Raleigh, North Carolina, protesting Martin Luther King Holiday, January 1986. *(George Littleton, SPLC)*

23. White Patriot Party march in Raleigh, North Carolina, protesting the Martin Luther King Holiday, January 1986. *(George Littleton, SPLC)*

24. Hugh Black at White Patriot Party march in Raleigh, North Carolina, protesting the Martin Luther King Holiday, January 1986. *(George Littleton, SPLC)*

25. March of the Invisble Empire Knights in Crawsfordville, Indiana, July 1986. *(UNK)*

26. Biker with torch during ceremony of the Christian Knights of KKK in Parkersburg, West Virginia, October 1987. *(Paul Lagann/Parkersburg Sentinel)*

27. Christian Knights of KKK march in Parkersburg, West Virginia, October 1987. *(Paul Lagann/Parkersburg Sentinel)*

28. Cross burning by the Christian Knights of KKK during ceremony in Parkersburg, West Virginia, October 1987. *(Paul Lagann/Parkersburg Sentinel).*

29. Aryan World Congress Meeting held by Aryan Nation at Hayden Lake, Idaho, July 1987. *(Jeff Green)*

30. Participants in Christian Knights of KKK rally in Philadelphia, Mississippi, March 1989.

31. Sign announcing KKK rally by Christian Knights in Philadelphia, Mississippi,
March 1989.

32. Christian Knights of KKK, Philadelphia, Mississippi, March 1989.

33. Aryan Nation march and rally in Pulaski, Tennessee, in October 1989.
(Tom Flanigan/Herald Tenn.)

34. March and rally of the Southern White Knights in Gainsville, Georgia, September 1989. *(D. K. Welch/SPLC)*

35. Southern White Knights, Gainsville, Georgia, September 1989. *(D. K. Welch/SPLC)*

36. Participants in Southern White Knights demonstration, Gainsville, Georgia, September 1989. *(D. K. Welch/SPLC)*

37. Skinheads participating in demonstration by the Southern White Knights in Gainsville, Georgia, September 1989. *(D. K. Welch/SPLC)*

38. Skinhead at Southern White Knights demonstration in Gainsville, Georgia, September 1989. (*D. K. Welch/SPLC*)

39. J.B. Stoner speaking at Southern White Knights rally, Gainsville, Georgia, September 1989. *(D. K. Welch/SPLC)*

40. Louis Beam, Richard Butler, and J.B. Stoner at Aryan Nations demonstration in Pulaski, Tennessee, October 1989. *(D. K. Welch/SPLC)*

1966. Initially willing to testify, he became reticent when investigators asked if the Mt. Dora Dunkers Club—for which he served as president—was in fact a front for the United Florida Ku Klux Klan. Huett "couldn't remember" joining the Klan, though he recalled taking several "similar" oaths in recent months. Despite his self-description as a trained observer, the chief "couldn't rightly say" if he had ever attended a Klan meeting in Florida or neighboring states. Pressed by the committee for a straight answer, Huett finally excused himself to consult legal counsel, complaining that "I didn't know you were going to give me the third degree, here." He was not recalled as a witness, but independent testimony established beyond a reasonable doubt the Dunkers Club's connection to the Klan. [38]

HUFFINGTON, JOE

Indiana's Klan pioneer in 1920, Huffington was soon replaced by Grand Dragon D.C. Stephenson. Four years later, he sided with Imperial Wizard Hiram Evans in a feud that led to Stephenson's defection from the parent Klan. [10]

HUGGINS, ALLEN P.

The "carpetbag" superintendent of schools in Monroe County, Mississippi, during Reconstruction, Huggins was flogged by Klansmen on March 9, 1871. He survived the attack, and not only refused to leave the county, but also prosecuted two Klansmen, whose confessions led to the arrest of twenty-six others. An army officer presented Huggins's shirt to Massachusetts Representative Ben Butler, who displayed it in speech before Congress on Southern atrocities, thus coining the term "waving the bloody shirt." [87]

HUIE, WILLIAM BRADFORD

An Alabama native and best-selling author, Huie was famous for his articles and books exposing the violent crimes of Klansmen and other white supremacists, which led to his home being periodically circled by Klan motorcades. In March 1966, Klansmen Lawrence Rainey and Cecil Price sued Huie for libel for his coverage of their involvement in a triple murder in Mississippi, but the case was eventually thrown out of court. Two years later, Huie's credibility was damaged when he reported that a racist conspiracy was responsible for the death of Dr. Martin Luther King. Huie later reversed himself and supported the lone-assassin theory, still allowing, however, for the possibility of a "small conspiracy" by "little men." [NYT 1966; 95]

HUMPHRIES, BAN

A black state legislator in Arkansas, during Reconstruction, Humphries was murdered by Klansmen in White County. The Democratic press blamed members of the Loyal League, and manufactured evidence to implicate blacks in the case. Detective Albert Parker was investigating the crime when he disappeared, killed by Klansmen in August 1868. [87]

HUMPHRIES, J.H.

A past president of the Bible-distributing Gideons, Humphries fought the 1920s Klan until he learned its doctrines and decided to enlist. "Now," he told the faithful, "I know better and am proud to belong to it." In fact, he was identified as the exalted cyclops of a klavern in Huntington, West Virginia. [10]

HUNNICUTT, JOHN L.

As a teenaged student in Greensboro, Alabama, Hunnicutt led the area's first Klan raid in early 1868, threatening the "carpetbag" teacher of a black school and terrorizing three black families "in regular old style." Local Democratic leaders provided horses for the raid, which succeeded in running the teacher out of Hale County. The young Klansmen were identified, and a grand jury was charged to indict them, but its foreman was one of those who sponsored the raid, and no criminal charges were forthcoming. A short time later, Hunnicutt organized a Klan den with the backing of "some of the best citizens" in Greensboro, publishing his first notices in March 1868. [87]

HUNT, HAROLD WHEELER

An elderly anti-Semite affiliated with the Aryan Nations in Hayden Lake, Idaho, Hunt has publicly advocated violence to rid the United States of Jews. In 1980, as publisher of the twice-weekly *National Chronicle*, he told an interviewer that his 1,400 subscribers "don't want a single sign of Jews or the scum that's along with them on this earth. Everything buried." [2]

HUNTER, C.M.
See *Hurst, Charlie.*

HUNTER, DEAN

A resident of Morrow, Georgia, Hunter was identified in November 1963 as an original incorporating officer of the Improved Order of the U.S. Klans, Knights of the Ku Klux Klan, Inc. [38]

HUNTERS CLUB

In 1965 congressional investigators identified this club as a front for the Shelby, North Carolina, klavern, United Klans of America. [38]

HUNTING CLUB

Evidence collected by the House Un-American Activities Committee identified this group as a cover for the Roseboro, North Carolina, United Klans of America. [38]

HURST, CHARLIE

A retired storekeeper in Pell City, Alabama, on February 22, 1950, Hurst was killed while defending his home from raiding Klansmen. Hurst's son was wounded during the exchange of gunfire. Enough evidence was left behind by Klansmen to identify several members of the band. Reverend Roy Heath, a Methodist minister from Talladega, was named as the wheelman. Heath committed suicide on February 26, his sons reporting that Grand Dragon Alvin Horn advised them not to discuss their father's comments on the day he died. Other suspects in the case included Klansmen Claude Lukes, Charles Carlisle, C.M. Hunter, and Louis Harrison, the exalted cyclops of the Pell City klavern and athletic director for the Avondale textile mills. Harrison cooperated with police by delivering a membership list for his klavern, and the trials proceeded that summer. On June 28, defendant Carlisle was convicted of manslaughter and sentenced to five years in prison. Hunter was still awaiting trial when he was stabbed at a local carnival by persons unknown on September 1. Pending murder charges against Horn were finally dismissed on October 13, 1952. [NYT 1950, 1952]

HUTCHINS, GUY

The band director at Camden (South Carolina) High School, Hutchins was abducted and whipped by Klansmen on December 28, 1956. An outspoken opponent of Klan violence, Hutchins was returning from a concert in Charlotte, North Carolina, when he blew a tire on the highway. He was fixing the flat when a party of Camden Klansmen arrived and carried him into the nearby woods, where he was whipped. Six Klansmen were arrested on January 3, 1957. [NYT 1957]

HUTTO, JIMMY DALE

A Houston, Texas, Klansman, Hutto became a local celebrity after he infiltrated the Students for a Democratic Society, serving as a police informant for two months in 1969. A year later, he was implicated in a Klan reign of terror against the Pacifica Foundation radio stations and other targets around Houston. Following a bomb threat to radio station KNUZ, Hutto and another Klansman were discovered in a car outside the building, possessing three rifles, ammunition, and flares. They were arrested, but both were later released without charges. On January 20, 1971, police, acting on an FBI tip, stopped Hutto's car twenty-five miles west of Houston. Allegedly bound for California and more Pacifica radio stations, Hutto was carrying a .45 caliber pistol and quantities of Klan literature at the time of his arrest. [12]

HYDRAS

In Klan parlance, hydras are the advisory officers chosen to serve a grand dragon. During Reconstruction, there were six, each one without individual titles. The modern Klan specifies nine hydras, including the grand klaliff, grand klokard, grand kludd, grand kligrapp, grand klabee, grand kladd, grand klarogo, grand klexter, and grand nighthawk. [43; 87]

I

IDAHO

Kleagles invaded Idaho from neighboring Washington in the 1920s, spreading their gospel of "Americanism" along the Snake River Valley, in the central and southern part of Idaho. Recruiters operated out of Lewiston and Boise, with klaverns identified in five other cities. The masked invasion of a black-owned home in Lewiston resulted in the issuance of shoot-to-kill orders on nightriders, but Idaho Klansmen were generally more pacific. (In one small town, the only Jewish family was included in all Klan activities as a matter of course.) A fading memory by the early 1930s, the Klan resurfaced briefly—and embarrassingly—in 1965, when James Venable announced the appointment of a new grand titan for his National Knights. The fledgling Klansman had applied by mail and was accepted, sight-unseen, to lead the one-man realm. This new grand titan turned out to be a black Catholic, who wasted no time in airing his charade for the media. Venable, of course, withdrew his nomination in disgust. By 1980, the neo-Nazi Aryan Nations had established its headquarters at a compound near Hayden Lake, and acts of violence against Jewish residents and other "enemies of the white race" have been recorded in the past decade. [2; 10; 84]

IDENTITY CHURCH MOVEMENT

Rooted in the 19th century British doctrine of "Anglo-Israelism," the Identity movement was transplanted to the United States by ex-Klansman Wesley Swift after World War II. Swift's Church of Jesus Christ Christian and affiliated groups preached the doctrine that God's chosen people—the "true Israel"—are the Teutonic, Scandinavian, and white Anglo-Saxon races of the world, those who had been earlier chosen for world domination in Adolf Hitler's "Master Race" philosophy. Both Klansmen and neo-Nazis found themselves attracted to this doctrine, which today has become an underlying theme connecting groups such as the Aryan Nations, Christian Defense League, Christian-Patriots Defense League, Posse Comitatus, the Mountain Church of Jesus Christ, the New Christian Crusade Church, various Klan factions, and the Covenant, the Sword, and the Arm of the Lord. Since Swift's death in 1970, prominent leaders of the movement include Richard Butler, Sheldon Emry, Dan Gayman, Robert Miles, Thomas Robb, James Warner, and Gordon Winrod. [2]

ILLINOIS

The modern Klan was well established in Chicago by 1921, posing as the Southern Publicity Bureau, and prospered despite official condemnation. There were eighteen klaverns in the Windy City by 1922, and 287 statewide a year later, with active membership numbered in the tens of thousands. Chicago's American Unity League was one of the earliest anti-Klan organizations, publishing the names of known (or suspected) Klansmen, but opposition in the southern end of the state was more direct. A virtual state of civil war prevailed in Williamson County, where pitched battles between "Kluckers" and "anti-Kluckers" claimed twenty lives between 1923 and 1926. National Guardsmen were called out eight times during that period, to restore order, and it was not until the violent death of each side's leader that a cease-fire was called. Elsewhere in the state, Klansmen were divided by the power struggle between William Simmons and Hiram Evans. By 1926, statewide membership had begun to decline. It did not fade completely, however. Illinois was noted as one of thirteen states where the Klan retained significant strength during the Great Depression, but formal disbandment in 1944 left the faithful without an organization.

James Venable attempted to rekindle the flames in 1967 with his National Knights, but eight of its identified members were Chicago policemen, who were fired and arrested after fellow officers uncovered their secret arsenal—including a bazooka—and the planned assassination of Mayor Richard Daley. In March 1975, Robert Shelton's United Klans of America, attempted to enlist members in Illinois, and reports of new Klan activity led to an investigation by the state legislature. Researchers discovered that Aurora Klansman Wilburn Foreman had been struggling to organize a klavern for the past eight years and had succeeded only after he had obtained advice from United Klans officials from neighboring Indiana. The United Klans held tiny organizational meetings in March and May, with members of an outlaw motorcycle gang among their audience, and an estimated 100 Klansmen were finally recruited statewide. Thirty of those followed Foreman in Robert Scoggin's Invisible Empire Knights, after quarreling with

Shelton into late May. By October 1976, no more than fifteen Illinois Klansmen were considered hard-core devotees to the cause. [10; 43]

IMMIGRANTS

As defenders of "100% Americanism," 20th century Klansmen have traditionally called for limitations or outright bans on immigration from Asia, Africa, Latin America, and southern and eastern Europe. Antipathy toward nonwhites and "foreign isms"—non-Protestant religions and "radical" politics—combined with the fear of economic competition to fuel the xenophobic fires from World War I until the present. Klansmen ardently supported the restrictive immigration laws passed between 1917 and 1929, ratified by the McCarran-Walter Act of 1952, but the relaxation of national origin restrictions in 1965 was viewed as one more symptom of a government dominated by Jewish communists. President Jimmy Carter's sweeping amnesty for illegal aliens was seen as the ultimate betrayal of "white America" by Klansmen. In 1976 and 1977, the Knights of the KKK mounted armed patrols along the U.S.-Mexico border from southern California to Texas, and it took a federal injunction to stop Texas Klansmen from harassing Vietnamese refugees in 1981. Most Klans still restrict their membership to native-born U.S. citizens, but the National Knights opened its doors to naturalized citizens in December 1974, and Dale Reusch's Invisible Empire Knights followed suit in October 1975. In general, moves such as the regional elimination of a standing bar on Catholics are symptomatic of desperate Klans seeking members and money. To date, there has been no evidence of naturalized U.S. citizens flocking to join the Klan. [10; 93]

IMPALA NO. 42

In 1965 congressional investigators identified this group as a cover for the Jackson, Georgia, klavern, United Klans of America. [38]

IMPERIAL CLUB NO. 27-1

A 1960s front for the Sebring, Florida, klavern, United Florida KKK, this group was exposed by the House Un-American Activities Committee in 1966. [38]

IMPERIAL GIANT

Theoretically reserved for retired imperial wizards in the United Klans of America, this honorary title has never been used, since founding wizard Robert Shelton still remains in office. [43]

IMPERIAL KLONCILIUM

In 1923, this title was applied to a group of six ranking Klansmen chosen to resolve the dispute between William Simmons and Hiram Evans over final ownership of the Klan, its regalia, and published rituals. In the modern United Klans of America, the kloncilium consists of fifteen genii serving as the imperial wizard's command staff. Members include the imperial klaliff, imperial klokard, imperial kludd, imperial kligrapp, imperial klabee, imperial kladd, imperial klarogo, imperial klexter, imperial klonsel, imperial nighthawk, and the five-man imperial klokann. [10; 43]

IMPERIAL REPRESENTATIVE

The acting grand dragon of a prospective realm, this officer is appointed by an imperial wizard to organize local Klansmen in sufficient numbers to elect state officers and obtain a realm charter. He may also be empowered to appoint kleagles, if that authority is not restricted to the imperial wizard. [43]

IMPERIAL TAX

Varying from one Klan to another, this "tax" constitutes the periodic dues paid by every Klansman in good standing. [43]

IMPERIAL WIZARD

Since 1915, this title has generally applied to the presiding officer of the Invisible Empire. He is the Klan's supreme chief executive, its military commander-in-chief, and (at least in the United Klans of America) chairman of the imperial kloncilium, consisting of his fifteen genii. Some Klans use other titles for their leader: a few cling to the original "grand wizard" designation used by Nathan Forrest during Reconstruction. Other Klan chiefs have proclaimed themselves "emperor," "grand emperor," or simply "president." In the late 1940s, Lycurgus Spinks set a new record for redundancy by dubbing himself the "imperial emperor" of his own tiny Klan. [10; 43]

IMPERIALE, ANTHONY

As leader of the vigilante North Ward Citizens' Committee in Newark, New Jersey, Imperiale admitted teaching karate to New Jersey Klansmen. In June 1967, the state's grand dragon announced that he had initiated Imperiale into the order on April 19, a claim that the Catholic Imperiale strenuously denies. [NYT 1967]

IMPROVED ORDER OF THE U.S. KLANS, KNIGHTS OF THE KU KLUX KLAN, INC.

Chartered in Georgia on November 7, 1963, this splinter group was organized by Lithonia resident E.E. George, after his ouster as imperial wizard of the U.S. Klans. Competing Klan leader James Venable served as attorney for the incorporating officers, and representatives of the Improved Order subsequently attended gatherings of Venable's National Association of Ku Klux Klan. At its peak strength, this faction boasted two klaverns in Georgia, two in Alabama, and three in Florida. Two Jacksonville, Florida, units disbanded in December 1964, and most of the others were inactive by January 1967, with an estimated 100 members clinging to the faith in Georgia. [38]

INDEPENDENT INVISIBLE KNIGHTS OF THE KU KLUX KLAN

In 1983 this splinter group was identified as one of two Klan factions active in Ohio. [2]

INDEPENDENT KLAN OF AMERICA

Indiana powerhouse D.C. Stephenson organized this splinter group in May 1924, after his publicized break with the Knights of the KKK, Inc. The move backfired, resulting in his belated banishment by Imperial Wizard Hiram Evans, while most Hoosier Klansmen and Klan politicians had remained loyal to imperial headquarters in Atlanta. In 1925, the Independent Klan solicited members in Ulster County, New York, without much success, and its efforts were soon doomed entirely by Stephenson's arrest and conviction of murder in the Madge Oberholtzer case. [10]

INDEPENDENT KLANS

See *Knights of the Ku Klux Klan of America.*

INDEPENDENT KNIGHTS OF THE KU KLUX KLAN

This faction was one of several splinter groups active in South Carolina during the 1950s following the Supreme Court's Black Monday decision on school integration. [38]

INDEPENDENT MISSISSIPPI KLAN

Organized in 1957, this splinter group was composed of defecting klaverns established earlier by the Association of Alabama Knights. Short-lived and relatively ineffective, the group had already disappeared when organizers from Louisiana's Original Knights arrived in the fall of 1963. [38]

INDEPENDENT NORTHERN KLANS, INC.

Based in Pine Bush, New York, this faction made headlines in 1976 when Grand Dragon Earl Schoonmaker and some of his followers were identified as state prison guards. New York Attorney General Louis Lefkowitz demanded the group's membership list under a 1920s anti-Klan state law requiring the public registration of members in oath-bound societies, but Schoonmaker resisted. On January 15, 1976, the state supreme court ruled in favor of the Klan, finding that its pledge was not an oath within the meaning of the statute. Publicity stirred local interest in the Klan, but Schoonmaker's fame was fleeting, and his group had disappeared by the time Anti-Defamation League investigators prepared a list of active Klans in 1983. [*NYT* 1976]

INDEPENDENT ORDER KNIGHTS OF THE KU KLUX KLAN

A Maryland splinter group reported active in 1987, the Independent Order Knights claimed fewer than 100 active members. [*NYT* 1987]

INDIAN RIVER HUNT CLUB

In 1965 congressional investigators identified this group as a cover for the Virginia Beach, Virginia, klavern, United Klans of America. [38]

INDIANA

Indiana was the success story of the 1920s Klan, and that success was due in large part to the charismatic personality of D.C. Stephenson, the state's Klan ruler. An established super-salesman before he joined the Klan, Stephenson ruled his realm with an iron fist, ultimately dooming the Hoosier Klan—and the national organization as well, according to some—when personal problems led to criminal court. The Klan began in Evansville, in 1920, and Stephenson's salesmanship had pumped membership up to an estimated 5,000 by early 1922. A year later, statewide membership was established at 300,000, with 40,000 Klansmen in Indianapolis alone. Stephenson's backstage role in the palace coup that unseated founder William Simmons earned him a powerful friend in Imperial Wizard Hiram Evans, and his reward was an appointment to manage a sub-empire consisting of twenty-three Northern and Midwestern states. Evans made the trip from Atlanta to Kokomo for Stephenson's July 1923 inauguration as grand dragon. Stephenson arrived fashionably late, alighting from an airplane declaring that he had been detained in Washington, D.C., conferring with the President on affairs of state. With their titanic egos in constant competition, Evans and Stephenson were quarreling bitterly by May 1924, prompting Stephenson to desert and organize his own Independent Klan of America. His "military machine" swept the state elections that year, electing a friendly governor and a majority of the state legislature, in addition to countless mayors and lesser officials. In Indianapolis, the new mayor signed a pledge to clear all civic appointments through Stephenson in advance, and other politicians were equally beholden, if less willing to commit their debts to writing. For all his local power, Stephenson's quarrel with Evans had split the Hoosier realm, with city officials and state senators falling out for Stephenson, and Klansmen in the legislature's lower house siding with Evans in Atlanta. The end came swiftly following Stephenson's arrest, conviction, and imprisonment for the 1925 murder of Madge Oberholtzer, a scandal that typified all of the seamy immorality Klansmen were pledged to oppose at the risk of their lives. Members deserted from coast to coast, as Stephenson began leaking details of Hoosier political corruption in a vain attempt to strike a bargain for leniency. By 1927, fewer than 7,000 dues-paying Klansmen remained in the state.

The Indiana Klan never recovered from Stephenson's fall, and Grand Dragon Walter Bossert was ridiculed when he unsuccessfully tried to run for the U.S. Senate in 1938. Rumbles of an Indianapolis Klan revival sent the state attorney general to court eight years later, filing suit to revoke the Klan's charter, along with those of such covers as the Horse Thief Detective Society, the Native Americans Club, the Fraternal Order of Rangers, the Modern Minutemen, the Loyal Liberty League, and the Rock of Freedom. But it was, in fact, unnecessary. In January 1967, Robert Shelton announced the appointment of William Chaney as Indiana's grand dragon, but congressional investigators found only a handful of Klansmen in the state, with no identifiable klaverns. Robed members paraded through Martinsville that July, and Klansmen are still suspected in the unsolved murder of Carol Jenkins, a black girl, in September 1968. For the most part, however, Indiana's new breed of Klansmen kept to themselves and caused few disturbances. Chaney broke with Shelton and the United Klans in May 1976, and in June 1977 he was elected to dual posts as imperial wizard for the new Confederation of Independent Orders and as national coordinator for the ambitious-sounding Northern and Southern Knights. A second conviction on bombing charges in November 1977, earned Chaney a prison term. Bill Wilkinson's Invisible Empire Knights was the next Klan to try its luck in Indiana, but membership remained low, the leadership sundered by personal rivalry. Grand Dragon Ken Taylor quarreled with Wilkinson's replacement, James Farrand, and was banished in October 1988, winning reinstatement only to resign and start his own organization. By August 1989, Taylor was billing himself as the imperial wizard, with his "national office" located in Crawfordsville. [10; 38; 43; 84]

INGE, BENJAMIN

A black state legislator during Reconstruction in Alabama, Inge was murdered by Klan nightriders. [93]

INGLE, HARRY

A Jacksonville, Florida, spokesman for the Knights of the KKK, Ingle told newsmen in 1957, "Applications are coming in so fast, we can't process them." [48]

INNOCENTS CLUB

A militant white supremacist group active in Louisiana during the 1868 election campaign, the Innocents Club cooperated with the KKK and Knights of the White Camellia to intimidate black voters. The club's activities were more specifically focused on politics than those of other contemporary racist groups, with little or no attention paid to black schools, miscegenation, or other "problems." It is believed that membership in the Innocents overlapped with the Klan and the Knights of the White Camellia in areas where two or more groups were simultaneously active. [87]

INTERSTATE KLANS, KNIGHTS OF THE KU KLUX KLAN

The Interstate Klans was organized in 1966, after Vernon Naimaster, acting grand dragon for the United Klans of America in Maryland, criticized Exalted Cyclops Xavier Edwards for recruiting members of the American Nazi Party into the United Klans. Based in Laurel, Maryland, Edwards promptly led his faithful Klansmen into a new organization, unofficially affiliated with George Rockwell's Arlington Nazis. The "interstate" title was adopted because members were also claimed in neighboring Virginia. (Interstate Klansmen were also known as the Maryland Knights of the KKK, not to be confused with the Maryland Knights organized in 1969 by United Klans defector Tony LaRicci.) Involved with the harassment of Roger Lee's New Era Bookshop in Baltimore, the Interstate Klans later sought help from New York Governor Nelson Rockefeller in repealing anti-Klan legislation and securing police protection for a robed march through Harlem. Neither plea was successful, and the Independent Klans faded into obscurity by the end of the decade. [NYT 1967; 38]

INTERNATIONAL BROTHERHOOD OF TEAMSTERS

In late November 1961, officers of this powerful labor union met with spokesmen for the United Klans of America to plot strategy for leader Jimmy Hoffa's upcoming Tennessee trial on charges of looting the union pension fund. Klansmen reportedly agreed to help intimidate witnesses and jurors, in return for Teamster "muscle" to be used for suppressing rival Klans. Hoffa's trial ended with a hung jury in December 1962, but he was subsequently indicted and convicted of jury tampering in the case. [79]

INVINCIBLE EMPIRE, KNIGHTS OF THE WHITE ROSE

In 1983 this tiny faction was identified as one of three Klan splinter groups claiming members in California. [2]

INVISIBLE EMPIRE

This term describes the overall geographical jurisdiction of a particular Klan organization, with "invisibility" referring to the presumed secrecy of membership, rituals, and operations. Members of the KKK are designated "citizens," with all nonmembers regarded as "aliens." Although theoretically the Invisible Empire covers the entire world, various restrictions are placed on membership. The Knights of Ku Klux Klan (1915-1944) required its members to be "native-born, white, Christian, gentile Americans." The modern United Klans of America still abides by those restrictions, but other groups have made allowances through the years, in the interest of gaining more recruits (and money) for the cause. Affiliated groups such as the Royal Riders of the Red Robe have been established for right-thinking "foreigners," while since the 1950s some Klans have agreed to admit Catholics and naturalized citizens. Expansion of various Klans into Austria, Canada, Chile, England, and Germany has also lowered the ban on foreign recruits, but Jews and nonwhites are still universally excluded. Within the United States, major Klans subdivide the Invisible Empire into realms, provinces, and klantons for purposes of administration. [10; 43]

INVISIBLE EMPIRE, KNIGHTS OF THE KU KLUX KLAN

The dominant Klan of the early 1980s was created in August 1975, following a rift in David Duke's Knights of the KKK. Based in Denham Springs, Louisiana, and led by Imperial Wizard Bill Wilkinson, the Invisible Empire Knights included between one fifth and one third of all active Klansmen by 1979, and remained dominant until membership began declining in 1983. Wilkinson's militance was a factor in the Klan's dramatic growth, typified by public displays of weapons and statements such as "These guns ain't for rabbit hunting: they're to waste people." The Invisible Empire Knights were adept at capitalizing on black civil rights demonstrations, provoking headline confrontations in Tupelo and Oklona, Mississippi, and in Decatur, Alabama, where Grand Dragon Roger Handley took maximum advantage of the Tommy Hines rape case. In July 1979, Wilkinson told the press, "The Klan's short-range goal at this time is separation of the races in America. Our long-term goal is repatriation of all colored races out of this country. We feel that this plan is feasible." Total membership was estimated between 2,000 and 2,500 in 1980, but autumn forays into Connecticut and Pennsylvania that fall evoked lukewarm responses. Wilkinson's hold on the Klan began to unravel in 1983, when the Nashville *Tennesseean* leaked documents naming him as an FBI informant.

In response, Wilkinson claimed he had revealed nothing that federal agents could not read in the press, but the damage was done. Disgruntled members further accused him of looting the Klan treasury and pandering to the media with tough talk that encouraged hostile attention from law enforcement agencies. James Farrand replaced Wilkinson near the end of the decade, but the Invisible Empire Knights membership continued to decline.
[*FOF* 1979; 2]

INVISIBLE EMPIRE, KNIGHTS OF THE KU KLUX KLAN

Unrelated to Bill Wilkinson's Klan of the same name, this group was organized on October 13, 1975, when five grand dragons deserted the National Knights, charging Imperial Wizard James Venable with mismanagement and senility. Venable retaliated by banishing the five and revoking their commissions as dragons, declaring, "They been runnin' over states creatin' trouble and gettin' in undesirable members, takin' in anybody who had $15." Ohio's Dale Reusch was elected imperial wizard of the new faction, supported by grand dragons Raymond Doerfler (Pennsylvania), John Howard (South Carolina), Tony LaRicci (Maryland), and W.B. Miller II (West Virginia). In an effort to attract new members, the Invisible Empire Knights opened its doors to women, children, Catholics, and naturalized U.S. citizens. By mid-1976, Jack Prins was identified as the Klan's new grand dragon for Canada, but this geographical expansion was not an indication of staying power. Overwhelmed by its Louisiana-based namesake, the new Invisible Empire Knights had disappeared entirely by 1983. [*NYT* 1975; 84]

INVISIBLE EMPIRE KNIGHTS OF THE KU KLUX KLAN

An independent splinter group reported active in New Jersey during 1987, the Invisible Empire Knights claimed fewer than 100 members. [*NYT* 1987]

INVISIBLE EMPIRE, KNIGHTS OF THE KU KLUX KLAN, REALM OF SOUTH CAROLINA

Its title notwithstanding, this faction had no connection with either of the two Klans that billed themselves as the Invisible Empire Knights. Founded in 1969 or 1970 by Robert Scoggin, following his banishment from the United Klans of America, this group was based in Spartanburg, South Carolina. The first apparent recruitment outside South Carolina occurred in May 1975, when Indiana Klansman Wilburn Foreman brought thirty defectors from the United Klans of America into the fold. A year later, Scoggin hosted his Conference of Eastern Dragons in South Carolina, hoping to promote the illusion of a far-flung organization. A survey of active Klan factions in 1983 revealed no trace of Scoggin's operation surviving in Spartanburg or elsewhere. [84]

INVISIBLE EMPIRE, UNITED KLANS, KNIGHTS OF THE KU KLUX KLAN OF AMERICA, INC.

An outgrowth of the failing U.S. Klans, this group was chartered in Georgia on February 21, 1961, with Robert ("Wild Bill") Davidson as imperial wizard and Calvin Craig as his Georgia grand dragon. Most of the early membership was drawn from U.S. Klans defectors in Georgia and Alabama, where Reverend Alvin Horn was recruited to lead the neighboring realm. Davidson's unusual commitment to nonviolence, typified by his reaction to Klan participation in the Athens, Georgia, university riots of 1961, led to his abrupt resignation on April 1. Calvin Craig immediately opened negotiations with Robert Shelton, leader of the militant Alabama Knights, and a merger was formalized on July 8, 1961, with the Klan's headquarters shifting from Atlanta to Shelton's home base in Tuscaloosa, Alabama. While Davidson's original title was used on the new Klan's incorporation papers, the Shelton-Craig operation has since been known as the United Klans of America, Inc., Knights of the Ku Klux Klan. [38; 93]

IOWA

The 1920s Klan began in Des Moines, and rapidly spread despite early and determined opposition from groups such as the American Legion. Numerous Protestant ministers were recruited as kleagles. Klansmen were inconvenienced by an anti-mask law, passed in 1923, but they scored local victories in the following year's school board elections, making it difficult for Catholic teachers to find employment in the state. Two years later, opposition to the Klan was out in force. In Des Moines, a mob armed with pitchforks and crowbars menaced assembled Klansmen, and retreated only when threatened with military force. By the end of the 1920s, the Klan had disappeared. [10]

ISBELL, JOEY

In July 1986, Isbell shot and killed a black teenager, Fahim Ahmad, at a carnival in Zion, Illinois. Witnesses at his murder trial testified that Isbell was shouting "Klan! Klan! Klan!" before he fired the fatal shot. [NYT 1986]

J

JACINTO CITY CITIZENS COMMITTEE FOR LAW AND ORDER

In 1965 congressional investigators identified this group as the cover for a Houston, Texas, klavern, United Klans of America. [38]

JACK ROBINSONS

A militant secret society also called the Robinson Club or the Robinson Family, this organization was founded in Pontotoc County, Mississippi, by Klansman and sheriff Tom Saddler in 1871. The immediate goal was a Democratic victory in that year's election, and Saddler ultimately recruited 1,500 soldiers for the cause in Pontotoc, Tippah, Chickasaw, and Monroe counties. Witnesses in Monroe County reported open cooperation between the Jack Robinsons and the KKK, along with a third group dubbed "the Johnsons." Despite a ready supply of weapons, their first resort was the economic boycott, pressuring merchants to join and support the Democratic Party. [87]

JACKSON, ANDREW

One of three "major" Klan organizers in modern Illinois, Jackson joined officers of the United Klans, the National States Rights Party, and the Devil's Advocates motorcycle gang for a May 1975 organizational meeting at the Kankakee Ramada Inn. Encouraged by the thirty-man turnout, he spent the summer trying to organize a United Klans klavern in Kankakee, without significant results. His recruits were few in number, and aside from the several undercover officers assigned to penetrate the Klan, fewer still turned out for periodic meetings. In August 1975, he led five Klansmen (including one state investigator) to Chicago for a joint demonstration with Frank Collin's neo-Nazis in Marquette Park. Jackson dropped out of sight for six months, resurfacing at Midlothian in early 1976 as the new Illinois grand dragon for James Venable's National Knights. Vigorous recruiting efforts brought no visible results, and by the end of August Jackson had fewer than ten dues-paying members on his rolls. [43]

JACKSON, ED

An intimate friend of Grand Dragon D.C. Stephenson in the 1920s, Jackson allowed that friendship to color his performance as Indiana's secretary of state. In that capacity, he received a wire from Stephenson—intercepted and published by the American Unity League—concerning the resignation of Indiana's Republican party chairman. Concerning a replacement, Stephenson instructed Jackson to "Permit no selection to be made and permit no one to be named until I have had an opportunity to confer with you." Elected governor with Klan support in 1924, Jackson was expected to grant executive clemency when Stephenson was convicted of killing Madge Oberholtzer the following year. His failure to intervene prompted a series of "leaks" from Stephenson, who revealed information about the Klan's political allies, including Jackson. He tried to describe a $2,500 check from Stephenson as payment for a horse, but few believed Jackson. Indicted for failing to report campaign contributions, Jackson was saved from conviction by the statute of limitations. His career in politics, however, was finished. [10]

JACKSON, HELEN

A prime attraction on the 1920s Klan lecture circuit, Jackson was one of several "escaped nuns" who delivered anti-Catholic speeches to credulous listeners. She had in fact escaped from a Catholic reformatory in Detroit, and her need for revenge, coupled with a profit motive, inspired her sermonettes on priestly debauchery. Jackson's "autobiography," *Convent Cruelties*, was a best-seller with Klansmen, and her public lectures were usually segregated by sex. Female audiences were regaled with details of the papal plot to brainwash their children in parochial schools, while men heard a more prurient version, complete with a display of small leather bags, allegedly used for conveying illegitimate newborns to the convent furnace moments after their arrival in the world. Not always well received, Jackson touched off riots in 1922, when her appearance at Brooklyn's First Baptist Church roused the ire of neighborhood Catholics. [10]

JACKSON, MATTHEW

A black resident of McComb, Mississippi, Jackson was the target of Klansmen who bombed his home on September 23, 1964. [38]

JACKSON, OPAL LEE

One of four black women shot and wounded by Klansman Marshall Thrash in Chattanooga, Tennessee, on April 19, 1980, Jackson survived the attack and pressed criminal charges against her assailant. [*AP*, April 20, 1980]

JACKSON, ROBERT

A black teenager in Prosperity, South Carolina, Jackson was jailed for disorderly conduct in the spring of 1965. Soon after his incarceration, a band of robed, hooded men entered the jail, threatening and beating Jackson in his cell. Two of the group—policeman Philip Plampkin and municipal night watchman L. Cornell Wise—were arrested April 8 and charged with second-degree lynching, a nonfatal incident of mob violence. [*NYT* 1965]

JACKSON, WHARLEST

As treasurer of the NAACP chapter in Natchez, Mississippi, Jackson participated in a boycott of white-owned stores after bombs crippled George Metcalfe in 1965. In early 1967, Jackson accepted a job, formerly held by a white man, as mixer of chemicals at the local Armstrong Tire and Rubber Company plant, where a number of Klansmen were also employed. On February 27, 1967, he was killed by a bomb set in his pickup truck, similar in all respects to the car bomb used on Metcalfe in August 1965. FBI agents linked the bomb to a Klan splinter group known as the Silver Dollar Group, but no prosecutions resulted. After the bombing, black activist Charles Evers led a procession to the Armstrong plant to "watch Jackson's killers" during the afternoon shift change, further protesting employment of Klansmen at the plant. [*Time*, March 10, 1967; *Newsweek*, March 13, 1967]

JACKSON COUNTY CITIZENS EMERGENCY UNIT

Based in Pascagoula, Mississippi, this paramilitary group was created by Sheriff James Grimsley in 1962, with members recruited from participants in the September university riot at Oxford. An estimated 400 members signed on at the Unit's peak of strength, drawing recruits from Biloxi and neighboring towns. A prime target of the Unit was Pascagoula newsman Ira Harkey, whose newspaper was subjected to boycotts, anonymous threats, and occasional gunfire in October and November 1962. Membership declined sharply after FBI agents launched an investigation of the shootings, and public opposition from AFL-CIO leaders caused many union men to abandon the group. Grimsley resigned as Unit leader to run for state office in 1963, but voters rejected his blatantly racist campaign. His replacement, a notorious saloon brawler, ran ninth in a field of eleven for county sheriff that year, but the winner tossed his hard-core constituents a bone by appointing the loser as one of his deputies. [37]

JACKSONVILLE SPORTS CLUB

In 1965 congressional investigators identified this club as the front for a Jacksonville, North Carolina, klavern, United Klans of America. [38]

JACOBS, LLOYD

A member of the United Klans in Durham, North Carolina, Jacobs ran against incumbent C.P. Ellis for the post of exalted cyclops in 1971, seeking a return to the traditional Klan posture versus Ellis's "radical" opposition to the local power structure. Ellis won with 60 percent of the vote (the usual winning margin in Klan elections is closer to 90 percent). When Ellis ran again in 1972, he was unopposed. [57]

JACOBS, MARVIN

A gas station attendant in Kankakee, Illinois, Jacobs was introduced at a May 1975 organizational meeting of the United Klans as the new exalted cyclops of a local klavern. Within a week of the announcement, he was forced out of office by rival Andrew Jackson, and subsequently resigned from the United Klans. [43]

JAMES, CHARLES E.

In August 1964 James was one of the original incorporators for the Adams County Civic & Betterment Association, later identified as a front for the Natchez, Mississippi, klavern, United Klans of America. [38]

JAPANESE-AMERICANS

As a highly visible West Coast minority, Japanese-Americans became a target for California Klansmen in the 1920s. Spokesmen for the invisible empire denied any intent of molesting Japanese farmers, but Klan newspapers stressed the "menace" of alien land ownership during 1923, and later correspondence stirred up anger at home, with reports that Klansmen were driving Japanese-Americans out of Sacramento and Sonoma counties. Antipathy toward Asians remained a fact of life in California through the Great Depression, reaching its climax with the internment of Japanese-Americans in concentration camps after Pearl Harbor. [10]

JARVIS, THOMAS J.

North Carolina's speaker of the house during Reconstruction, Jarvis was also identified as a prominent member of that state's KKK. [87]

JEFFERS, PERRY

A black farmer in Warren County, Georgia, during Reconstruction, Jeffers ignored Klan orders to vote Democratic in the 1868 election, insisting that he would campaign for Ulysses S. Grant. On the night of November 1, six Klansmen raided his home. Jeffers and his sons returned the gunfire, killing one Klansman and wounding at least three others. Retaliation came four days later, when a band of fifty to 100 Klansmen stormed the rural cabin. Jeffers and four of his sons hid in the woods while a fifth son, crippled from childhood, was shot eleven times and burned in a fire started with furniture from the house. Perry's wife was hanged from a nearby tree, but she was still alive when Jeffers cut her down after the Klansmen had departed. The raiders' leader was identified as Charles Wallace, editor of the Warrenton *Georgia Clipper* and a prominent spokesman for local Democrats. In the face of such opposition, Jeffers and his sons spent several nights in the Warrenton jail for their own safety, before deciding to flee the county. Their train was bound for South Carolina when Klansmen stopped it at Dearing and removed Jeffers and his sons for summary execution. One of his sons escaped, but Jeffers and the other three were killed. No effort was made to arrest the killers, although several were readily identified, including notorious triggerman Ellis Adams and the father of a Klansman killed in the first raid on the Jeffers homestead. [87]

JENA HUNTING & FISHING CLUB

In 1965 congressional investigators identified this club as a front for the Jena, Louisiana, klavern, Original Knights of the Ku Klux Klan. [38]

JENKINS, JAY

A special reporter for the Raleigh, North Carolina, *News & Observer*, Jenkins won a 1952 Sidney Hillman journalism award for his series exposing Klan activities in North Carolina. [*NYT* 1953]

JETER, COLUMBUS

A black resident of South Carolina, during Reconstruction, Jeter was whipped by Klansmen after he refused to buy a horse from a Klansman who demanded 20 percent interest on the price. [93]

JETT, IRA

See *Columbians, Inc.*

JOHN BIRCH SOCIETY

Organized at a December 1958 meeting in Indianapolis, Indiana, the John Birch Society was named for an obscure U.S. officer killed by Chinese communists in World War II and memorialized by Society members as "the first victim of World War III." Under the leadership of Massachusetts native Robert Welch, the Society adopted a conspiratorial view of history and current events that literally detected communists behind every major event of modern times. Franklin Roosevelt and Harry Truman had been dupes of the communists, the Society maintained, while President Dwight Eisenhower was described in print as a "dedicated, conscious agent of the Communist conspiracy." Such views meshed perfectly with those of the Citizens' Council and the Klan, promoting occasional cooperation that sometimes embarrassed the Society. In 1965, a California legislative committee noted increasing anti-Semitism in the Society's literature and lectures, with some Society bookstores openly stocking Minutemen guerilla warfare manuals. That same year, at a Chicago meeting of the Congress of Conservatives, Welch shared the dais with Lester Maddox and Edwin Walker, telling his audience that they should not hesitate to kill communists, because "if they are truly communists, they cannot be thought of as human beings." Selma's Sheriff Jim Clark joined the Society's lecture bureau a year later, and the Society openly cooperated with Klansmen in 1967 to organize a Florida branch of the American Independent Party. The Society's bookstore in Bakersfield, California, displayed pro-Klan literature on its shelves until the fact was publicized in 1968, at which time the material was withdrawn from circulation. Ironically, Delmar Dennis and other Society orators were simultaneously branding the KKK and National States Rights Party as communist fronts, created to discredit "legitimate" right-wing organizations, but the argument did not persuade some observers. [27; 28]

JOHN BROWN ANTI-KLAN COMMITTEE

Based in Austin, Texas, this group publicized KKK paramilitary training activities in Camp Puller, west of Houston, in November 1980. Adverse publicity surrounding the camp finally led to lawsuits and a federal injunction against the maintenance of "private armies." [AP, Nov. 25, 1980]

JOHNSON, DR. A.M.

A Republican state legislator during Reconstruction in Mississippi County, Arkansas, Johnson was murdered by Klansmen on August 26, 1868. [87]

JOHNSON, CARL

See Bellows, Jim.

JOHNSON, DONALD

One of three Michigan Klansmen charged with conspiring to shoot a black man who patronized a "white" Detroit bar, Johnson pled guilty to the charge in November 1980 and received a prison sentence of one to four years. [NYT 1980]

JOHNSON, E.G.

A state senator from Columbia County, South Carolina, during Recon-struction, Johnson received a Klan message warning him to resign or die in 1871. The note, penned after "sober deliberation in brotherhoods," further warned Johnson to keep the communication secret, but he disregarded the Klan's advice. Shortly after the message was published in a local newspaper, nightriders fired shots into Johnson's home. [87]

JOHNSON, REV. E.G.

See *Bellows, Jim.*

JOHNSON, FRANK M.

A federal judge in Montgomery, Alabama, Johnson issued the May 1961 injunction barring three Klans—the Alabama Knights, U.S. Klans, and Federated Ku Klux Klans—from any further violence aimed at interfering with the integrated Freedom Rides. Six years later, on April 25, 1967, his mother's home was bombed after Johnson ordered the desegregation of several Alabama schools. [*NYT* 1961, 1967]

JOHNSON, KATHERINE

One of four black women shot and wounded by Klansman Marshall Thrash in Chattanooga, Tennessee, on April 19, 1980, Johnson survived and pressed criminal charges against her assailant. [*AP*, April 20, 1980]

JOHNSON, LYNDON BAINES

The son of a 1920s Klan-fighter in Texas, Johnson hired ex-Klansman (and convicted killer) Philip Fox to manage his 1948 senate campaign, winning election in a race marked by numerous complaints of vote fraud. Elected Vice President of the United States in 1960, he was elevated to the White House following the assassination of John F. Kennedy in Dallas. As President, Johnson maintained his father's enmity toward the KKK, press-ing a reluctant FBI into action against the Klan in 1964 and denouncing the order six months later as a "hooded society of bigots," calling on Klansmen to resign and "return to a decent society before it is too late." [*NYT* 1965]

JOHNSON, PAUL

Elected governor of Mississippi with Klan support in 1963, Johnson was a diehard racist in the mold of predecessor Ross Barnett. (A typical Johnson campaign speech branded the NAACP as a collection of "Niggers, Apes, Alligators, Coons, and Possums.") Adverse publicity forced Johnson to dismiss several Klansmen from the state highway patrol in 1964, but he was generally more cordial to the hooded knights. After three civil rights workers vanished in Neshoba County in June 1964, Johnson told acquaintances, "Governor [George] Wallace of Alabama and I are the only two people who know where they are, and we're not telling." [42; 58]

JOHNSON, RICHARD

A Michigan Klansman, Johnson pled guilty in November 1980 to charges of harassing a black family and trying to drive them from their home in Romulus, Michigan. A prison term of one to four years was imposed by the court. [NYT 1980]

JOHNSON, RIVERS

A state senator from Duplin, North Carolina, Johnson led the fight against a 1923 anti-mask law, speaking on behalf of "25,000 red-blooded North Carolinians who are members of the Ku Klux Klan." He told fellow senators that "invisibility is the force of the empire," claiming that the KKK stood for "Protestant Americanism, free speech, free press, white supremacy, and the support of all law." Four years later, Johnson underwent a change of heart, joining Reverend Oscar Haywood to introduce a bill outlawing masks and membership in secret societies. Senators passed the bill, but it was killed by Klan supporters in the lower house. [10]

JOHNSON, THOMAS A.

A contractor in Wanaque, New Jersey, Johnson was angered by 1965 reports of local KKK activity, announcing plans to revive a 1920s anti-Klan organization, the Knights of the Flaming Circle. His proclamation sparked a rash of anonymous threats, and the "new" group never got off the ground, a victim of public apathy which also doomed the Wanaque KKK. [NYT 1965]

JOHNSON, WILLIS

A black resident of Newberry County, South Carolina, during Reconstruction, Johnson was whipped by Klansmen for voting the Republican ticket and distributing Republican ballots to his friends. [93]

JOHNSON, WOODROW

A mechanic from Whiteville, North Carolina, Johnson was lured from his home on December 8, 1951, and beaten by Klansmen for "drinking too much." Investigation traced the crime to the Association of Carolina Klans, and thirteen members were indicted by a county grand jury. Defendants included Early Brooks; Brock Norris; Henry Edwards (stepfather of the victim); Harvey Barfield; Ernest Ward; Lawrence Nivens; Ray Kelly; Rex Connor; Frank Lewis; Leroy Honeycutt; John Honeycutt, Jr.; Steve Edmond; and George White. At their trial in May 1952, eight Klansmen—including

Brooks, Kelly, Connor, Lewis, Edmond, White, and both Honeycutts—filed pleas of no contest and were sentenced to two years in jail. Klansmen Edwards, Barfield, and Ward received identical sentences on conviction, while Johnson, Norris, and Nivens were acquitted on all counts. [*NYT* 1952]

JOHNSTON, REV. EVALL G. ("PARSON JACK")

A leader of the Association of Georgia Klans in Columbus, Georgia, Johnston tried to organize a White Protestant Christian Party in August 1947, his membership applications urging recruits to prevent the United States from becoming "a mixed and mingled mass of –isms." Quarreling with Grand Dragon Samuel Green over money a few months later, Johnston resigned to start his own Original Southern Klans, Inc., in June 1948. Poor health was cited as the reason for his leaving in February 1949, and Alton Pate took over for Johnston. By 1952, editorials in Johnston's *Georgia Tribune* were questioning the Klan's ability to enforce segregation, and Johnston sold the paper in January 1953, to pursue his racist ministry full-time. Typical sermons suggested that Southern blacks should be "encouraged" to move north, but he was also interested in broader issues. Hosting an "anti-United Nations" convention at his Columbus Baptist Tabernacle, he invited Klan leaders Bill Hendrix and Tom Hamilton as guest speakers, but the high point was the reading of a telegram from Gen. Douglas MacArthur, expressing regret at his inability to attend. The gathering accomplished nothing, but it drew a round of praise from spokesmen for the fledgling National Association for the Advancement of White People. [25; 77]

JOHNSTON, JAMES DANIEL

See *Fitzgerald, Charlie.*

JOINER, LLOYD

In 1965 Joiner was among the first directors of the Anti-Communist Christian Association, identified as a front for the Original Knights of the KKK in Louisiana's 6th Congressional District. [38]

JOINER, NELSON

A black resident of Abbeville County, South Carolina, during Reconstruction, Joiner was selected as a delegate to the 1868 state constitutional convention. In June of that year, he was driven from the county by Klansmen, who burned his home to the ground. [87]

JONES, ARTHUR

As leader of the America First Committee, an offshoot of the American Nazi Party, Jones remained close to the parent organization and continued to advertise in their official magazine. [2]

JONES, BOB, SR.

A fundamentalist preacher in the 1920s, Jones never joined the KKK, but he publicly endorsed Klan principles and openly fraternized with Klansmen, thereby lending his prestige to the Invisible Empire. Following a three-week revival in Andalusia, Alabama, Jones gratefully accepted a Klan donation of $1,568, and he later maintained a judicious silence when Klansmen distributed recruiting literature to a church audience in Dallas, Texas. Bob Jones University, founded in Greenville, South Carolina, in 1927, remains a stronghold of fundamentalist religion and John Birch-style politics, staffed through the 1960s by Jones's descendants and supervised by people including Senator Strom Thurmond. In 1968, Dr. Bob Jones III reiterated the school's racial policy in a published interview, describing blacks as Biblical descendants of Ham, ordained by God to play the role of a "servant's servant." As Jones explained, "a Negro is best when he serves at the table, when he does that, he's doing what he knows how to do best. And the Negroes who have ascended to positions in government, in education, this sort of thing, I think you'll find, by and large, have a strong strain of white blood in them." [80; 93]

JONES, CALVIN E.

A Confederate veteran and one of six original Klansmen in Pulaski, Tennessee, Jones convened the first KKK meeting in the office of his father, Judge Thomas M. Jones. Later an attorney, Jones served the Pulaski Klan as a nighthawk. [87]

JONES, CLAYTON

A city court judge in Albany, Georgia, Jones addressed a local rally of the United Klans on July 7, 1963, urging Klansmen to "hurl back the black tide" in the United States. Striking a morbid note, Jones declared that he did not have long to live, adding, "But I hope that God will grant me the power to come back. And when I do, may I still see white faces in the positions of trust, not black faces." [NYT 1963]

JONES, H.H.

On February 29, 1960, Georgia Klansman H.H. Jones announced his election as imperial wizard of the Knights of the Ku Klux Klan, Inc., based in Jonesboro. According to Jones, representatives from seventeen southeastern and southwestern states had convened over the weekend to organize the new Klan, and a membership drive was planned for the North. Despite extravagant claims of 42,000 members, the Knights had disappeared by the time congressional investigators began their survey of active Klans in March 1965. [NYT 1960; 38]

JONES, H.J.

As exalted cyclops of College Park, Georgia, Klavern No. 297, Jones was elected imperial wizard of the U.S. Klans on October 26, 1963, in a surprise move unseating incumbent E.E. George. Jones was still in office as of January 1967, but his membership had shrunken to an estimated fifty Klansmen, and the U.S. Klans disappeared entirely by the end of the decade. [38]

JONES, HAMILTON C.

A resident of Charlotte, North Carolina, Jones joined the Klan in 1867 and was later identified as a high-ranking member, possibly the realm's grand dragon. At the same time, he was also a leader of the state senate, elected from Mecklenburg County. [87]

JONES, IREDELL

A Confederate veteran, Jones was one of ten Klansmen who founded the Klan in York County, South Carolina, in June 1868. He was later elected to serve as grand scribe for his den. [87]

JONES, JAMES FLOYD

See *White, Ben.*

JONES, JAMES ROBERTSON

A second-generation Klansman, Jones had trouble in the navy when he refused to salute black officers. Back in civilian life, he earned his living as a lightning rod salesman until June 1963, when he met with several former members of U.S. Klans and decided to approach Imperial Wizard Robert Shelton for affiliation with the United Klans of America. Shelton dispatched Robert Scoggin from South Carolina to coordinate an organizational meeting in mid-July, and eighty members were swiftly recruited for the new realm. Jones was first appointed as acting grand dragon for ninety days, then elected to a three-year term on August 17, with the United Klans' first statewide rally convened four days later. A dynamic salesman, Jones initiated mass recruiting drives that soon built up North Carolina to its mid-1960s status as the largest and most successful United Klans realm. Theoretically opposed to violence, Jones twice visited a black church in Elm City, cautioning elders against using integrated groups to paint the building. His warnings were ignored, and two Klansmen were arrested on July 14, when they tried to burn the church. Summoned before the House Un-American Activities Committee in October 1965, Jones was accused of financial irregularities including falsification of reports on the Klan's corporate income and "coercing" Klansmen into buying him a new Cadillac.

(His biggest money-makers were Klan robes, manufactured for $3.20 and sold to the faithful for $15.) Cited for contempt of Congress after he ignored subpoenas for various United Klans documents, Jones appealed his conviction and spent the intervening months on new recruitment. In September 1968, Rowan County's sheriff named Jones as a special deputy to help maintain order at a forthcoming Klan rally, but adverse publicity resulted in cancelation of the appointment. The outstanding contempt charges caught up with Jones in March 1969, and he was sentenced to a year in prison. By the time he emerged nine months later, the North Carolina realm was in chaos, with dissident leaders and splinter groups vying for power—some of which were secretly backed by the FBI—while the bulk of Klan membership disappeared. [10; 38]

JONES, KENNETH

A Wyoming state prison guard, Jones was fired in February 1988 for terrorizing black inmates by marching past their cells dressed in a Klan hood and robe. [NYT 1988]

JONES, TOM

A Georgia Klansman, Jones was one of five arrested in Lagrange during May 1961 for trying to block the integrated Freedom Rides. On May 29, he was convicted of loitering and fined $135. [FOF 1961]

JONES, WARREN

A black tenant farmer in Warren County, Georgia, Jones was promised a half-share of the crop he produced in 1869, hiring additional hands at harvest time. With the work complete, Jones's landlord reneged on his promise, threatening Jones with a Klan raid unless he stayed to work the land for free. Jones eventually fled to Atlanta, penniless, and later testified before a congressional panel probing Klan violence. [87]

JONES, WILLIAM

A white planter and enemy of the KKK in Obion County, Tennessee, during Reconstruction, Jones recruited black laborers and armed them when local authorities failed to suppress Klan raiders. When Klansmen raided his plantation, Jones and his workers responded with gunfire, killing one nightrider and wounding several others. Arrested on murder charges, Jones and several blacks were en route to the county jail when Klansmen ambushed the posse, killing two blacks and wounding three others. Jones escaped in the confusion and fled to Nashville, where he found sanctuary with friends. [87]

JORDAN, JAMES E.

See *Schwerner, Michael.*

JORDAN, OTIS

A black resident of Swainsboro, Georgia, Jordan was hospitalized after a Klan flogging on September 5, 1951. The beating was part of a KKK campaign to drive black residents from an integrated neighborhood. [*NYT* 1951]

JOSEPH E. JOHNSON CLUB NO. 61

In 1965 congressional investigators identified this group as a cover for the Marietta, Georgia, klavern, United Klans of America. [38]

JUDAY, ROBERT

A member of the Winter Garden, Florida, klavern, Juday was charged with perjury on June 3, 1953, regarding his testimony before a federal grand jury probing Klan violence since 1949. Independent evidence named Juday as a participant in the Klan beatings of victims Ivan Eilbeck and Albert Boykin. [*NYT* 1953]

JUNCTION CITY SPORTSMAN'S CLUB

A 1960s front for the Junction City, Louisiana, klavern, United Klans of America, this group was exposed by federal investigators in 1966. [38]

JUSTICE, JAMES M.

A Republican state legislator in Rutherford County, North Carolina, Justice was attacked by Klansmen at his home on the night of June 11, 1871. The raiders chopped through his front door with an ax, beat Justice unconscious, and dragged him through the streets of Rutherfordton, shouting and firing pistols. Despite a standing death sentence passed by their leaders, the Klansmen released Justice alive on his promise to support "the Southern cause." Instead, he had a dozen of the raiders arrested, including Klan leader Randolph Shotwell and his brother. [87]

JUSTICE KNIGHTS OF THE KU KLUX KLAN

A splinter group based in Chattanooga, Tennessee, this group was led by Imperial Wizard Bill Church in 1980. On April 20, 1980, Church and two of his followers were arrested in the shootings of several black women. Church and Klansman Larry Payne were acquitted, while Marshall Thrash was convicted on reduced charges, a verdict that touched off black riots in Chattanooga. [*NYT* 1980]

K

KAHL, GORDON

A North Dakota farmer, decorated and twice wounded in World War II, Kahl was financially ruined by falling wheat prices in the late 1960s. Casting about for a convenient scapegoat, he blamed the Jews and joined the radical Posse Comitatus, refusing to pay income tax after a 1970 "religious conversion" convinced him that the IRS was "sinful." For nearly a decade Kahl traveled the Midwest, lecturing right-wing audiences on the fine points of tax evasion and legal harassment of the federal government through nuisance lawsuits, taking time for occasional guerilla warfare courses sponsored by the Posse. In February 1983, federal marshals raided the sixty-three-year-old Kahl's home in Medina, North Dakota. Two officers were killed and four others wounded in the raid. Accomplices Yorivon Kahl (Gordon's son) and Scott Faul were later convicted on two counts of second-degree murder and six counts of assault, while Gordon went underground, hiding in the fortified home of Posse members Leon and Norma Ginter, near Smithville, Arkansas. Kahl penned letters to the Aryan Nations, describing his stand as a "Christian patriot." Authorities caught up with him on June 3, 1983, sparking an hour-long battle in which Kahl murdered Sheriff Gene Matthews. A smoke grenade hurled by one of the attackers touched off ammunition stored in the bunker, and Kahl was killed in the blast, and has become martyr of sorts for the racist right. [13]

KALENDAR

Developed by William Simmons to facilitate secret communications of scheduled meeting dates, the kalendar reckons years from the date of the

Klan's 20th century "reincarnation," with 1915 considered year I, and so forth. The twelve months are named Bloody, Gloomy, Hideous, Fearful, Furious, Alarming, Terrible, Horrible, Mournful, Sorrowful, Frightful, and Appalling. Weeks are variously dubbed Woeful, Weeping, Wailing, Wonderful, and Weird (in the case of a month with five weeks). Days of the week are labeled Dark, Deadly, Dismal, Doleful, Desolate, Dreadful, and Desperate. Thus, a July 4, 1990, greeting would be dated the Doleful day of the Woeful week of the Terrible month of the Year of the Reincarnation LXXV. [10; see also *Ku Klux Register*]

KAMELIA

This short-lived organization was created by William Simmons as the "official" KKK ladies' auxiliary after he was deposed by Imperial Wizard Hiram Evans in 1922. Infiltrating Oklahoma's White American Protestant Study Club, Simmons soon took control of the group and loaded the staff with his supporters, but the movement never caught on. Evans retaliated by forbidding Klansmen to associate with the Kamelia ladies, and Simmons finally agreed to disband the organization as part of a settlement reached in 1924. [10]

KANETA, EDWARD

See *Germany*.

KANGER, THOMAS

A resident of Palo Alto, Pennsylvania, Kanger was indicted on March 1, 1974—along with Roy Frankhouser and James Culbert—on federal charges of receiving, selling, and disposing of stolen explosives. [*NYT* 1974]

KANSAS

Klan kleagles first came to Kansas in 1922, planting their first klaverns along the Oklahoma border, and within two years a peak membership of nearly 100,000 had been achieved. Klansmen played an active vigilante role in Kansas, stopping cars on rural highways to search for contraband liquor, raiding homes around Emporia to catch "sinners" playing cards on Sunday afternoon. The mayor of Liberty was abducted and flogged for denying the KKK permission to meet in City Hall, and Klan candidates scored municipal victories in at least seven cities, including Wichita and Kansas City, in the 1923 elections. William Allen White, editor of the Emporia *Gazette*, was the Klan's most vocal and persistent enemy in Kansas, launching a shoestring gubernatorial campaign to publicize Klan corruption and violence in 1924. White failed to win election, but his larger goal was eventually realized, as mounting public opposition and internal dissension left the Kansas Klan in ruins by 1927. [10]

KAPPA BETA LAMBDA

Founded in the 1920s at the University of Michigan, this Klan-sponsored fraternity borrowed its initials from the phrase "Klansman Be Loyal." [10]

KARDINAL KULLORS

As indicated in the constitution of the United Klans of America, the Klan's kardinal kullors—utilized for banners and various robes denoting rank within the KKK—are white, crimson, gold, and black. Secondary kullors are gray, green, and blue. Only the imperial wizard is entitled to wear royal purple. Rival Klans generally ignore the United Klans ritual trappings, selecting colors for banners and robes on the basis of personal preference. [93]

KASPER, JOHN

While studying at New York's Columbia University, Kasper fell in love with the poetry of Ezra Pound, absorbing Pound's anti-Semitism intact and viewing the poet's commitment to a mental institution as political martyrdom. ("I think it is important to realize," Kasper once told reporters, "that almost 100 percent of psychiatric therapy is Jewish and that 80 percent of the psychiatrists are Jewish.") A protégé of John Crommelin, Kasper met Klan leader Asa Carter in April 1956 while managing Crommelin's unsuccessful senate campaign. A month later, Kasper organized the Seaboard White Citizens' Council in Washington, D.C., distributing literature that embarrassed many "legitimate" Council leaders. On August 23, 1956, he disrupted a meeting of the Virginia Council on Human Relations in Charlottesville, denouncing the members as "flat-chested highbrows," warning them, "We of the Citizens 'Councils have declared war on you people. We're going to run you out of town." A cross was burned outside the meeting hall, and several others followed over the next three weeks. Kasper logged his first arrest in Charlottesville, for distributing leaflets without a permit. Leaving town after his arrest, he arrived in Clinton, Tennessee, on August 25. School integration was soon arriving in Clinton, and Kasper delivered a series of fiery speeches in an attempt to stir up segregationists. Jailed again on August 27, he was bailed out the following day. On August 29, violence erupted in Clinton, and National Guardsmen and tanks were summoned to restore order. Kasper was again jailed, charged with inciting a riot, and remained in custody until September 6. Later in September, he addressed a rally of Carter's North Alabama Citizens' Council, welcoming robed Klansmen with the comment, "We need all the rabble-rousers we can get. We want trouble and we want it everywhere we can get it." Kasper called for "roving bands of fearless patriots" to remain alert, descending on any town threatened by imminent desegregation. Addressing a Klan rally at Warrior, Alabama, on October 6, Kasper shared the stage with Carter and Klansman

Ken Adams, who had been recently jailed for assaulting singer Nat "King" Cole in Birmingham. After a two-week trial in Clinton, Kasper was acquitted on November 20 to thunderous applause from the gallery. Two weeks later, police in Fairfax, Virginia, arrested Kasper on a reckless driving charge. His January 1957 appearance in Florida, complete with cross burnings and rumors of dynamite caches around Miami, prodded the state government into action. Summoned before a legislative investigating committee in March, Kasper ruefully confessed to dating black women when he lived in Greenwich Village, before Ezra Pound and Admiral Crommelin helped him see the light. Addressing a Klan audience at Chiefland, Florida, that month, Kasper urged them to spare no effort in support of his "segregation gospel." Members of an audience at Inverness were told, "God stamped ugliness on the face of the Jew for the same reason that he put rattlers on the snake." Kasper's antidote for liberal U.S. Supreme Court decisions was embodied in the oft-repeated slogan "Hang the nine swine." The Florida investigation harmed his reputation, however, and Klansmen were having second thoughts about a so-called Klan messiah who dated blacks on the side. On March 16, 1957, speakers at a Cleveland, Tennessee, Klan rally denounced Kasper as a "troublemaker" for his role in the violence at Clinton. Carter told reporters that the admission of inter-racial dating "will about fix Kasper in the South," claiming he had told Kasper "we didn't want him back in Alabama." A Tennessee chapter of the Citizens' Council organized by Kasper dissolved around the same time, and one segregationist leader proclaimed, "When John Kasper crossed the Mason-Dixon line, it set the cause of white supremacy back twenty years." John Crommelin was clearly in the minority when he told a Clinton audience, "You may not see it, and your children may not see it, but some day a statue will be erected on this courthouse lawn to John Kasper." The Klan disagreed, and Kasper was physically ejected from a Clinton Klan rally on May 11, 1957. Two months later, Kasper and six other defendants were convicted of violating a federal injunction barring interference with school integration in Clinton. Nashville Klansmen were willing to hand out pamphlets when Kasper addressed a small crowd on August 4, but police intervened and stopped the proceedings because of a lack of proper permits. Kasper surfaced on August 28 to announce publicly his harassment cam-paign against thirteen Nashville families whose children had enrolled in "white" schools. As reporters took copious notes, Kasper boasted that the blacks had been threatened with bombing or death unless the students were removed. Detectives took him at his word, and Kasper was arrested with twenty-six other suspects after bombers demolished the Hattie Cotton School on September 10. Subsequent conviction on federal charges earned him prison time, and Kasper was bound for a Florida jail in November, a copy of *Mein Kampf* in hand. Paroled in August 1958, he was met at the prison gates by a reception committee that included Admiral Crommelin, George Bright, John Hamilton, and Klan leader Bill Hendrix. Integration was still being hotly debated in the South, but Kasper had lost his edge. Hecklers outnumbered supporters at the Charlotte, North Carolina, courthouse on September 1, and Kasper needed a police escort in order to leave. Attaching himself to the National States Rights Party, Kasper persuaded a 1958 gathering to nominate John Crommelin for president in 1960, but the veteran anti-Semite was later bumped to the vice presidential slot in favor of unwilling candidate Orval Faubus. Belated riot charges from the Nashville bombings led to Kasper's arrest and conviction in 1960. He finished a six-month term on July 15, departing in a car festooned with rebel flags and "Kasper for President" stickers. His White House bid would have to wait, however. In 1964, he was nominated on the National States Rights Party ticket, with J.B. Stoner running for vice president. After receiving only 6,953 votes nationwide, Kasper soon disappeared from the public eye. [NYT 1956–1958, 1960, 1964; 14; 35; 50]

KEETON, WARD

Identified as a Dallas, Texas, police informant working in the local KKK and American Nazi Party, Keeton was killed by a bomb in January 1984. Two suspects, including one Klansman and a known Klan associate, were later charged with murder in the case. [NYT 1984]

KELLEY, FRANCIS

See White, Marlin.

KELLEY, R.B.

See Reeb, Reverend James.

KELLY, HARRY LEE

See Blackwell Real Estate.

KELLY, RAY

See Johnson, Woodrow.

KELLY, ROGER

Identified as grand dragon of the Pennsylvania KKK in 1988, Kelly was convicted of illegal cross burning in February 1988 and sentenced to six months probation by the court. [AP, Feb. 12, 1980]

KELLY, W.A.

A Union army veteran and active Republican in Tennessee during Reconstruction, Kelly was fired on and driven from his home by Klansmen in

1868. The raiders then lingered to abuse Kelly's wife, loot his home of cash, and drive a herd of cattle through his fields, destroying his crops. [93]

KELSO, DAVID

A member of Bill Wilkinson's Invisible Empire Knights, Kelso was shot and wounded in a clash with black demonstrators in Decatur, Alabama, on May 26, 1979. [NYT 1980]

KEMP, JOHN

A black Republican and coroner in St. Helena Parish, Louisiana, during Reconstruction, Kemp was targeted by the local Klan. Nightriders raided Kemp's home on October 29, 1868, dragged him outside and shot him to death before they beat his wife and searched his files for items of incriminating evidence. [87]

KEMPER FISHING LODGE

In 1965 congressional investigators identified this group as a cover for the Lake View, South Carolina, klavern, United Klans of America. [38]

KENNARD, ADAM

A black Union Leaguer-turned-Democrat, Kennard was also a deputy sheriff in Sumter County, Alabama, during Reconstruction. Kennard allegedly cooperated with the local KKK, and several times invaded Mississippi without legal authority in early 1871 to arrest black fugitives from criminal charges or labor contracts. On at least one occasion, traveling with armed whites identified as Alabama Klansmen, Kennard shot and wounded a fugitive while attempting to arrest him. The raids provoked a violent response from a group of Mississippi blacks, who dragged Kennard from a rented room and flogged him on one of his visits to Meridian in February 1871. Kennard identified the leader of the whipping party as Daniel Price, a white "radical," and Price was jailed pending trial. On the day of his preliminary hearing, Kennard appeared in Meridian with a dozen Sumter County Klansmen, calling for Price's blood. The hearing was postponed to prevent a riot, but the posse found three black fugitives in town, beat them, and then carried them back to Alabama on the next train. Kennard's illegal raids into Mississippi continued sporadically through the end of the year without further resistance. [87]

KENNEDY, JESSE C.

A prosperous Reconstruction mill owner and head of the Constitutional Union Guard in Lenoir County, North Carolina, Kennedy was one of twenty-five members indicted on murder and other charges in August 1869. [87]

KENNEDY, JOHN B.

A Confederate captain who was wounded three times and captured by Union forces in the Civil War, Kennedy was one of six original Klansmen in Pulaski, Tennessee. Tradition credits him with suggesting the addition of "klan" to the mystic "ku klux" prefix, for purposes of alliteration. As the first grand magi of the KKK, he participated in a Pulaski race riot in January 1869 that left one black man dead and several wounded while Klansmen emerged unscathed. [87]

KENNEDY, STETSON

A Florida native born in 1916, Kennedy traced his lineage to signers of the Declaration of Independence. His grandfather was a Confederate officer, and one of his uncles was a Klansman in the 1920s. Determined to succeed as an author, Kennedy moved from the WPA writer's project to a post as southeastern editorial director for the CIO's Political Action Committee in the late 1930s. He also worked for the Anti-Defamation League of B'nai B'rith and the Nonsectarian Anti-Nazi League, collecting inside information on the KKK. Using the alias John S. Perkins, Kennedy joined Sam Green's Atlanta klavern of the Association of Georgia Klans, sending back information to the Anti-Defamation League and columnist Drew Pearson, and published articles under his real name while Klansmen searched for the elusive informant. (Green offered a reward of $1,000 per pound for "the traitor's ass, FOB Atlanta.") When not embarrassing the Klan in print, Kennedy also leaked material to state attorney general Dan Duke, assisting in Duke's campaign to revoke the Klan charter. A member of several flogging parties, Kennedy prevented some crimes with advance warnings and began appearing in court as a prosecution witness. (He also furnished material to producers of the *Superman* radio program, launching the Man of Steel on a month-long battle against the Klan.) Kennedy soon took to the lecture circuit, and authored two books detailing his adventures with the KKK. In 1946, the House Un-American Activities Committee granted him a perfunctory interview, but documentary evidence on Klan violence was declined by the apathetic congressmen. When Kennedy publicly pushed for FBI action against the Klan, J. Edgar Hoover responded with a smear campaign, warning sponsors of a scheduled television interview that Kennedy was a "possible psychopathic case" who had participated in "various communist-inspired programs." Residing in Europe from 1953 to 1960, Kennedy settled in St. Augustine, Florida, on his return, launching a tutorial program for local blacks, paving the way for civil rights demonstrations in 1963 and 1964. Continuing his work into the 1980s, Kennedy exposed crucial new evidence of Klan-police involvement in the Harry Moore assassination, filing suit under the Freedom of Information Act to declassify FBI files on the case. [10; 93]

KENT, REV. GRADY

A black minister in Atlanta, Georgia, Kent was beaten by Klansmen in 1940 because his Ben Hill congregation was "making too much noise." [93]

KENTUCKY

A national anomaly, Kentucky was the only Union state to host an active Ku Klux Klan during Reconstruction. With blacks deprived of the right to vote until 1870 and barred from testifying against whites in court until 1872, the Kentucky Klan had little to do with politics, and most often served in a vigilante capacity, enforcing white supremacy and the group's own version of "community values." (Ironically, another major function of the KKK was guarding the illegal moonshine stills that some of its members operated.) Organized in 1868, the Klan usually rode in the Bluegrass region of the state, terrorizing blacks and Unionists in southwestern Kentucky, from Bowling Green to the Mississippi River. By July 1869, newspapers reported that twenty-five men had been lynched, with 100 others severely whipped or otherwise abused, inside a twenty-mile radius of Harrodsburg. Near Stanford, a black man who defended himself against nightriders and killed three Klansmen in the process was held for trial on murder charges. Most of the action was centered in Richmond and Madison counties by early 1870, as Klansmen offered resistance when the Fifteenth Amendment allowed blacks to vote. Black postal agents were a favorite target of Kentucky's Klan, but no one was immune. In March 1871, a published list detailed 116 specific outrages spanning the past three years, culminating in a jailbreak at the state capital. August's election sparked a violent race riot in Frankfort, and it was two months later, when prosecutions finally began, that order was restored.

The modern Klan invaded Louisville in 1921, when an Oklahoma kleagle operated briefly in the face of opposition from the mayor and police force. Pressure eventually drove the kleagle from town, pending a victory in the federal court of appeals. At the same time, however, klaverns began appearing in the Ohio River valley, moving eastward from Covington. Membership peaked around 1924, when Klansmen clashed with unionized miners in the Kentucky coalfields. Internal disputes over money and politics soon split the realm, and membership faded in the 1930s, with small chapters remaining near Ashland and Lexington. Rumors of a post-war revival sent Kentucky's attorney general to court in July 1946 to seek revocation of the charter of the group he described as a "lawless, seditious one of Nazi tendency, whose sole purpose is to create division and dissension in the United States," and cited the danger of the Klan as rooted in "orgies of lawlessness." The charter was revoked in September, and later efforts to resuscitate the realm were for the most part futile. Authorities rejected the Klan's offer to help police the Kentucky Derby in 1966, and although Klansmen received attention during the Louisville busing riots nine years later, the spontaneous outburst was not symptomatic of a statewide KKK revival. [NYT 1946, 1966, 1975; 10; 87]

KERNODLE, JAMES

See *American Conservative Party.*

KERR, JOHN

A Democratic ex-congressman and active Klansman in Yanceyville, North Carolina, Kerr was one of those arrested when Governor William Holden invoked martial law in 1870. [87]

KERR, MARTIN

A native of New Jersey, Kerr began his neo-Nazi activities in high school after reading a published interview with George Lincoln Rockwell. In the late 1960s and early 1970s he served as a group leader for James Madole's National Renaissance Party and edited the party's newsletter. While studying at Hofstra University on Long Island, Kerr received media coverage for displaying a Nazi flag in his dormitory window. Around the same time, he shifted allegiance from the National Renaissance Party to the National Socialist White People's Party (NSWPP), inserting ads for both organizations in the Hofstra campus newspaper. By 1976, Kerr was recognized as an organizer for the NSWPP, operating out of Washington, D.C. Six years later, his distribution of Nazi literature in Maryland prompted state legislators to consider a bill punishing purveyors of "defamatory material" with one year in jail and a $1,000 fine. The attendant publicity earned him a promotion as national spokesman for the NSWPP, announcing leader Matt Koehl's intention of shifting party headquarters to an unspecified midwestern location. [2]

KERSEY, JASON E.

A resident of Samsula, Florida, Kersey was elected grand dragon of the new United Florida KKK in June 1961. He held the office through early 1967, although declining health left subordinates in charge of the Klan after 1965. [38]

KERSEY, RICHARD

The son of Jason Kersey and kligrapp of the United Florida KKK, Kersey assumed most of the Klan's administrative duties in mid-1965, when his father became ill. [38]

KEYSTONE CLUB

In 1965 congressional investigators named this group as a cover for the Henderson, North Carolina, chapter, United Klans of America. [38]

KIDD, W.J.

Louisiana's grand dragon for the United Klans of America in the early 1970s, Kidd was replaced by Pete Holden in 1976. [84]

KILLEN, EDGAR RAY ("PREACHER")

A Philadelphia, Mississippi, sawmill operator, Baptist minister, and kleagle for the White Knights of the KKK, Killen was instrumental in establishing klaverns in Lauderdale and Neshoba counties during 1964. FBI informants described "Preacher" Killen as the leader of a party that assaulted black worshippers and burned the Mt. Zion Methodist Church on June 16, 1964, and as the mastermind of the plot to murder civil rights worker Michael Schwerner five days later. His trial on federal conspiracy charges in October 1967 resulted in a mistrial, and the charges were dismissed in 1973. Three years later, in an interview with Patsy Sims, Killen denied ever joining the Klan, but did admit to membership in the Americans for Preservation of the White Race. [84; 96]

KILLINGSWORTH, BOYD

See *McDanal, Mrs. Hugh*.

KIMBLE, JULES RICCO

An admitted Klansman in New Orleans, Kimble was also a key witness for District Attorney Jim Garrison's 1967 probe of the John Kennedy assassination. Kimble testified that he drove Jack Helm—former Louisiana grand dragon for the United Klans of America and later chief of his own Universal Klans—to the home of Minuteman and assassination suspect David Ferrie on the day after Ferrie's death, watching Helm remove a valise filled with papers that were taken to a bank safe deposit box. Kimble also claimed to have flown errands for the Minutemen to Montreal, Canada, working occasionally under contract for the CIA. The witness vanished briefly after giving Garrison his statement, and was traced by investigators to Atlanta and Montreal before his ultimate arrest as a material witness in Tampa, Florida. By that time, Canadian newsmen were speculating on a possible New Orleans link between Kimble and James Earl Ray in the murder of Dr. Martin Luther King, Jr. In 1978, a congressional committee probing both assassinations confirmed Kimble's "extensive criminal record" and Klan connections, but no link with the King assassination was established. The committee did not address Kimble's allegations concerning Ferrie and Helm. [21; 39]

KIMBRO, GEORGE B., JR.

As grand goblin of the 1920s Klan in Texas, Kimbro was assigned to supervise the activities of kleagles throughout the state. [10]

KINARD, WILLIAM

A member of Ancient City Gun Club in St. Augustine, Florida, Kinard was shot and killed on October 25, 1963, while riding with a gun in a Klan procession through a black neighborhood. NAACP officer Goldie Eubanks was indicted as an accessory to the crime. His son and three other blacks were charged with the murder. Three days after Kinard's death, nightriders retaliated by firing on two black homes, two nightclubs, and a grocery store. A hand grenade hurled at one of the nightclubs failed to explode. [70]

KINDLEY, ROBERT LEE

See *Caldwell, Lester.*

KING, REV. A.D.

As the brother of Martin Luther King, Jr., and a civil rights activist, King was a target for Klansmen in the 1960s. His home in Birmingham, Alabama, was damaged by a bomb on May 12, 1963, after a local Klan rally. Eyewitness Roosevelt Tatum told the FBI that he saw uniformed policemen plant the bomb, but no suspects were ever publicly identified. Another bomb, which failed to detonate, was found at King's house on March 21, 1965, but he had already returned to his native state of Georgia. [*NYT* 1965; 49]

KING, CECIL W.

A Parrish, Florida, citrus grower and longtime Klansman, King controlled the local American Independent Party at its formation in 1967. [*NYT* 1967]

KING, L.J.

A former Klan evangelist, King was the founder of the Book and Bible House in Decatur, Georgia, which was recognized as the nation's leading source of anti-Catholic literature in the early 1950s. Harking back to the days of "escaped nuns" in the 1920s, King specialized in such volumes as *Abolish the Nunneries and Save the Girls.* Prior to his death in 1952, King proclaimed that "God has specially sent me after the nunneries and the confessional box. Destroy these two institutions and Romanism is ended." [77]

KING, DR. MARTIN LUTHER, JR.

In 1956 King attained national prominence as a leader of the black boycott that finally desegregated buses in Montgomery, Alabama. On December 23, 1956, during the course of the boycott, a shotgun blast was fired into his home, and an unexploded bomb was found on his porch one month later. Moving on to lead the Southern Christian Leadership Conference, King led civil rights campaigns in Albany, Georgia, (1962); Birmingham, Alabama

(1963); St. Augustine, Florida (1964); and Selma, Alabama (1965). Various Klan factions talked about his execution, and some prepared plans for his assassination. In the late 1950s, Federated Klans leader William Morris allegedly offered competitors J.B. Stoner and Asa Carter $25,000 to murder King. Sidney Barnes and several other Mobile Klansmen visited Birmingham in 1963 with plans to shoot Dr. King, and Jack Brown, leader of the Dixie Klans in Chattanooga, tracked King through several states before his own death in 1965. In February 1965, Georgia Klansmen hired a gunman to murder King, but FBI agents warned King in advance. In early 1965, Mississippi's White Knights planned an ambush on Highway 19 between Philadelphia and Meridian, Mississippi. Again, the FBI was able to warn King, as informant Delmar Dennis told the FBI the details of the plan, which included a rifleman at each end of a particular bridge that had dynamite planted underneath should they miss. A year later, Klansmen in Natchez, Mississippi, kidnapped and murdered Ben White, an elderly black man, hoping that his funeral would lure King within rifle range. Ironically, it was during a confrontation that was not planned by Klansmen as a way of harming King that he received his most serious injury, when King led a Chicago protest march in August 1966. George Lincoln Rockwell and several robed Klansmen had incited their white audience to anger by the time King's marchers arrived, and the minister was struck in the head by a well-aimed brick that left him dazed and bleeding. Following King's Memphis assassination in April 1968, Klansmen were immediately suspected, and FBI agents checked twenty-five different reports linking various KKK factions to the murder. None of the reports conclusively linked the Klan to King's death, but suspicions of Klan involvement remained, bolstered by James Earl Ray's choice of Arthur Hanes as his first attorney. FBI informants maintain that Hanes received a contribution of $10,000 toward Ray's defense from the United Klans of America, and Ray chose Klansman J.B. Stoner to represent him a year later in his unsuccessful attempts to win a new trial. Congressional investigators who reviewed the case in 1978 found no substantial evidence of KKK involvement in King's death, but they did come across a rumor concerning New Orleans Mafia boss Carlos Marcello. Marcello allegedly had arranged the murder as a favor to the Klan, a reward for Klansmen helping him with labor trouble along the waterfront. [7; 33; 39; 49; 64; 95]

KINGSVILLE HUNT CLUB

In 1965 congressional investigators identified this club as a front for the Farmville, Virginia, klavern, United Klans of America. [38]

KIRK, GEORGE W.

A Tennessee native who commanded a Union Army regiment in the Civil War, Kirk was selected by Governor William Brownlow to lead the state's anti-Klan militia in 1868. Two years later, he was recruited to lead North

Carolina's militia in similar circumstances, during Governor William Holden's abortive war on the KKK. [87]

KITCHEN, FLOYD G.

See *American Conservative Party.*

KLABEE

The treasurer of a klanton, klabees are further designated by rank with the title of great klabee (at the province level), grand klabee (for a realm), and imperial klabee (for the national Klan). [43]

KLADD

As the conductor of a klanton, a kladd is the custodian of ritual paraphernalia, and he also introduces candidates for "naturalization." The office does not exist at the province level, but rank is otherwise designated by the titles of grand kladd (for a realm) and imperial kladd (at the national level). [43]

KLALIFF

The vice president of a klanton, klaliffs multiply as one ascends the Klan ladder of rank. At the province level, three great klaliffs serve as an advisory board for the great titan. The grand klaliff is vice president of a realm, while the imperial klaliff serves as second in command after the imperial wizard. [43]

KLAN

The smallest unit of the Invisible Empire, a klan is administered by an exalted cyclops and his twelve terrors presiding. To further confuse the issue, local units of the Constitutional Union Guard were also referred to as "klans" during Reconstruction. [43; 87; see also *Den*]

KLAN AIR FORCE

An innovation of the Mississippi White Knights, the Klan Air Force was organized to harass and terrorize civil rights workers during the Freedom Summer campaign of 1964. Its single appearance was logged in Indianola on October 22, when a small plane made several passes over a gathering of 250 persons, dropping flares and an explosive charge that rocked the building. In the wake of the "air raid," Police Chief Brice Alexander told newsmen that a similar plane or planes had been unloading flares and fireworks "all over Indianola" in recent days. [*NYT* 1964]

KLAN BERET

This paramilitary group was organized within Tony LaRicci's Maryland Knights around 1975 to provide Klansmen with monthly training sessions on martial arts, firearms, and explosives. [84]

KLAN HAVEN HOME

A 1920s Klan orphanage in Mannsville, New York, south of Watertown, this institution featured education in the fields of farming and "domestic science." [10]

KLAN KREST

An early symbol of KKK affluence, this was the $33,000 home purchased for Imperial Wizard William Simmons in an Atlanta suburb, when the Klan began turning a profit in 1920. [10]

KLAN OF THE NORTH

One of several groups targeted by Indiana Governor Ralf Gates's November 1946 crackdown, the group had already been inactive for years. Evidence remains hazy, but the title may be a simple variation on D.C. Stephenson's Independent Klan of America. [Indianapolis *Star*, Nov. 9, 1946]

KLAN SOFTBALL TEAM

Organized by the East Ridge, Tennessee, klavern of the Dixie Klans in 1957, this team was created to emphasize the KKK's "recreation side," casting the Klan as a "civic good." Three other teams withdrew from the Chattanooga league in protest that May when the Klan team was admitted, but the Klansmen remained, sporting red, white, and blue uniforms. They made it to the state playoffs in Nashville that August, but failed to bring home a trophy. For the record, all members of the team publicly denied being Klansmen. [*NYT* 1957]

KLAN YOUTH CORPS

Conceived by Bill Wilkinson to recruit younger members for his Invisible Empire Knights, the Klan Youth Corps operation included Camp My Lai, where paramilitary training was offered to children in 1980 and 1981. A teenaged New Jersey Klansman told *Junior Scholastic* that the Klan was trying to "get kids off the street and give them something to do," but adverse publicity finally closed down the camp. In May 1981, Wilkinson's youth director was one of six persons arrested for plotting to bomb a synagogue and Jewish businesses in Nashville, Tennessee. Across the state line, in Decatur, Alabama, teenagers wearing Klan t-shirts staged a public demonstration, burning a derelict bus to demonstrate their feelings on school integration. In Oklahoma City, high school students claiming membership in two Klan groups assaulted patrons of a gay bar, beating them with baseball bats. [93]

KLANBURGESSES

The published constitution of Mississippi's White Knights applied this title to the "lower house" of the Klan's theoretical "legislative branch," otherwise known as the Klongress. [38]

KLANKRAFT

This heading covers the practices and beliefs of Klansmen everywhere, incorporating all aspects of ritual, regalia and "klannishness"—the practice, where feasible, of trading and associating strictly with other Klansmen. Through the years, Klankraft has been encouraged by the sale of such "official" paraphernalia as belt buckles and jewelry, t-shirts and decals, records and tapes, jackknives, watches, and miniature "fiery crosses" (either bejeweled or electric). The proper attitude toward klannishness is maintained through periodic lectures and perusal of KKK literature. [10]

KLANTON

A subdivision of a province, a klanton is the domain of a klan, with an exalted cyclops and his twelve terrors presiding. [43]

KLANWATCH PROJECT

See *Southern Poverty Law Center.*

KLAPPROTT, AUGUST

See *German-American Bund.*

KLAROGO

As the inner guard of a klanton, the klarogo is roughly equivalent to a sergeant-at-arms. The office does not exist at the province level. Other rank designations include the grand klarogo (of a realm) and the imperial klarogo (for the national Klan). [43]

KLAVALIER KLUB

Described by infiltrator Stetson Kennedy as the Atlanta strong-arm squad for the Association of Georgia Klans, the Klavalier Klub was credited with the murder of Porter Turner and the February 13, 1946, flogging of a black hotel bellboy. State attorney general Dan Duke reported that the flogging squad had fifty members, chosen for their brawn and willingness to terrorize. Kennedy joined the Klub when the Klavaliers were assigned to ferret out a local informer—himself—and was told, "We Klavaliers serve as the secret police of the KKK and are entrusted with carrying out all 'direct-line' activity." He was ordered to buy a gun and was cautioned that the penalty for betrayal was "death at the hands of a brother." To minimize the risk of leaks, the Klavaliers took turns flogging a victim, thereby implicating all concerned, but Kennedy still managed to avert several beatings with timely advanced warnings, and later testified in court against his "brother" Klansmen. [*NYT* 1946; 93]

KLAVALIERS

As the paramilitary arm of the 1920s Wisconsin Klan, the Klavaliers offered to help Madison's mayor suppress crime, but their overture was rejected. Still, Klan infiltration of the police force was an open secret, with detectives utilizing information collected by Klavalier spies in minority neighborhoods to carry out raids and arrests. [10]

KLAVERN

Technically applied to the local headquarters of a klan, this term is often used interchangeably to describe the klan itself. [43]

KLEAGLE

In Klan parlance, a kleagle is an organizer or recruiter, appointed by the imperial wizard or his imperial representative to "sell" the KKK among nonmembers. Kleagles are generally paid on commission, receiving an established percentage of each recruit's klectoken. [43]

KLECTOKEN (OR KLECKTOKON)

The KKK initiation fee established by Imperial Wizard William Simmons in 1915 was generally stabilized at $10 before the inflationary 1970s. Prices now vary from group to group, but the United Klans of America manual stresses that payment is considered "a donation to its propagation and general fund and not in the sense of purchasing membership." [43]

KLEIN, CHARLES H.

As imperial kligrapp for the Association of Georgia Klans, Klein was second in command under Imperial Wizard Sam Roper. On July 27, 1951, he was arrested with Klansman James Knight on charges of bombing a black home in Klein's own Atlanta neighborhood. At his trial in January 1952, ex-Klansman Frank Castille testified that Klein had recruited him "to straighten out them Negroes on East Avenue," but jurors could not agree on a verdict, and a mistrial was declared on January 25. [*NYT* 1951–1952]

KLEIST, JOHN

A socialist attorney in Wisconsin and a perennial candidate for office in the 1920s, Kleist ran for a seat on the state supreme court in 1924 as both a Klansman *and* a Socialist. It did not significantly help, but he polled more votes than ever before on the straight socialist ticket. Disgruntled leftists later expelled Kleist from the Socialist Party because of his ties to the Klan. [10]

KLEXTER

Designated as the outer guard of a klan, the klexter is responsible for external security during regular meetings. The office does not exist at the province level. Each realm is served by a grand klexter, while the imperial klexter operates from KKK national headquarters. [43]

KLIGRAPP

As secretary of a klan or other jurisdictional unit, this title is further designated by rank to include the great kligrapp (at the province level), the grand kligrapp (of a realm), and the imperial kligrapp (for the overall Klan). [43]

KLIKON

Adapted from the word "icon," this title is applied to the "sacred picture" of a local klan, not specifically defined in any Ku Klux Klan constitutions. The picture most often reproduced on Klan literature and banners includes a robed Klansman on horseback, with or without a fiery cross, incorporating the name or initials of the particular Klan. [43]

KLINCK, EARL

See *Oberholtzer, Madge.*

KLIPOTH, SETH

A Detroit Klan spokesman, in June 1980 Klipoth applied for a joint parade permit in conjunction with the National Socialist Worker's Party, touching off violent demonstrations by leftist opponents at a city council meeting. [*AP,* June 27, 1980]

KLOKAN

An individual member of the klokann, this officer serves as an adviser, auditor, and investigator for his respective geographical unit. [43]

KLOKANN

The advisory board of a klan, serving as auditors and investigators, the klokann is composed of several members dubbed klokans. At the klanton and province levels, three members are selected for each board, with the latter body known as the great klokann. Five members are specified for the grand klokann (at the realm level), and the imperial klokann (at national headquarters). [43]

KLOKARD

Designated as the lecturer of a klan, the klokard has no counterpart at the province level. A grand klokard serves for the realm, while an imperial klokard is elected for the Invisible Empire at large. [43]

KLONGRESS

Described in official documents of Mississippi's White Knights as the Klan's legislative branch, the Klongress theoretically consisted of two houses, the Klonvocation and the Klanburgesses. Members of the Klonvocation were designated "senators," empowered to meet if and when called on by the Klanburgesses. The authoritarian control exercised by Imperial Wizard Sam Bowers suggests that the Klongress existed only on paper. [38]

KLONKLAVES

This designation is reserved for regular weekly meetings of a klan, held at the klavern. [43]

KLONVERSATION

A portion of the 1920s KKK initiation ceremony, this ritual briefing provided new recruits with the official Klan passwords and countersigns. [93]

KLONVERSE

In Klan parlance, the klonverse is a monthly province meeting, with the great titan presiding. [43]

KLONVOKATION

The national convention of a Klan, conducted annually, this gathering is omitted by smaller, geographically restricted factions. The constitution of Mississippi's White Knights broke with established tradition by applying this title to the upper house of a theoretical Klan legislative branch, otherwise known as the Klongress. [38; 43]

KLORAN

In 1915, William Simmons revised the prescript of the Reconstruction Klan to produce the Kloran, a ritual handbook for his own Knights of the KKK. The Kloran included songs, prayers, and various administrative details. Titles of the original Klan officers were altered in most cases to accommodate the mystic prefix "kl-". (As Simmons later told newsmen, "It was rather

difficult, sometimes, to make the two letters fit in, but I did it somehow.")
In 1953, Eldon Edwards made further revisions and published a new Kloran
for his own U.S. Klans. [93]

KLORERO

The annual statewide meeting of Klansmen from a particular realm, this
gathering is typically chaired by the grand dragon. [43]

KLUDD

The chaplain of a klan, this rank is occupied by an ordained Protestant
minister whenever possible. A great kludd offers prayers at the province
level, with a grand kludd serving the realm and an imperial kludd selected
for the Invisible Empire at large. [43]

KNIGHT, JAMES

See *Klein, Charles.*

KNIGHT HAWK, THE

A Klan periodical published in Atlanta during the early 1920s, *The Knight
Hawk* was edited by Texan Phil Fox prior to his 1923 murder conviction.
[10]

KNIGHTS OF AMERICAN PROTESTANTISM

A splinter group active in Wisconsin's Fox River Valley, this faction broke
away from D.C. Stephenson's Independent Klan of America in late 1924 or
early 1925. [10]

KNIGHTS OF LIBERTY

A New York anti-Klan group, the Knights of Liberty was organized in 1923
by a penitent ex-grand goblin. [93]

KNIGHTS OF MARY PHAGAN

Named for an Atlanta murder victim who was allegedly slain by Jewish
businessman Leo Frank, this group consisted of 100 lynchers who abducted
Frank from the state prison and hanged him on August 16, 1915. (Frank was
finally exonerated in 1982, by the deathbed statement of a witness who
perjured himself at the original trial.) The Knights earned the dubious
distinction as the first motorized lynch mob, transporting their victim to his
execution site by motorcade, rather than on foot or horseback. Georgia
kingmaker Tom Watson applauded Frank's lynching in the September 2
issue of his *Jeffersonian* magazine, calling for another Ku Klux Klan to be
formed to restore "Home Rule." On October 16, 1915, the Knights

ascended nearby Stone Mountain, lighting a gigantic cross that was reportedly visible throughout Atlanta. William Simmons filed a charter application for his Knights of the Ku Klux Klan ten days later, with the first Klan ceremony held atop Stone Mountain on Thanksgiving Eve. The Knights reportedly joined Simmons more or less en masse for his revival of the KKK. [93]

KNIGHTS OF THE AIR

Designed to recruit a Klan air force in the 1920s, led by C. Anderson Wright, this abortive program fell apart when financial support from imperial headquarters failed to materialize. [10]

KNIGHTS OF THE BLACK CROSS

A white supremacist group with significant Klan overlap, the Knights were organized in Franklin County, Mississippi, during early 1868. [87]

KNIGHTS OF THE BLAZING RING

A 1920s anti-Klan organization based in Pennsylvania, this group existed simultaneously with the Knights of the Flaming Circle. [93]

KNIGHTS OF THE CONFEDERACY

See *Dutton, Jerry.*

KNIGHTS OF THE FLAMING CIRCLE

Organized to fight the Klan in the late 1920s, the Knights of the Flaming Circle mimicked Klansmen by maintaining Klan-like rituals. Based in Pennsylvania, this group also established chapters in Ohio, New York, and New Jersey. At Steubenville, Ohio, members of the Knights assaulted Klansmen, pulling them from their cars to beat them in the street. The combination of violence and ritual ultimately doomed the organization, described by *The New York Times* as "just about as ridiculous as the Klan itself." When Thomas Jordan announced plans for the group's revival in December 1965, Klansmen countered with threats of violent retaliation. [*NYT* 1965; 93]

KNIGHTS OF THE FLAMING SWORD

Another short-lived Klan competitor, this group was created by William Simmons in 1924 following his ouster as imperial wizard. Chartered in Florida and funded by most of his $90,000 settlement from Hiram Evans, the group catered to dissatisfied Klansmen without much success. A band of KKK defectors in Hoboken, New Jersey, came close to joining, but decided not to when they learned that they would have to pay new initiation fees. The Knights disappeared while Simmons was convalescing from a February 1925 auto accident. [10; 93]

KNIGHTS OF THE GOLDEN EAGLE

A black-robed "action" unit, the Knights made their one and only public appearance with J.B. Stoner and representatives of United Florida KKK at a May 1964 rally in Jacksonville. [*NYT* 1964]

KNIGHTS OF THE GREEN FOREST

Organized in 1966, this militant splinter group was led by Imperial Wizard Dale Walton and was composed of defectors from the United Klans of America's Mississippi realm. The organization was apparently defunct by September 1969, when Walton was jailed for plotting the murder of civil rights activist Charles Evers. [*NYT* 1969; 38]

KNIGHTS OF THE KU KLUX KLAN (1955–?)

Identified as one of five Florida Klans organized after Black Monday, this group vanished during the general hysteria of the period. [6]

KNIGHTS OF THE KU KLUX KLAN (1955–?)

One of seven splinter groups reported active in South Carolina after Black Monday, this faction apparently dissolved by 1960, leaving no traceable history of itself behind. [6]

KNIGHTS OF THE KU KLUX KLAN (1956)

Chartered in Louisiana, this faction enjoyed a short and uneventful life, vanishing entirely by 1960. [38]

KNIGHTS OF THE KU KLUX KLAN (1964)

See *Fallaw, Eunice.*

KNIGHTS OF KU KLUX KLAN, FLORIDA

One of a half dozen Klan factions organized by Bill Hendrix since World War II, this group was founded around 1962, with its headquarters in Oldsmar. Congressional investigators identified ten dues-paying members in January 1967, reporting that the groups "only activity in the past five years has been its infrequent meetings." Even that minimal activity had ceased by the end of the decade. The Knights disappeared without a trace. [38]

KNIGHTS OF THE KU KLUX KLAN, INC. (1915-1944)

The Klan of the 20th century, the Knights were organized in November 1915, the brainchild of founder and Imperial Wizard William J. Simmons.

Five thousand members were recruited during the organization's first four years. In 1920, however, Simmons recruited publicists Edward Clarke and Elizabeth Tyler to spruce up the Klan's image, using modern salesmanship and old-fashioned bigotry in concert to build a large empire, almost overnight. By October 1921, there were 100,000 dues-paying Klansmen from coast to coast, and a halfhearted congressional probe of Klan violence only sparked new interest in the group. Under the shrewd guidance of Clarke and Tyler, itinerant kleagles bolstered the Klan's traditional message of white supremacy with appeals to regional prejudice and passion—anti-Semitism, anti-Catholicism, the mistrust of immigrants and "radicals," the vigilante enforcement of Prohibition, and community mores. By 1924, an estimated 3–5 million "aliens" had crossed the mystic threshold of the Invisible Empire, with active klaverns in each of the forty-eight states, but Simmons would not be around to reap the profits. Forced from power by a coup in 1922, he was replaced by Hiram Evans, a Texas dentist who ruled the Klan as his personal fiefdom until June 1939. By that time, with the country suffering the effects of the Great Depression, revelations of Klan violence and corruption had undermined public faith, and members were deserting by the thousands. Successor James Colescott tried to revive the failing Klan, expounding anti-communism and opposition to labor unions, but he was unable to reverse the trend. On April 23, 1944, slapped with a crushing IRS lien for $685,305 in unpaid back taxes, he ordered the Knights to disband. Local klaverns would survive from coast to coast, but this group would never attain its previous membership. Serene in his retirement, Hiram Evans watched the later crop of wizards come and go, commenting wryly that "You can't start a fire in wet ashes." [10]

KNIGHTS OF THE KU KLUX KLAN, INC. (1960)

Formation of this splinter group was announced by Imperial Wizard H.H. Jones on February 29, 1960, following a weekend conference in Atlanta that reportedly was attended by Klansmen from seventeen southeastern and southwestern states. Jones issued a preposterous claim of 42,000 members nationwide, adding that a new recruiting drive was planned for the North. What followed was silence, an indication that the Knights existed primarily on paper, or perhaps only in the wizard's fertile imagination. [NYT 1960; FOF 1960]

KNIGHTS OF THE KU KLUX KLAN, INC. (1975–)

Originally based in New Orleans, this faction was founded and led by realtor Jim Lindsay—alias "Ed White"—until his murder in June 1975. Louisiana Grand Dragon David Duke immediately took charge of the Knights, filing state incorporation papers that granted him, as a "founding member," the absolute right to determine Klan policy. By the end of the year, Duke had organized the largest Klan rally in a decade, luring an estimated audience of 2,700 to Walker, Louisiana. Operating from his base in Metairie, Louisiana, Duke became a fixture on television and radio talk shows, building the Knights into the dominant Klan in the United States by 1977, but dissension in the ranks soon fractured his empire. In San Diego, Grand Dragon Tom Metzger led his followers into a new California Knights of the KKK, and competitor Bill Wilkinson—a former Duke lieutenant—had more members in his Invisible Empire Knights by late 1979. Meeting with Wilkinson in July 1980, Duke offered to sell his mailing list for a lump sum of $30,000, but Wilkinson rejected the deal and gleefully publicized Duke's "betrayal." Resigning to head a new National Association for the Advancement of White People, Duke left the Knights in the hands of Alabama dragon Stephen Black, and the headquarters were shifted to Black's office in Tuscumbia. Black's subsequent arrest, conviction, and imprisonment for violation of federal neutrality laws for planning an invasion of Dominica left the Klan's leadership open. Klansmen Thomas Robb (of Metairie, Louisiana) and Stanley McCollum (of Tuscumbia, Alabama) claimed control of the Knights in Black's absence, and squabbled over control of the Klan newsletter and membership lists. The Knights turned out for a seven-Klan unity conference in Stone Mountain, Georgia, in September 1982, but the conference failed to unify. Robb appeared to hold the reins at a second Georgia gathering in 1983, but by that time the Knights had shriveled to the point of being more a curiosity than a threat. [2; 84]

KNIGHTS OF THE KU KLUX KLAN OF AMERICA

On August 23, 1949, fifty Klansmen from six Southern states gathered in Montgomery, Alabama, to merge their local factions into a stronger, more dynamic Klan. Participants included leaders of such obscure groups as the Independent Klans, Seashore Klans, Ozark Klans, Star Klans, River Valley Klans, and Allied Klans. The larger Federated KKK was pointedly excluded when the delegates cast their votes for Lycurgus Spinks as imperial emperor. Striving to impress the media with ridiculous claims of 650,000 members in Alabama, Mississippi, Missouri, and Louisiana, Spinks publicly claimed to represent "every Klansman in America," whether they knew it or not. The emperor's sole achievement was an autumn appearance on *Meet the Press*, which proved to be unintentionally hilarious. Following this appearance, his Knights abruptly dropped from the headlines. Spinks shifted the Klan's headquarters from Montgomery to Jackson, Mississippi, in March 1950, but he seems to have made the move on his own, and nothing more was heard from the Knights thereafter. [*NYT* 1949–1950]

KNIGHTS OF THE KU KLUX KLAN OF THE CONFEDERACY

Founded in Alabama during 1957, this splinter group was apparently distinct and separate from Asa Carter's Original KKK of the Confederacy, but no details of its leadership or activities are presently available. [6; 38]

KNIGHTS OF THE RISING SUN

A Klan-like group with overlapping membership, the Knights were active in Jefferson and Marion counties, Texas, during 1867 and 1868. Grand officers were sworn in on September 19, 1868, before an estimated audience of 1,500 persons, with members of the Seymour Knights participating in full uniform. William P. Saufley, chairman of Marion County's Democratic committee, was named grand commander of the Knights, and guest speakers included a black Democrat and other establishment notables. The Knights are credited with lynching two black prisoners in Jefferson, Texas, on October 4, 1868, as well as other random attacks on blacks and Republicans during that election year. Investigations by detectives and federal troops prompted numerous members to flee the state, some running as far as New York and Canada in their quest for sanctuary. Violence by the Knights declined by early 1869, although sporadic nightriding continued for several years. [87]

KNIGHTS OF THE WHITE CAMELLIA (1867-1869)

Organized in St. Mary Parish, Louisiana, in May 1867, this predecessor of the KKK was founded by Colonel Alcibiade DeBlanc in the French Creole territory west of New Orleans. Most of this group's members and activities were confined to that region, but by 1868 the organization had spread to western Alabama. In general, members of this group tended to be from the upper class and their organization maintained better discipline than the Klan, but the groups shared identical goals, and membership frequently overlapped. In Louisiana, the White Camellia was more widespread and somewhat less violent than the Klan, while its Arkansas chapter was regarded by locals as identical to the Razorback KKK. The White Camellia's charge to initiates proclaimed that the organization's "main and fundamental object is the MAINTENANCE OF THE SUPREMACY OF THE WHITE RACE in this Republic." A New Orleans convention formalized its constitution in June 1868, dividing the organization into councils administered by commanders, lieutenant commanders, guards, secretaries, and treasurers. Where sufficient members were recruited, each council was further subdivided into circles of fifty men and groups of ten. A provision was made for the establishment of a Supreme Council once the group had spread to five states, a goal it never reached. By November 1868, a majority of white men had enlisted in some South Louisiana parishes, with an estimated 15,000 members in New Orleans alone. (The 1870 census showed 32,000 white males residing in New Orleans.) For all its apparent strength, the group's activity fell sharply after the general carnage of the 1868 election, and more so in December, when a newspaper exposed the group's rituals, passwords, and other secrets. Some councils began calling themselves Caucasian Clubs after the January 1869 state convention, and the Knights of the White Camellia seems to have dissolved by early summer. [87]

KNIGHTS OF THE WHITE CAMELLIA (1934–1942)

Founded by Klansman George Deatherage in 1934, this fascist organization was based in St. Albans, West Virginia. After 1936, it shared quarters with another Deatherage creation, the American Nationalist Confederation, billed in its heyday as a coalition of seventy-two pro-Nazi fringe groups. This self-styled fuhrer's plan of burning swastikas in lieu of crosses never caught on, and his 1942 indictment for sedition—which ended in a mistrial—doomed any hopes of the group expanding. In 1949, years after its practical demise, this group earned a spot on the U.S. Attorney General's list of subversive organizations. [8]

KNIGHTS OF THE WHITE CAMELLIA (1950s)

One of the many Klan look-alikes founded by Florida Klansman Bill Hendrix, the new Knights of the White Camellia sometimes called itself the National Christian Church. Formation of the order was announced after Hendrix returned from a rally of various Klans in Montgomery, Alabama. Addressing one White Camellia audience, Hendrix set the group's tone: "Now, I don't want you good people to go around blowin' up buildings or temples, but the next time somebody does blow up a temple, I sure hope it is filled with Jews." Samples of the group's literature were covered when police raided the home of Wallace Allen, a National States Rights Party member charged in the October 1958 bombing of an Atlanta synagogue. When bombing suspect Richard Bowling was arrested on October 18, police found a letter from the "National Commander of the White Camillia [sic]." The group was last heard from two years later, in the late summer of 1960, when Florida journalists exposed a movement urging citizens to withhold their income taxes as a means to "get the chains of the beaurocrats off their necks." The anonymous literature was traced to a post office box in Oldsmar rented by Hendrix, who was by then facing federal prosecution for failure to report his income. A typical notice mailed from the box read "We intend to fight fire with fire. Smear with smear. We hope it does not take violence to win our country back from the US Extreme Court." [NYT 1958; 74]

KNIGHTS OF THE WHITE CAMELLIA (1980s)

In 1982, the Texas-based Original Knights of the Ku Klux Klan was renamed as the Knights of the White Camellia, in an apparent effort to spruce up the group's public image. The organization is now apparently defunct. [2]

KNIGHTS OF THE WHITE CARNATION

Organized in Tuskegee, Alabama, shortly after the Civil War, this group of nightriders anticipated the Alabama Klan in its raids against black "lawbreakers." The Knights were led by ex-Confederate General Cullen Battle, and the group may have been affiliated with the Knights of the White Camellia. Battle's group was absorbed by the KKK once Klansmen began to organize in Alabama. [87]

KNIGHTS OF WHITE CHRISTIANS

A short-lived, Klan-like group based in New Orleans, this faction was founded by Alvin Cobb soon after Black Monday. Apparently inactive by 1960, the Knights left no record of their operations behind. [61]

KNOWLES, JAMES ("TIGER")

See *Donald, Michael.*

KNOX, JAMES M.

One of three Murfreesboro, Tennessee, Klansmen who pled guilty to shooting at a home in December 1984, Knox maintained that the target house was being used for sales of illegal drugs in the neighborhood. [*NYT* 1984]

KOEHL, MATTHIAS, JR.

A fervent neo-Nazi since his high school days in Milwaukee, Koehl frequently distributed anti-Semitic literature in class and was known around Washington High as a member of a fascist youth group, the American Action Army. He graduated in 1952 and moved to New York City a year later to work for James Madole's National Renaissance Party. A 1953 report of the House Un-American Activities Committee names Koehl as leader of the National Renaissance Party's young elite guard in Manhattan. Tiring of New York City by year's end, he drifted back to the Midwest, maintaining his anti-Semitic contacts that included Dr. Edward Fields. Joining the National States Rights Party in 1957, he rose to the office of national organizer in 1958, roaming as far as New York and Chicago from his Milwaukee headquarters. A character witness at the George Bright bombing trial in Atlanta in 1959, Koehl was by then affiliated with the Fighting American Nationalists, recognized as a front for George Lincoln Rockwell's American Nazi Party. In 1962, Koehl formally resigned from the National States Rights Party to head the Nazi Party's Chicago chapter, earning himself a promotion to captain and a move to the home base in Arlington, Virginia, a year later. His performance as head of the Rockwell stormtroopers—a tiny squad of racist pickets—brought Koehl promotion to the rank of national secretary. Following Rockwell's assassination in August 1967, Koehl assumed command in Arlington, renaming the group the National Socialist White People's Party. (Despite the conviction of gunman John Patler in Rockwell's death, dissident Rockwell loyalists briefly circulated a rumor naming Koehl as wanted for the murder.) In 1982, the IRS filed a lien against Koehl's party for $37,000 in back taxes; Koehl responded that November by rechristening his group the New Order, announcing a headquarters move to the "more Aryan environment" of Cicero, Illinois. [2; 14; 90]

KOINONIA FARM

Founded in 1942 and named after the Greek word for fellowship, this racially integrated Christian commune near Americus, Georgia, remained unbothered until the U.S. Supreme Court issued its Black Monday ruling on school segregation in 1954. Thereafter, Koinonia Farm was a frequent target of violence by Klansmen and Klan sympathizers, seeking to disrupt life at the commune and force its residents to leave the state. The commune's roadside market was bombed on January 15, 1957, causing $5,000 damage, and seventy carloads of robed Klansmen visited the farm on February 24, offering to arrange a buyer for the land. Their proposal was rejected, and on March 22 shots were fired at the commune. Harassment of the commune continued through 1958. A boycott destroyed the commune's poultry business, houses were riddled with bullets, children were fired at and black families were threatened with death. A letter to the White House seeking federal intervention was routinely sent to Governor Marvin Griffin, who had been elected with Klan support. Griffin called the farm "a cancer on Georgia's fair soil," and accused the commune residents of shooting at themselves for the sake of publicity, and the local sheriff was unable to find any clues. The violence gradually subsided when Georgia Klansmen found new priorities—and targets—in the early 1960s. [*NYT* 1957–1958; 10]

KON KLAVE KLUB

In 1965 congressional investigators identified this group as a cover for the Quitman, Mississippi, klavern, United Klans of America. [38]

KONSOLIDATED KU KLUX KLANS OF THE INVISIBLE EMPIRE

This short-lived group was one of six organizations founded by Bill Hendrix in his continuing attempt to dominate Florida Klandom between 1949 and the early 1960s. [38]

KORMAN, ROBERT

A native of Florida, Korman was elected in September 1964 to serve as imperial klexter for the United Klans of America. [38]

KORNEGAY, MARSHAL ROBERT

A former Raleigh, North Carolina, insurance salesman with a record of "questionable business practices," Kornegay served as grand titan and grand klokard for the North Carolina realm of the United Klans before he was transferred and appointed as grand dragon of Virginia in August 1965. Establishing his headquarters at South Hill, Kornegay launched a massive recruiting drive in the southern part of the state, establishing thirty-two klaverns with an estimated 1,250 members by January 1967. Summoned before the House Un-American Activities Committee in October 1965, Kornegay remained silent as committee members dredged up his past, some of whom suggested that the move to Virginia had been encouraged by the exposure of insurance scams in North Carolina. Outside the hearing chamber, Kornegay was more talkative, telling reporters, "We need more mass killings in Selma, Alabama." Despite the tough talk, however, he seemed to draw a line where actual violence was concerned. When a black church was bombed in Richmond on October 5, 1966, Kornegay denounced the event as a "dastardly crime," offering Klan money and labor to help rebuild the chapel. In January 1967, Kornegay complained to Virginia's governor about ongoing FBI surveillance and "harassment," but the governor was unmoved, describing the local Klan as "obnoxious." [FOF 1966; NYT 1967; 38]

KOURIER, THE

This was one of several regional KKK magazines published during the 1920s. [10]

"KU KLUX ACTS"

By late 1869, it was apparent that state authorities in the South lacked the will or the ability to fight terrorism perpetrated by the KKK and allied groups. Accordingly, a series of federal Enforcement Acts were passed—known as the "Ku Klux Acts"—in an effort to stop the Klan. The first law, passed by Congress on May 31, 1870, sought to enforce the Fifteenth Amendment's grant of universal male suffrage by penalizing the bribery or intimidation of voters. (Section 6, of critical importance to a later generation, also banned conspiracy to deprive citizens of *any* legal right or privilege.) Although well-intentioned, the law was seldom used, and the 1870 elections saw violence against black voters in Alabama and Georgia. A second Enforcement Act, passed on February 28, 1871, tightened federal controls on election procedures, but its provisions had no direct relevance to the Klan. Finally, on April 20, 1871, Congress passed a Ku Klux Act designed to enforce the Fourteenth Amendment's guarantee of equal protection under the law. This bill made it a federal crime to "conspire together, or go in disguise upon the public highway, or upon the premises of another for the purpose . . . of depriving any person or any class of persons of the equal protection of the laws, or of equal privileges or immunities under the laws." In July 1871, the U.S. Attorney General issued a secret order for the prosecution of Klansmen to proceed across the South. By the end of the year, 600 Klansmen had been arrested in South Carolina, with 763 indictments in North Carolina, 200 in Mississippi, 130 in Alabama, and at least thirty in Georgia. Authorities in Kentucky and Florida lagged behind. Kentucky was overlooked primarily because it had not seceded from the Union. In Florida, a siege mentality prevented all but fourteen Klansmen to stand trial by the end of 1871, with one conviction. The first Klan trials were held in North Carolina in November 1871, with forty-seven defendants convicted of various crimes. In the same month, fifty-three South Carolina Klansmen filed guilty pleas, with five others convicted at trial, their sentences ranging from three months to five years in prison. A month later, twenty-eight Mississippi Klansmen pled guilty to murder charges and received suspended sentences in a deal with the court. By July 1872, sixty-five Klansmen sentenced to a year or more were serving time in the federal prison in Albany, New York, while others served their shorter sentences in Southern jails. That year witnessed over eighty convictions in North and South Carolina, with more than 2,000 indictments still pending by year's end. Mississippi authorities disposed of their cases with more alacrity, securing 265 convictions in 1872 with a promise of suspended sentences for any guilty plea, regardless of the offense. By August 1872, Washington had launched a program of selective pardons, and prosecutors were encouraged to drop any cases that did not involve a homicide. Eight months later, prosecutions were entirely suspended, except in the case of new crimes, and the wholesale dismissal of pending indictments began. By early 1874, 1,091 cases had been dismissed in South Carolina alone. Within a year, most convicted Klansmen had been paroled or pardoned, and in 1876 the U.S. Supreme Court declared that federal authorities were only empowered to punish civil rights violations committed by states, not individuals or private groups. Attempts to prosecute Klansmen under the Ku Klux Acts in modern times were restricted by the high court's ruling in a 1951 case, *United States* v. *Williams,* which stated that only a narrow range of federal rights—the right to life being specifically excluded—were protected by existing statutes. Interpretations of the *Williams* rule were finally relaxed after 1964, thus permitting the prosecution and conviction of Klansmen in the murders of civil rights workers. [97; 93]

KU KLUX KLAN (1866–1872)

The original Ku Klux Klan during Reconstruction was founded in Pulaski, Tennessee, sometime between December 1865 and August 1866. Reports of the event vary widely, including conflicting accounts by the principals involved, and no exact date can be established with any certainty. A modern plaque pegs the date, perhaps symbolically, as Christmas 1865, but better evidence was demonstrated by Klansmen themselves, when they celebrated their first anniversary with a gala parade on June 5, 1867. All sources agree that the original Klan was originally intended as a social organization with fun and frolic in mind. Its name was adapted from the Greek *kuklos*, or "circle," with "clan" tacked on and misspelled with a "k" for the sake of alliteration. The Klan's six founders—John Lester, James Crowe, John Kennedy, Calvin Jones, Richard Reed, and Frank McCord—were all Confederate veterans, well-educated, and from affluent families. Their penchant for outlandish costumes and nocturnal rambling, posing as ghosts to frighten local blacks and bedevil them with childish practical jokes, presumably had no sinister motivation in those early days. The advent of Radical Reconstruction, however, changed this, and diehard Confederates turned to the Klan as a vehicle for defeating black suffrage, maintaining white supremacy, and restoring Democratic rule to the prostrate South. A secret reorganizational meeting was convened at Nashville's Maxwell House Hotel in the spring of 1867, with Klansmen endorsing a new constitution (or prescript), laying the groundwork for a four-year guerilla war against the federal government in Washington. Nathan Bedford Forrest, a former slave trader and Confederate cavalry leader, was chosen as grand wizard of the new KKK, but his authority over local operations remained largely symbolic, with discipline—or the lack thereof—dependent on the strength and personalities of leaders in the individual Southern towns and counties. By October 1868, when Klan terrorism had reached its peak on the eve of the presidential election, an estimated 500,000 Klansmen were organized in the eleven ex-Confederate states and Kentucky. (One "inside" source placed 40,000 Klansmen in North Carolina alone.) Over the next three years, Klansmen and allies such as the Knights of the White Camellia would commit over 2,000 murders, in addition to innumerable floggings, castrations, rapes, brandings, shootings, and lesser assaults. Contrary to popular legend, Grand Wizard Forrest did not call Klansmen to disband in 1869, but he *did* issue a ban on masked violence, urging Klansmen to keep a low profile and save their ammunition for genuine "emergencies." Nightriding was finally curbed, by passage of new federal laws between May 1870 and April 1871 and the effort of congressional hearings held between May and December 1871. In fact, Klan activities in five Southern states had virtually ceased by the time the federal hearings convened, and the organization's ultimate demise had more to do with victory than fear of prosecution. Where Klansmen had ridden during Reconstruction, schools were destroyed and carpetbaggers driven out, black voters were terrorized, and Republican margins of victory were reduced or eliminated. In effect, the Klan had done what it had set out to do and, having outlived its usefulness to the Southern establishment, was encouraged to fade from the scene. [87]

KU KLUX KLAN OF AMERICA

See *Austria.*

KU KLUX KLAN OF FLORIDA, INC.

Chartered in September 1944 with its headquarters in Orlando, this was the oldest independent Florida Klan. Leaders included A.B. Taylor (of Orlando), A.F. Gulliam (of Clarcona), and H.F. McCormack (of Apopka). The group's strength was concentrated in central Florida, where it operated as an affiliate of Samuel Green's Association of Georgia Klans. Aside from a few scattered cross burnings and demonstrations, this group did not make headlines until July 1949, when the Groveland rape case produced an outbreak of violence against blacks that resulted in the deployment of National Guard units. The organization apparently dissolved, its members resigning or defecting to other Klans, before the Supreme Court issued its Black Monday ruling in 1954. [38]

KU KLUX KLAN OF THE CONFEDERACY

See *Original Ku Klux Klan of the Confederacy.*

KU KLUX RANGERS

A group of Reconstruction nightriders active around Sulphur Springs, Texas, the Ku Klux Rangers allegedly maintained a loose affiliation with the local Democratic Party. The group's theoretical link to the larger KKK remains unclear. [87]

KU KLUX REGISTER

A forerunner of the modern Klan Kalendar, the Ku Klux Register was established in the prescript of the original KKK. Curiously, although the Register allowed for twelve months and seven days, there was no provision for weeks, and only twelve hours are named, which must have created serious confusion in the announcement of gatherings. Months were designated as Dismal, Dark, Furious, Portentous, Wonderful, Alarming, Dreadful, Terrible, Horrible, Melancholy, Mournful, and Dying. Days of the week were named for colors: White, Green, Blue, Black, Yellow, Crimson, and Purple. The twelve designated hours were Fearful, Startling, Awful, Woeful, Horrid, Bloody, Doleful, Sorrowful, Hideous, Frightful, Appalling, and Last. Most dens apparently avoided confusion by ignoring the Register completely, using normal times and dates on their official notices and published warnings. [87]

KUBLI, K.K.

With Klan support, Kubli was elected speaker of the house in Oregon during 1923 (some critics maintained that his initials were his greatest political asset). A year later, Kubli's unsuccessful U.S. Senate race against incumbent Charles McNary helped divide the Oregon realm, since both candidates had strong Klan support. [10]

KUHN, FRITZ JULIUS

Born in Munich during 1895, Kuhn was thrice wounded in World War I. A devoted follower of Adolf Hitler and a participant in the Munich beerhall *putsch* of 1922, Kuhn afterward emigrated to the United States, working as a chemist at Detroit's Ford Hospital between 1928 and 1934. The visibility of Michigan's Klan and the anti-Semitic essays published by Henry Ford gave him hope for the U.S.'s future, and Kuhn became a naturalized citizen in 1934. Two years later, he merged a collection of tiny German-American Nazi groups—the Swastika League, Teutonia, and Friends of Hitler—into the German-American Bund. As führer of this new organization, Kuhn persistently sought cooperation with native U.S. groups, ranging from unresponsive Indian tribes to the more receptive Ku Klux Klan. Southern Klansmen were generally hostile to Nazi overtures in those days, but Klansmen along the East Coast were more receptive, and a joint Klan-Bund rally was conducted in New Jersey during August 1940. By that time, Kuhn was imprisoned in Sing Sing for a 1939 conviction for embezzling $14,000 from the Bund's treasury. After serving two and a half years in prison, he was released and deported to his native Germany. [93]

KUKLOS ADELPHON

A popular college fraternity founded at the University of North Carolina in 1812, Kuklos Adelphon soon spread throughout the South, declining in the 1850s and then disappearing entirely following the Civil War. Some historians believed Kuklos Adelphon to be the source of basic rituals and possibly the name adopted by the original Klansmen during Reconstruction. [93]

KURTS, DANIEL

A Dayton, Ohio, spokesman of the National Association for the Advancement of White People, Kurts published an article praising a 1953 gathering of Southern Klans in Columbus, Georgia. "You Klansmen have a great organization," he declared in print. "You have a right to be proud of it." [77]

KUSCH, JOSEPH

See *Hamm, Willie.*

L

LACKEY, GORDON

A Greenwood, Mississippi, Klansman, in May 1965 Lackey helped Byron de la Beckwith paint a black ring around the home of a local white man who hired "the wrong nigger" to paint the house white. [*NYT* 1966]

LACKEY, JAMES

See *Penn, Lemuel.*

LaCOSTE, RENE

A member of the New Orleans-based Universal Klans of America, LaCoste joined Imperial Wizard Roswell Thompson in a January 1972 demonstration at the local Robert E. Lee Memorial, resulting in an assault by Black Panthers armed with bricks. In September 1976, LaCoste was identified as a participant in demonstrations led by David Duke's Knights of the KKK. [84]

LADIES AUXILIARY OF THE SURF CLUB

In 1965 congressional investigators identified this group as a front for the United Klans of America's ladies auxiliary unit in Holly Ridge, North Carolina. [38]

LADIES CONFEDERATE DIXONS MILLS UNIT

A cover for the United Klans of America's ladies auxiliary in Dixons Mill, Alabama, this group was publicly exposed in 1965. [38]

LADIES CONFEDERATES

In 1965 this group was identified by federal investigators as a front for the Linden, Alabama, ladies auxiliary, United Klans of America. [38]

LADIES OF SAVANNAH

A 1960s cover for the Savannah, Georgia, ladies auxiliary, United Klans of America, this group was publicly identified in 1966. [38]

LADIES OF THE GOLDEN MASK

In the 1920s this organization served as the official ladies auxiliary for the Indiana KKK. [10]

LADIES OF THE INVISIBLE EMPIRE

A 1920s Klan auxiliary in Oregon, nicknamed "Loties," in 1924 this organization voiced its objections to domination by men. When a representative from Atlanta arrived at a local meeting and demanded that the Mother Counselor surrender the Loties charter and merge with the National Women of the Klan, he was surrounded and beaten with fists and handbags. The representative escaped, and few of the Loties remained in the Klan by year's end. [10]

LAKE WALES PIONEER CLUB NO. 5-4

A 1960s cover for the Lake Wales, Florida, klavern, United Florida KKK, this group was exposed in 1965. [38]

LAKEVIEW MEN'S CLUB

In 1965 congressional investigators identified this group as a front for the Locust Grove, Georgia, klavern, United Klans of America. [38]

LAKIN, REV. A.S.

A Northern Methodist missionary who moved to Alabama in 1865, Lakin was appointed president of the state university two years later. Arriving in Tuscaloosa to take up his duties, he was met by a mob of Klansmen who threatened his life, whereupon he fled the city and never returned. [87]

LAMBRIGHT, ODDIST J.

A Louisiana Klansman, Lambright was sentenced to prison in April 1983 after pleading guilty to acts of harassment against a radio executive in Oakdale. According to Lambright's confession, the target, a white man, was selected because his wife was black. [NYT 1983]

LANDERS, DON

See *Alexander, Henry.*

LANDRUM, ROY

See *Federated Ku Klux Klans, Inc.; McDanal, Mrs. Hugh.*

LANE, DANIEL

A white citizen of Georgia, during Reconstruction, Lane was whipped by Klansmen for hiring a black woman to work in his garden after she refused to work for another white man. [93]

LANE, DAVID EDEN

A resident of Denver, Colorado, Lane earned his living as a golf hustler and part-time real estate agent before he discovered anti-Semitism and the Christian Identity movement in the 1970s. It is not clear how Lane's career in real estate ended; some accounts report that his license was lifted for failure to deal with an interracial couple, while others maintain that Lane came to view real estate as part of the worldwide "Jewish conspiracy." He joined the local KKK and became an aggressive recruiter, and was banished by Fred Wilkins in the late 1970s for persistently mixing Nazi literature with the Klan pamphlets he was assigned to distribute. In 1981, Lane authored a pamphlet, *The Death of the White Race,* and was detained by police while distributing it on the street. Publicity surrounding his arrest led controversial radio host Alan Berg to book Lane as a guest on his show, and their verbal sparring produced an enmity that ultimately led to Berg's assassination three years later. In the meantime, Lane moved to Idaho, and served as a propagandist for the Aryan Nations, becoming propaganda minister of The Order when that militant faction was organized by Robert Matthews in 1983. Lane managed to avoid participation in The Order's several bank robberies, but he did try his hand at counterfeiting, and he drove the getaway car when Berg was murdered in Denver, in June 1984. Convicted for his role in Berg's death, he is currently serving a life term in prison, but incarceration has not prevented him from continuing to contribute to racist causes. In 1986, a new Lane pamphlet—*Identity: Under This Sign You Shall Conquer*—was distributed at Richard Butler's World Aryan Congress. A year later, Lane was one of thirteen charged with sedition, but was found innocent in April 1988. [13]

LANGE, OTTO

A railroad worker in Burleson County, Texas, Lange was killed when Klansmen raided his home on July 2, 1923. The nightriders also wounded Lange's daughter and pistol-whipped his elderly mother. [10]

LANGLEY, SARA

A resident of Stone Mountain, Georgia, Langley was identified as secretary-treasurer of the National Knights of the KKK in July 1965 when it applied for permission to operate in North Carolina. [38]

LANGSTON, DOROTHY

As executive secretary of the Freeport-based New York Committee for Justice, Langston received a threatening letter on April 5, 1946, signed "James H. Hanley, Great Kligrapp." The note marked New York's first reported Klan activity in nearly two decades. [NYT 1946]

LaRICCI, TONY

Born in Norfolk, Virginia, LaRicci lived in New Jersey until age ten, when his family moved to Baltimore. He joined the United Klans of America in 1965, and soon headed his own klavern as exalted cyclops. Within a year LaRicci had replaced Vernon Naimaster as imperial representative for the state. He sold his house at a loss when blacks moved into the neighborhood, and his turbulent United Klans career included LaRicci's arrest with four others for trying to kidnap a "drug pusher" who was in actuality an undercover police officer. Internal bickering prompted LaRicci to leave the United Klans in 1966, following Xavier Edwards into the new Maryland Knights of the KKK. By 1969, LaRicci was running this group, and followed the advice of United Klans defector Robert Scoggin by affiliating his splinter group with James Venable's National Knights. In October 1975, he was one of five grand dragons who resigned—or was banished—from the National Knights, creating a new organization, the Invisible Empire Knights, under Imperial Wizard Dale Reusch. Never satisfied with any arrangement for long, LaRicci briefed newsmen in 1976 on a new, unnamed coalition of right-wing groups in Maryland, of which the KKK would be an active part. With action in mind, he organized the paramilitary Klan Beret, but Grand Klaliff Will Minton tried to seize control of the realm in early 1977. LaRicci kept his job with some help from his friends, and September 1977 saw the Maryland Knights affiliated with William Chaney's Confederation of Independent Orders. LaRicci last made headlines in July 1978, when three of his Klansmen were convicted of attempting to bomb a Lochearn, Maryland, synagogue. [2; 84]

LAUCK, GARY REX ("GERHARD")

Born in Milwaukee and raised in Lincoln, Nebraska, Lauck's interest in Nazi philosophy began in adolescence, reading *Mein Kampf* at age 13 and deciding that "Adolf Hitler was the greatest man who ever lived." Enrolling at the University of Nebraska after high school, Lauck studied philosophy and German for two years before dropping out to organize his own *National*

Sozialistische Deutsche Arbeiter Partei—Auslands Organisation (National Socialist German Workers Party—Overseas Organization), more commonly known as the NSDAP-AO. Operating from a Lincoln post office box and backed by a handful of young disciples, Lauck is responsible for much of the neo-Nazi propaganda currently published in the United States and West Germany. In March 1981 West German authorities identified "Gerhard" Lauck as one of three main sources for Nazi posters and literature seized by police in that country, where such material has been outlawed since World War II. Lauck has traveled widely in West Germany, maintaining contact with neo-Nazi cells. In 1972, he was arrested in West Germany for distributing fascist literature. Two years later, authorities expelled him from the country after he delivered a speech on "Why Hitler is still so popular in the United States." In 1976, German police arrested him a second time, with a stash of 20,000 Nazi posters. A conviction earned him four months in prison and a permanent ban from West Germany. Granted immunity from prosecution in 1979, he returned long enough to testify for the defense at the trials of six European neo-Nazis charged with crimes of violence. Stateside, Lauck has been affiliated with the National Socialist Party of America, once holding the party's number two post until he was ousted in a power struggle with leader Harold Covington. [2]

LAUDERDALE, E.A.

A director of the Citizens' Council in Little Rock, Arkansas, Lauderdale and two other men—J.B. Sims and Jessie Perry—were arrested on September 10, 1959, in connection with a series of recent bombings. Local targets bombed on September 7 included the school board office, a construction firm owned by Little Rock's mayor, and a car owned by the city fire chief, whose men had used high-pressure hoses to break up recent segregationist riots. Two more alleged bombers, John Coggins and Gradon Beavers, were arrested September 11, after an explosives cache was found fourteen miles outside of town. Sims pled guilty on September 18, drawing a sentence of five years and a $500 fine. Perry was convicted on October 28, and sentenced to three years in prison. Lauderdale was convicted on November 28, 1959, with jurors recommending the same sentence applied to Perry. Gradon Beavers filed a guilty plea on October 13, 1960, receiving a sentence identical to that drawn by Sims. Testimony at Lauderdale's trial established the fact that the September bombings were planned at a KKK meeting. [*NYT* 1959–1960; 61]

LAURENS COUNTY, SOUTH CAROLINA

The scene of a Klan-inspired election riot in October 1871, Laurens County's racial situation was tense for months before violence finally exploded on October 19, 1871. Authorities were braced for trouble in the county seat in Laurensville, but white marauders instead staged their assault on the polls in Clinton, driving away a state constable stationed there as an observer. The constable mustered a company of black militia, but the troops withdrew the next morning. Their departure signaled a general massacre of blacks and "radicals." By October 22, an estimated 2,500 armed whites had invaded Clinton from the surrounding areas, hunting for blacks and Republicans. An estimated dozen victims were killed, including black legislator Wade Perrin and a newly elected white probate judge. [87]

LAWRENCE, GERALD

See *McComb, Mississippi.*

LEA, JOHN G.

A founder of the Reconstruction KKK in Caswell County, North Carolina, Lea admitted to being the one behind an 1870 plot to murder state Senator John Stephens. He personally led the murder party and was arrested, but a lack of evidence compelled his release while other Klansmen were bound over for trial. Lea wrote out a detailed confession in 1919, which was released after his death in 1935. [87]

LEAGUE OF ST. GEORGE

A European neo-fascist group active in the 1970s, the League sent representatives to New Orleans, Louisiana, for a September 1976 demonstration led by David Duke's Knights of the KKK. [84]

LEAZER, DONALD E.

Identified as grand kligrapp for the North Carolina realm, United Klans of America, Leazer was fined for carrying a concealed weapon in August 1965. A sixty-day jail sentence was suspended in the case. [38]

LEDFORD, DAVID

A member of the United Empire of the KKK, Ledford was arrested with Imperial Wizard Rocky Coker and "National Titan" Larry Owens on July 26, 1980, during racial disturbances in Chattanooga, Tennessee. Coker and Owens were later convicted of conspiracy and illegal possession of explosives in the case. [NYT 1980]

LEE, ELLIS

A Birmingham Klansman, Lee and accomplice Cranford Neal were captured and beaten by blacks who delivered them to police after a bungled house bombing on July 17, 1958. A third participant in the crime, Herbert Wilcutt, was arrested after Lee and Neal revealed his name. The three defendants told police that they had planned the bombing after a Klan meeting, selecting a home recently purchased from white owners by a black family. Several other bombings were planned, but the first charge went off prematurely, with disastrous results. Wilcutt was tried first, and convicted on December 5 despite his lawyer's plea that a guilty verdict would mean "you'll see Negroes spreading out like a cancer into every white community." On May 4, 1959, all three Klansmen were sentenced to three months in jail. [*NYT* 1958–1959]

LEE, EMORY ALLEN

See *McComb, Mississippi.*

LEE, H.D.

An ex-Confederate colonel, Lee was identified as a leading officer of the Reconstruction Klan in Cleveland County, North Carolina. In March 1871, he conferred with Rutherford County Klan leaders on means of reducing unauthorized nightriding. [87]

LEE, HENRY

A Mississippi Klansman, Lee wrote letters to acquaintances in 1964 claiming credit for building some of the bombs used against blacks and civil rights workers in McComb, Mississippi. Summoned before the House Un-American Activities Committee in February 1966, he refused to answer any questions on the subject, citing possible self-incrimination. [38]

LEE, HOWARD M.

A Bogalusa, Louisiana, firearms dealer and a member of the Original Knights of the KKK, Lee purchased 651 guns and over 21,000 rounds of ammunition for resale between May and August 1964, arranging bulk transfers of arms and ammunition to Klansmen in violation of federal law. Aside from the Original Knights, weapons were also traced to the United Klans of America and the White Knights in Mississippi. Arrested and charged with more than 216 violations of the Federal Firearms Acts, Lee was imprisoned at Texarkana, Texas, in 1965. [38]

LEE, KENNETH

See *Webster, Clyde.*

LEE, ROGER

As owner of the left-wing New Era Bookshop in Baltimore, Maryland, Lee became a target of harassment by the Interstate Klans in 1967. His store was picketed sporadically by Klansmen from February through March, and the target of acts of violence and vandalism, including a brick thrown through the shop's display window, a magazine rack overturned, the walls plastered with stickers reading "You are being watched by the Knights of the Ku Klux Klan," and an arson fire that caused $200 damage to the entryway. Lee's landlord finally ordered him to move because of concern expressed by neighboring merchants for their own shops. Baltimore's mayor tried to intervene – with the help of Klan leader Xavier Edwards – but Edwards was resolute. "Wherever the store goes," he declared, "they can expect to find the Ku Klux Klan." [NYT 1967]

LEE, RUFUS

A black resident of Conway, South Carolina, Lee was attacked by Klansmen at his rural home on November 9, 1950. Staging a predawn raid, the Klansmen dragged Lee and his two sons, Coolidge and Henson, from the house, stripping and beating both boys before they carried Lee away. A mile from the house Lee was flogged and had his hair cut off before the raiders fled. Questioned about possible involvement by his Association of Carolina Klans, Grand Dragon Tom Hamilton blamed the attack on "someone connected with the law." [NYT 1950]

LEE, WORTH T.

See *Lynch, John.*

LEE COUNTY IMPROVEMENT ASSOCIATION

In 1965 congressional investigators identified this group as a cover for Sanford, North Carolina, Unit No. 23, United Klans of America. [38]

LEECH, ALEX

A black militiaman in York County, South Carolina, during Reconstruction, Leech was shot by a gang of twenty to thirty Klansmen in 1871 and left in a roadside ditch. At an inquest packed with known Klansmen, a black witness testified that he dared not name the killers, fearing for his life. The presiding coroner joined Klansmen in laughing as the usual verdict of murder by "persons unknown" was returned. [87]

LELAND, BOBBY

Leland was named as Texas grand dragon for the National Knights of the KKK after presiding dragon Dan Smithers defected to join Dale Reusch's Invisible Empire Knights in October 1975. [84]

LENOIR FELLOWSHIP CLUB

In 1965 congressional investigators identified this group as a cover for the Kinston, North Carolina, klavern, United Klans of America. [38]

LENTZ, B.

A white Republican state senator in Alabama, Lentz and Representative R.E. Harris were taken from a train and whipped by Klansmen in October 1868. [87]

LEONARD, ARTHUR

A resident of Salisbury, North Carolina, Leonard served as North Carolina grand dragon for the United Klans of America between 1962 and early 1964, when he was replaced by James Robertson Jones. [38]

LESTER, JOHN C.

An ex-Confederate officer and one of six original Klansmen in Pulaski, Tennessee, Lester served as nighthawk for the first KKK den. Later an attorney and member of the Tennessee state legislature, he described the formation and early activities of the Klan in a book, *Ku Klux Klan: Its Origin, Growth and Disbandment,* published in 1884. He summarized the Klan's degeneration thus: "Secrecy was at first its strength. It afterwards became its greatest weakness. The devices and disguises by which the Klan deceived outsiders enabled all who were so disposed, even its own members, to practice deception on the Klan itself. It placed in the hands of its own members the facility to do deeds of violence for the gratification of personal feelings, and have them credited to the Klan." [87]

LEVIN, JOE, JR.

See *Southern Poverty Law Center.*

LEWALLYN, CECIL

An Alabama Klansman named by state investigators as one of the rioters who burned a Greyhound bus outside Anniston during the May 1961 Freedom Rides, Lewallyn pled the Fifth Amendment before federal judge Frank Johnson when questioned on May 30. Jailed for contempt for his refusal to say who advised him not to testify, Lewallyn spent two hours in a cell before returning to court and again refusing to testify, this time on advice from attorney J.B. Stoner. [NYT 1961]

LEWANDOWSKI, RALPH

A Chicago member of the National States Rights Party, Lewandowski was one of eight men indicted in Birmingham on September 23, 1963, for violent interference with court-ordered school desegregation. [FOF 1963]

LEWIS, CHARLES B.

A Klan troubleshooter in the 1920s, Lewis served as grand dragon of Michigan before moving on to charter a new realm in Wisconsin. In 1927 he was placed in charge of the troubled New York realm, but even his talent for diplomacy could not help it. [10]

LEWIS, FRANK

See *Johnson, Woodrow.*

LEWIS, HOWARD

An organizer for the National Knights of the KKK in Ohio, Lewis launched an April 1967 campaign to ban textbooks showing black and white children together. His targets included schools in Akron, Canton, and Cleveland, but the Klan's efforts to have "objectionable" books removed were unsuccessful. [*NYT* 1967]

LEWIS, THEO

See *Goodman, Jessie Lee.*

LIBERTY NET

A computer bulletin board maintained by the Aryan Nations for exchanging information with similar groups, the Liberty Net offers updates on pending rallies and conventions, along with prepared essays by recognized leaders of the white-supremacist Identity movement. Authors such as Louis Beam and Robert Miles supply the Liberty Net with an endless succession of essays on topics such as AIDS, "Are the Jews murdering Christian children once again?" and "We may need to round them up soon," and outlining plans for a national list of "known homosexuals," ready to be swept up in a massive dragnet "when the time comes." The bulletin board service offers both public and private material, with the "private" sector accessed by typing in a key phrase: Free America from the Zionist Occupational Government. [13]

LICTOR

In the early Reconstruction Klan, this title was applied to a guard of the den. With the passage of time, the designation was apparently replaced by, or used interchangeably with, that of the nighthawk. [93]

LILBURN MEN'S CLUB NO. 229

In 1965 congressional investigators identified this club as a front for the Dacula, Georgia, klavern, United Klans of America. [38]

LINDSEY, BEN B.   349

LIMESTONE DEBATING CLUB

A 1960s cover for a Wilmington, Delaware, klavern of the United Klans, this group was publicly identified in 1966. [38]

LIMESTONE FISHING CLUB

Federal investigators identified this group as a 1960s front for Beulaville, North Carolina, Unit No. 48, United Klans of America. [38]

LINCOLN COUNTY W.P. LODGE

In 1965 congressional probers named this group as a cover for the Lincolnton, North Carolina, klavern, United Klans of America. [38]

LINDERMAN, FRANK

An author and hotelman from Flathead Lake, Montana, Linderman once led the anti-Catholic American Protective Association. With Klan support, he won the Republican nomination for a 1924 senate race against Democratic incumbent Thomas Walsh. Klansmen mounted a subtle smear campaign against the Catholic Walsh, implying a conspiratorial connection with the Vatican. Linderman lost by a margin of 8,000 votes in the election. [10]

LINDSAY, JIM

A prosperous New Orleans realtor and man of many aliases, Lindsay was best known to local police as "James Lawrence." Under another alias, "Ed White," he founded and led the New Orleans-based Knights of the KKK until his murder in June 1975. Louisiana Grand Dragon David Duke was a pallbearer at Lindsay's funeral, assuming control of the Knights as national director or grand wizard. (Accounts vary on whether Duke assumed the leadership role shortly before Lindsay's death or immediately afterward.) Lindsay's estranged wife was tried and acquitted for his murder, blaming Lindsay's Klan connections, which had been unknown to her before his death. [84]

LINDSEY, BEN B.

A judge in Denver beginning in 1900, by the early 1920s Lindsey was an internationally recognized expert on family law and children's problems who had helped push more than a dozen child protection laws through the Colorado state legislature. In his 1924 reelection campaign, Lindsey was opposed by Klansman Royal Graham, who sought access to the voluminous children's court records for blackmail purposes. A strong opponent of the KKK, Lindsey won reelection in a year when Klansmen easily captured most other Colorado offices. When Graham filed suit, claiming that ballots were fraudulently marked for Lindsey in the Jewish districts of Denver, the case was thrown out of court. Graham's KKK attorney sued to recover his fee, and Graham committed suicide rather than face a state bar association probe of his Klan connections. Klansmen pursued the case, supplying an attorney for Graham's widow. Meanwhile, in January 1925, Grand Dragon John Locke was hauled into Lindsey's court and charged with conspiracy and kidnapping in the case of an underage boy coerced into marriage with threats of castration. Two years later, the Klan suit against Lindsey reached the Supreme Court of Colorado, where the ballots for an entire Jewish district were invalidated, and Lindsey had to step down. When the U.S. Supreme Court denied jurisdiction, Lindsey destroyed his secret files in a "shame bonfire" to keep them out of KKK hands. A few months later, Lindsey was disbarred on charges of accepting bribes in an earlier children's court case, and he departed for California. Colorado offered to reinstate his license in 1933, but Lindsey declined. A year later, he was elected to the Los Angeles superior court by the largest number of votes ever cast for that office and served with distinction until his death a decade later. [10]

LINGO, ALBERT J.

A native of southern Alabama, Lingo was president of a door manufacturing company before Governor George Wallace appointed him to lead the state police in 1963. A short time later, Lingo turned up on the dais at a United Klans of America rally, where he was introduced to the crowd as "a good friend of ours." In May 1963, he told Birmingham newsmen, "You can say that some of my best friends are nigras," but that friendship was seldom evident. Following a September 1963 church bombing that killed four black children in Birmingham, Lingo's troopers photographed every white person at the mass funeral, hoping in vain to blame civil rights workers for the bombing. When it became evident that Klansmen were responsible for the bombing, Lingo cooperated with Imperial Wizard Robert Shelton to finger members of the rival Cahaba River Group on charges of illegal dynamite possession. Lingo's second in command tried to stall the misdemeanor arrests, informing his boss that the Klansmen in question were prime suspects in an FBI investigation, but Lingo replied, "I don't know who their suspects are, and I don't care." In August 1965, Lingo procured a KKK bondsman for Klansman Tom Coleman, after Coleman shot civil rights workers Jonathan Daniels and Richard Morrisroe in Hayneville. State Attorney General Richmond Flowers accused Lingo of stonewalling the Daniels murder investigation and procuring perjured testimony in Coleman's defense, testimony that alleged that his victims were armed at the time they were shot. In 1966 Lingo ran for sheriff of Jefferson County, and visited a black church to address a meeting of the Southern Christian Leadership Council. He claimed that he had been singled out as a scapegoat for the violence in Selma the previous year. Newly registered black voters were not persuaded, however, and Lingo was soundly defeated at the polls that November. [15; 22; 63; 68]

LIPSTEIN, LEWIS

See *Gould, Barbara Ayrton.*

LITHONIA NO. 57 CLUB

In 1965 congressional investigators identified this group as a cover for the Lithonia, Georgia, klavern, United Klans of America. [38]

LITTLE COHAIRE IMPROVEMENT ASSOCIATION

See *Tar Heel Development Association.*

LITTLE HOLINESS CHURCH

Located at Dolly Pond, Tennessee, this church was invaded by Klansmen on a Sunday in 1949, with six members of the congregation blackjacked on accusations of neglecting their families. [10]

LITTLE RIVER CLUB NO. 27

In 1965 congressional investigators identified this club as a front for the Biscoe, North Carolina, klavern, United Klans of America. [38]

LITTLE RIVER ROD & GUN CLUB

A 1960s cover for the Dry Prong, Louisiana, klavern of the Original Knights, this organization was originally know as the Pollock Hunting & Fishing Club. [38]

LITTLE ROCK, ARKANSAS

A year after the school desegregation violence in Clinton, Tennessee, Little Rock became the focus of the civil rights movement. Governor Orval Faubus deployed National Guardsmen to bar black students from Central High School on September 4 while Klansmen screened *Birth of a Nation* in Little Rock. Riotous mobs became a daily fixture outside the school. A handful of blacks were finally admitted to Central High on September 23, with U.S. Army escorts that continued until late November. National Guardsmen remained until late May, but successful integration failed to soften white resistance. On August 12, 1959, firemen used high-pressure hoses to break up a disorderly segregationist march on the state capitol. Thirteen days later, two white youths were arrested for bombing a newly integrated high school. On August 27, two white women disrupted a school board meeting with tear gas grenades. On September 7, bombs damaged the school board office, the mayor's construction firm, and a car owned by the fire chief. E.A. Lauderdale and four others were charged with the bombings, and a cache of dynamite was found outside of town on September 11. Police announced that the blasts were planned at a Klan meeting. The home of a black student from Central High was bombed on February 9, 1960. A black defendant was subsequently charged and convicted. On July 12, 1960, Emmett Miller and two other nightriders were arrested while planting a bomb at Philander Smith College; hours later, another bomb damaged the school district warehouse. With the exception of one black defendant, all the adult bombers tried and convicted in Little Rock were affiliated with both the KKK and the Citizens' Council. His 1957 performance at Little Rock earned Orval Faubus an unwelcome presidential nomination on the National States Rights Party ticket in 1960. He polled 214,195 votes that November, despite his public rejection of the nomination. [61]

LITTLEJOHN, FRANK

The police chief of Charlotte, North Carolina, and a sworn enemy of the Klan since the 1920s, Littlejohn broke up a picket line when Klansmen protested a local showing of *Island in the Sun*, a film that depicted an interracial love affair. He also planted informants in the local KKK, which led to the arrest and conviction of five Klansmen for plotting to bomb a Charlotte school in 1959. [33]

LIUZZO, VIOLA GREGG

A white housewife from Detroit, Viola Liuzzo volunteered her services to the civil rights movement in Alabama. On March 25, 1965, she was assigned to transport carloads of demonstrators between Montgomery and Selma, the site of a protest. Around 8 p.m. that night, in the company of nineteen-year-old Leroy Moton, Liuzzo left Selma to retrieve another carload of blacks from Montgomery. A party of Klansmen overtook her car in Lowndes County and shot Liuzzo, whose vehicle swerved off the road as the nightriders sped away. One of four Klansmen in the car, Gary Rowe, was a paid informant of the FBI, and the killers were swiftly identified as Eugene Thomas, William Orville Eaton, and Collie Leroy Wilkins, Jr.—all of whom were members of Bessemer Klavern No. 20, United Klans of America. Unlike the Lemuel Penn murder case a year earlier, the Liuzzo slaying suspects were not suspended by Imperial Wizard Robert Shelton. Instead, they were paraded as heroes at Klan rallies from Alabama to North Carolina, signing autographs for the faithful while money was collected for their legal fees in a Whiteman's Defense Fund. (A separate United Klans Defense Fund was also established to bankroll the trial.) Wilkins was tried first in the case, with a mistrial declared on May 7, 1965, when the jury deadlocked 10–2 for conviction. Attorney Arthur Hanes took over the United Klans' defense team after Imperial Klonsel Matt Murphy died in a car crash that August, and Wilkins was acquitted at his second trial on October 22. (The all-white jury included six admitted white supremacists, including two identified members of the Citizens' Council.) Federal authorities filed charges against all three defendants under the Reconstruction Ku Klux Act, alleging conspiracy to violate Liuzzo's civil rights, and all three were convicted on December 3, 1965, drawing sentences of ten years each. Competing wizard James Venable publicly praised the verdict, declaring, "I've said all the time there's something wrong with some of our Klan leaders and some Klansmen." In Lowndes County, juries remained stubborn, and Eugene Thomas was acquitted of murder charges on September 27, 1966. Eaton died of a heart attack in March 1966, before his case came to trial. In the fall of 1978, a Lowndes County grand jury moved to indict Gary Rowe for Liuzzo's murder, but extradition from his new location was denied, and the case was not pursued. [FOF 1978; 38; 63; 68]

LIVINGSTON, WILLIAM KYLE, JR. ("SONNY")

A Montgomery, Alabama, Klansman, Livingston was charged with bombing the home of Reverend Ralph Abernathy in 1957, and then later released despite a signed confession admitting that he lit and threw the bomb. In 1961, on "street patrol" with twenty-five other Klansmen, he assaulted and beat a black woman with a baseball bat in sight of several policemen, but no charges were filed. (A photograph of the attack was published on the front page of a local newspaper the next day.) Employed as a Montgomery bail bondsman in January 1976, Livingston was arrested when he forced his way into police impound yard armed with a pistol to capture a bail-jumper. Again, no charges were filed. As State Attorney General Bill Baxley explained, "Livingston's got a bunch of buddies on the police department." On February 21, 1976, Livingston was charged with the January 1957 murder of a black man, Willie Edwards, but the count was dismissed two months later when a local judge ruled that the indictment was legally deficient because it failed to state the victim's cause of death. Prosecution witness Raymond Britt later said that he was "mistaken" in identifying Livingston as one of the killers. On August 11, 1979, when more than 100 members of Bill Wilkinson's Invisible Empire Knights were jailed following a march from Selma to Montgomery, Livingston helped them make bail. [NYT 1976; AP, Aug. 12, 1979; 84]

LOCKE, DR. JOHN GALEN

A Colorado physician denied membership in the Denver County Medical Association, Locke went on to practice in his own small hospital. An early member and state organizer of the 1920s Klan, he became Colorado's grand dragon in late 1923. The following year he occupied a private box at Denver's civic auditorium, when he supervised the Republican state convention. Soon after the November election, Locke ordered the abduction of a Denver hotelman's son and threatened the boy with castration if he refused to marry his pregnant girlfriend. (The boy chose marriage, which was performed on the spot.) When the boy's parents complained, Locke found himself in children's court before Judge Ben Lindsey, charged with conspiracy and kidnapping. IRS agents added to Locke's problems in the spring of 1925, charging him with evasion of back taxes spanning thirteen years. Claiming his financial records were "lost," Locke was fined $1,500 and given ten days in jail to reconsider the matter. More bad publicity followed when Governor-elect Clarence Morley, a Klansman, appointed Locke as his aide-de-camp, a colonel in the National Guard Medical Corps, and a ranking public relations/recruiting officer for the National Guard. Revelations that Locke had handpicked Denver's police chief in 1925 made headlines, and the newspapers gleefully echoed the grand dragon's order that Klansmen should refrain from acts of violence while he was in jail. Imperial headquarters requested Locke's resignation on July 1, 1925, but 20,000 Klansmen rallied in support of him. Surrendering his office later that summer, Locke made a halfhearted effort to organize the competing Minutemen, but the new movement never caught on. [10]

LOGAN, B.F.

The sheriff of Cleveland County North Carolina, during Reconstruction, Logan was also a leader of the local KKK, joining other officers in a fruitless call for moderation during the spring of 1871. That October, he fled the state to avoid arrest on federal charges. [87]

LOGAN, GEORGE W.

A North Carolina Unionist, superior court judge, and leading Republican in Rutherford County, during Reconstruction, Logan was a Klan target for harassment. His court term was once delayed by death threats, but he took the lead in asking for troops to hunt guilty Klansmen. A drunken raiding party went looking for Logan on the night of June 11, 1871, but he was out of town on business at the time. [87]

LOLLAR, COLEMAN A. ("BROWNIE")

A member of the Federated Ku Klux Klans, Lollar was identified as the ringleader of the terrorism in Birmingham, Alabama, in 1949. Once commissioned as a special deputy in Jefferson County, he was stripped of his badge by the sheriff after standing guard at an Adamsville Klan rally in June 1949. Witnesses identified Lollar as a member of the flogging party that brutalized Mrs. Hugh McDanal, Mary Henderson, Jack Alexander, and William Stevens. During his trial in the McDanal case in October 1949, Lollar admitted Klan membership while on the stand but denied any criminal activity. He was acquitted on October 29, to rousing applause from the spectator's gallery. [NYT 1949]

LOLLAR, RICHARD

See *Federated Ku Klux Klans, Inc.; McDanal, Mrs. Hugh.*

LONG, JACOB A.

A young attorney in Guilford County, North Carolina, during Reconstruction, Long was also identified as a member of the KKK, county leader of the White Brotherhood, and a commander in the local Constitutional Union Guard. In late 1869, he served as secretary for a Klan-dominated Conservative gathering that protested Republican moves against terrorism. Long was one of those arrested when Governor William Holden declared martial law in 1870. In December 1871, he was indicted, with seventeen other Klansmen, for the February 1870 murder of Wyatt Outlaw in Graham, North Carolina. [87]

LONG, ROBERT

See *Cheney, Turner.*

LOOMIS, HOMER L., JR.

See *Columbians, Inc.*

LOUISIANA

Louisiana pioneered the resistance to Radical Reconstruction with the Knights of the White Camellia, organized in May 1867, and the KKK, which arrived a year later. The two organizations worked hand-in-hand to terrorize blacks, white Republicans, and carpetbaggers. Most of the violence was politically inspired, accelerating in the weeks before the November 1868 presidential election. In Alexandria, the sheriff and 200 blacks armed with clubs successfully routed a Klan raiding party, but the outcome of most engagements reflected the armed superiority of the whites. An estimated thirty blacks were found floating dead in the river outside Shreveport in October 1868, and forty-two blacks were slaughtered in Caddo Parish the same month. Race riots occurred in New Orleans prior to the election, and white gunmen massacred 162 blacks in Bossier Parish. Congressional investigators later prepared a detailed body count of victims between April and November—1,081 murdered, 135 wounded by gunfire, and 507 whipped or otherwise assaulted. Republican margins dropped in the affected parishes, and Democratic election victories were generally followed by a swift decline in terrorism. By early 1869, the Knights of the White Camellia had effectively ceased to exist, and the Louisiana Klan followed suit a short time later.

In 1922 another outburst of violence made Louisiana the modern Klan's most notorious realm—a double murder at Mer Rouge, which attracted national attention. The governor complained to Washington that

Klansmen held his state in a grip of terror, controlling even the mails and telephones, rendering the indictment of Klansmen impossible. An FBI investigation failed to find any violations of federal law, but the publicity hurt, and an anti-mask law easily passed in the state legislature in 1924. Some ranking Klansmen supported the measure, in a bid to clean up the realm's image, and the result succeeded where prosecutors had failed, breaking the Klan from within. Membership was on the decline by 1926, and in the 1930s the surviving klaverns faced active hostility from the ruling political machine. In a state where "Kingfish" Huey Long could publicly threaten to lynch the imperial wizard, the Klan's future was limited at best.

Black Monday offered Louisiana Klansmen new hope in the late 1950s, and a local Knights of the KKK was incorporated in 1956, competing with the larger U.S. Klans. The most successful Klan organization in over thirty years was begun in 1960, as the Original Knights, solidifying its Louisiana base and branching out into neighboring Mississippi. The Original Knights would dominate Louisiana until the fall of 1964, when a three-way split in leadership permitted the United Klans of America to bid for members in the state. Endemic violence rocked Bogalusa during 1965, including the murder of a black policeman, but Louisiana legislators ignored the carnage. In July 1965, the state's Joint Legislative Committee on Un-American Activities cleared the KKK, calling it a "political action group" with "a certain Halloween spirit." The "impartial" researchers estimated state membership at 19,000, and uncovered no evidence of illegal acts. In summation, the Klan was found to be no more secretive than the Masons or Knights of Columbus, designed to express "frustration with the current national administration." Federal authorities disagreed, and sweeping injunctions were issued in December 1965, barring Klansmen from further attacks on black demonstrators around Bogalusa. By early 1967, combined membership of the United Klans and Original Knights was approximately 950.

The 1970s witnessed a short-lived revival of Louisiana klannishness, with David Duke's Knights of the KKK briefly dominating the national scene from its base in Metairie. Bill Wilkinson's Invisible Empire Knights opened a local klavern in Bogalusa during 1976, but the old days of riots and mass demonstrations were gone. The Knights barely survived following Duke's 1980 departure to head a new National Association for the Advancement of White People, but the news in Louisiana from then on would be Duke. In 1989, running as a Republican despite open opposition from party leaders, Duke was elected to the state legislature, to represent a New Orleans suburb. [2; 10; 38; 87]

LOUISIANA KNIGHTS OF THE KU KLUX KLAN

A short-lived independent faction, the Louisiana Knights was organized and led by Reverend Perry Strickland of Baton Rouge after his defection from the U.S. Klans in the winter of 1956. The group dissolved prior to the creation of the Original Knights in 1960. [38; 48]

LOUISIANA RIFLE ASSOCIATION

Between late 1960 and early 1964, the Original Knights of the KKK used this title as a cover for Klan bank accounts in Louisiana. [38]

LOUISIANA-ARKANSAS LAW ENFORCEMENT LEAGUE

A Klan front group, the League was created in 1922 as a vigilante patrol along the state border. [10]

LOUT, PETER, JR.

See *Pacifica Foundation.*

LOWE, CHARLES

See *Dahmer, Vernon.*

LOWE, CLIFTON E.

See *Dahmer, Vernon.*

LOWTHER, HENRY

A black Republican in Wilkinson County, Georgia, during Reconstruction, Lowther outraged Klansmen by suing several whites who owed him money. (He was also suspected of having an affair with a white female employer.) Klansmen visited his home during August 1871, in Lowther's absence, warning his wife to vacate the county within five days. Other local blacks organized and armed themselves to defend Lowther, but Klan leader Eli Cummins arranged for Lowther's arrest, with fifteen others, on trumped-up charges of assaulting another black. All the prisoners except Lowther were quickly released. Cummins visited the jail to offer Lowther a choice of castration or death. Choosing the former, Lowther was taken from the jail by a party of 180 Klansmen, carried to a nearby swamp, and castrated. Lowther survived and later fled to Macon, where he filed charges against his assailants. The Klan sent five men to kill Lowther, but he escaped to Atlanta. The charges against his attackers were dropped. Klansmen then spread a rumor that Lowther was castrated for having sex with his stepdaughter. [87]

LOYAL LEGION OF LINCOLN

An anti-Klan organization active in the 1920s, the Legion sometimes burned fiery "L's" to denote its presence in a given community. [10]

LOYAL LIBERTY LEAGUE

See *Indiana.*

LUCY, AUTHERINE

The first black coed at the University of Alabama, Lucy was enrolled on February 3, 1956, after a three-year court battle. Four crosses were burned around the Tuscaloosa campus on February 1, with another at a disorderly Klan rally on February 4. Campus rioting erupted on February 6, with crowds of students and adults shouting "To hell with Autherine!" and "Keep 'Bama white!" On February 7, Lucy was suspended indefinitely "for your safety and for the safety of the students and faculty members." A month later, sophomore Leonard R. Wilson, leader of the West Alabama White Citizens' Council, was expelled for his part in the February rioting. Four other students were suspended, and twenty others received less serious discipline. (Three students under investigation withdrew voluntarily from the university.) Lucy's suspension was subsequently altered to expulsion after she accused university administrators of complicity in the riot. On January 18, 1957, a federal court in Birmingham upheld her expulsion on grounds of "false, defamatory, impertinent and scandalous charges" against university leaders. [FOF 1956–1957]

LUKE, WILLIAM C.

A "carpetbag" member of the American Missionary Association and schoolmaster in Cross Plains, Alabama, during Reconstruction, Luke was lynched by Klansmen in 1871. Jailed with four black teaching assistants on trumped-up charges, Luke was removed from jail that night by Klansmen, who also hanged the other four prisoners. Before his death, Luke was allowed to write a letter to his wife and six children, later read before Congress by a Republican legislator in support of the proposed Ku Klux Acts. [93]

LUKES, CLAUDE

See *Hurst, Charlie.*

LUMBEE INDIANS

Rumored to be survivors of the 17th century Roanoke colony, Lumbee tribesmen comprise a significant minority in North Carolina's Robeson County. By the late 1950s, Robeson County's population included 40,000 whites, 30,000 Indians, 25,000 blacks, with a system of three-way school segregation to accommodate all races. In January 1958, Reverend James Cole's North Carolina Knights began to agitate against the Lumbees, burning crosses in Lumberton at an Indian home once occupied by whites and on the outskirts of Pembroke, where a Lumbee woman resided with white friends. A major rally was scheduled for January 18, despite warnings from the county sheriff and the Lumbee tribe, and Klansmen were heavily outnumbered by Indians on the night of the rally. Armed Lumbees routed the disorganized Kluxers with a tear gas grenade and a volley of gunfire, capturing Klan regalia and Cole's PA system. One Klansmen was found unconscious in a roadside ditch, and detained for public drunkenness. Sheriff Malcolm McLeod reportedly dispersed the Indians by warning that they might miss the television series *Gunsmoke,* if they didn't hurry home. In March 1966, Grand Dragon J.R. Jones announced that the United Klans would accept Lumbees as Klansmen, but no takers were identified. [*NYT* 1966; 10]

LUMPKIN, JAMES

An Alabama native and third-generation Klansman, Lumpkin joined the U.S. Klans at age eighteen. He later briefly joined Robert Shelton's Alabama Knights, before moving to Georgia and enlisting with the National Knights under James Venable. Employed as a textile mill foreman in Thomaston and serving as Georgia grand dragon for the National Knights, Lumpkin issued a controversial eleventh-hour endorsement of Lester Maddox in the 1974 gubernatorial primary. (Anxious to divorce himself from Klan support, Maddox blamed the endorsement on "dirty tricks" dreamed up by his opponent.) Lumpkin was later promoted to the rank of imperial klaliff, serving as Venable's second in command. [*NYT* 1974; 84]

LUNDAHL, BJOERN

The identified leader of a neo-Nazi Klan in Stockholm, Sweden, Lundahl was arrested with five of his disciples on May 13, 1965, charged with plotting to murder prominent local Jews. Investigation linked Lundahl's klavern to Horace Miller and the Aryan Knights, based in Waco, Texas. Klan literature and regalia was found in a search of Lundahl's home. In a related matter, a Stockholm policeman was suspended from duty on May 18 because of his ties to the Klan. [*NYT* 1965]

LUTHARDT, CHARLES

A segregationist candidate running for governor of Maryland in 1966, Luthardt addressed a Klan rally of 400 persons in a cow pasture thirty-five miles outside of Baltimore. Referring to blacks, he told assembled Klansmen, "I'm all for sending 'em back to Africa if I'm elected." [*Newsweek,* June 6, 1966]

LUTTERLOH, THOMAS

A physician and Klansman in Alamance County, North Carolina, during Reconstruction, Lutterloh privately admitted taking part in a December 1869 raid, during which he personally whipped a black man to death. [87]

LUTTERMAN, HARRY

In the 1920s Lutterman was identified as the Klan's grand dragon for Connecticut. [10]

LUTTRELL, ROY TALMADGE

One of twelve Klansmen called before a Miami federal grand jury in October 1952 probing local acts of terrorism against blacks and Jews, Luttrell escaped indictment when charges were issued three months later. [*NYT* 1952]

LYLE, J. BANKS

An ex-Confederate officer, South Carolina state legislator, and principal of Limestone College, Lyle was also the leader of Spartanburg County's Klan during a period of unparalleled Reconstruction brutality. In October 1871, immediately prior to state elections, Klansmen, including one Limestone College teacher who wore his academic gown without further disguise, closed local polls to prevent blacks from voting. Acts of violence, including several murders, were commonplace in the county, and Lyle later fled the state to escape arrest. He was never prosecuted for his crimes. [87]

LYNCH, CHARLES CONLEY

Born in 1913, Lynch joined Wesley Swift's Church of Jesus Christ Christian after his discharge from military service in World War II, and swiftly demonstrated the talent for oratory that earned him ordination as a preacher. Known as "Connie" to his friends, Lynch served the church in California for ten years before traveling in 1957. Driving a pink Cadillac and sporting a vest fashioned after a Confederate battle flag, Lynch became a regular fixture at Klan rallies and other segregationist gatherings across the country, returning to his California base and working as a plasterer between racial crises. An early member of the Minutemen, he also became California state organizer for the National States Rights Party in 1962, launching a friendship with attorney J.B. Stoner that would last the rest of his life. In autumn 1962, Lynch joined Jacksonville, Florida, Klavern 502 of the United Florida Ku Klux Klan but his talents were also available to competing factions. On October 13, 1962, he shared the stage with Robert Shelton when the United Klans of America rallied at Bessemer, Alabama. Five months later, on March 21, 1963, Lynch and two other National States Rights Party members were convicted of battery and disturbing the peace in California for assaulting a group of teenage restaurant patrons, wounding one youth with a gas-propelled gun. Released after paying a $1,200 fine, Lynch would be arrested later in 1963 in Memphis, Little Rock, and Gadsden, Alabama. Remaining flexible in his loyalties, Lynch kicked off a membership drive for the United Florida KKK that summer, appearing with

Shelton on August 17 for a United Klans rally in Spartanburg, South Carolina. A month later, addressing St. Augustine Klansmen on the subject of Birmingham's latest church bombing, Lynch proclaimed, "If there's four less niggers tonight, then I say good for whoever planted the bomb. We're all better off." The following spring, Lynch and Stoner were back in St. Augustine, working in concert against black civil rights demonstrators. "There's gonna be a bloody race riot all over this nation," Connie told one audience at the city's historical slave mart. "The stage is being set for the earth to get a bloodbath. When the smoke clears, there ain't gonna be nothin' left except white faces." On July 24, 1964, Lynch and Stoner were jailed for an illegal cross burning in St. Augustine, along with Florida Klansmen Barton Griffin, Bill Coleman, and Paul Cochran. In July 1965, Lynch and Stoner appeared together to address National States Rights Party rallies in Bogalusa, Louisiana, and Anniston, Alabama. At the latter gathering, on July 15, Lynch told his audience, "If it takes killing to get the Negroes out of the white man's streets and to protect our constitutional rights, I say, 'Yes, kill them!'" Following that rally, black resident Willie Brewster was murdered by nightriders and those arrested for Brewster's murder were defended by Stoner. In early 1966, Lynch made a West Coast tour for the National States Rights Party, appearing in Baltimore on July 28, where he denounced Mayor Theodore McKeldin as a "super-pompous jackassie nigger-lover." Lynch told the cheering crowd of 1,000, "To hell with the niggers, and those who don't like it, they can get the hell out of here." Another National States Rights Party rally was scheduled for the following day, but it was cancelled by an emergency injunction. On November 21, 1966, he was convicted and sentenced in Baltimore for inciting a riot, disorderly conduct, conspiracy to riot, and violation of city park rules. (A federal appeals court later overturned the conviction, accepting the free-speech arguments of Lynch's black attorney.) One of thirteen persons held on murder charges after a shootout at a National States Rights Party rally in Berea, Kentucky, left two men dead on September 1, 1968, Lynch was never brought to trial. A staunch supporter of Alabama's George Wallace, Lynch made numerous speeches supporting Wallace's presidential candidacy in 1968. Lynch died of heart disease in 1972. J.B. Stoner later told an interviewer, "Connie and I had a lot of fun." [3; 38; 84]

LYNCH, JOHN WILLIAM

As sheriff of Dade County, Georgia, Lynch was allegedly called to a black home in Hooker on April 2, 1949, with complaints of a wild party in progress. Seven blacks were arrested by Lynch and Deputy William Hartline, who promptly handed their prisoners over to a party of robed Klansmen for flogging. A federal grand jury was convened to investigate the case on August 3, 1949, and Grand Dragon Samuel Green formally banished the Trenton, Georgia, klavern of the Association of Georgia Klans five days later, citing its involvement in the beatings. The trial of twelve defendants, including Lynch and Hartline, opened on November 22, 1949, with five past or present Klansmen stricken from the list of prospective jurors. (One Klansman, James Berry, was seated as an alternate juror in the case.) Defense witnesses included Klan spokesman Sam Roper, who denied the existence of a Dade County klavern, and Walter Arp, self-proclaimed exalted cyclops for the state's seventh province, who acknowledged the presence of a provisional unit in the area. Prosecutors countered with testimony from Katherine Rogers, formerly Green's secretary, who identified Arp as the "cygraff" of Dade County's klavern, further recalling an order for ten Klan robes placed with imperial headquarters by defendant Terrell Wheeler. On November 28, witness Mamie Clay, owner of the home Lynch raided in April, testified concerning the police harassment she confronted after refusing to sell her home on demand from local whites. Following rejection of the first offer, she was jailed and later acquitted on charges of using her home as a brothel. Flogging victim Charles Roberts described how Sheriff Lynch ignored his pleas for help on April 2, and witness Worth Lee, who had been a Klansman in the 1920s, described watching Lynch consort with robed cross burners at the Clay home, afterward forcing victims into a Klansman's car. The prosecution rested on December 1, after introducing a statement from Lynch in which he admitted working with the Klan to "get this thing cleared up" by driving Mamie Clay from her home. On December 2, the judge directed verdicts of acquittal for defendants L.C. Spears and John Wilkins (city recorder for Trenton, Georgia) on grounds of insufficient evidence. Defendants Sam Peters and William Hartline admitted building a cross that was burned at Clay's home, but Hartline maintained that his presence at the time the Klansmen lit the cross was "a coincidence." A mistrial was declared on December 17, the jurors hopelessly deadlocked. Prosecutors pressed their case in new proceedings, convicting Lynch and Hartline of civil rights violations on March 9, 1950. Upon conviction, both defendants received the maximum penalty of one year in prison, with a fine of $1,000 each. No other Klansmen were convicted in the case. [NYT 1949–1950]

LYNCH, WOODROW W.

The proprietor of Lynch Chemical Company in Shelby, North Carolina, Lynch served as grand dragon for a local Klan splinter group, the Ancient Order, Invisible Knights of the Ku Klux Klan. On August 19, 1967, his chemical plant was bombed by persons unknown. The case remains unsolved. [NYT 1967]

LYNCHES RIVER HUNTING CLUB

In 1965 congressional investigators identified this group as a cover for the Lamar, South Carolina, klavern, United Klans of America. [38]

LYNCHING

Typically defined as the mob execution of an accused criminal without trial or other legal authority, lynching was a common practice of the Reconstruction KKK, but declined as a Klan activity—although never disappearing completely—in the 20th century. In retrospect, while lynchings typify the Ku Klux Klan's assertion of a "necessary" law-enforcement role in history, examination of the facts suggests that victims were selected on the basis of their race, as much as any real or fancied crime.

No final body count of victims is available from the chaotic period of Reconstruction, but the practice was clearly widespread in every Klan-infested state except Virginia, where nightriding was minimal and ceased entirely by the end of 1868. Elsewhere, Klansmen hanged or gunned down victims in prodigious numbers, with twenty-five lynchings reported from the neighborhood of Harrodsburg, Kentucky, alone, during a two-year period. Mass lynchings were not uncommon. Five black prisoners were killed by the Constitutional Union Guard at Kinston, North Carolina, in January 1869, and nine were lynched by Klansmen in Louisville, Georgia, two years later. In one lynching that occurred in Union, South Carolina, during January 1871, five black murder suspects were removed from jail and shot. Three of them survived their wounds, however, and a week later, 500 Klansmen descended on the jail, seizing ten blacks, and hanging eight of them before two others escaped.

While blacks accused of murder, rape, or arson were the Klan's chief victims during Reconstruction, others were selected on the basis of political affiliation or participation in militia drives against the KKK. Unionists and Republicans were frequently slain, without regard to race, including Dr. G.W. Darden in Georgia, Clinton Drake in Tennessee, and George Smith, who was lynched by the Knights of the Rising Sun in Texas. Not even Klansmen were immune from lynching. Members were hanged in Arkansas and Kentucky on suspicion of turning state's evidence against other Klansmen.

Lynching did not begin with the birth of the Klan, nor did it vanish with the order's dissolution in 1872. No reliable statistics are available prior to 1889, but the NAACP tabulated 3,224 lynchings between 1889 and the end of 1918, an average of 111 per year. Of those victims, 2,522 were black, 6 percent of which were dispatched by racist mobs without the slightest indication of a criminal offense. When a crime was charged, it ranged from rape and murder to window-peeping, disrespect toward whites, "disloyal remarks," and "frightening a white man's cow." Georgia had the largest number of lynchings, and incidents occurred outside of the South as well—in Wyoming, Oregon, and Maine.

It is, perhaps, no accident that one of Georgia's many lynchings—that of Jewish convict Leo Frank in 1915—paved the way for a revival of the Ku Klux Klan. Frank's lynchers called themselves the Knights of Mary Phagan, named after the child Frank allegedly abused and murdered. Taking a leaf from the novels of Thomas Dixon, the Knights participated in United States's first cross burning in October 1915, and most of the lynchers signed on for active duty when William Simmons chartered the new KKK a month later.

Despite the Klan's direct association with lynching, the modern Klan generally abstained from lynching. Only two clear-cut cases of Klan lynching were documented between 1915 and 1950 (the first lynch-free year in the United States): the execution of an accused bridge-burner in Arkansas and the 1923 hanging of Dallas Sewell, an Oklahoma black lynched on charges of "passing for white." Definitions of lynching have become more elastic since World War II, with civil rights groups including many crimes (such as the 1955 murder of Emmett Till) that involved no mob and no accusation of any crime. FBI agents found no evidence of organized Klan involvement with lynchings in the 1940s or the murder case of Mack Charles Parker in Mississippi in 1959. Some reporters identified the 1964 murder of civil rights workers Michael Schwerner, Andrew Goodman, and James Chaney as a lynching on the basis of Klan-police cooperation in the crime, but a more clear-cut case was the 1980 hanging of Michael Donald in Alabama, which resulted in the conviction (and death sentence) of several Klansmen. [10; 87; 93]

LYONS, JAMES F.

See *Dahmer, Vernon.*

LYONS, R.C.

See *Federated Ku Klux Klans, Inc.*

LYONS, ROBERT

Identified as a former Klansmen, Robert Lyons was forced to resign his post as Indiana's delegate to the Republican national committee in 1944. [10]

M

M. MURPHY CLUB

In 1965 congressional investigators named this club as a front for the Union, South Carolina, klavern, United Klans of America. The origin of its name remains obscure, but it may be a reference to late Imperial Klonsel Matt Murphy. [38]

MABRY, H.P.

A retired judge and ex-Confederate general, Mabry emerged as an officer of the Knights of the Rising Sun during Reconstruction in Texas. In the spring of 1869, he served as defense attorney for Knights members facing trial on murder charges, but he fled to Canada when one defendant turned state's evidence and identified Mabry as the leader of a mob that lynched carpetbagger George Smith in Jefferson in October 1868. [87]

MABRY, JESSE W.

See *Aaron, Edward; Cole, Nat.*

McADOO, WILLIAM GIBBS

A Georgia native, raised in Tennessee, McAdoo was the son-in-law of President Woodrow Wilson, and served as secretary of the treasury in World War I. A Democratic presidential contender in 1924, he won Klan support after a speech in Macon, Georgia, where a local Klan leader asked his opinion on the subject of religious freedom. McAdoo replied that he "stood four-square on the Constitution," avoiding any mention of the

Klan's anti-Catholic campaigns, and it was good enough to please Atlanta imperial headquarters. Rumors of closer Klan ties surfaced after McAdoo and Imperial Wizard Hiram Evans "coincidentally" appeared together at the resort of French Lick Springs, Indiana. McAdoo's chief opponents for the Democratic nomination were Catholic Al Smith and Oscar Underwood, an outspoken enemy of the Klan. The resultant floor fight in Madison Square Garden resulted in the compromise nomination of John W. Davis on the 104th ballot. McAdoo later served in the U.S. Senate, but his brief flirtation with the Klan continued to haunt him. In 1938, Republicans sought to defeat his reelection bid by producing an alleged lifetime Klan membership card made out in McAdoo's name. [10]

McAFEE, LEROY

A state legislator from Cleveland County, North Carolina, during Reconstruction McAfee was identified as KKK grand titan for his district. He played a leading role in the 1870 impeachment of Governor William Holden following Holden's attempt to crush the North Carolina Klan with armed force. In March 1871 McAfee conferred with top Klansmen from Rutherford County in an effort to curb the area's violence. His efforts were wasted, and McAfee was himself arrested by federal authorities in October 1871. Thirty years later, a nephew of McAffee's, Thomas Dixon, penned two novels that would help pave the way for a 20th century Klan revival. [87]

McBRIDE, CORNELIUS

An Irish immigrant and carpetbagger who taught a school for blacks during Reconstruction in Chickasaw County, Mississippi, McBride fled the area after he was roughed up and fired on by Klansmen. [93]

McBRIDE, HAROLD

See *Carter, Asa.*

McBRIDE, J.R.

A Greensboro, North Carolina, Klansman, McBride was arrested for burning a cross at the home of a local black family on July 15, 1967. [*NYT* 1967]

McCALL, CHARLES C.

While active in the Klan, McCall was elected as Alabama's state attorney general in 1926. Strong opposition greeted his appointment of Grand Dragon James Esdale as assistant attorney general, and McCall eventually withdrew the appointment, but he later joined Esdale in a libel suit against the Birmingham Age-Herald, after the paper printed quotes from Esdale in which he advocated flogging for those opposing the Klan. (The suit was dropped when defense attorneys began calling each member of the Birmingham klavern as witnesses in court.) In 1927, McCall broke with Governor Bibb Graves, a Klansman, when McCall attempted to prosecute flogging cases in Crenshaw County. Several convictions were obtained even though Graves cut prosecution funding to an average of fifteen dollars per case, and the exposure of these cases helped to break the Klan's power in Alabama. [10]

McCALL, HERSCHEL C.

A former Michigan lawyer who moved south and served as a deputy sheriff in Houston, Texas, McCall retired from law enforcement and served as Houston's grand titan in the early 1920s. He argued that a bit of violence was good for morale, and this exercise in logic led to his appointment as grand dragon of the state. A friend of would-be wizard Hiram Evans, McCall participated in the palace coup that ousted founder William Simmons from power in 1922. The reward for his loyal service was a transfer to Washington, D.C., where he served as the Invisible Empire's ambassador to the United States. [10]

McCALL, WILLIS V.

As sheriff of Lake County, Florida, between 1943 and 1973, McCall cultivated a reputation as a heavy-handed racist, friendly with the KKK and not averse to violating the civil rights of those constituents he viewed as "undesirables." The list of "undesirables" included union organizers, blacks, Indians, "liberals," and newsmen who insisted on reporting McCall's frequent resorting to violence. A staunch defender of the local citrus industry, he was accused throughout the latter 1940s of arresting, and occasionally beating, blacks who desired to quit their jobs at certain citrus companies. The sheriff's brand of justice first made headlines with the Groveland rape case in 1949, when he refused to let a lynch mob deal with two black suspects in his jail. Both defendants were convicted and sentenced to die, but the verdicts were overturned on appeal in November 1951, with a new trial ordered. Both men were handcuffed when the sheriff drove them back from Raiford to Tavares on November 6, but that did not prevent McCall from shooting them, one fatally, and then claiming self-defense. The headlines made McCall a celebrity, a role he enjoyed. In 1954, following the U.S. Supreme Court's ruling for nationwide school desegregation, McCall created a stir by ordering Indian farm workers Allen and Laura Platt to remove their five children from school in Mt. Dora. When school officials asked for proof that the Platts were black, McCall aimed an accusing finger at one of their daughters and said, "I don't like the shape of that one's nose." It was enough to satisfy the school board, and for the next twenty years McCall ruled Lake County as if it were his own private fiefdom. When President John F. Kennedy was assassinated in 1963, McCall refused to lower the courthouse flag, insisting that it would suffer costly damage from "flapping against the building." Illegal "White" and "Colored" signs were displayed in his office until a special court order removed them in 1971, and McCall was the only one of Florida's sixty-seven sheriffs to "consistently and adamantly" withhold uniform crime reports from higher authorities. On June 12, 1973, he was indicted for second-degree murder in the beating death of a black prisoner, a circumstance that did not prevent local Democrats from nominating McCall for his eighth term as sheriff three months later. Suspended from office by Governor Reubin Askew, McCall pursued his reelection campaign, but he was finally defeated by a narrow margin in the November election. The murder charge was eventually dropped, but McCall's name returned to the headlines eight years later, with revelations of new evidence in a double murder dating back to December 1951. In 1981, an ex-marine confessed to planting the bomb that killed NAACP official Harry Moore and his wife on Christmas Eve, describing the blast as a contract murder financed by the Klan. According to the confession, McCall provided cars for the murder party and picked up the bar tab for the victory celebration after Moore's death was confirmed. To date, no charges have been filed in the case. [*Life*, Nov. 17, 1973; 93]

McCAULEY, JOHN

A member of the Klan in White County, Arkansas, during Reconstruction, McCauley joined the Klan in April 1868 and later confessed to investigators, describing their group of 7,000 members. He confessed participation in the October 1868 murder of detective Albert Parker, who had been assigned to infiltrate the KKK, and testified for the prosecution at an 1871 murder trial that ended in the acquittals of all concerned. [87]

McCLELLAN, JAMES

An ex-Confederate officer and active Democrat in Jackson County, Florida, during Reconstruction, McClellan was sitting with local Klan leader James Coker on a hotel veranda in Marianna when sniper fire killed his daughter and left McClellan gravely wounded. The shooting followed the recent executions of several blacks by the Klan, and black constable Calvin Rogers was suspected by Klansmen of leading the attack, which had probably been aimed at Coker. The resulting violence claimed several black lives and the life of Jewish merchant Samuel Fleischman, killed by Klansmen after he ignored their orders barring him from Jackson County. [87]

McCLUSKEY, VALCUS C.

See *Federated Ku Klux Klans, Inc.*

McCOLLUM, RUBY

See *Adams, Dr. Clifford.*

McCOLLUM, STANLEY

A member of the Knights of the KKK in Tuscumbia, Alabama, McCollum and Klansman Thomas Robb were identified in 1982 as leaders of a dissident faction opposed to imperial headquarters in Louisiana. A unity meeting convened in Stone Mountain, Georgia, on Labor Day 1983 failed to resolve the quarrel, and membership in the Knights soon fell. [2]

McCOMB, MISSISSIPPI

An arena of brutal Klan violence during 1964, McComb was the scene of more than twenty-five bombings and acts of arson between April and September. On April 28, nightriders blasted the home of NAACP officer Curtis Bryant. On June 20, bombers struck two black homes, a black-owned barbershop, and the homes of two white men who had publicly denounced Klan violence. The homes of two black civil rights activists were bombed on June 22, and five days later a Molotov cocktail was hurled at a local moderate newspaper office. A black minister's son-in-law was beaten by nightriders on July 3, and a bomb destroyed a civil rights freedom house in McComb four nights later. Two rural black churches were damaged by arsonists on July 17 and 18, with two blacks assaulted during one of the attacks. On July 26, a bomb was thrown at the home of Curtis Bryant's brother, Charles. A black-owned market was bombed on August 15, and an attempt to firebomb a black home three nights later failed. On the same evening a civil rights worker was pursued by armed whites in a pickup. On August 23, a white friend of local blacks was abducted by five hooded men and held captive for three hours before his release. The night of September 7 was marked by five bombings that damaged black-owned property in the nearby communities of Auburn, Bogue Chitto, Summit, and Magnolia. In McComb two nights later, bombs damaged the home of black minister James Baker. On September 20, dynamiters struck another local church and the home of black civil rights activist Aylene Quinn. Bombings on September 23 damaged two black homes, including one owned by a former policeman. FBI agents arrested eleven McComb Klansmen in early October, seizing numerous guns and homemade bombs in the process. Federal indictments finally named nine defendants in the following cases: (1) for an attempted church-burning on July 18—Paul and Jimmy Wilson, and Murphy Duncan; (2) for the July 26 bombing of a black home—Paul and Billy Wilson, Hilton Dunaway, and Gerald Lawrence; (3) for the September 9 bombing of Baker's home—Paul and Billy Wilson; (4) for conspiracy in the bombing of Aylene Quinn's home—the three Wilsons, Murphy Duncan, John Westbrook, and Emory Lee. All nine entered pleas of guilty or no contest on October 23, 1964. Circuit judge William Watkins handed down terms of probation to all of the defendants, citing previous "undue provocation" by blacks. Violence continued around McComb in November 1964, with shots fired into the newspaper office that Klansmen had failed to burn down five months earlier. In 1965 congressional investigators established that the bombers were all members of the United Klans of America, assigned to various acts of violence after drawing lots in local klavern meetings. [38]

McCORD, FRANK O.

One of the six original Klansmen in Pulaski, Tennessee, McCord served simultaneously as the grand cyclops and editor of the Pulaski *Citizen*. He published the country's first KKK notice on March 29, 1867. A delegate to the Klan's April 1867 reorganization meeting in Nashville, he returned home to publish an April 19 account of the grand turk invading his newspaper office. "Awed into submission" by the appearance of the Klansman—McCord's good friend, James Crowe—he ran the notice of an upcoming den meeting in Pulaski. McCord addressed a public meeting at Christmas 1868 and denounced the mob violence in Pulaski. He briefly fled the area in early 1869, when Governor William Brownlow deployed militia units against the Klan. McCord returned to business as usual when the troops were withdrawn. [87]

McCORKLE, ALBERT

Identified as the grand dragon of Missouri in the mid-1970s, McCorkle attended Robert Scoggin's Conference of Eastern Dragons in 1976. [84]

McCORMACK, H.F.

See *Ku Klux Klan of Florida, Inc.*

McCORVEY, THOMAS CHALMERS

A Reconstruction member of the Knights of the White Camellia in Monroe County, Alabama, McCorvey later confessed participation in group intimidation of blacks during the summer of 1868, when he and others rode in disguise to frighten them out of voting. [87]

McCULLERS, JOHN HENRY

A black resident of Birmingham, Alabama, McCullers was beaten by Klansmen in June 1949, after being accused of adultery. [*NYT* 1949]

McCULLOUGH, CHARLES

A Klansman in Talladega, Alabama, McCullough was jailed in December 1981 on charges of stabbing three blacks. [*NYT* 1981]

McCULLOUGH, GROVER

See *Aaron, Edward.*

McDANAL, MRS. HUGH

A white resident of Birmingham, Alabama, Mrs. McDanal was targeted by local Klansmen in June 1949. Armed Klansmen broke into her home on the night of June 11, and whipped her on the front lawn, next to a burning cross. Klansmen threatened to burn her at the stake for allegedly selling whiskey and renting bedrooms "to bring men and women together," and for "dancing nude on her front porch." Struggling with her assailants, Mrs. McDanal tore off several hoods and identified some of the raiders. Alabama's attorney general denounced the Klansmen as "bums, hoodlums, and cutthroats." Investigation revealed that the raid occurred after a Klan meeting in nearby Adamsville, with three of the Klansmen identified as Coleman Lollar, Albert Swindle, and Roy Landrum. Lollar's trial opened on October 26, 1949, with Klansman Boyd Killingsworth naming Lollar as the leader of the raiding party. Mrs. McDanal repeated her identification of the defendant, but Lollar's attorney countered with charges of immorality, displaying photos of the victim walking nude in a cornfield. The jury acquitted Lollar on October 29, their verdict greeted by applause from the court. [NYT 1949]

McDANIEL, EDWARD LENOX

A Mississippi Klansman, McDaniel helped organize a klavern of the Original Knights in Natchez in early 1963. In December 1963, he was dumped from office—along with Douglas Byrd—on charges of mismanagement and misappropriation of Klan funds. Shifting allegiance to Sam Bowers and the White Knights in early 1964, McDaniel also secretly joined the United Klans of America later that year. McDaniel was expelled from the White Knights amid new charges of financial irregularity. Most Natchez Klansmen followed McDaniel into the United Klans, and he was appointed grand dragon for the state in September 1964. Familiar problems surfaced in August 1966, and McDaniel was ousted from his third consecutive Klan on accusations of financial irregularities. A public clash with Imperial Wizard Robert Shelton at a September 18 Klan meeting led to the formal dissolving of that Klan in October. By the mid-1970s, McDaniel had severed his Klan ties completely, and was reportedly friendly with Fayetteville's black mayor, Charles Evers. [NYT 1966; 38]

McDOWELL'S SPORTSMAN

In 1965 congressional investigators identified this group as a cover for the Marion, North Carolina, klavern, United Klans of America. [38]

McELVEEN, ERNEST RAY

See Moore, O'Neal.

McGHEE, REV. CHARLES D.

A Methodist minister and Klansman in St. Louis, Missouri, McGhee was reprimanded by Bishop W.B. McMurray for his Klan activities in September 1923. McMurray said, "If he wants to parade in a mask, that's his business, but I don't believe it will help his work as a disciple of Christ." McGhee countered by telling newsmen, "If it comes to a choice between the Methodist Church and the Klan, I shall choose the Klan." Removed from his pulpit a short time later, McGhee raged, "The Klan has your number, Bishop! We have had it for months. We know just where to find you and will attend to your case!" Despite the public threats, no action was taken against McMurray by the Klan. [93]

McGILL, RALPH

As editor of the Atlanta *Journal & Constitution*, McGill was a staunch opponent of the Klan and racial violence in general, a stance that made him a frequent target of picketing and threats by the Klan, the Christian Anti-Jewish Party, and similar groups. In 1939 McGill published a Catholic invitation for Imperial Wizard Hiram Evans to visit a new rectory, constructed in the Klan's former imperial headquarters, and his editorials helped launch a probe of Klan floggings and murders in 1939 and 1940. Beginning in 1946, McGill published Klan exposés by author Stetson Kennedy of the inherent violence of the new Association of Georgia Klans and its fringe competitors. In the 1950s, he continued his crusade for tolerance and moderation, lambasting the "respectable" Citizens' Councils as "a scrubbed-up cousin of the Klan." [10; 93]

McGINLEY, CONDE

A longtime ally of anti-Semites John Crommelin and Gerald L.K. Smith, McGinley published *Common Sense*, which provided Klansmen with much of their anti-Jewish propaganda in the 1950s and early 1960s. [14]

McGRIFF, COLBERT RAYMOND

A Georgia Klansman who was expelled from the United Klans of America after his arrest and conviction in an April 1964 shooting incident, McGriff joined other defendants in the case to organize the Vigilantes, a competing Klan-like group. A short time later, he joined James Venable's National Knights, rising to the rank of chief organizer and joining Klansman Earl Holcombe to create the super-militant Black Shirts. [38; 84]

McGRONE, FRANK

A black Job Corps supervisor in Edinburgh, Indiana, McGrone became a target for racist violence in September 1982, when his home and then his car were set afire in separate incidents. Later that month, he was lured to some nearby woods and ambushed by whites, who bound him and branded the letters "KKK" on his forehead and a single "K" on his chest. [*NYT* 1982]

McKELLAR, KENNETH

A Klansman and U.S. senator from Tennessee, McKellar was identified as a Klansman after he attended the Dyersburg wedding of Klan lobbyist W.F. Zumbrunn, in early 1925. [10]

McKINNEY, JAMES

Identified as the grand dragon of Illinois, McKinney was arrested in Centralia on September 1, 1980, and held for questioning in a series of burglaries spanning seven Illinois counties. Police retrieved stolen guns, dynamite, plastic explosives, furniture, and stereo equipment from the house McKinney shared with Klansman Robert Hansen, who was named as codefendant in the case. McKinney was convicted of burglary and theft, and sentenced to two concurrent three-year terms in jail. Hansen was sentenced to six months in jail and four years probation and a $4,000 fine. [*AP,* Sept. 2, 1980; 2]

McKOIN, DR. B.M.

As a leader of the KKK in Mer Rouge, Louisiana, McKoin declared a private war on crime in 1922, staging a phony attempt on his own life to dramatize the problem of criminal gangs in the area. Implicated in a double murder in August 1922, he entered Johns Hopkins Hospital in Baltimore, in order to escape arrest, but McKoin later waived extradition and returned to face a grand jury. No indictments were returned in the case. [10]

McMENNAMY, T.J.

A member of the Klan's Apopka, Florida, klavern, McMennamy was indicted on June 3, 1953, for perjury before a federal grand jury probing Florida violence since 1949. Witnesses before the grand jury named McMennamy as a member of the team that tried to kidnap NAACP attorney Franklin Williams in August 1949. [*NYT* 1953]

McMICHAEL, OBED

As leader of the White Brotherhood during Reconstruction in Guilford County, North Carolina, McMichael introduced the movement into neighboring Alamance County in 1868. [87]

McNAIR, DENISE

McNair was one of four black children killed in the bombing of Birmingham's 16th Street Baptist Church on Sunday, September 15, 1963. Klansman

Robert Chambliss was convicted of her murder and sentenced to life imprisonment in 1977. [NYT 1977]

McNAUGHT, DR. C.E.

An avid fraternalist and member of at least a dozen organizations besides the KKK, McNaught variously held office as Regimental Surgeon of the Patriarchs Militant and as Minnesota Grand Master of the International Order of Odd Fellows. In July 1930, while serving his second term as mayor of St. James, Minnesota, he was elected grand dragon of the tri-state realm that included Minnesota and the Dakotas. [10]

McNEELY, GEORGE

In 1965 McNeeley was identified as grand dragon of Arkansas for the United Klans of America. [38]

McPHAIL, ROYCE

Selected as the first grand dragon of Texas, United Klans of America, in December 1965, McPhail was barred from speaking at the University of Texas a month later. His tenure as grand dragon was short-lived, with McPhail abandoning his office by the fall of 1966. [NYT 1966; 38]

McRAE, DANDRIDGE

An ex-Confederate general and Reconstruction grand titan of the congressional district that included White, Jackson, and Independence counties, Arkansas, McRae fled to Canada in 1868 to escape murder charges. He returned to face trial in 1871 and he and his codefendants were acquitted, despite the testimony of Klan informant John McCauley. [87]

McRAE, THOMAS C.

Elected governor of Arkansas in 1922, McRae was not a member of the Klan, but he maintained a policy of "friendly neutrality" toward them, appointing a Klansman as his personal secretary to gain KKK support in future elections. [10]

MADDOX, CHARLES HOMER

A member of the U.S. Klans in the late 1950s, Maddox led dissatisfied Klansmen into a new Association of Georgia Klans in 1960, emerging as the group's imperial wizard. In September 1964, he affiliated the Georgia Klan with James Venable's Association of Ku Klux Klan and was named as klokard for the larger organization. By 1965, Maddox was identified as Georgia's grand dragon for the National Knights, telling one Klan audience, "We need to do a lot to stop these national politicians. A boy down in Texas did a lot already, remember?" His reference to the assassination of President John Kennedy evoked cheers and applause from the assembled Klansmen. [33; 38]

MADDOX, LESTER

An Atlanta restaurant owner and staunch segregationist, in 1960 Maddox was identified as the leader of a local white-supremacist group, Georgians Unwilling to Surrender (GUTS), which maintained friendly contact with the U.S. Klans under Grand Dragon Calvin Craig. A typical newspaper ad of his group read in part, "The mess we have this town in, it is a wonder that many more people are not going on an African hunt. . . . And, like a customer suggested, 'Why go to Africa for hunting when Atlanta could bear considerable hunting?'" A candidate for lieutenant governor in 1962, Maddox reportedly arranged Klan spokesman James Venable's endorsement of his opponent in the Democratic runoff election. As a result of that bargain, a newsletter signed by three Georgia Klan leaders was issued supporting candidate Peter Geer, but the trick backfired when Geer was elected. (Today, Maddox denies the story; Venable confirms it.) On July 4, 1964, Maddox shared the stage with Alabama Governor George Wallace and Calvin Craig at a segregationist rally in Atlanta, where several blacks in the audience were mobbed and beaten with metal chairs. In 1965, Maddox led a parade of some 2,000 whites, including Craig and other identified Klansmen, down Atlanta's Peachtree Street. Elected governor in 1966, Maddox appointed several known Klan sympathizers to important Democratic Party offices, but he also displayed a surprising generosity toward blacks. Listed as the front-runner in 1974's gubernatorial primary, Maddox's campaign was destroyed by an August 11 telegram that was given to UPI journalists one day before the election. The telegram offered the Klan's endorsement of Maddox and candidate J.B. Stoner (running for lieutenant governor as an avowed neo-Nazi) and was signed by James Lumpkin, Georgia grand dragon for the National Knights of the KKK, and called Maddox and Stoner the "best candidates who will fight for the return of true Americanism." Maddox branded the wire an example of campaign "dirty tricks," but Imperial Wizard Venable vouched for its authenticity. Maddox failed to win a majority in the election and was forced into a September runoff, where he was defeated. [NYT 1960, 1967, 1974; 82]

MADOLE, JAMES

Founder and leader of the National Renaissance Party in New York City, Madole was arrested in July 1963 following a brawl between blacks and party members at a New York diner. Police confiscated several knives, an ax, and a crossbow from a truck driven by group members, and Madole, Dan Burros, and another member were sentenced to ten days in jail. In 1968, Madole led his group into a formal alliance with Pennsylvania KKK units, the Minutemen, and the National Socialist White People's Party. [75]

MAGIC CITY LODGE

In 1965 congressional investigators identified this lodge as a front for the Florence, South Carolina, klavern, United Klans of America. [38]

MAGNOLIA SPORTSMAN CLUB NO. 10

In 1966 House investigators exposed this group as a cover for the Macon, Georgia, klavern, United Klans of America. [38]

MAHONEY, DR. WILLIAM J.

A diehard anti-Catholic, Mahoney was one of the Klan's most popular and most widely traveled orators in the 1920s. [10]

MAINE

Designated as part of a tri-state realm of the 1920s KKK, Maine was controlled by Grand Dragons Eugene Farnsworth and his successor, Dr. E.W. Gayer. The state's first klavern was organized in Bangor, where Farnsworth maintained a $60,000 estate, and by 1923 the Klan possessed sufficient strength to carry local elections in Sacco and Rockland. Political factionalism split the Klan along party lines between 1924 and 1928, resulting in mass resignations and a general decline in strength. In 1929, the mayor of Portland denied the Klan the use of city hall for a speech by Senator Tom Heflin, and no serious Klan activity has been reported since that time. [10]

MAITTON, HORACE

Identified as a KKK spokesman in Jacksonville, Florida, during 1964, Maitton told newsmen: "People in other parts of the country like to think of niggers as human beings because they have hands and feet. So do apes and gorillas have hands and feet. If a nigger has a soul, I never read about it in the Bible. The only good nigger is a dead nigger." [33]

MALLARD, ROBERT

A prosperous black salesman and owner of a thirty-two acre farm near Lyons, Georgia, Mallard was despised by the Klan for acting "too big" in the years following World War II. Returning from church with his wife and two other blacks on November 20, 1948, Mallard was ambushed by white gunmen, who blocked the lane with their cars and fired a shot through the windshield of Mallard's vehicle, killing him instantly. Sheriff R.E. Gray reported that Mallard's killers wore "white stuff," identified by his wife and the other survivors as Klan robes, without masks. Governor Herman Talmadge ordered the Georgia Bureau of Investigation to study the case, and Dr. Samuel Green announced that his Association of Georgia Klans would conduct its own investigation. Sheriff Gray, for his part, blamed the shooting on Mallard, declaring, "This Negro was a bad Negro, as I have had dealings with him. I further know that this Negro was hated by all who knew him." On November 27, Mallard's widow was arrested by the Georgia Bureau of Investigation at her husband's funeral and held on murder charges, while two other blacks and a white newsman were jailed as material witnesses. Lieutenant W.E. McDuffle told reporters, "I think the Ku Klux Klan has been wrongfully accused in this case." Charges against Mallard's widow were finally dismissed, and five whites were arrested on December 4. Two of those arrested were formally indicted six days later, but neither of them was convicted and the case remains "unsolved." [FOF 1948; NYT 1948]

MANN, ARTHUR

Identified as the exalted cyclops of Connecticut's first and largest klavern in the 1920s, Mann led a mass defection in January 1926, blasting Imperial Wizard Hiram Evans for corrupting the Klan in pursuit of cash, recruiting bad elements, and imposing an unpopular Michigan officer on Connecticut Klansmen. Connecticut Klandom never recovered from the rift, despite sporadic recruiting drives over the next sixty years. [10]

MANN, F. ALLEN

In 1958 Mann was identified as Illinois state chairman of the National States Rights Party. [65]

MANNESS, DAVID V.

A militant anti-Semite, Manness was arrested on February 1, 1969, in Prince Georges County, Virginia, for bombing a local synagogue. Police found Minutemen literature and an arsenal of twenty rifles, twenty-five pistols, several bombs, knives, and thousands of rounds of ammunition in his home. [NYT 1969]

MANUCY, HOLSTED R. ("HOSS")

A convicted bootlegger and outspoken segregationist in St. Augustine, Florida, Manucy served as leader of the Ancient City Hunting Club and of an informal group of racists known locally as "Manucy's Raiders." Questioned about his reported Klan ties, Manucy told newsmen, "I'm not a member of the Klan—I'm a Catholic—but I'm not knocking it, either. I think the Klan is a very good organization." On other occasions, he was more direct, declaring, "My boys are here to fight niggers." A contingent of the Ancient City Hunting Club marched in a St. Augustine Klan parade in 1963, and a year later the club fronted bail money for Klansmen arrested for rioting. A close friend of Klansman and National States Rights Party officer

J.B. Stoner, Manucy was publicly identified as a state officer of the United Florida KKK in 1965 during testimony before the House Un-American Activities Committee. [38]

MANY HUNTING & FISHING CLUB

In 1965 congressional investigators identified this group as a cover for the Many, Louisiana, klavern, Original Knights of the KKK. [38]

MARION COUNTY CATFISH CLUB

Testimony recorded by the House Un-American Activities Committee in 1966 identified this club as a front for the Marion, South Carolina, klavern, United Klans of America. [38]

MARION HUNTING & FISHING CLUB

In 1966 congressional investigators named this group as a front for the Marion, Louisiana, klavern, United Klans of America. [38]

MARS, GRADY

Passed over for promotion in favor of a black soldier, Mars resigned from the Army. In the early 1960s he was identified as North Carolina's grand klaliff for the United Klans of America. In 1965, he served as custodian of the Raymond Mills defense fund, established to aid Klansmen accused of bombings around New Bern. Mars refused to answer questions posed by the House Un-American Activities Committee in October 1965, and the experience left him despondent. On December 12, 1965, he committed suicide. [NYT 1965; 1]

MARSHLAR, STEVE

A member of the Greek Orthodox Church and owner of a Brookside, Alabama, cafe that served whites and blacks on a segregated basis, Marshlar became a target of KKK harassment in 1949. A gang of sixty Klansmen packed Marshlar's diner on the night of June 11, telling him, "We're tired of Catholics [sic] running this town. You've got to keep those niggers down." A Brookside patrolman was in the cafe at the time, but he made no effort to disperse the Klansmen. [NYT 1949]

MARTIN, JAMES

A white Republican state legislator from Abbeville County, South Carolina, Martin was murdered by Klansmen in 1868. [87]

MARTIN, JAMES G.

A member of Reverend James Cole's North Carolina Knights of the KKK, Martin was arrested for public drunkenness and carrying a concealed weapon on January 18, 1958. His arrest followed a riot by Lumbee Indians, that had routed Klan demonstrators near Lumberton. Convicted and sentenced on January 22, Martin also faced more serious charges in the same incident. On May 4, 1959, he pled guilty to inciting a riot and was fined $250. [*NYT* 1958–1959]

MARTIN, JIM

A prominent black Republican during Reconstruction in Alabama, Martin was killed by Klansmen near Union on March 31, 1870. [87]

MARTIN, MELVIN S.

See *Dahmer, Vernon.*

MARTIN, MURRAY H.

With Klansman Billy Skipper, Martin took command of Louisiana's Original Knights in early 1964, after leaders Royal Young and J.D. Swenson were banished for misappropriating Klan funds. By the fall, the Original Knights had suffered a three-way rift in its membership, with Klansmen in the Shreveport-Bossier City area remaining loyal to Martin and conducting financial transactions as the Christian Constitutional Crusaders. Leading his faction into affiliation with James Venable's National Association of Ku Klux Klan at the end of 1964, Grand Dragon Martin was appointed klokann chief for the larger organization. [38]

MARTIN, TERRY

See *Henson, Everett.*

MARTIN COUNTY LADIES IMPROVEMENT CLUB

In 1965 congressional investigators identified this group as the ladies auxiliary of a Klan front, the Martin County Sportsman Club. [38]

MARTIN COUNTY SPORTSMAN CLUB

A cover for Williamston, North Carolina, Unit No. 4, United Klans of America, this group was exposed by the House Un-American Activities Committee in 1965. [38]

MARTZ, LOUIS N.

A New Jersey Klansman, Martz was sentenced to three months in jail for burning crosses at a black housing project in Mercer County in early 1971.

The verdict was overturned by a state appeals court in June 1974, on grounds that the prosecutor made unnecessary appeals to racial feelings against Martz at his trial, thereby "inflaming" minority jurors. [*NYT* 1974]

MARYLAND

One of the Klan's least successful realms in the 1920s, Maryland still saw its share of nightriding violence. A philandering husband was beaten and branded in Hagerstown in 1922, but when another raiding party tarred and feathered several railroad workers, four Klansmen were sentenced to prison terms of seven years each. The realm was formally chartered in 1923, but local resistance continued. Baltimore residents rioted when one of the Klan's "escaped nuns" addressed the faithful at the First Baptist Church, and arsonists tried to destroy a former Presbyterian church where the Thomas Dixon Klan had its headquarters. Grand Dragon Frank Beall claimed seventy-two klaverns statewide, with an estimated 33,000 members, but the Klan never managed to make its presence felt in state politics. Beall's 1926 resignation, accompanied by angry denunciations of Atlanta imperial headquarters, soon ended Maryland's Klan.

An effort to revive the realm began in August 1965, when Grand Dragon Vernon Naimaster recruited for the United Klans of America. His efforts had borne little fruit by the following summer, when renegade Klansman Xavier Edwards and his loyal disciples were banished over their continuing flirtation with the American Nazi Party. Organizing his own Maryland Knights of the KKK, Edwards left Naimaster with four small klaverns and an estimated following of twenty-five members. The Maryland Knights were defunct by 1969, when United Klans of America Grand Dragon Tony LaRicci quarreled with Imperial Wizard Robert Shelton and adopted the same title for his own fledgling organization. Sporadic outbreaks of local violence and cross burning kept LaRicci's Klan in the news through the late 1970s, but there was no significant membership growth. In May 1981, three members of the militant Adamic Knights were convicted and sentenced to prison for plotting to bomb a Baltimore NAACP office. Around the same time, Klansman Richard Savina, leader of another Maryland splinter group, was imprisoned on similar charges, in an unrelated plot. A 1983 survey conducted by the Anti-Defamation League of B'nai B'rith found no identifiable Klan factions active in Maryland. [2; 10; 38; 84]

MARYLAND KNIGHTS OF THE KU KLUX KLAN (1966–1967)

Also known as the Interstate Knights of the KKK, this splinter group was created in 1966, after kleagle Xavier Edwards and some of his loyal disciples were banished from the United Klans of America. Their ouster was on the basis of close affiliation with the American Nazi Party, which at that time was regarded as subversive by United Klans of America imperial headquarters. Maintaining close ties with the Virginia-based Nazis through 1967, the Maryland Knights apparently disappeared sometime after Nazi leader George Lincoln Rockwell's assassination in August 1967. The group had ceased to exist by 1969, when Grand Dragon Tony LaRicci broke with the United Klans, adopting the Edwards faction's title for his own new splinter group. [38]

MARYLAND KNIGHTS OF THE KU KLUX KLAN (1969–80)

Created in 1969 when United Klans of America Grand Dragon Tony LaRicci split from Robert Shelton to form his own group. LaRicci's new group affiliated itself with the National Knights until an October 1975 disagreement with James Venable. LaRicci was one of five grand dragons banished. There was a failed attempt by Imperial Klaliff Will Minton to take control from LaRicci in early 1977. The Confederation of Independent Orders was formed in June 1977. Membership in the Maryland Knights declined sharply after July 1978, when three of LaRicci's Klansmen were convicted of trying to bomb a Lochearn synagogue. [2; 84]

MASON, JAMES

A former leader of the National Socialist Movement, Mason was identified in 1983 as the head of a National Socialist Liberation Front chapter in Chillicothe, Ohio. The latter organization, based in Louisiana, has claimed responsibility for acts of right-wing terrorism on the West Coast. [2]

MASON, CAPT. SIMPSON

An officer of the Arkansas state militia, Mason was killed in a Klan ambush in Fulton County on September 19, 1868. Several suspects were arrested in the case, and Klan leader N.H. Tracy fled the state to avoid prosecution. All but four of the defendants were eventually released, two of whom confessed under conditions that local Democrats called torture. The informants, L.D. Bryant and Uriah Bush, were taken from custody by masked riders while en route to Salem, Arkansas, and were executed. The two other Klansmen, who had been implicated by Bryant and Bush, were soon released for lack of evidence. [87]

MASSACHUSETTS

The modern Klan has a traumatic history in Massachusetts, where its first appearance in the 1920s was opposed by the Masonic Lodge, most elected officials, and Catholic citizens who often resorted to vigilante acts. Klansmen enjoyed their warmest reception in Worcester, where they met in the local Shrine building and were sometimes invited to address the Exchange Club. The rest of the state, however, proved to be less hospitable. In 1923, the Massachusetts House passed a resolution denouncing the KKK as a danger to U.S. freedom, and a year later the state Democratic convention voted a plank that condemned the Klan by name. During 1924 and 1925, a series of bloody riots occurred in Worcester County, where the Klansmen found themselves outnumbered. Other outbreaks occurred in Norfolk, Middlesex, and Essex. In Westwood, twenty Klansmen were injured by a stone-throwing mob. Framingham police jailed seventy-nine Klansmen and confiscated an arsenal of weapons from them after five men were shot near a local Klan rally. By 1928 the beleaguered Klan had disappeared in Massachusetts.

Stirrings of a Klan revival occurred a half-century later, when opposition to court-ordered busing sparked angry white demonstrations in South Boston. Louisiana Klansman David Duke visited the riot scene in 1974 and was greeted with placards proclaiming "This is Klan Country." But local racism did not translate into a new Klan revival. Although ethnic tensions remain in Boston, the Klan's assistance is apparently unwelcomed. [*NYT* 1974; 10]

MASSEL, SAM

A prominent Atlanta Jew who was elected to serve as the city's vice mayor, Massel was marked for murder in 1965 by a Klan faction dubbed the "Secret Six." FBI agents uncovered the plot and warned Massel, thus discouraging the conspirators from carrying out their plan. Running for mayor of Atlanta in October 1969, Massel was again targeted for Klan harassment. A cross was burned on his lawn and a brick was tossed through a window of his home. Massel was elected and tried, unsuccessfully, to ban J.B. Stoner's racist political ads from local radio and television in 1972. The Federal Communications Commission ruled in Stoner's favor, and the campaign spots were allowed to run, complete with its references to "kikes" and "niggers." [*NYT* 1969; 33; 84]

MASSENGALE, PAT

Identified as a member of the Klan in Hattiesburg, Mississippi, Massengale was charged with obstructing justice and attempted jury tampering in the Vernon Dahmer case. His 1969 trial ended in a hung jury. In September 1969, he was arrested on federal firearms charges, accused of illegally transferring a submachine gun to Klansman Bobby Haywood of Tupelo as part of a plot to kill civil rights activist Charles Evers. [*NYT* 1969]

MATTHEWS, DAVID WAYNE

See *Greensboro, North Carolina.*

MATTHEWS, J.L.

The white proprietor of a theater for blacks in Atlanta, Georgia, Matthews was beaten by Klansmen in 1940 after he refused to fire a black employee marked for ostracism by the KKK. [93]

MATTHEWS, L.E.

See *Blackwell Real Estate.*

MATTHEWS, OTIS

A black financial secretary and assistant business agent for the International Woodworkers of America in Laurel, Mississippi, Matthews was abducted and whipped by hooded Klansmen in November 1964. The assault followed a federal court order demanding an end to racial job discrimination at the local Masonite plant. [24]

MATTHEWS, ROBERT JAY

Born in Texas in 1953, by his early teens Matthews was known as a fanatical right-wing racist, organizing a group of tax protesters in his local high school. He would later claim that the move cost him admission to West Point. Seeking escape from ethnic minorities, he moved to remote Metaline Falls, Washington, in the early 1970s and began corresponding with the Aryan Nations, the National Alliance, and other neo-Nazi groups. A reading of *The Turner Diaries* persuaded Matthews to organize a small private army, The Order, which recruited ex-Klansmen David Lane and Frank Silva upon its formation in 1983. Matthews was reportedly the mastermind behind a string of robberies and other violent crimes—including the June 1984 assassination of Alan Berg—which ultimately sent sixty-eight right-wing militants to jail. Surrounded by FBI agents on Whidbey Island in Puget Sound in early December 1984, Matthews was shot and killed after a thirty-six hour siege. [13]

MAYFIELD, EARL B.

A former Texas state railroad commissioner, in 1922 Mayfield became the first active Klansman elected to the U.S. Senate. His opponent in the crucial Democratic primary was Klansman R.L. Henry, who had been officially endorsed by Atlanta imperial headquarters, but Mayfield carried the election by appealing to state Klan leaders. Assured of Mayfield's support in Washington, the Texans let Henry, who ran openly as a Klansman, draw the anti-Klan flack, while Mayfield remained quiet about his own Klan membership. In the general election, Republican leaders tried to have Mayfield stricken from the ballot on the grounds that his KKK oath meant Mayfield was not actually a Democrat. The effort failed, and Mayfield defeated his Republican opponent, 264,000 to 130,000. A last-ditch Republican effort failed to prevent Mayfield from taking his Senate seat in 1923, and a year later he was named to the Klan's strategy board for the Democratic national convention in New York City. In 1925 Mayfield was a featured guest of honor at the Dyersburg, Tennessee, wedding of Klan lobbyist W.F. Zumbrunn. Three years later, public with sentiment running against Klansmen in Texas, Mayfield sought reelection by publicly disavowing the Klan and backing Catholic Al Smith for president, but his scheme failed. [10]

MEADOW IMPROVEMENT ASSOCIATION

In 1965 congressional investigators identified this group as a cover for a unit of the United Klans of America, serving the towns of Benson and Dunn, North Carolina. [38]

MEADOWS, WILLIAM R.

A black resident of Claiborne Parish, Louisiana, Meadows was chosen as a delegate to the state's constitutional convention in 1868. He was murdered by Klansmen on May 6 of that year. [87]

MEANS, RICE

A Klansman and Denver's city attorney, Means was elected to fill a U.S. Senate vacancy in 1924. In July 1925, he was suspended from the Klan by Grand Dragon John Locke for siding with imperial headquarters in a struggle for control of the Colorado Klan. In 1926, Means led the Klan's slate in the Republican primary, losing his bid for a full Senate term. [10]

MECKLENBURG SPORTSMAN CLUB

In 1966 congressional investigators identified this club as a front for the Charlotte, North Carolina, klavern, United Klans of America. [38]

MELTON, QUIMBY, JR.

As editor of the Griffin, Georgia, *Daily News*, Melton penned an editorial denouncing a July 1960 cross burning at the home of a local black family, leading to the arrest of two nightriders. Klansmen retaliated by burning a cross at the editor's home three nights later, on July 25. [NYT 1960]

MEN OF JUSTICE

A vigilante group of white supremacists during Reconstruction in Alabama that was organized in 1867, the Men of Justice merged with Alabama's KKK a year later, disappearing as a separate entity. [87]

MENDEZ-RUIZ, JUAN

A Mexican national, Mendez-Ruiz was thumbing rides in southern California when a Klan "border patrol" picked him up in April 1978. The Klansmen held him captive, threw away his passport and other identification, then delivered him to the Border Patrol as an illegal alien. Klansman Carl Shipton was subsequently convicted in federal court for violating the victim's civil rights and drew a one-year prison term. [NYT 1979]

MENDOSA, MICHAEL

The founder of a Klan unit in Richmond, California, Mendosa was sentenced to a six-year prison term in February 1982 following his conviction of firing shots into a black housing project. The presiding judge described Mendosa's actions as part of a pattern in "which he seeks to advance one group over another through violence." [2]

MEN'S CLUB OF STRONG COMMUNITY

In 1965 congressional investigators identified this group as a cover for the Strong, Arkansas, klavern, United Klans of America. [38]

MERHIGE, ROBERT, JR.

See *Hudgins, Robert.*

MERIDIAN, MISSISSIPPI

On March 6, 1871, a preliminary hearing was scheduled for three defendants charged with making incendiary speeches at a black gathering two days earlier. The accused included white Republican William Dennis, Warren Tyler (the white teacher at a local school for blacks), and black state legislator Aaron Moore. As court convened, the gallery was filled with armed Klansmen, including many from neighboring Alabama who had been summoned as reinforcements for the occasion. When defendant Tyler called a witness to impeach the testimony of white prosecution witness James Brantley, Brantley advanced on Tyler with a raised walking stick, and shots rang out in the courtroom. Presiding Judge Bramlette and two blacks were killed, with Tyler and several other persons wounded. Friends of Tyler tried to hide him in a nearby store, but Klansmen tracked him down and riddled him with bullets. William Dennis, also wounded, was jailed in "protective custody," but his guards withdrew that night and Klansmen entered the jail, and murdered him. Mobs roamed the city over the next few days, killing and mutilating blacks at random, failing to locate Aaron Moore, who had escaped from the court unharmed. Moore had safely made his way to Jackson. Meanwhile, Klansmen burned his home and an adjacent Negro church to vent their rage. A grand jury met in April to investigate the riot, binding six defendants over for trial on charges of unlawful assembly, assault, and intent to kill. All six were acquitted, but one Alabama Klansman was convicted of raping a black woman during the riot. Subsequent state and federal probes failed to produce any further convictions. [87]

MERIWETHER, MINOR

A St. Louis attorney, Meriwether made headlines in 1909 when he claimed to have served as the Klan's grand scribe under Nathan Bedford Forrest. His claim proved impossible to verify. [87]

MER ROUGE, LOUISIANA

Located in Morehouse Parish, Mer Rouge was the scene of a 1922 double murder that embarrassed the national Klan and prompted thousands of members to resign. A local Klan leader, Dr. B.M. McKoin, launched a "cleanup" drive in Morehouse that year, dramatizing his case by firing several shots into his own car and claiming a murder attempt. Klansmen blamed two locals, Watt Daniel and Tom Richards, who had publicly denounced the Klan and were once caught spying on a Klan gathering. Abducted and accused of the McKoin attack, they denied the shooting, and both men were released with stern warnings. Threats failed to silence their criticism of the KKK, however, and Klansmen struck again. On August 24, as most of the population was returning from a barbecue and baseball game in Bastrop, they were met by a roadblock set up by Klansmen. Klansmen cut the phone lines linking Bastrop and Mer Rouge as other Klansmen abducted Daniel, Richards, their fathers, and a male companion. The prisoners were bound and driven to a nearby clearing in the woods. Two of them were flogged before Daniel broke away, ripping off the mask of a Klansman he recognized before being recaptured. Both of them were carried deeper into the woods, where they vanished without a trace. In early September, an emissary from Governor John Parker visited Washington, D.C., with complaints that the KKK controlled police, the telephones, and mail throughout his state. A team of federal agents was dispatched, but produced no evidence resulting in indictments. Repeated pleas for help from Parker and his attorney general were ignored by Washington authorities, who saw no grounds for further federal intervention in the case. Meanwhile, state investigators reported that the missing bodies had been dumped in one of the deep lakes dotting Morehouse Parish, and the governor dispatched troops to drag the lakes under armed guard. Late one night, a dynamite charge was detonated in Lake Lafourche by persons unknown, perhaps in an effort to destroy evidence, but the blast had the opposite effect: two decomposing bodies rose to the surface. An autopsy identified the bodies as Richards and Daniel, revealing that both men had been crushed to death under a road grading machine. While two grand juries failed to indict the killers—the dramatic federal arrests depicted by actor James Stewart in The FBI Story never occurred—the resulting publicity from the case led many nonviolent Klansmen to resign their membership, costing the KKK thousands of dollars in annual dues. [10]

METCALFE, GEORGE

A black employee of the Armstrong Tire and Rubber Company in Natchez, Mississippi, Metcalfe also served as president of the local NAACP chapter until August 27, 1965, when he was crippled by a car bomb. Following the blast, Klansmen and blacks were enjoined from marches through Natchez, but lawsuits restored the rights of both groups to hold public demonstrations. FBI agents traced the Metcalfe bombing to Klansmen in the Silver Dollar Group, but no prosecutions resulted. [NYT 1965; 96]

METTERT, LARRY

A Merced, California, Klansman, Mettert was convicted of boarding a local school bus in April 1981 and threatening an integrated group of children with a gun. [NYT 1981]

METZGER, TOM

Raised a Catholic in his native Indiana, Metzger moved to Los Angeles in 1961 and found work as a television repairman. Affiliated with the John Birch Society in the early 1960s, he eventually broke with the group because, as he explained, "I soon found out you could not criticize the Jews." In search of a new movement, Metzger briefly led his own White Brotherhood in California prior to joining David Duke's Knights of the KKK in 1975. A move to San Diego coincided with Metzger's appointment as California grand dragon for the Knights, and in the summer of 1979 he organized Klan patrols of the Mexican border, searching for illegal aliens. Metzger's KKK security guards dressed in black uniforms and helmets, carrying clubs, chemical Mace, and black-lacquered plywood shields in public demonstrations, clashing with police and anti-Klan hecklers on several occasions. (In one such melee in Oceanside, seven persons were injured in street fighting.) Defecting from the Knights in the summer of 1980, Metzger formed his own California Knights of the KKK, launching a series of protests against Vietnamese refugees living in San Diego. That fall, he entered politics as a Democratic congressional candidate, his radio spots urging voters to "Let me raise a little hell for you." The appeal resulted in a surprise primary win for Metzger, polling 33,000 votes, but November's election saw little improvement on that total: the Republican opponent's 254,000 votes overwhelmed Metzger's 35,000. Two years later, after publicly renouncing his Klan connections, Metzger launched a U.S. Senate race that won him 75,593 votes, an estimated 2.8 percent of all votes cast that year in California. After retiring from politics, Metzger organized the White American Political Association, later renamed as the White Aryan Resistance ("WAR"). Metzger's son John, a frequent guest on television "tabloid" talk shows, leads the White Aryan Resistance Youth ("WARY"), with both groups based in Fallbrook, California. WAR and WARY have been instrumental in organizing disaffected skinheads for the neo-Nazi cause, and federal officers allege that neo-Nazi groups have returned the favor, underwriting Metzger's organization with cash from bank robberies carried out in 1980. In December 1983, Metzger was one of fifteen men arrested—including Aryan Nations leader Richard Butler—for illegal cross burnings in the Lakeview Terrace district of Los Angeles. According to Metzger, the twenty-foot crosses were burned in honor of a white policeman killed by blacks six months earlier. [2; 13]

MICHIGAN

A late-blooming realm for the 1920s Klan, Michigan did not reach its peak membership until mid-decade, with an estimated 80,000 members enrolled. Pioneer kleagles pretended to represent the "National Research Bureau" until their realm was finally chartered by imperial headquarters, and official resistance soon developed, with a state anti-mask law enacted during 1923. Once again, however, Klansmen were their own worst enemies, quarreling incessantly over cash and policy decisions. In 1926, Muskegon's exalted cyclops was arrested for mailing a bomb that killed three persons, and his conviction produced mass resignations in the state. Within three years, the Klan had nearly disappeared, and retired from politics and public demonstrations.

In the late 1960s, organizers for the United Klans of America tried to rekindle interest in Michigan with a brisk recruiting drive. In 1967 congressional investigators found three active klaverns in Genesee and Wayne counties, boasting an estimated 200 members, and Michigan Klansmen were active in the American Independent Party a year later, backing the presidential campaign of Alabama Governor George Wallace. The realm was loosely governed from imperial headquarters in Alabama, until Robert Miles was appointed grand dragon in 1969. Indicted in 1971 for bombing ten Pontiac school buses, Miles resigned from the United Klans a year later and founded the Mountain Church of Jesus Christ, maintaining close affiliations with assorted Klans and neo-Nazi factions. In addition to his "church," two other Klans—the Michigan KKK and the White Knights of the KKK—were reported active on a small scale in the state during the mid-1980s. [2; 10]

MICHIGAN KU KLUX KLAN

In 1983, the Michigan KKK was identified as one of three Klan factions locally active in the state. [2]

MIDWAY CLUB

In 1965 congressional investigators identified this group as a cover for West Columbia, South Carolina, Unit No. 5, United Klans of America. [38]

MIGLIONICO, NINA

A moderate member of the Birmingham, Alabama, city council, Miglionico was targeted by Klansmen, who planted a bomb at her home on April 1, 1965. [*NYT* 1965]

MILAM, DENNIS

In late 1974 and early 1975, Milam was identified as one of three pioneer Klansmen promoting expansion of the United Klans of America in Illinois. An April 1975 clash with fellow Klansman Wilburn Foreman escalated into a verbal war with United Klans national headquarters after Milam described Imperial Wizard Robert Shelton as "stupid" and "out of his mind" for appointing Foreman imperial representative in Illinois. Virtually ostracized by the United Klans leadership, Milam launched one-man recruiting campaigns around Kankakee, Chicago, and Cicero with negligible results. Grudgingly appointed kleagle in August 1975 with direct orders from Shelton to avoid adverse publicity, Milam was banished from the United Klans three months later, following a Danville speech in which he denounced blacks as subhumans and deserving of treatment as animals. [43]

MILES, ROBERT EDWARD

A New York City native and self-described racist, Miles settled in Cohoctah, Michigan, in 1953 and was employed as a traffic safety engineer and manager of a local insurance company. Appointed as grand dragon for the United Klans of America in 1969, he left his insurance job the following year, claiming company harassment because of his KKK connections. In 1970 Miles launched an abortive campaign for the office of Michigan secretary of state. On August 30, 1971, explosions destroyed ten buses scheduled for use in court-ordered school desegregation in Pontiac, Michigan. Ten days later, FBI agents arrested Miles and five other Klansmen on federal conspiracy charges, alleging that the plot was hatched during a July Klan meeting in Lake Odessa, Michigan. These arrests, based on testimony from an informant inside the Michigan Klan, preempted the bombing of a local power station, scheduled as a diversion for a mortar attack on Pontiac's surviving school buses. Miles and four others were indicted by a federal grand jury in October 1971, with all five convicted in May 1973. Miles was also convicted for his part in the tarring and feathering of a Michigan high school principal, earning additional prison time of nine years on both counts. (The state of Michigan, meanwhile, filed bombing charges against the five convicted defendants and three other suspects.)

While his case wound its way through the courts, Miles was briefly appointed to serve as imperial kludd of the United Klans, a post he held until his resignation in 1972. Founding his own racist group in Lansing, the Mountain Church of Jesus Christ, Miles assured the faithful that "I am still, always was, and always will be a Klansman." The "church" was forced to do without its "pastor" until 1979, when Miles was released from prison, but Sunday services featured armed guards and fiery crosses in the best KKK tradition. Free on parole, Miles organized a front group called "Unity Now," promoting Michigan appearances by Klan leaders Robert Shelton, Stephen Black, and Edward Fields. Another "church" affiliate, the "Free Association Forum," has imported speakers such as J.B. Stoner and leaders of the neo-Nazi American Nationalist Party. In the summer of 1982, Miles addressed members of the Aryan Nations in Idaho and appeared at a KKK unity rally near Stone Mountain, Georgia. His persistent affiliation with militant Nazis led to his indictment on federal sedition charges in 1987, but Miles and twelve other defendants were acquitted by jurors in Fort Smith, Arkansas, on April 7, 1988.

In June 1989, Miles announced his retirement from the racist cause to care for his ailing wife. He left the faithful with instructions that "the torches now must be lighted elsewhere. New hands, younger hands, more merciless and totally fanatical holders of the torches will appear. Instead of merely raising the torches as guideposts atop of the walls, the new hands will turn the prairies and fields into beacons of flame and firestorm. My work is done. After us, the true wildfire of the raging barbarian!" [NYT 1971, 1988; From the Mountain, May-June 1989; 2]

MILES, URIEL

A Birmingham, Alabama, member of the United Klans in the 1960s, Miles became a target of domestic harassment under the FBI's COINTELPRO campaign. In 1976, Miles and his wife Laura filed suit against the FBI for disrupting their marriage, citing a series of classified memos released under the new Freedom of Information Act. One federal memo, dated August 25, 1966, identified Miles as a Klansman and a heavy drinker, suspected of adultery and neglecting his family. Another memo, dated September 9, 1966, approved the mailing of an anonymous letter to Miles, with a carbon copy to Imperial Wizard Robert Shelton, which read: "I know what sorry things you have been doing lately and how you have neglected and mistreated your family. You and I are sworn to put an end to just such lowdown and sorry carrying on as you have been doing. I have put up with it as long as I'm going to. I'm letting the imperial wizard know about you. If he don't do something, or you don't straighten up and act right, me and some of your buddies are going to learn you a lesson." FBI headquarters ordered the Birmingham field office to "post the letters in the area of Miles' Klan activity and take all the usual precautions to insure they cannot be associated with the bureau." [84]

MILLER, EMMETT E.

A founder and onetime president of the Citizens' Council in Little Rock, Arkansas, Miller also served as a KKK recruiter in the late 1950s. On July

12, 1960, Miller and his accomplice Robert Parks were arrested by FBI agents while planting a bomb at integrated Philander Smith College in Little Rock. Another accomplice, Hugh Adams, was jailed later the same day. Federal agents had watched Adams deliver dynamite to Miller and Parks five days earlier at a meeting in West Memphis, thereafter making their first arrests under an anti-bombing provision of the new 1960 Civil Rights Act. Two hours after the arrests, bombs damaged a school warehouse and two black-owned homes in Little Rock. Federal charges in the case were dismissed in October 1960, based on the lack of evidence that the explosives had been transported across state boundaries. Three months later, a local grand jury indicted Miller on misdemeanor charges of conspiracy to commit a felony; Adams and Parks were never charged by the state. In May 1961, the U.S. Justice Department requested the dismissal of Miller's charge, refusing to expose informants planted in the local Klan. By May 1962, Miller had joined the National States Rights Party, emerging as the leader of units in Little Rock and West Memphis. [*NYT* 1960; 61]

MILLER, GEORGE

See *Grainger, Ben.*

MILLER, GEORGE THAXTON

A third-grade dropout from Alabama, Miller served nine months in federal prison in the 1920s after being convicted of bootlegging and shooting a deputy sheriff during his arrest. Paroled by 1926, he joined the KKK that year, after an uncle introduced him to the hooded order. Six months later, he was dragged from home and beaten by a gang of fellow Klansmen, charged with tipping off a neighbor who was marked for flogging by the local klavern. In 1927 he was again ambushed by Klansmen while en route to warn a white Butler County couple of an impending raid. Battered and peppered with birdshot during the melee, Miller resigned from the Klan, but later assaulted individual Klansmen on two occasions, "just to let them know to leave me alone." (His sympathy did not extend to blacks. Tried and acquitted on charges of killing one Negro in the 1920s, Miller later admitted slaying "a couple" of blacks during his time with the Klan.) By 1967, Miller owned a service station, supermarket, diner, and a feed and grist mill in Luverne. The Klan demanded that he fire a black employee, Willie McDonald, who had recently been whipped for enrolling his son in a "white" school. Miller rejected the ultimatum, and Klansmen launched a five-year boycott and terror campaign that ultimately cost Miller $95,000, as well as most of his remaining friends in the neighborhood. When the Justice Department filed suit against the Crenshaw County klavern, United Klans of America, for interfering with school desegregation, Miller was called to testify before Judge Frank Johnson, admitting his violent record of shootings and assaults under cross-examination by defense attorneys. [84]

MILLER, GLENN, JR.

A career soldier, Miller was discharged from the army after twenty years for distributing Nazi literature to an undercover intelligence officer. Affiliated with the National Socialist Party of America in the 1970s, he subsequently founded the Carolina Knights of the KKK, based in his home town of Angier, North Carolina. (The Carolina Knights were subsequently renamed the Confederate Knights, and in 1985 became known as the White Party of America.) Members of both groups were linked with the November 1979 murders of five communist demonstrators in Greensboro, but Miller was not charged in that case. A year later, Miller's Klan allegedly received financial contributions from another neo-Nazi group, The Order, banking several thousand dollars stolen from banks in the Pacific Northwest. In April 1980, the National Socialist Party and Miller's Klan celebrated their first annual "Hitlerfest" on land owned by Miller, in Benson, North Carolina, in honor of Adolf Hitler's birthday. In September 1982 Miller attended a Klan unity meeting in Stone Mountain, Georgia, consorting with rival leaders such as Edward Fields, Robert Miles, Stephen Black, and James Venable. Four years later, Miller was convicted of operating a paramilitary training camp in North Carolina, but he was free on bond in April 1987, pending appeal of his conviction, when he and fourteen other racist leaders were indicted on federal charges of sedition after publicly declaring war against the government of the United States. Traced to Ozark, Missouri, on April 30, 1987, Miller was arrested with three other men. In September 1987, Miller pled guilty on charges of mailing threatening letters and stockpiling illegal weapons. His sentence—six months in prison, with three years probation—was affirmed on appeal in February 1989. [NYT 1980, 1987, 1989; 2; 13]

MILLER, HORACE SHERMAN

A disabled veteran of World War I and self-styled dragon of the Aryan Knights of the KKK based in Waco, Texas, Miller compensated for his nonexistent stateside membership by mailing literature to neo-Nazi groups around the world. Linked by mail with Klan activities in Austria, Chile, and the Swedish racist group led by Bjoern Lundahl, Miller also urged a boycott of the Ford Motor Company and the makers of Phillip Morris and Marlboro cigarettes because of their corporate contributions to the National Urban League. [10; 74]

MILLER, JACOB

A mason living near Tuscaloosa, Alabama, during Reconstruction, Miller lost his son to KKK assassins in June 1869. The boy's body was found weeks later beneath a heavy boulder in the North River. [87]

MILLER, SHERWOOD

See *Grainger, Ben.*

MILLER, WALLACE

A police officer and member of the White Knights in Meridian, Mississippi, Miller testified as a prosecution witness at the 1967 trial of Klansmen charged with killing civil rights workers Michael Schwerner, Andrew Goodman, and James Chaney. According to Miller's testimony, he was informed of the murder plot in advance, and took no action to prevent the three men from being killed. [96]

MILLER, WILLIAM B., II

A jeweler from Huntington, West Virginia, Miller was identified in 1976 as the Maryland grand dragon of the Invisible Empire Knights led by Dale Reusch. [84]

MILLER, WILLIAM F.

A resident of Cincinnati, Miller was identified in early 1964 as the founder and president of the National Association for the Advancement of White People. On August 25, 1964, he announced plans to disband the group, charging that it had been "taken over by the Ku Klux Klan." [*NYT* 1964]

MILLER, WILLIAM J.

See *Aaron, Edward.*

MILLIKEN, CARL S.

One of the 1920s Klan's first Colorado recruits, Milliken also served as Colorado secretary of state and second in command of the Denver klavern. He later damaged Klan prestige by resigning in the middle of a clash between Grand Dragon John Locke and imperial headquarters in Atlanta. [10]

MILLIS, MARION W.

As the sheriff of New Hanover County, North Carolina, Millis was subpoenaed to testify before the House Un-American Activities Committee in 1965. Millis admitted joining the United Klans of America, along with six of his deputies, but maintained that he made the move to gather intelligence on Klan activities in his area. Despite the sheriff's assertion, congressional investigators demonstrated that Millis filed no surveillance reports on the Klan during his tenure. He did store Klan literature and dues in his office safe, however, leading the Committee to describe him as an "ideological member" of the United Klans. Despite public exposure of his Klan ties, Millis was reelected as sheriff in 1966. [38]

MILLS, LETTY

A black resident of Reconstruction Walton County, Georgia, Mills and several members of her family were flogged by Klan nightriders. She identified one of the raiders, but local authorities refused to prosecute. [87]

MILLS, RAYMOND DUGUID

Identified as the exalted cyclops of the New Bern, North Carolina, klavern, United Klans of America, Mills was arrested by FBI agents on January 29, 1965, in connection with the bombing of a black-owned funeral home and two cars. Also arrested in the case were Klansmen Edward and Laurie Fillingame. The three pled guilty to the bombing of Oscar Dove's mortuary in June 1965 and received suspended sentences. Grand Dragon J.R. Jones announced the banishment of Mills following his guilty plea, but congressional investigators discovered that Mills was never actually dropped from the United Klans membership rolls. [38]

MILTEER, JOSEPH ADAMS

A native of Quitman, Georgia, Milteer was identified in 1963 as a Klansman and functionary of the National States Rights Party. On November 9, 1963, he met with police informant Willie Somersett in Miami, discussing a forthcoming visit by President John F. Kennedy. Somersett delivered a tape recording of the conversation to federal authorities, including Milteer's discussion of plans to shoot Kennedy "from an office building with a high-powered rifle," using a "patsy" to cover the crime. According to Milteer, "They will pick up somebody within hours afterwards, if anything like that would happen, just to throw the public off." Secret Service agents canceled the Miami visit, and Kennedy moved on to Dallas, Texas, where he was slain in a shooting remarkably similar to Milteer's plan. The day after Kennedy's death, Milteer met with Somersett in a Jacksonville, Florida, railroad depot, telling Somersett, "Everything ran true to form. I guess you thought I was kidding you when I said he would be killed from a window with a high-powered rifle." Asked if he was guessing, Milteer replied, "I don't do any guessing." FBI agents questioned Milteer on November 27, 1963, and recorded his denial of any threats against the president. Despite the Somersett tapes, Milteer's possible involvement in the assassination was not pursued by the FBI or the Warren Commission. [95]

MIMS, CECIL BELTON

In 1967 Mims was identified as a member of the grand council of the Association of South Carolina Klans. [38]

MINER, ROY

A salesman of fraternal regalia and exalted cyclops of the Minneapolis Klan in the 1920s, Miner ran for mayor in 1923. As part of his campaign, the KKK recruited a female jail inmate to testify that she had been intimate with the incumbent mayor, and her published story was distributed around Minneapolis. A grand jury found the document criminally libelous, and Miner was sentenced to jail with four other Klansmen. [10]

MINNESOTA

The Klan's banner year in Minnesota was 1923, marked by Roy Miner's mayoral campaign—and subsequent conviction of criminal libel—in Minneapolis. From that point on, however, membership declined rapidly. By July 1930, only 500 active Klansmen cast their ballots for a new grand dragon selected to rule a consolidated tri-state realm that included Minnesota and the Dakotas. [10]

MINTON, WILL

A former grand klaliff of the Maryland Knights under Tony LaRicci, Minton tried to oust LaRicci as grand dragon in the spring of 1977. The power play was unsuccessful, and LaRicci banished his rival in September 1977. [84]

MINUTE MEN OF THE WEST

An anti-Klan group organized in San Francisco during 1923, the Minute Men apparently limited their activities to publicity and nonviolent protest. [93]

MINUTEMEN (1920s)

Created by ex-Grand Dragon John Locke in Denver following his break with the national Klan in 1925, the Minutemen failed in its effort to recruit disaffected Klansmen nationwide. Klan leaders signed on in Dane and Madison counties, Wisconsin, and recruiters also solicited members in Ulster County, New York, but the group soon disappeared due to a lack of interest. [10]

MINUTEMEN (1959-1973)

A paramilitary anti-communist organization founded by Robert DePugh in Norborne, Missouri, in 1959, the Minutemen stockpiled illegal weapons while openly recruiting members from various KKK and neo-Nazi groups. In October 1966, nineteen members were jailed for conspiracy on the eve of scheduled raids against various "leftist" targets in New York. Two years later, the organization was publicly linked with William Hoff and Paul

Dommer, two associates of the Klan and National States Rights Party who had been convicted of conspiracy and violent acts against blacks. Dennis Mower, the number two Minuteman in California, was a close friend of Imperial Wizard Sam Bowers and an ordained minister in Wesley Swift's Church of Jesus Christ Christian; one of his business cards was found on Klansman Thomas Tarrants after a 1968 shootout with police in Meridian, Mississippi. The political arm of DePugh's private army was the Patriotic Party, created on July 4, 1966; in 1970, the party backed Robert Bagwell, a former Klan and National States Rights Party member, as a candidate for congress in New York. In 1971 police informants reported a membership overlap between the Minutemen and the Universal Klans in Louisiana, including shared facilities for training in guerilla warfare. As one Klan spokesman declared, "We won't need the National Guard if a race riot breaks out around here. We'll wipe them out with the Minutemen." In Pennsylvania Grand Dragon Roy Frankhouser combined membership in the Minutemen and the United Klans of America, stating: "We work independently, but we also complement each other, and the lines of communication are always open between us. We've got the same enemies, the same friends, and the same goals. We're fighting under different leadership, but we're fighting together just the same." (Frankhouser also proudly called the Minutemen a "terrorist organization.") After his release from federal prison in 1973, DePugh announced the formation of a new Patriots' Inter-Organizational Communications Center designed to unite various right-wing groups. As late as 1980 the "new" group was still distributing stickers bearing the old Minutemen logo. [2; 46; 67; 90]

MISSISSIPPI

The Reconstruction KKK invaded Mississippi in the spring of 1868 but remained less active than in other states until the new "radical" constitution was approved in November 1869. Contemporary racist groups, including Heggie's Scouts, the Washington Brothers, and the Knights of the Black Cross, were short-lived, their membership disbanded or absorbed by the Klan as the violence escalated in 1870. In Lauderdale County, two black county supervisors were murdered by Klansmen in separate attacks, and several black women were whipped on accusation of "entertaining" white men. Klan violence was generally concentrated in the eastern border counties of Monroe, Chickasaw, Lowndes, Noxubee, Winston, Kemper, and Lauderdale, where reinforcements from Alabama were readily available. Reconstruction violence climaxed in the spring of 1871 with a concerted campaign against black schools, and nightriding declined rapidly after federal arrests began in June.

In the 1920s, Mississippi Klansmen were less militant than their brethren in neighboring states. The KKK possessed no real political strength above the local precinct level, and even that was rapidly fading by 1924. Ex-Klansman Theodore Bilbo was elected governor in 1928, but his inauguration heralded no revival of the Klan. When the state legislature proposed an anti-mask law that year, the Jackson *Daily News* editorially advised legislators, "Don't kick the corpse."

Following the U.S. Supreme Court's Black Monday ruling on school desegregation in 1954, Mississippi gave birth to the first Citizens' Councils, but the modern KKK was slower to revive. Newsman Ira Harkey reported Klan activity around Pascagoula in September 1954, with members probably linked to one of neighboring Alabama's several Klan factions. The Association of Alabama Knights established several Mississippi klaverns in 1956, which broke from the Alabama Knights to form the Independent Mississippi Klan a year later, but the movement failed to draw dynamic leaders or substantial membership.

Late in 1963, the Louisiana-based Original Knights recruited some 300 Klansmen in Mississippi, but quarrels over money and power led to the expulsion of leaders Douglas Byrd and E.L. McDaniel by December. Byrd led most of the Mississippi Klansmen into his new White Knights two months later, with McDaniel briefly hanging on, simultaneously flirting with the larger United Klans of America. Sam Bowers assumed control of the White Knights in April 1964, molding it into the most violent faction of the 1960s, responsible for at least ten murders and scores of bombings between 1964 and 1968. By the spring of 1964, the United Klans also had a strong foothold in Mississippi, with an estimated 750 members divided among seventy-six klaverns. The White Knights maintained numerical superiority with a peak membership of some 6,000 Klansmen, but state and federal prosecutions thinned the membership to an estimated 400 hard-core fanatics by early 1967. Throughout the troubled 1960s, fickle Mississippi Klansmen continually shifted their allegiance from the White Knights to the United Klans and back again, with affiliated groups including the Americans for Preservation of the White Race, the Knights of the Green Forest, and the militant Silver Dollar Group. The extreme violence of the 1960s seems to have affected Klan activity in the 1970s and 1980s; since the mid-1970s, rumors of Klan revivals in Mississippi have not been substantiated. [10; 38; 84; 87]

MISSISSIPPI CONSTITUTION PARTY

A front group for the White Knights of the KKK organized in 1965, this group was short-lived and generally inactive. [59]

MISSOURI

St. Louis was the 1920s headquarters for Klan recruitment in the Mississippi Valley, and kleagles prospered in Missouri, drawing support from numerous Protestant ministers. (At least one Klan evangelistic service was conducted in the House of Representatives Building in the state capital.) There was reportedly a Klan flogging near Warrensburg in 1921, and the Klan engaged in some inconclusive political maneuvers the following year. One of the Klan's 1922 recruits was future President Harry Truman, but he soon resigned in disgust and made his way to the White House despite Klan opposition. Membership was already declining in 1924, although some units clung to life through the early years of the Great Depression before vanishing. Modern Klan activities in Missouri are apparently limited to sporadic meetings of the New Order Knights, an independent faction created in 1982 or 1983 with fewer than 100 members in 1987. [2; 10]

MISSOURI KNIGHTS OF THE KU KLUX KLAN

A modern independent splinter group, the Missouri Knights created a controversy in neighboring Kansas during February 1988 when a spokesman was invited to speak on a student radio station at the state university campus in Lawrence. University administrators postponed the broadcast after protests; the Knights, meanwhile, announced their own plans to purchase time on cable television. [NYT 1988]

MITCHELL, GERHART

Identified as a New Jersey exalted cyclops in the United Klans of America, Mitchell led his Klansmen in a clash with the Jewish Defense League in Hightstown in April 1971. Mitchell's subsequent rejection of legal aid in the case prompted several of the defendants to resign from the United Klans. [NYT 1971]

MITCHELL, JOHN MAX

In April 1964 Mitchell and Klansman Colbert McGriff founded a violent splinter group known as the Vigilantes, based in Barnesville, Georgia. Members of the group later formed the hard-core nucleus of a Barnesville klavern of the National Knights. [38]

MITCHELL, PARREN J.

A Maryland congressman, Mitchell was the target of a Klan bombing plot in the summer of 1978. Three alleged conspirators—all of whom were members of the Confederation of Independent Orders, Knights of the KKK—were convicted and sentenced to jail or probation on charges related to the attempted bombing of a Maryland synagogue. [2]

MIXON, FRED HOWARD

A white resident of Soperton, Georgia, Mixon was abducted by five Klansmen in July 1950, whipped, and ordered to leave town under threat of death. After recovering from his wounds, Mixon promptly moved to Savannah. [NYT 1950]

MIXON, O.C.

Congressional investigators identified Mixon as the host of an October 1961 bombing seminar sponsored by the United Klans of America and conducted near Macon, Georgia. Instructors William Anderson and William Crowe taught assembled Klansmen how to build time bombs and create intense fires inside a car "faster than anyone can get out." [*NYT* 1965]

MODERN DEMOCRATS

See *Shoemaker, Joseph.*

MODERN MINUTE MEN

See *Indiana.*

MOHR, GORDON ("JACK")

A retired army colonel, Mohr was a paid lecturer for the John Birch Society between 1969 and 1980, when he resigned to join the Citizens Emergency Defense System. Operating from the Louisville, Illinois, headquarters of founder John Harrell, Mohr escalated his verbal and printed attacks on Jews and other minorities, hosting "freedom festivals" that included firearms instruction and guerilla warfare training. Klansmen and Klan allies attending the various "freedom festivals" include William P. Gale, Robert Miles, Kerry Noble, and Jim Ellison. [2]

MONROE HUNTING & FISHING CLUB

In 1965 congressional investigators identified this group as a cover for the Monroe, Louisiana, klavern, United Klans of America. [38]

MONTANA

The 1920s Klan began violently in Montana, with a flogging in Warland and cases of intimidation around the state, but it soon calmed. The realm was officially chartered in September 1923. The Billings klavern took out large newspapers ads in 1923, denying it was anti-Negro, anti-Jew, or anti-Catholic, but the Klan opposed Catholic Senator Thomas Walsh in the 1924 election, solely on the basis of his religion. Although voters finally rejected the Klan campaign of bigotry, the count was close enough to encourage Klan recruiters, and Imperial Wizard Hiram Evans visited Billings after the election. Grand Dragon Lew Terwillinger persuaded the Chamber of Commerce to throw a banquet in Evans' honor, but the fete was not indicative of wide support. Within a year, membership was declining rapidly in the state, and the Klan had disappeared by 1930. [10]

MONTGOMERY, ALABAMA, BUS BOYCOTT

A pivotal campaign in the modern civil rights movement, the Montgomery bus boycott was triggered by the December 1955 arrest of Rosa Parks, a black woman, for her refusal to vacate a "white" seat on a municipal bus. In the preceding twelve months, similar incidents had resulted in the arrests of four other women and two children, with one man shot and killed by police for ignoring a bus driver's order to change seats. Montgomery blacks, who comprised 40 percent of the city's population and 70 percent of its daily bus passengers, responded with a boycott of city buses, demanding immediate desegregation as the price of their continued patronage. Montgomery Mayor W.A. Gayle and Police Commissioner Clyde Sellers responded by publicly joining the Citizens' Council and blacks countered by creating the Montgomery Improvement Association (a forerunner of the Southern Christian Leadership Conference), led by a young Reverend Martin Luther King, Jr. Violence followed, with King's home bombed on January 30, 1956; three days later, a second blast hit property owned by civil rights activist E.D. Nixon. On February 10, Mississippi Senator James Eastland addressed a local rally of the Citizens' Council. Scurrilous pamphlets were distributed asserting the white man's "inalienable" rights to life, liberty, and "the pursuit of dead niggers." Klansmen held a rally on September 8, drawing 1,200 spectators to the local ball park. Fiery crosses preceded another rally, scheduled for November 10, but the mayor denied Klansmen a permit and ordered them out of town. Three days later, the U.S. Supreme Court affirmed a lower court's order requiring desegregation of city buses, and Klansmen launched an illegal forty-car motorcade through Montgomery's black district, cutting the procession short when the residents watched the procession instead of cowering behind drawn blinds. Violence escalated following the Court's ruling, and 1,000 persons turned out for a November 24 Klan rally at a race track outside of town. Nightriders fired a shotgun blast into King's home on December 23, and snipers fired on two buses the day after Christmas. On December 27, Klan leader Asa Carter announced plans for white Minutemen to patrol buses and enforce segregation. The following day, a single bus was fired on twice in the space of one hour, with a black woman wounded in both legs. A fourth bus was damaged by gunfire on December 31, and bombers celebrated the new year by touching off blasts at three black churches and the homes of two activist ministers on January 10, 1957. (The drowning of black deliveryman Willie Edwards on January 23 was considered accidental until a Klansman confessed to the slaying and named alleged accomplices in 1976.) On January 27, a bundle of dynamite failed to explode at King's home, while another bomb damaged a black-owned gas station and the adjacent living quarters. Five Klansmen were arrested the following day, with William Livingston and James York facing capital charges for the January 10 bombing of Reverend Ralph Abernathy's home; other KKK defendants included Henry Alexander and Raymond Britt. Montgomery's police chief publicly blamed the Klan for local bombings on February 10, citing confessions signed by York and Livingston. At their trial, defense attorneys blamed civil rights workers for planting the bombs in a bid for sympathy and publicity. White jurors acquitted both Klansmen despite their confessions, and three others were freed without trial in a general amnesty that also dismissed charges filed against various blacks during the boycott. The last boycott-related violence was recorded on September 5, 1957, when nightriders ambushed a black activist minister, Reverend J.W. Bonner, on his way home from Prattville. Bonner escaped unharmed. [NYT 1955–1957]

MONTICELLO MEN'S CLUB

In 1965 congressional investigators identified this group as a front for the Monticello, Arkansas, klavern, United Klans of America. [38]

MOORE, AARON

See Meridian, Mississippi.

MOORE, CHARLES

The editor of the Florence, South Carolina, Morning News, Moore was assaulted on August 13, 1955, when he asked a group of robed Klansmen why they were burning a cross. A policeman witnessed the incident, but refused to intervene because the cross was being burned on private property. Marking the first public Klan demonstration since the imprisonment of Grand Dragon Tom Hamilton, the incident came eighteen months after Governor James Byrnes announced that the Klan "no longer exists" in South Carolina. [NYT 1955]

MOORE, CHARLIE EDDIE

See Dee, Henry.

MOORE, CLAYTON

A black resident of Greenwood, South Carolina, Moore was flogged by Klansmen on December 5, 1950, for "insulting a white woman." His son shot and killed one of the attackers; thirteen others were identified and pled guilty to conspiracy on February 12, 1951. One defendant got two years probation for turning states evidence; the remaining twelve defendants were sentenced to one-year jail terms. [NYT 1951]

MOORE, HARRY

A black Florida superintendent of public education, NAACP leader, and executive secretary of the Progressive Voters' League, Moore was killed when a bomb exploded in the bedroom of his Mims, Florida, home on

December 25, 1951. (Christmas was also Moore's silver wedding anniversary; his wife Harriet died from her injuries a week after the blast.) Following Moore's murder, Klan leader Bill Hendrix issued the usual denials of KKK involvement, saying: "Moore was a good fellow who was trying to help his race, but he just found out he was going about it wrong." Investigation revealed that floor plans of Moore's home were displayed and discussed at Klan meetings, but no indictments were forthcoming. In 1978, ex-marine Raymond Henry confessed his role in the crime to a Florida civil rights leader. According to Henry's statement, he was on furlough at Ft. Pierce, Florida, shortly before Christmas 1951, when a Wauchula policeman approached him with an offer of $2,000 to help Klansmen build a bomb and plant it in Moore's house. Sheriff Willis McCall promised to provide cars and pick up the bar tab for a victory celebration after the blast. The murder was reportedly accomplished by Henry, his police contact, and six local Klansmen, all under the age of twenty-three. A confederate called at Moore's house on Christmas Day while his wife was visiting relatives, and Moore was lured away on the pretext of helping the stranger locate a relative in the neighborhood. In Moore's absence, the killers picked a lock, crept inside, and placed the bomb under his bed. The explosives were detonated ten minutes after Moore and his wife turned out their lights for the evening. FBI agents took Henry's statement in 1978 but maintained that the statute of limitations had lapsed for prosecution of a federal civil rights charge. Journalist Stetson Kennedy filed suit to obtain files on the case in 1981, under the Freedom of Information Act, but FBI spokesmen refused to divulge any information. Appeals were filed by Kennedy, the NAACP, and ABC News in 1983, but the case remains unresolved. [10; 93]

MOORE, JERE

A newspaper editor in Milledgeville, Georgia, Moore was the target of cross burnings in 1949, after he published editorials attacking the KKK. [25]

MOORE, DR. JOHN A.

A Klansman and state legislator from Reconstruction Alamance County, North Carolina, Moore publicly described the KKK as "a good thing for poor men" that would "protect their families from the darkies." [87]

MOORE, O'NEAL

One of the first black deputies hired in Washington Parish, Louisiana, Moore was patrolling near Bogalusa on June 3, 1965, when he was killed by rifle fire from a passing pickup truck. Another black officer, Creed Rogers, was wounded by a shotgun blast in the same attack. Suspect Ernest McElveen was arrested an hour later, in Tylertown, Mississippi, with two pistols, one of which was described by the local sheriff as recently fired. McElveen waived extradition on June 4 and was jailed in Bogalusa, and promptly retained attorney Ossie Brown, who later defended the Original Knights against federal lawsuits stemming from violence around Bogalusa. On June 6, nightriders fired six shots into the home of a white deputy, Doyle Holliday, assigned to investigate Moore's slaying. Prosecutors ultimately released McElveen for lack of evidence, and his Klan affiliation remains speculative, but congressional investigators publicly identified one of his relatives, D.D. McElveen, as a member of the local Klan's "wrecking crew." [NYT 1965; 38]

MOORE, ROGER

An ex-Confederate officer, Moore introduced the KKK to Wilmington, Virginia, in March 1868. According to his own testimony, he traveled to Raleigh, North Carolina, for his own initiation into the Klan prior to signing up recruits in his home town. [87]

MORATTO, PAUL W.

See *Pacifica Foundation.*

MOREHOUSE HUNT AND GUN CLUB

Identified as a front for Klan activity around Bastrop, Louisiana, this group maintained a rural clubhouse booby-trapped with explosives that injured juvenile trespassers in October 1967. Investigation of the incident exposed this group's KKK connection. [NYT 1967]

MORGAN, JOHN T.

An ex-Confederate general, Morgan was identified as the grand dragon of Reconstruction Alabama. [93]

MORGAN, LAWRENCE GENE

See *Greensboro, North Carolina.*

MORGAN, M. WESLEY

An upholsterer in Atlanta, Georgia, Morgan was one of the original officers in the U.S. Klans when that group was founded in 1955. Listed as imperial klaliff during 1957, he subsequently joined Calvin Craig and other defectors in founding the United Klans of America during 1961. [38; 48]

MORGAN, P.L.

A ranking officer in the Louisiana-based Original Knights of the KKK, Morgan was also elected klaliff for the National Association of Ku Klux Klan in September 1964. [38]

MORLEY, CLARENCE J.

A Klansman and criminal court judge in Denver who deliberately stacked his juries with Klansmen, Morley was elected governor in 1924. He used his inaugural address to call for a ban on undesirable aliens and sacramental wine, afterward appointing Grand Dragon John Locke as his aide-de-camp and a colonel in the National Guard. Morley tried to appoint fifty-two Klansmen as unsalaried auxiliary Prohibition agents, but the state civil service commission blocked the appointments. The Colorado Klan retaliated by trying (unsuccessfully) to abolish the state's civil service system. [10]

MORRIS, HOUSTON P.

Launching his Klan career as an officer of the Louisiana-based Original Knights, Morris lost his bid for internal promotion in the fall of 1964, promptly defecting to begin his own splinter group, christened the Original Ku Klux Klan of America, Inc., chartered in January 1965. Three months later, he presided at a rally in Hamburg, Arkansas, where black-robed Klansmen threatened a police officer and pursued a carload of newsmen who took "unauthorized" photos. (Morris referred to the black-clad group as "our political action committee.") Following that incident, Morris withdrew from the Original KKK, leading several Arkansas and Louisiana klaverns into Robert Shelton's United Klans of America. [NYT 1965; 38]

MORRIS, WILLIAM HUGH

A Birmingham, Alabama, roofing contractor and a Klansman since 1924, Morris emerged as grand wizard of his own Federated Ku Klux Klans in June 1946. By 1949, Morris claimed a total of 30,000 members in sixty-five klaverns, an assertion that rival Lycurgus Spinks conceded as correct—if each of Morris's Klansmen was counted fifteen times. A rash of floggings in the spring of 1949 prompted Alabama Attorney General A.A. Carmichael to denounce the Federated Klans as a group of "bums, hoodlums, and cutthroats." A state anti-mask bill was passed in June, and Morris was jailed the following month for refusing to give a grand jury his membership list. Morris initially claimed that the list had been "stolen," and remained in jail for sixty-seven days before he satisfied the court by "recreating" an abbreviated list from memory. In December 1949, Morris met with Klan leaders Bill Hendrix and Tom Hamilton in Montgomery, Alabama, to create the governing body of a national KKK—excluding Sam Roper's Association of Georgia Klans—but the movement never took hold. On the same day that Hendrix was fined for mailing obscene postcards in Florida, Morris was arraigned in Alabama for mailing "obscene, lewd, lascivious, filthy and indecent" pamphlets. By 1963, he was living in Georgia, newly affiliated with James Venable's National Knights of the KKK. Selected as imperial klaliff and a member of that group's imperial kloncilium in 1965,

Morris was also the alleged target of an assassination plot that year, sponsored by Ohio Klan "empress" Eloise Witte. Police informants have accused Morris of hiring New Orleans gangsters to execute the 1968 assassination of Dr. Martin Luther King, but a 1979 congressional report on the assassination found no evidence to substantiate those claims. [*NYT* 1949; 10; 38; 39]

MORRISON, AARON

A onetime KKK organizer in New Jersey, Morrison was arrested in 1980 for firing rifle shots into the home of a black family in Barnegat Township. Klan associates Karl Hand and James Morrison (Aaron's stepbrother) were charged in the same incident, and all three filed guilty pleas in January 1981. Hand was sentenced to six months in jail, while James Morrison received a fine and a brief jail term on reduced charges. Aaron Morrison withdrew his guilty plea and was convicted at his trial. His three-month jail sentence was suspended in March 1983. [2]

MORRISON, JAMES

See *Morrison, Aaron.*

MORRISROE, RICHARD

See *Daniels, Jonathan.*

MORTON, ERNEST GLENN

A Klansman in Apopka, Florida, Morton was indicted in June 1953 on charges of perjury stemming from his testimony before a federal grand jury probing local violence since 1949. According to FBI agents, Morton confessed knowledge of an August 1949 kidnapping plot aimed at NAACP attorney Franklin Williams, but he later recanted his story before the grand jury. [*NYT* 1953]

MOSELEY, GEORGE VAN HORN

An associate of professional anti-Semite Gerald L.K. Smith, affiliated with the KKK and various U.S. Nazi groups in the 1930s, Moseley was commanding general of the U.S. Third Army until his retirement in 1938 at age sixty-three. Theoretically linked with an abortive plot to assassinate President Franklin Roosevelt and overthrow the U.S. government, Moseley was not among the twenty-eight defendants indicted for sedition in 1942. Still active in fascist politics after World War II, he cooperated with Edward Fields on a Free Emory Burke Committee in Atlanta, Georgia, in 1946. [*NYT* 1946; 8]

MOSS, EMANUEL B.

See *Dahmer, Vernon.*

MOSSY-BACKS

A Unionist, anti-Klan vigilante group, the Mossy-Backs were active in Fayette County, Alabama, for several months in the latter half of 1869, waging guerilla warfare against numerically superior Klan units. The activities of the Mossy-Backs initially encouraged the county sheriff to arrest Klan nightriders, before resistance to the KKK in Fayette County was effectively crushed in 1871. [87]

MOTON, LEROY

See *Liuzzo, Viola.*

MOUNTAIN CHURCH OF JESUS CHRIST

A Klan splinter group based in Cohoctah, Michigan, and led by former Grand Dragon Robert Miles, the Mountain Church is considered a major bulwark of the Christian Identity movement. Federal authorities accused Miles and his church of receiving illicit "donations" during 1980, in the form of money from bank robberies conducted by The Order, but a jury acquitted Miles and twelve other defendants of sedition charges in April 1988. The church's link with various Klan and neo-Nazi groups is undeniable, however, with Miles listed as a guest speaker at gatherings of the Aryan Nations and similar organizations around the country. Conversely, the church has sponsored Michigan speaking engagements by Robert Shelton, Edward Fields, J.B. Stoner, and other well-known Klan activists. In April 1982, members of the fascist Euro-American Alliance participated in meetings at the Cohoctah farm, and Klansman Roy Frankhouser served as pastor of the Mountain Church in Reading, Pennsylvania. In 1989 Miles announced his retirement from active duty to care for his ailing wife, and the full impact of his withdrawal remains to be seen. [2; 26]

MOWER, DENNIS

A member of the paramilitary Minutemen, Mower was tried in Springfield, Missouri, in 1967, on charges of possessing and transporting unlicensed machine guns. He was defended by Bertrand Comparet, an attorney noted for his frequent representation of National States Rights Party members. A friend of White Knights Imperial Wizard Sam Bowers, and an ordained minister of Wesley Swift's anti-Semitic Church of Jesus Christ Christian, by 1971 Mower was recognized as the second-ranking Minuteman in California. One of his business cards, bearing the slogan "The wages of sin is death," was found on Klansman Thomas Tarrants after a 1968 shootout with police in Meridian, Mississippi. Prior to Wesley Swift's death in 1970, Mower cooperated with the minister of hate in organizing front groups such as the Southern California Freedom Councils, the Friends of Rhodesia, the California Anti-Communist League, and the Christian Nationalist Alliance. [90]

MUELLER, L.A.

As grand kleagle of Washington, D.C., in the 1920s, Mueller was the official host for the Klan's massive 1925 parade down Pennsylvania Avenue. Mueller assured a Klan crowd that "it will not rain – God won't let it ," before a cloud burst soaked the audience.[10]

MULDROW, H.L.

An attorney in Starkville, Mississippi, during Reconstruction, Muldrow founded the local KKK. In his professional capacity, he served as defense counsel for Klansmen charged in a series of attacks that drove one carpetbagger, a Methodist minister named McLachlen, from the area in 1871. Repeated postponements eventually scuttled the case, and local Klan supporters showed their appreciation by electing Muldrow to the House of Representatives. [87]

MULLIGAN, E.

The white teacher of a school for blacks in Madison County, Alabama, during Reconstruction, Mulligan was abducted by Klansmen and forced to witness the whipping of his two black assistants. When the floggers announced it was his turn, Mulligan bolted, narrowly escaping. [93]

MUNROE, A.

An attorney in Kinston, North Carolina, during Reconstruction, and a member of Lenoir County's Constitutional Union Guard, Munroe participated in the lynching of five black prisoners in Kinston in January 1869. He was one of twenty-five Union Guard members indicted and held for trial on various charges in August 1869, their prosecution effectively ending terrorism in Lenoir County. [87]

MUNSELL, CHARLES

The son of an Albany, New York, newspaper editor, Munsell tempted fate by enrolling at the University of Alabama, in Tuscaloosa, in 1870. He subsequently fled the state after a threatening note from the Klan was pinned to his door with a dagger. Klan intimidation succeeded in closing the Republican-dominated university that year, but it reopened in 1871 under a less partisan leadership. [87]

MURDER

Violence came easy to Reconstruction Klansmen, most of whom were recently discharged from Confederate service in the Civil War, and the Klan was responsible for a large number of deaths during its five-year guerilla war against Radical Republican rule in the South. Passage of time, inadequate records, and partisan law enforcement have made an accurate tabulation of murders impossible, but well-documented cases include at least 109 victims in Alabama, more than ninety deaths in Arkansas, 235 in Florida, seventy-four in Georgia, at least eighty-six in Kentucky, and over forty deaths in Tennessee. Klansmen in the Carolinas are credited with an average of one murder per month during Reconstruction, but they frequently outdid themselves: thirty-five homicides were recorded in South Carolina during the first six months of 1871. No general tabulation exists for Mississippi, but Kemper County Klansmen reportedly killed thirty-five persons between 1869 and 1871. Texas and Louisiana, meanwhile, were abandoned to virtual anarchy. Of 1,035 murders recorded in Texas between late 1865 and July 1868, nearly half involved black victims, and all but fifty-eight were committed by whites. In Louisiana, 1,081 persons were slain during the 1868 presidential campaign, and no accurate records are available thereafter. While most of the Klan's victims were blacks, carpetbaggers, or active Republicans, at least three Klansmen were executed as police informants, and another in Tennessee was hanged by members of his own den for killing the wrong Negro on a nocturnal raid.

The modern KKK has been relatively nonviolent when compared with its Reconstruction ancestor, but homicide remains a part of Klan activity. Between the 1915 KKK revival and disbandment of the parent organization in 1944, at least eighty victims died in violent incidents related to the Klan; fully one quarter of those were slain in Illinois, where Klansmen fought pitched battles with bootleggers in Williamson County. Ten people died in Texas (including eight men who were reportedly burned at the stake in ceremonial style). The post-war period was relatively quiescent, with only four documented Klan murders between 1946 and 1953, but the activities of KKK associates in law enforcement—including Florida's Sheriff Willis McCall and Atlanta patrolman "Trigger" Nash (credited with the slayings of thirteen blacks)—suggest that the total may be seriously understated.

The black civil rights movement sparked a new wave of violence in the South, with eighty-six race-related murders documented by the Southern Regional Council between 1954 and 1968. At least thirty of those slayings were directly linked to members and associates of the various Klans or the National States Rights Party, and lethal violence continued into the 1970s, with five communist protestors murdered by Klansmen and neo-Nazis in Greensboro, North Carolina, in 1979. Murderous loners such as Fred Cowan and Joseph Franklin, both of whom had histories of membership in several racist groups, accounted for at least another eighteen murders. New militance in the 1980s, culminating in a string of bank robberies, assassination attempts, and a public declaration of war against the "Zionist Occupational Government" in Washington, produced at least a dozen homicides related to the KKK or neo-Nazi movements. With Klan and neo-Nazi membership reduced to small bands of hard-core fanatics at the turn of the decade, continued violence appears to be inevitable. [10; 87; 93]

MURPHY, MATTHEW HOBSON, JR.

Appointed as imperial klonsel for the United Klans of America after James Venable resigned in 1963, Murphy achieved national prominence two years later with his defense of Klan suspects in the Viola Liuzzo murder case. In May 1965 he won a mistrial for triggerman Collie Leroy Wilkins after branding FBI witness Gary Rowe "a traitor and a pimp and an agent of Castro." Looking forward to a retrial, Murphy toured the South with his clients, addressing triumphant United Klans rallies in North Carolina and elsewhere. On August 21, 1965, Murphy was killed in a car accident north of Tuscaloosa, Alabama. His duties were taken over by Birmingham's ex-mayor Arthur Hanes. [NYT 1965]

MURPHY, ROBERT PATRICK

Identified as Delaware's grand dragon in 1965, Murphy was arrested by state police that November in connection with a shooting incident near Hartley. Additional charges were filed in connection with weapons found in Murphy's car at the time of his arrest. [NYT 1965]

MURRAY, ALBERT

The Democratic sheriff of Reconstruction Alamance County, North Carolina, Murray was also a member of the Constitutional Union Guard who enlisted his deputies in the group. Identified as the chief of Union Guard camp #4, Murray displayed remarkable apathy in his pursuit of nightriders. [87]

MURRAY, HAROLD

A North Carolina Klansman, Murray was fired from his job as clerk of Charlotte's city building inspection department when he became grand dragon of the North Carolina Knights. In December 1971, a federal court ruled that the city had violated Murray's constitutional rights by dismissing him on the basis of his Klan membership, and the city was told to settle the issue with Murray's attorneys. [NYT 1971]

MYERS, CECIL WILLIAM

A militant Georgia Klansman and yarn-plucker by trade, Myers was a member of the United Klans of America at the time of his August 1964 arrest on charges of murdering Lieutenant Colonel Lemuel Penn, a black. Suspended by United Klans leaders pending a dismissal if indicted, Myers and other defendants were acquitted by an all-white jury on September 4, 1964. With codefendant Joseph Sims, Myers joined James Venable's National Knights, spearheading activities of the militant Black Shirts within that organization. On October 13, 1965, he was arrested in Crawfordsville, Georgia, for assaulting a black photographer. Five days later, also in Crawfordsville, he was among seven Black Shirts jailed for assaulting a black. On July 8, 1966, Myers and Sims were convicted in federal court on charges of violating Lemuel Penn's civil rights when they took his life. Myers was sentenced to the statutory ten-year maximum, and served his time in Pennsylvania. [*NYT* 1964–1966; 38]

MYERS, H.E.

See *Caldwell, Lester.*

N

NACIREMA, INC.

Organized in Cobb County, Georgia, in 1960, Nacirema—"American" spelled backwards—was an organization comprised of past and present Klansmen disappointed by the lack of violent action in their respective Klans. (Members of the National States Rights Party were also welcome.) The group first drew police attention in Atlanta in 1963, when a local prostitute informed a city detective that her boyfriend had recently asked her to wash his black robe, remarking, "I thought those Klan boys wore white ones." Investigation revealed Nacirema's hard-core membership as a group of sixty racist fanatics linked with 138 bombings in eleven states since the U. S. Supreme Court's Black Monday ruling. The group's literature was stamped with a heading that read, "God the Segregator Knows Best—For You, Me, and All the Rest!" Police managed to infiltrate an October 1961 training session near Macon, Georgia, where twenty-six racists were instructed in the manufacture of bombs and booby traps. Leaders of Nacirema were identified as William Anderson and William Crowe, both members of the United Klans who boasted long police records. Those in attendance at the seminar included United Klans Imperial Wizard Robert Shelton and Georgia Grand Dragon Calvin Craig, along with lesser Klansmen described by police as including several with physical deformities and/or histories of sexual perversion. Two members of Nacirema were seen in Birmingham, Alabama, on September 14, 1963—the day before a church bombing killed four black children—and authorities suggested that the group was planting bombs for money on behalf of other racist groups. As Atlanta Police Captain Everett Little explained, "These fellas were the real hoods of the whole racist movement, guys who would take a contract to blow up a place, just like an underworld hood would take a contract to kill a man." [38; 60]

NAIMASTER, VERNON

Identified in 1965 as Maryland's acting grand dragon for the United Klans of America, Naimaster lost his job as a Baltimore city bus driver after the state NAACP president called for his ouster and the driver's union—two thirds black—threatened a wildcat strike. Naimaster's lawsuit against the NAACP failed in court, but he retained his Klan ties, emerging as Maryland's grand titan in 1966. In May 1966, he addressed a small rally near Baltimore on the subject of blacks, declaring: "Before they take over this country, there's going to be an awful lot of bloodshed. I hope to God this won't happen. But I'm gonna keep fighting. The only thing that is gonna stop me is a bullet." In fact, poor recruiting did the trick, and before year's end, Naimaster had been replaced by activist Tony LaRicci. [*Newsweek,* June 6, 1966; 38; 84]

NALLS, REV. L.A.

A Baptist minister and a 1920s Klansman in Crenshaw County, Alabama, Nalls supervised the flogging of a divorced farmer and the divorcée with two children whom he married. After the beating, Nalls told the woman: "Sister, you were not punished in anger this evening; you were punished in a spirit of kindness and correction, to set your feet aright and to show your children how a good mother should go." Nalls took up a collection from the floggers, giving the woman $3.50 and a jar of Vaseline for her wounds. Nalls later fled to Texas, when Alabama's attorney general—himself a Klansman—launched an investigation of the recent whippings. [10]

NANCE, JAMES

A resident of Reconstruction Georgia, Nance was whipped by Klansmen for reporting the murder of a black man by one of his white neighbors. [93]

NANCE, SILAS

The city marshal during Reconstruction in Jefferson, Texas, Nance doubled as an active member of the Knights of the Rising Sun. He was identified as a member of the party that murdered George Smith in jail on October 4, 1868. [87]

NANSEMOND & SUFFOLK HUNT CLUB

In 1965 congressional investigators identified this group as a cover for a Virginia klavern, United Klans of America, including Klansmen from Holland and Suffolk. [38]

NASH COUNTY CHARTER SERVICE

This front group for Nash County, North Carolina, Unit No. 1, United Klans of America, was publicly identified by the House Un-American Activities Committee in 1966. [38]

NASH, "TRIGGER"

An Atlanta policeman and member of the Association of Georgia Klans following World War II, Nash sometimes addressed gatherings of Nathan Bedford Forrest Klavern No. 1. At one klavern meeting, recorded by informant Stetson Kennedy and delivered to the media in November 1948, Nash, nicknamed for his "itchy trigger finger," was singled out for praise after killing his thirteenth black "in the line of duty." According to Kennedy's notes, Nash "got up and made a talk and said he hoped he wouldn't have the honor of killing all the niggers in the South and he hoped the people would do something about it themselves." [10; 93]

NATHAN, DR. MICHAEL

See *Greensboro, North Carolina.*

NATIONAL ALLIANCE

A Klan-Nazi hybrid based in Washington, D.C., the National Alliance was organized in 1969 as an outgrowth of the recently defunct Youth for Wallace movement. Originally called the National Youth Alliance and conceived as "a fighting movement" determined to "liquidate the enemies of the American people," it was initially managed behind the scenes by Willis Carto, anti-Semitic founder and head of the Liberty Lobby. Mutinous American Nazis broke with Carto a year later, adopting the group's present name, and control temporarily passed to William Pierce, former editor of the *National Socialist World,* and author of *The Turner Diaries.* A persistent source of anti-Semitic and racist literature, the Alliance was denied federal tax exemption in 1979, an IRS judgment upheld on appeal in 1981 and 1983. The final court ruling declared that the National Alliance was not an educational organization, but rather one which "repetitively appeals for action, including violence . . . to injure persons who are members of named racial, religious, or ethnic groups." Members have participated in gatherings hosted by Klansman Robert Miles and his Mountain Church of Jesus Christ in Cohoctah, Michigan. One noteworthy recruit was Robert Matthews, founder of The Order, who died in a 1984 shootout with federal agents. [2; 13]

NATIONAL AMERICAN SOCIALIST RENAISSANCE PARTY

A small neo-fascist movement based in Queens, New York, this group was publicly exposed in January 1960 when three members—perhaps its entire membership—were arrested for plotting to attack Jews in neighboring Fresh Meadows. The defendants included twenty-one-year-old John Wallace, twenty-year-old Hugh Barlow, and sixteen-year-old Richard E. Phelps. On January 15, all three were hit with treason charges carrying a mandatory death penalty, but the counts were later plea bargained down to lesser felonies. [FOF 1960]

NATIONAL ANTI-KLAN NETWORK

Created in 1979 from a conference of thirty concerned groups, including the Anti-Defamation League and NAACP, the Atlanta-based network collected information on Klan activities for public dissemination. Led by coordinator Lyn Wells, the network organized support groups for Klan victims and helped them address their grievances to the proper authorities, and sponsored national and regional conferences on racial violence. In 1980, private attorneys were retained to sue members of the Justice Knights charged with shooting five black women in Chattanooga, Tennessee, after the U.S. Justice Department refused to intervene. In January 1986, the network changed its name to the Center for Democratic Renewal, continuing operation under the leadership of Reverend C.T. Vivian. [93]

NATIONAL ASSOCIATION FOR THE ADVANCEMENT OF WHITE PEOPLE

Rendered irresistible to racists by the success of the NAACP, this title has been applied to at least five separate organizations in as many decades. Dayton, Ohio, spokesman Daniel Kurts openly praised the KKK in a 1951 editorial, declaring: "You Klansmen have a great organization. You have a right to be proud of it." Following the U. S. Supreme Court's Black Monday decision, a small, ineffectual, and short-lived NAAWP was reported active in South Carolina, but no details of its career have survived. By 1959, the group had surfaced in Baltimore, led by anti-Semite Bryant Bowles, who was fond of addressing Klan rallies prior to his conviction and imprisonment on murder charges. Around the same time, a NAAWP chapter in Milford, Delaware, gathered enough support to upset ongoing school desegregation, as the local authorities vacillated under pressure and reversed their decision to comply with the U.S. Supreme Court's ruling. Revived in Cincinnati during 1964 and led by racist agitator William Miller, the new NAAWP disbanded in August. Miller complained that his group had been "taken over" by Klansmen. Most recently, the title was applied to a group organized by ex-Klansman David Duke in July 1980 and based in Louisiana, and is still active at this writing. [2; 45; 93]

NATIONAL ASSOCIATION OF KU KLUX KLAN

Organized by James Venable after his split from the United Klans of America in late 1962 or early 1963, the National Association was a loose-knit collection of local, independent Klans, with Venable serving as chairman and assisted by ranking officers from the other groups in various capacities. Over the next four years member groups included the Association of Arkansas Klans, the Association of Georgia Klans, the Association of South Carolina Klans, the Dixie Klans, Venable's own National Knights, the Original Knights, the U.S. Klans, and the United Florida KKK. Congressional investigators estimated total membership below 1,200 in early 1967, and all affiliated factions except the National Knights were defunct by the early 1970s. [2; 38]

NATIONAL CHRISTIAN CHURCH

A front group for the Florida Klan activities of leader Bill Hendrix reported active in 1960, the "church" used the same Oldsmar, Florida, post office box used by his Knights of the White Camellia. [74]

NATIONAL CHRISTIAN CONSERVATIVE SOCIETY

Based in Cleveland, Ohio, and led by Robert Annable, this group was identified as working closely with Ohio Klansmen in the spring of 1967. [5]

NATIONAL CHRISTIAN DEMOCRATIC PARTY

See *Carlson, Gerald.*

NATIONAL CHRISTIAN KNIGHTS

Organized in North Carolina during 1957, the National Christian Knights ran into trouble with the law in February 1958 when Grand Wizard Lester Caldwell and two other Klansmen were jailed for bombing a school near Charlotte. Two other Klansmen were acquitted in the same case, the arrests resulting from investigative work by Charlotte Police Chief Frank Littlejohn. [*FOF 1958;* 38]

NATIONAL CHRISTIAN PARTY

Identified as a Klan front in Oklahoma, this group was reported active during 1973 and 1974. No details of its activities survive. [26]

NATIONAL COMMITTEE TO FREE AMERICA FROM JEWISH DOMINATION

Founded by George Lincoln Rockwell in Arlington, Virginia, this group was a forerunner of the American Nazi Party. Lengthy correspondence with Wallace Allen, a Georgia member of the National States Rights Party, was discovered during police investigation of an October 1958 synagogue bombing in Atlanta. [*NYT 1958*]

NATIONAL EMANCIPATION OF OUR WHITE SEED

An association of racist/right-wing groups founded by anti-Semite and ex-high school principal Dan Gayman, this group had passed to other hands by 1976, setting up shop in Knoxville under the leadership of Tennessee Klansman Reverend Buddy Tucker. By the late 1980s, its headquarters had shifted to Louisiana. A similar name was briefly adopted by neo-Nazi followers of Robert Matthews in 1983 before they decided to call themselves The Order. [13; 84]

NATIONAL INTELLIGENCE COMMITTEE

A fictitious group created on paper by the FBI in 1967, the Committee was part of an ongoing federal campaign to disrupt the powerful United Klans of America in North Carolina. Under the Committee aegis a letter was mailed to Carolina Klansmen announcing the suspension of Imperial Wizard Robert Shelton and Grand Dragon J.R. Jones on charges of mishandling Klan funds. When Shelton and Jones denied the existence of any such group in the United Klans, FBI informant George Dorsett countered with a story that the Committee was organized in 1964 "by the people to protect them from the leadership" and that its origins were so secret that even Shelton was ignorant of its birth. As revealed in an FBI memo, publicized in 1975: "The so-called supersecret NIC referred to in these articles is a fictitious organization originated and controlled by the Bureau in our continuing program to disrupt the Klan on a nationwide scale. The purpose behind this fictitious committee is to circulate misleading information which will continue to neutralize and disrupt the Klan and discredit Klan leaders." [84]

NATIONAL KNIGHTS OF THE KU KLUX KLAN

Chartered in November 1963 by James Venable, a lifelong Klansman and ex-imperial klonsel for the United Klans of America, the National Knights is a loose-knit organization with little control exercised outside of Georgia by its aging imperial wizard. Embarrassed by the mail-order recruitment of a black Catholic as Idaho's grand titan in 1965, Venable managed to plant klaverns in five states despite adverse publicity. But his membership remained marginal. In 1967 congressional investigators estimated total membership at roughly 100 Klansmen, with another thousand affiliated through other factions, via Venable's National Association of Ku Klux Klan. By the mid-1970s, Venable claimed grand dragons in forty states, but FBI reports acknowledged active membership in only eight of those states. Most of those bailed out in 1975, when Dale Reusch and other defecting dragons led the bulk of Venable's members into the new Invisible Empire Knights. The group survives, holding occasional small rallies in a pasture near Stone Mountain, Georgia, owned by Venable's family, but total membership was well below 100 in 1987. [2; 38; 84]

NATIONAL KOURIER

Published in the 1920s, the *Kourier* was one of several racist periodicals circulated during the national Klan's most prosperous period. [10]

NATIONAL KU KLUX KLAN

The short-lived National Klan was identified as one of seven groups active in South Carolina during the late 1950s following the U.S. Supreme Court's Black Monday ruling on school integration. [6; 38]

NATIONAL ORDER OF KNIGHTS OF THE KU KLUX KLAN, INC.

A post-World War II splinter group, the National Order voluntarily surrendered its Georgia charter in June 1947 in return for the state's dismissal of outstanding felony counts. [*NYT* 1947]

NATIONAL PARTY (CANADA)

A Canadian neo-Nazi organization, in 1980 the National Party joined U.S. Klansmen in Raleigh, North Carolina, at a gathering sponsored by the National Socialist Party of America. [2]

NATIONAL PARTY (U.S.A.)

Created by then-student David Duke at Louisiana State University, the National Party was an outgrowth of Duke's earlier White Youth Alliance. Sporting Nazi-style uniforms, party members were blamed by police for sparking violence at two racially troubled New Orleans high schools during the 1971–1972 school year. In an interview with journalist Patty Sims, Duke described the party as "a Klan that wasn't called a Klan." [84]

NATIONAL RENAISSANCE PARTY

A small neo-Nazi group founded by James Madole and based in New York City, this group actively recruited Klansmen, including Frank Rotella, Dan Burros, and Roy Frankhouser. Madole, Burros, and another member served ten days in jail after brawling with blacks at a New York restaurant in July 1963; a search of their truck revealed weapons, including several knives, an ax, and a crossbow. The party was embarrassed in 1965 when members Dan Burros and Robert Burros (no relation) were identified as being Jewish. In July 1967, a party rally at the Newburgh, New York, courthouse touched off two days of black rioting that led to seventy arrests. A year later, the *NRP Bulletin* headlined the party's formal alliance with delegates from the Minutemen, the National Socialist White People's Party, and Frankhouser's Pennsylvania Klan. Frankhouser and fourteen other members were jailed after a New York City demonstration in April 1971, and the party apparently disbanded in the mid-to-late 1970s. [*NYT* 1971; 75]

NATIONAL SOCIALIST LEAGUE

Founded in 1974 by defecting members of the National Socialist White People's Party, this San Diego-based NSL is unique in restricting its membership to homosexual Nazis. Led by veteran anti-Semite Russell Veh, the group distributes membership applications declaring NSL's "determination to seek sexual, social, and political freedom." [2]

NATIONAL SOCIALIST LIBERATION FRONT

Founded in 1969 by Joseph Tomassi, former West Coast leader of the American Nazi Party, the Front has earned a reputation as one of the United States' most violent neo-Nazi splinter groups. Prior to his 1975 assassination by a member of the rival National Socialist White People's Party, Tomassi claimed that his Front was responsible for the bombing of a California Socialist Workers Party office. After Tomassi's death, Californian David Rust ran the group until his conviction and imprisonment on federal firearms charges. In March 1981, ex-Klansman Karl Hand defected from the National Socialist Party of America to head up the group, which he describes as "a revolutionary movement that has repudiated mass tactics and has instead embraced armed struggle and political terrorism." Despite relocation of its headquarters to Metairie, Louisiana, the Front retains a strong California flavor. A June 1985 phone call claimed credit for acts of anti-Semitic vandalism at the Studio City home of actor Ed Asner. [*NYT* 1985; 2]

NATIONAL SOCIALIST MOVEMENT

Based in Cincinnati, Ohio, this group was led by James Mason until he resigned to lead the Chillicothe chapter of the National Socialist Liberation Front. With Robert Brannen at the helm, the National Socialist Movement established small but active chapters in Detroit, Michigan, and Ashton, Rhode Island, distributing swastika stickers bearing the slogan "Off the Jew-Capitalist Pigs." A typical pamphlet is emblazoned with swastikas and a hand holding a cocked revolver, reading: "The future belongs to the few of us still willing to get our hands dirty. POLITICAL TERROR . . . It's the only thing they understand. Build the National Socialist Revolution through Armed Struggle." Violence erupted at a Detroit city council meeting in June 1980 when local Movement leader William Russell joined Klansman Seth Klipoth in requesting a parade permit; ten persons were arrested after Klansmen and neo-Nazis were assaulted by members of the Detroit Anti-Klan Coalition and the Revolutionary Socialist League. In November 1982, the Movement's McKenzie, Tennessee, unit filed a $3.2 million lawsuit against Carroll County officials, claiming members had been "arrested and railroaded" as part of a conspiracy "to stop all Nazi activity in the state." The arrests had included charges of malicious mischief, following a teenage spree of swastika-daubing, in addition to a charge of parole violation and possession of a sawed-off shotgun by an adult Movement captain. A federal court dismissed the suit in 1983. [*NYT* 1980; 2]

NATIONAL SOCIALIST PARTY OF AMERICA

Founded in Chicago during 1970, this group was the brainchild of Frank Collin, lately expelled from the National Socialist White People's Party upon discovery of his Jewish ancestry. Limited in membership to an average of 100 neo-Nazis over the next decade, the party drew national attention in 1977 and 1978 with its threats to hold rallies in Skokie, a Chicago suburb occupied by Jewish Holocaust survivors and their families. A year of legal wrangling finally permitted the group to hold a "monster rally" in Chicago's Marquette Park. Twenty-five neo-Nazis appeared, outnumbered by hecklers and police. Other publicized marches in the summer of 1978 were held in St. Louis and Florisant, Missouri. Leadership of the group passed to Harold Covington in 1980, after Collin was convicted and sentenced to prison for sexually abusing children. Its national headquarters was shifted to Covington's home state of North Carolina, where Klansmen joined the group for a "Hitlerfest" in April 1980, celebrating his birthday. (Covington deemed the rally "a success" even though only fifty people managed to attend.) Later in 1980, the group began courting Canadian racist groups, including the National Party, the Western Guard, and a Canadian branch of the KKK. Upon Covington's resignation in April 1981, Michael Allen assumed command of the party, and its national headquarters returned to Chicago. A few months later, Nebraska Nazi Gary Lauck announced the group's merger with his own Lincoln-based splinter group, the NSDAP-AO, and his *New Order* tabloid continued to function as the National Socialist Party of America's official newsletter through 1983. Despite intergroup cooperation and the announced merger, however, the party still lacked members. James Burford took over in 1982, and promptly renamed the group the American Nazi Party. [2]

NATIONAL SOCIALIST WHITE PEOPLE'S PARTY

The recognized successor to George Lincoln Rockwell's defunct American Nazi Party, this group was founded by Matthias Koehl soon after Rockwell's 1967 assassination. Struggling into the early 1980s with only 100 hard-core members and several hundred dues-paying "official supporters," the party maintained its headquarters in Arlington, Virginia, while operating small chapters in Illinois, Ohio, Minnesota, Wisconsin, and California. Arlington Place Books, the party's official publishing house, produced most of the racist books authored by ex-Klansman James Warner in the 1970s. In November 1982, Koehl announced a new name for the group, the New Order, and a plan to shift party headquarters to some unspecified point in the Midwest. [2; 84]

NATIONAL SOCIALIST WHITE WORKERS PARTY

Founded in the mid-1970s by San Francisco Nazi Allen Vincent, this group gained national publicity in 1977 by opening its Rudolf Hess Bookstore in a heavily Jewish neighborhood. Local controversy and sporadic Nazi lawsuits continued through the end of the decade, culminating in the April 1980 police revocation of an "incomplete" permit granting group members permission to meet in the San Francisco Civic Center. [*AP*, April 11, 1980; 2]

NATIONAL STATES RIGHTS PARTY

The "ideal" merger of Klan and Nazi philosophies, the National States Rights Party (NSRP) was organized in 1958 in Knoxville, Tennessee, by twenty veterans of the short-lived United White Party. Founder Edward Fields borrowed the party's thunderbolt emblem from the Columbians, Inc., who in turn had lifted it from Hitler's SS. In March 1960, National States Rights Party delegates convened in Dayton, Ohio, and nominated Arkansas Governor Orval Faubus as the party's presidential candidate and ex-Admiral John Crommelin for vice president. Despite Faubus's public repudiation of the party, its slate polled 214,195 votes in November, and a National States Rights Party congressional candidate earned 65,000 votes in Alabama in 1962, more than half of them from Birmingham. A year later, the party launched a South-wide "Fire Your Nigger" campaign, designed to drive blacks out of the South. In September 1963, during Birmingham's race riots, the murder of black youth Virgil Ware was traced to two white teenagers photographed at NSRP headquarters hours before the shooting. One of the three Klansmen linked with a fatal church bombing that sparked the 1963 riots was also an NSRP member; eight more—including Fields, J.B. Stoner, and James Warner—were indicted by a federal grand jury on September 22, 1963, for stoning an integrated, occupied school. (The presiding judge also reported attempts to intimidate the grand jury.) A 1963 California legislative report called the NSRP "more potentially dangerous than any of the American Nazi groups, as it is interested in activities that are far more vigorous and direct." Its national headquarters was moved to Birmingham in 1964, and joint rallies with the KKK were held near Selma that year. In March 1964, NSRP delegates met in Louisville and nominated John Kasper and J.B. Stoner for president and vice president respectively, but the slate won only 6,957 votes nationwide, marking the party's last national effort. Active in racial violence near St. Augustine, Florida, in 1964 and Bogalusa, Louisiana, in 1965, the NSRP was, ironically, denounced by spokesmen for the John Birch Society as a group of communist provocateurs. Willie Brewster, a black man, was shot and killed after a July 1965 rally in Anniston, Alabama, and one rally participant was jailed for the murder. A year later, NSRP members joined Klansmen and American Nazis for a rally in Cambridge, Maryland, but their motorcade was dispersed by police.

Party rallies were banned in Baltimore in the summer of 1966 after speeches by Connie Lynch, the NSRP's "official policy speaker," touched off anti-black riots. In August 1966, an NSRP officer and an Ohio Klan leader were arrested during an unauthorized rally in Chicago; associate George Lincoln Rockwell managed to escape before police arrived. Gunfire erupted at a rally in Berea, Kentucky, in September 1968, with one black man and one NSRP member killed in the exchange; Connie Lynch was one of the thirteen suspects briefly detained for investigation of murder charges. Named as national chairman of the party in 1969, J.B. Stoner campaigned unsuccessfully to become governor of Georgia in 1970. A year later, he opened a new party headquarters in Marietta, after thirteen years of housing "beneath the proper dignity needed to present us in a highly professional light to the public." Defeated once more in his 1972 senate race, Stoner remained as chairman of the party until January 1983, when he resigned to enter prison for his conviction for a 1958 church bombing in Alabama. Reverend R.B. Montgomery was named as his successor, but he was soon replaced by chairman W. Eugene Wilson. The party's flirtation with foreign Nazis has combined with continuing activism at home, and as recently as February 1986 Klansmen and NSRP members were jailed for assaulting a civil rights worker in Cobb County, Georgia. Its size estimated at 1,000 members, the NSRP mails its monthly *Thunderbolt* newsletter to 15,000 subscribers, making it the most widely read periodical in the Invisible Empire. [*NYT* 1963, 1986; 2]

NATIONAL VIGILANCE ASSOCIATION

Chartered in Washington, D.C., around 1923, this group was the most effective anti-Klan group of the 1920s. Local chapters pressed for state anti-mask laws, and a federal law banning mob violence. In the group's first two years of operation, anti-mask laws were passed in Arizona, Idaho, Illinois, Louisiana, Minnesota, New Mexico, North Dakota, and Oklahoma. [93]

NATIONAL WHITE AMERICANS PARTY

A short-lived neo-Nazi group, it joined Klansmen and the Defensive Legion of Registered Americans for a joint rally in Stone Mountain, Georgia, on July 4, 1962. [*NYT* 1962]

NATIONAL WOMEN OF THE KU KLUX KLAN

A 1920s Klan auxiliary organization based in Atlanta, the National Women of the Klan was created to absorb regional female auxiliaries and drain their money into the imperial treasury. Robbie Gill Comer, wife of Arkansas's grand dragon, was appointed to lead the group as a payoff for her husband's support of Hiram Evans in the 1922 coup that ousted Imperial Wizard William Simmons. At the state level, the men's organization received a portion of the women's initiation fees, and ranking Klansmen increased their take by having their wives appointed as kleagles. Mishandling of the women's group produced frequent rebellion in the ranks, as when a national officer barged into a Portland, Oregon, meeting of the Ladies of the Invisible Empire, demanding immediate surrender of their records and merger with the women's group; he was beaten with fists and purses by the outraged "Loties," and was rescued from the screaming mob before they had a chance to cause him further harm. In Pennsylvania, male leaders fought to wrest control of the profitable Klan Haven orphanage from the Klanswomen in charge, and continued meddling produced uprisings around the state. Swindled out of their share of profits from a jointly sponsored boat ride on the Delaware, ignored when they sought punishment for an officer accused of immoral conduct with two Klanswomen, auxiliary units in Philadelphia and Chester, Pennsylvania, resigned en masse. [10]

NATIONAL YOUTH ALLIANCE

See *National Alliance.*

NATIONS, MOODY

See *Federated Ku Klux Klans.*

NATIVE SONS OF THE SOUTH

A Reconstruction white supremacist group with known Klansmen on the rolls, it was reported active in Noxubee and Lowndes counties, Mississippi, during 1871. [87]

NEAL, COY

A member of the United Klans of America, Neal was appointed as kleagle at large for the Louisiana realm in 1967. [38]

NEAL, CRANFORD

See *Lee, Ellis.*

NEALEY, J.D.

See *Flowers, Evergreen.*

NEASON, JOHN

A resident of Reconstruction South Carolina, Neason was whipped by Klansmen for allowing blacks to hold meetings on his property. [93]

NEBRASKA

The 1920s Klan established its first Nebraska den in Omaha, and soon spread statewide, with over 40,000 Nebraskans enrolled as members of the

Invisible Empire. Five thousand Klansmen resided in Lancaster County, the location of the state's capital in Lincoln, but the KKK still faced strong opposition in the state. Omaha's mayor banned Klan parades in the early days of organization, and the Klan's big political drive in 1926 resulted in sweeping defeats for their candidates. Scattered klaverns were still present in 1930, but membership was on the wane, and the Nebraska Klan's marginal influence had already faded.

NELSON, SCOTT MONROE

A resident of Houston, Texas, Nelson was identified as the imperial wizard of the Texas Fiery Knights in 1974, sparking controversy in April when he announced his political support for Jack Terry, a black candidate running for justice of the peace. In November 1974, Nelson spoke for the Klan's radical fringe in withdrawing support from the future political aspirations of Alabama's George Wallace, declaring, "He is not as white as he was in 1968. His mind has deteriorated, I'm sorry to say, along with his body." In January 1975, Nelson adopted "White" as a second middle name, announcing, "I want to include the most beautiful word in the English language in my name." In 1976, Nelson was selected by James Venable's National Knights as their vice presidential candidate, running with Ohio Klansman Dale Reusch. [*NYT* 1974–76]

NEUSE HUNTING CLUB

In 1965 congressional investigators identified this group as the cover for a Kinston, North Carolina, klavern, United Klans of America. [38]

NEUSE RESCUE SERVICE

Another Kinston, North Carolina, front group for the United Klans of America, it served as a cover for Neuse Unit No. 41. [38]

NEVADA

Its sparse population discouraged the 1920s Klan from mounting a major recruitment drive, and the Klan never really took hold in Nevada. Reno's klavern claimed 1,800 members on paper—roughly 15 percent of the adult male population—but only 200 Klansmen turned out for the unit's only public demonstration. In the early 1980s, a new Nevada KKK was identified as a one-man operation, attempting to recruit teenagers by scattering leaflets at local high schools. [2; 10]

NEVADA KU KLUX KLAN

See *Nevada.*

NEVER CLUB

Drawing its name from the classic 1960s segregationist battle cry, this club was identified in 1965 as a front for the United Klans of America located in Smithfield, Virginia. [38]

NEW, FRED K.

An attorney in Columbus, Georgia, and publisher of the racist weekly *Georgia Tribune*, New was also a member of the Association of Georgia Klans. In March 1948, he addressed a rally at Pine Mountain, where Jim Bellows was assaulted by masked Klansmen. Three months later, he joined Alton Pate and "Parson Jack" Johnston to form the Original Southern Klans, Inc. [25]

NEW CHRISTIAN CRUSADE CHURCH

Closely affiliated with the Christian Defense League, this "church" was founded by James K. Warner around 1975, while Warner was serving as Louisiana grand dragon for David Duke's Knights of the KKK. The following spring, Warner left his Klan post to handle church affairs full-time. The congregation's supervisor in Los Angeles was identified as "Reverend" Richard Norton, identified as an associate of J.B. Stoner and the National States Rights Party in Maryland during 1966. [2; 84]

NEW EMPIRE KU KLUX KLAN

In 1983, the New Empire KKK was identified as one of three militant splinter groups active in North Carolina. It had vanished from the scene when a new survey of Klans was completed in 1987. [2]

NEW HAMPSHIRE

The 1920s Klan was strongest around Rochester, on the border with Maine, where Dr. E.W. Gayer established his regional headquarters after replacing Eugene Farnsworth as grand dragon of the tri-state realm. Even so, most of the Klan's northeastern action was centered in neighboring Maine, and New Hampshire was generally unreceptive to the KKK.

NEW HANOVER COUNTY IMPROVEMENT ASSOCIATION, INC.

In 1965 congressional investigators identified this group as a cover for the Wilmington, North Carolina, klavern, United Klans of America. [38]

NEW JERSEY

The modern Klan invaded New Jersey from Pennsylvania and New York in early 1921, establishing its first strongholds in Passaic, Bergen, Essex, Union, and Morris counties, with outposts on the Pennsylvania border near

Trenton and Camden. Grand Dragon Arthur Bell hailed from Bloomfield, but his greatest concentration of members lay further south, in Monmouth County. Early opposition was voiced by merchants in Asbury Park after Klansmen tried to block the tide of Catholic and Jewish tourists from New York, but Protestant ministers staunchly supported the KKK throughout the state. In Zarephath, members of the Pillar of Fire Church signed on en masse, and in May 1923 they came close to becoming Klan martyrs when they were besieged and stoned by anti-Klansmen at Bound Brook. Three months later, Perth Amboy was rocked by a series of anti-Klan riots, but adversity only made New Jersey Klansmen more tenacious. A divisive element in state politics, the Klan failed to gain any victories, and membership was waning by 1927, when Imperial Wizard Hiram Evans paid a visit to inspire the faithful. One of thirteen states with significant Klan numbers in the 1930s, New Jersey was embarrassed when Klansmen held joint rallies with the German-American Bund in 1940. The realm folded when a federal tax lien closed imperial headquarters in 1944.

Two years later, with new stirrings in the South, the New Jersey Klan attempted a comeback, but the state attorney general moved to lift its charter in July, and the state supreme court filed an official judgment of ouster in October 1946. Twenty years elapsed before the United Klans of America attempted to begin another Klan in New Jersey, under Grand Dragon Frank Rotella, but a scheduled rally was canceled in May 1966 when South Carolina's Robert Scoggin failed to appear for the keynote address. Rotella announced his resignation from the United Klans in June, moving on to head his own Nazi group, and by 1967 congressional investigators described New Jersey Klan membership as "negligible," with no active klaverns identified. Sporadic stirrings were reported through the 1980s, with a local White Knights of the KKK identified in 1983 and the tiny Invisible Empire Knights in 1987, but membership remained marginal, overlapping with various neo-Nazi splinter groups. [2;10]

NEW MEXICO

The 1920s Klan endured a lackluster existence in New Mexico, beset by stern opposition. In 1924, the state Democratic convention adopted a resolution stating that the KKK did violence to the spirit of U.S. institutions, and Republicans were hardly more receptive to the hooded knights. By 1931, scattered klaverns barely clung to life in a state that had at that time a Jewish governor and where 80 percent of the population consisted of Hispanic Catholics. [10]

NEW ORDER

See *National Socialist White People's Party*.

NEW ORDER, KNIGHTS OF THE KU KLUX KLAN

Organized in Georgia during 1980 and led by veteran racist Edward Fields, the New Order Knights were active in Polk County in November 1980, harassing Hispanic residents. In September 1982, and again in 1983, Fields and the New Order Knights joined leaders of seven other Klans in unity conferences held in Stone Mountain, Georgia. No trace of the group remained when a survey of Klans was completed in 1987. [2]

NEW ORDER OF KNIGHTS OF THE KU KLUX KLAN

A St. Louis, Missouri, splinter group, organized and led by Reverend James L. Betts in 1976, the New Order reaped local publicity in March 1976, when police rejected Betts's offer of forty Klansmen to help patrol city streets against crime. A group of Missouri-based New Order Knights have been reported active as recently as 1987, with fewer than 100 members on the rolls. [NYT 1976, 1987]

NEW ORLEANS KU KLUX KLAN

A local splinter group active in 1971 and 1972, the New Orleans KKK was led by Imperial Wizard H. Boswell Thompson. [NYT 1972]

NEW RIVER FISHING CLUB

In 1966 this club was identified by congressional investigators as a front for a Beulaville, North Carolina, klavern, United Klans of America. [38]

NEW RIVER RIFLE CLUB

In 1965 the House Un-American Activities Committee identified this group as a cover for the New River, Louisiana, klavern, Original Knights of the Ku Klux Klan. [38]

NEW SOUTH FREEDOM FIGHTERS

In March 1987, this group sent letters to newsmen in San Antonio, Texas, claiming credit for the alleged murder of two illegal aliens near Ozona, which were designed to protest amnesty provisions of a new federal immigration act. No bodies were recovered at the scene, and the group has not been heard from since. [NYT 1987]

NEW YORK

New York City is the recognized capital of everything the modern KKK detests, but kleagles did their best to purify New York in the 1920s, creating a furor in the fall of 1922 by distributing Klan literature at Manhattan's largest Baptist church. In Brooklyn, Klansmen gathered in the city traffic court after hours, with Exalted Cyclops Wilson Bush presiding from the judge's bench, and the district attorney affirmed their right to peaceably assemble on city property. As the KKK began to spread, the state passed a bill outlawing masks and secret membership, along with Klan use of the mails or participation in politics, and the law's constitutionality was affirmed by the U.S. Supreme Court in 1928. In the meantime, Klansmen tried to incorporate themselves as a fraternity, Alpha Pi Sigma, but their ruse was quickly uncovered. Klan marches sparked fighting in Elmira in the summer of 1923, but recruitment continued, and by early 1924, one in every seven residents of Suffolk County was a Klansman. They patrolled Long Island highways, raided bootleg stills, drove a Jewish merchant out of Hicksville, and burned crosses at Columbia University when a black student enrolled. Support was slipping by 1926, and a year later, two persons died in Manhattan anti-Klan riots. Still, the Invisible Empire remained in New York through the 1930s, with twelve active klaverns in New York City. When imperial headquarters disbanded in 1944, the local membership consolidated into four dens—Brooklyn, Queens, the Bronx, and Staten Island—going underground.

Klansmen were quick to surface after World War II, but official resistance continued, and the Klan's state charter was revoked in July 1946, with a sentence of six months in jail and a $10,000 fine for espousing racist beliefs. The state attorney general reported that an informer inside the New York Klan had obtained a list of 1,100 members and information linking local chapters to the Association of Georgia Klans. New York officers were identified as Wilson Bush, a political leader, publicist, and ghost writer; James Wagner, Brooklyn kligrapp of the Richmond Hill unit; and Clarence Herlth, also of Richmond Hill, a grand titan and the link to the Georgia-based national Klan. Horace Demarest, doubling as a Klan officer and the Republican leader in Queens, was stripped of his job as deputy state motor vehicle commissioner when his Klan ties were discovered, and threats of further prosecution effectively dispersed the New York Klan by year's end.

Two decades later, ex-Nazi Dan Burros was appointed as New York king kleagle for the United Klans of America, presiding over two Manhattan klaverns before his suicide in October 1965. Burros was replaced by another Nazi stalwart, William Hoff, under the supervision of Pennsylvania Grand Dragon Roy Frankhouser. In 1967 congressional investigators found one klavern struggling to survive in Queens, with an estimated twenty-five hard-core members. A new splinter group, the Independent Northern Klans, was organized in Pine Bush in the early 1970s, with Grand Dragon Earl Schoonmaker and most of his followers employed as state prison guards, but the movement had disbanded by the decade's end. [NYT 1946; 10; 84]

NEWBERRY, JAMES DOUGLAS

Identified as Georgia's grand klabee for the United Klans of America, Newberry was accused by congressional investigators of withdrawing money from the United Klans' Atlanta bank account and using it for his personal expenses. In 1968 he was elected to a seat on Atlanta's model cities program with Grand Dragon Calvin Craig. Both Klansmen agreed that race was not an issue in their election, stressing a desire for racial harmony and cooperation. [NYT 1968; 38]

NEWEY, GEORGE

See *England.*

NEWPORT FELLOWSHIP CLUB

In 1965 congressional investigators identified this group as a cover for the Morehead City, North Carolina, klavern, United Klans of America. [38]

NEWTON, YOUNGER

See *Heritage Enterprises, Inc.*

NIGHT RIDERS

An elite, black-robed group of Klansmen recruited for violent missions around Bellaire, Ohio, in the 1920s, this group was organized by Dr. William J. Shepard. The uniforms were reportedly an object of envy among other Klansmen at the KKK's Buckeye Lake Konklave in 1925. [10]

NIGHT RUN

A slang designation employed by some Klansmen, particularly members of the defunct Invisible Empire Knights under Dale Reusch, this term describes a shorter-than-average black robe, worn for concealment and easy running during nocturnal raids. [84]

NIGHTHAWK

In the Reconstruction Klan, two nighthawks were selected to serve as assistants for the grand cyclops of each den. In most modern Klans, the title denotes a courier at various levels, with further designation dependent on rank. Thus, a nighthawk serves at the klavern level, a great nighthawk for the province, a grand nighthawk at the realm level, and an imperial nighthawk operates from national headquarters. [43; 93]

NIGUS, DAVID

The sheriff of Brown County, Kansas, Nigus was found dead in Hiawatha in September 1983. Authorities described his death as accidental, but a member of the Posse Comitatus referred to the case as a right-wing assassination. [NYT 1983]

NIVENS, LAWRENCE

See *Johnson, Woodrow.*

NIX, DEAVOURS

A ranking member of Mississippi's White Knights under Sam Bowers, Nix was selected to lead that group's Klan Bureau of Investigation in June 1965. Nine months later he was arrested in connection with the nightrider slaying of Vernon Dahmer, and a cache of weapons was seized at his home by arresting officers. Indicted on federal civil rights charges in the Dahmer case in February 1967, Nix was jailed again in November on charges of helping to kidnap prosecution witness Jack Watkins. A mistrial was declared at his civil rights trial in May 1969. In 1978, congressional investigators probed alleged links between Nix, the White Knights, and the 1968 assassination of Dr. Martin Luther King, but no evidence was found to substantiate the charge. [*NYT* 1967; 38; 39]

NIX, SYBIL

A resident of Laurel, Mississippi, and the wife of Klansman Deavours Nix, Sybil served as secretary-treasurer for a Klan front group, Americans for Preservation of the White Race. In 1968 she also served as Mississippi treasurer for the American Independent Party during the George Wallace presidential campaign. [17]

NOBLE, CHARLES R.

See *Dahmer, Vernon.*

NODINE, JOHN

An elderly veteran of the War of 1812, residing in Rutherford County, North Carolina, Nodine was whipped by Klansmen for voting the Republican ticket in 1871. [87]

NORMAN, FRANK

A union organizer and member of the International Labor Defense Committee in Lakeland, Florida, Norman was abducted by Klansmen in April 1934 and was never seen again. He is presumed to be a murder victim, but the case remains officially unsolved. [93].

NORRIS, BROCK

See *Johnson, Woodrow.*

NORRIS, JOHN C.

The Republican sheriff of Warren County, Georgia, during Reconstruction, Norris requested troops for use against the local KKK in 1868. Ambushed by Klansmen in December 1868, he was wounded several times, but survived to identify three of the gunmen as Klansmen James Cody and his two brothers. Partially crippled by his wounds, Norris refused to step down as sheriff, but he took the advice of friends and declined to prosecute his assailants. In the spring of 1869, he visited Atlanta with a new request for troops; local Conservatives took advantage of his absence to declare the sheriff's office vacant and appointed a Klansman in his place. With a special commission signed by the governor and a U.S. general affirming his position, Norris returned from Atlanta with troops to make the ruling stick. Driven out of the county by Klan threats that fall, Norris returned in January 1870 with a new federal commission as sheriff. A month later, he foolishly accepted a $5,000 I.O.U. in return for his promise to limit the arrests of Klansmen, and he received payments totaling $3,250 before he was arrested on bribery charges. Removed from office by the army and returned to Atlanta in irons pending military trial, Norris eventually won dismissal of the case, but Klansmen struck back with a new warrant, and Norris was jailed on charges of false arrest. He remained in Atlanta, finally spared from extradition and certain conviction by a gubernatorial pardon. [87]

NORTH ALABAMA CITIZENS' COUNCIL

Organized by Asa Carter in October 1955, this radical splinter group was denounced by competing councils for excluding Jews. Three leading officers stepped down in February 1956 after Carter demanded the resignation of the state university's president for permitting the brief enrollment of black coed Autherine Lucy. Several members of the Council attacked singer Nat "King" Cole during a Birmingham performance in April 1956, and Carter promptly organized a White People's Defense Fund to cover the attackers' legal expenses. Within a year, Council membership and goals were interchangeable with those of Carter's Original KKK of the Confederacy. [61]

NORTH AMERICAN ALLIANCE FOR WHITE PEOPLE

An Ohio white supremacist group reported active in the spring of 1967, it was known to cooperate with Ohio Klansmen. [NYT 1967]

NORTH CAROLINA

A haven for the KKK since Reconstruction, North Carolina was first invaded between December 1867 and March 1868. At the time, three overlapping paramilitary groups were active in the state, including the White Brotherhood, the Constitutional Union Guard, and the Invisible Empire—generally understood to be a formal designation for the state's Klan, with ex-governor Zebulon Vance serving as grand dragon. Republican victories in the fall 1868 elections produced a sharp upswing in nightriding violence, with members of the Constitutional Union Guard dominating activities in Jones, Duplin, and Lenoir counties. Governor William Holden's policy of conciliation and appeasement generally defused Union Guard violence in late 1869 and early 1870, but Klan nightriding escalated in other parts of the state, particularly in Alamance County, where membership in the KKK and White Brotherhood were virtually identical. In the face of mounting violence, Republican newspapers called for a stern vigilante response, and scattered groups of blacks retaliated for nocturnal raids with strategic acts of arson, torching the barns of known or suspected Klansmen. By March 1870, Governor Holden was prepared to declare a state of armed insurrection in Alamance County, and the subsequent expansion of martial law provoked a Conservative revolt, earning Holden the dubious distinction as the first governor in the United States to be impeached and removed from office, in March 1871. Klan violence continued during and after Holden's trial before the state legislature, reaching its peak in Cleveland, Gaston, Lincoln, and Rutherford counties, adjacent to the most chaotic regions of South Carolina. Interaction between the two state Klans was commonplace, with hit teams trading off to frustrate witnesses, finally requiring military enforcement of the federal Ku Klux Acts, between October 1871 and February 1872, to suppress Klan terrorism in the state.

The modern Klan spread quietly and quickly through the state, with Superior Court Judge Henry Grady named as grand dragon when the realm won its charter in 1922. A year later, the North Carolina KKK boasted an estimated 25,000 members, and a proposed anti-mask law was defeated in the state legislature. Sporadic violence and vigilante activity was reported throughout the state—Lumberton's police chief led the mob that flogged two white women on charges of abusing their husbands—but Grady generally managed to restrain his Klansmen, channeling their energies into rallies and local politics. In 1927, imperial headquarters decided that Grady was exercising too much restraint over the rank and file; presented with a package of proposed anti-black and anti-Catholic legislation in January 1927, the grand dragon refused to play along, denouncing the bills as "silly, unseemly, and unconstitutional." Imperial Wizard Hiram Evans responded by banishing Grady, but the move backfired, as sixty-six of the state's eighty-six klaverns disbanded in protest. Scattered units remained during the Great Depression, but general disbandment ended the North Carolina Klan in 1944.

In 1949, wholesale grocer Thomas Hamilton defected from the Association of Georgia Klans to create the Association of Carolina Klans, launching a reign of terror that culminated in mass state and federal arrests in 1952. In February 1952, Hamilton and eleven of his followers—including the police chief of Tabor City, North Carolina, and the ex-police chief of Fair Bluff—were indicted on federal kidnapping charges for dragging two South Carolina victims across the state line for a flogging. Ten of the eleven were convicted and sentenced to prison, but Hamilton's problems continued. In July 1952, state authorities rounded up seventy-one Klansmen for a trial on 180 felony charges arising from twelve flogging incidents. Hamilton was among the sixty-three Klansmen convicted, and drew another four-year prison term.

The U.S. Supreme Court's Black Monday ruling on school segregation helped resuscitate the Klan in 1954, and North Carolina witnessed a proliferation of competing splinter groups by 1960. The Georgia-based U.S. Klans was dominant in terms of membership, but local factions tried to compensate with militant reactions to demands for equal rights. Brothers Arthur and Joseph Bryant were jailed for illegal possession of dynamite in 1955, before their fledgling Klan could gather more than a token following. In 1956, U.S. Klans defector James "Catfish" Cole founded his own North Carolina Knights, facing national humiliation in 1958 when his Klansmen were routed by armed Lumbee Indians in Robeson County. The National Christian Knights were organized in 1957 and disbanded in February 1958 when three members were convicted of bombing a school in Charlotte. Meanwhile, the black-shirted Chessmen were active in the Richfield area, harassing employers who dared to hire blacks.

Greensboro, North Carolina, was the birthplace of the black sit-in movement in February 1960, but North Carolina Klansmen lagged behind their comrades in other Southern states, with the dominant U.S. Klans crippled by the death of Imperial Wizard Eldon Edwards in August 1960. The fledgling United Klans of America began in consolidating local dens in 1962 and 1963, with James R. Jones appointed as grand dragon in 1964. Within a year, successful recruiting drives gave North Carolina the Klan's highest state membership, with an estimated 7,500 members organized in 192 active klaverns—more than double the number in any other state. (James Venable's National Knights ran a distant second, with one small klavern in the town of Wilson.) Sporadic violence was reported during 1965, with Exalted Cyclops Raymond Mills and two other Klansmen arrested for bombings around New Bern in January 1965, and in August Klan-inspired riots in Plymouth led to Governor Dan Moore dispatching state troopers to restore order.

The late 1960s were a time of dissension in the North Carolina Klan. In 1967, United Klans defector George Dorsett joined Cole to organize a new Confederate Knights of the KKK—with secret backing from the FBI— but their effort was short-lived. J.R. Jones was sentenced to a year in prison for contempt of Congress in 1969, and the choice of Joseph Bryant as acting grand dragon in his absence suggested that the quality of talent available to leaders of the United Klans was lacking. A July 1969 shootout with blacks in Swan Quarter landed Bryant and sixteen other Klansmen in jail on charges of inciting a riot, and two months later Bryant abandoned the United Klans entirely, leading most of his remaining followers into a new splinter group, the North Carolina Knights. Unable to control the rank and file, Bryant was soon banished in favor of Virgil Griffin. By 1978, Griffin was negotiating with leaders of the National Socialist Party of America to create a United Racist Front in North Carolina, and members of both groups were charged with the November 1979 murders of five Communist Workers Party members in Greensboro.

North Carolina Klansmen remained militant and divided in the 1980s, with active groups including the White Knights of Liberty, the Federated Knights of the KKK, and the New Empire KKK. Succeeding Virgil Griffin as head of the North Carolina Knights, Glenn Miller emerged as North Carolina's preeminent Klansman, and around 1980 he changed his group's name to the more expansive Carolina Knights, openly affiliating with the Aryan Nations and other neo-Nazi groups around the country. As Miller began accumulating federal indictments by 1985, his Klan sought cover behind a bewildering rapid-fire series of name changes, emerging at various times as the Confederate Knights, the Southern National Front, and the White Patriot Party. The United Klans maintained a minimal following through the end of the decade, and another competing faction, the Christian Knights, were estimated to have fewer than 100 active members in 1987. [2; 10; 38; 84; 87]

NORTH CAROLINA KNIGHTS OF THE KU KLUX KLAN (1956–1958)

A splinter movement of the U.S. Klans, this faction was organized by James "Catfish" Cole, reaping its main—and final—publicity from a disastrous, and unsuccessful, confrontation with Lumbee Indians in Robeson County in 1958. [NYT 1957–1958; 38]

NORTH CAROLINA KNIGHTS OF KU KLUX KLAN (1969–1980)

Organized by Joseph Bryant and Edward Dawson in September 1969, the North Carolina Knights was born from a quarrel between Bryant—then acting grand dragon for the United Klans of America—and acting Imperial Wizard Melvin Sexton. On September 16, Bryant led his followers in a public demonstration, nailing their United Klans membership cards to a cross and burning them. Bryant was soon deposed in favor of militant Virgil Griffin, who led the North Carolina Knights into a working alliance with the National Socialist Party of America, to create a so-called United Racist Front. Members of both groups were charged (and ultimately acquitted) in the 1979 murders of five communist demonstrators in Greensboro. Griffin's successor, Glenn Miller, subsequently sought to expand his operation by renaming his group the Carolina Knights of the KKK. [NYT 1969; 10; 84]

NORTH DAKOTA

Klansmen in North Dakota avoided violence in the 1920s, but reports of nightriding and murder in other realms led to the passage of a 1923 anti-mask law covering any citizen over the age of fifteen. As the state senator from Richland County declared while debating the bill, "We don't want conditions in North Dakota to become such that a man must carry a pistol to be safe." A two-hour speech by the state's ranking Klansman, Reverend Halsey Ambrose, backfired, producing a heavy vote in favor of the law. Still, the Invisible Empire managed to survive and took an active role in local politics. Klan candidates did well across the state in 1924, and two years later made a clean sweep of municipal offices in Ambrose's home base of Grand Forks. Despite such victories, however, Klansmen found no enemies of any consequence among North Dakota's overwhelmingly white and Protestant population. Its membership waned during the Great Depression, vanishing entirely with national disbandment in 1944. The 1980s witnessed a small-scale resurgence of far-right activity, spearheaded by the Posse Comitatus, and violence erupted in February 1983 when Posse member Gordon Kahl murdered two U.S. marshals near Medina. Despite the Posse's close affiliation with various KKK and neo-Nazi groups, its localized appearance in North Dakota in no way signals a revival of the Klan in North Dakota. [2; 10]

NORTH FLORIDA KLAN

See *Fallaw, Eunice.*

NORTHEAST GUN CLUB

In 1965 congressional investigators identified this group as a cover for the Monroe, Louisiana, klavern, Original Knights of the Ku Klux Klan. [38]

NORTHERN AND SOUTHERN KNIGHTS OF THE KU KLUX KLAN (1949–1952)

An outgrowth of the disintegrating Original Southern Klans, this faction was created by Bill Hendrix in June 1949 at a Florida rally that drew 1,000 Klansmen, including delegations from Alabama and Georgia. The group was based in Jacksonville, where an August 1949 klonvocation saw Hendrix installed as the Klan's national adjutant, serving under an anonymous "Permanent Emperor Samuel II," soon replaced by an imperial wizard known only as "Number 4-006800." (There seems to be little doubt now that both of these superior officers were figments of Hendrix's active imagination.) The group's unofficial paper, *The Southern Gospel*, was published by A.C. Shuler in River Junction, Florida. [25]

NORTHERN AND SOUTHERN KNIGHTS OF THE KU KLUX KLAN (1977–?)

Created and led by William Chaney, in affiliation with his Confederation of Independent Orders, this group was described as a loose alliance of independent Klans in twenty-six states, with Northern and Southern subdivisions. Each affiliated Klan paid $100 a year, regardless of membership, and local groups were guaranteed complete autonomy, without interference from national headquarters. The resultant combination was too relaxed to survive, and no trace of the organization remained when a national survey of Klans was completed in 1983. [84]

NORTHERN INDEPENDENT KU KLUX KLAN OF NEW YORK

An independent splinter group led by Earl Schoonmaker and his wife Janice, based in Pine Bush, New York, the Northern Independent Klan reaped national publicity when Schoonmaker was fired from his job as a state prison guard in 1975. Journalists lost interest as his appeal made its way through the courts, and no record of the group's dissolution survives, but it vanished sometime prior to a national survey of Klans conducted in 1983. [NYT 1975; 2]

NORTON, BOBBY JOE

A Tennessee member of the Confederate Vigilantes, Knights of the KKK, Norton was convicted and sentenced to five years in prison for his role in the May 1981 attempted bombing of a Nashville synagogue. [2]

NORTON, RICHARD

A spokesman for the National States Rights Party, Norton was banned from Baltimore, along with agitators Connie Lynch and Joseph Carroll, after their rallies sparked white rioting against blacks in August 1966. In November 1966, Norton was sentenced after his conviction for inciting a riot, disorderly conduct, conspiracy to riot, and violation of city park rules. A decade later, relocated in Los Angeles, he emerged as a local organizer for James Warner's New Christian Crusade Church. [NYT 1966; 84]

NOSSER, JOHN

As the politically moderate mayor of Natchez, Mississippi, in the 1960s, Nosser became a target of Klan violence after his refusal to adopt a strict segregationist stance. A bomb blast damaged his front lawn on September 25, 1964, and arsonists leveled his supermarket on New Year's Eve 1965. Ironically, a 1965 congressional investigation named both of Nosser's sons as Klansmen. [NYT 1964–1965; 38]

NOTTOWAY CLUB

In 1965 congressional investigators identified this group as a cover for the Emporia, Virginia, klavern, United Klans of America. [38]

NUSSBAUM, PERRY E.

A Jackson, Mississippi, rabbi, Nussbaum was targeted for violence by the White Knights of the KKK in 1967. His synagogue was bombed in September, and nightriders bombed his home on November 21. Suspects in the first bombing included Joe Denver Hawkins, his son, Joe Daniel Hawkins, and Klansman J.L. Harper, but no indictments were returned and the case remains officially unsolved. [NYT 1967; 96]

OAKVILLE OUTDOOR SPORTS CLUB

In 1965 congressional investigators identified this group as a cover for a Chesapeake, Virginia, klavern, United Klans of America. [38]

OBERHOLTZER, MADGE

A young schoolteacher in Hagerstown, Indiana, Oberholtzer met Grand Dragon D.C. Stephenson at the January 1925 inaugural banquet honoring Governor Ed Jackson. While living with her parents, a few blocks from Stephenson's mansion in Irvington, she agreed to several dates but firmly rebuffed the Klansman's push for a more intimate relationship. On the night of March 15, 1925, Stephenson called Madge at home to arrange an urgent meeting, dispatching Klan bodyguard and ex-policeman Earl Gentry to escort her for the short walk over. Madge did not return until the afternoon of March 17, carried into the house by a stranger who said she had been injured in "an auto accident." A physician found bruises and bite marks all over her body, with her breasts lacerated, and chunks of flesh missing from her genitals. According to Madge, Stephenson and Gentry had plied her with liquor at Stephenson's home, after which the grand dragon and Gentry forced her to board a train for Chicago. On board, in their private compartment, Stephenson tore off her clothes, raped her, and gnawed on her body in a drunken frenzy. Rising early on March 16, as the train stopped in Hammond, Indiana, the party checked into a local hotel. There, Madge tried to shoot herself with Stephenson's gun, but he disarmed her, ordering Gentry to clean her wounds. After breakfast, Stephenson's chauffeur took

Madge shopping in Hammond, where she secretly purchased deadly mercuric chloride tablets instead of makeup. Back at the hotel, she gulped the poison and soon began vomiting blood. Stephenson panicked, driving her back to his home but refusing to summon a doctor, telling his flunkies, "I've been in worse messes than this before and got out of it." Madge dictated a sworn statement to authorities on March 28. She suffered kidney failure on April 8, and died six days later. Indicted for murder, Stephenson claimed an elaborate frame-up, and his attorney sought to dismiss Madge's death as simple suicide. Jurors disagreed, and he was convicted of second-degree murder, drawing a life sentence. Publicity surrounding the case, including courtroom revelations of Stephenson's alcoholism and sexual proclivities, was instrumental in the decline the Indiana Klan. [10; 93]

O'BERRY, CLARENCE

A white resident of Slidell, Louisiana, O'Berry was flogged by nightriders in 1965 on accusations of neglecting his family. John Gipson and two other members of the Original Knights were indicted in the case. [38]

OCALA HUNT CLUB

Also known as Sportsman's Club No. 3, this group was identified in 1965 as a cover for the Ocala, Florida, klavern, Improved Order of the U.S. Klans. [38]

ODD BROTHERS CLUB NO. 16 AND NO. 33

In 1965 congressional investigators identified these clubs as front groups for two Dillon, South Carolina, klaverns, United Klans of America. [38]

ODINIST RELIGION AND NORDIC FAITH MOVEMENT

A California fringe group led by National States Rights Party member James Warner in 1971, this group taught mystic Aryan supremacy as a forerunner of Warner's New Christian Crusade Church. Unrelated to Warner's movement, New York Klansman Dan Burros also worshipped Odin, prior to his nominal Christian conversion on joining the United Klans of America. [90]

ODOM, WILLIE

A grocer in Sumter, South Carolina, Odom was shot to death while leaving a local rally of Robert Scoggin's Invisible Empire of the KKK in September 1970. The incident occurred after guards tried to confiscate a tape recorder from United Klans member Walter Brown, ordering Brown to leave the rally site when he refused to surrender the recorder. Brown was on his way, with Odom, his wife, and two sons following in a separate car, when guards made a new attempt to stop them. Odom opened fire with a pistol, and was killed when the guards fired back. Scoggin and nine others were briefly charged with conspiracy to commit robbery and as accessories after the fact in a murder. [NYT 1970]

O'DONNELL, PAT

See *American Unity League.*

OHIO

Overshadowed by the action in neighboring Indiana, Ohio still took honors as the Klan's most populous realm in the 1920s. Kleagles first opened their shop in Cincinnati in the summer of 1920, and within three years they claimed an estimated half million recruits, with 50,000 Klansmen each in the cities of Akron and Columbus. The Buckeye realm was chartered in 1924 under Grand Dragon Clyde Osborn, but opposition was growing despite the massive turnout at public Klan rallies and marches. In Steubenville, hostile Knights of the Flaming Circle dragged Klansmen from their cars and beat them, but recruiters used such attacks to further boost membership. For all its numerical strength, the Ohio Klan's forays into politics produced only a handful of lackluster municipal victories. By 1925, the membership was slipping, but the movement had spread too far to die quickly. Hanging on as one of the Klan's top thirteen realms during the Great Depression, it was not until general disbandment in 1944 that the Ohio Klan ceased to exist.

In the mid-1960s, James Venable brought his National Knights to Ohio, planting small klaverns in Cincinnati, Columbus, and Oregonia. Volatile members imported dynamite from Georgia and debated political assassinations, but did not follow through. Robert Shelton's United Klans of America offered Venable some competition in 1966 and 1967, establishing four klaverns with an estimated 100 members between them, and Venable fired back with an April 1967 campaign to ban so-called integrationist textbooks from public schools in Akron, Canton, and Cleveland. The National Knights was still active—albeit with few members—in 1975 when Grand Dragon Dale Reusch led defectors from several states into his new Invisible Empire Knights. Opponents in Columbus rioted against the fledgling Klan in July 1977, and it had vanished by 1980, dissident splinters surviving into the 1980s as the Independent Invisible Knights and the Ohio Knights of the KKK. The only Klan group in Ohio by 1987, the Ohio Knights claimed fewer than 100 members in the state. [5]

OHIO KNIGHTS OF THE KU KLUX KLAN

Reported active through the 1980s, this local splinter group claimed fewer than 100 active members in a 1987 census of surviving Klans. [NYT 1987]

OHIO WHITE NATIONALIST PARTY

A one-man, Toledo-based outlet for neo-Nazi propaganda, this party was founded in 1970 and led by Russell Veh. Its disappearance coincided with Veh's move to California, where he organized a group of homosexual Nazis that called itself the National Socialist League. [2]

OKALOOSA HUNTING & FISHING CLUB

Created as the cover for a Monroe, Louisiana, klavern of the Original Knights, this group kept its name when members defected en masse to the United Klans of America in 1965. [38]

OKLAHOMA

Kleagles brought their message to Oklahoma a short time after William Simmons organized the modern Klan in 1915, and by 1921 the imperial wizard numbered one in every twenty Oklahomans as followers. The Klan spirit was evident in Tulsa's bloody race riot in 1921, when more than thirty blacks died, and in the installation of the vice president of the state university as grand dragon of the realm. Klansmen flogged radical labor organizers near Atoka and Bald Knob, with numerous other assaults aimed at "correcting" personal behavior. Opposition did exist, however, and anti-Klan supporter Jack Walton was elected governor in 1922 with mass support from labor unions and Klan-fearing Catholics. A new outbreak of violence the following summer prompted Walton to impose martial law in Henryetta and Tulsa, but the local citizens resented his methods and reacted furiously when troops were called out to bar the state legislature from meeting to consider Walton's impeachment. Courts upheld the legislature's right to meet, and Walton's removal from office was a foregone conclusion. Despite its victory, the Klan was its own worst enemy in Oklahoma, and membership was declining by 1926, dropping from an estimated peak of 100,000 to 20,000 in 1928. Neither party welcomed Klan support in that year's election, and by the end of the Great Depression the Klan had disappeared from Oklahoma.

OLD DOMINION CLUB

In 1965 congressional investigators identified this group as a cover for the Danville, Virginia, klavern, United Klans of America. [38]

OLD HICKORY CLUB

In 1966 congressional investigators named this club as a front for Klavern No. 1 of the Chattanooga-based Dixie Klans, Knights of the KKK, Inc. [38]

ONSLOW COUNTY IMPROVEMENT ASSOCIATION

Organized as a cover for a Jacksonville, North Carolina, klavern, United Klans of America, this group was publicly exposed in 1965. [38]

ORBISON, CHARLES

An Indiana Klansman in the 1920s, Orbison also won recognition as a judge, former state Prohibition director, and leader of the Indiana Klan's Democratic wing. In 1923 he was named a member of the imperial kloncilium, created to settle the ongoing feud between William Simmons and Hiram Evans. Orbison was considered for grand dragon in 1926, following the murder conviction of D.C. Stephenson, but Evans named him imperial klaliff instead. [10]

ORDER, THE

Also known as the Bruder Schweigen or Silent Brotherhood, this militant offshoot of the Aryan Nations was inspired by, and named for, a fictional right-wing terrorist group in *The Turner Diaries*. Founder Robert Jay Matthews discovered the novel and became acquainted with its author, William Pierce, during his affiliation with the anti-Semitic National Alliance, later drifting into the Aryan Nations compound at Hayden Lake, Idaho. When neither group proved militant enough to satisfy his urge for action, Matthews attempted to make fiction a reality, recruiting allies from various racist groups and penal institutions around the country. As finally consti-tuted, The Order represented a cross section of far-right groups. The twenty-odd identified members included Matthews, Tom Martinez, and William Soderquist from the National Alliance; Dan Bauer, Denver Parmenter, Randy Duey, Bruce Pierce, and David Tate from the Aryan Nations; David Lane, Frank Silva, and Randall Evans from Colorado and California branches of the KKK; Andrew Barnhill, from the Covenant, Sword, and Arm of the Lord; and Gary Yarborough, a professional criminal recruited by the Aryan Brotherhood while serving time in an Arizona prison. In their first raid in April 1983, members of The Order robbed a Seattle, Washington, pornography theater of $369, but something was clearly missing. On December 20, 1983, Matthews robbed a Seattle bank of $25,900, but an indelible dye pack exploded during his getaway, ruining much of the cash. On January 30, 1984, Bruce Pierce and Gary Yarborough raided a bank in Spokane and escaped with $3,600. Their luck improved on March 18, when a four-man team robbed $43,000 from an armored car in Seattle. On April 22, members of The Order bombed a Seattle pornography theater, phoning another threat to the same establishment a day later, thereby diverting police while they robbed another armored car and fled with $500,000 in cash. Pierce and Kemp bombed a synagogue in Boise, Idaho, while Duey and Barnhill—dubbed "Mr. Closet" for his passion for stalking gay men—began assaulting homosexuals in Portland, Oregon. On

June 18, 1984, a hit team from the Silent Brotherhood assassinated Alan Berg in Denver, Colorado, emulating their fictional heroes in *The Turner Diaries* with the random murder of a Jewish radio host. The group attempted counterfeiting, with results so poor that Bruce Pierce and Tom Martinez were promptly arrested and jailed. On July 19, 1984, the group netted $3.6 million from an armored car in Ukiah, California. Only $600,000 of that money was accounted for, and authorities believe that large sums of the money were distributed to leaders of the racist right. Named (but never formally charged) as recipients of unlawful donations were Tom Metzger ($250,000–$300,000), Glenn Miller ($300,000), Louis Beam ($100,000), William Pierce ($50,000), Richard Butler ($40,000), and Robert Miles ($15,300). Once in custody, Tom Martinez was persuaded to turn state's evidence against his comrades, and sweeping federal indictments were issued, ultimately leading to sixty-three arrests in seventeen states. Acting in concert with FBI agents, Martinez arranged a meeting with Matthews and Yarborough in Portland, Oregon, on November 24, 1984; Matthews escaped in the ensuing shootout, but Yarborough was captured and held for trial. The following day, thirteen members of The Order issued an eight-page Declaration of War against the U.S. government, vowing to kill all politicians, judges, journalists, lawmen, bankers, and soldiers who got in their way. As the statement proclaimed, "The current system of government does not fit into God's law. The whole government structure is suspect. Our task is to establish God's law as the law of the land. If it be war, so be it." Twelve days later Matthews died in a shootout with FBI agents on Whidbey Island, in Puget Sound. Arrests continued through the following spring, with trial commencing for ten Order defendants in June. All were convicted in September, and drew federal prison terms ranging from forty to 120 years. Investigation of The Order and its various associations led to federal indictments of fourteen prominent racists on sedition charges in 1987. Klansman Glenn Miller ultimately pled guilty to reduced charges and was sentenced to prison, while the remaining thirteen defendants—including Miles, Beam, Butler, Richard Snell, and five known members of The Order—were acquitted by a federal jury in Ft. Smith, Arkansas, in April 1988. [13; 85; 93]

ORDER OF ANTI-POKE NOSES

An anti-Klan society, organized in 1920s Searcy County, Arkansas, this group declared itself "opposed to any organization that attends to everyone's business but its own." Spokesmen expressed confidence in elected leaders who "do not need to be eternally prodded by the Ku Klux Klan." [93]

ORDER OF PALE FACES

A white supremacist organization formed in Columbia, Tennessee, in 1867, the Pale Faces were generally considered to be synonymous with Klansmen.

The group was divided into camps, with thirty-four reported active in Tennessee by October 1868, when a Grand Camp, or state convention, was convened in Columbia. Grand Wizard Nathan Bedford Forrest admitted joining the order in 1867 in Memphis, but his congressional testimony remained ambiguous about whether the Pale Faces and the KKK were identical. Spokesmen for the order denied Klan affiliations in letters to the press, but known Klansmen such as Forrest and murder victim John Bicknell demonstrably belonged to both groups at the same time. [87]

ORDER OF THE RATTLESNAKE

One of several front groups organized by Florida Klan leader Bill Hendrix in the late 1950s and early 1960s, this order was disbanded sometime prior to 1961. No record of its activities remains. [38]

OREGON

Klan recruiters came to Oregon via California in the spring of 1921, stressing anti-Catholicism in their public speeches, despite the relatively small number of Catholics in Oregon. By 1922, Klansmen had found widespread success in state politics, and Governor Ben Olcott told that year's conference of governors, "We woke up one morning and found the Klan had about gained political control of the state. Practically not a word had been raised against them." Klan power centered around Portland and the headquarters of Grand Dragon Fred Gifford, who claimed an estimated 25,000 followers statewide by early 1923. In that year the Klan pushed for the passage of laws aimed at banning parochial schools, but Catholics and Seventh-Day Adventists defeated the effort. An emasculated version of the bill was ultimately passed, only to be declared unconstitutional in 1926. By that time, Klan membership and prestige were already fading, and the Klan could only help their senatorial candidate in the 1926 election by publicly endorsing his opponent. [10]

ORIGINAL KNIGHTS OF THE KU KLUX KLAN

Created in 1962 from remnants of the Texas-based Original KKK, the Original Knights was led by J.D. Swenson, serving in the dual capacity of grand dragon and national kleagle. In early 1963 Royal Young was named imperial dragon of the group, but recruitment was limited to Louisiana until the fall of 1963, when the Original Knights branched out into Mississippi and Arkansas. An estimated 300 members were recruited in Mississippi, under Douglas Byrd and E.L. McDaniel, but factional disputes and alleged mishandling of funds prompted Swenson to banish both state officers in December 1963. Mississippi Klansmen responded by resigning en masse to join the new White Knights in February 1964. In Arkansas, the Original Knights established small klaverns near Crockett and El Dorado, but the group's overtures were poorly received, and the units soon dissolved. Dissension continued in Louisiana, with Young and Swenson ousted on charges of financial mismanagement in early 1964. Murray Martin and Billy Skipper took control of that troubled realm, with an understanding that elections for permanent officers would be held in six months. Klansman Houston Morris was promised a top position in the group following those elections, but the Skipper-Martin faction used their time to undercut Morris's following, with political in-fighting producing a three-way split in the Original Knights that fall. Morris and his loyal followers in Monroe, Louisiana, left the group to charter the short-lived Original KKK of America in January 1965. A second faction, led by Charles Christmas and Saxon Farmer, began as the Anti-Communist Christian Association in December 1964, participating in violence around Bogalusa that led to the issuance of federal injunctions a year later. Loyalists of the Martin-Skipper faction had their greatest strength near Shreveport and Bossier City, where they sometimes hid behind the cover name of Christian Constitutional Crusaders. By October 1965 the competing United Klans of America was the dominant Klan faction in Louisiana, with membership in the Original Knights plunging from its 1964 peak of 1,000 to an estimated 250 Klansmen in January 1967. By 1974, when young David Duke began proselytizing for the competing Knights of the KKK, no trace of the Original Knights remained. [38; 84]

ORIGINAL KU KLUX KLAN

Organized and led by Dallas Imperial Wizard Roy E. Davis in 1959, the Original KKK began recruiting in Arkansas that summer, and planted klaverns in Louisiana in 1960. The group apparently dissolved during 1962, with its Louisiana realm surviving as the Original Knights of the KKK. [33; 38; 84]

ORIGINAL KU KLUX KLAN OF AMERICA

A product of dissension in the Louisiana-based Original Knights, the Original KKK of America was created in the fall of 1964 by Klansman Houston P. Morris. Morris secured a state charter for his Klan in January 1965, but internal problems continued, and he resigned as imperial wizard in late April. Two months later, Morris and the bulk of his former membership defected to Robert Shelton's United Klans of America. The Original KKK survived as a separate entity through the fall of 1965, disappearing early in 1966. [38]

ORIGINAL KU KLUX KLAN OF THE CONFEDERACY

A violent Alabama splinter group organized by Asa Carter in 1956, the Original KKK of the Confederacy was an outgrowth of Carter's militant North Alabama Citizens' Council. The group was noted for its strident anti-

Semitism and for Nazi-style, brown shirt uniforms. In their dual capacities, Carter's Klansmen participated in February 1956 riots resulting from black coed Autherine Lucy's attempt to enroll at the University of Alabama, and assaulted black singer Nat "King" Cole during his performance at a Birmingham auditorium. Their most notorious crime was the 1957 castration of Edward Aaron, a black man who had been selected at random for a local KKK initiation ceremony. This episode landed four Klansmen in prison for twenty-year terms. The group was further damaged when Carter shot and wounded two of his followers during an angry dispute over money and power. The group apparently dissolved sometime in early 1958. [10; 55]

ORIGINAL SOUTHERN KLANS, INC.

A product of dissension in the Association of Georgia Klans, the Original Southern Klans was chartered in Muscogee County, Georgia, in June 1948. Members of two large Association of Georgia Klans klaverns—in Columbus and Manchester—defected en masse to create this new faction led by Grand Wizard Alton Pate, a twenty-three-year-old veteran of World War II. Backing Pate, were "Parson Jack" Johnston and Fred K. New. Their stated goals: maintenance of the "Southern white man's political superiority" and prevention of interference from "any inferior minority group." Their major plans included the creation of a Klan radio station, a newspaper printing plant, and a textile factory for the manufacture of robes, but none were ever realized. Only two issues of the group's paper *The Klansman* were published, and its meetings drew miniscule crowds. Expansion into Alabama was marked by an incident in Phoenix City, where fifteen hooded members invaded a courtroom and staged a demonstration in the jury box. Georgia Klans leader Samuel Green called the Original Knights a "bolshevik Klan," and the group was included on the U.S. Attorney General's list of subversive organizations in 1949. A Florida chapter, led by Bill Hendrix, was created after the demise of Georgia imperial headquarters, to emerge as the new Northern and Southern Knights of the KKK. [NYT 1948; 25; 38]

ORMANDSVILLE LOYAL FELLOWSHIP ASSOCIATION

In 1965 congressional investigators identified this group as a cover for the Ormandsville, North Carolina, klavern, United Klans of America. [38]

ORWICH, WILLIAM G.

A linotype operator and former officer of the John B. Gordon klavern in Hialeah, Florida, Orwich was one of twelve Klansmen called before a federal grand jury probing local terrorism in October 1952. Two months later he was charged with two counts of making false statements to the FBI. Orwich told federal agents he had resigned from the KKK in 1946, but the investigation proved he was active as late as 1951. He also falsely denied attending strategy sessions with his fellow Klansmen. [NYT 1952]

OSBORN, CLYDE W.

A Youngstown, Ohio, attorney and 1920s Klansman, Osborn became grand dragon when the Ohio realm was chartered in 1924. By his own admission Osborn saw the Klan primarily as a means of electing a Republican president, while making money on the side. Before the end of the year, he was replaced as grand dragon by Gilbert Taylor. [10]

OSTWALT, FARRELL

A security guard for the United Klans of America in Charlotte, North Carolina, Ostwalt was an unsuccessful candidate for city council who became an outspoken critic of other United Klans factions in the state. His home was bombed by persons unknown in August 1968. [NYT 1968]

OTWELL, B.G.

A member of the 1920s Klan in Georgia, Otwell emerged in 1946 as the exalted cyclops of East Atlanta's Post No. 213, Association of Georgia Klans. When State Attorney General Dan Duke filed suit to revoke the Klan's charter in Georgia, Otwell was named as one of the ranking leaders. [NYT 1946]

OTTO, GEORGE

A Houston Klan leader, Otto led a march by thirty-one Klansmen to the state capitol in Austin in November 1965 to protest anti-war activities by the Students for a Democratic Society. The small rally broke up when 2,000 University of Texas students drowned out Klan speakers by singing football songs. In early 1966 congressional investigators identified Otto as a kleagle and co-leader (with William Drennan) of the Texas realm, United Klans of America. [FOF 65; 38]

OUACHITA PARISH HUNTING & FISHING CLUB

In 1965 congressional investigators identified this group as a cover for a Monroe, Louisiana, klavern, United Klans of America. [38]

OUR FISHING CLUB

In 1966 this club was identified as the front for a Baltimore, Maryland, klavern, United Klans of America. [38]

OUTEN, CHARLES

See *Dayvault, Wayne.*

OUTLAW, WYATT

A black town councilman and head of the local Union League during Reconstruction in Graham, North Carolina, Outlaw was the first prominent victim of Klan violence in Alamance County. Klansmen dragged him from his home on the night of February 26, 1870, and hanged him from a tree near the county courthouse. (A note left at the mayor's house threatened him with a similar fate.) Eighteen Klansmen, including county chief Jacob A. Long, were indicted for the murder by federal authorities in December 1871, but none were ever brought to trial. [87]

OUZTS, THURMAN

A Montgomery, Alabama, Klansman, Ouzts was one of four individuals named in Judge Frank Johnson's May 1961 restraining order to prevent Freedom Ride violence. [FOF 1961]

OVERTON, HAROLD

A Klansman since 1922, based in Wilkinson, Indiana, Overton was appointed Indiana king kleagle for the Association of Georgia Klans in October 1946. In a November 8, 1946, interview, he claimed to operate with a secret council of five, including a banker, a businessman, a labor leader, a farmer, and a city councilman—all anonymous. Overton also alleged that the Association of Georgia Klans was active in sixty of Indiana's ninety-two counties, stressing a program of "no rough stuff" and minimal cross burnings, with robes worn only at rallies. [Indianapolis Star, Nov. 8, 1946]

OWENS, LARRY

Identified as national titan for the United Empire, Knights of the KKK, Owens was arrested with Imperial Wizard Rocky Coker and another Klansman during July 1980 racial disturbances in Chattanooga, Tennessee. Coker and Owens were both convicted on charges of possessing explosives and conspiring to commit an illegal act, with Owens receiving a jail term of three to six years on each charge. [AP, July 28, 1980; 2]

OXFORD, JAMES

A Reconstruction Georgia Klansman, Oxford was jailed in Sparta on murder charges, but a band of disguised Klansmen liberated him from custody. Convicted of a second murder in 1871, he was sentenced to hang in Washington County. Klansmen declined to intervene on his behalf the second time. [87]

OXFORD, MISSISSIPPI

Home to the University of Mississippi—"Ole Miss"—Oxford became a civil rights battleground when federal courts ordered the admission of black student James Meredith in September 1962. In Pascagoula, Sheriff James Grimsley issued a radio appeal for volunteers to block Meredith's enrollment. Grimsley and his chief deputy led fifty-five men to Oxford in a charter bus, picking up twenty more en route. From Dallas, former General Edwin Walker announced: "It is time to move. We have talked, listened, and been pushed around far too much by the anti-Christ Supreme Court. Now is the time to be heard—10,000 strong from every state in the union." Walker flew to Jackson, Mississippi, on September 29, meeting reporters and calling for "a national protest against the conspiracy from within." That same day 3,000 whites gathered for a courthouse rally in Shreveport, Louisiana, laying plans for a caravan of 150 cars from Shreveport and sixty from Monroe to meet at Tallulah the next morning, to proceed from there to Mississippi. Edward Fields wired Governor Ross Barnett from Birmingham, declaring that the National States Rights Party would "place our lives and fortunes at the disposal of your supreme authority as governor of the sovereign state of Mississippi." Also in Birmingham, Eastview Klavern No. 13, United Klans of America, ordered its members to assemble on September 28 and to be ready to travel. From Anniston, Alabama, the Dixie Klans wired Barnett that hundreds of members "are on stand-by alert for your call to protect the sovereign state of Mississippi." Barnett tried to discourage this out-of-state "help," but was unsuccessful. Walker reached the campus at 9 p.m. on September 30, and state highway patrolmen pulled out ten minutes later, with sporadic sniper fire beginning around 9:30. A force of 166 U.S. marshals was surrounded in the campus lyceum, while rioters roamed the campus at will, beating a Texas newsman and his wife with metal pipes and breaking benches to gain chunks of concrete to lob at the marshals. Rioter Ray Gunter was killed by a stray bullet during the melee, and French journalist Paul Guihard was shot to death execution-style behind a dormitory, hundreds of yards from the main riot scene. Rioters tried to ram the marshals' line with a bulldozer, a car, and a firetruck. State police aided the rioters, trying to block National Guardsmen from entering and marshals from leaving to get more tear gas, threatening an ambulance driver with arrest if he left the campus carrying wounded U.S. marshals. Conversely, the troopers refused to stop convoys of armed racists, except when one group of 250 men was advised to split into smaller bands and enter the campus at different points. Of 166 U.S. marshals on the scene, 160 were injured, twenty-eight of them wounded by bullets. Sixty National Guardsmen reached the campus at 10:30 p.m. and had to fight their way in, suffering forty casualties from shotgun blasts or thrown objects. Five more hours passed before the regular army arrived. Three thousand federal troops and federalized guardsmen were required to suppress the riot. Of the

200 rioters arrested, only twenty-four were students at Ole Miss; the rest came from Alabama, Georgia, Louisiana, Tennessee, Texas, and various Mississippi towns. The state issued no indictments, but federal authorities indicted Melvin Bruce, an ex-Nazi from Decatur, Georgia, and three men from Pritchard, Alabama. With Klansman J.B. Stoner serving as defense counsel, one indictment was dismissed, and the other three defendants were acquitted. Governor Barnett blamed "trigger-happy" marshals for the violence, exonerating his own administration and criminally negligent state police. In January 1963 a federal grand jury refused to indict Edwin Walker and six other alleged conspirators for inciting the riot. [18; 52; 83]

OZARK KLANS

See *Knights of the Ku Klux Klan of America.*

P

PACE, REV. EDWARD

A black minister in Gadsden, Alabama, Pace was shot and killed in his home in November 1973, shortly after a downtown Christmas parade a few blocks away. Klansman Bruce Botsford was convicted of second-degree murder four months later, signing a statement that he was "acting under the sanction of the United Klans of America" when he shot Pace. Botsford later repudiated his confession on the witness stand, claiming that police threatened to put him in a "cell full of niggers" if he refused to sign the document. Witness Charles Battles testified that he and other Klansmen, including Aubrey Eugene Arledge and his son Ricky Arledge, were standing in the yard outside Klan headquarters, across from Pace's home, when Botsford and Ricky Arledge crossed the street, knocked on the door, and shot Pace when he answered. In his confession Botsford said that he did not know Pace, but was told that the minister's home served as headquarters for the Black Panther Party. Ricky Arledge subsequently claimed to be an FBI informant, naming his father as the mastermind behind Pace's murder; in April 1974, jurors deadlocked in the case of Aubrey Arledge, voting 7–5 for conviction, and a mistrial was declared. [NYT 1974]

PACIFICA FOUNDATION

Based in California, this foundation operated a chain of radio stations known for their liberal politics and public airing of unpopular beliefs. Station KPFT began operation in Houston, Texas, during February 1970 and soon became the target of Klan harassment; its transmitter was bombed in May. The new station, fortified with sandbags against further attacks, was bombed again on October 6, in what police called a "very professional" strike. On January 21, 1971, Klansman Jimmy Dale Hutto was arrested in Texas while en route to California and other Pacifica targets with a carload of weapons and KKK literature. In June 1971 a Texas grand jury indicted four Klansmen—Louis Beam; Peter Lout, Jr.; Jimmy Dale Hutto; and Paul Moratto—in connection with a local reign of terror. Hutto and Moratto were already charged with conspiracy to bomb Pacifica radio stations in California, and the list continued to grow. The enumerated crimes in Houston included two bombings at KPFT, a March 1971 bombing of the local Socialist Party headquarters, a bombing at the Family Hand Restaurant (where "hippies" apparently ate), in addition to the bombings of a motorcycle shop and an architect's office. When KPFT went back on the air after repairs, it picked up the broadcast of "Alice's Restaurant" at the exact point where transmission was interrupted by the bombing in October 1970. [12]

PACTOLUS HUNTING CLUB

In 1965 congressional investigators identified this group as a cover for Unit No. 162, United Klans of America, in Pactolus, North Carolina. [38]

PAGE, ALEC

A black resident of Reconstruction Monroe County, Mississippi, Page was murdered by the KKK in 1871. Twenty-eight Klansmen were charged with the crime and treated to a hero's welcome—complete with firing cannons—when they were released on bond. Legal expenses were paid for the accused by popular subscription. All twenty-eight pled guilty in December 1871, whereupon they were released with suspended sentences. [87]

PAGE, HUBERT A.

Appointed in 1961 as the first Alabama grand dragon for the United Klans of America, Page served until March 1964, when he was replaced by Robert Creel. [38]

PALMETTO KNIGHTS OF THE KU KLUX KLAN

Organized in the late 1950s, the Palmetto Knights was one of several factions active in South Carolina after the U.S. Supreme Court's Black Monday decision. [38]

PARADISE NO. 115

In 1965 congressional investigators identified this group as a cover for the Winder, Georgia, klavern, United Klans of America. [38]

PARKER, ALBERT H.

The first of eleven detectives hired by Arkansas Governor Powell Clayton to infiltrate the Reconstruction Klan, Parker entered White County in August 1868, posing as a cattle buyer and hoping to join the Ku Klux den in Searcy, thereby discovering the killers of Ban Humphries and the attempted assassins of State Senator Stephen Wheeler. Parker disappeared without a trace two months later, and his fate remained unknown until March 1870, when Klansman John McCauley confessed to participating in his murder. As McCauley explained, Klansmen grew suspicious when Parker never bought any cattle; his death was ordered by KKK leaders including Grand Titan Dandrige McRae and Grand Giant Jacob Frolich. Parker's body had been dumped in an abandoned well. McRae and Frolich sought to avoid prosecution—McRae fled to Canada—but both returned for a farcical trial in 1871, with all the defendants acquitted despite the testimony from McCauley and another Klansman who turned state's evidence. [87]

PARKER, C.L.

Identified as a Florida grand dragon, Parker announced in October 1953 that his Klan was discarding its robes and rituals, opening the ranks to "all races, creeds or colors"—on a strictly segregated basis. [FOF 1953]

PARKER, ERNEST

A member of the White Knights in Morgantown, Mississippi, Parker was called before the House Un-American Activities Committee in January 1966 and refused to answer questions concerning the use of his barge to dump the bodies of murder victims Henry Dee and Charlie Moore. [38]

PARKER, LEWIS

A Klansman and farmer from Hartselle, Alabama, Parker was a member of the jury that failed to reach a verdict on KKK defendants charged with burning a Freedom Ride bus near Anniston. On November 28, 1961, he was jailed for perjury after denying Klan membership during the process of jury selection. [NYT 1961]

PARKS, LEROY

See *Philpot, Kate.*

PARKS, ROBERT LLOYD

See *Miller, Emmett.*

PARNELL, BEVERLY ANN

A black resident of Meridian, Mississippi, Parnell was reported missing by her family in June 1982. A month later, her lifeless body was found in an abandoned warehouse, with the initials "KKK" painted in red on the floor nearby. [NYT 1982]

PATE, ALTON E.

Named as imperial wizard of the Original Southern Klans in June 1948, Pate held office as a nominal leader, reportedly controlled by Fred New and "Parson Jack" Johnston. [25]

PATLER, JOHN

A member of the American Nazi Party, Patler toured the South with Dan Burros in May 1961, protesting integrated Freedom Rides with the party's "hate bus." That fall, Patler and Burros defected to form their own two-man American National Party in New York City, publishing a magazine entitled KILL!. Back in the Nazi fold by August 1966, Patler joined George Lincoln Rockwell and robed Klansmen for joint rallies in Chicago's Marquette Park, urging "white revolution" against local civil rights demonstrators. In March 1967, Patler was fired by Rockwell for creating dissent between light- and dark-skinned Nazis at party headquarters in Arlington, Virginia. Five months later, Patler shot Rockwell to death at a local laundromat, and was ultimately sentenced to prison. [75]

PATRICK, N.W. ("PAT")

The police chief of Saraland, Alabama, Patrick was arrested with six fellow Klansmen in September 1958, charged with burning a cross at the home of a Mobile minister and destroying political posters prior to the May 6 Democratic primary in Saraland. Sheriff Ray Bridges made the arrests, describing the Saraland police station as a center of Klan activity in Mobile County. According to Bridges, the arrests were also "definitely" linked with the August 1958 shotgun slaying of Mayor Oscar Driver, but none of the prisoners were charged in that case. [NYT 1958]

PATRIOTIC LEGAL FOUNDATION

The brainchild of Houston attorney Kirk D. Lyons, this foundation was conceived as "an ACLU-type organization to serve the needs and concerns of the 'Patriotic Movement.'" In 1989, Lyons corresponded with the Aryan Nations, the Mountain Church of Jesus Christ, and other neo-Nazi groups, soliciting donations of office equipment and other material support to make his group a functioning reality. Among the cases listed as "priority concerns," Lyons included an inquest into the death of Posse Comitatus member Gordon Kahl, the legal defense of four Aryan Nations marchers arrested in

Pulaski, Tennessee, in October 1989, and intervention in a lawsuit filed against California Klansman Tom Metzger by the Southern Poverty Law Center. [*From the Mountain*, Nov.–Dec. 1989]

PATRIOTIC LEGAL FUND

Organized by lawyer J.B. Stoner in 1969, this group solicited funds for the legal defense of James Earl Ray, who was then appealing his conviction in the murder of Martin Luther King, Jr. [31]

PATRIOTIC PARTY

See *Minutemen (1959–1973)*.

PATRIOTS INTERORGANIZATIONAL COMMUNICATIONS CENTER

Established at the August 1975 national klonvocation of the United Klans, held in Lakeland, Florida, this ambitious coalition of far-right groups was jointly led by United Klans of America Imperial Wizard Robert Shelton and Minutemen founder Robert Bolivar DePugh. Headquarters for the group was established in DePugh's home town of Norborne, Missouri, but evidence suggests that the Communications Center existed mainly on paper, its goals of uniting the racist right wing unrealized. [43]

PATTERSON, JAMES A.J.

A resident of Reconstruction Alamance County, North Carolina, and county chief of the Constitutional Union Guard, Patterson organized the county's first Union Guard "klan" in September 1868, with three more formed in June 1869. [87]

PATTERSON, REV. JOE

The pastor of the Lindon (Alabama) Baptist Church, Patterson resigned after church deacons protested his plan to admit black worshippers. A cross was burned at his home and the house was stoned by nightriders on June 14, 1963. [NYT 1963]

PATTERSON, JOHN

After serving as Alabama's state attorney general from 1955 to 1958, Patterson entered the 1958 gubernatorial race as one of thirteen candidates. To boost his campaign Patterson solicited votes from members of the KKK, posting letters on official stationery that asked for support in the name of "a mutual friend, Mr. R.M. (Bob) Shelton"—who was then grand dragon for the Alabama realm of the Georgia-based U.S. Klans. During the campaign, Klansmen ripped down competing posters and assaulted volunteers employed by other candidates, including one man who was shot in the scalp with a staple gun. Patterson was elected, and Shelton, a salesman for the B.F. Goodrich Company at the time, received a million-dollar order from the state as a reward for his support. Shortly after Patterson's inauguration, the state legislature introduced a measure to expand Alabama's mental health facilities, a move opposed by Shelton on grounds that the National Mental Health Association was "linked with the communists." Patterson echoed Shelton's concerns from the state house, and the bill died on the assembly floor. A rift between Patterson and the KKK developed in August 1959 over Patterson's support for the presidential candidacy of liberal John F. Kennedy. On August 10, a thirty-two-man delegation from the Alabama Knights called on the governor, led by an imperial kladd from Prattville, branding Patterson a tool of the "communist-Jewish integrators." Patterson allayed their fears with a promise that "if a school in Alabama is integrated, it will be over my body." In December 1960, he told newsmen, "You're going to have rioting on your hands if they try forced integration here," adding, "I'll be one of the first ones stirring up trouble, any way I can." In May 1961, when integrated freedom riders entered Alabama, Patterson promised an escort of police cars and helicopters, then abruptly withdrew security as the buses approached Montgomery. Dismissing the resultant Klan riots—"I can't guarantee the safety of fools"—Patterson ordered his state police to terminate their "working relationship" with the FBI, following up with a June 16 announcement that any trooper found cooperating with federal agents on a probe of racial violence would be fired. Patterson's final break with the Klan occurred when President John F. Kennedy nominated Charles Merriwether, Patterson's 1958 campaign manager, to head the Export and Import Bank, thereby drawing more flack from Shelton for his "liberal" associations. Forbidden by law from succeeding himself in office, by 1962 Patterson had no further need for Klan electoral support, and he retired from public life with his segregationist record more or less intact. [14; 17; 68]

PAUL REVERE HISTORICAL SOCIETY

In 1965 congressional investigators identified this group as a cover for Jacksonville Klavern No. 502 of the United Florida KKK. [38]

PAULEN, BEN

A 1920s Klansman and Kansas politician, Paulen owed his 1924 gubernatorial nomination to KKK supporters. With the nomination secured, he quickly killed discussion of a Republican anti-Klan plank, deflecting journalistic questions with bland denials of membership in the KKK "at this time." Despite spirited opposition from anti-Klan forces, he was elected governor in November 1924. [10]

PAYNE, LARRY

A member of the Tennessee-based Justice Knights of the KKK, Payne was arrested on April 19, 1980, charged with shooting four black women in Chattanooga. His acquittal three months later touched off widespread rioting by black residents of Chattanooga. [*AP*, April 20, 1980; July 23, 1980]

PEARL RIVER GUN & ROD CLUB

In 1965 congressional investigators identified this club as a front for the White Knights of the KKK in Crossroads Community, Mississippi. [38]

PEARL RIVER HUNTING & FISHING LODGE NO. 1028

In 1966 the House Un-American Activities Committee identified this group as a cover for the Pearl River, Louisiana, klavern, Original Knights of the KKK. [38]

PEARSON, DREW

A nationally syndicated newspaper columnist, Pearson announced on June 16, 1946, that Klansmen had threatened to kill him if he delivered a scheduled speech in Stone Mountain, Georgia. Pearson planned to proceed, but owners of the property forbade his appearance, and he spoke instead from the steps of the state capitol, introduced by Governor Ellis Arnall. Opposing the 1946 gubernatorial campaign of Eugene Talmadge, Pearson reported that Talmadge had promised Atlanta Exalted Cyclops Sam Roper a post as leader of the Georgia Bureau of Investigation, with a collateral vow that "all race problems will be left up to the Klan" under Talmadge's administration. Five years later, Pearson was the target of a vulgar cartoon—depicting the columnist disappearing into a toilet labeled "American Pot for Communists and Stooges"—which earned Florida Klansman Bill Hendrix a $700 fine on conviction of criminal libel. In the late 1960s, Pearson continued his drive against militant racists with a series of columns exposing links between the the far-right Liberty Lobby, led by Willis Carto, and various other Klan or neo-Nazi groups. [*NYT* 1946; 10]

PECK, JAMES

A participant in the integrated Freedom Rides, Peck was severely beaten by Birmingham Klansmen on May 14, 1961. In 1983, he sued the FBI over its failure to prevent the attack, and a federal court awarded him $25,000 damages in February 1984. [93]

PECORARO, CLARA

A New Orleans native and reputed kung fu expert, Pecoraro joined the Knights of the KKK around 1973, rising to the rank of Klan security chief under David Duke. [84]

PEDEN, ALONZO

A Klansman and son of the sheriff during Reconstruction in Giles County, Tennessee, Peden also served his father as an appointed deputy. In his KKK capacity, he was identified as a leader of harassment aimed at Republicans and members of the Union League around Pulaski. [87]

PEDEN, BRYANT

Elected as sheriff of Giles County, Tennessee, during Reconstruction, Peden was recognized as a Klan sympathizer, although his actual membership was never conclusively established. Peden publicly insisted that blacks were still slaves, despite the outcome of the Civil War, and boasted of whipping his black employees, offering ex-slave owners ten dollars a head for their human "property." Peden's son and deputy, Bryan, was a known Klansman active in harassment of KKK enemies around Giles County. [87]

PEDIGO, AMOS

A Tennessee Klansman, Pedigo was elected to serve as imperial nighthawk of the United Klans in September 1964. [38]

PEE DEE GUN CLUB

In 1965 congressional investigators identified this group as a cover for the Darlington, South Carolina, klavern, United Klans of America. [38]

PEEK, JAMES

A white restaurateur in Montgomery, Alabama, Peek became a target of KKK harassment after he replaced three white waitresses with black waiters in September 1959. Klansmen warned him three times to reverse his decision, plastering the door of his establishment with KKK stickers and once packing the cafe with fifty Klan members in protest. On September 12, Peek met Klansman William Horton in the parking lot of a deserted shopping center, killing Horton with a shotgun blast when he reached for a concealed pistol. Charged with murder, he was acquitted in May 1960, on a plea of self-defense. A year later, Klansmen reportedly tried to firebomb Peek's home during an outbreak of general violence sparked by the integrated Freedom Rides. [NYT 1959–1961]

PELLEY, WILLIAM DUDLEY

While serving as a volunteer with Japanese troops in Siberia in 1918, Pelley became convinced that Jews were responsible for the Bolshevik revolution. Once back home in Asheville, North Carolina, he founded the pro-Nazi Silver Shirts the day after Adolf Hitler took power in Germany. A profitable sideline was Pelley's nonexistent Galahad College, allegedly based in Asheville, with sales of unregistered stock resulting in a felony conviction. In 1936, Pelley moved to Seattle, Washington, and ran for president on the Christian Party ticket, backed by Nazi funds. His campaign slogan, "Christ or Chaos," was further illuminated when he told a local gathering of the German-American Folk Union that "the time has come for an American Hitler and a pogrom." Recognized as a friend of prominent Klansmen during the Depression, Pelley was instrumental in advising Michigan Klan leaders to enter politics, and his North Carolina publishing house was a reliable source of anti-Semitic literature for Klansmen and Nazis. One of twenty-eight far-rightists indicted for sedition in July 1942, he was freed when a mistrial ended the case in November 1944. [8; 10]

PENDER COUNTY IMPROVEMENT ASSOCIATION

In 1965 congressional investigators identified this group as a cover for a klavern of the United Klans, serving Klansmen in Currie and Atkinson, North Carolina. [38]

PENN, LEMUEL

The black director of adult and vocational education in Washington, D.C., Penn also served as a lieutenant colonel in the U.S. Army Reserve. On July 11, 1964, while driving home from summer training exercises at Ft. Benning, Georgia, he was shot and killed by nightriders on the highway near Colbert. FBI agents arrested four members of the United Klans on August 8, and Grand Dragon Calvin Craig announced their automatic suspension, pending banishment if indicted on criminal charges. Klansmen Joseph Sims, Cecil Myers, and James Lackey were charged with murder on August 25, based on statements collected from Lackey, Herbert Guest, Claude Bennett, Denver Phillips, and Thomas Folendore. Their trial began on August 31, and while Lackey refused to testify, his confession was entered in evidence, along with another statement repudiating the first. Herbert Guest, an illiterate dropout, accused FBI agents of tricking him into signing a false confession, claiming that they did not "read it right" before he signed. Defense attorneys harped on Lackey's alleged mental illness and an FBI payment of $3,000 that followed his confession, branding the prosecution as "carpet-bagging administration of justice." "Never let it be said," one lawyer exclaimed, "that a Madison County jury converted an electric chair into a sacrificial altar on which the pure flesh of a member of the human race was sacrificed to the savage, revengeful appetite of a raging mob." An all-white jury acquitted the defendants of murder on September 4, with Sims, Myers, their wives, and attorneys joining several jurors in a victory dance before they retired to celebrate at the local klavern. Pleased with the verdict, Klansman James Venable declared: "You'll never be able to convict a white man that kills a nigger what encroaches on the white race of the South." In

1966 federal authorities filed civil rights charges against Myers, Sims, Lackey, Guest, Phillips, and George Turner. When verdicts were returned that July, Myers and Sims were found guilty and sentenced to ten years in prison; their four codefendants were acquitted on all counts. [33; 40; 88]

PENNSYLVANIA

The KKK invaded Pennsylvania in the late summer of 1921, recruiting around Philadelphia and Chester counties before kleagle F.W. Atkins absconded with the realm's treasury and membership records. Anti-Klan rioting in Carnegie left one Klansman dead in 1923, Imperial Wizard Hiram Evans remarking that the incident should be worth 25,000 new recruits. By the end of 1924, order had been restored to the Invisible Empire in western Pennsylvania, with an estimated 125,000 Klansmen on the rolls, but chaos reigned in the eastern half of the state. Membership in eastern Pennsylvania peaked at 100,000 the following year, and Klansmen saw their share of action in the form of floggings, abductions, and minor riots. Two policemen were shot and wounded at a Klan meeting on the Haverford campus, in Lower Marion, but Klansmen remained their own worst enemies in the late 1920s. Members became suspicious of Grand Dragon Sam Rich's handling of Klan funds, and the quarrel spread to imperial headquarters in Atlanta, leading to the creation of rival splinter groups. Wizard Evans retaliated with a civil suit in federal court against the renegades, but evidence of Klan violence persuaded a judge that the KKK had not come into court with the requisite "clean hands," and injunctive relief was denied. The rebel groups lingered briefly, and Pennsylvania remained as one of the KKK's thirteen significant realms during the Great Depression. But the glory days of the Pennsylvania Klan had already past.

In August 1946 Governor Edward Martin requested FBI assistance in probing rumors of a statewide Klan revival, but no active units were uncovered. Two more decades would elapse before the United Klans of America arrived in Pennsylvania, establishing a fifty-man klavern in Reading under Grand Dragon Roy Frankhouser. A dedicated anti-Semite, Frankhouser recruited most of his troops from the Minutemen and American Nazi Party, surviving into the early 1980s despite his numerous arrests and the public disclosure of his role as an FBI informant. In 1983, marginal activity by an independent White Knights of the KKK was reported in Pennsylvania, replaced four years later by the White Unity Party, which claimed fewer than 100 active members. [2; 10; 38]

PEOPLE'S MOVEMENT

A West German neo-fascist group, the People's Movement sent representatives to join David Duke's Knights of the KKK in public demonstrations around New Orleans in September 1976. [84]

PEPPER, GEORGE

A city bus driver in Fontana, California, Pepper was identified as leader of the local Klan in July 1980. While admitting his membership and rank, he denied KKK participation in recent cross burnings and violence against local blacks, including the murder of a black woman. As Pepper remarked, "Cross burning's been going on around here for years, but it ain't us. The Klan ain't into burning crosses in niggers' yards, 'cuz it's just a totally different meaning to us. It's a religious ceremony." In spite of this disclaimer, one Fontana Klansman was awaiting trial for pointing a rifle at a Hispanic policeman at the scene of a cross burning, and authorities noted that many local Klansmen were drawn from the ranks of motorcycle gangs,

PERKINS, DEFOREST

Appointed grand dragon of Maine in 1926, Perkins was implicated with Governor Owen Brewster and Imperial Wizard Hiram Evans in a plot to swing a special senate election in favor of the Klan's candidate by accusing his opponent of illegal overspending in the state primary. [10]

PERKINS, W.O.

An Alabama cabinetmaker and member of the United Klans, Perkins was elected to serve as imperial kligrapp in September 1964, holding that office until he replaced Frederick Smith as imperial klabee the following summer. [38]

PERNIC, WILLIS

See *Hall, Reverend Enell.*

PERRIN, WADE

A black state legislator during Reconstruction in South Carolina, Perrin was one of a dozen Republicans killed by rioting Klansmen in Laurens County in October 1870. [87]

PERRY, J.W.

Doubling as the grand dragon of Rhode Island and Connecticut in the 1920s, Perry was charged with perjury before a Rhode Island state legislative committee probing the Klan's involvement in politics during 1927. He was acquitted at his trial in the winter of 1928. [10]

PERRY, JESSIE RAYMOND

See *Lauderdale, E.A.*

PERRY, SAMUEL

A black resident of Orlando, Florida, Perry became a target of Klan violence in October 1950. A cross was burned at his home on October 7, and arsonists destroyed the house four days later. White neighbors responded by collecting money to rebuild the Perry home. [NYT 1950]

PETERS, SAM

See *Lynch, John.*

PETERSON, ERIC

A member of the Original Knights and owner of the Pearl River Towing Company in Sun, Louisiana, Peterson earned a yearly income of $300,000 in the 1960s, operating from land rented to him by the federal government for $35 a month. [38]

PETERSON, JIM

As mayor of Soperton, Georgia, in the late 1940s, Peterson was an outspoken enemy of the KKK. Alerted by reports of robed men prowling the streets on May 21, 1949, Peterson accosted Klansmen Malcolm Braddy and Joe Greene near his home, ripping their masks off in a scuffle that landed the Klansmen in jail. Continuing his rounds, Peterson surprised three more Klansmen, unmasking John Edge, a night watchman for the state highway department, before Edge's two companions escaped in a hail of police gunfire. President Harry Truman praised Peterson's action, while Grand Dragon Samuel Green threatened legal action. Disorderly conduct charges filed against the three Klansmen were dismissed on June 13, 1949, and loitering charges were thrown out of court on July 28. [NYT 1949]

PETTIE, VIRGIL

An Arkansas Klansman and state delegate to the 1924 Democratic national convention in New York City, Pettie also served on the Klan's private strategy board during the convention. Despite his KKK membership, he was subsequently elected as a member and treasurer of the Democratic National Committee. [10]

PETTUS, EDMUND W.

A member of the Reconstruction Klan in Alabama, Pettus testified before a congressional committee investigating Klan violence in 1871. A bridge named in his honor outside of Selma was the scene of a "Bloody Sunday" clash between Sheriff Jim Clark's mounted posse and black civil rights marchers on March 7, 1965. [93]

PHELPS, COY RAY

A San Francisco Nazi, Phelps planted bombs at two local synagogues, a rabbi's home, and two other buildings in 1985. Only one of the bombs exploded, and physical evidence led police to Phelps's home, where a search turned up more explosives and literature published by the KKK and Aryan Nations. Phelps's van was decorated with a bumper sticker issued by the Invisible Empire Knights of the KKK. [NYT 1985]

PHILLIPS, DENVER

A member of the United Klans in Athens, Georgia, Phillips was accused of firing shotgun blasts into a black home on June 20, 1964, blinding victim John Clink in one eye. Jailed on charges of assault with intent to kill, he was never brought to trial. A month later, Phillips signed a statement implicating Klan suspects in the murder of another black man, Lemuel Penn. [38; 40]

PHILPOT, KATE

A black resident of Dawson, Georgia, Philpot became a target for Klan violence on September 5, 1962, several days before the state's Democratic primary election. A band of masked Klansmen stormed her house one night, and Philpot's daughter returned their gunfire, fatally wounding Leroy Parks. Authorities ruled the killing justifiable, and six other nightriders were convicted on October 19 on charges that included assault, riot, shooting into an occupied dwelling, and violation of Georgia's anti-mask law. [NYT 1962]

PHILPOTT, TOM

A reporter for the Army Times, Philpott authored a 1979 article summarizing a Defense Department report that recorded some type of Klan activity in every Army command. The same document reported that U.S. Air Force officers were concerned about Klan activities on bases in Germany. [93]

PICHETT CLUB

In 1965 congressional investigators identified this group as a cover for a Lawrenceville, Virginia, klavern, United Klans of America. [38]

PICKETT, A.C.

An ex-Confederate officer and Reconstruction Klansman in Woodruff County, Arkansas, Pickett led a force of 200 insurgents that threatened to attack state militiamen in Augusta in December 1868. Militia officers broke up the group by seizing hostages and vowing to destroy the town in the event of an attack. Pickett later led a delegation to visit Governor Powell Clayton and denied any Klan activity in Woodruff County, but Clayton countered by producing a list of known members, with Pickett's name at the top. Once home, Pickett convened a public meeting on December 19, 1868, at which 400 locals signed a pledge to assist authorities in curbing terrorism. [87]

PICKLE, WILLIAM

See *Blackwell Real Estate*.

PIERCE, PAUL, JR.

In 1977 Pierce was identified as grand titan for Bill Wilkinson's Invisible Empire Knights in Louisiana's 6th Congressional District. [84]

PIERCE, WILLIAM

An ex-member of the John Birch Society, Pierce defected to join the American Nazi Party in Arlington, Virginia, winning a position as editor of George Lincoln Rockwell's *National Socialist World*. A ranking officer of the party after Rockwell's 1967 assassination, Pierce moved on to command the Washington-based National Alliance in 1970 when it broke with Willis Carto's Liberty Lobby. In 1978, as "Andrew Macdonald," Pierce authored *The Turner Diaries*, a futuristic racist novel that inspired several of his followers to create The Order five years later. Federal officers maintain that Pierce received $50,000 from The Order's 1984 bank robberies as a "reward" for writing the book, but he denies the charge and was never tried as an accomplice to their crimes. His National Vanguard Press, based in Arlington, remains a leading outlet for far-right and neo-Nazi literature, most of which praises Adolf Hitler, whom Pierce refers to as "The Great One." [2; 13]

PIKE, ALBERT

An ex-Confederate general and editor of the Memphis *Appeal* during Reconstruction, Pike was also identified as an early Klansman and co-author of the KKK's original prescript. [87]

PIN HOOK IMPROVEMENT ASSOCIATION

In 1966 congressional investigators identified this group—also known as the Cape Fear Fishing Club—as a cover for the Wallace, North Carolina, klavern, United Klans of America. [38]

PINE GROVE HUNTING & FISHING CLUB

In 1966 the House Un-American Activities Committee identified this group as a cover for the Pine Grove, Louisiana, klavern, Original Knights of the KKK. [38]

PINE VALLEY LODGE

Also known as Pine Valley No. 99, this group was identified in 1965 as a front for the Buford, Georgia, klavern, United Klans of America. [38]

PINEDALE SADDLE CLUB

In 1965 congressional investigators identified this group as a front for Guilford County Unit No. 10, United Klans of America, based in Greensboro and Pleasant Garden, North Carolina. [38]

PIONEER SPORTSMAN CLUB

The front for a Covington, Georgia, klavern of the United Klans, this group was publicly identified in 1965. [38]

PIRES, ROBERT

A member of the Aryan Nations indicted for bombings in Idaho, Pires shot and killed white supremacist Kenneth Shray near Baltimore, Maryland, in August 1986. He later pled guilty to the murder and was sentenced to prison. [NYT 1986]

PITT COUNTY CHRISTIAN FELLOWSHIP CLUB

Also known as Benevolent Association Unit No. 53, this club was identified in 1965 as a front for the Greenville, North Carolina, klavern, United Klans of America. [38]

PITT COUNTY IMPROVEMENT ASSOCIATION

In 1965 congressional investigators identified this group as a cover for Farmville, North Carolina, Unit No. 37, United Klans of America. [38]

PITTS, BILLY ROY

A member of the Mississippi-based White Knights, Pitts was jailed in March 1966 on charges of murdering black civil rights activist Vernon Dahmer. A year later, he was charged with kidnapping Jack Watkins, a prosecution witness in the Dahmer case. Pitts ultimately pled guilty to arson and murder in state court, receiving a life sentence on March 8, 1968. A guilty plea for civil rights charges earned him five years in a federal prison, and Pitts dropped from sight after serving that term. He was never taken into custody by state authorities to serve his life sentence, an apparent payoff for his testimony against other Klansmen charged in the case. Hostile Klansmen reportedly traced him to Louisiana following his disappearance, but authorities refuse to comment. [NYT 1967–1968, 1972; 96]

PLAMPKIN, PHILIP

See *Jackson, Robert.*

PLOGGER, WILLIAM H.

One of five Chicago policemen identified as Klan members in December 1967, Plogger was dismissed from the force in lieu of facing criminal charges based on stockpiles of illegal weapons and alleged murder plots aimed at various civic leaders. [*NYT* 1968]

POINSETTIA UNIT 101

Operating as a cover for the Jacksonville, Florida, klavern, Improved Order of the U.S. Klans, this group disbanded in December 1964, and was revived a few months later as the front for a local unit of the United Klans. [38]

POLLOCK HUNTING & FISHING CLUB

See *Little River Rod & Gun Club.*

POPE, HENRY H.

An ex-Union officer and sheriff of St. Mary's Parish, Louisiana, during Reconstruction, Pope was murdered by Klansmen in an October 1868 attack that also claimed the life of a local judge, Valentine Chase. [87]

POPULIST PARTY

A political arm of the 1980s Christian Identity movement, this anti-Semitic group is also known as the American Populist Party. Led by chairman Bill Baker and vice chairman Jim Yarborough and well-financed by the far-right Liberty Lobby, the party succeeded in placing candidates on the ballot in fourteen states during the 1984 national elections. [13]

PORTER, WILLIAM H.

A Tennessee Klansman, Porter pled guilty in a December 1984 shooting incident that damaged a home in Murfreesboro. He was sentenced to sixty days in jail and eighteen months of supervised probation for his crime. [*NYT* 1985]

POSSE COMITATUS

A volatile blend of survivalism, neo-Nazi politics, and the Christian Identity faith, this movement dates from 1969, when an aging veteran of the Silver Shirts, Henry Lamont Beach, founded the first known chapter in Portland, Oregon. Beach's group was variously called the Sheriff's Posse Comitatus or the Citizens' Law Enforcement Research Committee, and it was soon joined by the U.S. Christian Posse Association, organized in Glendale, California, by anti-Semite William Potter Gale. In essence, Posse Comitatus—literally, "power of the county"—draws its inspiration from the post-Civil War Possee Comitatus Act, which forbade federal troops from intervening to enforce domestic laws. Posse members recognize no elected officials above the county sheriff, and even that authority is disregarded if a sheriff is suspected of cooperating with the "Zionist Occupational Government" in Washington, D.C. Devoid of any meaningful nationwide organization, local Posse units have been identified in California, Colorado, Delaware, Idaho, Illinois, Kansas, Michigan, Nebraska, North Dakota, Oregon, Texas, Washington, and Wisconsin. Overlapping membership with KKK and neo-Nazi groups is common, and Klan leader David Duke once told the press: "We work with the Posses whenever we can. We get their material and funnel it to our groups." Entranced by nuisance suits against the government and ill-conceived tax protest movements, Posse members were active enough by the mid-1970s to prompt creation of a special IRS Illegal Tax Protester Program. In 1980 federal agents identified 17,222 dedicated tax protesters, with that number leaping to 49,213 in 1982 and 57,754 in 1983. One such Posse stalwart, Gordon Kahl, murdered two federal marshals trying to arrest him for tax evasion in February 1983, and killed a county sheriff before officers killed Kahl four months later. Dedicated survivalists, Posse members stockpile weapons and will use them. In May 1982 eight members—including a known Klansman—were jailed for plotting to kill a federal judge and bomb the IRS office in Denver, Colorado. In September 1983, a Kansas member described the "accidental" death of Sheriff David Nigus in Hiawatha as a right-wing assassination conducted by the Posse. In October 1984, Nebraska Posse member Arthur Kirk died in a shootout with a sheriff's SWAT team after declaring his farm a sovereign county under Posse dictates. Beginning in the late 1970s, Colorado Posse leader John Grandbouche persuaded members to adopt a widespread barter scheme, theoretically avoiding income tax by delivering all their wealth to a National Commodities and Barter Association, which converted the money into gold or silver bullion stored in fortified "warehouse banks." In 1985 federal officers raided five such facilities in Colorado, Iowa, Minnesota, and South Dakota, seizing ten tons of silver bullion collected on behalf of an estimated 20,000 participants in the scheme. An estimated $250,000 in gold bullion and thousands of documents were seized in a raid on Grandbouche's office, but a federal judge ordered the bullion returned. In July 1986 Colorado Posse member Roderick Elliott was convicted on theft charges for embezzling funds "donated" by midwestern farmers as part of a similar barter arrangement. [NYT 1982–1983; 2; 13]

POTER, OLAF

In 1977, Poter was identified as a giant of David Duke's Knights of the KKK in St. Bernard Parish, Louisiana. [84]

POTITO, REV. OREN

A St. Petersburg, Florida, member of the National States Rights Party, Potito managed John Crommelin's 1962 Alabama gubernatorial campaign. In October 1962 he was arrested in Oxford, Mississippi, while organizing protests against integration of the state university. A cache of firearms was recovered from his car. By 1964 he was leading the eastern conference of Wesley Swift's Church of Jesus Christ Christian, declaring that his church had formed guerilla warfare units to "defend the country in case of a takeover." [67; 90]

POTTLE, E.H.

A prominent attorney during Reconstruction in Warrenton, Georgia, Pottle served as lawyer for the local KKK and was recognized as having influence over the organization. In 1870 he was a prime mover in the trumped-up bribery prosecution of anti-Klan Sheriff John Norris. [87]

POTTS, "PREACHER"

A black garage employee of Klansman Herbert Guest in Athens, Georgia, Potts was dispatched by Guest to retrieve a stalled car from a rural highway in May 1964. Arriving at the scene of the alleged breakdown, he was accosted by Klansman and flogged. On his return to the garage, Guest met Potts with a smile and asked, "Your tail sore, Preacher? You want a cushion to sit on?" [40]

POULNOT, EUGENE

See *Shoemaker, Joseph.*

POWELL, REV. EUGENE

A Methodist minister in Fair Bluff, North Carolina, Powell became a target of Klan threats after inviting a black quartet to sing at his church in 1952. The continued harassment ultimately forced him to leave town, following a nervous breakdown. [NYT 1952]

POWELL, MRS. LEWIS

A black resident of Reconstruction Hickman County, Tennessee, Mrs. Powell was shot and killed by Klansmen as an active member of the Union League. [93]

POWELL, LUTHER

The Klan's pioneer in Oregon during 1921, Powell signed up 100 members in Jackson County during his first week of operation, later moving on to serve as king kleagle in Washington and Idaho, with his headquarters in Spokane. There, he established a Klan newspaper, *The Watcher on the Tower*, and helped create the Royal Riders of the Red Robe. Near the end of the decade he moved to Alaska and tried his hand at KKK recruiting there without success. [10]

PRICE, CECIL RAY

An active member of the Mississippi White Knights and deputy sheriff in Neshoba County under Sheriff Lawrence Rainey, Price was identified as a participant in the plot to murder civil rights activist Michael Schwerner in June 1964. After arresting Schwerner, James Chaney, and Andrew Goodman on a spurious traffic charge, Price released them from the county jail, then stopped their car a second time and delivered the trio to a White Knights murder party. Indicted with Rainey on federal charges of beating black mechanic Kirk Culbertson and fracturing his skull, Price was also one of twenty-one Klansmen charged in the Neshoba County triple murder. Following his arrest in that case, he said it took him an hour to get to work, "I had to spend so much time shaking hands." In 1967, Price ran for sheriff in Neshoba County, reminding voters how he and Rainey had worked to "maintain a buffer between our people and the many agitators who have invaded our county," adding, "You can be sure that I will be ready to serve you in the future." Defeated at the polls, he was also convicted on civil rights charges in October 1967, drawing a sentence of six years in federal prison. Appeals stalled his incarceration until 1970, and he was released in 1974, finding work as a truck driver for a local oil distributor. [42; 84]

PRICE, JACK

See *Columbians, Inc.*

PRIDE SPORTSMAN LEAGUE

In 1965 congressional investigators identified this group as a cover for the Pride, Louisiana, klavern, Original Knights of the Ku Klux Klan. [38]

PRIDMORE, LAWRENCE GENE

See *Greensboro, North Carolina.*

PRINS, JACK

A native of Holland, Prins worked on guidance systems for the German V-1 and V-2 rockets during World War II. He emigrated to Canada after the war and found work as a truck mechanic, enduring numerous brushes with the law related to his racist, anti-Semitic activities. Named as Canada's grand dragon for the Invisible Empire Knights under Dale Reusch, Prins also served as leader for the White Confederacy of Understanding, and was active in the Toronto-based Western Front. In a 1976 interview with journalist Patsy Sims, he explained his belief that "The root of all evil is the Jew." [84]

PRITCHETT, JOE

See *Aaron, Edward.*

PROGRESSIVE PARTY

A left-wing third party that ran Henry Wallace as its presidential candidate in 1948, the Progressive Party drew flack from Klansmen across the South after Wallace refused to address racially segregated rallies. Angry demonstrations were organized by militant whites in North Carolina and elsewhere, with Klansmen in Knoxville, Tennessee, timing a rally to coincide with Wallace's appearance at a local black church. Progressive Party meetings were disrupted by hecklers and showers of fruit in Charlotte and Hickory, North Carolina, on August 31, 1948. In the November 1948 general election Wallace polled 1,156,103 votes nationwide, running 23,000 behind Dixiecrat candidate Strom Thurmond. [*NYT* 1948]

PRO-SOUTHERNERS

A Georgia-based white supremacist organization and suspected Klan front, the Pro-Southerners were led by Harry Pyle, an ex-Klansman from Memphis, until factional rifts led to his resignation and the group's breakup in March 1956. During its brief existence, the group was headquartered in Ft. Pierce. [*NYT* 1956]

PROTESTANT WAR VETERANS OF AMERICA

Founded by Edward J. Smythe in 1946, this group was publicly identified by Georgia State Attorney General Dan Duke as a Klan front. [10]

PROVINCE

In Reconstruction Klan terminology, the province was equivalent to a county, with a grand giant presiding over KKK affairs. In the modern Klan, province replaces the obsolete Reconstruction term "dominion," generally referring to the congressional district but more flexible, adapted to larger and smaller areas based on the needs of the Klan. The modern ruling officer is the great titan. [43; 87]

PRUITT, DR. E.P.

A Birmingham, Alabama, physician, Pruitt was named president of the Federated Klans when it incorporated in July 1946. Three years later, with

Imperial Wizard William Morris in jail, Pruitt ordered the Klan to unmask. Enraged, Morris declared that Pruitt had "overstepped his authority" and "accepted" the doctor's resignation. [25]

PRYOR, RALPH

An ex-policeman in Wilmington, Delaware, Pryor was appointed to serve as Delaware's grand dragon for the United Klans of America on July 31, 1965, at a rally intended to start a mass recruiting drive in the state. By mid-November, he was voicing his dissatisfaction with the United Klans to newsmen, citing mismanagement of funds and a prevalence of rabid neo-Nazis in the northern membership. As evidence of the latter charge, Pryor cited a recent gathering in Rising Sun, Maryland, complete with straight-armed fascist salutes from the dais, which struck him as "more like a Nazi funeral than a Klan rally." Pryor initially agreed to testify before the House Un-American Activities Committee but later changed his mind, telling reporters, "If I testify, some day they are going to find me in Selma, Alabama, with thirty bullet holes in me, and that killer is going to get off scot free." Pryor formally resigned from the United Klans in January 1966, and was replaced by Bennie Sartin. [NYT 1965; 38]

PUCKETT, CHARLES J.

An Alabama Klansman, Puckett pled guilty in January 1980 to charges of intimidating and injuring two black ministers at a Muscle Shoals restaurant. He was sentenced to a year in prison for the crime. [2]

PULASKI, TENNESSEE

Recognized as the birthplace of the Reconstruction KKK, Pulaski still harbors a touch of mystery concerning the date of that event. The founding fathers of the Klan agreed that their first meeting took place in the office of Judge Thomas M. Jones, father of charter member Calvin Jones, but they were never clear about the date. James Crowe would later place the gathering some time in the fall or winter of 1865–1866, while John Lester remembered the date as May 1866, the date accepted as accurate by the modern United Klans of America. Reconstruction Klansmen held their first anniversary parade on June 5, 1867, but historians turned the clock back in May 1917, when the United Daughters of the Confederacy unveiled a memorial plaque at the building that once housed Judge Jones's office, listing the names of the six founders and dating the Klan's birth from Christmas Eve 1865. James Venable's National Knights regard the latter date as accurate, and they dispatched nine delegates for a centennial celebration in Pulaski on December 24, 1965. For their part, leaders of the United Klans convened a bicentennial rally in the city on May 27, 1976, suggesting a birthdate for the KKK that seems impossibly precise. Racist groups continue to "honor" Pulaski with public demonstrations from time to time, most recently with the appearance of 175 marchers from the Aryan Nations in October 1989, despite Mayor Stacey Garner's comment that "Pulaski is *not* the 'home' of the Ku Klux Klan. The small band of KKK marchers have come in from other places and, like you, they are not welcome here." [*NYT* 1989; 87; 93]

PURYEAR, WILLIAM

A black resident of Reconstruction Alamance County, North Carolina, Puryear witnessed the February 1870 murder of Wyatt Outlaw and identified two Klansmen involved in that crime. A short time later, he was taken from his home and killed by nightriders, his body weighted and dropped in a nearby mill pond. [87]

PYLE, HARRY WILLIAM

A retired Memphis house painter and ex-Klansman, identified as national chairman of the segregationist Pro-Southerners, Pyle resigned his post in March 1956, at age seventy-five, after internal policy disputes tore the group apart. [*NYT* 1956]

QUEENS OF THE GOLDEN MASK

Created by Grand Dragon David Stephenson in 1922, this group served as the official ladies' auxiliary for the Indiana Klan. Stephenson used the organization as his personal rumor mill—dubbed the "poison squad"—and boasted that telephone links could transmit rumors from Evansville to Gary within twenty-four hours. [93]

QUICK, DAVID

See *Caldwell, Lester.*

QUILTING CLUB

In 1965 congressional investigators identified this group as a cover for the ladies' auxiliary of the Roxboro, North Carolina, klavern, United Klans of America. [38]

QUINN, AYLENE

A black resident of McComb, Mississippi, active in civil rights work, Quinn was attacked by members of the United Klans, who firebombed her home on September 20, 1964. [38]

R.H. VOLUNTEERS OF AMERICA

In 1965 congressional investigators identified this group as a cover for the Rock Hill, South Carolina, klavern, United Klans of America. [38]

RAINBOW CLUB

In 1965, congressional investigators identified this club as a front for the ladies auxiliary of the Pink Hill, North Carolina, klavern, United Klans of America. [38]

RAINEY, LAWRENCE A.

Hired as a policeman in Canton, Mississippi, Rainey transferred to the Philadelphia, Mississippi, force two years later, where he killed black resident Luther Jackson in October 1957. When a female friend of Jackson denounced Rainey for the unprovoked shooting, she was beaten by Rainey and the Philadelphia police chief. In 1961 Rainey became a deputy under Sheriff Ethel Barnett; in May 1962, with Barnett and another deputy, Rainey shot and killed a handcuffed black, Willie Nash, and claimed self-defense. Elected Neshoba County sheriff in 1963, Rainey campaigned on a promise to "handle the niggers and the outsiders" expected during 1964's Freedom Summer. Local blacks were so intimidated by Rainey that he once cleared a black county fair of 300 people by simply walking into the room and standing there until everyone drifted away. In 1964 Rainey and deputy Cecil Price were indicted by federal authorities for beating black mechanic Kirk Culbertson and fracturing his skull. A member of the Mississippi White

Knights, Rainey was further accused of complicity in the June 1964 murders of civil rights workers Michael Schwerner, James Chaney, and Andrew Goodman, but he was acquitted by a federal jury in October 1967. He became something of a local celebrity, praised by Circuit Judge O.H. Barnett as "the bravest sheriff in America." Rainey was also featured as a guest speaker at rallies of the United Klans in Mississippi, and he was greeted with loud applause at a meeting of the state sheriff's association. Following his 1967 retirement and acquittal in the Schwerner case, Rainey found work as a private security guard, working, ironically, for a black supervisor. [19; 84]

RALEY, JOHN

A Klansman and town constable during Reconstruction in Warrenton, Georgia, Raley participated in the March 1869 lynching of Dr. G.W. Darden, a local Republican activist. That spring, Raley was appointed sheriff of Warren County in a Conservative move to replace anti-Klan Sheriff John Norris, who was temporarily out of the county on official business. One of six Klansmen arrested by Norris and federal troops in June 1869 and charged with Darden's murder, Raley was released on bond and never came to trial. [87]

RAMSEY, H.C.

While serving as a klaliff in Louisiana during 1922, Ramsey took part in the campaign to replace Imperial Wizard William Simmons with Texas newcomer Hiram Evans. In the wake of the successful coup, Ramsey was rewarded with an appointment as imperial klaliff, and was stationed in Atlanta. [10]

RAMSPECT, ROBERT

One of the earliest Klan recruits in 1915, Ramspect later represented Georgia in the U.S. House of Representatives. [10]

RANCH GUN CLUB

In 1965 congressional investigators identified this group as a cover for the Clayton, North Carolina, klavern, United Klans of America. [38]

RANDOLPH, B.F.

A black chaplain in the Union army, Randolph settled in Orangeburg, South Carolina, during 1864, and remained after the Civil War to become an active Republican and state senator for Abbeville County. In that capacity he helped establish black schools and chapters of the Union League, becoming one of the state's most prominent Republicans. On October 1,

1868, he was shot and killed by three Klansmen at a railroad station near Cokesbury. One of the killers later confessed, but no one was prosecuted for the crime. [87]

RANDOLPH, RYLAND

A bitter racist, Randolph moved to Tuscaloosa, Alabama, in 1867 and bought the local *Independent Monitor*, publishing his paper with the masthead: "White Man—Right or Wrong—Still the White Man!" In December 1867, he printed an editorial calling for armed resistance to Radical Reconstruction, and Klansmen made their first local appearance on December 30, carrying Randolph off into mock captivity. Generally acknowledged as the Tuscaloosa cyclops, Randolph began printing KKK warning notices in March 1868, his troops resorting to violence when simple threats failed. In 1901 Randolph fondly recalled how blacks were "thrashed in the regular antebellum style, until their unnatural nigger-pride had a tumble, and humbleness to the white man reigned supreme." Never one to stand on the sidelines of a scrap, Randolph once waded into a fight between a white man and two blacks, stabbing one of the blacks "in self-defense." On another occasion, he allegedly confronted a mob of 100 angry blacks and scattered them by brandishing a pistol. His penchant for street brawling led Democratic leaders to shun Randolph by mid-1868, but Klansmen remained loyal, and a mob of them joined with him to break up a local Republican meeting prior to that year's presidential election. A candidate for the state legislature, Randolph was victorious in 1868 and again in 1870. His crowning "achievement" was a campaign of intimidation aimed at Republican staffers and students at the state university in Tuscaloosa, which succeeded in closing the school for a short time in 1870. In April 1870, armed with a pistol and Bowie knife, Randolph carried his war to the streets, stalking Professor Vernon Vaughan, but he met student William Smith instead. A nephew of Alabama's governor, Smith was quicker on the draw than Randolph, killing an elderly bystander and wounding his target in one leg. Subsequent amputation of the wounded limb seemed to quench Randolph's zeal for armed struggle, and a June 1870 editorial declared: "It is now time, we are free to announce, for murders and assassinations to cease." A year later, while testifying before Congress, Randolph was moved to say that the once honorable Klan had lately fallen into low and violent hands. [87]

RARICK, JOHN

A district court judge from St. Francisville, Louisiana, Rarick ran against incumbent twelve-term congressman James Morrison in the 1966 Democratic primary. Morrison accused Rarick of being a Klansman, and Rarick responded with a $500,000 libel suit, rolling on to defeat his opponent before the case was settled. Newsmen revealed that Morrison's charges had prompted FBI surveillance of Rarick, and a 1973 report confirmed his previous occupation as exalted cyclops of a klavern in St. Francisville. [*NYT* 1966, 1972; 71]

RAWLS, LOUIS

As mayor of Bogalusa, Louisiana, elected in 1970 and 1974, Rawls accepted the KKK's endorsement in his second campaign, remarking that, "The blacks don't vote for me, anyway." When the Invisible Empire Knights opened their local klavern on Good Friday 1976, Rawls participated in the ribbon-cutting ceremony, accepting a Klan hood and certificate of honorary membership from Imperial Wizard Bill Wilkinson. [84]

RAWLS, SARAH

See *Ford, Benton.*

RAY, JERRY

A brother of James Earl Ray, Jerry attached himself to National States Rights Party headquarters in Savannah, Georgia, when J.B. Stoner took over the 1969 appeals of his brother's conviction for killing Dr. Martin Luther King. Serving as Stoner's chauffeur and personal bodyguard, Ray spent his free time selling copies of the group's newspaper, later emerging as campaign manager for Stoner's 1970 gubernatorial race. In July 1970, he shot and wounded teenaged Nazi Stephen Donald Black during an attempted burglary at National States Rights Party headquarters, and jurors acquitted him of attempted murder four months later. [*NYT* 1970]

REALM

In both the Reconstruction and modern Klans, a realm is equivalent to a state, administered by a grand dragon. The term is never applied to smaller geographical units, although the 1920s saw the term occasionally applied to larger areas, when membership in one state was insufficient to justify an imperial charter. Thus, the states of Maine, Vermont, and New Hampshire were considered a single realm. [43; 87]

REAVIS, HENRY

An ex-judge in Gainesville, Alabama, Reavis served as an attorney and local leader of the Reconstruction Klan, enrolling members at his law office. [87]

RED BLUFF HUNTING CLUB

In 1965 congressional investigators identified this group as a cover for a Bennettsville, South Carolina, klavern, United Klans of America. [38]

RED CAPS

In 1868 this title was applied to Klansmen active in nightriding around Humphreys County, Tennessee, west of Nashville. [87]

RED RIVER CLUB

In 1965 the House Un-American Activities Committee identified this group as a front for Bennettsville, South Carolina, Unit No. 19, United Klans of America. [38]

RED WOOD LODGE

In 1966 congressional investigators identified this lodge as a front for Kings Mountain, North Carolina, Unit No. 35, United Klans of America. [38]

REDWINE, CLIFFORD

An Indiana Klansman, Redwine was charged with bombing a black-owned Indianapolis home in July 1980. Authorities identified him as a suspect after he boasted to friends about the bombing, claiming he had "killed eight niggers." [NYT 1980]

REEB, REV. JAMES

A Unitarian minister from Boston active in civil rights work, Reeb was fatally beaten in Selma, Alabama, when racists attacked him and two other ministers on March 9, 1965, outside the Silver Moon Cafe. Four suspects were jailed the next day, with murder charges ultimately filed against William Hoggle, R.B. Kelley, and Elmer Cook. State Attorney General Richmond Flowers linked all three suspects to the United Klans of America, although that group had no active klavern in Selma. The city attorney allowed their release on modest bail over strenuous objections from Police Chief Wilson Baker. On March 25, a few hours prior to Viola Liuzzo's murder, one of the Reeb defendants met several Birmingham Klansmen in Selma's Silver Moon Cafe, where Klansman Eugene Thomas introduced him to FBI informant Gary Rowe as a close friend. In parting, the defendant—never publicly identified—said, "You all go do your job. I already done mine." In a March 27 news conference, United Klans Imperial Wizard Robert Shelton called the Reeb and Liuzzo deaths part of a "trumped-up plot to destroy the right wing in America," claiming that Reeb "had been dying of cancer before he ever came to Alabama." Judge James Hare, best known for his public statement that blacks never attain an IQ above 65, spent forty minutes addressing a local grand jury on the Reeb case, recounting Selma's troubles and proclaiming that federal officers "selected Selma for assassination back in the fall of 1963." In Hare's opinion, local whites had shown "unbelievable restraint" in the face of "fantastic and terroristic" acts by blacks and "self-appointed saints" drawn from the Northern clergy. In spite of Hare's diatribe, the panel still indicted the three defendants on April 15, and their trial opened on December 7, 1965. Each prospective juror was asked if racial prejudice would influence his verdict, and three were seated after standing mute, the court treating their silence as a negative response. In fact, one chosen juror was the brother of a crucial defense witness, but the prosecutor failed to object or move for a mistrial. Four critical eyewitnesses were unavailable as the trial convened. Two had left Alabama, another was ruled mentally incompetent, and the last— formerly accused with the three defendants—refused to testify on grounds of possible self-incrimination. Jurors deliberated for ninety minutes, during which an unprecedented off-the-record visit from Sheriff Jim Clark occurred, before acquitting the three defendants on December 10. [NYT 1965; 63]

REED, CHARLES

See *Hattie Cotton School.*

REED, JOHN C.

When a local Klan den was organized in Oglethorpe County, Georgia, during April 1868 in order to save the South from "Africanization," Reed was appointed to serve as grand giant. In that capacity, he led a nocturnal parade through black neighborhoods prior to the presidential election, and two years later spearheaded teams of Klansmen that prevented blacks from casting ballots in the state elections. His subsequent testimony dated local KKK disbandment from late 1870, although nightriding continued well into 1871. [87]

REED, RICHARD R.

One of six original Klansmen in Pulaski, Tennessee, he served as the organization's first lictor, equivalent to a sergeant at arms. [87; 93]

REEVES, FRED

See *Dollar, William.*

REISNER, HARVEY

Identified as the exalted cyclops of an Apopka, Florida, klavern in 1952, Reisner was indicted for perjury in June 1953 on the basis of false answers given before a federal grand jury probing local terrorism. Evidence collected by the panel named Reisner as a participant in the beatings of Klan victims Ivan Eilbeck and Albert Boykin. [NYT 1953]

RESTER, ROBERT T.

While serving as city attorney for Bogalusa, Louisiana, Rester was also publicly identified as a member of the Original Knights of the KKK and a registered agent of a known Klan front, the Anti-Communist Christian Association. Frequent acquittals of local Klansmen, coupled with vigorous prosecution of black civil rights activists around Bogalusa, prompted questions about Rester's fitness for office in 1965, precipitating federal intervention and a lawsuit enjoining Klansmen against further interference with civil rights demonstrations. [38]

REUSCH, DALE

An auto worker in Lodi, Ohio, who doubled as grand dragon for the National Knights for the state, Reusch ran for sheriff in Medina County in 1968 and 1972. Defeated in those campaigns, he ran for governor as a write-in candidate in the 1974 Democratic primary, and lost again. In September 1974, a spokesman for the National Knights announced that he would be their presidential candidate in 1976, with Texas Klansman Scott Nelson as his running mate. By early 1975 Reusch was involved in a campaign to rescue Ohio textbooks from the taint of "government indoctrination and nationalized education." Quarreling with Imperial Wizard James Venable that October, he led four other dissident dragons into the new Invisible Empire Knights, proclaiming that Catholics and naturalized U.S. citizens would be welcomed as recruits. In February 1976 Reusch filed as a vice presidential candidate in West Virginia's Democratic primary, voicing his hopes for the number-two spot on a ticket headed by Alabama Governor George Wallace. Despite his claims of control over Klan votes in eighteen states, Reusch was solidly trounced in 1976, and again in his 1978 bid for the office of lieutenant governor. By 1980 the Invisible Empire Knights were reported as defunct and disbanded, the title usurped by Bill Wilkinson's more militant, action-oriented Klan. [NYT 1974–1976; FOF 1978]

REYNOLDS, EDWIN

An unemployed machinist and United Klans recruiter in New Jersey, Reynolds was dismissed from his post by Pennsylvania's grand dragon on charges of adultery, misusing Klan funds, abusing narcotics, and "being a member of an anti-Christian cult." Klan spokesmen charged that Reynolds "set aside our oath and substituted his own, requiring everyone to swear allegiance to Hitler." In retaliation, Reynolds organized his own White Knights of the KKK in New Jersey, maintaining friendly contact with the American Nazi Party, but the small membership dwindled to nine identified Klansmen after his 1980 arrest on charges of rape, filed by a female member of the Jewish Defense League. Prior to his trial, Reynolds announced the group's disbandment, urging his handful of loyalists to join David Duke and the Knights of the KKK. Pressed for comments on the case, he replied, "I will say only that I am innocent, Heil Hitler." Jurors ultimately agreed, and Reynolds was acquitted of all charges, but his moment in the Klan spotlight had already passed him by. [10]

REYNOLDS, JAMES

A New Orleans Klansman, Reynolds was arrested in June 1966, for his role in a series of firebombings targeting churches, homes, and businesses between March and May 1965. [NYT 1966]

RHODE ISLAND

The 1920s Klan claimed roughly 15,000 members in Rhode Island, but they were never politically strong, and membership had fallen below 1,000 by the early part of 1926. In March 1928, the state's Klan gained headlines when the Providence *Journal* reported that Klansmen had taken over three companies of the state militia, packing the ranks and funding acquisition of weapons that included a machine gun. With Klansmen in control, all new recruits in the suspect companies were forced to join the KKK—at fifteen dollars a head—as their price of admission. Grand Dragon J.W. Perry was called before a state legislative commission to explain the situation, and members of the KKK militia were officially disarmed by order of the governor. By 1930, statewide membership had plunged below 100, and the Rhode Island Klan soon vanished entirely. [10]

RHODY, ROBERT MICHAEL

Identified as an associate of the KKK in San Diego, California, Rhody was convicted with Exalted Cyclops Orville Watkins of firing shots into homes owned by Mexican-Americans in April 1977. [2]

RICCIO, BILL

A member of the Aryan Nations, Riccio once served as a state leader for Bill Wilkinson's Invisible Empire Knights of the KKK, and was also identified as an officer in the White Knights of Alabama. Riccio was one of several Klansmen charged with assaulting black demonstrators in Decatur, Alabama, in 1979, during riots linked to the rape trial of black defendant Tommy Lee Hines. A convicted felon, Riccio drew a term of two years in federal prison during April 1985, after his conviction of possessing firearms in violation of his parole terms. [NYT 1985]

RICH, SAM

A native of Kentucky, Rich was dispatched to western Pennsylvania as the Klan's resident kleagle in 1921, followed by his subsequent appointment as grand dragon. He was present, with Imperial Wizard Hiram Evans, at the Carnegie riot scene where Klansman Thomas Abbott was shot and killed in 1923. Two years later, Allegheny County Klansmen filed complaints against Rich with imperial headquarters, noting the dragon's irregular handling of cash and internal discipline. Evans ignored the dissidents at first, but finally convened a tribunal when they threatened to bypass Atlanta and choose their own dragon. Even with friends on the panel, Rich lost out, to be replaced by Reverend Herbert Shaw. [10]

RICHARDS, TOM

See *Mer Rouge, Louisiana.*

RICHARDSON, ALFRED

A black resident of Reconstruction South Carolina, Richardson was despised by Klansmen for his ownership of land and his successful management of a grocery store. Local whites warned him that Klansmen "say you are making too much money and they do not allow any nigger to rise that way," but Richardson refused to leave the area. A short time later, he was flogged by Klansmen on an accusation of "voting the radical ticket." [93]

RICHARDSON, CARL

See *Grainger, Ben.*

RICHARDSON, FRIEND W.

An ally of the 1920s California Klan, Richardson was elected governor in 1922 with KKK support. In public, the governor always hedged on the question of personal Klan membership, and spokesmen for the Invisible Empire helped keep his secret. When the question was raised by Klansmen themselves at a Sacramento klavern meeting, the grand dragon replied, "I just don't like to say as to that, boys. I can say this: Richardson is all right." Following Richardson's inauguration, Sacramento's kludd was appointed to serve as chaplain for the state senate. [10]

RICHARDSON, JULE C.

See *Flowers, Evergreen.*

RICHBURG SPORTSMAN CLUB

In 1965 congressional investigators identified this group as a front for Chester, South Carolina, Unit No. 32, United Klans of America. [38]

RIDDLEHOOVER, CHARLES B. ("RIP")

A Ft. Lauderdale, Florida, Klansman, Riddlehoover quarreled with Grand Dragon Donald Cothran in mid-1965 and led other dissidents in defecting from the United Klans of America that October, emerging as grand dragon of the new United Knights of the KKK. Riddlehoover was barely installed in his new office when Miami police arrested him for a traffic violation, adding concealed weapon charges when they removed a pistol from the grand dragon's possession. [38]

RIDLEY, REV. CALEB

An Atlanta minister and imperial kludd of the 1920s Klan, Ridley brought the KKK unfortunate publicity when he was jailed for drunk driving in 1921. Three years later, he was a member of the imperial kloncilium appointed to mediate the ongoing dispute between William Simmons and Imperial Wizard Hiram Evans. [10]

RIGHTS OF WHITE PEOPLE

A North Carolina splinter group led by ex-marine Leroy Gibson, this group was described by police as "more dangerous than the Klan." Members patrolled the streets of Wilmington, North Carolina, during black riots in October 1971, with Gibson telling newsmen: "We're going where the trouble is and do some shooting if we have to. We'll destroy them all if necessary." Gibson's rallies drew several hundred armed whites, and the group's periodic convoys through black neighborhoods produced a citywide ban on the public display of firearms. Wilmington Police Chief H.E. Williamson complained that half of his seventy-six man force was tied up following the group's members around town to avert acts of violence. Gibson responded by offering paramilitary training courses for white high school students, announcing that: "We have as many as 2,000 white men in Wilmington who are willing to settle the trouble right now. If it weren't for the Wilmington police, the blacks in there would have been destroyed by now." [NYT 1971]

RIOTS

Best known for their furtive, nocturnal assaults, Klansmen are not averse to turning out en masse and attacking their enemies in daylight, if the odds seem favorable. Conversely, members of the modern KKK have frequently been targets of mob violence by opponents who are not content to stand aside and watch the Klan convene in public. By the early 1980s, Klansmen were more likely to be mobbed than to do the mobbing.

The Reconstruction Klan staged some spectacular uprisings, typically gearing the "spontaneous" action to coincide with local elections or the public trials of black and "radical" defendants. Klan rioters killed one black and wounded several more in Pulaski, Tennessee, in January 1868, and their Georgia comrades joined the fray in Camilla in September 1868, leaving seven blacks dead and another thirty injured. During the October 1870 elections, twelve blacks were killed by rioting Klansmen in Laurens County, South Carolina, with four others massacred and fifty wounded in a similar incident in Eutaw, Alabama. No precise casualty figures were recorded for the Klan's "hunt" around Meridian, Mississippi, in March 1871, but two whites were killed that August when local Klansmen staged an election riot in Frankfort, Kentucky.

Members of the 1920s KKK were quick to learn that violence was a two-edged sword, especially in the Northern states. One man was killed in a battle between Klansmen and Klan opposition in Smackover, Arkansas, and Sheriff Bob Buchanan was publicly censured after his interruption of a Klan parade touched off bloody violence in Lorena, Texas, leaving one man dead and several others—including Buchanan himself—seriously wounded. As kleagles pushed north of the Mason-Dixon Line, they frequently encountered violent opposition from Catholics, labor unions, and outraged immigrants—but never, it is interesting to note, from blacks. In 1921, Klansmen were mobbed in Steubenville, Ohio, a performance repeated two years later in Youngstown. In 1923 there were outbursts of anti-Klan rioting in Lancaster, Lilly, and Carnegie, Pennsylvania—with Klansman Thomas Abbott killed in the latter clash—with similar attacks recorded in Bound Brook and Perth Amboy, New Jersey. Violence against Klansmen continued in 1924, with riots in Binghamton and Hicksville, New York; Waukesha, Wisconsin; Berlin and Westwood, Massachusetts; and in South Bend, Indiana, where Notre Dame students beat and unmasked Klansmen prior to a scheduled parade. Des Moines, Iowa, was the scene of an anti-Klan riot in 1926, as was New York City in 1927. Ex-senator Tom Heflin was pelted with stones in 1928 when he tried to deliver an anti-Catholic speech in Brockton, Massachusetts.

More traditional racist violence surfaced in the 1940s, with robed Klansmen turning out to bar black families from Detroit's Sojourner Truth housing project in 1942, and closing ranks with white police to terrorize black residents of Columbia, Tennessee, four years later. Groveland, Florida, was the scene of near-anarchy in 1949, after a white woman accused several black men of rape. Florida Klansman Bill Hendrix claimed credit for the 1949 riot in Peekskill, New York, against black singer Paul Robeson, but there was no evidence of actual KKK involvement.

The U.S. Supreme Court's Black Monday ruling on school segregation precipitated a new wave of Southern violence in the 1950s, with Klansmen turning out for school riots in Clinton, Tennessee, and Tuscaloosa, Alabama. Members of the KKK in Little Rock, Arkansas, undoubtedly participated in local mob scenes the following year, but militant Klansmen reserved most of their energy for a series of bombings. In August 1960, Jacksonville members of the Florida Knights clashed with black demonstrators in riots known as "Ax Handle Saturday," after the number of bludgeons employed by rampaging Klansmen. In 1961 Klansmen were jailed for their participation in riots at the state university in Athens, Georgia, while police in Alabama collaborated with Klansmen and members of the National States Rights Party to arrange violent welcomes for the integrated Freedom Rides. A year later, militant racists from six states rallied to greet black student James Meredith in Oxford, Mississippi, leaving two men dead and over 200 injured in rioting at the state university. Between 1964 and 1966, agitators J.B. Stoner and Connie Lynch toured the nation as a two-man "riot squad," leaving their mark in St. Augustine, Florida; Bogalusa, Louisiana; and Baltimore, Maryland. Illinois Klansmen closed ranks with George Lincoln Rockwell's American Nazi Party for riots in Chicago in 1966, and the same year brought school integration to Grenada, Mississippi, where lawmen stood aside and watched members of the United Klans assault black children in the street.

In the 1970s and 1980s, Klansmen once again traded off as both the instigators and targets of mob violence. Charismatic Klansman David Duke visited South Boston in 1974, proclaiming it "Klan country" when local whites rioted against court-ordered busing to achieve school integration, and more traditional outbreaks were recorded in the South. Bill Wilkinson's Invisible Empire Knights and the independent Southern White Knights were linked with attacks on black demonstrators in Decatur, Alabama; in Forsyth County, Georgia; and in Tupelo and Oconee, Mississippi. At the same time, Imperial Wizard Dale Reusch was mobbed by anti-Klan demonstrators during a speech in Columbus, Ohio, in September 1977, and other Klan factions faced violent harassment from Oxnard, California, to Detroit and Washington, D.C. Today, Klansmen and their allies in the neo-Nazi movement have as much to fear from their opponents as beleaguered blacks and "radicals" once had to fear from the Klan. [10; 87; 93]

RITTENHOUSE, D.M.

A Philadelphia Klansman, Rittenhouse led dissident Klansmen who filed a receivership suit against imperial headquarters in 1923, charging Imperial Wizard Hiram Evans with financial waste and mismanagement. The suit was finally dismissed in November 1923, on grounds that the complaint was an internal matter for the KKK to handle on its own. [10]

RIVER VALLEY KLANS

See *Knights of the Ku Klux Klan of America.*

RIVERS, E.D.

A Klan lecturer in the 1920s, Rivers was elected governor of Georgia in 1936 and 1938. Imperial Wizard Hiram Evans was appointed as a "lieutenant colonel" on the governor's staff, a reward for his political support in a deal that allowed Evans to sell asphalt and paving material to the Georgia Highway Board without competitive bids. The covert arrangement led to felony prosecutions in 1940, by which time Rivers had also drawn heat for his pardon of Klansman and convicted killer Philip Fox. [10]

RIVERSIDE SPORTSMAN CLUB

In 1965 congressional investigators identified this group as the cover for a Wendell, North Carolina, klavern, United Klans of America. [38]

ROBB, THOMAS ARTHUR

A self-styled "pastor" from Harrison, Arkansas, Robb received national notoriety in 1980 and 1981 when he was identified as the national chaplain for the Knights of the KKK, led by Don Black. In November 1982 he led thirty Klansmen to Washington, D.C., for a demonstration against proposed laws granting amnesty to illegal aliens, an outing that resulted in two hours of rioting by KKK opponents. Identified as a prominent spokesman for the Christian Identity movement, Robb was also the driving force behind a September 1983 unity meeting in Stone Mountain, Georgia, involving representatives of half a dozen independent Klans. [2]

ROBERTS, ALTON WAYNE

A member of the Mississippi White Knights under Sam Bowers, Roberts was convicted of federal civil rights violations in October 1967 for his participation in the 1964 murders of Michael Schwerner, Andrew Goodman, and James Chaney. He was still free on appeal in 1968 when a new rash of bombings and arson terrorized parts of Mississippi, and Jewish residents of Meridian raised a $38,500 reward for information leading to the arrest and conviction of the bombers. Roberts and his brother, Raymond, pocketed over $30,000 for their role in setting up a confrontation between Meridian police and two nightriders that resulted in the death of Klanswoman Kathy Ainsworth and the capture of Thomas Tarrants. [96]

ROBERTS, CHARLES

See *Lynch, John.*

ROBERTS, CHARLES MACON

A Chattanooga, Tennessee, Klansman, Roberts assumed leadership of the Dixie Klans after Imperial Wizard Jack Brown died in 1965. [38]

ROBERTS, JAMES W.

In 1965 Roberts pled guilty to stealing military explosives from Ft. McClellan, Alabama, near Anniston, and giving them to Kenneth Adams, an officer of the Klan and National States Rights Party. Adams was acquitted at his trial on charges of receiving stolen property in January 1966. [FOF 1966]

ROBERTS, RAYMOND

See *Roberts, Alton Wayne.*

ROBINSON, COY

A resident of Lancaster, South Carolina, Robinson was identified in 1966 as a member of the five-man grand council that controlled the Association of South Carolina Klans. [38]

ROBINSON, DORSEY

A black sawmill worker in Columbus County, North Carolina, Robinson was flogged by members of the Association of Carolina Klans in late 1951, having been accused of public drunkenness and cursing in front of a white woman. Several Klansmen were indicted by a local grand jury in March 1952. [*NYT* 1952]

ROBINSON, J.T.

The police chief of Natchez, Mississippi, Robinson was arrested by the county sheriff in December 1965 on a warrant sworn out by Grand Dragon E.L. McDaniel, charging Robinson with failure to enforce the state's anti-boycott law against blacks. [*NYT* 1965]

ROBINSON, JAMES

A member of the National States Rights Party, Robinson was jailed for assaulting Dr. Martin Luther King at a Selma, Alabama, hotel in January 1965. A sixty-day jail sentence and $100 fine failed to keep him out of trouble, and two months later he was arrested for assaulting an FBI agent on Highway 80 east of Selma. The agent, who had been attacked while photographing a group of whites in the act of beating a black man, identified Robinson as one of the assailants who assaulted him and stole his camera. Robinson was punished with a $27 fine. [64; 88]

ROBINSON, WILL

A black resident of Soperton, Georgia, Robinson was dragged from his home and flogged by four carloads of robed Klansmen in July 1950. The local sheriff reported three other whippings in the preceding two weeks, but declined to investigate because FBI agents were already working on the case. [*NYT* 1950]

ROCHESTER, MARSHALL ANDREW

See *Cruell, Claude.*

ROCK OF FREEDOM

See *Indiana*.

ROCKWELL, GEORGE LINCOLN

An amateur artist in his college days, Rockwell was introduced to *Mein Kampf* and the fantasies of another failed painter while attending rallies conducted by anti-Semite Gerald L.K. Smith in the early 1950s. Blaming his academic and economic failures on the Jews, Rockwell moved south to work for the United White Party in 1957. By 1958 he was leading his own National Committee to Free America from Jewish Domination, based in Arlington, Virginia, corresponding with other racists, including National States Rights Party member and accused synagogue bomber Wallace Allen. Arlington remained Rockwell's base of operations when he founded the American Nazi Party, doubling as leader of the American Party of the World Union of Free Enterprise Socialists in 1959, leading a tiny delegation to Chicago for joint meetings with the black separatist Joint Council on Repatriation. In July 1960 Rockwell was arrested with Dan Burros, James Warner, and fourteen other Nazis after a rally on the Mall in Washington, D.C., degenerated into random brawling. Dissension on the racist fringe barred Rockwell from the National States Rights Party's 1964 presidential convention, with Edward Fields describing Rockwell as "a known leftist." Not to be outdone, Rockwell entered the 1964 presidential primary race in Wisconsin, but the only resident who volunteered to represent the Nazi cause was ultimately disqualified on grounds that he had never registered to vote. A year later, Rockwell ran for governor in Virginia as a candidate of the so-called White Majority Party, and he was a spectator during the House Un-American Activities Committee hearings on the KKK. Robed Klansmen stood shoulder to shoulder with Rockwell for riotous gatherings in Chicago the following year, but his own party was torn by internal dissension. Lieutenant John Patler was dismissed by Rockwell in 1966 for stirring up animosity between dark- and light-skinned Nazis, but Patler had the last word. On August 26, 1967, he lay in wait for Rockwell at an Arlington laundromat, killing Rockwell as he emerged from his car. During Rockwell's tenure, members of the American Nazi Party doubled as ranking officers for the United Klans of America in Delaware, Maryland, New York, New Jersey, and Pennsylvania. [38; 75; 78]

ROEDER, MANFRED RICHARD KURT

A disbarred West German attorney and notorious neo-Nazi, Roeder has been deeply involved in anti-Semitic propaganda and terrorism on two continents since the mid-1970s, when he organized the Liberation Movement of the German Reich and an affiliated group, the German Citizens' Initiative, with offices in both West Germany and the United States.

Claiming service in the Hitler Youth during 1945, Roeder has been publicly linked with organizations as diverse as the Palestine Liberation Organization and the National Socialist White People's Party. In 1976 he was fined $1,200 and sentenced to seven months in jail (suspended), for distributing a pamphlet called *The Auschwitz Lie*, which refuted claims that Nazis killed 6 million Jews in World War II. Later the same year, he spent five weeks in the United States, including an appearance at the World Conference of National Socialists, sponsored by James Warner's New Christian Crusade Church. Fleeing West Germany in November 1977, Roeder surfaced in South Africa and then in Washington, D.C., in the summer of 1978 to visit anti-Semite William Pierce at the offices of his National Alliance. In the summer of 1980, Roeder attended a conference of the Aryan Nations in Hayden Lake, Idaho, residing with Reverend Richard Butler during his visit. Before returning to Germany, he also met with Klan leaders David Duke and Bill Wilkinson, picking up speaker's fees for his lectures to several KKK gatherings. As 1980 drew to a close, Roeder was linked with a series of bombing attacks perpetrated by the German Action Groups in West Germany, including raids against Holocaust memorials, a home for Ethiopian refugees in Loerrach, and a Hamburg shelter for Vietnamese "boat people." Two Vietnamese were killed in one firebombing, and two Ethiopians were seriously wounded in a separate incident. Sentenced to thirteen years in prison, Roeder maintains regular contact with racist groups in the United States, and his wife is a regular visitor to the Aryan Nations compound, where she was presented with a special award in July 1982. [2]

ROGERS, CALVIN

A black constable during Reconstruction in Marianna, Florida, Rogers was a repeated target of Klan violence in 1869 and 1870. Klansmen tried to kill him for the first time at a picnic for blacks on September 20, 1869, but missed, killing two other members of the crowd instead. Two blacks were gravely wounded on September 29, and unknown gunmen retaliated three days later, firing on Klan leader James Coker at a local hotel. The snipers missed, wounding Colonel James McClellan and killing his daughter, who were seated near the intended target. Klansmen blamed Rogers for the attack, launching a week-long "hunt" that claimed several black lives around Marianna. Rogers was murdered the following spring. [87]

ROGERS, ERNEST AND CHRISTINE

A brother and sister who lived in Lake View, South Carolina, Ernest and Christine Rogers were abducted from their separate homes and flogged by Klansmen in 1953. Because they were driven across the state line, FBI agents were assigned to the case, and fourteen members of the Association of Carolina Klans were jailed on federal kidnapping charges in November 1953. Defendants in the case included: E.P. Harrington; his son, P.M.

Harrington; Forrest Walters; Claudis Hardee; Elbert Blanton; James Rowell; Benjamin Royals; George Skipper; Rufus C. Gardner; his sons, Rufus and Woodrow Gardner; Mack Arnette; Crayton Snipes; and Marsden Barfield. [*NYT* 1953]

ROGERS, JOHN PAUL

Identified as Florida grand dragon for the United Klans of America, Rogers ran for a seat on the Polk County school board in 1972, polling 7,000 votes to his opponent's 12,000. In May 1976, when local Boy Scouts withdrew from their own Memorial Day parade rather than march beside Klansmen, Rogers accused the Scouts of "prejudice and bigotry." A month later, in Lake Wales, Rogers paid $1,000 to a local black man for his role in helping police crack a reign of terror by black home invaders, linked to a series of rapes, robberies, and at least one murder—all aimed at white families— between October 1975 and January 1976. (The informant, an ex-convict who infiltrated the gang on behalf of law enforcement, accepted the cash.) Last heard from in the autumn of 1976, Rogers launched another losing political campaign, this time for a seat in the U.S. House of Representatives. [*NYT* 1976; 84]

ROGERS, KATHERINE

See *Lynch, John.*

ROGERS, LESLIE

The owner of a janitorial service in Atlanta, Georgia, Rogers infiltrated the local Klan and National States Rights Party in September 1957, feeding information back to agents of the FBI. In his capacity as a National States Rights Party member, Rogers traveled with George Bright and Billy Branham to greet John Kasper on his release from federal prison. Klan leaders suspended Rogers after an October 1958 synagogue bombing in Atlanta, suspecting Rogers of informing to police or the Anti-Defamation League of B'nai B'rith, and their suspicions were confirmed when he surfaced as a prosecution witness at George Bright's bombing trial. [*NYT* 1958]

ROGERS, LOUIS J.

A resident of Lisbon, Connecticut, Rogers chaired a local committee supporting George Wallace's presidential candidacy in 1968. In August 1968, he was one of six Minutemen charged with conspiracy to commit arson and assault with intent to kill, following an armed raid on a pacifist camp in Voluntown, which left four Minutemen, a state trooper, and a female camper wounded by gunfire. [17]

ROGERS, DR. SAMUEL

See *Shoemaker, Joseph.*

ROGERS, WALTER

A member of the United Florida KKK, Rogers was elected to serve as kladd for James Venable's National Association of Ku Klux Klan in September 1964. [38]

ROPER, SAMUEL W.

An Atlanta policeman and member of the 1920s Klan, Roper headed the Georgia Bureau of Investigation in 1941 and 1942, under Governor Eugene Talmadge. In 1946 he emerged as second in command of the Association of Georgia Klans, doubling as nighthawk for Grand Dragon Samuel Green and as exalted cyclops of Oakland City Post No. 297 in Atlanta. When Green died of a heart attack in August 1949, Roper moved into control of the Georgia Klans, which he described as "an educational outfit." De-emphasizing violence and intimidation, Roper saw his Klan dwindle in size, retreating into a two-room headquarters located over a poultry market. In 1949, Roper joined forces with rival Klan leader Lycurgus Spinks, thus serving as both grand dragon of the Georgia Klans and imperial wizard of the new Associated Klans of America. Roper and both of his tiny splinter groups had vanished from the scene by the time the U.S. Supreme Court's Black Monday decision on school segregation revived the Invisible Empire in 1954. [10; 25]

ROSE, E.M.

An active Republican and county treasurer in York County, South Carolina, during Reconstruction, Rose used his Yorkville office as headquarters for a black anti-Klan militia in early 1871. Klansmen came looking for him that February, but he escaped through a window and sought refuge with federal troops. [87]

ROSE, DR. M.W.

See *Royal Riders of the Red Robe.*

ROSECRANS, WILLIAM STERLING

A member of the United Florida KKK and recognized "close associate" of Klan leaders in northern Florida, Rosecrans participated in the February 1964 theft of dynamite from two construction sheds in Jacksonville. The dynamite was used in the bomb that damaged the home of George Gilliam, a black resident whose grandson had recently enrolled in a "white" school, on February 16. Fellow Klansmen drove Rosecrans to St. Augustine after the bombing and helped him find work under an alias, but Klansman Holstead Manucy, leader of the Ancient City Gun Club, turned Rosecrans over to authorities on March 4, seeking a cash reward offered for the arrest of persons responsible for recent bombings on the strike-bound Florida East Coast Railroad. A polygraph examination cleared Rosecrans of the railroad bombings, but he confessed in the Gilliam case and filed a guilty plea on March 13, drawing a seven-year prison term. His confession implicated five other Klansmen in the bombing, but death threats induced Rosecrans to withdraw his promise of testimony, and the other defendants were acquitted at trial in July and November 1964. [NYT 1964; 10; 38]

ROSELAND HUNTING CLUB

In 1965 congressional investigators identified this group as a cover for the Roseland, Louisiana, klavern, Original Knights of the KKK. [38]

ROSENBERG, JIMMY MITCHELL

As "Jimmy Mitchell," Rosenberg joined the 1970s New York Klan and spoke at various rallies, including one in Gamber, Maryland, where he described his plans for joining the Rhodesian army to preserve apartheid. In 1976, he broke his cover, admitting that he was Jewish and claiming that Pennsylvania Grand Dragon Ray Doerfler recruited him to infiltrate the Anti-Defamation League of B'nai B'rith as a Klan spy. The story was confirmed by New York dragon Earl Schoonmaker, but Doerfler denounced Rosenberg as an Anti-Defamation League member sent to spy on the KKK. [84]

ROSS, MIKE

A resident of Macon, Georgia, employed by the Congress of Industrial Organizations as a recruiter for "Operation Dixie," Ross became a target for Klansmen who raided his home in 1947, causing his pregnant wife to suffer a miscarriage. [94]

ROTELLA, FRANK

A Roman Catholic and graduate of Hofstra University in New York, Rotella was appointed to serve as New Jersey king kleagle for the United Klans of America in July 1965, simultaneously holding office as state director of the National States Rights Party, in addition to active membership in the American Nazi Party and the National Socialist American Party. Suspended from his job with the New York City Welfare Department in October 1965 when his Klan links were publicized, Rotella was fired a month later. In early December he was subpoenaed by a grand jury probing Klan activities in Paterson, New Jersey. Four months later, when he announced plans for a rally near Bridgeton, a police infiltrator told newsmen that the number of Jersey Klansmen was so small that they "could meet in a telephone booth." In fact, only six of an estimated ninety or so members were able to afford Klan robes for the rally on May 13, at which Rotella and his five disciples were arrested for violating state fire laws (by burning a cross) and carrying concealed weapons. Rotella resigned from the United Klans of America without explanation in June 1966, resurfacing on November 5 when he led seventy-five men in a cross burning ceremony outside of Cedarville, heralding creation of a new splinter group, the White Crusaders of the North. [*NYT* 1965–1966]

ROTON, RALPH •

An Alabama member of the United Klans and a leader of that group's Klan Bureau of Investigation, Roton was appointed to serve as the United Klans of America's imperial investigator in late 1961. He approached Governor George Wallace for a job in early 1963 and was hired by the Alabama Legislative Commission to Preserve the Peace, investigating the "communist roots" of recent racial strife. In that capacity, he reported both to the state and the KKK, including an active role in the investigation of a September 1963 church bombing that killed four black children in Birmingham. Summoned to testify before the House Un-American Activities Committee in 1965, Roton admitted membership in a Montgomery klavern for the proceeding six years. [18; 38]

ROUND HILL FISHING CLUB

In 1965 congressional investigators identified this group as a front for the Landrum, South Carolina, klavern, United Klans of America. [38]

ROUNDTREE, TOM

A black resident of York County, South Carolina, during Reconstruction, Roundtree served as a spokesman for other local blacks and promised to resist the KKK if nightriders came for him. In December 1870, a gang of sixty Klansmen, including some from North Carolina, raided Roundtree's home, shot him, and cut his throat. [87]

ROWAN SPORTSMAN'S CLUB

In 1966 congressional investigators identified this group as a cover for North Carolina Unit No. 1, United Klans of America, including Klansmen from Salisbury and Spencer. [38]

ROWBOTTOM, HARRY

An Indiana congressman elected with Klan support in 1924, Rowbottom paid his political debt by promising to let Grand Dragon D.C. Stephenson name all recipients of patronage jobs. [10]

ROWE, GARY THOMAS

A resident of Birmingham, Alabama, and self-styled barroom brawler, Rowe was recruited by FBI agents as a paid Klan informant in late 1959 or early 1960. Over the next five years, he earned an estimated $20,000 from his federal contacts, who reportedly covered up his involvement in acts of violence and encouraged him to seduce Klan wives as part of the FBI's COINTELPRO disruption campaign. A member of Robert Shelton's Alabama Knights in May 1961, Rowe forewarned FBI agents of impending Klan-police collusion in connection with attacks on the integrated Freedom Rides, and he participated in the subsequent Birmingham riots, suffering a neck wound when a black man slashed him with a knife in self-defense. (The FBI paid Rowe's medical bills and kicked in a $125 bonus for the day's "services.") When Shelton organized the United Klans of America two months later, Rowe stayed on as a member of Eastview Klavern No. 13, recognized as Alabama's single most violent den. A regular participant in Klan "missionary work" through the early 1960s, including numerous assaults and beatings of innocent blacks, Rowe was variously suspected of participation in a 1963 church bombing which killed four children, the firebombing of black millionaire A.G. Gaston's home, and the fatal shooting of a black man during a 1963 race riot. (In the latter case, Rowe admitted the killing to state authorities, insisting that his FBI contact ordered him to "just sit tight and don't say anything about it." Bureau spokesmen describe the charge as an "absolute falsehood.") In March 1965, Rowe was one of four Birmingham Klansmen dispatched to patrol around Selma, Alabama, resulting in the murder of civil rights worker Viola Liuzzo. Breaking cover to testify in that case, Rowe was later relocated by FBI agents, complete with a new identity to protect him from anticipated Klan reprisals. In 1976, Alabama State Attorney General Bill Baxley considered using Rowe as a witness against church bomber Raymond Chambliss, but his testimony was rejected after polygraph tests implicated Rowe in the fatal blast and several other 1963 explosions. (Baxley suggests that Rowe was either present when Chambliss planted the bomb or had advance knowledge of the crime, wrongly believing the timer was set to explode when the church was vacant, instead of during crowded Sunday services.) In July 1978, the U.S. Justice Department launched an abortive probe to determine whether Rowe participated in illegal acts of violence while serving on the FBI payroll, and the same year saw him indicted by state authorities for Viola Liuzzo's murder, which was technically unsolved because an all-white jury acquitted three Klansmen in 1965. Georgia's governor approved Rowe's extradition to Alabama in February 1979, but the case was ultimately dismissed. In the fall of 1979, the NBC television network presented a highly fictionalized account of Rowe's exploits in the Klan, with ex-football star Don Meredith in the title role. [68; 76]

ROWELL, JAMES

See *Rogers, Ernest and Christine.*

ROWLEY, EWELL

While serving as principal of a junior high school in Slidell, Louisiana, in 1963, Rowley doubled as exalted cyclops of the Pearl River klavern, Original Knights of the KKK. Summoned to testify before the House Un-American Activities Committee in January 1966, he refused to answer questions on the grounds of possible self-incrimination. [38]

ROXBORO FISHING CLUB

In 1965 congressional investigators identified this group as a cover for the Roxboro, North Carolina, klavern, United Klans of America. [38]

ROYAL ORDER OF THE PURPLE DOG

See *Yellow Dog.*

ROYAL RIDERS OF THE RED ROBE

Based in Portland, Oregon, this affiliate of the 1920s KKK was created to serve naturalized citizens who qualified for Klan membership in other respects. Organized by kleagle Luther Powell and Dr. M.W. Rose, a naturalized U.S. citizen from Canada, the group was led by a grand dragon, offering "a real patriotic organization to all Canadians, Englishmen, and other white, gentile, Protestants" who failed to meet the KKK's strict limitation to native-born U.S. citizens. A Vancouver chapter was launched by Reverend Keith Allen in 1924, and the group was also reported active in Colorado, later merging with the American Krusaders. [10]

ROYALS, BENJAMIN

See *Rogers, Ernest and Christine.*

RUCKER, ELZA

An officer of the National States Rights Party, Rucker was killed in a shootout with blacks at a rally outside of Berea, Kentucky, in September 1968. [*NYT 1968*]

RUSSELL, KATHERINE

A Miami resident and vice president of the Edison Center Civic Association, Russell allegedly consulted with local Klansmen to prevent blacks from moving into Carver Village, a housing project, in 1951. She reportedly helped organize Klan motorcades around the housing project that summer, including a robed demonstration at one building that was bombed on September 22. Hailed before a federal grand jury in October 1952, she denied involvement in the reign of terror, and was indicted for perjury two months later. [*NYT* 1952]

RUSSELL, RICHARD B.

Chief justice of Georgia's state supreme court in the 1920s and a recognized friend of the KKK, Russell was dissuaded from launching a 1924 senate race when Klansmen told him that they were backing incumbent William Harris. As a reward for his patience, Russell was nominated by Governor Clifford Walker, a Klansman, to serve as chancellor of the state university, but angry student protests killed the nomination. In 1926, Klan support was insufficient to help Russell win his race against incumbent Senator Walter George, but he eventually found a seat in the upper house, once advocating that all blacks should be bussed into Northern states. A recognized power in the field of military appropriations, Russell stood fast with his fellow Southerners as an opponent of civil rights legislation in the 1960s. [81]

RUST, DAVID C.

Following the murder of Joseph Tomassi by a rival Nazi in 1975, Rust assumed Tomassi's role as leader of the National Socialist Liberation Front. Convicted and sentenced to prison for federal firearms violations, he was subsequently replaced by Karl Hand, Jr. [2]

S

S.S. ACTION GROUP

Also known as the Security Services Action Group, this Michigan-based neo-Nazi group was founded in 1979 as the Detroit chapter of the National Socialist Movement. Leaders John Moriarty and Edward Dunn broke from the National Socialist Movement later that year, recruiting an estimated fifty members for a series of pugnacious demonstrations in 1980 and 1981. In August 1981 the S.S. Action Group and the Ku Klux Klan obtained permits for a joint rally in Detroit's Kennedy Square, prompting local far-left organizations to merge as The Committee Against Klan/Nazi Terror. Eight persons were jailed in the confrontation, as hecklers overran police lines to assault the small band of fascists and Klansmen. By 1982 violence had become a staple ingredient of S.S. Action Group rallies, with neo-Nazis on the receiving end of eggs, stones, and bricks when they turned up in Ann Arbor, Detroit, and Birmingham, Michigan. Similar outbreaks were recorded in March 1983, again at Ann Arbor, and a month later in Cleveland, when eight members of the group staged a joint rally with the United White Party. Members of the S.S. Action Group have also attended cross burning demonstrations in Cohoctah, Michigan, on the farm maintained by Klansman Robert Miles and his Mountain Church of Jesus Christ. [2]

SADDLER, TOM

As exalted cyclops of the KKK during Reconstruction in Pontotoc County, Mississippi, Saddler led a group that tried unsuccessfully to abduct school superintendent Robert Flournoy in May 1871. Six months later, Saddler was elected to serve as county sheriff. [87]

SADEWHITE, MICHAEL DESMOND

As "Michael Desmond," FBI informant Sadewhite infiltrated the United Klans of America in 1966, rising to the rank of king kleagle in Delaware and Pennsylvania and maintaining links with the Klan in Virginia as well. Pennsylvania Grand Dragon Roy Frankhouser recruited Sadewhite into the Minutemen, and he provided further information on that group before resigning in 1967, worried that Klansmen were growing suspicious. He moved to Kansas City under his own name, where FBI agents persuaded him to join a Missouri branch of the Minutemen, posing as an ex-Klansman in search of the "right organization." Sadewhite finally broke cover that August, describing his activities from a new post as news director for radio KUDL in Kansas City. [46]

SAFRIT, NOLAN

See *Dayvault, Wayne.*

ST. AUGUSTINE, FLORIDA

The oldest city in the United States became a target for civil rights activists in 1959, when Dr. R.N. Hayling settled there and became the local NAACP director. In 1961, Hayling encouraged sit-ins by black college students, and Klansmen reacted violently, once locking several demonstrators inside a variety store and beating them with ax handles. On September 19, 1963, Hayling and three other blacks were caught spying on a Klan rally. All four of them were severely beaten before Sheriff L.O. Davis arrived on the scene. Four Klansmen were charged with assault and released on $100 bond, but the case took an ironic turn when Davis charged the black victims with assaulting their Klan assailants. (All four were convicted, after a pistol was planted in Hayling's car.) In late October 1963, a young Klansman was shot and killed during an armed parade through a black neighborhood; NAACP officer Goldie Eubanks was one of four blacks charged with complicity in the slaying, but all were ultimately cleared. In January 1964 the car owned by black parents with children enrolled at a "white" school was burned at a local PTA meeting. A month later, arsonists destroyed the home of another black family whose child was enrolled at a "white" school, and nightriders fired into Dr. Hayling's home on February 8, killing the family dog. In March, a day after restaurateur John Kalivos served four black sit-in demonstrators, vandals smashed the windows of his home, his automobile, and his business. A black minister's car was burned after a civil rights rally was held in his church, and a black man enrolled in adult classes at a "white" school was beaten on his way home from class. Dr. Martin Luther King arrived to lead protest marches in late May, and Klansmen staged their first assault on the marchers May 28, wading in with pipes and chains as blacks knelt to pray at the historic slave market. Police parted ranks to let the Klansmen through, and several newsmen were also beaten in the melee. By that time, Sheriff Davis had recruited over 100 special deputies from the United Florida KKK and its local front group, the Ancient City Gun Club, giving white rioters free reign while black demonstrators were penned in an eight-foot-square "sweat box." (In one riot, a deputy was observed offering his billy club to a Klansman with the remark, "Here, want to use this for a few minutes?") King called St. Augustine "the most lawless community that we've ever worked in," with Sheriff Davis banning nocturnal protests while Klansmen patrolled the streets in radio-equipped cars, relying on the presence of attorney J.B. Stoner to secure their swift release in the unlikely event of an arrest. Violence escalated as nightriders surrounded a beach cottage rented by King's Southern Christian Leadership Conference, riddling the structure with gunfire, and one of King's aides narrowly escaped death when snipers pumped bullets into his car. On June 9, Judge Bryan Simpson enjoined Sheriff Davis from banning night marches, and Klansmen retaliated the next evening, breaking through police lines, hurling bricks and jugs of sulphuric acid, mauling blacks and reporters before they were finally dispersed by tear gas and police dogs. On June 12, gunmen fired into the home of a black teacher, and J.B. Stoner led a parade through black neighborhoods that night, exhorting his followers that, "we whites deserve more rights, not less. When the constitution said all men are created equal, it wasn't talking about niggers." Klan agitator Connie Lynch arrived on June 24, and the following day was marred by St. Augustine's worst racial violence in a century. Authorities released five Klansmen when a mob chanted, "Turn 'em loose!" and Governor Farris Bryant risked a citation for contempt of court on June 26 by renewing the ban on nocturnal parades. Four days later, King departed for Atlanta, proclaiming "victory" in St. Augustine, but nothing appeared to have changed. Four blacks were beaten on July 17, one of whom was hospitalized, after seeking service at a segregated restaurant. Dr. Hayling was successful that month in his bid for a federal injunction, banning further violence by Holstead Manucy's Ancient City Gun Club and affiliated groups, but Klansmen remained eager for action. Hundreds gathered for a rally on the city outskirts on July 24, and the newly integrated Monson Motor Lodge was firebombed shortly after they dispersed. The same night, authorities jailed five Klansmen for an illegal cross burning, with defendants including Stoner, Lynch, Barton Griffin, Bill Coleman, and Jacksonville Klan leader Paul Cochran. In hearings before Judge Simpson, Sheriff Davis was forced to produce a list of his special deputies, which included convicted bootlegger Holstead Manucy, as well as Klansmen Barton Griffin, Robert Gentry, and Donald Spegal. (All were identified as members of the United Florida KKK, in spite of denials from the sheriff that any Klansmen were employed as deputies.) Violence finally subsided near the end of the month, and a committee of the Florida legislature issued a report on July 31, charging the National States Rights Party with most of St. Augustine's recent unrest. [3; 7; 10; 38; 64]

SAMPSON, BILL

See *Greensboro, North Carolina.*

SAND HILL HUNTING CLUB

In 1965 congressional investigators identified this group as a cover for the Mount Olive, North Carolina, klavern, United Klans of America. [38]

SANDHILL STAG CLUB

In 1966 the House Un-American Activities Committee identified this group as a front for Richmond County Unit No. 32, United Klans of America, based in Rockingham, North Carolina. [38]

SANTEE SPORTSMAN CLUB

A front for the St. Stephen, South Carolina, klavern, United Klans of America, this group was publicly identified in 1965. [38]

SAPOCH, ABRAHAM

See *Wright, William.*

SARTIN, BENNIE

A resident of Elkton, Maryland, Sartin replaced Ralph Pryor as Delaware grand dragon of the United Klans in early 1966. That April, Delaware State Attorney General David Buckson described Sartin as "just a puppet goose-stepping along behind [Pennsylvania Grand Dragon Roy] Frankhouser." [*NYT* 1966]

SAUCIER, JACK

A resident of Monroe, Louisiana, Saucier was identified as secretary-treasurer for the Original Ku Klux Klan of America, Inc., when that group was incorporated in January 1965. [38]

SAUFLEY, WILLIAM P.

Elected leader of the Knights of the Rising Sun, on September 19, 1868, Saufley led the mob that lynched Captain George Smith at Jefferson, Texas, two weeks later. He left town "on business" in early December, a day before federal authorities started arresting the lynchers, and he was never apprehended, his "business" taking Saufley through the Indian Territory, and then to New York. [87]

SAUNDERS, WILLIAM L.

An ex-Confederate officer, Saunders also served as editor of the Wilmington, North Carolina, *Journal*, a Democratic paper that helped call the local Klan into existence during March 1868. Several sources name Saunders as the state's grand dragon during Reconstruction. [87]

SAVAGE, FRED

An ex-detective and professional strikebreaker from New York City, Savage was brought to Atlanta by William Simmons as the Klan's chief investigator. A participant in the 1922 plot to oust Simmons in favor of contender Hiram Evans, Savage pretended that his "sources" had word of a plan to "attack Simmons's character" at that year's klonvokation when his name was announced for renomination as imperial wizard. Savage told Simmons that his men had orders to kill the insurgent Klansmen, whereupon the wizard agreed to accept Evans as his "temporary" replacement, as a means of averting bloodshed and scandal. With Evans firmly in control of imperial headquarters, Savage was installed as the Klan's chief of staff. [10]

SAVINA, RICHARD LEE

Identified as the leader of a Maryland Klan faction, Savina was one of ten persons arrested by federal agents in May 1981, charged with firearms violations and conspiracy to bomb the NAACP headquarters in Baltimore. Conviction on three counts earned him a fifteen-year prison term. [*NYT* 1981]

SAWYER, B.F.

As Reconstruction editor of the Rome, Georgia, *Courier*, Sawyer was an ardent apologist for the KKK, but his public stance did not protect him from abuse. Accosted on a city street at midnight, February 6, 1871, he was forced to dance at gunpoint for the amusement of Klansmen returning from a nocturnal raid. [87]

SCAIFE, DOROTHY

Identified as a staff sergeant in the Veterans for Victory Over Communism, Scaife participated in paramilitary training courses in Camp Puller, near Houston, prior to the facilities closing in December 1980. While admitting that any Klansman was welcome to attend the training sessions, she told journalists, "We make it very clear he's not to wear his insignia or talk about it." [*Newsweek*, Dec. 15, 1980]

SCALAWAGS

In Reconstruction parlance, "scalawags" were Southern whites who sided with the Union in the Civil War or those who supported the Republican Party and black civil rights after 1865. Along with Northern carpetbaggers, scalawags were special targets of the original KKK, regarded as traitors to their race and native land. [87]

SCARBOROUGH, W.W.

A deputy sheriff in Fulton County, Georgia, Scarborough doubled as exalted cyclops of Atlanta's East Point klavern in 1939 and 1940. Jailed after a series of local whippings claimed at least three lives, he admitted calling out Klan floggers "whenever someone wasn't doin' like he ought to." Scarborough and seven other Klansmen, including two other deputies, were convicted on various felony charges. All of them were later pardoned by Governor Eugene Talmadge. [93]

SCHENCK, DAVID

An attorney during Reconstruction in Lincolnton, Georgia, Schenck joined the Klan in neighboring Gaston County, in October 1868. Fourteen months later, he recruited various friends into a Lincoln County den, bent on averting outbreaks of black arson and lawlessness. [87]

SCHMIDT, ROBERT

See *Cheney, Turner.*

SCHOONMAKER, EARL

Employed as a teacher at the medium-security Eastern New York Correctional Facility in Napanock, Schoonmaker served as grand dragon for the Northern Independent KKK of New York. In December 1974 he was suspended from his job on the basis of charges filed by Nancy Loorie, head of vocational services for the prison, who claimed that Klansmen had threatened her life, vandalized her car and office, and set fires in the cells of black inmates. Superintendent Jerome Peterson denied the charge of office vandalism, declaring further that out of six fires recorded since September 1974, only one was considered suspicious—and that was blamed on prison inmates, not the KKK. Not even the inmates blamed the Klan, which made its first appearance at the prison that September. Loorie claimed to have seen a membership list naming fifteen to twenty Klansmen among 400 prison employees, but Charles Krom, spokesman for a council representing 248 correctional officers, called the charges irresponsible. Schoonmaker was fired on December 23, 1974, and his wife Janice was asked to resign her post as director of the Pine Bush school board, following the exposure of her role as a KKK officer, but she refused to step down voluntarily. In 1976,

Schoonmaker attended Robert Scoggin's Conference of Eastern Dragons, and a year later he was listed as imperial klokard for the new Confederation of Independent Orders, led by William Cheney. [NYT 1974–1975; 84]

SCHREFFLER, FREDERICK

Once a member of the United Klans in Pennsylvania, Schreffler resigned after a quarrel with Exalted Cyclops Gerhart Mitchell, branding Keystone Klansmen as "scrapbook heroes" while he signed on with the White Christian Crusaders. He was arrested with three other Crusaders in Hightstown, New Jersey, on weapons charges, following a 1971 clash with members of the militant Jewish Defense League. [NYT 1971]

SCHWERNER, MICHAEL

A Northern volunteer for Mississippi's Freedom Summer of 1964, Schwerner made his headquarters in Meridian and was known to members of the militant White Knights. Plans for his execution were already underway when Schwerner and black civil rights worker James Chaney drove to Ohio on June 14, to attend an orientation meeting held by the Council of Federated Organizations at the Western College for Women in Oxford. There they met New York volunteer Andrew Goodman, and he returned with them to Meridian on June 20. Meanwhile, the White Knights had put their murder plan in motion, hoping to lure Schwerner into Neshoba County, where the sheriff's department was staffed and controlled by Klansmen. On June 16 raiders attacked the Mt. Zion Methodist Church, near Philadelphia, beating black worshippers and burning the church. Schwerner, Chaney, and Goodman visited the site on June 21, and were subsequently arrested "for speeding" by deputy—and Klansman—Cecil Price. Released that evening after paying a $20 fine, the three were stopped a second time by Price, delivered to a waiting party of Klansmen, and shot to death, their bodies buried under a nearby earthen dam. Schwerner's burned-out car was found June 23 in a swamp on the local Choctaw reservation, but state authorities treated the disappearance as a hoax or publicity stunt, and massive searches proved fruitless until Klan informants began talking for money. The corpses were unearthed on August 4, 1964, and FBI agents arrested twenty-one Klansmen in December 1964. Alleged members of the murder party were named as Cecil Price, Jimmy Lee Townsend, Horace Doyle Barnette (who later confessed), James Jordan (who also confessed), Jimmy Arledge, Travis Barnette, Billy Wayne Posey, Alton Wayne Roberts, Jerry Sharpe, and Jimmy Snowden. Charged with having knowledge of the plot were Sheriff Lawrence Rainey, Patrolman Otha Neal Burkes, Meridian Klan leader Frank J. Herndon, Neshoba County Klan leader Edgar Ray Killen, Olen Burrage (owner of the burial site), Herman Tucker (a contractor who built the dam), Oliver Warner, Jr. (owner of a Meridian store where the killers bought gloves), James Harris, and Bernard Akin. Klansmen charged with misprision of a felony included Earl Akin (Bernard's son) and Tommy Horne. At a December 10 preliminary hearing, U.S. Commissioner Esther Carter threw out Doyle Barnette's confession and dismissed all charges against the twenty-one suspects. The FBI rearrested sixteen of the Klansmen and Philadelphia Patrolman Richard A. Willis on January 16, but Judge Harold Cox dismissed federal felony charges on February 25, ruling that the seventeen defendants could only be tried on a misdemeanor count of conspiracy to deny the right to be free from summary punishment. In June, the Justice Department announced plans to proceed with the case, but Judge Cox ordered dismissal of new charges in late September, on the grounds that the indicting grand jury had excluded blacks and women. A new grand jury indicted eighteen Klansmen on civil rights charges in February 1967, adding Imperial Wizard Sam Bowers and Ethel "Hop" Barnett (former and future sheriff of Neshoba County) to the list. Dropped from the original list of twenty-one defendants were Townsend, Warner, Otha Burkes, and James Jordan—the latter having filed a guilty plea and turned state's evidence against the other Klan defendants. The federal conspiracy trial opened on October 9, 1967, with Meridian Police Sergeant Wallace Miller testifying that he was told in advance of the White Knights plot against Schwerner. Verdicts were returned on October 20, with seven Klansmen convicted. Bowers and Roberts were each sentenced to ten years, Price and Posey to six years, while Arledge, Snowden, and Horace Barnette drew three years each. Defendants Akin, Willis, Burrage, Harris, Herndon, Rainey, Tucker, and Travis Barnette were acquitted on all counts. Mistrials were declared in the cases of E.G. Barnett, Edgar Killen, and Jerry Sharpe, with charges dismissed against the trio in January 1973. The guilty verdicts were affirmed on appeal in July 1969, and the U.S. Supreme Court refused to hear the case in February 1970, clearing the way for convicted Klansmen to serve their prison time. [42; 96]

SCOGGIN, ROBERT

A member of the U.S. Klans in South Carolina, Scoggin worked his way up from exalted cyclops to grand titan and grand dragon of the realm before defecting to the United Klans of America in July 1961. As a charter officer of the United Klans, he was named to serve as imperial kladd while retaining his post as South Carolina's grand dragon; he also presided over North Carolina Klansmen until J.R. Jones was elected grand dragon of that state in 1963. Under Scoggins, the United Klans enjoyed steady growth in South Carolina, increasing its number of klaverns from twenty in 1964 to a minimum of fifty by the end of 1966. At the same time, Scoggins also managed to line his own pockets, depositing $15,690 for one year in personal bank accounts, while declaring only $574 in income. A tough-talking leader, Scoggin condoned formation of a paramilitary faction known as the "Underground," designed to train Klansmen in preparation for violent action, but his realm experienced few actual incidents. In

October 1965, the House Un-American Activities Committee exposed his record of drunk driving convictions and fraudulent billing of the Veteran's Administration for exaggerated war injuries, but Scoggin stood fast on the Fifth Amendment, drawing a one-year sentence for contempt of Congress in March 1968. Paroled in December 1969, he returned to find statewide membership shrunken by some 40 percent under acting grand dragon Harry Gilliam. Public quarrels with Gilliam and Imperial Wizard Robert Shelton soon forced Scoggin out of the United Klans, and in 1970 he founded his own Invisible Empire, Knights of the KKK, Realm of South Carolina. In September 1970, with nine other Klansmen, Scoggin was jailed for conspiracy to commit robbery and as an accomplice after the fact in a murder, charges arising from the death of rival Klansman Willie Odom at a rally near Sumter, South Carolina. Charges against Scoggin were dismissed in time for him to serve as a middleman, coordinating the merger between United Klans defector Tony LaRicci's Maryland Knights and James Venable's National Knights of the KKK. In August 1975, Scoggin visited Louisville during a school busing controversy, sharing the dais at joint rallies with Klansmen David Duke, James Warner, and Phillip Chopper. In the spring of 1976 he convened the Conference of Eastern Dragons in South Carolina, and Scoggin's subsequent three-way struggle with Dale Reusch and Bill Wilkinson, vying for leadership of various independent Klans, led to a curious unity conference in June 1977. When the smoke cleared, all three contestants had lost out to Hoosier Klansman William Chaney, chosen to command the new Confederation of Independent Orders. [38; 84]

SCOTT, LUTHER HARDY

A resident of Texarkana, Arkansas, Scott was identified in 1967 as the ranking officer of the Association of Arkansas Klans in Miller County. [38]

SCOTT, PARKIE

A resident of Oregonia, Ohio, Scott was identified in 1965 as Ohio's kleagle for the National Knights of the KKK. In August 1965, he launched a two-day recruiting drive at a farm south of Cleveland, complaining that many potential members were barred from the rally by police roadblocks. In September 1966, he announced plans to picket the Montgomery County fairgrounds during a scheduled visit by President Lyndon Johnson. [*NYT* 1965–1966]

SCOTT, SID

See *Flowers, Evergreen.*

SCUTARI, RICHARD JOSEPH

A member of The Order and its hard-core inner cell, the Bruder Schweigen (Silent Brotherhood), Scutari was nicknamed "Mr. Black" by his fellow Nazis, after the black belt he had earned as an expert in karate. Identified as a member of the Order hit team that murdered Alan Berg in June 1984, Scutari also participated in a Ukiah, California, armored car robbery the following month, with Nazi gunmen netting $3.6 million in cash. Testimony secured from militants in custody led to Scutari's indictment on April 12, 1985, on federal charges of racketeering, conspiracy, and transportation of stolen money across state lines. A few days later he was hit with additional charges of interfering with interstate commerce by means of threats and violence. Scutari had already gone into hiding by that time, and his name was added to the FBI's Ten Most Wanted list on July 11, 1985. Arrested eight months later in San Antonio, Texas, he pled guilty to racketeering charges in April 1986, and was sentenced to a term of sixty years in federal prison. Authorities in Denver encouraged Scutari to turn state's evidence against triggermen David Lane and Bruce Pierce in the Berg slaying, but Scutari refused to testify for the prosecution, and his own pending murder charges were ultimately dismissed in the interest of economy. In April 1987, Scutari was one of fourteen neo-Nazis indicted on federal sedition charges, but jurors in Ft. Smith, Arkansas, acquitted all fourteen in April 1988. In a published letter from prison, Scutari told the faithful: "Many have disagreed with the methods of the Bruder Schweigen. I offer no apologies except for having failed to meet our goals. At least we were not afraid to take on the Beast. For those of you who truly believe in Yaweh our God and our King, Jesus the Christ, it is time to follow our example. The Bruder Schweigen has shown you the way. Learn from our mistakes, succeed where we failed." [13; 85]

SEALE, JAMES FORD

See *Dee, Henry.*

SEARCHLIGHT, THE

One of several Klan periodicals published in the 1920s, *The Searchlight* was edited in Atlanta by J.O. Woods. Its editorials backed William Simmons in his power struggle with Hiram Evans during 1923 and 1924, with publication continuing at least through the 1928 presidential campaign. [10]

SEASHORE KLANS

See *Knights of the Ku Klux Klan of America.*

SEAWELL, MALCOLM

The chief prosecutor of Carolina Klansmen charged with acts of terrorism in the early 1950s, Seawell won convictions against Grand Dragon Tom Hamilton and numerous others on various felony charges. He later served as chairman of North Carolina's state elections board in 1965–1966, and in January 1966 he was appointed by the governor to head a new anti-Klan committee, which included representatives from the State Bureau of Investigation, the motor vehicles commissioner, the state attorney general, the revenue commissioner, and the state director of administration. [*NYT* 1966]

SECRET SIX

A Klan action squad in Georgia, the Secret Six plotted a series of high-profile assassinations in 1965, targeting Morris Abrams (head of the American Jewish Committee), Atlanta Vice-Mayor Sam Massel, and a white Southern clergyman. FBI agents warned the prospective victims, and none of the attacks was carried out. [33]

SEGAL, DONALD

See *Gilliam, George.*

SELLERS, CLAYTON

A white farmer residing in Whiteville, South Carolina, Sellers was lured from home and whipped by Klansmen in late 1951, accused of beating his elderly mother and making her "stay in the backhouse." The flogging was interrupted when Sellers's wife drove off the Klansmen with rifle fire. [*NYT* 1952]

SELMA, ALABAMA

The seat of Dallas County, in the heart of Alabama's "Black Belt," Selma became a target for civil rights activists in February 1963 with the inauguration of a two-year drive to register black voters. Sheriff Jim Clark responded to the "invasion" by donning a "NEVER" lapel pin and recruiting white civilians—including alleged Klansmen—as members of a special posse designed to cope with demonstrations. So violent were Clark's deputies that Mayor Joe Smitherman brought ex-police captain Wilson Baker out of retirement in early 1964 and appointed him chief of police in an effort to curb the beatings of blacks and civil rights workers inside the city limits. Clark's closest friend and supporter, meanwhile, was Circuit Judge James Hare, whose racial theories were summarized in his remark, "Most of your Selma Negroes are descended from the Ibo and Angola tribes of Africa. You could never teach or trust an Ibo back in the slave days, and even today I can spot their tribal characteristics. They had protruding heels, for instance." While congressional investigators found no active klavern of the KKK in Dallas County, Alabama's grand dragon lived only fifty miles away, in Demopolis, and Klansmen joined members of the National States Rights Party for public rallies around Selma in the summer of 1964. National States Rights Party member James Robinson assaulted Dr. Martin Luther King at a local hotel in January 1965, and two months later he was jailed again, for attacking an FBI agent on Highway 80, east of Selma. Out-of-town Klansmen were seen on the streets with increasing frequency after Colonel Al Lingo's state troopers killed Jimmy Lee Jackson, a black civil rights activist, in nearby Marion on February 18. During the melee that claimed Jackson's life, Clark turned up at Lingo's side, telling newsmen, "Things got a little too quiet for me over at Selma tonight, and it made me nervous." On March 7, 1965—memorialized as "Bloody Sunday"—state troopers and Clark's posse attacked civil rights marchers on the Edmund Pettus bridge. Sixteen persons were hospitalized and fifty were injured. (In 1966, Lingo claimed that the assault was personally ordered by Governor George Wallace.) Two days later, Reverend James Reeb was fatally beaten by racists in Selma; his assailants, allegedly Klansmen or close associates of the KKK, were later acquitted by an all-white jury. Another civil rights worker, Viola Liuzzo, was shot and killed by members of the United Klans in neighboring Lowndes County on March 25. Violence around Selma ultimately proved counterproductive for segregationists, leading to the electoral defeat of Clark and Lingo in 1966, along with the conviction of three Klan defendants on federal charges linked to the Liuzzo murder. [20]

SEMET, ERNEST

One of five Chicago policemen identified as Klansmen in December 1967, Semet was forced out of his job in lieu of prosecution on conspiracy and federal firearms charges. [NYT 1968]

SESSUM, CECIL VICTOR

An exalted cyclops of the Mississippi White Knights, Sessum was arrested in connection with the arson-murder of black civil rights worker Vernon Dahmer in March 1966. Eight months later additional charges were added, naming Sessum as a participant in the abduction of prosecution witness Jack Watkins, and Sessum was one of twelve Klansmen indicted by a federal grand jury in February 1967 on charges of conspiring to violate Dahmer's civil rights. Convicted of murder in the case, he was sentenced to life imprisonment in March 1968. [NYT 1968; 96]

7-11 SPORTSMAN CLUB

In 1965 congressional investigators identified this group as a cover for the Americus, Georgia, klavern, United Klans of America. [38]

7-1 CLUB

A front for the Orlando klavern of the United Florida Ku Klux Klan, this club was publicly exposed in 1965. [38]

772 CLUB

Also know as Southside Sportsman Club No. 39, this group was identified in 1965 was a front for the Mecklenburg County, Virginia, klavern, United Klans of America, serving Klansmen in Boydton and South Hill, Virginia. [38]

SEWARD, WILLIAM

A Tennessee native and ex-Klansman, Seward was abducted by Klansmen in February 1981, accused of being a government informer, and covered with yellow paint and feathers before he was pushed from a moving car. A week later, he was secluded under guard after police learned of a contract on his life. Two Klansmen were later charged with kidnapping in the case. [NYT 1981]

SEXTON, MELVIN

An Alabama member of the United Klans and next-door neighbor of Imperial Wizard Robert Shelton in Tuscaloosa, Sexton was appointed to serve as imperial kligrapp in the summer of 1965. Four years later, he filled in for Shelton as acting imperial wizard, during Shelton's incarceration for contempt of Congress, and his performance sparked a major revolt in the North Carolina realm. Accused of pocketing money from a defense fund established on behalf of Klansmen jailed following a July 1969 shootout at Swan Quarter, North Carolina, Sexton dismissed the complaints and sought to chastise his accusers. As a result, Klansmen Joe Bryant and Edward Dawson led substantial numbers of Carolina Klansmen in defecting from the United Klans to form their own rival organization. [38; 84]

SEYMOUR KNIGHTS

A white terrorist group organized prior to the 1868 elections in Louisiana, the Seymour Knights were named after New York Governor Horatio Seymour, nominated that year as the Democratic Party's presidential candidate. Investigators noted a heavy overlap of membership between the Seymour Knights, the KKK, and the Knights of the White Camellia. Unlike the Klan, this group apparently dissolved at the end of the year's anarchic political campaign. [87]

SHAFFER, H.F.

A disciple of anti-Semite Gerald L.K. Smith and exalted cyclops of a Chambersburg, Pennsylvania, klavern, Shaffer filled the mails with pamphlets and "open letters" inviting "white Gentile Protestants" to join his Franklin County unit in 1952 and 1953. One pamphlet, *America for Americans*, read in part: "It is and always will be the earnest endeavor of the Knights of the Ku Klux Klan to preserve this great Nation for its native born through Christ Jesus our Criterion of Character." [77]

SHAFFER, JAMES F.

See *Federated Ku Klux Klans, Inc.*

SHAKERS

A religious minority targeted by Reconstruction Klansmen in Bowling Green, Kentucky, in the spring and summer of 1868, the Shakers suffered more than $250,000 in property damage when nightriders burned down several buildings owned by members of the sect. [87]

SHAMROCK SOCIETY

See *Forbes, Ralph P.*

SHARPE, JERRY

See *Schwerner, Michael.*

SHAVER, CLIFTON

See *Dayvault, Wayne.*

SHAVER, ROBERT GLENN

An ex-Confederate general and resident of Reconstruction Jackson County, Arkansas, Shaver granted a press interview in 1911, claiming past service as the grand dragon of Arkansas. No documentary proof was forthcoming, and some historians reject Shaver's claim. [87]

SHAW, REV. HERBERT C.

A Tennessee native and virulent anti-Catholic, Shaw served as a Baptist minister in Erie, Pennsylvania, during the 1920s. In 1925, he was appointed by Imperial Wizard Hiram Evans to serve as the state's grand dragon, overruling protests from Pennsylvania Klansmen who wanted to choose their own leader. Reverend Shaw embarrassed many Klansmen with his violent tirades against Catholics and blacks, but he retained the staunch support of imperial headquarters. In the autumn of 1926, Evans responded to new complaints from the ranks by banishing one dissident spokesman and lifting charters of eight local klaverns, filing suit for an injunction to bar their continuing use of the Klan name and regalia. The Keystone Klansmen fought back in court, aware that plaintiffs in such a lawsuit must come into court with "clean hands." Testimony from ex-wizard William Simmons and other witnesses documented the sordid tale of Klan violence and financial corruption, ending in dismissal of the imperial suit. [10]

SHAW, IAN

An engineering inspector in London, England, Shaw was identified as a KKK recruiter in May 1957. As he told the press, "We aim at putting down subversives. We fight social evils like the vile prostitution in London's west end." When Klansmen were blamed for the dismissal of Trinidad laborer Dick Henderson, fired from his job in London after whites refused to work with him, Shaw called the incident "a hoax to frighten communists." [*Newsweek*, May 13, 1957]

SHEARHOUSE, I.T. ("TED")

A member of the 1960s Association of Georgia Klans, Shearhouse was elected to serve as kligrapp and klabee for the National Association of Ku Klux Klan in September 1964. [38]

SHELTON, ROBERT MARVIN

The son of a Tuscaloosa, Alabama, grocer and Klansman, Shelton briefly enrolled at the state university, but a lack of money forced him to drop out and abandon his plans for attending law school. He joined the Air Force in 1947, and was stationed in Germany, where he was outraged at the spectacle of black servicemen dating white women. Back in Tuscaloosa, Shelton found work at the B.F. Goodrich plant and joined the U.S. Klans, rising through the ranks until personal conflict with Grand Dragon Alvin Horn prompted him to defect and organize his own Alabama Knights. In 1958, Shelton's support for gubernatorial candidate John Patterson landed Goodrich a $1.6 million contract with the state, and Shelton was promoted to a traveling sales job that covered the South, but he was fired in 1961 for devoting too much time to the KKK. In May 1961, he was one of four Klan leaders named in Judge Frank Johnson's injunction barring violent interference with the integrated Freedom Rides. Two months later, Shelton merged his Alabama Knights with Georgia Klansmen led by Calvin Craig and Carolina units under Robert Scoggin, creating the United Klans of America. Within a month, demolition courses and other paramilitary training were offered to United Klans members in Georgia, as Shelton's group cooperated with the ultra-violent Nacirema, Inc. In 1962, Shelton backed another political winner in Alabama Governor George Wallace, and the following year saw Shelton's father named as a colonel on Wallace's staff. Called as the House Un-American Activities Committee's first witness in a 1965 probe of the KKK, Shelton refused to produce Klan records, standing fast on the Fifth Amendment as he declined to answer 158 questions. Independent evidence showed that Shelton and his wife had drawn money from a United Klans front, the Alabama Rescue Service— including checks forged under fictitious names—with the money used to pay personal bills, put gas in Shelton's Cadillac, and purchase diamond rings.

Charged with contempt of Congress, Shelton was convicted before future Watergate Judge John Sirica in September 1966, drawing the maximum penalty of one year in prison and a $1,000 fine. Paroled in November 1969, he vowed a new drive to free America from "the infected black carcass that's dragging us down to the low morals and disruption that's in this nation today," but the United Klans had withered in his absence, under the inept handling of acting imperial wizard Melvin Sexton. A national speaking tour in November 1970 failed to revitalize the Klan, although Shelton claimed success in Michigan and Pennsylvania. The speeches were vintage Shelton, including a remark to an audience in Forrest City, Arkansas, that "Negroid is like hemorrhoid: they're both a pain." In spite of the declining membership throughout the Invisible Empire, Shelton's United Klans remained one of the dominant groups through the 1980s, with an estimated 4,000 members in 1983. Still relatively "strong" with 1,500 members in 1987, the United Klans was crippled by a lawsuit connected to the murder of black teenager Michael Donald, resulting in forfeiture of the Klan's Tuscaloosa headquarters to settle the unpaid claim. [2; 10; 38]

SHEPARD, REV. BRUCE

An Episcopal minister in Bogalusa, Louisiana, Shepard was the target of a KKK cross burning in December 1964, after he invited moderate Arkansas congressman Brooks Hays to speak at his church. Klansmen also threatened to bomb the church, and Shepard's bishop barred him from making nocturnal home visits, based on the danger of possible ambush. [34]

SHEPARD, M.L.

A Republican leader during Reconstruction in Jones County, North Carolina, Shepard organized several hundred blacks into an armed, anti-Klan militia in the spring of 1869. His pleas for regular troops and protection fell on deaf ears in the state capital, but Shepard remained in Jones County after other Republicans fled the area. On August 16, 1869, Shepard and two other men were shot dead by Klansmen while working at his Trenton sawmill. [87]

SHEPARD, DR. WILLIAM J.

A 1920s Klan leader in Bellaire, Ohio, Shepard also doubled as the city health officer. In 1925, he led a group of black-robed Night Riders, organized as a local action squad, to a statewide Klan gathering at Buckeye Lake. Eleven years later, records confiscated by police linked Shepard to a local chapter of the Black Legion, although he denied any connection with the group. [10]

SHEPPARD, REV. CLIFFORD

A black minister in Evergreen, Alabama, Sheppard was one of four Negroes kidnapped and flogged by Klansmen on August 8, 1957. [NYT 1957]

SHERER, MARK J.

A North Carolina Klansman said to have fired the first shot in a November 1979 massacre of five unarmed communist demonstrators in Greensboro, Sherer was acquitted of murder charges in 1980. Four years later, conviction on lesser charges related to the same incident saw him committed to a community treatment center for six months, with a further term of five years probation. [NYT 1979–1980, 1984]

SHIPTON, CARL LEROY

See *Mendez-Ruiz, Juan.*

SHOEMAKER, JOSEPH

A Vermont native and member of the socialist Modern Democrats, Shoemaker moved to Tampa, Florida, in the 1930s, working for municipal reform and organization of labor unions. His efforts infuriated local cigar manufacturers dependent on cheap labor in an area where numerous civic employees were also members of the KKK. A city fireman joined the Modern Democrats, reporting back to both policemen and the Klan, with the result that lawmen raided a party gathering on November 30, 1935, arresting Shoemaker, Eugene Poulnot, Dr. Samuel Rogers, and three others (including the spy). Shoemaker, Poulnot, and Rogers were questioned by detectives, then driven to a waterfront warehouse where Klansmen were waiting. All three prisoners were beaten and tarred; Shoemaker also had his genitals mutilated with a hot poker and his leg thrust into a bucket of boiling tar. Shoemaker died nine days later. National protests forced an investigation, with Police Chief R.G. Tittsworth personally exonerating his men, but when a grand jury handed down indictments in the case, Tittsworth was one of those named, along with kleagle Fred M. Bass and six Tampa policemen. Cigar manufacturers raised $100,000 bail for the defendants, and a crucial witness "committed suicide" prior to the trial, with defense attorneys concentrating their attack on the politics of the victims. Despite damaging testimony from Tampa's chief of detectives and several other policemen, two trials resulted in the acquittal of Bass and Tittsworth; five patrolmen were later convicted and sentenced to four years in jail. [10; 93]

SHORES, ARTHUR

A black attorney in Birmingham, Alabama, Shores became a target of Klan harassment after representing plaintiffs in a school desegregation case. His home was bombed by nightriders on August 20, 1963, and again on September 4. The second blast touched off a riot, leaving one person dead and eighteen injured. The attorney's home was bombed for a third time on March 21, 1965. [NYT 1963, 1965]

SHORT, REV. JIMMY

As pastor of the Caaba Heights Church in Birmingham, Alabama, Reverend Short angered racist members of his congregation in 1959 by publicly declaring that blacks are human beings. In late July, seventy-five hooded Klansmen protested the comment by burning a cross at Short's church. [*NYT* 1959]

SHOTWELL, RANDOLPH A.

A young Confederate veteran and son of a Presbyterian minister, Shotwell joined the Reconstruction Klan soon after it was organized in Rutherford County, North Carolina. He briefly published the Democratic *Vindicator* in Rutherfordton during 1868, and moved to Asheville, where he edited another paper, which went bankrupt. A bitter racist and self-professed heavy drinker, Shotwell was restless for action after the Civil War, and his Asheville sojourn saw him wounded in a street fight with a U.S. district attorney, whom Shotwell sought to punish for prosecuting local Klansmen. Back in Rutherford County, he spent his time with other drunken ruffians and was elected chief of the county's Klan when it was organized in the spring of 1871. Shotwell's alcoholism and self-imposed distance from his 300 members made him an ineffective leader, although his Klansmen were responsible for raping several women and whipping numerous blacks. The den's biggest raid was conducted against white Unionist Aaron Biggerstaff, two weeks after Shotwell's installation as leader, but it was apparently carried out without his knowledge or approval. Klansmen later testified that Shotwell organized a June 1871 raid that trashed the offices of a Republican newspaper, the Rutherford *Star*. Shotwell, with his brother and ten other members, was arrested, and convicted and sentenced to federal prison in September 1871. Once in jail, he volunteered to testify against other Klansmen while filling his diaries with attacks on the "traitors" who testified against him in his own case. Years later, he would blame local violence on "reckless young country boys" whom he was never able to control. [87]

SHROPSHIRE, WESLEY

A plantation owner and target of KKK harassment during Reconstruction in Chattooga County, Georgia, Shropshire was despised for his Unionist and Republican sympathies, and for encouraging black tenants to build a school on his land in 1871. Several blacks were whipped on his plantation, and Shropshire was repeatedly threatened, but he prevailed on his tenants to remain, and the school was allowed to operate without further interference. [87]

SHULER, REV. A.C.

A native of Virginia and pastor of the Los Angeles Trinity Methodist Church in the early 1920s, Shuler increased church membership fivefold in the space of three years. Obsessed with rooting out sin and civic corruption, he engaged in brawls with saloonkeepers and once waited all night to catch the sheriff emerging from a local whorehouse, driving him from office with sermons and protests. On the subject of the KKK, Shuler declared that "Good men everywhere are coming to understand that the Klan is dangerous only to the lawless and un-American elements within our midst." Grateful Klansmen responded in kind, rallying behind Shuler in the face of competition from rival evangelist Aimee Semple McPherson. In 1921, he began publishing a racist tabloid, *The Crusader*, which was still being successfully published in 1949. He relocated to Jacksonville, Florida, during 1946, where he tried unsuccessfully to launch a local chapter of the neo-Nazi Columbians, Inc. In 1950, he was identified as the imperial kludd for Sam Roper's Association of Georgia Klans, briefly publishing the *American Klansman* for that group. As pastor emeritus of the Central Baptist Church in Jacksonville, he also published the unofficial monthly of the Northern and Southern Knights, attacking Jews and other targets of Klan animosity. In August 1950, Shuler announced that he was leaving the KKK to have more time for preaching and the publication of a "religious patriotic magazine." Following the U.S. Supreme Court's Black Monday ruling on school segregation, he was reported active in the Florida Citizens' Council movement. [25; 61; 77]

SHUTTLESWORTH, REV. FRED

A black minister and civil rights activist in Birmingham, Alabama, Shuttlesworth was a frequent target of Klan violence in the 1950s and 1960s. His home was destroyed by a bomb on Christmas Day 1956, injuring five persons. Bombs struck his church in June 1958, January 1962, and December 1962. Twenty-two years after the fact, Klansman and National States Rights Party leader J.B. Stoner was convicted and sentenced to prison for the 1958 church bombing. [*NYT* 1958, 1962, 1980]

SIBLEY, J.D.

A Republican state senator from Madison County, Alabama, Sibley became a target of Klan harassment in January 1869. Persistent death threats caused him to seek refuge at an army post near Huntsville, where Klansmen briefly laid siege to the camp, blockading access roads to prevent his escape. [87]

SICKLES, CHARLES WILLIAM

Identified as the leader of Maryland's small but militant Adamic Knights of the KKK, Sickles was one of ten persons jailed by U.S. Treasury agents in May 1981 and charged with federal firearms violations and plotting to firebomb a Baltimore NAACP headquarters. His June indictment listed twenty separate felony counts, and Sickles was convicted four months later, drawing a five-year prison term. [2]

SILVA, FRANK

A recognized leader in the California KKK, Silva joined The Order in late 1983 or early 1984, operating a message center that helped neo-Nazi bank robbers communicate. In April 1985 he was arrested by FBI agents at Bentonville, Arkansas, a sizeable cache of weapons retrieved from his car. Five months later in Seattle, he was one of ten Order defendants convicted on federal racketeering charges. Silva was sentenced to a forty-year prison term. Despite incarceration and dismal prospects for parole, he was chosen to lead the shrunken Order, and reportedly continues to solicit new members from his cell. [13; 85]

SILVER DOLLAR CAFE

A popular hangout for Klansmen in Elwood, Indiana, during the 1970s, the Silver Dollar featured walls scarred by bullet holes during a KKK campaign to purge the neighborhood of drug dealers. Inside, a white hood adorned antlers mounted on one wall, above a sign that read: "This is Klan Country." [WRTV-News, Indianapolis, Indiana, Sept. 29, 1977]

SILVER DOLLAR GROUP

Drawing its members from Adams County, Mississippi, and neighboring Concordia Parish, Louisiana, this group was composed of Klansmen drawn from the White Knights, the United Klans of America, and the Original Knights of the KKK. Disgruntled at the "lack of guts" displayed by their respective Klans—typified by a ninety-day moratorium on violence, ordered by White Knights Imperial Wizard Sam Bowers after the murder of Michael Schwerner, James Chaney, and Andrew Goodman—the dissident Klansmen agreed to form a secret, hard-core group committed to the violent defense of segregation and white supremacy. Members of the group identified themselves by carrying silver dollars minted in the year of their respective births, and rural "family picnics" were combined with demolition seminars, including practice on the fine technique of wiring dynamite to the ignition of a car. At its peak, the group included an estimated twenty members, who prided themselves on being "the toughest Klansmen in Mississippi or Louisiana." The group's first victim was Frank Morris, a black shoe repairman in Ferriday, Louisiana, suspected of dating white women, who was fatally burned in an arson attack on his shop, December 10, 1964. FBI agents also suspected Silver Dollar members in the August 1965 bombing that crippled George Metcalfe in Natchez, and a second Natchez blast that killed Wharlest Jackson in February 1967. No one was ever prosecuted for the crimes, leading one FBI agent to remark, "Perhaps the perfect crime is one in which the killers are known, but you can't reach them for lack of substantive evidence." [96]

SILVER SHIRTS

Organized by anti-Semite William Dudley Pelley the day after Adolf Hitler took power in Germany, this group was bankrolled by rich Jew-haters and sales of literature issued by Pelley's Fellowship Press in Asheville, North Carolina. (Congressional investigators established that Pelley received more than $166,000 in donations between September 1937 and July 1939.) Racist Gerald L.K. Smith was an early recruit who conducted street rallies and traveled under the protection of a self-styled "Silver Shirt storm troop." Overlapping membership with the KKK and the Black Legion was common in midwestern states, and Pelley was known to confer with Michigan Klan leaders on political strategy from time to time. Pelley's abortive presidential campaign in 1936 paid off for the group in plenty of free publicity, attracting like-minded racists from around the country. One prominent member was Reverend W.D. Riley, founder of the World's Christian Fundamentals Association in Minneapolis, and director of the Northwestern Bible Seminary. Another active Silver Shirt promoter was Joseph Jeffers, pastor of the Kingdom Temple in Los Angeles, who studied in Germany and Italy during 1938, returning with tales of his personal chats with Benito Mussolini and Josef Goebbels. In 1939 Jeffers ran a Silver Shirt promotional film at his temple, narrated by recruiter Roy Zachary, who told the audience he was willing to kill President Franklin Roosevelt "if nobody else will." That spring, Jeffers and his wife of nine months were scandalized when journalists revealed their sponsorship of sex orgies involving "unconventional practices while naked for the entertainment of house guests." Elsewhere, Silver Shirt recruiter Walter Bailey Bishop was also affiliated with Father Charles Coughlin's anti-Semitic Christian Front, and U.S. Representative Jacob Thorkelson was a frequent guest speaker at the group's public rallies. The group disbanded following Pelley's indictment and abortive trial on sedition charges during World War II. [8]

SIMKINS, W.S.

A Reconstruction leader of the KKK and Young Men's Democratic Club in Jackson County, Florida, Simkins later served as a professor of law at the University of Texas. In his later years, Simkins published memoirs claiming that his group played on black superstition without resorting to physical violence, a claim undermined by the county's phenomenal record of racist murders and other acts of terrorism. [87]

SIMMONS, SAMUEL

A black victim of the Reconstruction Klan in South Carolina, Simmons ran afoul of Klansmen when, at his landlady's request, he traded her horse to a white neighbor, for a mule. The neighbor subsequently demanded his mule back, and Klansmen were called to whip Simmons when he refused to cancel the swap. [93]

SIMMONS, WILLIAM JOSEPH

An Alabama native born in 1880, Simmons claimed—perhaps falsely—that his father was a member of the Reconstruction KKK. He joined the army at age eighteen and saw action in the Spanish-American War before returning to civilian life in 1900 as a circuit-riding Methodist preacher, working the backwoods of Alabama and Florida. In 1912 Alabama's Methodist Conference defrocked Simmons on grounds of inefficiency and "moral impairment," and he briefly worked as a salesman before becoming a fraternal organizer and recruiter. Simmons soon became the youngest "colonel" in the Woodmen of the World—a title he used for the rest of his life—and within two years he was earning $15,000 annually from the lodge. He joined numerous other lodges and at least two different churches, and described himself as "a fraternalist" when asked his profession. In 1915 an October cross burning by the Knights of Mary Phagan and publicity surrounding the Atlanta screening of the film *Birth of a Nation* inspired Simmons to revive the KKK on Thanksgiving night. Two dozen charter members joined him for a cross burning atop Stone Mountain, Georgia, but the Knights of the KKK, Inc., began slowly, drawing only a few thousand members by 1919. The following year Simmons hired publicists Edward Clarke and Elizabeth Tyler to promote the Klan, whose efforts were assisted by press exposures of Klan violence in September 1921 and congressional hearings a month later. Simmons was the star of the hearings held before the House Rules Committee, mounting the witness stand on the third day of testimony. "If this organization is unworthy," he urged the panel, "then let me know and I will destroy it, but if it is not, let it stand." Turning to the gallery of spectators, he asked them "to call upon the Father to forgive those who have persecuted the Klan," then collapsed to the floor in a swoon. Membership applications flooded Klan headquarters in the wake of his performance, and Simmons later declared that "Congress made us." By 1922 ambitious subordinates had their eyes on the imperial throne. Dallas Klansman Hiram Evans huddled with chief of staff Fred Savage, Louisiana klaliff H.C. Ramsey, and grand dragons D.C. Stephenson (Indiana), H.C. McCall (Texas), and James Comer (Arkansas) to solicit their backing for a palace coup. Simmons was preparing for the Klan's first klonvokation, where he was scheduled for confirmation as imperial wizard, when he received a pre-dawn visit from Savage and Stephenson. The pair claimed knowledge of a plot by dissident Klansmen to attack Simmons's character on the convention floor, Savage vowing that his men had orders to kill the traitors where they stood. Seeking to avert bloodshed and scandal, Simmons reluctantly accepted Evans as his "temporary" replacement, receiving a new—and meaningless—title of "emperor for life." Perusing the new constitution, approved by klonvokation delegates, Simmons found that the emperor's powers had been omitted, relegating him to the status of an impotent figurehead. He retaliated by organizing Kamelia, a group catering to Klanswomen, but its membership never matched that of the Knights. An April 1923 court order granted Simmons control of the KKK, but Evans loyalists slipped away with crucial documents and $107,000 in cash before he could resume control. The power struggle dragged on until February 1924, when a final settlement gave Simmons $90,000 in return for disbandment of Kamelia and his promise to refrain from further competition or harassment of the KKK. He died in poverty in Luverne, Alabama, in 1946. [10]

SIMS, J.B.

See *Lauderdale, E.A.*

SIMS, JOSEPH HOWARD

A Georgia member of the United Klans, Sims traveled the South in 1963 and early 1964, participating in violent demonstrations in Birmingham, Alabama, and St. Augustine, Florida. In March 1964 police confiscated a pistol from Sims, after he threatened and assaulted an elderly black man in an Athens, Georgia, cafe. Five months later he was arrested as a suspect in the murder of black victim Lemuel Penn, and suspended from the United Klans by Grand Dragon Calvin Craig, pending permanent banishment if indicted. An all-white jury acquitted Sims and codefendant Cecil Myers of murder charges on September 4, 1964, by which time both men had allied themselves with James Venable's National Knights of the KKK. As charter members of a militant action squad, the Black Shirts, Sims and Myers were arrested in October 1965 in Crawfordsville, Georgia, for assaulting a black photographer. Days later, Sims, Myers, and five other Black Shirts were again jailed, this time for attacking a black farmer outside of Crawfordsville. Convicted of federal conspiracy charges in the Penn case, Sims and Myers were sentenced to ten-year prison terms in July 1966. An additional ten years was added to Sims' sentence, after he pled guilty to assault with intent to kill in the May 1966 shooting of his wife. [38; 40; 88]

SINCLAIR, JOYCE

A black resident of Robeson County, North Carolina, Sinclair was kidnapped, raped, and murdered on Halloween 1985. Her body was discovered near the site of a local Klan rally. The only witness to the crime was

Sinclair's four-year-old daughter, who described the killer as "a white man wearing white." [*NYT 1985*]

SIPSEY SWAMPERS

A violent faction of the Reconstruction Klan, active in western Tuscaloosa County, Alabama, this group was named after the local swamp where they held their secret gatherings. Responsible for numerous crimes in Tuscaloosa and adjacent counties, the Sipsey Swampers lost two of their own men in April 1869 during a three-day "hunt" which also left two blacks dead, several others wounded, and a number of black homes burned. [87]

SISENTE, ROBERT J.

Identified as the commander of Camp Puller, west of Houston, Texas, in 1980, Sisente offered paramilitary training to campers, including teenagers inducted without parental approval. Sisente's wife held the rank of sergeant at the camp. Media pressure forced it to close in December 1980. [*Newsweek*, Dec. 15, 1980]

SKINHEADS

A relatively new phenomenon, "skinhead youths" are noted for their short, sometimes shaved, hair, steel-toed boots, and fondness for "white power" rock music. Across the country they have organized themselves in loose-knit gangs with names such as Romantic Violence (Chicago), White American Skin Heads (Cincinnati), Christian Identity Skins (Las Vegas), Reich Skins (Los Angeles), and Confederate Hammer Skins (Dallas). Closely affiliated with the various Klans and neo-Nazi groups, the skinheads provide ready recruiting for adult racist cliques (four skinheads were publicly inducted into the American Knights of the KKK in Modesto, California, in October 1987) and there is evidence of manipulation by older racists Louis Beam, Richard Butler, Tom Metzger, and others. On their own, skinheads have proven themselves capable of random violence. In October 1986 police in Portland, Oregon, intercepted a gang of skinheads armed with knives, baseball bats, and pipes en route to a popular teen hangout, and in November 1988, skinhead Kenneth Mieske—nicknamed "Ken Death"— was charged in the beating death of an Ethiopian national. (Conviction, in June 1989, brought Mieske a life sentence.) Ybor City, Florida, was the scene of more skinhead violence in October 1986, with five skinheads arrested for assaulting patrons leaving a punk rock nightclub, and Orlando police reported problems with skinhead gangs the same year, until the "real hard-core, criminal element types" were jailed on traditional felony charges and the leather cliques melted away. In 1986 and 1987, authorities in Dallas, Texas, arrested various skinheads for robbery, assault, and narcotics violations. Cincinnati skinheads published newspaper advertisements in

September 1987, calling for recruits to "smash Red, Jew and Black power." A month later, police in Los Angeles jailed eight Reich Skins on charges including attempted burglary, vandalism, and using unlawful violent acts to affect political change; several weapons were seized during the arrests, along with quantities of racist literature from groups such as Tom Metzger's White Aryan Resistance. Providence, Rhode Island, was the scene of skinhead vandalism in October 1987, with swastikas and the legend "Skins Rule" spray-painted on public buildings. A month later, three Los Angeles skinheads were arrested for swerving their car toward a group of Hispanic children, and the same month saw a Chicago skinhead leader jailed for vandalizing three synagogues and thirteen Jewish shops on the forty-ninth anniversary of Kristallnacht. In October 1988 a gang of skinheads in the Greenwich Village area of New York City assaulted a white man who objected to their racial slurs, and attempted to throw his infant child down the steps of a subway station before police arrived and took four gang members into custody. A month later, after Klansmen canceled a Philadelphia rally in the face of hostile demonstrations, skinheads brawled with hecklers at Independence Hall. Aside from the October 1988 murder in Portland, skinheads were also blamed for the death of another black man that year, in Reno, Nevada. Much in the news during 1989, skinheads staged a minor riot on the Geraldo Rivera television show and reportedly assaulted talk-show personality Morton Downey, Jr., in a San Francisco airport restroom. In April 1989 Richard Butler hosted a three-day skinhead conference at the Aryan Nations compound in Idaho, with Klan leaders that included Louis Beam, Thom Robb, and Kim Badynski. A month later, in LaVerne, California, four skinheads attacked an Iranian couple, mistaking them for Jews, and October 1989 found skins marching side by side with Aryan Nations members in Pulaski, Tennessee. No past or present Klansman has shown more continuing interest in skinhead recruitment than California's Tom Metzger, openly soliciting teenaged allies through his son, John, identified as the leader of a group variously calling itself the White Student Union, the Aryan Youth Movement, the WAR Youth, or the WAR Skins. [*NYT* 1986–1989]

SKIPPER, BILLY

With Murray Martin, Skipper assumed control of the Louisiana-based Original Knights in early 1964, operating publicly as the Christian Constitutional Crusaders. Skipper remained loyal to Martin when a three-way rift broke up the Klan that autumn, with most of their declining membership drawn from Shreveport and Bossier City. [38]

SKIPPER, GEORGE

See *Rogers, Ernest and Christine.*

SKIPWORTH, J.K.

A Confederate veteran and mayor of Bastrop, Louisiana, before World War I, Skipworth emerged as exalted cyclops of Bastrop's Klan in the early 1920s. Unable to control the membership, he was effectively dominated by Dr. B.M. McKoin, with unrestrained violence leading to a notorious 1922 double murder at Mer Rouge. Investigation of the slayings failed to implicate Skipworth, but he was fined $10 for raiding an illegal still without authority. A year later he led a delegation to Atlanta, backing William Simmons in his ongoing power struggle with Imperial Wizard Hiram Evans. [10]

SLAUGHTER, G.H.

A black delegate to the Texas constitutional convention in 1868, Slaughter was targeted for execution by the Knights of the Rising Sun. Gunmen raided his home on October 4, but Slaughter escaped unharmed. [87]

SLIGH, GEORGE

A defector from the Georgia realm of the U.S. Klans, Sligh was an original incorporator in February 1961 of the Invisible Empire, United Klans, Knights of the Ku Klux Klan of America, Inc. [38]

SMITH, ALFRED EMANUEL

As the Catholic governor of New York, a product of Tammany Hall, and an outspoken critic of Prohibition, Al Smith stood in opposition to every major tenet of the 1920s KKK. Klan headquarters did all they could to derail his Democratic presidential nomination in 1924. As the convention approached, front-runner Senator Oscar Underwood had already betrayed his Alabama heritage by blasting the Klan as "a national menace," and with Smith as the alternative, Klansmen were forced to throw their considerable weight behind Californian William Gibbs McAdoo. Trouble began on the second day of the convention in New York's Madison Square Garden, when a nominating speaker for Underwood denounced un-American groups in general, specifically naming "the hooded and secret organization known as the Ku Klux Klan." For over an hour delegates hooted and cheered, some parading in the aisles, while fistfights broke out between Klansmen and anti-Klansmen in the Missouri and Colorado delegations. Behind the scenes a special Klan strategy board worked overtime to defeat a campaign plank that would have denounced the KKK by name, and they ultimately defeated the measure by a single vote. So divisive was the Ku Klux issue that the convention was hopelessly split on its more crucial business of naming a candidate; delegates required 103 ballots before all the major contenders were set aside in favor of compromise candidate John William Davis. (Smith, who had placed second on the first ballot, with 241 votes to

McAdoo's 431, received only seven in the final count.) As H.L. Mencken described the disastrous convention: "The battle that went on between the Kukluxers and their enemies was certainly no sham battle. There were deep and implacable hatreds in it. Each side was resolutely determined to butcher the other. In the end, both were butchered—and a discreet bystander made off with the prize." (In the anticlimactic November elections, most Klansmen jumped to the Republican Party and incumbent Calvin Coolidge, incensed by Davis's passing remarks on racial equality.) By 1928, Klan membership had declined to the point that Smith was unbeatable in his second bid for the Democratic nod, winning nomination on the convention's first ballot. Even Klansmen were changing their minds about Smith, and several Atlanta Klansmen were expelled that year for refusing to pledge against Smith. In Alabama, Senator Hugo Black, a Klansman, openly campaigned for Smith, and state voters gave the New Yorker a narrow majority. Another Klan senator, Tom Heflin, stood fast in opposition to Smith's candidacy, warning New York Klansmen of Smith's plan to tie the United States to "the tail of the Roman Catholic kite." In the Dakotas, Klan literature carried the slogan "Swat Smith and put Heflin in the White House," and a Methodist minister in Paterson, New Jersey, was jailed for illegally distributing Klan posters that read "Men and Women, Keep the Roman Menace Out." The importance of Smith's religion in the final balloting—an 83 percent landslide in favor of Republican Herbert Hoover—is difficult to assess, but the Invisible Empire was relegated to a marginal role in the campaign. Smith's final bid for the Democratic nomination in 1932 was reportedly doomed by the defection of underworld backers (including Meyer Lansky and "Lucky" Luciano) to the Roosevelt camp, while Klansmen were preoccupied with maintenance of their own dwindling ranks. [10; 93]

SMITH, BOB

Identified as a leader of the National States Rights Party in Mobile, Alabama, Smith was arrested with seventeen-year-old Thomas Tarrants in the summer of 1964. A search of their vehicle resulted in Tarrants being charged with possession of a sawed-off shotgun. [NYT 1964]

SMITH, DAVID

The son of Alabama's Reconstruction governor and a student at the state university in Tuscaloosa, Smith became a target of harassment during Klansman Ryland Randolph's vendetta against the school between 1868 and 1870. A typical warning note, delivered in 1870, read in part: "You nor no other damned son of a damned radical traitor shall stay at our university. Leave here in less than ten days, for in that time we will visit the place and it will not be well for you to be found out there." Smith took the hint, and the school was subsequently closed, reopening in 1871 under new, Conservative management. [87]

SMITH, FREDERICK

An Alabama Klansman, Smith served as imperial klabee for the United Klans of America between September 1964 and the summer of 1965, when he was replaced by W.O. Perkins. [38]

SMITH, GEORGE W.

A New York native and ex-Union officer, Smith settled in Jefferson, Texas, after the Civil War. As a Republican carpetbagger who befriended blacks—and who was elected to the 1868 state constitutional convention by black voters—he became an early target for the Knights of the Rising Sun. On the night of October 3, 1868, Smith was jailed after trading shots with a gang of would-be assassins. Rising Sun lynchers invaded the jail on October 4, and Smith reportedly killed one of them before others burst into his cell and shot him. [87]

SMITH, GERALD LYMAN KENNETH

A notorious anti-Semite, Smith launched his career in 1933, when he and his wife joined William Dudley Pelley's Silver Shirts. Smith briefly toured the Midwest as a self-styled spokesman for the group, accompanied by a Silver Shirt "storm troop," but he soon parted company with Pelley, settling in Shreveport, Louisiana, as pastor of the King's Highway Church. He soon attached himself to "Kingfish" Huey Long, but Smith's attempt to capture Long's political machine in 1935, following Huey's assassination, was foiled by cronies closer to the throne. A year later, Smith was back in the thick of far-right politics, as Father Charles Coughlin sponsored William Lemke for president on the National Union for Social Justice ticket, and Dr. Francis Townsend launched a personal bid for office on his Share-the-Wealth plan. By the summer Smith was billing himself as a "contact man for the Union Party, director of the Townsend organization, a keynote speaker for Father Coughlin and supporter of Lemke for President." He also found time to share the dais at one grass roots convention with Georgia Governor Eugene Talmadge, while organizing the Committee of One Million as a "nationalist front against Communism"—interpreted by journalists as an effort to "seize the government of the United States." In the late 1930s Smith tried to purchase X-Ray from Klansman Court Asher, but Asher refused to sell. In 1940 Smith operated from Detroit, where voters rejected his bid for a U.S. Senate seat. In November 1946, Georgia State Attorney General Dan Duke announced that Smith and his associates were forging ties with the modern Klan, and at least one notorious Klansman, Wesley Swift, was retained by Smith as a bodyguard, prior to striking off on his own with the Church of Jesus Christ Christian and the Christian Defense League. Settling in Arkansas, Smith had established his own Christian Nationalist Crusade by the turn of the decade, using its political arm, the Christian Nationalist

Party, to run for president in 1952 and 1956. (He polled less than 15,000 votes nationwide.) Through the 1960s and early 1970s, Smith's editorials openly supported the KKK and Citizens' Councils in their resistance to court-ordered desegregation, and his anti-Semitic literature was a staple of far-right distributors, ranging from the Klan and National States Rights Party to the more moderate John Birch Society. One of Smith's close associates, W. Henry MacFarland, Jr., was linked with James Madole's National Renaissance Party in the early 1960s, and ex-lieutenant Kenneth Goff openly campaigned on behalf of Robert DePugh's Patriotic Party in 1966. Attorney Bertrand Comparet—who served at various times as legal counsel for the Christian Nationalist Crusade, Swift's Christian Defense League, the National States Rights Party, and members of the Minutemen—remained into the 1980s, penning editorials on behalf of the Aryan Nations. [8; 25; 27; 28; 29]

SMITH, HAZEL BRANNON

As publisher of the moderate *Northside Reporter* in Jackson, Mississippi, Smith was a natural target for Klan harassment in the 1960s. A cross was burned at her Lexington home in 1960, and the newspaper office was wrecked by a bomb on August 27, 1964. Ten days later, at a state executive meeting of the militant White Knights, a grand giant reported that Jackson Klansmen had asked for permission to eliminate Smith. The request was tabled indefinitely, when it was discovered that she was visiting New Jersey at the time. [*NYT* 1964]

SMITH, JERRY PAUL

One of six Klan and neo-Nazi defendants charged in the November 1979 murders of five Communist Workers Party members in Greensboro, North Carolina, Smith was acquitted by an all-white jury in November 1980. Days later, he reported an attempt on his life, allegedly trading shots with unknown gunmen while driving near Maiden, North Carolina. As the local sheriff told newsmen, "We're not sure if it was an attempt on his life, or it could have been a prank." Honored at a 1981 banquet of the National States Rights Party, Smith ran (unsuccessfully) for sheriff in Lincoln County, North Carolina, the following year. In August 1984, he was jailed for assaulting a referee at a Lincoln County high school sporting event. [*NYT* 1979–1980, 1984; 93]

SMITH, JOHN

A 1920s Klansman in Herrin, Illinois, Smith owned the automotive garage that served as unofficial KKK headquarters. During local elections in November 1926, Smith challenged Catholic voters at the polls and was assaulted by a precinct worker. The fight, broken up by sheriff's deputies, sparked violence as local bootleggers stormed Smith's garage, battling with Klansmen barricaded inside. The raiders then drove past a Masonic temple where voting was in progress, firing on assembled Klansmen and touching off another firefight that left five men dead. The outburst resulted in National Guard units being summoned to Herrin for the eighth time in four years. [10]

SMITH, RANDALL WILEY

A member of the Georgia-based New Order Knights, Smith beat black teenager Tim Carey with brass knuckles in Cedartown, in April 1984. Nearly eighteen months later, in September 1985, he assaulted another black youth, this time in Villa Rica, Georgia. [NYT 1984–1985]

SMITH, RAY

An exalted cyclops of the United Klans in McComb, Mississippi, Smith led one of two klaverns responsible for a series of bombings in 1964. [38]

SMITH, SANDI

See Greensboro, North Carolina.

SMITH, WILLIAM RAY

See Dahmer, Vernon.

SMITH, WOODROW

A black resident of Chattanooga, Tennessee, Smith became a target for Klan violence after purchasing a home formerly occupied by whites. The house was bombed by nightriders on July 23, 1949. [NYT 1949]

SMITH AND WESSON LINE

A nickname applied to the Mason-Dixon Line by Klansmen after World War II, the label hinted at the armed response awaiting "outside agitators" in the South. [10]

SMITHERS, DAN

A warehouse supervisor in Beaumont, Texas, Smithers claims to have served as a Houston policeman for one year, but the department refuses to verify his story. A defector from the United Klans of America, he shifted allegiance to the National Knights and was appointed to serve as grand dragon of the Texas realm, with his wife named as Texas queen kleagle. Both retained their titles when they switched to Dale Reusch's Invisible Empire Knights in 1975, with Smithers later doubling as imperial klaliff for the Confederation of Independent Orders. [84]

SMYTHE, EDWARD JAMES

As founder of the Protestant War Veterans of America and an associate of the German-American Bund, Smythe helped organize an August 1940 rally in New Jersey, where Klansmen mingled freely with Bundists and Smythe shared the dais with Grand Dragon Arthur Bell. Smythe also wrote a weekly column for *X-Ray*, published by Klansman Court Asher. One of twenty-eight American fascists charged with sedition in July 1942, he escaped conviction when a mistrial was declared two years later and prosecutors dropped the case. Following the 1946 reelection of Georgia Governor Eugene Talmadge, Smythe announced plans to open a Southern headquarters of his Protestant War Veterans in Atlanta sometime after January 1947, but the move was stymied when Talmadge died prior to the inauguration. Meanwhile, State Attorney General Dan Duke launched an investigation of the organization, calling it a front for the KKK. [10]

SNEADS FERRY FELLOWSHIP CLUB

In 1965 congressional investigators identified this group as a cover for United Klans of America Unit No. 154, in Sneads Ferry, North Carolina. [38]

SNELL, RICHARD WAYNE

A member of the Covenant, the Sword, and the Arm of the Lord, Snell shot and killed black state trooper Louis Bryant in 1983 after a routine traffic stop near DeQueen, Arkansas. Investigation disclosed that the automatic weapon used in the murder was supplied to Snell by the group's leader, James Ellison. Convicted and sentenced to life imprisonment on a charge of first-degree murder, Snell was also one of thirteen white supremacists charged with federal sedition counts in 1987. A jury in Ft. Smith, Arkansas, acquitted him of those charges in April 1988. [13]

SNELSON, EARL

Identified as the grand dragon of California in the late 1930s, under Imperial Wizard James Colescott, Snelson maintained his state headquarters in Long Beach. [10]

SNIPES, CRAYTON

See *Rogers, Ernest and Christine.*

SNYDER, RAY J.

See *California.*

SOCIAL NATIONALIST ARYAN PEOPLES PARTY

Organized in Post Falls, Idaho, in 1979, this tiny neo-Nazi splinter group was the brainchild of ex-convict Keith Gilbert, who had served five years in California prisons for wounding a black man with gunfire and stockpiling dynamite with the aim of assassinating Dr. Martin Luther King. The party's most notorious member, however, is "Lieutenant" Frank Spisak, a transvestite serial killer who was sentenced to death in 1983 for three murders in Cleveland, Ohio. [*People,* Aug. 29, 1983]

SONS OF DEMOCRACY

In the 1960s this was a Plymouth, North Carolina, front for the United Klans of America. [38]

SONS OF LIBERTY

An affiliate of the American Nazi Party led by James K. Warner in the late 1960s, the Sons of Liberty staged occasional joint demonstrations with neo-Nazis around Los Angeles. Surviving into the 1980s as an adjunct of Warner's New Christian Crusade Church, the group was based in Metairie, Louisiana, as of December 1989. [90]

SOPHIA REBELS CLUB

In 1965 congressional investigators identified this group as a front for the Sophia, North Carolina, klavern, United Klans of America. [38]

SOUTH CAROLINA

Klansmen in South Carolina trace their roots to February 1868, when Governor Benjamin Perry issued a call for white men to organize militant Democratic Clubs to defend white supremacy. The KKK made its first public appearance a month later in York County, with pranks and threats escalating into violence with the approach of November's presidential election. In the autumn of 1868, nightriding was concentrated in twelve northeastern counties, especially Abbeville. Klansmen in Abbeville County murdered two state legislators that fall, and some 80 percent of the county's black voters were barred from casting their ballots on election day. (By comparison, about half of the registered blacks were allowed to vote in nearby Anderson and Laurens counties.) In the wake of Republican victories in November, Governor-elect Robert Scott warned that further terrorism might provoke another civil war, and Klansmen for the most part kept a low profile over the next two years, with South Carolina having the least violence of any realm except Virginia. The violence resumed in 1870, however, typified by the bloody riot in Laurens County, as Conservatives launched their drive to recapture the state government. In York County, where an estimated 1,800 of the region's 2,300 white men were loyal

Klansmen, authorities recorded eleven murders and more than 600 assaults between November 1870 and September 1871. With Klansmen beyond the control of their nominal leaders, federal force and prosecutions under the new Ku Klux Acts were required to suppress the Klan in 1872.

In the early 1920s, South Carolina was the last of ten realms chartered under Imperial Wizard William Simmons, with modern Klansmen most active in the coastal terraces and piedmont, generally making little headway in the coastal plains. Charleston was hostile enough that a 1923 mayoral candidate based his campaign on pleas for public sympathy, claiming that he had been victimized by the KKK. Voters in Columbia elected a Klansman as mayor three years later, but in the absence of noteworthy enemies, the decade produced few reports of actual violence. This changed in 1939 and 1940, with Greenville and Anderson counties recognized as strongholds of the declining Klan population. Klansmen stood fast against organized labor in the state, and Greenville police joined ranks with the Klan to prevent registration of black voters in 1940. Several Klansmen were convicted of flogging a white man in Anderson County, and their Greenville County brethren twice raided a Negro Youth Administration camp in Fountain Inn, whipping residents and posting signs that read: "Niggers, Your Place is in the Cotton Patch."

South Carolina units were represented when Dr. Samuel Green organized the Association of Georgia Klans in 1946, but Grand Dragon Tom Hamilton bailed out three years later, creating his own Association of Carolina Klans. Although headquartered in South Carolina, Hamilton's Klansmen raided freely on both sides of the state line between 1950 and 1952, a circumstance that landed them in trouble with both state and federal authorities on kidnapping charges. Hamilton and nine other Klansmen were sentenced to federal prison, ending the terror, with the grand dragon and sixty-two others later convicted on state felony charges.

In 1954, the U.S. Supreme Court's Black Monday decision on school integration helped revive the dormant Carolina KKK, with Eldon Edwards and his U.S. Klans facing spirited opposition from splinter groups that included the Association of South Carolina Klans, the South Carolina Knights of the KKK, the National Ku Klux Klan, the Independent Knights, and the Palmetto Knights. In July 1961 Grand Dragon Robert Scoggin defected from the U.S. Klans and led most of his followers into the new United Klans of America, recruiting an estimated 800 members in fifty klaverns by late 1966. (Another 250 Klansmen belonged to the dwindling Association of South Carolina Klans, affiliated with James Venable's National Association of Ku Klux Klan.) Despite rumors of bombing seminars and Scoggin's support for a hard-core militant group dubbed the "Underground," South Carolina witnessed few incidents of actual violence in the 1960s.

Imprisoned for contempt of Congress in 1969, Scoggin served his time in federal prison and returned to find statewide membership shrunken by some 40 percent under the negligent management of acting grand dragon Harry Gilliam. Forced out of the United Klans after quarrels with imperial headquarters, Scoggin founded his own Invisible Empire, Knights of the KKK, Realm of South Carolina in 1970, briefly facing murder charges that September after a member of the United Klans was killed at a rally near Sumter. In 1976, Scoggin convened a Conference of Eastern Dragons in his home state, but the rally did not presage any widespread Klan revival. An independent faction, the Federated Knights, were reported active in both Carolinas through the early 1980s, but by 1987, only a small contingent of the United Klans survived in South Carolina. [10; 38; 87]

SOUTH CAROLINA KNIGHTS OF THE KU KLUX KLAN, INC.

An independent splinter group organized after the U.S. Supreme Court's Black Monday decision in 1954, it was one of at least six Klan factions operating in South Carolina during the late 1950s. [38]

SOUTH DAKOTA

North Dakota Klansman F. Halsey Ambrose attempted to sign up recruits in South Dakota, but his efforts met with little apparent success in the 1920s. In 1928, with membership declining nationwide, anti-Catholic Senator Tom Heflin was forced to cancel a scheduled appearance in South Dakota when local Klansmen were unable to provide him with an audience. [10]

SOUTH HILL "85" CLUB

In 1965 congressional investigators identified this group as the cover for a Mecklenburg, Virginia, klavern, United Klans of America, serving Klansmen in La Crosse and South Hill. [38]

SOUTH PIKE MARKSMANSHIP ASSOCIATION

In 1966 the House Un-American Activities Committee identified this group as a front for McComb, Mississippi, Unit No. 700, United Klans of America. Members of this klavern were identified as participants in a series of local bombings during Mississippi's Freedom Summer of 1964. [38]

SOUTH ROWAN GUN CLUB

A front for the Landis, North Carolina, klavern, United Klans of America, this group was publicly exposed in 1965. [38]

SOUTHERN CALIFORNIA FREEDOM COUNCILS

See *Swift, Wesley.*

SOUTHERN CONFERENCE ON BOMBING

Organized in response to a series of forty-six racial bombings between January 1957 and May 1958, this organization was the brainchild of Jacksonville, Florida, mayor Haydon Burns. Lawmen from twenty-one Southern cities participated in the effort, compiling dossiers on known racists and anti-Semites, collecting rewards that ultimately totaled $55,700. FBI agents declined to participate, but members of the conference reportedly infiltrated an August 1958 convention of the National States Rights Party, also keeping watch on the KKK and the Florida-based Knights of the White Camellia. [65]

SOUTHERN GENTLEMEN, INC.

A semi-secret racist organization based in Baton Rouge, Louisiana, the Southern Gentlemen existed briefly in the wake of the U.S. Supreme Court's Black Monday decision in an attempt to marshal resistance against public school integration. [61]

SOUTHERN KNIGHTS OF THE KU KLUX KLAN

Led by Florida Klansman Bill Hendrix, the Southern Knights met with spokesmen of the Federated Klans and the Association of Carolina Klans in January 1950, issuing a joint declaration of war on "hate groups" such as the NAACP and B'nai B'rith. In the late 1950s, it survived as one of five Florida Klans resisting racial integration. [6]

SOUTHERN NATIONAL FRONT

One of several names applied to Glenn Miller's Carolina Knights of the KKK during the turbulent 1980s, this particular name surfaced around 1986, after the group tried its hand as the White Patriot Party. Its estimated total membership was between 250 and 300 in 1987. [NYT 1987]

SOUTHERN POVERTY LAW CENTER

Organized in Montgomery, Alabama, in 1971, by attorneys Joe Levin, Jr., and Morris Dees, the Southern Poverty Law Center (SPLC) is a non-profit organization dedicated to educational projects and the legal defense of indigent minorities. In December 1980 the SPLC created its Klanwatch Project, collecting information from 13,000 periodicals and bringing Klansmen to court on civil suits whenever possible, seeking to bankrupt the various Klans and cripple them with bad publicity. As investigator Bill Stanton declared of his opponents, "They thrive on secrecy. A Klansman looks at a courthouse the way a vampire sees a crucifix." In 1980 the SPLC filed suit against Bill Wilkinson and his Invisible Empire Knights seeking $43 million in damages for a 1979 Klan assault on black demonstrators protesting the rape trial of Tommy Lee Hines in Decatur, Alabama. By 1982, SPLC investigators had produced Klan witnesses, reactivating a dormant federal probe of conspiracy allegations in the case. (Wilkinson filed bankruptcy in January 1983, complaining that the SPLC's legal actions were costing him $10,000 a month.) In 1981, the SPLC filed lawsuits against Louis Beam's Texas realm of the Klan, winning federal injunctions against harassment of Vietnamese refugees, and a 1982 court action closed Beam's paramilitary training camps, prompting him to flee Texas and take up residence with the Aryan Nations, in Idaho. In Idaho Beam established a computer bulletin board declaring that Dees had "earned two death sentences," and members of The Order were planning to carry out his execution when FBI agents cornered and killed their leader, Robert Matthews, in the state of Washington. In July 1983 arsonists nearly destroyed the SPLC office in Montgomery. In 1985, Klansman Joe Garner, an associate of Beam, pled guilty in the firebombing and was sentenced to prison. A 1984 lawsuit filed by the SPLC in Alabama resulted in the closings of more Klan guerilla training camps, and North Carolina Klan leaders were jailed the following year for violating court injunctions against paramilitary activity in that state. In 1987 SPLC investigators produced evidence that led to the conviction of three United Klans members in the 1981 murder of black youth Michael Donald, and a subsequent lawsuit resulted in a $7 million judgment against the United Klans, forcing sale of the Klan's new headquarters in Tuscaloosa, Alabama. Another lawsuit, filed against the Invisible Empire Knights and Southern White Knights of the KKK, cost Klansmen close to $1 million in damages based on their 1987 assault on black demonstrators in Forsyth County, Georgia. In August 1989, FBI agents reported a new plot against Dees, conceived by Georgia Klansmen, and the SPLC's chief counsel responded with plans for a lawsuit against California Klansman Tom Metzger, charging his White Aryan Resistance with complicity in recent crimes committed by gangs of teenaged skinheads. [*Los Angeles Times Magazine*, Dec. 3, 1989; 93]

SOUTHERN PUBLICITY ASSOCIATION

See *Clarke, Edward.*

SOUTHERN PUBLICITY BUREAU

In 1921 this name was used as a cover for the first Klan chapter in Chicago, Illinois. [10]

SOUTHERN WHITE KNIGHTS OF THE KU KLUX KLAN

A Georgia-based splinter group, this faction was organized in 1985 by Dave Holland, former grand dragon for the National Knights and an associate of Glenn Miller's White Patriot Party. A resident of Lawrenceburg, Georgia, boasting numerous arrests for drunk driving, assault, and child molestation, Holland described his new Klan as "the most militant white racist organization in the South." Holland's Klansmen sought to prove that claim in January 1987, when they joined members of the Invisible Empire Knights to assault black protesters in Forsyth County, Georgia, but the move backfired in a lawsuit filed by the Southern Poverty Law Center, resulting in an October 1989 judgment of $940,400 against the two Klans and various individual members. Holland was personally ordered to pay damages in the amount of $50,000. The judge also required the convicted Klansmen to attend classes on race relations, to be taught by members of the Southern Christian Leadership Council. [NYT 1989]

SOUTHERNERS, THE

In the early 1970s this group was identified as a front for the racist Assembly of Christian Soldiers, Inc., active in Mobile, Alabama, between 1972 and 1974. [23; 26]

SOUTHLANDS SPORT CLUB OF FAIR BLUFF

Identified as a cover for the violent Columbia County, North Carolina, klavern of Tom Hamilton's Association of Carolina Klans, this club was decimated by mass prosecutions in 1952. [10]

SOUTHSIDE BEAGLE CLUB

In 1965 congressional investigators identified this group as a cover for the Burkeville, Virginia, klavern, United Klans of America. [38]

SOUTHSIDE HANDCRAFT CLUB

In 1966 the House Un-American Activities Committee exposed this club as the front for a Richmond, Virginia, klavern, United Klans of America. [38]

SPEARS, REV. JAMES

A resident of Decatur, Alabama, Spears was elected to serve as Alabama grand dragon for the United Klans of America in June 1966, replacing William Brassell. Three years later, he was one of seventeen Klansmen arrested after a shootout with blacks in Swan Quarter, North Carolina. In 1976, he was elevated to the rank of imperial kludd for the United Klans. [38; 84]

SPEARS, L.C.

See Lynch, John.

SPENCER, WILLIAM OLIVER

See *Caldwell, Lester.*

SPENCER CLUB

In 1965 congressional investigators identified this group as a front for the Goochland, Virginia, klavern, United Klans of America. [38]

SPINKS, LYCURGUS

After ten years of preaching in Arkansas and the Carolinas, Spinks began calling himself a doctor and switched to sexology, giving lectures "For Men Only," with special matinees "For Women Only." He once toured the South in a lecture series in which he billed himself as the reincarnation of George Washington. In 1947 he ran for governor of Mississippi, receiving 4,344 votes of the 350,000 cast, and he did just as poorly in two subsequent races for state tax collector. He was associated with the Federated Knights of the Ku Klux Klan, Inc., until prosecutions began to fragment that group. On August 8, 1949, Klansmen from six states met at Montgomery, Alabama, to form the Knights of the KKK of America, naming Spinks as their leader. Spinks claimed a membership of 650,000 although the leader of a rival Klan organization said that Spinks was wizard "over himself and one other guy." Spinks claimed to represent every Klansman, whether they knew it or not. In October 1949, he appeared on NBC's *Meet the Press* for what turned out to be an unintentionally hilarious appearance: Spinks said that he thought that Jesus Christ was a Klansman, and later stated that blacks in the South "know that the best friend they've got on earth is the Knights of the Ku Klux Klan." South Carolina sought to extradite Spinks for charges of banking irregularities when he served as a receiver in that state, but Governor Bilbo refused to obey the order. On September 17, 1950, Spinks claimed that he was cutting all Klan ties because his great dream of one large Klan had "turned into a nightmare." [25; 33]

SPISAK, FRANK, JR.

A homosexual transvestite and virulent neo-Nazi living on Cleveland's near east side, Spisak was known for hoisting a swastika banner in his window on holidays and blaring Adolf Hitler's Nuremberg speeches into the street. He was considered harmless by his neighbors, however, until September 1982 when police were called to act on complaints of Spisak firing a pistol from his apartment window. Subsequent ballistics tests, prompted by an anonymous phone call, identified Spisak as the triggerman in a six-month series of shootings that had claimed three lives. Once in custody, Spisak eagerly confessed to the murders of two blacks and a white maintenance man whom he mistook for a Jew. His object, as he later testified, was "to kill as many [blacks and Jews] as I could before I got caught. One thousand, one million, the more the better." Convicted and sentenced to death in August 1983, Spisak told the judge: "Even though this court may pronounce me guilty a thousand times, the higher court of our great Aryan warrior god pronounces me innocent. I do hereby set the example for our loyal Aryan nation. Many more will come after me. Heil Hitler!" Only after Spisak's conviction and sentencing were his links to the neo-Nazi underground revealed. From Idaho, ex-convict Keith Gilbert, founder of the Social Nationalist Aryan People's Party, claimed that Spisak was a lieutenant in his small group, and that Spisak was "acting under direct orders of the party" when he launched his private "search and destroy" missions in Cleveland. The orders, according to Gilbert: "Kill niggers until the last one is dead." [*People,* Aug. 29, 1983]

SPORTS, INC.

Identified as the front for a Miami, Florida, klavern in 1950 and 1951, this group was linked with the harassment of black residents in the Carver Village housing project and other local targets. [*NYT* 1952]

SPORTSMAN CLUB

In 1965 congressional investigators identified this group as a cover for the Rosehill, North Carolina, klavern, United Klans of America. [38]

SPORTSMANS CLUB

In 1966 the House Un-American Activities Committee identified this club as a front for Pickens, South Carolina, Unit No. 4, United Klans of America. [38]

SPORTSMAN'S CLUB NO. 3

See *Ocala Hunt Club.*

SPORTSMAN'S LAKESIDE LODGE

A front for the Hillsboro, North Carolina, klavern, United Klans of America, this group was publicly identified in 1965. [38]

STALLWORTH, CLARKE

A reporter for the Birmingham *Post,* Stallworth was investigating a 1949 cross burning in nearby Sumiton, Alabama, when two men lured him into a store and assaulted him, one of them hurling a hammer at Stallworth before he escaped. Klansmen Roscoe Fowler and Glen Godfrey were arrested in the incident. [*NYT* 1949]

STANLEY, DAVID

A Canadian member of the National States Rights Party, Stanley was one of eight of that group's activists indicted for violent interference with school integration in Birmingham, Alabama, in September 1963. Two years later, while addressing a Canadian government panel that denied him use of the mails for distributing hate literature, he denied membership in the party but admitted serving as its Canadian representative. [FOF 1963; 84]

STANLY IMPROVEMENT ASSOCIATION

In 1965 congressional investigators identified this group as a cover for the Albemarle, North Carolina, klavern, United Klans of America. [38]

STANTON, RICHARD

A Chicago policeman, identified as a member of the National Knights in December 1967, Stanton was allowed to resign in lieu of prosecution on charges of stockpiling illegal weapons and allegedly plotting to assassinate Mayor Richard Daley. [NYT 1967]

STAPLETON, BEN

A 1920s Colorado Klansman, Stapleton was elected mayor of Denver in 1923. Once in office, he appointed Klansmen to numerous city jobs, beating back a recall attempt in 1924. One of eight ranking Klansmen suspended by Grand Dragon John Locke for siding with imperial headquarters in a July 1925 power struggle, he was defeated in his bid for reelection. [10]

STAR KLANS

See *Knights of the Ku Klux Klan of America.*

STARLING, JACOB

A member of the Union League and victim of the Reconstruction Klan in Moore County, North Carolina, Starling was abducted by Klansmen in the fall of 1869 and branded in several places with the letters "UL." [87]

STATES RIGHTS PARTY

Also known as Dixiecrats, this third-party movement nominated South Carolina's Strom Thurmond for president in 1948, with Mississippi Governor Fielding Wright as his running mate. Two months before the party's grass roots convention, Wright endeared himself to Klansmen with a radio speech urging blacks desirous of social equality to "make your home in some state other than Mississippi." Noteworthy delegates to the convention included J.B. Stoner (recently fired as a Tennessee kleagle for being "too extreme") and anti-Semite Gerald L.K. Smith. The Dixiecrat platform mingled racism and regional outrage at the decline of Southern influence in national politics, with Thurmond blaming President Harry Truman's civil rights program on "demands of the parlor pinks and the subversives" and describing the Fair Employment Practices Commission as "hatched in the brains of communists." Klansmen did their best to help the party slate while subverting the left-wing Progressive Party in Southern precincts, and Thurmond ran third in November's election, polling 1,169,021 votes nationwide. [61]

STECK, DANIEL

A Democratic senator from Iowa elected with Klan support in 1924, Steck was challenged by opponent Smith Brookhart prior to taking his seat. At the resultant Senate hearing Steck denied any link with the Klan, but his attorney of record was Klan lobbyist W.F. Zumbrunn, who earlier had helped seat a Klan senator from Texas. Indiana and Ohio Klansmen pressured their members on the elections committee, and Steck was allowed to take his seat. [10]

STEPHENS, ED

Identified as Georgia grand dragon of the Invisible Empire Knights in 1989, Stephens participated in a January 1987 Klan assault on black demonstrators in Forsyth County, Georgia. Named as a defendant in a civil suit filed by the Southern Poverty Law Center, Stephens was ordered to pay $30,000 damages in October 1989, with a further stipulation that he attend classes in race relations to be taught by the victims of his attack. [NYT 1989]

STEPHENS, JOHN W.

A Unionist "scalawag" and Republican state senator from Reconstruction Caswell County, North Carolina, Stephens outraged local bigots by treating blacks as equals. In May 1870, while meeting with Democratic sheriff and Klansman Frank Wiley, Stephens was lured to a woodshed behind the county courthouse, where Klansmen stabbed and strangled him to death. His body was discovered the next day, and Klansmen mounted a virulent campaign of character assassination, accusing Stephens of everything from chicken theft to killing his mother and making it look like an accident. The full story of his murder was not revealed until 1935, with the release of a deathbed confession by John Lea, founder of the Caswell County Klan and leader of the execution team. [87]

STEPHENS, ROBERT J.

An informant for the Columbus, Ohio, police department, Stephens infiltrated the National Knights of the KKK in 1964, listing himself as an officer when the Ohio realm was incorporated that October. (Two months later, he petitioned the secretary of state to have his name removed from the incorporation papers.) In February 1966 he told the House Un-American Activities Committee of a Klan plot to dynamite buildings and sewers in Columbus in an attempt to start race riots. According to Stephens, a cache of explosives found outside of town was transported from Stone Mountain, Georgia, and was supplied by a group of National Knights that included Joseph Sims and Cecil Myers. Stephens also named Klansman (and convicted robber) Daniel Wagner as being involved in plots to kill various dissident Klansmen and national celebrities in 1964. [38]

STEPHENS, THOMAS

A resident of Athens, Georgia, and an ex-member of Clarke County Klavern No. 244, United Klans of America, Stephens appeared as a surprise prosecution witness at the 1966 federal conspiracy trial of Klansmen Cecil Myers and Joseph Sims. His testimony described Myers and Sims boasting of Lemuel Penn's murder in July 1964. Both defendants were convicted by the jury. [NYT 1966]

STEPHENSON, DAVID CLARKE

A Texas native born in 1891 who dropped out of elementary school, Stephenson was working as a printer in Oklahoma when he joined the National Guard to serve in World War I. Discharged as a lieutenant, he moved to Evansville, Indiana, in 1920, selling coal and recruiting members for veterans organizations. Indiana's first klavern was organized in Evansville that year, and he soon took control from founder Joe Huffington. His program for Klan building included appeals to Protestant clergy and to law and order in the form of legalized vigilantes, and the organization of an all-female "poison society," the Queens of the Golden Mask. By early 1922, membership had topped 5,000, and Stephenson was selected for a key role in Hiram Evans's drive to replace Imperial Wizard William Simmons. The coup was accomplished, and Stephenson was rewarded with the command of a sub-empire spanning twenty-three Northern and midwestern states, recruiting thousands of members each week in Indiana alone. Stephenson revived the dormant Horse Thief Detective Society as his private Klan police force, and Klansmen had sufficient strength to make him the "old man" of Indiana politics by early 1923. Hiram Evans came north for Stephenson's inauguration as grand dragon that year in Kokomo's Malfalfa Park, but their alliance soon foundered due to Stephenson's boundless ambition. Relying for support on the political apparatus that he called his "Military Machine," Stephenson formally resigned his state and national Klan titles in September 1923, looking forward to a 1926 senate race and a bid for the White House in 1928. As an alternative to serving under Evans, Stephenson convened a special convention in May 1924, and was elected by his followers as grand dragon of the new Independent Klan of America. Evans responded by supporting Huffington in a move that banished Stephenson from the Invisible Empire, and a bomb destroyed Stephenson's yacht at its moorings in Toledo, Ohio. (Stephenson blamed the explosion on "yellow-livered Southerners who hate everything that is pure throughout the state of Indiana.") In November 1924, Klan votes helped elect Indiana's governor, the mayor of Indianapolis, and countless lesser officials, but control of the state legislature was split, with Evans loyalists dominating the lower house and Stephenson's supporters the upper chamber. As a result, few bills were passed, but Stephenson remained confident of the future until March 1925, when he was charged with murder in the rape and slaying of Madge Oberholtzer. Conviction brought a life sentence, but Stephenson hung on in hopes of a gubernatorial pardon, which never came. Disgusted with his former "friends," the ex-dragon retaliated by leaking information linking various public officials to the KKK, and widespread scandals produced a series of bribery trials. Indianapolis Mayor John Duvall was among those convicted of hiding Klan contributions, and a Muncie judge who doubled as a Klan lecturer was impeached by a unanimous vote of the state assembly. Friends of the Klan who escaped prosecution soon found themselves voted out of office in the backlash of Stephenson's disclosures, and the sordid details of his trial cost the national KKK thousands of members. Paroled to the custody of Oklahoma relatives in March 1950, Stephenson vanished five months later and was traced to Minneapolis by FBI agents, who found him working as a printer. A year of legal wrangling saw him returned to Indiana and prison in 1951, and he was paroled for a second time in December 1954. Settling in Seymour Indiana, he married his third wife in 1958, but soon abandoned her and disappeared until 1961, when he was jailed for assaulting a teenage girl in Independence, Missouri. Charges were dropped on the condition that he leave the state, and Stephenson became a drifter, finally settling in Jonesboro, Tennessee, where he wed his fourth wife in 1964. Upon his death in June 1966, Stephenson's widow professed shock when informed of her husband's notorious past. [10; 93; see also *Oberholtzer, Madge*]

STERLINGTON HUNTING & FISHING CLUB

Identified as a cover for the Sterlington, Louisiana, klavern, Original Knights of the KKK, this title was retained when the unit defected en masse to the United Klans of America, in early 1964. [38]

STEWART, ALECK

A black resident of Monroe County, Mississippi, Stewart was whipped by Reconstruction Klansmen when he tried to sue his white employer for overdue wages. [93]

STEWART, DONALD

See *Dayvault, Marx*.

STILLINGS, PAUL

See *Adamic Knights of the Ku Klux Klan*.

STIREWALT, JOHN

An admitted Klansman, Stirewalt was elected sheriff of Rowan County, North Carolina, in 1966. He publicly resigned from the KKK when he took office, but in September 1968 he swore in Grand Dragon J.R Jones as a special deputy after Jones warned the sheriff of possible trouble at a forthcoming rally in Salisbury. Stirewalt's appointment of Jones was rescinded after media exposure produced a public outcry. [*NYT* 1968; 84]

STOBALL, GEORGE

A Reconstruction Klansman in Columbia County, Georgia, Stoball cultivated a reputation as a nightrider, his notoriety paving the way for election to the state legislature. [87]

STODDARD, LOTHROP

The 1920s exalted cyclops of Massachusetts Provisional Klan No. 1, Stoddard also authored a popular volume on white supremacy, *The Rising Tide of Color*, which warned that "the white race will be absorbed and fused with those of darker color, unless precautionary measures are taken" by cutting off immigration from Southern and Eastern Europe. [10]

STOKES, WILDA IRA

A resident of Enterprise, Alabama, Stokes accosted two youths at a local shopping center in July 1984, raving about his Klan connections and his plan to "burn out" the home of Judge Warren Rowe. The incident ended with Stokes assaulting both boys, clubbing them with a beer bottle. Ironically, Judge Rowe was assigned to preside over the case. Upon conviction, Stokes was sentenced to a one-year jail term. [*NYT* 1984]

STONE MOUNTAIN, GEORGIA

Rivaling Pulaski, Tennessee, as a Klan mecca, Stone Mountain was the sight of the first two cross burnings on U.S. soil. In October 1915, a month before the modern KKK was revived, members of a lynch mob called the Knights of Mary Phagan burned a cross atop the mountain, visible from nearby Atlanta, and "Colonel" William Simmons was impressed enough to duplicate their feat on Thanksgiving night, when he convened the first gathering of the 20th century Klan. The initial group of fifteen recruits allegedly included two Reconstruction Klansmen, along with several Knights of Mary Phagan. In the 1920s, sculptor-Klansman Gutzon Borglum carved a Confederate memorial on the mountain's face, as a forerunner to his later work on Mt. Rushmore. In the spring of 1946, Samuel Green celebrated the emergence of his Association of Georgia Klans with a rally at Stone Mountain, and Imperial Wizard Eldon Edwards followed suit in September 1956, summoning members of his U.S. Klans for the largest rally since World War II. In July 1962, eighty-five state troopers tried to bar 800 members of the United Klans, led by Imperial Wizard Robert Shelton and Grand Dragon Calvin Craig, from gathering on state property, but police lines were overrun after a brief exchange of stones and tear gas. Governor Ernest Vandiver announced that he would use National Guardsmen, if necessary, to prevent future trespass on Stone Mountain, but Klansman James Venable's family owned land at the foot of the mountain, allowing Klansmen limited contact in spite of the official ban. In 1964, members of Venable's National Knights staged a victory celebration at Stone Mountain following the acquittal of Cecil Myers and Joseph Sims on charges of murdering Lemuel Penn. The Venable property continued in use through the late 1970s for the Klan's annual Labor Day celebrations. [10; 93]

STONER, JACK

An Alabama Klansman, Stoner was sentenced to one year in prison for burning a cross at the home of black Montgomery County Commissioner John Knight in 1983. Stoner named his accomplices in the crime as Klansmen Joe Garner, Tommy Downs, and Charles Bailey. [NYT 1983]

STONER, JESSE BENJAMIN

A Georgia native born in 1924, Stoner endured a grim childhood. At age five, Stoner lost his father. A few years later, Stoner was stricken with crippling polio. At age sixteen his mother died. Exempted from wartime military service by his limp, Stoner joined a Chattanooga unit of the KKK in 1942, and was soon promoted to kleagle by Imperial Wizard James Colescott. Obsessive anti-Semitism had become the center of his life, and in 1944 Stoner fired off a petition to Congress, urging the passage of a resolution declaring that "Jews are the children of the Devil." In 1945 he organized the Stoner Anti-Jewish Party, advocating legislation that would "make being a Jew a crime, punishable by death." Interviewed in 1946, he described Adolf Hitler as "too moderate," declaring that his own neo-Nazi party would eliminate Jews via gas chambers, electric chairs, firing squads, or "whatever seems most appropriate." At the same time, Stoner remained active in the KKK, joining Samuel Green's Association of Georgia Klans in the post-war era. (Klan-watcher Stetson Kennedy listened to one of Stoner's near-hysterical speeches before an Atlanta klavern, calling for the death of all American Jews, and emerged convinced that Stoner was "stark raving crazy.") In 1948 Stoner campaigned for a Tennessee congressional seat, polling 541 votes out of 30,000 cast. In January 1950 Sam Roper's Associated Klans of America expelled Stoner from Klavern No. 317 after he urged fellow Klansmen to drive all Jewish residents from Chattanooga. Moving to Atlanta, Stoner finished law school and teamed with Edward Fields, once a member of the Columbians, Inc., to organize the Christian Anti-Jewish Party in 1952. In 1954, Stoner and four party members picketed the White House with anti-Semitic placards. Sharing law offices with Klansman James Venable near the end of the 1950s, Stoner rallied with like-minded Jew-haters to create the National States Rights Party (NSRP) in May 1958; two of those present were later charged with the October bombing of an Atlanta synagogue, and police named Stoner as the possible source of dynamite used in the blast. In July 1959 Stoner proclaimed himself "archleader" and imperial wizard of the new Christian Knights of the KKK, based in Louisville, Kentucky, where Fields had once worked as a chiropractor. In August and September 1959, Stoner and Fields joined forces to oppose integration of Miami's Orchard Villa School, and Jesse made headlines again in October 1959, denouncing the rival U.S. Klans as "Jew-dominated." By June 1960 his Christian Knights were doing business from Atlanta, using the same post office box rented for the Christian Anti-Jewish Party eight years earlier. Named by journalists as a member or close associate of Nacirema, Inc., Stoner lectured a Birmingham, Alabama, NSRP audience on the proper construction of time bombs in July 1963. That September, he returned to Birmingham in time for a church bombing that killed four black children, and on September 23 he was one of eight NSRP members indicted for violent interference with local school desegregation. (Stoner was also present in March and April 1965, when a new series of bombs was discovered in Birmingham.) Between January and November 1963 Stoner joined Klansmen Connie Lynch, Gene Fallaw, and Don Cothran for a series of rallies in Jacksonville, Florida, where Klansmen were openly encouraged to shoot blacks and engage in other violent acts. June 1964 found Stoner in St. Augustine, Florida, teaming with Lynch, Holstead Manucy, and the United Florida KKK to harass black demonstrators being led by Dr. Martin Luther King. Nominated as the NSRP's vice presidential candidate in 1964, Stoner and his running mate, notorious anti-Semite John Kasper, polled a total of 6,957 votes nationwide. Traveling widely with Lynch over the next year, Stoner agitated Klansmen in Bogalusa, Louisiana, and NSRP members in Anniston, Alabama, where black victim Willie Brewster was shot and killed by nightriders following the rally. Brought before the House Un-American Activities Committee in February 1966, Stoner refused to answer any questions but infuriated congressmen with an editorial branding committee chairman Edwin Willis as "part ape." In 1970, Stoner ran for governor of Georgia on the NSRP ticket, but gathered less than 3 percent of the registered electorate. Two years later, he polled 40,600 votes in a race for the U.S. Senate, and 71,000 Georgians supported

Stoner in his 1974 bid to become lieutenant governor. In September 1977, already gearing up for another gubernatorial campaign, Stoner was indicted by a Birmingham grand jury for his role in a 1958 church bombing. Campaigning vigorously in the knowledge that his election would permit him to deny his own extradition, Stoner scored a limited victory when the FCC ruled that Georgia television stations were forbidden from censoring his racist political announcements. For a period of several weeks, voters were subjected to film clips of Stoner denouncing integration as "a nigger plot" to seduce white women and proclaiming that "You can't have law and order and niggers, too." Stoner ran third, and was finally extradited to Alabama in January 1980. Ex-policeman Tom Cook, identified by FBI agents as a 1960s liaison man between the KKK and Birmingham Police Commissioner "Bull" Connor, appeared as a witness for the prosecution, detailing Stoner's connections with local militants. Jurors convicted Stoner on May 14, and he was sentenced to the maximum ten-year term. Stoner told the court: "This confirms my conviction that this is a Jew-dominated country with no freedom for white Christians." A month later, Stoner sued the Georgia state Democratic party over its ruling that a felony conviction and impending jail term barred him from challenging incumbent Senator Herman Talmadge in the August primary race. A federal court upheld his right to appear on the ballot, but Stoner ran fifth in a field of six candidates, with fewer than 20,000 votes. His bombing conviction was upheld on appeal in April 1982, and nine months later he formally resigned from the NSRP, forfeited his $20,000 bond, and went underground as a fugitive, remaining at large until his surrender in May 1983. Paroled in November 1986, Stoner immediately resumed his racist activities, and in 1989 he was identified as the leader of a new organization, the Crusade Against Corruption, based in Marietta, Georgia. [2; 10; 38; 84]

STONEWALL JACKSON NO. 1

Established as a front for the Jacksonville, Florida, klavern, Improved Order of the U.S. Klans, this group disbanded in late 1964 and shifted its affiliation to the United Klans of America. [38]

STORK CLUB

In 1965 congressional investigators identified this group as a cover for the Canton, Mississippi, klavern, United Klans of America. [38]

STOVALL, BILL GUYTON

A white navy veteran and resident of Birmingham, Alabama, Stovall was dragged from his home by robed Klansmen in June 1949, carried to a nearby wooded area, and given twenty lashes with a belt. The Klansmen were angry with Stovall for letting his wife take a job, thus leaving their children "neglected." [Newsweek, July 11, 1949]

STRAIGHT ARROW NO. 17

In 1965 congressional investigators identified this group as a front for the Cumming, Georgia, klavern, United Klans of America. [38]

STRANGE, DAMON

See *Brewster, Willie.*

STRAYER, REV. JOHN

A minister of the United Brethren Church in Westmoreland, Pennsylvania, and exalted cyclops of the local 1920s KKK, Strayer was a spokesman for Klansmen opposed to the selection of Grand Dragon Herbert Shaw. In the fall of 1926 he was banished by Imperial Wizard Hiram Evans for opposing the will of national headquarters. [10]

STRICKLAND, CAREY

A Wilmington, North Carolina, member of the United Klans, Strickland was identified as an incorporating officer of the New Hanover County Improvement Association in June 1964. [38]

STRICKLAND, HORACE

See *Grainger, Ben.*

STRICKLAND, PAUL

A resident of Athens, Georgia, and a member of the United Klans, Strickland fired shotgun blasts into the homes of local blacks on June 20, 1964, wounding two persons. Arrested with Herbert Guest and Denver Phillips, he paid a fine of $105 for firing guns inside the city limits. An additional charge of assault with intent to kill was never prosecuted. [40]

STRICKLAND, REV. PERRY E.

A resident of Baton Rouge, Louisiana, and founder of the Central Baptist Mission, Strickland resigned from the U.S. Klans in 1956 in a quarrel over finances. The quarrel began at a large rally in Atlanta, where Strickland was appalled by the accounting methods of Imperial Wizard Eldon Edwards. ("They just told us the Klan had a balance of $300.") Strickland chartered his own independent Louisiana Knights of KKK that same year, telling journalists: "The NAACP is backed by Jew money. Catholic Archbishop [Joseph] Rummel came out for integration, but most Catholics won't go along with him. Some Catholics tried to join us but we turned them down. We need a white, Protestant group based on American principles." [48]

STRICKLAND, PITTMAN FOY

See *Grainger, Ben.*

STRUDWICK, FREDERICK N.

An attorney and Reconstruction Klan leader in Orange County, North Carolina, Strudwick was later elected to the state legislature. In December 1869 he led a party of Klansmen from Orange and Chatham counties on a raid intended to kill Republican state senator T.M. Shoffner at his home in Alamance County, but a friend of Shoffner's foiled the raid by telling Klansmen that their target was away from home. Shoffner subsequently fled the area to save his own life. [87]

STUDDARD, ELIZABETH

A resident of Lynn Park, Alabama, Studdard was attacked in her home by seventy-five to 100 Klansmen in the spring of 1949. The raiders captured Studdard, her daughter, the daughter's boyfriend, and a male boarder, giving the women four lashes each with a belt, while the men received eight lashes apiece on vague accusations of "immorality." [*NYT* 1949]

STYLES, HAL

A 1920s Klan leader in the Jamaica district of Queens, New York, Styles lost a 1944 congressional race when his Klan ties were revealed. [10]

SUMMER, W.A.

A South Carolina Klan leader, Summer was listed in 1977 as an officer of the Confederation of Independent Orders. [84]

SUMMERFIELD FELLOWSHIP CLUB

In 1965 congressional investigators identified this group as a cover for the Belleview, Florida, klavern, United Klans of America. [38]

SUMMERFIELD SEWING AUXILIARY

This organization was the 1960s women's auxiliary for the Summerfield Fellowship Club. [38]

SUMTER SPORTSMANS CLUB

In 1966 the House Un-American Activities Committee identified this group as a front for Sumter, South Carolina, Unit No. 10, United Klans of America. [38]

SUPPLY IMPROVEMENT ASSOCIATION

In 1965 congressional investigators exposed this group as a cover for Unit No. 28, United Klans of America, in Supply, North Carolina. [38]

SUPREME CYCLOPEAN COUNCIL

A Reconstruction Klan-like group in Memphis, Tennessee, this organization was crushed by Memphis police in April 1868 when twenty members were arrested outside their den, at Hernando and Beale streets. Various disguises and the council's constitution were seized at the same time. While members considered themselves Klansmen, their constitution was less sophisticated than the KKK's Nashville prescript, outlining a committee on assassination and requiring members to swear that "should I ever betray a secret, or a member of the Brotherhood, I hope that all the social relations which I now enjoy may be sundered, that honesty in the men or virtue in the females may not be known in my family and generation, and that all who own my name shall be branded as dogs and harlots." Council members also promised that, upon receiving orders from their leaders, "should I be even in the embraces of my wife, I will leave her to obey them." [87]

SURRATT, JACKSON

A South Carolina Republican, Surratt was flogged by Reconstruction Klansmen in 1871 "for voting the radical ticket." [93]

SURRY COUNTY SPORTSMAN CLUB

In 1965 congressional investigators identified this group as a front for the Mount Airy, North Carolina, klavern, United Klans of America. [38]

SWANSBORO-WHITE OAK FISHING CLUB

Established as a cover for the Swansboro, North Carolina, klavern, United Klans of America, this group was exposed in 1966. [38]

SWARTZ HUNTING & FISHING CLUB

Organized as a front for the Swartz, Louisiana, klavern of the Original Knights, this group defected en masse to the United Klans of America in 1965. [38]

SWENSON, JOHN D.

A resident of Bossier City, Louisiana, described by congressional investigators as the "modern father of the Klan" in Louisiana, Swenson served as grand dragon and national kleagle for the Original Knights of the KKK. Assisted by Royal V. Young, Swenson recruited new members in Mississippi and Arkansas, but charges of financial irregularities surfaced in late 1963, with

Swenson and Young accused of hiding Klan assets in the name of the Louisiana Rifle Association. Before surrendering control in early 1964, Swenson burned Klan records, allegedly to prevent their falling "into the hands of the enemy—the communists." Authorities countered with suggestions that Swenson hoped to lose the evidence of profits earned from the sale of Klan robes, but Swenson refused to discuss the subject when he was called before the House Un-American Activities Committee, in January 1966. [38]

SWIFT, REV. WESLEY A.

An ex-chauffeur and bodyguard for Gerald L.K. Smith, Swift also served as a KKK rifle team instructor in the 1940s before founding his Church of Jesus Christ Christian in 1946. Claiming an improbable 1.5 million members in the United States (and another 1 million abroad), Swift regaled his small congregation with the message that "All Jews must be destroyed." (Until passage of time proved him wrong, he was also fond of telling the faithful: "I prophesy that before November 1953, there will not be a Jew in the United States, and by that I mean a Jew that will be able to walk or talk.") In October 1950 Swift traveled to Utah with Gerald Smith to aid in a smear campaign against Senator Elbert Thomas, defeated in his bid for a fourth term. While in Salt Lake City, Swift and Smith visited Governor J. Bracken Lee, emerging with announcements that Lee supported their anti-Semitic campaigns. Over the next two months, Swift and Smith marshaled opposition to the appointment of Anna Rosenberg as assistant secretary of defense in charge of manpower; on December 5, they presented the Senate Armed Services Committee with "proof" of her alleged communist ties. Back at home in Lancaster, California, Swift fabricated a baffling network of paper organizations, considered the West Coast's strongest neo-Nazi element by 1953. Over the years, members of the KKK, National States Rights Party, Minutemen, and California Rangers were welcomed into leading positions with Swift's church, lending their talents to such diverse enterprises as the Christian Defense League, the Southern California Freedom Councils, the Friends of Rhodesia, the California Anti-Communist League, and the Christian Nationalist Alliance. A pioneer of the Christian Identity movement in the United States, Swift "ordained" ministers including Connie Lynch, Dennis Mower, and Oren Potito to spread his gospel of anti-Semitism and white supremacy. Following Swift's death in 1970, leadership of the church passed to Richard Butler, and the group—alternately dubbed the Aryan Nations—shifted its headquarters to Idaho in 1976, following a mass seizure of illegal weapons (including machine guns and napalm) from a bunker near Lancaster. [2; 29; 90]

SWINDLE, ALBERT

See *Federated Ku Klux Klans, Inc.; McDanal, Mrs. Hugh.*

SWORD OF CHRIST

See *Forbes, Ralph P.*

T

TACKETT, ELMER

A Michigan security guard for the United Klans of America, diagnosed as terminally ill in March 1974, Tackett had two weeks to live when he issued a statement designed to "clear my conscience" in the August 1971 bombing of school buses in Pontiac. Tackett claimed to be the only one responsible for the bombing, which had already resulted in jail terms for Grand Dragon Robert Miles and four other Klansmen. Authorities were unimpressed with Tackett's last-minute revelations, and the convicted defendants were left to serve out their time. [NYT 1974]

TALBOT, JOE

See *Bellows, Jim.*

TALMADGE, EUGENE

A three-term governor of Georgia (1933–1936 and 1941–1942), Talmadge made no secret of his personal racism in campaign appeals to the KKK and its sympathizers. Standing firm against New Deal civil rights initiatives, "Ol' Gene" cherished brief presidential hopes in January 1936, when he shared the dais with Gerald L.K. Smith at a grass roots convention of Southern Democrats in Macon, Georgia, but an unseasonable snowfall and a luke-warm political response doomed the campaign in its infancy. Talmadge never acknowledged membership in the Klan, but in December 1941, while pardoning eight Klansmen jailed the year before on flogging charges, he admitted whipping a black man in his younger days. "I wasn't in such bad company," Talmadge told his audience. "The Apostle Paul was a flogger in his life." Defeated by protégé Ellis Arnall in 1942, Talmadge joined forces with Major John Goodwin of the state highway patrol to organize a secret "patriotic" society called Vigilantes, Inc., which maintained open affiliation with the Klan's Georgia realm. Attempting a comeback in 1946, Talmadge placed his campaign strategy in the hands of Roy Harris, speaker of the Georgia House and later an officer of the Citizens' Council and a staunch supporter of George Wallace in national politics. Together, they campaigned on a promise to restore the white primary, discarded by

Arnall, and to "put inspectors at the state line to look into every sleeping car and see that there's no mixing of the races." After one Talmadge rally in Soperton, the angry crowd rushed off to destroy a black church. Branded a Klansman by columnist Drew Pearson, Talmadge denied the charge, describing himself as the "only candidate in Georgia who wasn't a Klansman." At the same time, he was willing to venture an opinion on the Klan, stating that he "approved of any good order if it is handled right." In September 1946, Talmadge ran second in the popular voting, but won the election due to Georgia's archaic county unit system, which guarantees each county two electoral votes, regardless of population. Stricken by a liver ailment prior to his inauguration, Talmadge died on December 21, 1946. The most impressive wreath at his funeral bore a ribbon emblazoned with the letters "KKKK"— for Knights of the Ku Klux Klan. [8; 10; 81]

TALMADGE, HERMAN

The son of Georgia governor Eugene Talmadge, Herman appeared as a guest speaker at Grand Dragon Samuel Green's 1948 birthday party, staged in the Atlanta Municipal Auditorium. The audience cheered his remark that Georgia was fortunate to have Klansmen "ready to fight for the preservation of our American traditions against the communists, foreign agitators, Negroes, Catholics and Jews," and Green returned the favor in that election year, boosting Talmadge for governor as "the man who will put Georgia back in the white man's column." On March 2, robed Klansmen paraded through Wrightsville, warning that "blood will flow in the streets" if blacks sought equality "through the force of federal bayonets," and none of the town's 400 registered blacks turned out to vote next morning in the Democratic primary. Similar tactics were noted in Swainsboro, Mt. Vernon, and Jeffersonville, where cross burnings, threatening letters, and distribution of small cardboard coffins labeled "KKK" convinced most black voters to remain at home. The Association of Georgia Klans publicly endorsed Talmadge in August, following his pledge to maintain white supremacy, and Green used the opportunity to inflate his own membership by promising 100,000 votes. At the same time, state registrars were busy striking some 588 black voters from the rolls on various technicalities, and one black, Isiah Nixon, was shot dead after casting a ballot in September, his killer acquitted on a farfetched plea of self-defense. Klansmen turned out in force for mass demonstrations prior to the general election, and Talmadge was swept into office at age thirty-five, the youngest governor in the United States. Although Talmadge pled ignorance of the fact when questioned by newsmen, Green was rewarded on November 17 with an appointment as a lieutenant colonel and aide-de-camp on the governor's staff. Klan support for Talmadge became a major issue in the 1950 gubernatorial race, with opponent M.E. Thompson calling for an anti-mask law, blaming recent acts of terrorism on "allies of the Talmadge machine who specialize in violence and use fear as their weapon." Talmadge fired back by branding Thompson "a friend of the Negroes, a friend of civil rights, and a friend of the FEPC," a broadside that carried the day in November. Anticipating the U.S. Supreme Court's Black Monday decision, Talmadge introduced a constitutional amendment to place Georgia's school system under private control, thus protecting it from federal interference. In 1951, with Green dead and the Klan greatly weakened, Talmadge demonstrated his adaptability by pushing for passage of the anti-mask law his cronies had killed a year earlier. By 1956, he was on his way to the U.S. Senate and a long career of opposition to civil rights legislation, which ended in the 1980s when he stepped down to seek treatment for chronic alcoholism. [29; 81]

TAR HEEL DEVELOPMENT ASSOCIATION, SAMPSON COUNTY

Previously known as the Little Coharie Improvement Association, this group was identified in 1965 as a cover for the Salemburg, North Carolina, klavern, United Klans of America. [38]

TARRANTS, THOMAS ALBERT, III

A Mobile, Alabama, native, anti-Semite, and proficient bomb-maker by adolescence, Tarrants was recalled by local police as "a thorn in our side ever since he was seventeen years old." The youngster's first encounter with far-right politics came in 1963, with his exposure to John Birch Society literature during the Goldwater presidential campaign, and he began making regular trips to National States Rights Party headquarters in Birmingham, where leader Edward Fields allegedly mistrusted his rabid antipathy toward Jews. In the summer of 1964, Tarrants was packing a sawed-off shotgun when he was arrested by Mobile police in the company of National States Rights Party officer Bob Smith. Tarrants participated in the harassment of blacks and Jews around Mobile, maintaining loose ties with the Klan and National States Rights Party, but he did not become a formal member until 1967, when he moved to Mississippi and signed on with the militant White Knights. A self-styled "guerilla for God," he was arrested for reckless driving in Collins, Mississippi, in December 1967; Imperial Wizard Sam Bowers was a passenger and police found an illegal submachine gun in the car. Unknown to authorities, Tarrants was also involved in a series of bombing and arson incidents in Mississippi in late 1967 and early 1968, leading Meridian Police Chief Roy Gunn to issue a shoot-to-kill order in March 1968. Three months later, on June 29, he was ambushed by police sharpshooters while trying to plant a bomb at the Meridian home of Meyer Davidson. Tarrants sustained thirty wounds in the battle, which also killed Klanswoman Kathy Ainsworth. Four days later, after tracing the bullet-riddled getaway car to Klansman Joe Daniel Hawkins, Chief Gunn announced that Klansmen had "vowed open warfare on law enforcement officers," adding: "We've accepted the challenge." (Subsequent evidence revealed that Klansmen Alton and Raymond Roberts had collected $34,000 in rewards for arranging the ambush, with another $2,000 pocketed by an ex-FBI agent serving as the middleman.) Indicted with Hawkins for conspiracy on November 14, 1968, Tarrants was convicted two weeks later and sentenced to thirty years in prison. Although he was never charged in other crimes, Chief Gunn called Tarrants the prime suspect in a series of bombings, including a Jackson synagogue blast on September 18, 1967 ($25,000 damage); the Jackson home of a white administrator at Tougaloo College, bombed October 6; the parsonage of St. Paul's Church in Laurel, where the black pastor doubled as head of the NAACP, bombed on November 15; the Jackson home of a white minister active in civil rights, blasted four days later; the home of Rabbi Perry Nussbaum in Jackson, bombed November 21; a Meridian synagogue, dynamited in May 1968; and the Florence home of a black civil rights worker's widow, bombed June 6. Following his conviction, Tarrants briefly escaped from the Parchman prison farm, assisted by other White Knights, but he was soon recaptured. Paroled in December 1976, he enrolled at the University of Mississippi and professed to be a born-again Christian, his "guerilla" days behind him. [84; 96]

TATE, DAVID

A member of the Aryan Nations and The Order, Tate was a fugitive from federal racketeering charges in April 1985 when he was stopped by highway patrolmen for a routine traffic check near Branson, Missouri. Tate emerged from his car firing a submachine gun, killing Patrolman Jimmie Linegar and wounding Patrolman Allen Hines. Seized by FBI agents a week later at the Arkansas compound of the Covenant, the Sword, and the Arm of the Lord, he was subsequently convicted of murder and sentenced to life imprisonment. [13]

TAYLOR, A.B.

See *Ku Klux Klan of Florida, Inc.*

TAYLOR, EDGAR

A Baton Rouge welder and gas station attendant, Taylor was identified as the Louisiana grand dragon of the U.S. Klans in 1957. In a statement to newsmen that spring, he outlined the Klan's purpose as follows: "The niggers are the main thing with us now. We are not fighting Jews and Catholics except where they help the niggers." [65]

TAYLOR, GILBERT

An ex-congressman from Huron County, Ohio, Taylor succeeded Clyde Osborn as Ohio's grand dragon of the KKK in 1924. [10]

TAYLOR, KEN

Identified as Indiana's grand dragon of the Invisible Empire Knights in 1988, Taylor was banished by Imperial Wizard J.W. Farrands that September, and reinstated a month later by a special tribunal of dragons in Georgia. With the meager victory in hand, Taylor promptly resigned in an effort to disassociate himself and Hoosier Klansmen from what he termed the Farrand "cult" of neo-Nazis and youthful skinheads. In November 1988 he launched a campaign to become coroner of Montgomery County with the remark that "I can't lose." Voters proved him wrong, and a year later, there was still no sign of the "new constitution" promised to Indiana Klansmen in November 1988. [NYT 1988; Correspondence with author]

TAYLOR, JOHN ROSS

A Canadian anti-Semite, Taylor toured Europe in the late 1920s and came home with an inordinate fondness for Nazis. In 1937 he ran unsuccessfully for elective office on an anti-Semitic platform, later emerging as an active member of the Canadian Klan and the Western Guard. Along the way, he endured numerous brushes with the law, and in 1965 Canadian authorities terminated his use of the mails to distribute anti-Semitic literature, including publications of the National States Rights Party. Taylor's rural farmhouse was allegedly used for right-wing paramilitary training exercises in the 1960s, and in 1973 he shared the dais at a Georgia National States Rights Party convention with rabble-rousers Buddy Tucker and Byron de la Beckwith. Three years later, Taylor attended Klan rallies in New Orleans (with David Duke) and in Charleston, West Virginia (with Dale Reusch). In July 1983 he visited Hayden Lake, Idaho, for an annual gathering of Klansmen and neo-Nazis sponsored by the Aryan Nations. [2; 84]

TAYLOR, WOODFORD

A Virginia state prison guard, Taylor was one of five persons jailed for illegal cross burning in Richmond during January 1967. Spurred by two incidents on New Year's Day, the arrests spearheaded a new crackdown on Klan activities ordered by Governor Mills Goodwin. [NYT 1967]

TAYLOR TOWN HUNTING CLUB

In 1965 congressional investigators identified this group as the cover for a Bernice, Louisiana, klavern, United Klans of America. [38]

TENNESSEE

As the cradle of the Reconstruction KKK, Tennessee witnessed the Klan's birth in Pulaski in the spring of 1866, and its reorganization into a paramilitary movement the following April in Nashville. Grand Wizard Nathan Forrest conducted both his Klan and railroad business from

Memphis, sharing the Klan administrative duties with Grand Dragon George Gordon, another ex-Confederate general. Phenomenal expansion followed the Klan's first public demonstrations, and Forrest claimed a minimum of 40,000 members in the state by March 1868. Membership overlapped with that of the Pale Faces and other like-minded groups, but the bona fide KKK possessed its greatest strength in central and western Tennessee. Maury County was the center of violent action in the state, with Klansmen raiding black homes and confiscating 400 guns in February 1868 alone, killing several persons and whipping many others, including one man who received a total of 900 lashes. With Unionist "scalawag" William Brownlow in the governor's mansion, Tennessee was spared the indignity of military occupation following the Civil War, but Klansmen still took out their anger on Radical Republicans and blacks. In July 1868 the state legislature responded with a new militia bill, prompting Forrest and Gordon to head a committee of thirteen Confederate generals—all Klansmen—who pledged to maintain law and order if the militia was restrained. It seemed to work, briefly, and new violence flared on the eve of November's presidential election. Republicans still carried the state, but President U.S. Grant's winning margin was 18,000 votes shy of Governor Brownlow's in December 1867, and Klansmen in several western counties escalated their nightriding after the election. By January 1869, even conservative Democrats were fed up, and Nathan Forrest issued his only proclamation as grand wizard on January 25, banning further Klan demonstrations without direct orders from a grand giant or higher officer, and commanding that disguises be "entirely abolished and destroyed." Brownlow was unconvinced, and declared martial law in nine counties on February 24, but he departed to fill a vacant U.S. Senate seat the same day, and his successor withdrew the troops on February 27. In August 1869 Conservatives recaptured the state legislature, and Tennessee's Klan evaporated with the last traces of Radical Reconstruction.

In the 1920s, the Klan's strength was concentrated in the eastern and western corners of the state, but the new Invisible Empire never challenged its predecessor in numbers or zeal. Klansmen made their great political efforts in 1923, pushing hard in the Memphis and Chattanooga municipal elections, but Klan candidates were defeated in both cities. Membership had already peaked by the time the ballots were counted that year, and the realm suffered a precipitate decline, except in Chattanooga, where stubborn units hung on through the Depression and World War II. Sporadic floggings were reported in the late 1940s, and a Jewish merchant was driven from Chattanooga by cross burnings, but the Tennessee Klan lacked a real issue until 1954, when the U.S. Supreme Court's Black Monday decision challenged the time-honored system of school segregation. John Kasper and Alabama's Asa Carter helped foment violence in Clinton, when local schools were ordered to desegregate in 1956, and Eldon Edwards already had units of his U.S. Klans in place. The Chattanooga faction defected in

October 1957 to become the rival Dixie Klans, whose participation in a statewide softball tournament made national headlines.

The 1960s failed to gather the same response in Tennessee as in adjoining states, but the Klan was by no means inactive. Grand Dragon Raymond Anderson represented the United Klans of America after mid-1961, with an estimated 225 members split among ten klaverns, but he had no major enemies or targets to use to encourage further growth. Anderson's closest competitor, the Dixie Klans, survived until 1970 with 150 members in four klaverns, loosely affiliated with James Venable's National Association of Ku Klux Klan. By 1980, armed resistance had been relegated to the Justice Knights and a competing splinter, the United Empire Knights, with several Klansmen jailed in Chattanooga for the April drive-by shootings that wounded several blacks. Acquittals and plea bargains sparked black rioting in July 1980, but Imperial Wizard Rocky Coker's 1986 murder conviction ended the United Empire Knights as a viable force. Meanwhile, members of the long-established United Klans of America were jailed for arson in Knoxville in 1982 and for shooting a black man suspected of dealing drugs in Rutherford County in 1984. At this writing, the KKK's most enduring link with Tennessee remains Pulaski, its birthplace and mecca, which still draws yearly pilgrimages from assorted Klans, the Aryan Nations, and skinhead gangs. [2; 10; 87]

TENSAS SPORTSMAN CLUB

In 1965 congressional investigators exposed this club as a front for the Tensas Parish, Louisiana, klavern, Original Knights of the KKK. [38]

TERBECK, DONALD

A resident of DeKalb County, Georgia, Terbeck was arrested in December 1982 for wounding a black man with rifle fire outside a local restaurant. In custody, Terbeck denied Klan membership, but witnesses recalled him distributing "Klan calling cards" outside the restaurant, and he was defended at his trial by Imperial Wizard James Venable. [NYT 1982]

TERRY, CHARLES R.

A Chattanooga grocer and Klansman, Terry was indicted on three felony and six misdemeanor counts in February 1949 stemming from his participation in a raid by seventy-five robed Klansmen on a reputed gambling club at Lookout Mountain. [NYT 1948]

TERWILLINGER, LEW

In the 1920s, Terwillinger served as Montana's grand dragon for the Knights of the KKK, Inc. [10]

TEXAS

Freewheeling violence was an established tradition in Texas before the Civil War, and it became worse with the advent of Reconstruction. Summarizing the situation for acquaintances in 1867, General Philip Sheridan remarked that if he owned both Hell and Texas, he would rent Texas out and move to Hell. Authorities recorded 1,035 murders in the state between April 1865 and July 1868, one-third of which were committed in 1868. Nearly half the known victims were black, and 833 of the murders were committed by whites, despite the fact that whites outnumbered blacks in Texas by roughly twenty to one. The KKK made one of its earliest appearances at Marshall in April 1868, and the movement spread swiftly in the eastern region of the state, avoiding Indian territory and the southern horn, where Mexicans lived in greater numbers. The Klan's Clarksville debut was marked by an assault on a black school party, but the worst violence was noted in counties bordering Arkansas and Louisiana; in the Red River counties, federal officers noted that whites had begun to massacre blacks "from the pure love of killing." Klansmen were not alone in the carnage by any means, but they did their part, assisted after the fall of 1868 by the Knights of the Rising Sun. Jefferson and Marion counties were the heart of operations for both groups, boasting rabid Democratic newspapers that included the *Ultra Ku Klux*. Military courts were convened for thirty-seven accused lynchers in early 1869, and although only six were convicted, the prospect of arrest and prison prompted the Knights to disband. By September, another twenty-nine convictions before courts-martial had led most Klan units to follow suit.

Texas was the first chartered, self-governing realm of the modern KKK, but the initial quality of its recruits in 1920 degenerated over the next two years, with widespread violence reported by the time membership peaked at 200,000 in 1922. From its Houston launching pad, the Klan spread statewide, administered by Grand Dragon A.D. Ellis, with Grand Titan Hiram Evans in Dallas pulling many of the strings from Province No. 2. Over 500 violent acts were credited to Texas Klansmen by 1922, when Evans muscled Imperial Wizard William Simmons out of power and moved his headquarters to Atlanta, and Klansmen were ready for something new. Politics was the answer, and the Invisible Empire scored some local victories—including the capture of the sheriff's offices in Jefferson and Travis counties—but a backlash was developing. The KKK became a major issue by 1924, with Miriam "Ma" Ferguson winning election as the nation's first female governor on a stern anti-Klan platform. By 1926, sporadic prosecutions and continued bad publicity—including published reports of eight men burned alive in a ritual ceremony—had cost the Klan thousands of members. In Dallas, membership was estimated at 1,200, down from a peak of 13,000, and there were less than 18,000 Klansmen in the Texas realm. The eventual disbandment in 1944 may well have come as a relief.

Surviving Texas Klansmen faced a challenge in the years immediately after World War II. Dallas was marked by a spate of home bombings in

1949, but Texas Klansmen were relatively silent after the U.S. Supreme Court's Black Monday decision five years later. Horace Miller's Aryan Knights may have established correspondence with neo-Nazis in Europe and Latin America, but it was still a two-man operation being run from Miller's home in Waco. Dallas Klansman Roy Davis made a more ambitious effort near the end of the decade with his Original KKK, but control of the movement had passed to other hands—and other states—by mid-1960. Even Robert Shelton's dominant United Klans had difficulty on the Texas front, with three grand dragons between the summer of 1965 and early 1966, all in pursuit of an estimated 200 dues-paying members.

Texas Klansmen saw a bit more action in the early 1970s, with future Klan luminary Louis Beam leading the Houston faithful in terrorist campaigns against local leftists, pornography outlets, and the Pacifica network's radio stations. Affiliated with David Duke's Knights of the KKK by the end of the decade, Beam was also a prime mover in the harassment of Vietnamese refugees in 1980 and 1981, until lawsuits filed by the Southern Poverty Law Center forcibly restrained his troops. A year later, further injunctions closed Beam's paramilitary training camps, and he fled north to Idaho, seeking refuge with the Aryan Nations. In the vacuum created by his passing, the independent Original Knights sought protection in diverse identities, changing their name to the Knights of the White Camellia by 1983, and again to the Camellia White Knights by 1987. Still, Texas Klansmen retain their potential for violence: Dallas police informant Ward Keeton was killed by a bomb in January 1984, after providing information on the local KKK and American Nazi Party. [2; 10; 87; 93]

TEXAS EMERGENCY RESERVE

Organized by Grand Dragon Louis Beam to promote paramilitary training for Klansmen and like-minded racists, this group maintained camps on the swampy flats near Galveston and at other locations around the state. In 1980, the Reserve was linked to the operation of Camp Puller, where students were required to study *The Turner Diaries* as part of their training. The project was scrapped in June 1982, after the Southern Poverty Law Center filed suit under an obscure Texas law banning private armies, winning an injunction against further training sessions. The defeat prompted Beam to move to Idaho, where he joined the Aryan Nations and issued "two death sentences" against the Southern Poverty Law Center's chief counsel, Morris Dees. [93]

TEXAS FIERY KNIGHTS OF THE KU KLUX KLAN

Based in Houston and led by Klansman Scott Nelson in the early 1970s, the Fiery Knights created a minor sensation in April 1974 when they announced support of a black candidate for justice of the peace in Precinct 6. The group was loosely affiliated with James Venable's National Knights, and Nelson was named as a prospective 1976 vice presidential candidate for that group. [*NYT* 1974]

THOMAS, EUGENE

A Fairfield, Alabama, steelworker and member of Bessemer Klavern No. 20, United Klans of America, Thomas was identified in March 1965 as the driver of the car involved in the ambush slaying of civil rights worker Viola Liuzzo. FBI agents seized an illegal sawed-off shotgun from his possession during the Liuzzo murder investigation, but Thomas remained undaunted, posing as a hero before Klan audiences in Alabama and North Carolina that May. On December 3, 1965, he was convicted on federal conspiracy charges in the Liuzzo case and sentenced to the maximum ten-year penalty. In February 1966 a consecutive two-year sentence was added after his conviction of a federal firearms charge. Despite the verdicts in federal court, a state jury—consisting of eight blacks and four whites—acquitted Thomas of murder charges in September 1966. His bid for parole was denied in April 1973. [*NYT* 1965–1966, 1973]

THOMAS, ROBERT

Named by FBI informant Gary Rowe as Alabama's grand titan for the United Klans of America, Thomas allegedly relayed orders from Imperial Wizard Robert Shelton that dispatched a Klan hit team to Montgomery and Selma, Alabama, on the day civil rights worker Viola Liuzzo was murdered. Defense witnesses in his federal conspiracy trial placed Thomas at a veterans club near his home when the murder occurred, and he was acquitted of all charges. Described by the House Un-American Activities Committee as "one of the most influential members of the United Klans of America in Alabama," Thomas refused to answer any questions when he appeared before that panel in February 1966. [*NYT* 1965; 38]

THOMAS, S.J.

See *Bailey, S.G.*

THOMAS, WILLIAM

A member of the Covenant, the Sword, and the Arm of the Lord, Thomas was one of several of that group's associates linked to the November 1983 bombing of a gas pipeline along the Red River in Arkansas. [*NYT* 1983]

THOMASVILLE BROTHERHOOD CLUB

In 1965 congressional investigators identified this group as a cover for the Thomasville, North Carolina, klavern, United Klans of America. [38]

THOMPSON, REV. DONALD A.

A Unitarian minister and secretary of the Mississippi Council on Human Relations, Thompson was critically wounded by shotgun blasts outside his Jackson, Mississippi, apartment building in August 1965. Klansmen were suspected, but never charged, in the attack. Three months later a new series of death threats persuaded Thompson to leave the state. [*NYT* 1965; 70]

THOMPSON, H. ROSWELL

Identified in 1971 as imperial wizard of Louisiana's Universal Klan—also known as the Fraternal Order of the Klan—Thompson was assaulted and injured by three brick-wielding Black Panthers in January 1972 while marching in a birthday parade for Confederate General Robert E. Lee. Prior to his death in 1976, Thompson entered and lost four gubernatorial campaigns, also running for mayor of New Orleans and various lesser offices. [*NYT* 1972; 84]

THOMPSON, JERRY

A reporter for the Nashville *Tennesseean*, Thompson infiltrated David Duke's Knights of the KKK in November 1979, going public a year later with his story of internal back-biting and financial chicanery. [*NYT* 1980]

THOMPSON, ROBERT

A Georgia member of the United Klans, Thompson was elected to serve that group as imperial klaliff in September 1964. [38]

THORNHILL, J. EMMETT ("POOL HALL")

Identified as a leader of the United Klans in McComb, Mississippi, Thornhill hosted a public appearance by Imperial Wizard Robert Shelton in the spring of 1964. [*NYT* 1964]

THORNTON, LESTER

See *Dahmer, Vernon.*

THRASH, MARSHALL

A Chattanooga Klansman identified as a member of the Justice Knights, Thrash was jailed with two other Klansmen in April 1980 on charges of wounding four black women—Viola Ellison, Lela Evans, Opal Jackson, and Katherine Johnson—in a drive-by shooting. All three defendants faced charges of assault with intent to kill that July; two were acquitted, but Thrash was convicted on reduced charges of simple assault and battery (two counts) and simple assault (one count), and sentenced to eight months in jail and a $225 fine. Announcement of the relatively lenient verdict sparked black riots in Chattanooga. [*NYT* 1980]

TILLERY, J.P.

See *Carter, Asa.*

TIPPINS, BILL

A white victim of Tennessee Klansmen, Tippins was flogged on July 3, 1949, while a grand jury was investigating similar cases. [*Time,* July 25, 1949]

TIPTON COUNTY COMMUNITY CENTER

In 1965 congressional investigators identified this group as a cover for the Covington, Tennessee, klavern, United Klans of America. [38]

TITTSWORTH, R.G.

See *Shoemaker, Joseph.*

TITUS, REV. GEORGE

In the 1920s Titus served as exalted cyclops for the Klan in South Bend, Indiana. [93]

TOLLIVER, KEN

A reporter for the Greenville *Delta Democrat-Times*, considered Mississippi's most influential voice of moderation in the 1960s, Tolliver wrote a May 1964 article accusing the Americans for Preservation of the White Race of using boycotts to keep "white" businesses segregated. A month later, Tolliver received an anonymous phone call declaring: "We have read your article on the Americans for the Preservation of the White Race, and we understand you plan to do a series. We want you to know that we know how to take care of you if you do." Less than an hour later, the same man called back, adding, "We forgot to tell you that we've killed other people. You wouldn't be the first." [4]

TOMASSI, JOSEPH

A West Coast leader of the American Nazi Party, Tomassi went on to organize the National Socialist Liberation Front after George Lincoln Rockwell was murdered in 1967. Eight years later, in an ironic replay of the Rockwell assassination, Tomassi was himself eliminated by a member of the rival National Socialist White People's Party. [2]

TONEY, PIERCE

An Atlanta union organizer active in the Congress of Industrial Organizations, Toney became a target for Klan harassment when he tried to recruit workers at the Scottdale Mill, owned by the Georgia Savings Bank & Trust Co., in 1937. When threats failed to stop his recruitment, he was abducted and beaten by Klansmen who told him, "Now, I guess you'll let that damned union alone. We're going to break up all these damned unions." [93]

TOP SAIL FISHING ASSOCIATION

In 1965 congressional investigators identified this group as a cover for the Holly Ridge, North Carolina, klavern, United Klans of America. [38]

TOWN & COUNTRY SPORTSMAN CLUB

Created as a front for the Durham, North Carolina, klavern, United Klans of America, this group was publicly exposed in 1966. [38]

TRACY, N.H.

A prominent planter and leader of the Reconstruction Klan in Fulton County, Arkansas, Tracy was a prime suspect in the September 1868 ambush murder of militia Captain Simpson Mason. He fled the county to avoid arrest, and his farm was occupied by troops within a week, fortified against Klan assaults. [87]

TRAWICK, PAUL

As editor of the weekly *Jasper* (Alabama) *Union News*, Trawick was threatened by Klansmen in 1949 for "meddling in Klan affairs." [*Newsweek,* July 11, 1949]

TREADWAY, F.N.

A veteran of the Confederate Army and sheriff in Fayette County, Alabama, during Reconstruction, Treadway sided with the Mossy-Backs in their anti-Klan struggles between 1869 and 1871. Treadway was the target of threats, and masked demonstrations as well as gunfire attacks on his home. Treadway persuaded the federal government to make arrests in October 1871, but most of the suspects had been forewarned and escaped. [87]

TRENT COMMUNITY CLUB

In 1965 congressional investigators identified this group as the front for a Kinston, North Carolina, klavern, United Klans of America. [38]

TRI-CITY LODGE

Established as a cover for the Dinwiddie County, Virginia, klavern, United Klans of America, this unit served Klansmen from Ettrick and Petersburg in the 1960s. [38]

TRI-COUNTY SPORTSMAN CLUB

In 1966 the House Un-American Activities Committee exposed this club as a front for Rocky Mount, North Carolina, Unit No. 24, United Klans of America. [38]

TRIPLE ACE CLUB

A front for the Faison, North Carolina, klavern, United Klans of America, this club was publicly exposed in 1965. [38]

TRIPLE-S SUPER SECRET SOCIETY

A 1920s Klan unit in Pennsylvania, this group was patterned after the Ohio Night Riders, and created with an eye toward violent action. Members wore black robes, with a skull and cross bones in addition to the usual KKK insignia. [10]

TRI-STATE KU KLUX KLAN

Reported active in 1970, this faction was based in the region where Delaware, Maryland, and Pennsylvania converge. Members were allegedly responsible for a December 1970 raid on Phoenix Center, a controversial students' center at the University of Delaware, whose occupants were active in civil rights and anti-war protests. With their faces darkened like commandos, Klansmen ransacked the house, smashed telephones and appliances, then fled after burning a five-foot cross on the lawn. [NYT 1970]

TRI-VALLEY SPORTSMAN CLUB

In 1965 congressional investigators identified this group as a cover for the Vero Beach, Florida, klavern, United Klans of America. [38]

TROSPER, DON

An insurance salesman from Danville, Illinois, Trosper helped Bernard Gustiatus organize a local chapter of the United Klans in July 1975. A month later, he attended the Klan's national klonvokation in Lakeland, Florida, returning home with a personal determination to unify the splintered Illinois realm. In September 1975 Trosper hosted a statewide meeting of United Klans loyalists in Urbana, but support from imperial headquarters was not forthcoming, and the realm continued its aimless drifting, torn by factionalism and personal spite. [43]

TRUMAN, HARRY S

A haberdasher from Independence, Missouri, Truman paid his dues to the 1920s KKK on the eve of a primary race for a judgeship in eastern Jackson County. Sources differ on whether he was actually initiated as a Klansman;

Truman insists that he demanded, and received, his money back when he became disgusted with the Klan's anti-Catholic and anti-Semitic doctrines. In any case, he cherished no love for the KKK during the remainder of his political career, and Klansmen despised him as President (1945–1952) on the basis of his liberal civil rights policies, including the integration of the armed forces and sponsorship of the Fair Employment Practices Committee. [10]

TUCKER, REV. BUDDY

A right-wing minister from Knoxville, Tennessee, identified as a prominent spokesman for the Christian Identity cult, Tucker shared the stage with Klansman Byron de la Beckwith at a 1973 convention of the National States Rights Party. Three years later, identified as leader of the Louisiana-based National Emancipation of Our White Seed, he found time to address Robert Scoggin's Conference of Eastern Dragons in Greenville, South Carolina. In the 1980s, Tucker was also affiliated with Dan Gayman, pastor of Missouri's anti-Semitic Church of Israel. [2; 84]

TUCKER, GARY A.

A retired Birmingham bus driver and former member of a Klan faction known as the Cahaba River Group, Tucker approached FBI agents in October 1988 to confess his involvement in a September 1963 church bombing that killed four black girls. Klansman Robert Chambliss had been convicted in the case eleven years earlier, but Tucker maintained his silence until he was diagnosed as suffering from terminal cancer. In his final interview, he expressed a desire to clear his conscience before he died. His confession marked the fourth public identification of a Klansman linked with the fatal blast; the others included Chambliss, Charles Cagle, and John Hall. [FOF 1988]

TULLS MILL RECREATION CLUB

In 1965 congressional investigators identified this group as a cover for the Deep Run, North Carolina, klavern, United Klans of America. [38]

TURKEY CREEK ROD & GUN CLUB

Created as a front for the Turkey Creek, Louisiana, klavern, Original Knights of the Ku Klux Klan, this group was exposed in 1965. [38]

TURNER, ABRAM

A black Republican during Reconstruction in Georgia, Turner was elected to the state legislature in December 1870 and murdered by Klansmen a short time later. A special election was held to choose his successor, and rioting whites insured a Democratic victory the second time around. [87]

TURNER, GEORGE

A black farmer and resident of Crawfordsville, Georgia, Turner was forced off the road in October 1965 and threatened with guns by three carloads of Klansmen, including Cecil Myers and Joseph Sims. [NYT 1965]

TURNER, GEORGE HAMPTON

An Athens, Georgia, Klansman and member of the Black Shirts, Turner was arrested with Cecil Myers, Joseph Sims, and his brother, Horace Turner, after assaulting black motorists near Crawfordsville in October 1965. Police seized six sawed-off shotguns, five pistols, four wooden clubs decorated with swastikas and the letters "KKK," a heavy chain welded to a swivel handle, and seventy-five rounds of ammunition. Tried with Sims and Myers in 1966 on federal conspiracy charges related to the murder of Lemuel Penn, Turner was acquitted on all counts. [38]

TURNER, HORACE

See *Turner, George Hampton.*

TURNER, JOSIAH

A Klan apologist and Democratic editor of the Raleigh, North Carolina, *Sentinel,* Turner was active in suppressing news of Reconstruction terrorism. When blacks were murdered in the area, Turner printed editorials accusing Union League members of killing each other in an effort to frame white Democrats. In private conversations, he praised the KKK as a political tool of the Democratic Party. Turner was arrested by the state militia during Governor William Holden's 1870 anti-Klan campaign, but prosecutors were unable to substantiate criminal charges. [87]

TURNER, PORTER FLOURNOY

A black cab driver in Atlanta, Georgia, Turner was stabbed to death by persons unknown and dumped on the lawn of a DeKalb County physician. The dormant investigation was reopened in August 1945 after Klavalier Klub members boasted of the murder, but no prosecutions resulted. [NYT 1946]

TURNER DIARIES, THE

A racist fantasy novel written in 1978 by "Andrew Macdonald," the pen name of National Alliance leader William Pierce, *The Turner Diaries* opens in 1991 and presents an apocalyptic vision of the United States enslaved by the Jewish international conspiracy. Under the new regime, whites are legally compelled to mate with other races, until the population becomes "a swarming horde of indifferent mulatto zombies," while enforcement of the

"Cohen Act" confiscates firearms from law-abiding patriots in a series of brutal coast-to-coast raids. Survivalist hero Earl Turner signs on with a white revolutionary clique, The Organization, to set things right, and one of his first missions is a bombing raid that leaves 700 persons dead in the ruins of FBI headquarters. Members of The Organization gleefully bomb synagogues, pornographic theaters, and homosexual hangouts, financing their raids with armed robbery and destabilizing the economy via sophisticated counterfeiting schemes. Along the way, Turner feels obliged to murder interracial couples and assault "degenerates" at every turn, gaining momentum toward the "Day of the Rope," when 60,000 "race traitors" are executed nationwide. In due time, he is invited to join The Order, an elite inner circle of The Organization, and cheerfully embarks on a suicide mission, guiding a nuclear warhead into impact on the Pentagon. By 1981, Pierce's novel was required reading for members of Klansman Louis Beam's Texas Emergency Reserve, and the fiction became reality in 1983, when militant disciples of the National Alliance and the Aryan Nations merged to create The Order in Washington State. *The Turner Diaries* served as a working blueprint for Robert Matthews and company, but Earl Turner's "heroic" exploits turned pathetic in the hands of mere mortals. Half-baked counterfeiting schemes produced currency so inferior that several members of The Order were immediately jailed, and their "Day of the Rope," in June 1984, resulted only in the death of Denver radio host Alan Berg. At this writing, Pierce's novel is offered for sale by various racist groups, including David Duke's National Association for the Advancement of White People. [13; 85]

TUSCALOOSA, ALABAMA

The presence of an active Ku Klux Klan and the University of Alabama have made for a volatile mix since Reconstruction, when Exalted Cyclops Ryland Randolph launched a campaign to purge the school of "radical" students and professors. Intimidation closed the university in 1868 and again in 1871. Anti-Republican riots and various "unsolved murders" (many of them perpetrated by a hard-core group of Klansmen dubbed the Sipsey Swampers) produced various calls for martial law between 1868 and 1871, but troops were not forthcoming. It was left for Ryland Randolph's own extremism, including street fights, to undermine the local Klan. Gravely wounded in a March 1870 gun battle, Randolph lost a leg and emerged from surgery a changed man, warning his Klansmen in June that "it is now time, we are free to announce, for murders and assassinations to cease." Still, a bit of the old spark remained, and when rioting Klansmen massacred blacks in Eutaw, Alabama, in October, Randolph editorialized that "a row occasionally does no little good."

Klansmen in Tuscaloosa County may or may not have participated in the January 1917 lynching of a black rape suspect, but their klavern held on and engaged in occasional nightriding until 1926, when state prosecutions for flogging encouraged the group to disband. Three decades later, Tuscaloosa was the seat of Robert Shelton's Alabama Knights, and Klansmen demonstrated with a vengeance when black coed Autherine Lucy enrolled at the state university in February 1956. In July 1961, Tuscaloosa became imperial headquarters for Shelton's new United Klans of America, recognized as the nation's dominant Klan through the early 1970s. Although klaverns in Birmingham recruited more members and the North Carolina realm would ultimately outnumber Alabama, Tuscaloosa remained the seat of the action, with Shelton reigning over an Invisible Empire that spanned nineteen states.

Elected governor in 1962 with Klan support, George Wallace tried to fulfill his campaign promises the following June by "standing in the schoolhouse door" to prevent integration of the state university. He failed, but numerous Klansmen were on hand to applaud his performance, and six Birmingham Klansmen—including William Keith, Herman Cash, Herbert Reeves, Ellis Denesmore, Gary Rowe, and Charles Cagle—were arrested by state troopers with a carload of weapons that included carbines, shotguns, pistols, bayonets and nightsticks, dynamite and hand grenades, a submachine gun, and a bazooka with six rounds of ammunition. The Klansmen were later released without bond, after Shelton threatened to "tear the damn jail down a bar at a time," and a friendly circuit judge returned the confiscated weapons, advising the nightriders to "use them well." In October 1963, a series of bombings around the university campus were traced to members of the Alabama National Guard, and five weekend warriors were indicted in January 1964. A year later, Shelton reportedly launched a harassment campaign against Reverend P.Y. Rogers, leader of the Tuscaloosa Citizens for Action Committee, distributing the minister's home phone number to Klansmen with orders to call around the clock, saying nothing when the telephone was answered. Declining fortunes in the 1970s and 1980s failed to drive the United Klans from Tuscaloosa, but an act of violence outside of Tuscaloosa may have changed this. In 1987, after several Klansmen were convicted in the death of a black Mobile teenager, Michael Donald, the Southern Poverty Law Center filed suit against Shelton's Klan and won a $7 million judgment that resulted in the sale of the United Klans' new two-story headquarters for roughly half its estimated value. Since the judgment, United Klans recruiting is reportedly at a standstill, and the Klan remains without a home. [10; 87]

TUTTLE, DOUGLAS

Arrested on weapons charges by New York State Police following a routine traffic stop near Stormville in October 1989, Tuttle identified himself as the grand dragon of Indiana, a post simultaneously claimed by Ken Taylor. He was held in lieu of $10,000 bond. [*Indianapolis Star,* Oct. 2, 1989]

211 POINTERS CLUB

In 1965 congressional investigators identified this group as a cover for Southern Pines, North Carolina, Unit No. 63, United Klans of America. [38]

TYLER, ELIZABETH

Edward Clarke's partner in the Atlanta-based Southern Publicity Association, Tyler was arrested with Clarke in 1919, half-dressed and intoxicated, in a bawdy house; each paid a $5 fine on conviction of disorderly conduct. In 1920 her son-in-law joined the KKK, and Tyler was introduced to Imperial Wizard William Simmons, and retained in June in an effort to boost sluggish recruiting. Tapped for interviews as membership climbed past the 100,000 mark, Tyler told newsmen that Jews feared the Klan because Klannishness "teaches the wisdom of spending American money with American men." Exposure of the 1919 arrest, in 1921, sparked dissension in the ranks of an order pledged to defend chastity and morality; Ed Clarke responded by commissioning a phony attempt on Tyler's life, to portray his partner and the KKK as victims of "un-American" persecution. Still, many Klansmen resented Tyler's prominent role in the group, which barred women from membership, and she was pressured to resign in 1922, citing her daughter's illness and a need for rest. She married a prominent Atlanta businessman the following year, around the same time that Klan leaders canceled Clarke's contract "for the good of the order." [10]

TYLER, WARREN

See *Meridian, Mississippi.*

TYRELL COUNTY MEN'S CLUB

In 1965 congressional investigators identified this group as a cover for the Columbia, North Carolina, klavern, United Klans of America. [38]

TYSON, LEE

A white sharecropper in Horry County, South Carolina, Tyson was flogged by six robed Klansmen in December 1951 on accusations of skipping church and neglecting his family. The county sheriff reported five more recent whippings—all of the victims white—with the Association of Carolina Klans responsible. [NYT 1952]

U.S. KLANS OF GEORGIA

Organized in September 1953 by Atlanta Klansman Eldon Edwards, this group consisted primarily of remnants from the old Association of Georgia Klans. In October 1955 Edwards went national, renaming his organization the U.S. Klans, Knights of the KKK, Inc. [48]

U.S. KLANS, KNIGHTS OF THE KU KLUX KLAN, INC.

Chartered on October 24, 1955, this group was the brainchild of Atlanta Klansman Eldon Edwards. He revised and copyrighted the rituals authored by William Simmons, thus claiming a "direct link" to 1920s Klan while denouncing competitors as "outlaws and counterfeiters." Samuel Green, Jr., served as attorney for the group, with Klansmen William Daniel and M. Wesley Morgan listed as incorporating officers. In September 1956 Edwards presided over the largest Klan rally since World War II, in Stone Mountain, Georgia, and by 1959 he had an estimated 15,000 members in ten states, with his greatest strength concentrated in Alabama, Georgia, Louisiana, and South Carolina. A major recruiting drive in March 1960 was marked by simultaneous cross burnings across the South, but Edwards was stricken with a fatal heart attack five months later. The late wizard's widow sought to replace him with Klansman E.E. George, but the membership chose Robert "Wild Bill" Davidson in defiance of her wishes, and a bitter power struggle ensued. In February 1961 Davidson and Georgia grand dragon Calvin Craig defected from the U.S. Klans, leading a majority of active members into the new Invisible Empire, United Klans, Knights of the KKK of America, Inc. Finally installed as imperial wizard, E.E. George presided during the May 1961 Freedom Rides when his Klan was named in a federal injunction barring riotous violence against demonstrators in Alabama. George held the post until October 1963, when dissident members of Georgia's College Park Klavern No. 297 accused him of financial irregularities, holding a special klonvokation to elect H.J. Jones as the new imperial wizard. It was a Pyrrhic victory, at best, with Klavern 297 abandoned as George and all the other active klaverns created a new Improved Order of the U.S. Klans. In January 1967 congressional investigators counted fifty Klansmen in the U.S. Klans, its membership still on the decline. [10; 38]

UDGREEN, ARTHUR F.

A Miami Klansman, Udgreen was indicted in December 1952 on one count of making false statements to the FBI during a probe of racial terrorism. In his statement to federal agents, Udgreen denied participation in local beatings, but evidence linked him with a July 1951 assault in Miami. [*NYT* 1952]

UNDERGROUND, THE

Organized by Klansman Furman Williams of Gaffney, South Carolina, this group comprised a secret action squad within the South Carolina realm of the United Klans. Tacitly encouraged by Grand Dragon Robert Scoggin, members of the Underground stockpiled weapons and gathered to practice marksmanship in the mid-1960s, but no evidence exists to link the group with specific acts of violence. [*NYT* 1965; 38]

UNDERWOOD, OSCAR

An Alabama senator who sought the Democratic presidential nomination in 1924, Underwood angered Klan leaders that spring by calling the KKK "a national menace." "It is either the Ku Klux Klan or the United States of America," he declared. "Both cannot survive. Between the two, I choose my country." His opposition to the Klan was a major issue at the party's national convention in July, and with Catholic Al Smith as the other prominent candidate, Klansmen were forced to throw their weight behind Californian William Gibbs McAdoo in an acrimonious battle that resulted in the nomination of compromise candidate John Davis. [93]

UNION LEAGUE

A Northern patriotic society organized during the Civil War, the Union League spread to the South in the post-war years, enlisting blacks and white Unionists in a Republican political machine. Regarded by Southern Democrats as a radical terrorist group, desirous of arming blacks for self-defense or worse, the League became a major target of Klan harassment during Reconstruction. Numerous members were threatened, whipped, or killed across the South, and at least one member was branded by Klansmen with the group's initials. [87]

UNITED COALITION AGAINST THE KLAN

Organized in Wrightsville, Georgia, in May 1980, this group staged a series of street demonstrations, accusing local cops of condoning Klan violence after an April courthouse melee that injured nine persons. [*AP*, May 3, 1980]

UNITED CONSERVATIVE COALITION OF ALABAMA

See *Wallace, George.*

UNITED CONSERVATIVES OF MISSISSIPPI, INC., NO. 1

In 1965 congressional investigators identified this group as the cover for Unit No. 702 of the United Klans, serving Klansmen in Poplarville and Crossroads Community, Mississippi. [38]

UNITED EMPIRE, KNIGHTS OF THE KU KLUX KLAN

A Tennessee splinter group led by Imperial Wizard Rocky Coker, this Klan was linked with July 1980 racial disturbances in Chattanooga. Coker and two other members were arrested that month for rioting and illegal possession of explosives. The Klan apparently disbanded after Coker's 1984 arrest and subsequent conviction on murder charges in Dunlap, resulting in a sentence of death. [*AP*, July 28, 1980; *NYT* 1984]

UNITED KLANS OF AMERICA, INC., KNIGHTS OF KU KLUX KLAN

On July 8, 1961, five hundred Klansmen from seven states gathered in Indian Springs, Georgia, with the majority representing Robert Shelton's Alabama Knights and Calvin Craig's Georgia-based Invisible Empire, United Klans, Knights of KKK. Shelton's forceful personality and uniformed eight-man security guard were so impressive that he was named imperial wizard by acclamation, presiding over a new Klan that retained Craig's Fulton County charter. The group's headquarters soon shifted to Tuscaloosa, Alabama, and Shelton set about building the nation's dominant Klan, with klaverns identified in nineteen states by 1966. Shelton professed distaste for the neo-Nazi movement in those days, but at least five of his appointed grand dragons—in Delaware, Maryland, New Jersey, New York, and Pennsylvania—were acknowledged members of the American Nazi Party. Imperial headquarters adopted a similar ambiguous attitude toward violence, urging Klansmen to adopt civil disobedience tactics while Shelton and Craig attended 1961 demolition courses sponsored by Nacirema, Inc., and Shelton shared the stage with violent rabble-rouser Connie Lynch in Bessemer, Alabama (October 1962) and in Spartanburg, South Carolina (August 1963). United Klans members accused of murder were banished from the Klan in July 1964, but those charged in an identical case eight months later were treated as heroes in Alabama and North Carolina by their fellow Klansmen. In spite of conflicting signals from the top, the United Klans' record of violence is well established. A partial listing of incidents follows:

July 1962—Stone Mountain, Georgia: Shelton and Craig lead a mob of Klansmen that overruns police lines to hold an illegal rally on state property.

June 1963—Tuscaloosa, Alabama: Six members are arrested with an arsenal of weapons, including a bazooka, but a circuit judge returns the guns to the Klansmen, urging them to "use them well."

September 1963—Birmingham, Alabama: United Klans members are linked with a series of bombings, including one in which four children are killed. Shelton tries to divert police attention by fingering members of a rival splinter group. In 1977, ex-Klansman Raymond Chambliss is convicted of murder and sentenced to life.

April 1964—Griffin, Georgia: Five members hold a crowd at bay with guns during an illegal cross burning. Jailed for disorderly conduct, all five forfeit bond by failing to appear for trial. Their weapons are returned by court order.

June 1964—Athens, Georgia: Four members are charged with firing shot-guns into a black-owned home, wounding two persons. Two of the defendants are convicted and fined.

July 1964—Colbert, Georgia: Lemuel Penn is ambushed and killed by Klansmen. Two ex-members of the United Klans are convicted of federal conspiracy charges in 1966 and sentenced to prison.

October 1964—McComb, Mississippi: Nine United Klans members plead no contest on multiple bombing charges. Their jail terms are suspended by the judge on grounds that they were "unduly provoked" by their black victims.

January 1965—New Bern, North Carolina: Three members are jailed on bombing charges. All plead guilty in June and receive suspended sentences.

March 1965—Selma, Alabama: Reverend James Reeb is beaten to death by a gang of racists, who are later identified as members or close associates of the United Klans.

March 1965—Lowndes County, Alabama: Civil rights worker Viola Liuzzo is shot and killed by United Klans members, two of whom are sentenced to federal prison later that year.

August 1965—Hayneville, Alabama: Civil rights worker Jonathan Daniels is shot and killed by a member of the United Klans.

August 1965—Plymouth, North Carolina: Numerous members participate in local race riots, assaulting and stabbing black civil rights demonstrators.

October 1965—Crawfordsville, Georgia: Grand Dragon Calvin Craig is jailed for assaulting a black protest marcher.

July 1967—Salisbury, North Carolina: Eleven members are arrested in a series of local racist bombings.

July 1969—Swan Quarter, North Carolina: Members engage in a shootout with blacks at a rally site. Grand Dragon Joe Bryant and Imperial Kludd James Spears are among seventeen Klansmen arrested.

August 1971—Pontiac, Michigan: Bombers destroy ten school buses. Grand Dragon Robert Miles and four other members are convicted of the crime.

Spring 1979—Talladega County, Alabama: Federal authorities charge twenty United Klans members with shooting at black homes; three defendants plead guilty, with ten others convicted and sentenced to jail.

March 1981—Mobile, Alabama: Black teenager Michael Donald is stabbed and strangled to death. Six years later, three United Klans members are convicted and sentenced for his murder.

July 1982—Knoxville, Tennessee: Two United Klans members are charged with burning a black family's home.

December 1984—Rutherford County, Tennessee: United Klans members are jailed for shooting a black man whom they suspected of dealing drugs.

April 1985—St. Petersburg, Florida: Three United Klans members are the first men arrested under Florida's new Anti-Paramilitary Training Act. All are convicted in 1986.

Membership in the United Klans has fluctuated wildly, from an estimated 15,000 in early 1967 to some 1,500 twenty years later. The biggest decline began in 1969, when Shelton and two of his strongest grand dragons were sentenced to prison for contempt of Congress and Calvin Craig resigned from the Klan to escape a similar fate. By the time of their parole in 1970, the Carolina realms were in total disarray, prompting both dragons to resign in disgust. Shelton sought to revitalize the United Klans with a national speaking tour, debating mergers or cooperative ventures with David Duke, Robert DePugh, and John Harrell's Christian Patriots Defense League. Still tied (with the Invisible Empire Knights) for honors as the nation's largest Klan in the 1980s, the United Klans maintained marginal pockets of strength in Alabama, Florida, the Carolinas, Kentucky, Virginia, and Indiana. Recruiting was stalled in 1987, when a civil suit resulting from the Donald murder produced a $7 million judgment against the United Klans, with Shelton's Tuscaloosa headquarters sold for a down payment on the outstanding bill. [2; 10; 38; 84; 93]

UNITED LADIES CLUB

In 1965 congressional investigators identified this group as a cover for the ladies auxiliary of the Amelia, Virginia, klavern, United Klans of America. [38]

UNITED NORDIC CONFEDERATION

A neo-Nazi splinter group dedicated to "unifying and purifying the Nordic people," the Confederation was exposed on January 18, 1958, when leader George Leggett and six of his stormtroopers were arrested on weapons charges in New York City. According to police, the seven fascists intended to finance their *putsch* by robbing a bank in the Kew Gardens area of Queens. At age twenty-one, Leggett was the oldest member of the group. His teenaged disciples included neo-Nazis Brian Casey, Bryan Colgan, Jay Page, William Schultz, Joseph Wagner, and George Zack. [*FOF 1958*]

UNITED PROTESTANT ALLIANCE

A 1920s anti-Catholic group in Queens, New York, the Alliance held meetings at the Klan-owned Triangle Ballroom in Richmond Hill, where speakers such as Senator Tom Heflin regaled the faithful with tales of papist perfidy. In retrospect, this group was probably a simple front for the New York KKK. [10]

UNITED RACIST FRONT

Organized in Greensboro, North Carolina, in 1978, this group sought to merge local Klansmen and neo-Nazis. [10]

UNITED SOCIAL CLUB

In 1965 congressional investigators identified this group as a front for the Savannah, Georgia, klavern, United Klans of America. [38]

UNITED STATES v. WILLIAMS

In this 1951 case, the U.S. Supreme Court ruled that the Reconstruction-era Ku Klux Acts were limited in application to violations of certain narrowly defined federal rights. The decision drastically curtailed use of the old laws during the next fourteen years, with judges using it to block federal prosecution of Klansmen in the murders of Lemuel Penn and Michael Schwerner. Prosecution was allowed in the 1965 Viola Liuzzo case because the protest march preceding her death was a peaceable assembly to petition for redress of grievances, conducted under the approval of a federal court order. In 1966, Justice Department appeals overturned lower rulings in the Penn and Schwerner cases, resulting in further prosecutions and convictions of guilty Klansmen. [93]

UNITED WHITE PARTY

A forerunner of the National States Rights Party, this group counted Chattanooga Klansman Jack Brown and future American Nazi George Lincoln Rockwell among its supporters in 1957. [78]

UNIVERSAL KLANS

Also called "The South," this Louisiana splinter group was organized by Jack Helm in March 1967 when he deserted from his post as grand dragon for the United Klans of America. The Klan's small membership consisted of United Klans defectors and affiliated Minutemen, with the two groups maintaining a joint guerilla training camp in St. Bernard Parish, located fifty miles from New Orleans. A small train (purchased from a New Orleans amusement park) carried Klansmen and Minutemen from a farmhouse— stocked with American Nazi Party literature and a portrait of Nazi "martyr" Horst Wessel—through the woods to a hidden rifle range. Led by Roswell Thompson in 1972, the group also maintained a fortified storehouse, containing what one investigator called an "enormous supply" of rifles, ammunition, dynamite, and grenades. [38; 90]

UPCHURCH, Z.R.

One of Edward Clarke's key men in promoting the 1920s Klan, Upchurch created a scandal when he resigned in disgust, charging that Clarke kept Imperial Wizard William Simmons constantly drunk while looting the Atlanta treasury. [93]

UPTOWN REBELS

A Chicago youth gang affiliated with the American Nazi Party, the Uptown Rebels were linked with the separate murders of victims Henry Hampton and Kevin Zornes in 1985. [NYT 1985]

UTAH

The 1920s Klan in Utah concentrated on anti-Catholicism, wisely ignoring the state's Mormon majority, but diplomacy produced no great windfall of members, and there is no evidence of nightriding or political activity. "Success" for Klansmen in Utah consisted of retaliating for passage of an anti-mask law with legal action that barred Santa Claus from Salt Lake City's 1925 Christmas parade. Several thousand Klansmen turned out for a rally in Provo that year, but interest and members soon declined, the Klan's potential still unrealized. Wesley Swift and Gerald L.K. Smith maintained some contact with Utah's governor in the early 1950s, and ex-Klansman Joseph Franklin brought his one-man war to Salt Lake City in the late 1970s, but such incursions presaged no revival of the Utah realm. In

1986, residents of Hurricane were briefly plagued by threats and racist vandalism, carried out by teenaged members of a small band calling itself the Socialist Anarchist Nazi Remnant, a title that fairly summarized the general confusion of Klan affairs in Utah. [*NYT* 1986; 10]

VAIL, ED
See *Culbreath, Lee.*

VAIL, JAMES
See *Culbreath, Lee.*

VAIL, VERNON
A defector from the Maryland Knights, Vail was identified as grand dragon of his own splinter group in the fall of 1976. His thirty followers were branded as "misfits" by established Klan leaders, and Vail finally severed his connection with the group in March 1977, after William Aitcheson was jailed for various acts of intimidation. Disgusted with the whole affair, Vail told reporters that the case had "set the Klan back fifty years." [84]

VALPARAISO UNIVERSITY
A college in Indiana once known as the Harvard of the West, it went bankrupt in 1923 and was purchased by the Klan under D.C. Stephenson, with plans of making it "100 percent American." The purchase was blasted by the press, the New York *Call* asking if the school's "kurrickulum" would include courses in flogging or tarring and feathering. Hiram Evans refused to fund the project, however, which led to outbursts from Stephenson, who, pointing out that the sculpting project was funded by the Klan on Stone Mountain, Georgia, stated that Atlanta "donated $100,000 to erect a monument to the memory of rebels who tried to destroy America, yet they

refused to give a single dollar for Valparaiso University to help educate the patriots of the North who saved the Union for posterity, unsullied from the contamination of Southern traitors." [93]

VANCE, JAMES

See *Fellowship Forum*

VANCE, ZEBULON

A former governor of North Carolina, Vance served as the state's grand dragon during Reconstruction. [93]

VAN LOON, REV. OREN

A resident of Berkeley, Michigan, Van Loon was abducted from his home by nightriders on June 30, 1924. Twelve days later, he was found near Battle Creek, delirious, with the letters "KKK" branded on his back. [*NYT* 1924]

VARNADO, JERRY

A white millworker in Bogalusa, Louisiana, Varnado was abducted, pistol-whipped, and flogged by hooded Klansmen in April 1964, for allegedly failing to support his family. [*NYT* 1965]

VARNADO SPORTSMANS CLUB

In 1965 congressional investigators identified this group as a cover for the Varnado, Louisiana, klavern, Original Knights of the KKK. [38]

VEH, RUSSELL RAYMOND

A native of Toledo, Ohio, Veh was identified in 1970 as "leader" of the one-man Ohio White Nationalist Party in 1970, renamed the American White Nationalist Party in 1971. In July 1971, he was indicted for using false names in an ill-conceived plot to swindle the Book of the Month Club and various magazine publishers out of free reading material; convicted of mail fraud in August 1972, Veh was placed on three years probation. Relocating to southern California in mid-1973, Veh has been identified since 1974 as leader of the National Socialist League, the only clique of avowed Nazi homosexuals in the United States. [2]

VENABLE, JAMES R.

Perhaps the ultimate Klansman, Venable is the product of a true Klan family, including his father and several uncles. In 1915, the Venable Brothers granite company—then the owner of Stone Mountain, Georgia—allowed William Simmons to use the mountain for a ceremony inaugurating the 20th century KKK. Years later, when state authorities took over the mountain, Venable's family retained a pasture at its base, ideal for rallies and cross burnings. Venable himself had been a Klansman for three years when he graduated from Georgia Tech engineering school in 1927; three years later, he completed law school in Atlanta and entered private practice, always ready to defend his fellow Klansmen or affiliated racists when they stepped outside the law. Friendly with a procession of imperial wizards from Hiram Evans to Eldon Edwards, Venable also served three terms as mayor of Stone Mountain. In 1946 he joined the Association of Georgia Klans under Dr. Samuel Green, and ten years later he surfaced as imperial klonsel for the U.S. Klans. Sharing law offices with J.B. Stoner in the late 1950s, Venable scored national headlines defending accused synagogue bomber George Bright in 1958. When the U.S. Klans was split by dissension in early 1961, Venable retained membership in that group while simultaneously joining its successor, holding the rank of imperial klonsel in the new United Klans of America. In 1962 Venable launched his own Defensive League of Registered Americans, retaining his post with the United Klans until 1963, when he left to organize the National Knights. That group, in turn, was one of eight independent factions loosely united under Venable's umbrella organization, the National Association of Ku Klux Klan. (His other diverse organizations included the Committee of One Million Caucasians to March on Washington and the Christian Voters and Buyers League, organized with United Klans defector Wally Butterworth.) Apparently more militant than his competitors, Venable told a 1964 audience that if Southern schools were integrated, "we'll close them up; we'll burn them up, if it comes to that." In May 1965 he attended a Klan gathering in Montgomery, Alabama, where participants agreed "not to participate in castration, but if it was necessary to liquidate someone to prove the Klan was not kidding, this would be done." That same year his National Knights also included a hard-core "elite" faction, the Black Shirts, which welcomed Klansmen expelled from the United Klans following their arrests on murder charges. Appearing before the House Un-American Activities Committee in February 1966, Venable told congressmen that he would "like to retract" and "apologize" for pamphlets he had published attacking the manufacturers of kosher food. In 1975, five of Venable's grand dragons quarreled with their leader, accusing him of mismanagement and senility before they defected en masse to create the Invisible Empire Knights under Dale Reusch. The National Knights was considered moribund by 1978, except for annual cross burning picnics on Venable's land near Stone Mountain, but the veteran Klansman made a new bid for prominence in 1982 and 1983, hosting successive Labor Day unity conferences attended by representatives of seven rival Klans. The result was a loose-knit Confederation of Klans, with Venable listed as a ranking officer, but continued dissension prevented the group from attaining real strength. No trace could be found of the Confederation or the National Knights by 1987, but Venable remained active, allegedly huddling with leaders of the Southern White Knights and the Invisible Empire Knights before their members assaulted black demonstrators in Forsyth County, Georgia. Venable's relative status in the movement was reflected by the fact that he was not named among the various defendants in a subsequent damage suit filed by the Southern Poverty Law Center. [2; 10; 38; 84]

VENANGO GANG

A group of 1920s Pennsylvania Klansmen recruited as nightriders, the Venango Gang specialized in smearing buildings with cow dung. [10]

VENUS RESCUE SERVICE

In 1965 congressional investigators identified this group as a cover for the Venus, Florida, klavern, United Klans of America. [38]

VERMONT

In the 1920s, Eugene Farnsworth was the Northeast's preeminent Klansman, organizing units in Vermont, New Hampshire, and Maine. Most of his Vermont recruits hailed from the northern part of the state, with some impressive mid-decade rallies recorded in Morrisville and Montpelier. Bad publicity caused members to desert en masse, after a kleagle was jailed for robbing St. Mary's Cathedral in Burlington. Decades of inactivity ended with reports in 1982 of a small klavern struggling to survive, burning crosses in Concord and threatening black residents in Burlington. For his part, the grand dragon denied any link between his Klan and illegal activity, blaming the outbreak on "young people doing what they think the Klan would approve of." [NYT 1982; 10]

VERNADO, DEVAN

A Klansman in Bogalusa, Louisiana, Vernado was twice appointed to sit on the city housing authority in 1965, over protests from the black community. [NYT 1965]

VETERANS FOR VICTORY OVER COMMUNISM

See *Camp Puller.*

VICKS, RAYMOND C.

A resident of Indianapolis, Vicks was identified in February 1947 as an associate of the Columbians, Inc., commissioned by Henry Loomis to start a local chapter of the neo-Nazi group. No evidence of actual recruiting was uncovered by authorities. [NYT 1947]

VICTORIA HUNT CLUB

In 1965 congressional investigators identified this group as a cover for the Victoria, Virginia, klavern, United Klans of America. [38]

VIDALIA SPORTSMAN'S CLUB

Created as a front for the Vidalia, Louisiana, klavern, Original Knights of the Ku Klux Klan, this group was publicly exposed in 1965. A year earlier, several members of the klavern had cooperated with Klansmen from neighboring areas to organize the violent Silver Dollar Group. [38; 96]

VIETNAMESE REFUGEES

In the wake of the United States' 1972 military withdrawal from South Vietnam and that nation's capture by communist troops three years later, thousands of anti-communist refugees sought sanctuary and a new life in the United States. One particular area of settlement was the gulf coast of Texas, where hundreds of Vietnamese fishermen arrived with their families in the late 1970s. The immediate target of racial prejudice, they were also accused of jeopardizing "white" jobs and "ruining" the Gulf of Mexico by netting too many fish and shrimp. In 1980, a Seabrook, Texas, Klansman was charged with burning several boats owned by Vietnamese fishermen, and the harassment continued into early 1981, with four cross burnings and five more arson attacks on Vietnamese. In February 1981, white fishermen began harassing Vietnamese shrimpers in the neighborhood of Galveston. Grand Dragon Louis Beam coordinated the movement, publicly setting fire to a small craft at one rally, as "a lesson to Klansmen on how to properly burn a shrimp boat." A month later, one of the Vietnamese boats went up in flames, and robed Klansmen began armed patrols of Galveston Bay. White fishermen equipped one vessel with a small cannon and a hanging effigy, firing their deck gun during cruises and occasionally stopping at the homes of Vietnamese fishermen. Crosses were burned at homes and on the docks, with one dock owner, accused of doing business with Vietnamese, receiving death threats signed by the Knights of the KKK. Asian victims turned to the Southern Poverty Law Center for help, and attorney Morris Dees filed suit against the Klan in April 1981, with testimony from expert witnesses to prove that the bay had not been damaged or overfished. When Beam appeared for his deposition with a pistol, Dees demanded federal protection and a psychiatric examination for the witness. In May 1981, a sweeping federal injunction barred Klansmen from patrolling or even wearing their robes within sight of Vietnamese residents, and a permanent ban on acts of violence or intimidation was issued four months later. The legal defeat was a pivotal first step in driving Louis Beam out of the Klan and out of Texas to the militant Aryan Nations compound in Hayden Lake, Idaho. [NYT 1980–1981; 93]

VIGILANTES

A Georgia splinter group organized in May 1964, the Vigilantes was founded by Klansmen Colbert McGriff and John Max Mitchell near Barnesville, Georgia. Originally members of the United Klans, McGriff, Mitchell, and three other members resigned following their April 24 arrest on weapons and cross burning charges in Griffin, Georgia. Their new group openly espoused violence against blacks, subsequently forming the nucleus of a Barnesville klavern, National Knights of the KKK. Colbert McGriff also subsequently participated in the creation of the militant Black Shirts. [38]

VIGILANTES, INC.

Organized by Georgia's ex-governor Eugene Talmadge, following his electoral defeat in 1942, this group was billed by its supporters as a "secret, patriotic white man's organization." With Talmadge as the figurehead and guiding light, actual leadership fell to Major John Goodwin, of the Georgia Highway Patrol, based in Atlanta. Investigator John Carlson had trouble obtaining the Vigilantes' address, until he finally asked a local klavern of the KKK, reporting that the two groups cooperated closely in their "patriotic" work. [8]

VINCENT, ALLEN

A resident of San Francisco, Vincent organized the National Socialist White Workers Party in the mid-1970s, gaining publicity for the group in April 1977 when he opened his Rudolf Hess Bookstore in a heavily Jewish neighborhood. Later that year he was embroiled in a new controversy, when journalists revealed that the city was renting a public park clubhouse to his group, for meetings that excluded blacks and Jews. In February 1978 Vincent tried to keep his group in the limelight by filing a $28 million lawsuit against San Francisco's mayor and various other defendants, charging abridgement of his civil rights, but the suit was dismissed eight months later. Vincent's group survived into the 1980s, but no link was established between the party and outbreaks of racist violence in 1984 and 1985. [2]

VINCENT, ROBERT

A black resident of Roanoake Rapids, North Carolina, Vincent was jailed for assault with a deadly weapon in November 1966, after sniper fire wounded two persons at a local Klan rally. [NYT 1966]

VINCENT, WILLIE

A black resident of southern Florida, Vincent was murdered by Klansmen and dumped from a speeding car in 1951. [Newsweek, Jan. 7, 1952]

VINSON, E.L.

See *Cole, Nat ("King").*

VIRGINIA

The Reconstruction Klan surfaced in Virginia during March and April 1868, its published notices exciting controversy over several weeks, but there was no evidence of widespread organization. Sporadic nightriding was reported in Lee County between June and December 1868, but Klansmen in the state otherwise remained quiescent, as the state never passed under Radical Republican control. The 1920s KKK faced widespread opposition in Virginia, and established political leaders were uniformly hostile to the Klan, but localized strength was developed in the southeastern part of the state, where there were reports of scattered raids and floggings. Stubborn units hung on into the 1930s, neither growing nor fading away, and Virginia was, ironically, listed as one of thirteen states with significant numbers of Klansmen during the Great Depression. National disbandment finished the realm in 1944, and two decades would pass before kleagles could reestablish themselves in the state. Virginia politicians coined the term "massive resistance" in response to the U.S. Supreme Court's Black Monday decision on school integration in 1954, but white residents were satisfied to let the Citizens' Council do their fighting for them, rather than resort to the more "vulgar" KKK. Grand Dragon Sandy Coley launched a new recruiting effort for the United Klans of America in the spring of 1965, but it took another year and the appointment of Marshal Kornegay to gather an estimated 1,250 Klansmen in thirty-two Virginia klaverns. Elected officials remained hostile, and a spate of 1966 cross burnings prompted Governor Mills Goodwin to offer a reward for the arrest of those responsible. Five cross burners were jailed in January 1967, including a woman and a state prison guard, but Kornegay's complaints of harassment fell on deaf ears, with Goodwin denouncing the Klan as "obnoxious." Still, the Invisible Empire remained in Virginia, the United Klans maintaining small, local pockets into the 1980s. In November 1982, a leader of the independent Justice Knights was jailed in Amelia County on charges of raping a seven-year-old girl, and Richmond Klansmen were blamed for harassing black residents in August 1984. [10; 38; 87]

VIRGINIA HUNTING CLUB NO. 1039

In 1965 congressional investigators identified this group as a cover for the South Boston, Virginia, klavern, United Klans of America. [38]

VIRGINIA ROD & GUN CLUB

Organized as the front for a Richmond, Virginia, klavern, United Klans of America, this club was publicly exposed in 1965. [38]

VITTUR, CLIFF

An Atlanta Klansman in the 1940s, Vittur was identified by Stetson Kennedy and Drew Pearson as the "chief ass-tearer" for Klavern No. 1, Association of Georgia Klans. Following his public exposure in Pearson's syndicated column, several vehicles at Vittur's trucking firm were burned by arsonists. [93]

WADE HAMPTON CLUB

In 1965 congressional investigators identified this group as a cover for Greenville, South Carolina, Unit No.1, United Klans of America. [38]

WAGNER, DANIEL

An Ohio member of the National Knights, Wagner testified before the House Un-American Activities Committee in February 1966 while free on bail from an armed robbery charge. He told congressmen that he and Columbus Klan leader Vernon Gilliam—also charged with robbery—had transported dynamite from Georgia to Ohio with the aim of launching a "civil war" in 1965. Georgia suppliers of the dynamite allegedly included Klansmen Joseph Sims and Cecil Myers. Wagner also recounted conversations with Klan "empress" Eloise Witte, concerning alleged plots to murder President Lyndon Johnson, Vice President Hubert Humphrey, Dr. Martin Luther King, and others. Reportedly supplied by Witte with a rifle and pistol, Wagner was instructed to "practice on Negroes as a sniper to prove yourself and help the white race." Witte denied the accusations in her own sworn testimony, branding Wagner a "psychopath" and a "mentally disturbed loudmouth." [38]

WAGNER, JAMES

See *New York.*

WAGONER, BOBBY

See *Dayvault, Wayne.*

WAKE FOREST RESTORATION SERVICE

In 1965 congressional investigators identified this group as a cover for the Wake Forest, North Carolina, klavern, United Klans of America. [38]

WALDROP, ROBERT

See *Cruell, Claude.*

WA-LIN-DA BEACH CLUB

In 1966 congressional investigators exposed this club as a front for the Andrews, South Carolina, klavern, United Klans of America. [38]

WALKER, CLIFFORD

A Georgia Klansman and the state's attorney general, Walker was elected governor in 1922 on his promise to suppress reports of Klan nightriding. As he told the KKK's national convention that year, "I am not going to denounce anybody. I am coming right here to your leaders and talk to you." In 1924, Atlanta newsmen broke the story of Walker's secret trip to Kansas City to address a conference of ranking Klansmen on the topic of "Americanism." When he declined comment on the story, reporters dubbed him "Kautious Kleagle Kliff." In 1926, after two terms as governor, Walker retired from public life. [10]

WALKER, EDWIN A.

A major general in the U.S. Army, Walker resigned his commission in 1961 after he was disciplined for illegally distributing far-right literature to his troops in Europe. Retired to Texas, where he flew a Rhodesian flag outside his home, Walker became a favorite guest speaker for groups such as the John Birch Society and the Citizens' Council. When a federal court ordered a black student's admission to the University of Mississippi in 1962, Walker issued a national call to arms, personally supervising—and, according to some sources, leading—the subsequent riot in Oxford, Mississippi. (Federal authorities declined to indict Walker in January 1963.) In February 1964, Walker appeared in a Jackson, Mississippi, courtroom to shake hands with Klansman Byron de la Beckwith, after his first mistrial in the murder of Medgar Evers. A year later, the ex-general was working with Royal Young, former imperial wizard of the Original KKK of America, and addressed a Chicago "Congress of Conservatives," sharing the dais with Lester Maddox and Birch Society founder Robert Welch. On that occasion, Walker told his cheering audience that there were "more good Americans in the Ku Klux

Klan" than in the liberal Americans for Democratic Action. In September 1965, Walker appeared at the Henry Grady Hotel in Atlanta, where he promised another crowd that there "will be a KKK in the U.S.A. longer than there will be an LBJ." [*NYT* 1965; 28; 52]

WALKER, JOHN A., JR.

As a U.S. Navy warrant officer, Walker befriended Bill Wilkinson when they worked together as cryptographers aboard the *USS Bolivar*. He later joined Wilkinson's Invisible Empire Knights of the KKK and helped his former shipmate recruit other naval personnel, forming active klaverns aboard the *USS Concord* and at least five other ships. (On one occasion, a cross was burned on the mess deck of the aircraft carrier *America*.) In May 1985, Walker was arrested on charges of spying for the Soviet Union, the evidence suggesting that he had helped KGB agents decipher more than a million coded messages since 1968. With several friends and members of his family, Walker pled guilty in 1986 and received a sentence of life imprisonment. [93]

WALKER, MORRIS

A member of the Association of Carolina Klans, Walker was convicted in three flogging cases and sentenced to a six-year prison term in July 1952. [*NYT* 1952]

WALLACE, CHARLES

A Confederate veteran and editor of the *Georgia Clipper*, Wallace doubled as a leader of the Reconstruction KKK in Warren County, Georgia. An avid street brawler, he killed a black man in one fight and suffered serious knife wounds in another, complementing the five wounds he sustained during his military service. In November 1868, Wallace led the Klan party that was responsible for the murder of the wife and son of intended victim Perry Jeffers. Four months later he was shot and killed in a personal dispute with Republican activist G.W. Darden in Warrenton. Klansmen soon retaliated for the slaying by abducting Darden from jail and killing him. [87]

WALLACE, DAVID

See *Holder, James.*

WALLACE, GEORGE CORLEY

An Alabama jurist in 1953, Wallace was the first Southern judge to issue an injunction barring removal of Jim Crow signs from public railway terminals. Five years later, he tried a new angle in his first gubernatorial campaign, courting NAACP support and attacking candidate John Patterson's link with the Alabama Knights of the KKK. In a typical speech,

Wallace cautioned voters that "If the Klan should now succeed in electing Patterson governor, the triumph might well lead to a revival of the Klan as the controlling political force in Alabama. Patterson chatters about the gangster ghosts in Phenix City, while he himself is rolling with the new wave of the Klan and its terrible tradition of lawlessness." Appearing on stage with a bed, Wallace entertained crowds by lifting the covers and asking, "Who is down there between the sheets with you, John? Are you in bed with the Ku Klux Klan?" November's balloting sent Patterson to the statehouse with a healthy majority, and Wallace complained: "They out-niggered me that time, but they'll never do it again." He refused to supply the U.S. Civil Rights Commission with voter lists from his county, cheerfully pleading guilty to charges of contempt, but Judge Frank Johnson discovered that Wallace had delivered the records secretly, staging his own trial as a publicity stunt. With Patterson barred by law from succeeding himself in office, Wallace began courting Imperial Wizard Robert Shelton for Klan support in the 1962 election. That September, he dispatched Al Lingo to Oxford, Mississippi, to observe the state university riots against integration, but Wallace's effort to block desegregation in Tuscaloosa fizzled the following spring. Still, Klansmen admired his pugnacious style, and they were showered with rewards for their political support. Al Lingo was named to lead the state police, while veteran Klansman Asa Carter emerged as the governor's special assistant and sometime speechwriter. Robert Shelton's father was appointed as a colonel on Wallace's staff, and two of Alabama's leading rightists found seats on the Textbook Selection Committee, working overtime to screen authors for "possible connections with communist-front organizations." (Approved textbooks, meanwhile, were delivered by the American Southern Publishing Co., which also produced *The Fiery Cross* for Shelton's United Klans of America.) When journalists reminded Wallace that the KKK was also on the government's subversive list, Wallace replied that he was only interested in authors who "front for commies." Wallace was barely in office before United Klans lobbyists began pushing for a constitutional amendment to permit his reelection in 1966, and the governor responded by promoting Ralph Roton, head of the Klan Bureau of Investigation, to a state position as investigator of racial disorders. (Wallace later called the appointment "an accident.") In September 1963, nine days before a Birmingham church bombing killed four black children, Wallace told a cheering audience: "What this country needs is a few first-rate funerals, and some political funerals, too." In an apparent reference to nightriding Klansmen, he said that whites resisting integration "are not thugs—they are good working people who get mad when they see something like this happen." After the fatal bombing, Wallace first tried to blame "unknown black perpetrators," then fell silent as Lingo's state troopers arrested three Klansmen on misdemeanor charges. In 1964's congressional election, the United Conservative Coalition of Alabama—composed of spokesmen for the KKK, the Citizens' Council, and the John Birch Society—distributed a half-million sample ballots, omitting the name of moderate Representative Carl Elliott, a Wallace opponent; by the time Elliott learned of the trick it was too late, and he lost the election. In July 1964, Wallace shared the stage at an Atlanta gathering with Lester Maddox and Grand Dragon Calvin Craig, denouncing new civil rights legislation while blacks in the audience were beaten with chairs. Mississippi's militant White Knights sent money to Wisconsin for Wallace's 1964 presidential primary race, but the governor scrubbed a third-party campaign in favor of Republican Barry Goldwater, with Al Lingo serving as Goldwater's chauffeur on visits to Alabama. As a sidebar to the 1964 campaign, the U.S. Bureau of Public Roads accused Wallace of forcing an Alabama engineering firm to hire Robert Shelton as a do-nothing "agent" for $4,000, his fee the price of their success in bidding for state contracts. In 1965 the Klan launched another drive to amend the state constitution in Wallace's favor, but their plea fell on deaf ears, and his wife was forced to run for governor in George's place. Questioned about the United Klans' solicitation of funds for Lurleen's campaign, Wallace told newsmen, "I'm glad to get support from anyone except gangsters and communists." By early 1967, Wallace had his eyes fixed on the White House, the United Klans distributing matchbooks with a Klan membership application inside, the covers reading: "Draft George Wallace for President." When Wallace visited Pennsylvania that year, his security guards were provided by Grand Dragon Roy Frankhouser. Back in Tuscaloosa, Robert Shelton told his followers, "We made him governor and we must make him president," but *The Fiery Cross* was more reserved. "Governor Wallace may never be President," the paper editorialized, "but the psychological impact upon our enemies of this possibility is our greatest word weapon, and we dare not let this great man fade from the national scene." Xavier Edwards, leader of the Maryland-based Interstate Klans, cabled Wallace his "100 percent support," and Georgia's J.B. Stoner declared, "Our slogan is the same as in 1964: Governor George C. Wallace—Last Chance for the White Vote!" Prior to his 1967 assassination, George Lincoln Rockwell chimed in with the advice that "Wallace, while not a Nazi, is close enough that, as president, he would probably preserve our nation and race." Plain-clothes Klansmen frequently served as security guards when Wallace hit the campaign trail in 1968, and their leaders kept busy behind the scenes in the American Independent Party. In California, two rival committees supported the Wallace campaign—one led by William Shearer, head of the state's Citizens' Council, the other chaired by veteran anti-Semite Opal Tanner White. In Lisburn and Norwalk, Connecticut, the governor's campaign was managed by members of the paramilitary Minutemen facing criminal charges for attempted murder. In Memphis, Tennessee, the party was led by Richard Ryn, later a defense attorney for James Earl Ray in the murder of Dr. Martin Luther King. In Eutaw, Alabama, Wallace was caught shaking hands with Robert Shelton at a party fundraiser, but his bodyguards promptly seized the film from ABC network photographers. In November's balloting, Wallace and running mate Curtis LeMay polled 9,446,167 votes, paving the way for a smooth gubernatorial race in 1970. That spring, brother Jack Wallace paid for a twenty-four page campaign biography in *The Fiery Cross*, and George's official party newsletter carried the banner headline, "Unless Whites Vote on June 2, Blacks will Control the State." Elected to his second term in a near-landslide, Wallace played no favorites among Klansmen, appointing Louisiana Klansman David Duke as an honorary colonel in the Alabama militia. In 1972, when Judge Frank Johnson ordered steps to integrate the state police, Wallace stalled new hiring to the point of creating a critical manpower shortage. Making a new bid for the White House that spring, Wallace was shot and crippled by Arthur Bremer at a party rally in Laurel, Maryland, on May 15. Klan support for Wallace had largely evaporated by 1976, with the United Klans mounting a halfhearted draft movement. Imperial Wizard Dale Reusch still cherished hopes of a Wallace campaign, but Texas Klansman Scott Nelson withdrew his support, complaining that Wallace was "not as white as he was in 1968. His mind has deteriorated, I'm sorry to say, along with his body." [10; 17; 30; 42; 61; 63; 81; 84]

WALLACE, HENRY

See *Progressive Party*.

WALLACE FELLOWSHIP CLUB

In 1965 congressional investigators identified this group as a cover for the Wallace, North Carolina, klavern, United Klans of America. [38]

WALLER, WILLIAM L.

Prior to his 1971 election as governor of Mississippi, Waller served as defense counsel for Klansman Charles Wilson, during his appeal of a conviction and life sentence for the murder of Vernon Dahmer. In December 1972, a KKK informant told newsmen that he had campaigned for Waller's opponent the year before, when the candidate promised to free all imprisoned Klansmen within a year of his inauguration. Waller allegedly countered with a guarantee of freedom in six months, and carried the election with Klan support. The new governor did, however grant ex-client Wilson two ninety-day furloughs from prison, back to back, before finally admitting him to a work release program at the Southern Mississippi State Hospital. [*NYT* 1972]

WALRAVEN, GERALD

A Texas spokesman for the United Klans of America, Walraven was interviewed on Houston radio station KTRH in 1965. He was paid for his appearance on the program, the check returned endorsed by Nazi leader George Lincoln Rockwell, complete with a swastika stamp. [53]

WALTON, DALE

Once exalted cyclops for the United Klans of America in Tupelo, Mississippi, Walton emerged as imperial wizard of the Knights of the Green Forest when that group was organized in 1966. In September 1969 he was arrested for his role in a conspiracy to murder black gubernatorial candidate Charles Evers. A search of Walton's car revealed six guns, and he was arrested for carrying concealed weapons. [NYT 1969]

W-A-M-B-A

In 1965 congressional investigators identified this group as a cover for the United Klans of America ladies auxiliary in Morganton, North Carolina. The acronym remains unexplained. [38]

WAMBLE, ABRAHAM

A black minister and political activist during Reconstruction in Mississippi, Wamble was abducted by Klansmen and shot seven times in the head. [93]

WARD, ERNEST

See Johnson, Woodrow.

WARD, HAROLD

A Wyoming prison guard, Ward was fired in February 1988 for terrorizing black inmates by parading past their cells in full Klan regalia. [NYT 1988]

WARD, ROSCOE

See Webster, Clyde.

WARD 10 HUNTING CLUB

In 1965 congressional investigators identified this group as a cover for the Winnfield, Louisiana, klavern, United Klans of America. [38]

WARE, JAMES

A black teenager residing in Birmingham, Alabama, Ware was shot and killed while riding his bicycle on September 15, 1963, shortly after a local church bombing killed four black girls. His assailants, two white youths on a motorcycle, were traced through photographs that showed them collecting literature at National States Rights Party headquarters, and both were arrested the following day. One pled guilty to manslaughter, and the other was convicted at trial; both received seven-month jail terms, suspended, and were released on probation. [63]

WARE, JORDAN

A black resident of Reconstruction Floyd County, Georgia, Ware was visited by Klansmen at his home, beaten and robbed on charges of addressing a white woman as "wife." [87]

WARING, J. WAITES

A federal judge in South Carolina, Waring struck down the state's white primary as unconstitutional in 1947. After his Charleston home was stoned by nightriders in October 1950, Waring told the press, "You can expect this sort of thing in South Carolina. It's a state dominated by the Klan—a crime-committing Klan that goes unpunished." [NYT 1950]

WARNER, JAMES KONRAD

As an early member of the American Nazi Party, Warner was arrested with George Lincoln Rockwell, Dan Burros, and fourteen other brownshirts when a July 1960 demonstration in Washington, D.C., degenerated into street fighting. Three years later, a National States Rights Party member, Warner was among eight men indicted for violent interference with school desegregation in Birmingham, Alabama. Following Rockwell's assassination, Warner served for a time as editor of the National Socialist Bulletin, published by the National Socialist White People's Party. In 1968 he organized the pro-Nazi Sons of Liberty in southern California, a group that survives to this day in Metairie, Louisiana. Along the way, Warner's links with militant fascist groups earned him a spot on the Secret Service list of persons considered dangerous to the president of the United States. In September 1976, while serving as Louisiana grand dragon and national information director for the Knights of the KKK, he was jailed with leader David Duke during a New Orleans demonstration. Early the following year Warner resigned from the Klan to work full time for his own New Christian Crusade Church, an arm of the Christian Identity movement. Closely affiliated with the "church" was Warner's Christian Defense League, organized in 1977 for whites desirous of "fighting back" against the "Satanic Jewish conspiracy." He remained active through the 1980s, publishing editorials that warned U.S. Jews to "keep their big noses out of our racial and religious affairs." [2; 78; 84]

WARREN, FULLER

An active Klansman prior to World War II, Warren altered his racial views after he "helped to fight a war to destroy the Nazis—first cousins to Klansmen." Elected governor of Florida in 1948, he announced a plan to outlaw the KKK in January 1949, following a forty-three car Klan motorcade through Tallahassee. (Of six Klan drivers jailed for improper license tags, four were Georgians.) Warren publicly denounced the KKK as "hooded hoodlums, sheeted jerks, and covered cowards," but his best efforts failed to suppress a wave of Klan terrorism spanning the next three years. [*NYT* 1948–1949]

WARREN COUNTY IMPROVEMENT ASSOCIATION

In 1965 congressional investigators identified this group as a cover for Warren County, North Carolina, Unit No. 30, United Klans of America, serving Klansmen in Norlina and Warrenton. [38]

WARREN WOMEN'S IMPROVEMENT ASSOCIATION

Created as a front for the ladies auxiliary of the United Klans in Norlina, North Carolina, this group was publicly exposed in 1965. [38]

WARSAW FELLOWSHIP CLUB

In 1966 congressional investigators identified this group as a cover for the Warsaw, North Carolina, klavern, United Klans of America. [38]

WARTHEN, PERRY

Identified as leader of the Chico Area National Socialists in California, Warthen recruited youthful members for acts of harassment and vandalism, nocturnal shootings, and the stockpiling of weapons. In 1982 he was linked with two separate homicides, one of which was a case in September in which teenage neo-Nazi Joseph Hoover was shot eight times in the head, two days after giving information on the group to Chico police officers. Conviction on a murder charge consigned Warthen to prison for life without parole. [*NYT* 1982]

WARWICK MENS CLUB

In 1965 the House Un-American Activities Committee exposed this club as a front for the Southampton County, Virginia, klavern, United Klans of America, serving Klansmen in Franklin and Newport News. [38]

WASHINGTON, HUGH

A black resident of Summit, Mississippi, Washington was targeted by members of the United Klans, who bombed his home in September 1964. [38]

WASHINGTON COUNTY FELLOWSHIP CLUB

Created as a cover for the Creswell, North Carolina, klavern, United Klans of America, this group was exposed by congressional investigators in 1965. [38]

WATERS, H. FRANKLIN

A federal judge in Ft. Smith, Arkansas, Waters was the target of a 1985 assassination plot by members of the Covenant, the Sword, and the Arm of the Lord. [NYT 1985]

WATKINS, JACK

An ex-convict, Watkins was a prosecution witness in the Vernon Dahmer murder case. In an effort to prevent him from testifying, Klansmen kidnapped Watkins and attempted to intimidate him by driving him to a secluded area and beating him and threatening him with a gun, also ordering him to testify that Sam Bowers was with him at the time of the murder. Watkins refused to be intimidated, but the Klansmen released him anyway, their theory being that an ex-convict would not go to the police. But Watkins did go to the police, as did one of the Klansmen who had kidnapped him. Arrests made in March 1967 included that of Klan attorney Travis Buckley, who threatened Watkins for implicating him. Buckley was convicted in February 1968 following a two-day trial. The jury deliberated for only two hours. [Newsweek, Feb. 23, 1968; NYT 1967–1968]

WATKINS, ORVILLE WADE

The exalted cyclops of a California klavern, Watkins was convicted in April 1977 of shooting at several Hispanic homes in the San Diego area. [NYT 1977]

WATKINS, WILLIAM H.

See Blackwell Real Estate.

WATLEY, SMITH

A black resident of Reconstruction Tallapoosa County, Alabama, Watley filed charges against the Klansmen who whipped him in 1871, but all were acquitted after producing alibi witnesses. [87]

WATSON, THOMAS E.

An early Populist reformer in Georgia, Watson campaigned for the state legislature in 1882 with black support, demanding free black schools and condemning the brutal convict lease system, and lost. During his unsuccessful election campaign of 1892, fifteen of Watson's black supporters were murdered by whites. He accepted the Populist vice presidential spot four years later and again lost. Acknowledging that he could not command black votes, Watson finally bid farewell to the agrarian revolt and joined the move to strip Southern blacks of the franchise. The move changed Watson's luck, propelling him from the state assembly to the House of Representatives and

U.S. Senate, where he served until his death in 1922. On the side, he published two xenophobic tabloids, *Watson's Magazine* and the *Weekly Jeffersonian,* which were ultimately banned from the mails as obscene material. A staunch advocate of lynching in his post-Populist days, Watson declared, "When mobs are no longer possible, liberty will be dead." Seemingly obsessed with interracial sex, he denounced blacks as a "hideous, ominous national menace," while Jews were damned as "moral cripples" with "an utter contempt for law and a ravenous appetite for the forbidden fruit—a lustful eagerness enhanced by the racial novelty of the girls of the uncircumcized." Playing no favorites, he also hated Catholics, calling the Pope "Jimmy Cheezy" and the confessional a "sink of perdition," manned by "libidinous priests" whom Watson dubbed the "wolves of Rome." A typical article, published in 1911, proclaimed: "At the confessional, the priest finds out what girls and married women he can seduce. Having discovered the trail, he wouldn't be human if he did not take advantage of the opportunity." Continuing in the same vein, Watson sermonized that "no man can imagine a woman who could maintain her self-respect after being compelled to act as a sewer pipe for a bachelor priest's accumulation of garbage." Black priests were the worst of all, as noted by *Watson's Magazine* in April 1912. "Heavens above!" Watson wrote, "Think of a Negro priest taking a vow of chastity and then being turned loose among women. It is a thing to make one shudder." When young Mary Phagan was slain in 1915, Watson convicted suspect Leo Frank in print, attributing her death to a "filthy perverted Jew of New York." After Frank was lynched by the Knights of Mary Phagan, Watson penned an editorial calling for "another Ku Klux Klan . . . to restore HOME RULE." No evidence exists that Watson joined the modern Klan, but he was clearly an admirer, and his magazines provided Klansmen with substantial aid and comfort in the early days. [33; 93]

WATSON HUNTING CLUB

In 1965 congressional investigators identified this group as a cover for the Watson, Louisiana, klavern, Original Knights of the Ku Klux Klan. [38]

WAYNE COUNTY IMPROVEMENT ASSOCIATION

In 1965 congressional investigators identified this group as a cover for Goldsboro, North Carolina, Unit No. 38, United Klans of America. [38]

WAYNE COUNTY SEWING CIRCLE

Created as a front for the Pikeville, North Carolina, ladies auxiliary, United Klans of America, this group was publicly exposed in 1965. [38]

WEAKLAND, ALFRED CHARLES

A county leader of the militant Adamic Knights, Weakland was one of ten persons arrested by U.S. Treasury agents' raids conducted in Maryland, New Jersey, and Pennsylvania during May 1981. Indicted on federal firearms charges, he pled guilty and was sentenced to four months in jail. [NYT 1981]

WEAVER, GERALD E.

A member of the White Patriot Party, Weaver was convicted in September 1985 and sentenced to six months in jail for carrying firearms on a Klan march through Forest City, North Carolina. [NYT 1985]

WEBB, J.S.

The sheriff of Reconstruction Rutherford County, Tennessee, Webb was dragged from his Murfreesboro home by Klansmen in April 1868 and threatened with lynching if he did not resign his post. He refused, and although Klansmen later whipped his brother, they never challenged Webb again. [87]

WEBER, MARK

A freelance writer and German translator from Portland, Oregon, Weber traveled in Europe and Africa before settling in Washington, D.C., in 1977. By May 1978 he was established as news editor of the *National Vanguard*, published by William Pierce's neo-Nazi National Alliance. Since the summer of 1979, in cooperation with the far-right Liberty Lobby, Weber has specialized in articles and speeches "exposing" the "myth" of the Nazi Holocaust. As he wrote in December 1979: "A careful examination of the origins of the 'holocaust' legend in the famous Nuremberg Trials and other 'war crimes' trials reveals just how fraudulent the entire story really is." In June 1981 Weber took up the case of convicted German terrorist Manfred Roeder, imprisoned for participation in a series of bombings that killed two persons and gravely wounded several others. As Weber views the case: "His violations of the law are purely political in nature. In America his actions would be considered completely legal expressions of opinion protected by the Constitution. Not crimes. Men and women sentenced for such 'crimes' in the Soviet Union are praised by American politicians and newspapers as courageous 'dissidents.' Roeder's case is no different." [2]

WEBSTER, CLYDE

A Greensboro, North Carolina, Klansman, Webster was sentenced to six months on a road gang in October 1958 after his conviction with codefendant Roscoe Ward of hurling bottles through the windows of an office occupied by black NAACP officer Kenneth Lee. Each defendant also received a ninety-day suspended sentence for smashing the windows of Lee's barbershop, in protest of his admission as the first black student at the University of North Carolina. In July 1967 Webster was arrested with fellow Klansman J.R. McBride for burning a cross at a black home in Greensboro. [*NYT* 1958, 1967]

WEIR, JAMES D.

A British subject, Weir was whipped by Jackson County, Alabama, Klansmen during April 1869. The attack brought protests from U.S. Secretary of State Hamilton Fish and the British minister in Washington, D.C. [87]

WELLS, LYN

See *National Anti-Klan Network.*

WESLEY, CYNTHIA

Wesley was one of four black girls killed when Klansmen bombed Birmingham's 16th Street Baptist Church on September 15, 1963. Ex-Klansman Robert Chambliss was convicted of murder in the case fourteen years later. [84]

WEST, GENE

A former grand dragon of Texas, West was jailed in San Antonio in May 1985 with his son, Joe, and accomplice James Cornelius on federal charges of manufacturing and possessing illegal drugs. Another son, Michael , was subsequently charged in an unrelated arson case. [*NYT* 1985]

WEST, J.W.

As editor of the Laurel, Mississippi, *Leader-Call,* West took a courageous stand by criticizing racial violence in the same town where Imperial Wizard Sam Bowers made his home and headquarters for the militant White Knights of the KKK. Forced to moderate his stand after the newspaper's office was bombed in 1964, West said, "Anything we write about Bowers will be strictly from the court record. We don't want to fool with him." [84]

WEST, THOMAS

The sheriff of Reconstruction Jackson County, Florida, West resigned in March 1871 after numerous threats from the Klan and a daylight assault on the street. [87]

WEST CARROLL RIFLEMAN CLUB

In 1965 congressional investigators identified this group as a cover for the West Carroll Parish, Louisiana, klavern, Original Knights of the KKK. [38]

WEST COLUMBIA CLUB

Established as a front for the West Columbia, South Carolina, Klavern No. 335, Association of South Carolina Klans, this group was publicly exposed in 1965. [38]

WEST DUPLIN BOATING & FISHING CLUB

Also known as the Enterprise Club or Harmony Club, this group was identified in 1966 as a cover for Clinton, North Carolina, Unit No. 46, United Klans of America. [38]

WEST MELBOURNE FELLOWSHIP CLUB

In 1965 congressional investigators identified this group as a cover for the Melbourne, Florida, klavern, United Klans of America. [38]

WEST ORANGE SPORTSMAN'S LODGE NO. 7-3

Established as a front for the Apopka, Florida, klavern, United Florida KKK, this group was publicly exposed in 1966. [38]

WEST VIRGINIA

The 1920s Klan dabbled in the political affairs of both major parties in West Virginia and scored some noteworthy victories on both sides. Mine owners recruited Klansmen as coalfield strikebreakers, but members of the growing United Mine Workers held their own in rough-and-tumble confrontations. Several Catholic teachers were fired at the Klan's insistence in Clarkson, and Mingo County Klansmen threatened to use force to keep black champion Jack Johnson from boxing there. Adverse publicity resulted, however, when robed raiders in Logan County accidentally killed a white woman. An owner of the pro-Klan Fellowship Forum was elected governor in 1928, and several klaverns made it through the 1930s, the realm disbanding in 1944. The post-war years were, ironically, barren for Klan recruiters in West Virginia, although ex-kleagle Robert Byrd tried to introduce the Association of Georgia Klans to his home state in 1946. The bombing of a newly integrated school in 1958 was not the sign of a great Klan revival, and none of eighteen active Klans claimed West Virginia units in the 1960s. A small klavern was reported active in 1980 and was responsible for a rash of cross burnings near Beckley and Clarksburg, and for hounding Reverend Michael Curry from his Smithburg home in June after he refused to let a Klansman speak from the pulpit of his church. Scattered incidents continued into the

1980s, with cross burnings reported in Wheeling in 1983 and another in Princeton in 1985. [*NYT* 1980, 1983, 1985; 10]

WESTERN FRONT

Founded in 1965 by Walter White, Jr., the husband of Opal Tanner White, this anti-Semitic organization worked closely with Gerald L.K. Smith until his death. In the 1980s, White and company remained active in Hollywood, California, publishing racist tracts and newsletters that exposed the farfetched "Jewish conspiracy." [2]

WESTERN GUARD

A Canadian anti-Semitic group based in Toronto, the Western Guard maintains close ties with U.S. and Canadian Klan units, counting Canadian Klansmen Jack Prins, John Ross Taylor, and Wolfgang Droege among its active officers. Links have also been established with the National States Rights Party, with J.B. Stoner appearing as a guest speaker at a Western Guard banquet in 1974. Members participated with David Duke in New Orleans Klan demonstrations in September 1976, and delegates were dispatched to Raleigh, North Carolina, in 1980 for the first annual convention of the National Socialist Party of America. [2; 84]

WHANGS

A short-lived anti-Klan group, the Whangs were Tennessee blacks who armed and organized in response to Klan terrorism in the spring of 1868. Grand Dragon John Gordon publicly called on the group to disband, ordering his Klansmen to break them up "at any cost," and the order was apparently effective. [87]

WHATLEY, ANDREW

A white youth living in Americus, Georgia, Whatley was shot and killed while stoning black motorists during a July 1965 race riot. Grand Dragon Calvin Craig led members of the United Klans in a protest preceding Whatley's funeral, at which five blacks were mobbed and beaten by whites. The Klan organized a memorial march for Whatley on August 8, with seventy Georgia Klansmen and others from Florida counted among the 700 participants. Cecil Myers and Joseph Sims were on hand for the parade and subsequent rally, with Craig and Imperial Wizard Robert Shelton addressing a crowd of 1,000 persons. [*NYT* 1965]

WHEAT, G. CLINTON

A Los Angeles Klansman, Wheat hosted a series of closed meetings at his home in 1963 and 1964 in which members of the Christian Defense League plotted illegal attacks on Castro's Cuba. Moving to northern California in 1965, Wheat vanished three years later when New Orleans District Attorney Jim Garrison issued warrants for his arrest as a material witness in the assassination of President John F. Kennedy. [90]

WHEELER, STEPHEN

A Republican state senator from White County, Arkansas, Wheeler was the target of a bungled Klan murder attempt in the summer of 1868. [87]

WHEELER, TERRELL T.

See *Lynch, John.*

WHITE, ALMA BIRDWELL

The most active and prolific fundamentalist minister of the 1920s, White founded the Pillar of Fire Church and established forty-nine active branches, with headquarters at the religious community at Zarephath, New Jersey. She openly endorsed the Klan as an ally in her church's war on "modernism" and sin, publishing a magazine, *The Good Citizen*, which denounced Catholics as "toe kissers" and "wafer worshippers." In a typical editorial, she wrote: "We hail the K.K.K. in the great movement that is now on foot, as the army divinely appointed to set the forces in operation to rescue Americanism and save our Protestant institutions from the designs of the 'Scarlet Mother.'" When Klan orators visited White's church in Bound Brook, New Jersey, for a widely publicized organizational meeting in May 1923, hundreds of angry townspeople surrounded the church and showered it with stones, smashing windows and furniture, and damaging parked cars before a small detachment of police cleared an escape route. Despite the setback and continuing opposition, Alma White remained the only leader of a U.S. Protestant denomination to openly praise the KKK. [10]

WHITE, BEN CHESTER

A black resident of Kingston, Mississippi, elderly Ben White was abducted by Klansmen on June 10, 1966, shot sixteen times and nearly decapitated by a shotgun blast. Following the discovery of his body two days later, one Mississippi Klan leader telephoned FBI agents to deny involvement in the crime, but inside information led to the June 14 arrest of Klansmen Claude Fuller, Ernest Avants, and James Jones. At Jones's trial in April 1967, the Adams County sheriff read a statement in which Jones admitted that White was killed by the Klan's Cottonmouth Moccasin Gang to divert attention from James Meredith's one-man "march against fear" and to lure Dr. Martin Luther King to Natchez, Mississippi, to be killed. The proceedings ended in a mistrial on April 10, and Ernest Avants was acquitted of murder charges eight months later, persuading a jury that White was already dead when he fired his shotgun at the corpse. White's relatives pursued the killers with a civil suit for wrongful death and they were victorious in November 1968 when a federal court assessed $1,021,500 in damages against Avants, Fuller, Jones, and the White Knights of the Ku Klux Klan. [*NYT* 1967–1968]

WHITE, EDWARD

See *Lindsay, Jim.*

WHITE, EDWARD D.

A member of the Reconstruction KKK in New Orleans, White later served as chief justice of the U.S. Supreme Court. Following a 1915 meeting with Thomas Dixon, White gave his personal endorsement to the film *Birth of a Nation*, thus helping to clear the way for the movie's nationwide release. Weeks later, when violence greeted the film's opening in Boston and New York City, he tried to rewrite history, curtly denying the "rumors" of his endorsement. [93]

WHITE, GEORGE

See *Johnson, Woodrow.*

WHITE, J.M.

See *Alexander, Henry.*

WHITE, MARLIN

A white resident of Talladega, Alabama, White and his wife were flogged by Klansmen in May 1961 for letting a black maid discipline their children. Eight Klansmen were arrested in the case, with Francis Kelley sentenced to an eight-year prison term that October. [*NYT* 1961]

WHITE, ROBERT L.

A Maryland member of the Confederation of Independent Orders, White was accused by state police of organizing a special Klan unit "with the intent and purpose of engaging in illegal violent acts aimed primarily at religious and ethnic targets." In July 1978 he was convicted with two codefendants in the attempted bombing of a Lochearn, Maryland, synagogue. Authorities maintain that White's Klansmen also planned to bomb the home of Representative Parren Mitchell. [*NYT* 1978]

WHITE, STEVEN

A freelance writer and Klansman in Philadelphia, White resigned from the United Klans of America in March 1971, blaming the exodus of some 300 Klansmen on "paranoia" over FBI informants. White and his wife organized the White Christian Crusaders, publicly disavowing violence. In 1971 he was employed at the Philadelphia campaign headquarters of mayoral candidate Frank Rizzo, also proclaiming his group's support for George Wallace and the American Independent Party. [NYT 1971]

WHITE, WALTER

See *Western Front.*

WHITE, WILLIAM ALLEN

As editor of the Emporia *Gazette,* White was a leading opponent of the 1920s KKK in Kansas. His editorials blasted the Klan as an "organization of cowards" led by "moral idiots," further proclaiming that the "picayunish cowardice of a man who would substitute clan rule and mob law for what our American fathers have died to establish and maintain should prove what a cheap screw outfit the Klan is." In 1923 White embarrassed the Klan by publishing a list of delegates to its statewide convention, and a year later he launched an independent gubernatorial campaign against Klan candidate Ben Paulen. Although White polled almost half of Paulen's final tally in November, he viewed the race primarily as a chance to "clear the atmosphere" with a campaign designed to "get out and spit in the face of the Klan." In his 1927 obituary of the Kansas realm, White wrote, "Dr. Hiram Evans, the Imperial Wizard of the kluxers, is bringing his imperial shirttail to Kansas this spring. He will see what was once a thriving and profitable hate factory and bigotorium now laughed into a busted community." [10]

WHITE AMERICA, INC.

An Arkansas resistance group, assisted by the Mississippi Citizens' Council, White America mounted a series of anti-desegregation protests that closed schools in Hoxie, Arkansas, for three weeks during August 1955. [45]

WHITE AMERICAN POLITICAL ASSOCIATION

Organized by California Klansman Tom Metzger following his defeat in a 1980 congressional race, this association was designed to promote "pro-white" candidates for public office. Describing its restricted membership, Metzger told newsmen, "I wouldn't knowingly allow a Jew to belong. Judaism is a conspiracy against all races." In the mid-1980s, the group was supplanted by Metzger's new White Aryan Resistance. [2]

WHITE ARYAN RESISTANCE

Described by founder Tom Metzger as "an association dedicated to the struggle of the white working people," this group was organized in the mid-1980s to replace Metzger's White American Political Association. The alleged recipient of at least $250,000 stolen by members of The Order in

1984, Metzger escaped indictment when other neo-Nazi leaders were charged with sedition in April 1987, and he still denies participation in any unlawful conspiracy. Metzger's son, John, manages affairs for the White Student Union, also known as the Aryan Youth Movement, WAR Youth, and WAR Skins, recruiting skinheads. Metzger's "Race and Reason" television talk show is available to subscribers on more than fifty cable systems in at least a dozen states, and he is linked to racist groups across the country by computer, through the Aryan Nations Liberty Net. In October 1989, the Southern Poverty Law Center filed suit against the Metzgers for alleged complicity in the death of an Ethiopian immigrant, beaten to death by skinheads in Portland, Oregon, hours after Metzger's agents harangued a local racist gang on the need for violent action against blacks. [*Los Angeles Magazine,* Dec. 3, 1989]

WHITE BAND

Organized by Exalted Cyclops Robert Bing in the early 1960s, this unit was created as a paramilitary action squad within Clayton County (Georgia) Klavern No. 52, United Klans of America. According to congressional investigators, the White Band's primary aim was "to plan and execute acts of harassment and intimidation against Negroes." Members were extensively trained in firearms, demolition, judo, and karate. [38]

WHITE BROTHERHOOD

A Reconstruction terrorist group organized in 1868, the White Brotherhood was largely confined to North Carolina, where it shared space and members with the KKK and the Constitutional Union Guard. Local units were designated as "camps," which were administered by captains, and there was no evidence of active authority higher than the county chiefs, who also served as captains of "grand camps." The Brotherhood was especially strong in Alamance County, where its members included the sheriff, his deputies, and all of the county's state legislators. Ranking officers joined Union Guard leaders and a few Klan spokesmen to call for disbandment in 1870 during Governor William Holden's militia war against organized nightriders, and the Brotherhood apparently dissolved that year. [87]

WHITE CAPS (1888–1903)

First organized in Crawford and Harrison counties, Indiana, where settlers from Tennessee—including veterans of the Reconstruction Klan—had put down roots, the White Caps quickly spread as disconnected bands with purely local operations and objectives. In Indiana and Ohio White Caps served primarily as vigilante "regulators," while the Georgia faction spent its time protecting moonshine stills. In northern Texas, the group's victims were mostly black, while Republicans bore the brunt of White Cap attacks in New Mexico. In southwestern Mississippi units sprang up in 1892–1893, and again ten years later, driving black tenants from land that had been seized from whites in bank foreclosures. Historians generally consider the White Caps a "bridge" between the first and second Klans, paving the way for 1920s KKK activity in areas untouched by the Reconstruction model. [87; 93]

WHITE CAPS (1965)

A front for the militant White Knights, the White Caps were responsible for the circulation of leaflets in Natchez, Mississippi, and Ferriday, Louisiana, during April 1965, accusing various locals of homosexuality or cohabiting with blacks. [38]

WHITE CHRISTIAN CRUSADERS

A Pennsylvania splinter group organized by Steven White and his wife in March 1971, the Crusaders consisted of defectors from the United Klans of America. Explaining his unit's paramilitary garb, White said, "We designed a uniform to look like the stormtroopers of Germany thirty years ago, to wake people up." The group publicly disavowed violence, but four members were arrested on weapons charges in Hightstown, New Jersey, after a street clash with the Jewish Defense League. White's troopers were also active in supporting Frank Rizzo for mayor of Philadelphia and George Wallace in his second presidential bid. [NYT 1971]

WHITE CHRISTIAN PROTECTIVE AND LEGAL DEFENSE FUND

See *Bowers, Samuel; Greaves, Elmore.*

WHITE CITIZENS' COUNCIL

See *Citizens' Council.*

WHITE CITIZENS OF RANDOLPH

In 1965 congressional investigators identified this group as a cover for the Asheboro, North Carolina, klavern, United Klans of America. [38]

WHITE CITIZENS OF WHITSETT

Created as the front for a Randolph County, North Carolina, klavern of the United Klans, serving Klansmen in Julian and Whitsett, this group was publicly exposed in 1965. [38]

WHITE CONFEDERACY OF UNDERSTANDING

A Canadian racist group, it was led by Klansman Jack Prins in 1976. [84]

WHITE CRUSADERS FOR GOD AND COUNTRY

Suspected as a front group for Frank Rotella's White Crusaders of the North, this group distributed posters claiming responsibility for a series of fifteen cross burnings near Salem, New Jersey, between December 1966 and April 1967. [*NYT* 1967]

WHITE CRUSADERS OF THE NORTH

Based in Cumberland County, New Jersey, this brainchild of ex-Klansman Frank Rotella was unveiled in a November 1966 cross burning ceremony outside of Cedarville and was attended by seventy-five members. [*NYT* 1966]

WHITE HERITAGE KNIGHTS OF THE KU KLUX KLAN

A California splinter group reported active in 1983, this faction had dissolved by the time a new survey was completed four years later. [2]

WHITE KNIGHTS OF ALABAMA

A militant splinter group active in the 1980s, this Klan listed Bill Riccio as an officer in 1985. No trace of it remained in 1987 when a new survey of the Invisible Empire had been completed. [*NYT* 1985, 1987]

WHITE KNIGHTS OF THE KU KLUX KLAN (MISSISSIPPI)

A product of dissension in the Louisiana-based Original Knights, this militant faction was organized in Brookhaven, Mississippi, in February 1964 under the leadership of Natchez Klansman E.L. McDaniel. The White Knights allegedly claimed their first victim on February 29, murdering a black man near Centreville accused of romantic involvement with a white woman. A brief power struggle in April 1964 left Sam Bowers in charge of the group, with McDaniel moving on to serve as Mississippi grand dragon for the rival United Klans of America. In a dramatic show of strength, the White Knights burned crosses in sixty-four of Mississippi's eighty-two counties the night of April 24, and members gathered near Raleigh, Mississippi, on June 7 to plot their strategy for the upcoming Freedom Summer. Over the next four years, White Knights compiled an unrivaled record of violence, including the publicized murders of victims Henry Dee and Charles Moore; Michael Schwerner, James Chaney, and Andrew Goodman; Vernon Dahmer; and Ben Chester White. (The death of a White Knights defector was ruled "accidental" in 1965, despite evidence of crushing blows to the victim's skull.) A 1964 Klan leaflet warned civil rights workers: "We are not going to sit back and permit our rights to be negotiated away by a group of Jewish priests, bluegum black savages and mongrelized money worshippers. We will buy you a ticket to the Eternal if you insist." To that end, White Knights participated in an estimated eighty beatings and thirty-five shootings in 1964, while bombing or burning thirty-seven churches and thirty-one other buildings across Mississippi. Another twenty-six churches were destroyed between 1965 and mid-1968, while random assaults, drive-by shootings, and other acts of harassment continued. Front groups such as the White Caps and Americans for Preservation of the White Race were sometimes employed to mask Klan activities, and Bowers also commissioned a Klan Air Force to shower explosives and fireworks on civil rights meetings in the fall of 1964. Membership peaked at 5,000 in mid-1965 and declined to an estimated 1,500 by January 1966 as federal arrests began to decimate the ranks. The only modern Klan in which the imperial wizard sought to control and direct violence from the top, personally selecting targets for arson, bombing, and murder, the White Knights were uniquely vulnerable to conspiracy prosecutions. By 1966 FBI agents reported that 488 members had turned informant, providing inside information on the Klan, and eighteen Klansmen were indicted on federal charges stemming from the Schwerner case in February 1967. Sam Bowers was one of seven Klansmen convicted and sentenced to prison in October 1967, and was already facing further charges—with sixteen others—for the death of Vernon Dahmer. In November 1968 a federal court in Vicksburg awarded damages of $1,021,500 to relatives of Ben White, naming the White Knights and three individual Klansmen as parties to his wrongful death. Christmas 1968 saw another member jailed for shooting at the home of P. Rayfield Brown in Monroe, Louisiana, but the gunman was freed on a legal technicality in February 1969. Considered defunct with Bowers in prison, the group was allegedly revived within days of his March 1976 parole, but informed sources placed the total membership at about a dozen hard-core Klansmen. [84; 93; 96]

WHITE KNIGHTS OF THE KU KLUX KLAN (IOWA)

An independent splinter group reported active in 1983, the Iowa White Knights disbanded sometime prior to 1987. [2]

WHITE KNIGHTS OF THE KU KLUX KLAN (MICHIGAN)

Yet another independent faction claiming this popular title, the Michigan White Knights were active in the early 1980s, disbanding sometime between 1983 and 1987. [2]

WHITE KNIGHTS OF THE KU KLUX KLAN (PENNSYLVANIA)

An independent splinter group reported active in 1983, the Pennsylvania White Knights disbanded sometime prior to 1987. [2]

WHITE KNIGHTS OF LIBERTY

Led by Klansman Joe Grady, this Greensboro, North Carolina, faction ignored a challenge from the Communist Workers Party that provoked a deadly shootout in November 1979, but its members were not averse to occasional violence. In July 1985, one of the White Knights pled guilty to harassing blacks in Alexander and Iredell counties, turning state's evidence to help convict several of his comrades. Eleven months later, another member was jailed in Nash County, North Carolina, for brandishing firearms at participants in an NAACP parade. [*NYT* 1985–1986; 2; 10]

WHITE KNIGHTS OF THE NEW JERSEY KU KLUX KLAN

Organized in the late 1970s by ex-kleagle Edwin Reynolds—dismissed by Pennsylvania's grand dragon on charges of adultery, misuse of Klan funds, and membership in "an anti-Christian cult"—the New Jersey White Knights were friendly with local Nazis to the point of conducting joint rallies. The already small membership shrank to an estimated nine Klansmen after Reynolds was accused of raping a Jewish informant, and Reynolds announced the unit's dissolution, proclaiming: "The White Knights of the New Jersey Ku Klux Klan, after a twenty-two-month history of television shows, countless interviews, street demonstrations, intense recruitment, and court injunctions, will proudly disband for the best interest of the Klan movement in New Jersey." Surviving members were urged to join David Duke's Knights of the KKK, described by Reynolds as "the future of the Klan and the white race," but a few apparently stood fast. A remnant of the White Knights was reported still active in 1983, but it disbanded sometime prior to 1987. [2; 10]

WHITE LEAGUE

A paramilitary racist group, including many former Klansmen in its ranks, the White League staged a bloody coup against the Republican government of Louisiana in September 1874, leaving 27 dead and 105 wounded in the streets of New Orleans. Federal troops suppressed the rebellion, but it marked the effective end of Radical Reconstruction in Louisiana, with Democrats recapturing the statehouse two years later. [87]

WHITE MAJORITY PARTY

See *Rockwell, George Lincoln.*

WHITE MAN'S LEAGUE

Conceived by Emory Burke in November 1949, this one-man effort to replace the Columbians, Inc., was based in Atlanta, Georgia, during its brief existence. [25]

WHITE PATRIOT PARTY

In 1985 Klansman Glenn Miller adopted this title for his Confederate Knights of the KKK, formerly known as the Carolina Knights. In July 1985, nine members were jailed for a series of violent assaults on blacks in Bell Glade and West Palm Beach, Florida; one defendant pled guilty and received a year's probation, while the others entered into plea bargains with the prosecution. (The Florida chapter was reportedly formed "just for something to do" after members had heard a Miller radio speech.) In another July 1985 incident, party members were charged with harassing a black businessman in Fayette County, Georgia. Two months later, member Gerald Weaver was convicted of carrying firearms during a racist parade through Forest City, North Carolina. Miller was convicted of violating injunctions against paramilitary training in July 1986, forfeiting his appeal bond to remain at large as a fugitive. In January 1987, three men were killed and two others critically wounded when White Patriot Party members raided a bookstore in Shelby, North Carolina, and Miller was captured in Missouri three months later, seized with an arsenal of weapons and three fellow party members. Meanwhile, the group sought cover in another name change, emerging as the Southern National Front, with an estimated 250 to 300 members, but its future was jeopardized in September 1987 when Miller pled guilty on federal charges and agreed to turn state's evidence against his fellow "patriots." [NYT 1985–1987]

WHITE PATRIOTS

In 1965 congressional investigators identified this group as a cover for the Brantley, Alabama, klavern, United Klans of America. [38]

WHITE PEOPLE'S COMMITTEE TO RESTORE GOD'S LAWS

Listing Klansman Thomas Robb as its director in 1983, this group was identified as an adjunct to the Arkansas-based Church of Jesus Christ. [2]

WHITE PEOPLE'S DEFENSE FUND

See *Carter, Asa.*

WHITE PEOPLE'S MARCH FOR FREEDOM

In 1965 congressional investigators identified this group as a front for the Ashland, Mississippi, klavern, United Klans of America. [38]

WHITE PROTESTANT CHRISTIAN PARTY

See *Johnston, Evall.*

WHITE ROSE SOCIETY

A racist vigilante group that predated the Reconstruction Klan in Noxubee County, Mississippi, the White Rose Society remained active into 1871, raiding alongside the KKK, with apparently overlapping membership. [87]

WHITE STUDENTS UNION

Based in Fallbrook, California, this organization is also variously known as the Aryan Youth Movement, the WAR Youth, and the WAR Skins. Leader John Metzger is the son of California Klansman Tom Metzger, and the White Students Union serves as an adjunct for the elder Metzger's White Aryan Resistance, recruiting neo-Nazi skinheads and others. In 1989 John Metzger and his followers staged a minor riot on the set of Geraldo Rivera's television talk show. [*Los Angeles Times Magazine,* Dec. 3, 1989]

WHITE UNITY PARTY

Identified as a Pennsylvania splinter of the KKK, this party claimed fewer than 100 active members in 1987. [*NYT* 1987]

WHITE YOUTH ALLIANCE

See *Duke, David.*

WHITEHEAD, TOM

Identified as the exalted cyclops of the Athens, Georgia, klavern in 1964, Whitehead collected funds for the defense of Klansmen charged with murdering Lemuel Penn that July, despite the fact that they were allegedly suspended from the United Klans of America. [38]

WHITEMAN'S DEFENSE FUND

Created by Imperial Wizard Robert Shelton in March 1965, this front group for the United Klans of America collected money to defray the legal expenses of Klansmen charged with the murder of Viola Liuzzo. [3]

WHITMAN, R.L.

See *Columbians, Inc.*

WICKSTROM, JAMES

A resident of Wisconsin and an outspoken member of the Posse Comitatus, self-proclaimed "national director of counterinsurgency for the United Posses of America," Wickstrom served a short prison term following his

1983 conviction for impersonating a federal officer. His early parole was made contingent on a promise to desist from further political activity. [13]

WIDE AWAKE CLUB

A Louisiana white supremacist group organized during the 1868 election campaign, the Wide Awake Club cooperated with Klansmen, the Innocents, and Knights of the White Camellia to harass black voters. On October 25 members joined the Knights in murdering seven blacks in Algiers, Louisiana. [87]

WIDE AWAKES

A group of Tennessee blacks who armed themselves against the Klan in the spring of 1868, the Wide Awakes apparently disbanded that July, after Grand Dragon John Gordon called on his Klansmen to scatter such bands "at any cost." No actual violence was traceable to this or similar groups in Tennessee. [87]

WILCUTT, HERBERT

See *Lee, Ellis.*

WILDER'S GOLF CLUB

In 1965 congressional investigators identified this group as a cover for the Selma, North Carolina, klavern, United Klans of America. [38]

WILDWOOD SEWING AUXILIARY

Established as a front for the women's auxiliary of the Wildwood, Florida, klavern, United Klans of America, this group was publicly exposed in 1965. [38]

WILDWOOD SPORTSMAN CLUB

In 1965 the House Un-American Activities Committee exposed this club as a front for the Wildwood, Florida, klavern, United Klans of America. [38]

WILEY, FRANK A.

A Klansman elected to serve as sheriff during Reconstruction in Caswell County, North Carolina, Wiley lured State Senator John Stephens into a courthouse trap in May 1870, where he was murdered by Klansmen. Afterward, Wiley claimed that Stephens was last seen alive in the company of "an unknown Negro." Arrested in July after Governor William Holden invoked martial law against the KKK, Wiley was never brought to trial. [87]

WILKES COUNTY CLUB NO. 301

In 1965 congressional investigators identified this group as a cover for the Washington, Georgia, klavern, United Klans of America. [87]

WILKINS, COLLIE LEROY, JR.

A Fairfield, Alabama, auto mechanic and member of the United Klans, Wilkins was arrested in Hueytown in 1964 for carrying an illegal sawed-off shotgun in the car. His guilty plea on federal firearms charges earned Wilkins a one-year suspended sentence with two years probation on the condition that he remain within the judicial district at all times. Beginning in February 1965 he was identified as a participant in violent acts against the W.S. Dickey Clay Manufacturing Company, in Bessemer, and in March he was jailed as the triggerman in the murder of civil rights worker Viola Liuzzo. His first trial on the murder charge in May resulted in a hung jury, and a second jury acquitted him in October. Two months later, Wilkins was convicted on federal charges in the Liuzzo case, with codefendants Eugene Thomas and William Eaton, drawing the maximum sentence of ten years. With an appeal of that conviction pending, Wilkins was consigned to prison on his previous firearms conviction, a federal judge ruling that the trip from Birmingham to Lowndes County, where Liuzzo was shot, violated terms of the Klansman's probation. His bid for parole on the Liuzzo conviction was denied in April 1973. [*NYT* 1965–1966, 1973; 38]

WILKINS, FRED

A native of Birmingham, Alabama, residing in Lakewood, Colorado, Wilkins was briefly suspended from his job as a fireman in 1979 after publicly threatening the life of radio host Alan Berg. The incident resulted in Wilkins's arrest on a charge of felony menacing, and also publicized his role as leader of the local KKK. Proud of the fact that his father and grandfather were Alabama Klansmen, Wilkins told an interviewer in 1980 that "the Klan tries to teach racial pride. If you define a racist as someone who loves his race, then I am one. But I'm not against other races." [85]

WILKINS, JOHN

See *Lynch, John.*

WILKINSON, ELBERT CLAUDE ("BILL")

A native of Galvez, Louisiana, Wilkinson graduated from high school at age sixteen and immediately joined the navy, serving as a cryptographer aboard the nuclear submarine *USS Simon Bolivar*. He retired from the service after eight years and settled in Denham Springs, Louisiana, joining David Duke as Louisiana grand dragon for the Knights of the KKK and editor of the

Klan's *Crusader* magazine. In 1975 Wilkinson quarreled with Duke over disposition of Klan funds, and defected to organize his own Invisible Empire Knights. In the spring of 1976 he was a featured speaker at Robert Scoggin's Conference of Eastern Dragons in South Carolina. A year later he vied with Scoggin and Dale Reusch for control of various independent Klans, meeting at a special Unity Conference, but William Chaney emerged as leader of the new Confederation of Independent Orders. By late 1980 Wilkinson had perfected a recruiting technique that his rivals denounced as "ambulance chasing," gaining new members in areas where racial tension would be making headlines. His single hottest case in 1979 involved the Decatur, Alabama, rape trial of black suspect Tommy Lee Hines, which reached its climax in a riot that led to four persons being shot. In the spring of 1979, he scored another media coup by recreating the 1965 civil rights march from Selma to Montgomery, Alabama, with Klansmen trooping over highways where black marchers had traveled a quarter of a century before. Yet another recruiting gimmick was Wilkinson's Klan Youth Corps, which offered paramilitary training to teenagers until media exposés drove the operation out of business. By 1980 Wilkinson's membership had outstripped Duke's following, and Wilkinson finished off his rival that summer by exposing Duke's offer to sell his membership list for a one-time payment of $35,000. Still, the wizard's glory days were numbered. In 1981, the press revealed that Wilkinson had been employed by federal agents as a paid informer since 1974, an act of treachery that led substantial numbers of his Klansmen to desert. In January 1983 Wilkinson was forced to declare bankruptcy after being faced with an IRS lien for back taxes and a crippling lawsuit filed by the Southern Poverty Law Center stemming from the 1979 Decatur riots. Passing the reins to Connecticut grand dragon J.W. Farrands, Wilkinson wistfully advised him that "everyone should try Chapter 11." In March 1983, Wilkinson and six of his comrades were convicted of disturbing the peace in Hammond, Louisiana, charges stemming from a riotous demonstration in December 1982. [2; 10; 93]

WILLIAMS, ALLEN A.

A black state legislator from Tuscaloosa County, Alabama, Williams was dragged from his home and beaten by Klansmen in the spring of 1868. [87]

WILLIAMS, BILL

Once the grand dragon of the Association of Arkansas Klans, Williams served as exalted cyclops for the group's Pine Bluff klavern in early 1967. [38]

WILLIAMS, ELDRED

With accomplice Howard Bentcliffe, Williams was jailed for an illegal cross burning in Levittown, Pennsylvania, in September 1958. He pled guilty to the charge and paid a $50 fine. [NYT 1958]

WILLIAMS, FRANKLIN

A black NAACP lawyer assigned to the defense team in the Groveland, Florida, rape case, Williams was the target of a Klan kidnapping attempt in August 1949. While driving back from court on August 4, accompanied by another attorney and two black newsmen, Williams was pursued by Klansmen in a wild chase from Tavares to Orlando. In June 1953, a federal grand jury indicted Klansmen William Bogar, Emmett Hart, T.J. McMennamy, and Ernest Morton for their roles in the conspiracy. [*NYT* 1953]

WILLIAMS, FURMAN DEAN

A Gaffney, South Carolina, member of the United Klans, Williams was identified in 1965 as the founder of a violent KKK faction known as The Underground, organized and trained with the approval of Grand Dragon Robert Scoggin. Williams was called to testify before the House Un-American Activities Committee in February 1966, and declined to answer on the grounds of possible self-incrimination. [38]

WILLIAMS, GEORGE LEONARD

A Greenville, North Carolina, member of the United Klans in 1965, Williams told congressional investigators that Klansmen were instructed to purchase firearms in areas where no permits or registration was required. Dispatched to Plymouth, North Carolina, to fight black demonstrators in August 1965, he suffered a minor bullet wound in the ensuing riot, with the Klan covering his medical expenses. Williams recalled seeing 1,000 Klansmen in Plymouth during the clash, and he resigned in disgust after Grand Dragon J.R. Jones told the press that no Klansmen had been involved. [38]

WILLIAMS, JIM

An ex-captain of the black militia during Reconstruction in York County, South Carolina, Williams was dragged from his home and hanged by Klansmen on the night of March 6, 1871. His murder nearly sparked a riot by members of his militia company, who threatened to massacre the county's white population before being restrained. [87]

WILLIAMS, JOSEPH JOHN

An admitted leader of the Reconstruction KKK in Leon County, Florida, Williams commanded 400 members—a force equal to half of the county's registered Democratic voters. [87]

WILLIAMS, LONDELL AND TAMMY

A Missouri carpenter and his wife linked to the Covenant, the Sword, and the Arm of the Lord, the Williamses were jailed in Belleville, Illinois, in May 1988 for allegedly conspiring to murder black presidential candidate Jesse Jackson. In custody, Londell Williams boasted of his militant connections, insisting that Covenant members had supplied him with an automatic rifle before he began stalking Jackson along the campaign trail. [NYT 1988]

WILLIAMS, ROBERT

A black ex-marine and leader of a militant NAACP chapter in Monroe, North Carolina, Williams chartered his group with the National Rifle Association in 1957 to obtain guns and ammunition to defend against Klan nightriders. Guards at his home exchanged gunfire with raiders on January 18, 1958, and violence resumed in August 1961, when participants in the integrated Freedom Rides visited Monroe. On the night of August 26, armed blacks barricaded their streets and repelled Klan raiders with rifle fire, briefly sheltering an innocent white couple who inadvertently drove into the cross fire. Local authorities charged Williams with kidnapping on August 28, prompting him to flee the country and seek refuge in Cuba. Upon his return to the United States, several years later, he was acquitted on all counts. [93]

WILLIAMS, W.J.

A resident of Vernado, Louisiana, Williams was listed as an early director of the Anti-Communist Christian Association. [38]

WILLIS, RICHARD A.

A Philadelphia, Mississippi, police officer, Willis was charged in February 1965 with violating the civil rights of Klan victims Michael Schwerner, James Chaney, and Andrew Goodman. [86]

WILLOW SPRINGS RESTORATION ASSOCIATION

In 1965 congressional investigators identified this group as a cover for the Willow Springs, North Carolina, klavern, United Klans of America. [38]

WILLS VALLEY HUNTING CLUB

Established as a front for the Fort Payne, Alabama, klavern, United Klans of America, this group was publicly exposed in 1965. [38]

WILMINGTON 10

In February 1971, confronted by white opposition in their efforts to erect a memorial for Dr. Martin Luther King, young blacks in Wilmington, North Carolina, planned a boycott of local schools. Reverend Eugene Templeton allowed them to meet in his Gregory Congregational Church, a move that resulted in death threats for Templeton and armed motorcades through black neighborhoods, accompanied by random blasts of gunfire. Templeton's request for police protection was denied, and Reverend Ben Chavis led a march to city hall to ask the mayor to impose a curfew on nightriders, which was also denied. Blacks then erected street barricades, and repelled armed assaults on six consecutive nights. One raider was killed and one black was killed by police before North Carolina's governor dispatched National Guardsmen to raid the fortified Gregory Congregational Church. The Klan and a militant offshoot, the Rights of White People, were threatening further violence when a white-owned grocery store was firebombed around the corner from Grace Congregational. Chavis and nine other blacks were indicted for conspiracy that spring, their case transferred to Pender County when prosecutors admitted a fair trial would be impossible in Wilmington. As the trial opened, the presiding judge refused to let defense attorneys question the racial beliefs of prospective jurors, ruling that Klan membership was no impediment to impartial service. All ten defendants were subsequently convicted, their case becoming a local cause célèbre. [73]

WILSON, BILLY EARL

A resident of McComb, Mississippi, recruited for the United Klans of America by cousin Paul Dewey Wilson, Billy Earl was one of nine bombers convicted in October 1964. His jail sentence, however, was suspended on grounds of "provocation" by the Klan's victims. Specific evidence linked Wilson to explosions at the homes of James Baker, Charles Bryant, and Aylene Quinn. In January 1966 Wilson testified before the House Un-American Activities Committee, describing how Klansmen drew lots to determine their targets before bombing raids. [38]

WILSON, CHARLES CLIFFORD

A member of the White Knights in Mississippi, Wilson received a local Jaycees distinguished service award in 1968, three days before his indictment in the murder of black civil rights worker Vernon Dahmer. Convicted and sentenced to life imprisonment in January 1969, Wilson sparked new controversy in 1972 when he was admitted to a work release program by Governor William Waller, who had been Wilson's attorney during the appeal of his conviction. The inmate's work assignment was particularly curious—Wilson was assigned to the Southern Mississippi State Hospital in Laurel (formerly Klan headquarters), where he worked primarily with poor blacks. Investigation revealed that Wilson had spent only a short time in prison, due to long furloughs granted by Governor John Bell Williams and his successor. Immediately prior to placing Wilson in the work release program, Waller had granted his former client two consecutive ninety-day furloughs. [NYT 1972]

WILSON, FRED LEE

A convicted gambler with arrests dating from 1949, Wilson served as North Carolina's grand klabee for the United Klans of America in 1964. [38]

WILSON, JIMMY PRINSTON

See *McComb, Mississippi.*

WILSON, PAUL DEWEY

Identified as leader of a Mississippi Klan front known as the South Pike Marksmanship Association, Wilson was one of nine United Klans members convicted of bombings near McComb, Mississippi, in October 1964. Specific evidence linked Wilson with a bombing that damaged the home of Aylene Quinn, and an arson attack that destroyed the Sweet Home Missionary Baptist Church. His jail sentence was suspended by the presiding judge on grounds of "undue provocation" by his victims. [38]

WILSON, WILLIAM EUGENE

A Jacksonville member of the United Florida KKK, Wilson was acquitted in November 1964 on charges of bombing George Gilliam's home after Gilliam's grandson enrolled at a "white" school. In 1965 he served simultaneously as exalted cyclops for the United Florida KKK's Jacksonville klavern and as director of the National States Rights Party in Duval County. In June 1983, he was named national chairman of the National States Rights Party, following J.B. Stoner's incarceration on bombing charges. [*NYT* 1964; 2; 38]

WILSON COUNTY IMPROVEMENT ASSOCIATION

In 1965 congressional investigators identified this group as the cover for Wilson County Unit No. 31, United Klans of America, serving Klansmen in Lucama and Wilson, North Carolina. [38]

WINFIELD, ROOSEVELT

A black shop steward for the Congress of Industrial Organizations, and employed by Pan American Airways in Miami, Florida, Winfield was driving to work on August 5, 1946, when he was forced off the highway by three men wearing black hoods and robes. Introducing themselves as spokesmen for "the boys," the raiders warned Winfield that "regardless of the union, you can't buck up with white people." He was cautioned to quit the union, or else "we'll give you a chance to drink up part of the water in the bay." CIO officers blamed Klansmen for the incident. [*NYT* 1946]

WINNFIELD HUNTING & FISHING CLUB

In 1965 congressional investigators identified this group as a cover for the Winnfield, Louisiana, klavern, Original Knights of the KKK. [38]

WINROD, GORDON

An ex-Lutheran minister, repudiated by the Missouri Synod of the Luthern Church over his anti-Semitic activities in 1960, Winrod served as national chaplain of the National States Rights Party in 1962. Leaving that position after six months, he moved on to found Our Savior's Church in Gainesville, Missouri, a forum from which he advocates "killing all Jews" as a solution to the problems of the United States. [2]

WINSMITH, DR. JOHN

A prominent Republican during Reconstruction in South Carolina, Winsmith was armed and ready when Klansmen raided his home in March 1871. He suffered seven wounds during the shootout, and while no Klansmen were hit, Winsmith was not bothered again. [87]

WINTER, PAUL

A leader of the 1920s Klan in Philadelphia, Winter alienated members with his pompous attitude and seamy private life, including an adulterous love affair with the wife of a Triple-S Super Secret Society leader. Dissident Klansmen brought him up on charges in 1925, but Imperial Wizard Hiram Evans sided with Winter, and his opponents lacked the necessary three-fourths majority vote to remove him from office. Winter retaliated for the attack by banishing his accusers and disbanding the Warren G. Harding Klan in Philadelphia, whereupon other klaverns resigned en masse. Evans finally transferred Winter to Queens, New York, in a bid to salvage the Philadelphia klaverns, but his effort was unsuccessful. [10]

WISCONSIN

The modern Klan was organized in the fall of 1920, among Milwaukee business and professional men, conducting its first formal meeting aboard a U.S. Coast Guard cutter. Membership continued to grow through 1924, with heavy recruiting among Masons finally easing the state's hostile Grand Master out of office. A surprising number of Milwaukee Socialists also joined, and Madison's mayor appointed Klansmen to a special bootleg squad, policing stills in Little Italy. The KKK did well in local elections in Oshkosh, Racine, Kenosha, and Chippewa County, but state officials generally stood in opposition to the Invisible Empire. Klansman Dan Woodward polled 40,000 votes in his 1924 Senate race, but still lost to popular Progressive incumbent Bob La Follette. Internal dissension led to schisms in the late 1920s and early 1930s, with splinter groups draining most of the realm's active membership, and no surviving klaverns were identified in early 1932. No significant Klan organization has been reported from Wisconsin since that time, despite Robert Shelton's premature appointment of a grand dragon in the mid-1960s, but Wisconsin has emerged as a haven for Posse Comitatus in recent years. Shawano County sheriff's deputies reported themselves "outgunned" in a confrontation with Posse members in 1981, after sniper attacks on teams of highway surveyors, and two members were jailed in December 1981 for setting fire to a state Department of Natural Resources building at Columbia Park, near Pipe. Sporadic vandalism and violent harassment of minorities has continued since that time, including synagogue attacks in Mequo and Milwaukee. In 1985 deputies raided a Posse compound near Tigerton, seizing a cache of 30 guns, 40,000 rounds of ammunition, pipe bombs, and hand grenades. [10; 38]

WISE, L. CORNELL

See *Jackson, Robert.*

WITTE, ELOISE

A Cincinnati resident, Witte proclaimed herself "grand empress" of the Klan in the mid-1960s, simultaneously presiding over the ladies auxiliary of James Venable's National Knights and a Cincinnati chapter of the National States Rights Party. In 1966, congressional witness Daniel Wagner named Witte as the instigator of abortive murder plots against President Lyndon Johnson, Vice President Hubert Humphrey, Dr. Martin Luther King, KKK Grand Emperor Hugh Morris, and her own husband. She allegedly furnished Wagner with firearms, telling him to "practice on Negroes as a sniper, to prove yourself and to help the white race." King's assassination was scheduled to occur during a speech at Antioch College, with Wagner ordered "to shoot King and make sure he was dead." (Wagner was apparently the second choice for the assignment, chosen only after a hit man—hired for $25,000—allegedly backed out of the job.) As far as killing politicians was concerned, Wagner suggested that "blowing up the White House would be appropriate, and she agreed." This was too much, even for Wagner, and he denied ever taking the White House plan seriously. Witte testified before the House Un-American Activities Committee in February 1966, denouncing her accuser as a "psychopath" and a "mentally disturbed loudmouth." She pled the Fifth Amendment, rather than disclose the names of fellow Klansmen, but admitted her house had been "like Grand Central Station" for "at least fifteen Klan groups" trying to gain a foothold in Ohio. [38]

WOLDANSKI, PAUL F.

A Robinsville, New Jersey, Klansman, Woldanski was convicted and sentenced to three months in jail for burning crosses at black housing projects in Mercer County in early 1971. On June 21, 1974, the verdict was overturned by a state appeals court, which found that Woldanski's prosecutor had made unnecessary appeals to racial feelings against Klansmen, "inflaming" minority jurors. [*NYT* 1974]

WOMACK, MELVIN

A black resident of Winter Garden, Florida, Womack was dragged from his bed, beaten, and shot to death by Klansmen on March 31, 1951. [*Newsweek,* Jan. 7, 1952]

WOMEN

Conceived as a masculine organization, pledged to protect "white womanhood" from insult (or worse) at the hands of minorities, the Ku Klux Klan has honored its goal more often in the breach than in observance. Women—white and otherwise—have been frequent targets of Klan violence through the years, including torture, floggings, gang rape, and murder. Females were absolutely excluded from the Reconstruction Klan, but numerous "ladies' auxiliary" units appeared in the 1920s as Klan leaders sought to maximize profits. Deposed imperial wizard William Simmons tried to compete with his own brainchild on the distaff side, organizing Kamelia for Klanswomen in 1923, but the movement was doomed by mismanagement and a 1924 financial agreement requiring Simmons to desist from competition with the KKK. In the North, Indiana Grand Dragon D.C. Stephenson used the Queens of the Golden Mask as a political rumor mill, his personal "poison society," specializing in behind-the-back character assassination. Elsewhere, regional women's groups such as the Women of the KKK (in Pennsylvania) and the Ladies of the Invisible Empire (in Oregon) suffered from meddling by the male-dominated National Women of the KKK, sometimes deserting en masse rather than surrendering their treasuries to imperial headquarters. Klanswomen were still relegated to auxiliary units in the 1960s, with the United Klans constitution specifying that "Every applicant must not only be 'white' and a 'Gentile,' but also a 'male.'" Some units, however, granted their women more active roles in the war against blacks and Jews. In Ohio, Eloise Witte served as a kind of den mother for the National Knights, dubbing herself "grand empress" of the Klan, and nightrider Kathy Ainsworth died in a shootout with police in Meridian, Mississippi, in June 1968. In the 1970s, David Duke's Knights of the KKK offered greater opportunities for Klanswomen, including various leadership roles. Top-ranking sisters of the sheet included Sandra Bergeron and "Gladys X," reigning as giants in Jefferson Parish, Louisiana, and Nashville, Tennessee, respectively, while Clara Pecoraro served as security chief for the Knights. Duke once claimed that 40 percent of his membership was female, and while secrecy makes verification impossible, this new prominence of women in Klan ranks is generally attributed to a decline in overall numbers. By definition, Klansmen remain ultra-conservative chauvinists, and although female members of the Aryan Nations have been jailed for active participation in bank robberies and other violent crimes since 1985, they are still regarded primarily as "life-bearers," receptacles for the precious "white seed." [*NYT* 1975; 10; 84]

WOMEN'S ACTIVITY CLUB

In 1965 congressional investigators identified this group as a cover for the Portsmouth, Virginia, ladies auxiliary, United Klans of America. [38]

WOOD, ROLAND WAYNE

See *Greensboro, North Carolina.*

WOODLE, ROY

A bricklayer and self-ordained minister, Woodle served as grand kludd for the North Carolina realm of the United Klans until 1965, when he resigned to appear as a cooperative witness before the House Un-American Activities Committee. While Woodle supported the Klan's racist doctrines, he had grown disgusted at the personal enrichment of ranking officers, including the use of shills to stimulate generous donations at public rallies. As Woodle told the committee, "The way I see it, they come into town this month, have a rally, get all the money you can get, and get out, and say, 'Now you folks work hard, get all the members you can. We will be back next year for another rally.' And then on other occasions, I saw poor men on the side, can't hardly pay their bills, supporting it, and [Klan leaders] promising you, 'We are going to give you the victory. We are going to stand. We are going to stand,' but ain't nobody found out what they are going to stand for." [38]

WOODS, JIM

A black resident of Reconstruction Chester County, South Carolina, Woods served as captain in an all-black militia unit organized in February 1871 to counteract Klan terrorism. Klansmen raided his home on the nights of March 4 and 5, with one nightrider wounded and several disguises captured by the black defenders. On the morning of March 6, armed blacks marched into Chester, the county seat, and fortified the railroad depot as their new headquarters. A brief skirmish that night persuaded the blacks to withdraw on March 7, and they retreated to a church five miles away. By that time, hundreds of whites had rallied "in self-defense," including numerous Klansmen, with reinforcements arriving from North Carolina. Routed by superior numbers, the blacks were taken into protective custody by Chester County's sheriff and later returned to their homes unmolested, while news of the "Chester riot" inflamed white paranoia for miles around. [87]

WOODS, WOODROW

Identified as a grand titan of the United Florida KKK, Woods shared the stage with J.B. Stoner at a Jacksonville, Florida, Klan rally in May 1964. [NYT 1964]

WRECKING CREW

Generally consisting of six Klansmen appointed by the klokan of a klavern, the "wrecking crew" is an action squad, entrusted with whippings, cross burnings, and arson. Depending on the preference of their members, such "elite" groups have also been dubbed the "Secret Six," the "Ass-tear Squad," and "Holy Terrors." [38]

WRIGHT, ANDERSON

A black Republican activist in Jefferson, Texas, Wright was jailed on October 3, 1868, after he witnessed a shootout between George Smith and gunmen from the Knights of the Rising Sun. Rising Sun members lynched Smith the next day, and Wright fled the state. Traced by the military, he was escorted back to Jefferson on a steamboat, accompanied by a lone army officer, but Wright's escort grew careless one night, allowing four men to assault him before Wright jumped overboard and swam to a nearby army base. Returned to Jefferson under heavy guard, he testified at the murder trial of twenty-three defendants, a trial that resulted in six convictions. [87]

WRIGHT, GREER P.

A white tenant farmer and house painter in Columbus County, North Carolina, Wright was lured from his home and whipped by Klansmen in December 1951. Three months later, a county grand jury indicted several members of the Association of Carolina Klans. [NYT 1952]

WRIGHT, WILLIAM

A black resident of York County, South Carolina, Wright was flogged and had his house burned by Klansmen in October 1869. Protests from Wright's landlord led to the formation of a black militia company, under the command of a white officer. Wright identified Klansman Abraham Sapoch as one of his assailants, but Sapoch was discharged after producing alibi witnesses. He then retaliated by having Wright jailed on charges of perjury and false arrest, with eventual conviction sending Wright to prison. [87]

WYATT, WILLIAM

An elderly state Republican senator from Lincoln County, Tennessee, Wyatt was dragged from his home by Klansmen one night in the spring of 1868, then pistol-whipped and left unconscious in the yard. [87]

WYDNER, DAVID

A Boston native, Wydner moved to Baton Rouge, Louisiana, in the 1970s to manage a Klan bookstore for David Duke's Knights of the KKK. Held on charges of armed robbery in 1976, he escaped from jail in Baton Rouge and was declared a fugitive from justice. [84]

WYOMING

The 1920s Klan found little interest from the people of Wyoming, and Imperial Wizard Hiram Evans was embarrassed when he planned to visit the state in 1924. Casper Klansmen could not fill the meeting hall, and when deacons of the First Christian Church discovered who was coming to their auditorium, they canceled the date. There were scattered incidents of masked racial violence in the mid-1980s, but it by no means heralded a revival of the KKK. [10]

XAVIER, PETER

An associate of Bill Hendrix in the Florida-based Southern Knights, Xavier was ejected from St. Petersburg with his mentor in December 1960 when they tried to counterpicket against black protesters. [*NYT* 1960]

X-RAY, THE

Published by Muncie, Indiana, Klansman Court Asher, *The X-Ray* was a source of anti-Semitic propaganda in the 1930s and 1940s, one of its weekly columnists during World War II being Edward James Smythe. Gerald L.K. Smith once tried to buy out the magazine, but Asher refused to sell. A typical 1941 editorial proclaimed: "The word 'democracy' is the weapon of scoundrels and the refuge of fools. Every political pap-sucker seeking public office takes it to his breast, every war monger and public liar uses it as a shield to deceive the unwary. No thank you. Before this matter is ended a great many Americans will not like the taste of 'democracy.'" [10]

YARBOROUGH, GARY LEE

See *Order, The.*

YELLOW DOG

An informal hazing ritual and test of loyalty practiced in some units of the United Klans, the "yellow dog" initiation typically involves pranks similar to those found in some college fraternities. (Some Klansmen, for example, describe swallowing a raw oyster with a string attached, then having it pulled back from their stomachs as a test of nerve.) When practiced by imperial officers, such hazing is called the "Royal Order of the Purple Dog." As Imperial Wizard Robert Shelton told journalist Patsy Sims, "It gives you an opportunity to see how much a man can take, if he's going to do what you tell him to do." [84]

YELLOW JACKETS

A Klan-like group, with apparent overlapping membership, the Yellow Jackets participated in nightriding around Humphreys County, Tennessee, in the spring of 1868. [87]

YORK, JAMES

A Montgomery, Alabama, Klansman jailed for the 1957 bombing of Ralph Abernathy's home, York was released without a trial after two other Klansmen were acquitted in a different bombing. In 1976 he was indicted with three codefendants for the January 1957 murder of Willie Edwards, but the charges were soon dismissed when the key prosecution witness confessed mistaken identification of one suspect. [*NYT* 1976]

YORK COUNTY KLAN

One of seven groups reported active in South Carolina after the U.S. Supreme Court's Black Monday decision, this faction apparently disappeared by the end of the 1950s. [6]

YOUNG, ALEX

A Louisville, Kentucky, policeman who joined the KKK and later formed his own right-wing clique on the side, Young was charged with various crimes in 1986. Testifying at his trial in May, he described Klan infiltration of the Louisville police force as extensive. [*NYT* 1986]

YOUNG, ROYAL VIRGIN, SR.

An early member of the Louisiana-based Original Knights, Young served as "imperial dragon" in 1963, helping J.D. Swenson expand the organization into neighboring Mississippi. Ousted from the Original Knights in early 1964 on charges of financial irregularity, Young drifted into the Original KKK of America, Inc., and was briefly identified as imperial wizard of that group before resigning in April 1965 to work with retired general Edwin Walker, in Texas. Summoned to testify before the House Un-American Activities Committee three months later, Young was generally cooperative, but used the Fifth Amendment to avoid discussion of his links with a Louisiana Klan faction known as the American Royal Rangers. [*NYT* 1965; 38]

YOUNG, S. GLENN

Dismissed from the Prohibition Bureau for his violent and erratic behavior, Young took command of a crusading klavern in Herrin, Illinois, during 1923. Sporting a paramilitary uniform, twin .45s on his belt, and often carrying a submachine gun, Young led his raiders into private homes, roughing up the opposition in his war against bootleggers and other "undesirables." In the winter of 1923–1924, his strike force closed more than 100 speakeasies, and gathered hundreds of prisoners, with French and Italian immigrants receiving so much attention that both nations filed formal complaints in Washington. Tried for assault and battery, Young packed the courtroom with armed Klansmen and won a swift acquittal from intimidated jurors. In May 1924, Young was ambushed on the highway by gangsters, and gravely wounded, his new bride blinded by shotgun pellets. Grieving Klansmen ambushed the hit team, beginning an open war in "Bloody Williamson" County. National Guardsmen were called out eight times in the space of four years, as the violence between Klansmen and anti-

Klansmen claimed twenty lives. Young was expelled from the KKK in 1925, but his Klansmen were loyal, and the raiding continued. Sheriff George Galligan appointed a leading anti-Klan gunman as his chief deputy, and a showdown was inevitable. When it came, in a local tobacco store, Young and the deputy managed to kill each other, along with two innocent bystanders. A cease-fire was grudgingly imposed in April 1926, following battles on election day that left several men dead or wounded. [10]

YOUNG MEN'S DEMOCRATIC CLUBS

A front group for the Reconstruction Klan in Florida, where Klansmen rarely called themselves the KKK by name, the Young Men's Democratic Clubs were reported active during the 1868 election campaign and for a short time afterward. [87]

YOUNG MEN'S SOCIAL CLUB

In the 1960s, this title was used as a cover for klaverns of the United Klans in Bessemer and Dora, Alabama. Both groups were publicly exposed by the House Un-American Activities Committee in 1965. [38]

YOUNT, JAMES

A defense witness in the murder trial of Klansman Cecil Sessum, Yount was jailed for perjury in March 1968, after denying previous membership in the White Knights of the KKK. [*NYT* 1968]

Z

ZIMMERLEE, JOHN H., JR.

See *Columbians, Inc.*

ZUMBRUNN, WILLIAM F.

A native of Missouri, Zumbrunn served as the Klan's attorney and legislative lobbyist in Washington, D.C., during the 1920s. In 1923 he helped Texas Klansman Earl Mayfield take his seat in the U.S. Senate, beating a challenge filed before the Senate Elections Committee, and he repeated the performance with Iowa senator Daniel Steck a year later. Mayfield and Tennessee senator Kenneth McKellar were guests of honor at Zumbrunn's wedding in November 1924. The following year Zumbrunn was dispatched to Colorado, aiding the ouster of dissident grand dragon John Galen Locke. Hoping for a presidential appointment as ambassador to Mexico in 1925, Zumbrunn was furious when someone else was appointed. In 1928, with Imperial Wizard Hiram Evans, Zumbrunn tried to block the Democratic nomination of vice presidential candidate Joseph Robinson after Robinson denounced religious bigotry and supported the presidential candidacy of Al Smith. [10]

BIBLIOGRAPHY

For reasons of space and for the reader's convenience, sources for individual entries are generally noted in the text by numbers coordinated to the alphabetized list below. Exceptions include the following:

Facts on File : "FOF" followed by the year of a specific volume.

New York Times Index : "NYT" followed by the year of a specific volume.

Associated Press articles : "AP" followed by the date.

United Press International articles : "UPI" followed by the date.

Other newspapers or magazines : Title followed by the date.

1. Alsop, Stewart. "Portrait of a Klansman." *Saturday Evening Post* (April 9, 1966).

2. Anti-Defamation League of B'nai B'rith. *Extremism on the Right.* New York: ADL, 1983.

3. Armbrister, Trevor. "Portrait of an Extremist." *Saturday Evening Post* (August 12, 1964).

4. Atwater, James. "If We Can Crack Mississippi . . ." *Saturday Evening Post* (July 25, 1964).

5. Bartimole, Roldo S., and Murray Gruber. "Cleveland: Recipe for Violence." *The Nation* (June 6, 1967).

6. Bartley, Numan. *The Rise of Massive Resistance.* Baton Rouge: Louisiana State University Press, 1969.

7. Bishop, Jim. *The Days of Martin Luther King, Jr.* New York: Putnam, 1971.

8.   Carlson, John Roy. *Under Cover.* New York: E.P. Dutton, 1943.

9 .   Carter, Hodding. *So the Heffner's Left McComb.* New York: Doubleday, 1965.

10.   Chalmers, David M. *Hooded Americanism.* New York: Franklin Watts, 1981.

11.   Chester, Lewis. *An American Melodrama.* New York: Viking Press, 1969.

12.   Chriss, Nicholas. "Bombs to the Right of Them." *The Nation* (February 22, 1971).

13.   Coates, James. *Armed and Dangerous: The Rise of the Survivalist Right.* New York: Hill & Wang, 1987.

14.   Cook, James G. *The Segregationists.* New York: Appleton-Century-Crofts, 1962.

15.   Cornwell, Bill. "The Birmingham Bombers, 1963–1976." *The Nation* (September 4, 1976).

16.   Donner, Frank J. *The Age of Surveillance.* New York: Knopf, 1980.

17.   Dorman, Michael. *The George Wallace Myth.* New York: Bantam, 1976.

18.   ———. *We Shall Overcome.* New York: Dell, 1964.

19.   Evers, Myrlie. *For Us, The Living.* New York: Ace, 1967.

20.   Fager, Charles. *Selma, 1965.* New York: Scribner, 1974.

21.   Flammonde, Paris. *The Kennedy Conspiracy.* New York: Meredith Press, 1969.

22.   Flowers, Richmond. "Southern Plain Talk About the Ku Klux Klan." *Look* (May 3, 1966).

23.   Foley, Albert S. "New 'Church,' Old Klan." *America* (October 21, 1972).

24.   Foner, Philip S. *Organized Labor and the Black Worker.* New York: Praeger, 1974.

25. Forster, Arnold. *A Measure of Freedom*. New York: Doubleday, 1950.

26. ———, and Benjamin Epstein. *The New Anti-Semitism*. New York: McGraw-Hill, 1974.

27. ———. *The Radical Right*. New York: Vintage Books, 1967.

28. ———. *Report on the John Birch Society*. New York: Vintage Books, 1966.

29. ———. *The Troublemakers*. New York: Doubleday, 1952.

30. Frady, Marshall. *Wallace*. New York: World Publishing Co., 1968.

31. Frank, Gerold. *An American Death*. New York: Bantam, 1972.

32. Friedman, Leon. *Southern Justice*. New York: World Publishing Co., 1965.

33. Gillette, Paul, and Eugene Tillinger. *Inside the Ku Klux Klan*. New York: Pyramid Books, 1965.

34. Good, Paul. "Klantown, USA." *The Nation* (February 1, 1965).

35. Gordon, Arthur. "Intruder in the South." *Look* (February 19, 1957).

36. Haas, Ben. *KKK*. Evanston, Ill.: Regency Books, 1963.

37. Harkey, Ira B. *The Smell of Burning Crosses*. Jacksonville, Ill.: Harris-Wolfe, 1967.

38. House Committee on Un-American Activities. *The Present-Day Ku Klux Klan Movement*. Washington, D.C.: U.S. Government Printing Office, 1967.

39. House Select Committee on Assassinations. *The Final Assassinations Report*. New York: Bantam, 1979.

40. Huie, William B. "Murder: The Klan on Trial." *Saturday Evening Post* (June 19, 1965).

41. ———. *Ruby McCollum*. New York: New American Library, 1956.

42. ———. *Three Lives for Mississippi*. New York: New American Library, 1968.

43. Illinois Legislative Investigating Committee. *Ku Klux Klan.* Chicago: Illinois Legislative Investigating Committee, 1976.

44. Ingalls, Robert P. *Hoods.* New York: Putnam, 1979.

45. Javits, Jacob K. *Discrimination USA.* New York: Washington Square Press, 1962.

46. Jones, J. Harry. *The Minutemen.* New York: Doubleday, 1968.

47. Kempton, Murray. "Trial of the Klansman." *New Republic* (May 22, 1965).

48. Knebel, Fletcher, and Clark Mollenhoff. "Eight Klans Bring New Terror to the South." *Look* (April 30, 1957).

49. Lane, Mark, and Dick Gregory. *Code Name "Zorro."* Englewood Cliffs, N.J.: Prentice-Hall, 1977.

50. Lewis, Anthony. *Portrait of a Decade.* New York: Bantam, 1965.

51. Long, Margaret. "The Imperial Wizard Explains the Klan." *New York Times Magazine* (July 5, 1964).

52. Lord, Walter. *The Past That Would Not Die.* New York: Pocket Books, 1967.

53. Lowe, David. *Ku Klux Klan: The Invisible Empire.* New York: W.W. Norton, 1967.

54. Martin, Harold H. "The Trial of 'DeLay' Beckwith." *Saturday Evening Post* (March 14, 1964).

55. Martin, John B. *The Deep South Says "Never."* New York: Ballantine, 1959.

56. Martin, Ralph G. "The CIO Takes a Long Lease in the South." *New Republic* (January 13, 1947).

57. McConville, Edward. "The Prophetic Voice of C.P. Ellis." *The Nation* (October 15, 1973).

58. McCord, William. *Mississippi: The Long, Hot Summer.* New York: W.W. Norton, 1965.

59. McIlhany, William H. *Klandestine*. New York: Arlington House, 1975.

60. McMillan, George. "New Bombing Terrorists of the South Call Themselves Nacirema . . . American Spelled Backward." *Life* (October 11, 1963).

61. McMillen, Neil R. *The Citizens' Council*. Chicago: University of Illinois Press, 1971.

62. McWilliams, Carey. "The Klan: Post-War Model." *The Nation* (December 14, 1946).

63. Mendelsohn, Jack. *The Martyrs*. New York: Harper & Row, 1966.

64. Miller, William. *Martin Luther King, Jr.* New York: Weybright & Tally, 1968.

65. Murphy, Robert J. "The South Fights Bombing." *Look* (January 6, 1959).

66. Muse, Benjamin. *Ten Years of Prelude*. New York: Viking Press, 1964.

67. Norden, Eric. "The Paramilitary Right." *Playboy* (June 1969).

68. O'Reilly, Kenneth. *Racial Matters*. New York: Macmillan, 1989.

69. Overstreet, Harry and Bonaro. *The FBI in Our Open Society*. New York: W.W. Norton, 1969.

70. Parker, Thomas F. *Violence in the United States, 1956–67*. New York: Facts on File, 1974.

71. Peirce, Neal R. *The Deep South States of America*. New York: W.W. Norton, 1973.

72. Perlmutter, Nathan. "Bombing in Miami." *Commentary* (June 1958).

73. Pinsky, Mark. "North Carolina Blots Its Record." *The Nation* (October 11, 1975).

74. Randel, William Pierce. *The Ku Klux Klan: A Century of Infamy*. New York: Chilton, 1965.

75. Rosenthal, A.M., and Arthur Gelb. *One More Victim*. New York: New American Library, 1967.

76. Rowe, Gary Thomas. *My Undercover Years With the Ku Klux Klan*. New York: Bantam, 1976.

77. Roy, Ralph Lord. *Apostles of Discord*. Boston: Beacon Press, 1953.

78. Shapiro, Fred C. "The Last Word (We Hope) on George Lincoln Rockwell." *Esquire* (February 1967).

79. Sheridan, Walter. *The Fall and Rise of Jimmy Hoffa*. New York: Saturday Review Press, 1972.

80. Sherill, Robert. *The Accidental President*. New York: Pyramid Books, 1967.

81. ———. *Gothic Politics in the Deep South*. New York: Grossman, 1968.

82. ———. "Strange Decorum of Lester Maddox." *The Nation* (May 1, 1967).

83. Silver, James. *Mississippi: The Closed Society*. New York: Harcourt, Brace & World, 1966.

84. Sims, Patsy. *The Klan*. New York: Stein & Day, 1978.

85. Singular, Stephen. *Talked to Death: The Murder of Alan Berg and the Rise of the Neo-Nazis*. New York: Beech Tree, 1987.

86. Sobel, Lester. *Civil Rights, 1960–1966*. New York: Facts on File, 1967.

87. Trelease, Allen W. *White Terror*. New York: Harper & Row, 1971.

88. Tully, Andrew. *The FBI's Most Famous Cases*. New York: Dell, 1965.

89. Turner, William W. *The Police Establishment*. New York: Tower Books, 1969.

90. ———. *Power on the Right*. Berkeley, Calif.: Ramparts Press, 1971.

91. Ungar, Sanford J. *FBI*. Boston: Little, Brown, 1975.

92. Velie, Lester. "The Klan Rides the South Again." *Colliers* (October 9, 1948).

93. Wade, Wyn Craig. *The Fiery Cross*. New York: Simon & Schuster, 1987.

94. Wallace, Henry. "Violence and Hope in the South." *New Republic* (December 8, 1947).

95. Weisberg, Harold. *Frame-Up*. New York: Outerbridge & Dienstfrey, 1969.

96. Whitehead, Don. *Attack on Terror*. New York: Funk & Wagnalls, 1970.